Foreign Policy
in World Politics

CONTRIBUTING AUTHORS

Robert J. Art
Vernon V. Aspaturian
Josef Joffe
Robert J. Lieber
Roy C. Macridis
Riordan Roett
Nadav Safran
Robert A. Scalapino
Françoise de la Serre
Bengt Sundelius
Allen S. Whiting

Foreign Policy in World Politics: States and Regions

Seventh Edition

Roy C. Macridis, Editor
Brandeis University

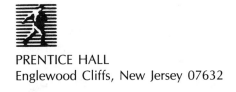

PRENTICE HALL
Englewood Cliffs, New Jersey 07632

LIBRARY OF CONGRESS
Library of Congress Cataloging-in-Publication Data

Foreign policy in world politics : states and regions / Roy C.
Macridis, editor. -- 7th ed.

Includes bibliographies and index.
ISBN 0-13-325481-X
1. International relations.   I. Macridis, Roy C.
JX1391.F65 1989
327--dc19   88-17836
                                                        CIP

Editorial/production supervision and
 interior design: *Jenny Kletzin*
Cover design: *Ben Santora*
Manufacturing buyer: *Peter Havens*

 © 1989, 1985, 1976, 1972, 1967, 1962, 1958 by Prentice-Hall, Inc.
A Division of Simon & Schuster
Englewood Cliffs, New Jersey 07632

Printed in the United States of America

10 9 8 7 6 5 4 3 2 1

ISBN 0-13-325481-X

Prentice-Hall International (UK) Limited, *London*
Prentice-Hall of Australia Pty. Limited, *Sydney*
Prentice-Hall Canada Inc., *Toronto*
Prentice-Hall Hispanoamericana, S.A., *Mexico*
Prentice-Hall of India Private Limited, *New Delhi*
Prentice-Hall of Japan, Inc., *Tokyo*
Simon & Schuster Asia Pte. Ltd., *Singapore*
Editora Prentice-Hall do Brasil, Ltda., *Rio de Janeiro*

Contents

Preface

The first edition of this volume appeared in 1958. This seventh edition, some thirty years later, is presented with the knowledge that "comparative foreign policy" has become a recognized field of study and both the editor and the authors share a sense of accomplishment in having contributed to it.

We have maintained the original format with some modifications. We continue with our essays on the major countries of our world—Great Britain, France, the Federal Republic of Germany, China, Japan, the Soviet Union, and the United States. We have updated all these essays and added a brief chronology of major foreign policy landmarks since the end of World War II for each nation covered. We have grouped in Part Two our regional studies on the Middle East, Latin America, the European Community, and we have added a new study on Scandinavia. We felt that in this manner the new edition can be used to supplement courses in international politics as well as comparative politics.

Again, as with previous editions, my warmest thanks to all contributors—old and new. Special thanks to Jenny Kletzin of Prentice Hall who supervised the editing and publication of this volume. My thanks also to the many colleagues who have written to me on different occasions with their comments and suggestions.

Roy C. Macridis
Belmont, Massachusetts

Introductory Remarks

In all our essays in this volume we discuss the historical background of the various countries we survey and the accumulated political experience and "memory" in terms of which problems are assessed and decisions are made. They constitute the "elements of foreign policy" in terms of which the foreign policy "patterns" are shaped. In each and every essay we discuss the foreign policy-making institutions and the role of political elites in the shaping and implementation of foreign policy objectives. Finally, we present a framework in terms of which foreign policy decisions can be evaluated and, in many cases, attempt to give an evaluation ourselves.

The elements of foreign policy may be thought of in terms of concentric circles. At the center are certain elements that are more or less material in character. Some of these are relatively permanent, such as geography and natural resources. Others, like the economic, industrial, and military establishments, are more responsive to change and human manipulation. Then there are human factors, largely quantitative in the case of population, and qualitative as regards national character, social structure, national morale, political institutions and experience, and an effective tradition of diplomacy. From these elements and the instrumentalities of the policy-making process, the substance of foreign policy derives.

The Elements of Foreign Policy

A. *The relatively permanent material elements*
   1. Geography
   2. Natural Resources
      a. Minerals
      b. Food production
      c. Energy and power
B. *Less permanent material elements*
   1. Industrial establishment
   2. Military establishment
   3. Changes in industrial and military capacity
C. *The human elements: quantitative and qualitative*
   1. Quantitative—population
   2. Qualitative
      a. policy makers and leaders
      b. The role of ideology
      c. The role of information

The Foreign Policy-making Process

A. *The governmental agencies*
   1. Executive (that is, prime minister, relevant ministries, and interministerial or interdepartmental organizations)
   2. Legislature (including relevant committees)
B. *The nongovernmental agencies*
   1. Political parties
   2. Interest groups
   3. Media of communication
   4. Characteristics of public opinion

Patterns of Foreign Policy
Evaluation of Foreign Policy

PATTERNS OF FOREIGN POLICY

A "pattern" implies the existence of goals to be realized and the mechanisms and practices through which such goals are realized. Above all, the term connotes the existence of intellectual equipment—something like a filter mechanism or lens—through which policymakers look at the outside world, sift information that comes in, and take steps that relate to the goals of the nation-state. A military coup in Ethiopia; uncertainty about the future regime in Portugal; invasion of northern Cyprus by the Turks—these are events that mean different things to different nations and their policymakers. They are events that are viewed in terms of the goals of their respective nation-states. As a result reactions to them will differ from one state to another.

Objectively speaking no nation-state can expect to realize fully all its goals all the time. There are irreducible goals that are associated with clear-cut patterns of action and reaction. They generally involve the minimum requirements of security and defense as defined by the policymakers and the nation's political elite. Not much compromise is possible. The Soviets' reaction to an effort on the part of Poland to join NATO is obvious. They will use force rather than allow it. The reaction of the U.S.A. to the installation of Soviet missiles on Cuban territory is equally certain. The harder and clearer the definition of minimum and irreducible goals and the means of action to bring them about, the higher the level of predictability in international relations and, as a result, the stability of the international system. In contrast, the situation in the Middle East is highly volatile because of the *lack* of clear-cut goals and of anticipated forms of action on the part of the various protagonists. Another illustration was the war in Korea in 1951 that may have originated in the inadvertent remarks made earlier by Secretary of State Dean Acheson according to which South Korea was not within the perimeter of U.S. defense.

There are, however, goals that call for adjustment and compromise. They are what a nation-state considers desirable but not indispensable. They do not directly involve matters of security and survival but rather the expansion or consolidation of power. Such goals may be graded on a scale of priorities beginning with what is of particular importance and ending with those that can be dispensed with under pressure. For instance, a former secretary of defense in France, an ardent Gaullist, defined the goals of France to be the security of Europe, the avoidance of "certain dominations" in the Mediterranean, in Africa, and in "certain parts of the world where our flag flies." Obviously this implied a ranking of interests and goals in which Europe, North Africa, French-speaking Africa, and "certain parts" of the world would be ranked in that order.

How are patterns shaped? There is one and only one answer: by history. And by this we mean the existence over a long period of time of analogous, if not identical, reactions to analogous, if not identical, stimuli. It is only then that a "pattern" becomes firmly crystallized. It involves a goal shared widely by the elites, and it is associated with an equally accepted set of actions to bring it about. In the discussion of the individual foreign policies of the countries we cover, we identify basic patterns and indicate the force they have acquired over a given period of time.

As technological, economic, strategic, and political changes occur, and the international environment becomes transformed, two major dangers are ever-present. We have already mentioned one, that is, the political elite may remain blind to these changes and follow patterns that were valid under different conditions in the past. The elites become ensnared in the stereotypes of the past and assume that the *same* goals are to be implemented by the *same* actions. The second danger is equally ever-present. Elites—and not only in democracies—may divide sharply on goals and means. A division may lead either to inaction or to sudden changes that create an element of unpredictability and instability.

There is a need for careful analysis of the existing patterns, their scope, their intensity, the conditions under which they change, and the penalties—both for the nation-state and the international community—that result from prolonged rigidities and from divisions among the elites.

EVALUATION OF FOREIGN POLICY

As the student goes through the analysis of the foreign policy-making of individual countries, he or she unavoidably is concerned with evaluating them. Have the policymakers made a "good" or a "bad" decision? Has the foreign policy pursued by a given country been "successful" or "unsuccessful"? In terms of what criteria and what canons shall we judge and render a verdict? The intense debate that went on over U.S. policy in Vietnam, just as in France over Indochina and Algeria, clearly demonstrates that clear-cut and objective tools for analysis and judgment are not always available.

To begin with, there is the perennial problem of "good" and "bad"—that is, of *normative* criteria and goals. Such goals generally indicate the overall commitment of a society to a way of life, and naturally influence policy-making and foreign policy as well. American isolationism was based squarely on normative considerations—primarily the belief that the American way of life was distinct and superior to those of the European countries, and that any involvement in their affairs and any involvement on their part in the affairs of the American continent would "contaminate" and perhaps corrupt the American democracy. By the same token, many French political leaders and intellectuals believed that the French colonies were a major challenge for the dissemination of the French culture and the French language through which the "natives" would be assimilated to a higher and better way of life.

The student generally is inclined to be very sympathetic to foreign policy analysis in terms of basic ethical criteria. This is not, however, an easy job—nor is it analytically satisfactory. The first difficulty is that of agreeing on ethics. For those who consider an ethical principle more important than human life, outright destruction in its name is preferable to peace; for those who consider communism a danger far outweighing the well-being of any given generation, war and sacrifice is above that of welfare and well-being; for those who consider democracy and an open society more valuable than one man's life, again, war and destruction may be inevitable to preserve what is so highly valued. In other words, it is not always easy to find people agreeing on the highest normative goal. In a pluralistic universe, then, judgment and evaluation in terms of ethical considerations is hazardous and highly unpredictable. We prefer and we suggest here a more instrumental approach to the evaluation of foreign policy. It is based on the assumption that, at least for the time being, nation-states are here to stay and that their foreign policy must be evaluated in terms of the success and failure to implement the goals they pursue. In the international community each and every state is allotted some power which alone, or in combination with others, allows it to keep its autonomy and way of life or, conversely, prevents its destruction by others. The international community has been in this sense a world of power relations differing in degree rather than in kind from domestic politics.

An analysis based upon power must also take into consideration that it is not an end in itself. It is an instrument for preserving a national community and its way of life. Its use, therefore, must always be subjected to this test: Does it preserve the national community? Does it enhance its security and well-being? Is its use consistent with the basic interests of the national community? The analysis we suggest, therefore, involves a number of steps *before* we confront the thorny ethical question of what is "right" and "wrong." We propose simply to suggest a set of instrumental criteria in terms of which "success" or "failure," or at least a discriminating bill of particulars, can be determined.

The steps we try to pursue are the following:

1. We must first provide a clear description of the predicament—what exactly was the predicament or, rather, how was the predicament perceived. In other words, we must determine why a certain situation was or is considered by policy-makers to be a predicament.
2. The next step, related to the first, is to make an effort to assess the flow of information and intelligence that goes into the formation of the perception of the policymakers: Is there only one source? Which one? Are there many sources? Do they provide the same facts and figures, or do they differ? If they differ, how are differences resolved in accepting one set of information flows and rejecting another?
3. This leads us to our third required piece of information: Which governmental units are most responsible for coping with the predicament? And if it falls (at least technically) within the jurisdiction of more than one, what types of intergovernmental and interunit arrangements exist to allow for a concerted action?
4. At this stage, assuming that the nature and perception of the predicament, the information sources, and the particular governmental units and procedures are known, we need to have a clear statement and description of the action resulting from the decision actually made—for

example an ambassador was recalled; economic aid was offered; an official was bribed; the marines were dispatched.

5. A knowledge of the action taken (or contemplated) must be coupled, at least when analyzing democratic foreign policy-making, with the possession of an unambiguous declaration of the anticipated consequences of the action or decision. The simpler and the smaller the number of consequences anticipated, the easier the evaluation. The greater the number and the more complex the goal, the more difficult the assessment—unless one is able to peel off the rhetoric that often accompanies a decision from its substance, or unless we can establish a set of priorities for goals ranging from the imperative ones through the desirable ones down to the least-expected but simply hoped-for. Such priority assessments are not always easy to make, for the time dimension within which policies are implemented constantly forces reconsideration and reshuffling of priorities.

Only after the above steps have been carefully followed can the analyst survey the actual consequences that flowed from the policies made and arrive at a very quiet, and always highly qualified, verdict.

Our frame of analysis, in other words, is *instrumental,* relating means to ends and linking the two by study of decision-making procedures and intermediate steps. It is based on a power theory of international politics in which the ultimate analysis of "success" and "failure" can be measured in terms of the plusses and minuses in the increments of power and influence for a given nation.

To summarize: Foreign-policy evaluation involves assessment of the goals of a given country; analysis of the various predicaments that seem to endanger these goals; an examination of the instrumentalities (policies) pursued to alleviate the predicaments; a careful examination of the manner in which such policies were formulated, with regard to both the predicament involved and the manner in which the policy was to be implemented; an account of the major governmental organs responsible for the implementation of a policy; a careful examination of the availability of alternate means and instrumentalities (were they considered? were they rejected after being considered, and if so, why?); and finally, an assessment—that is, did the policy as formulated and implemented bring about the desired goals?

GENERAL BIBLIOGRAPHY

ALLISON, GRAHAM T. *Essence of Decision: Explaining the Cuban Missile Crisis.* Boston: Little, Brown, 1971.

ARON, RAYMOND. *A Century of Total War.* Garden City, N.Y.: Doubleday, 1954.

———. *Peace and War: A Theory of International Relations.* Garden City, N.Y.: Doubleday, 1966.

AXELROD, ROBERT. *The Structure of Decision: The Cognitive Maps of Political Elites.* Princeton, N.J.: Princeton University Press, 1976.

BERGSTEN, C. FRED, and LAURENCE R. KRAUSE. *World Politics and International Economics.* Washington, D.C.: Brookings Institution, 1975.

BOULDING, KENNETH. *Conflict and Defense.* New York: Harper & Row, 1961.

BROWN, SEYOM. *The Causes and Prevention of War.* Boston: St. Martin's Press, 1987.

CARNESALE, ALBERT, et al. *Living with Nuclear Weapons,* Bantam Books, NY, 1983.

DESTLER, I. M. *Presidents, Bureaucrats, and Foreign Policy.* Princeton, N.J.: Princeton University Press, 1972.

GILPIN, ROBERT. *War and Change in World Politics.* Cambridge: Cambridge University Press, 1981.

GOLDTHORPE, JOHN H., ed. *Order and Conflict in Contemporary Capitalism.* Oxford: Clarendon Press, 1984.

HALPERIN, MORTON H. *Bureaucratic Politics and Foreign Policy.* Washington, D.C.: Brookings Institution, 1974.

The Harvard Nuclear Study Group (A. Carnesale, Paul Doty, Stanley Hoffmann, Samuel P. Huntington, Joseph S. Nye, Jr., Scott D. Sagan). *Living with Nuclear Weapons.* Cambridge, Mass.: Harvard University Press, 1983.

JARVIS, ROBERT. *Perceptions and Misperceptions in International Politics.* Princeton, N.J.: Princeton University Press, 1976.

KAPLAN, MORTON A., ed. *New Approaches to International Relations.* New York: St. Martin's Press, 1968.

KEGLEY, CHARLES W., JR., EUGENE R. WITTKOPT, eds. *The Nuclear Reader: Strategy, Weapons, War.* New York: St. Martin's Press, 1985.

KEOHANE, ROBERT. *Power and Interdependence: World Politics in Transition.* Boston: Little, Brown, 1977.

KEOHANE, ROBERT, and JOSEPH J. NYE, eds. *Transnational Relations in World Politics.* Cambridge, Mass.: Harvard University Press, 1972.

KISSINGER, HENRY, ed. *Problems of National Strategy.* New York: Praeger, 1965.

MORGENTHAU, HANS J. *Politics Among Nations,* 4th Ed. New York: Knopf, 1967.

NICOLSON, HAROLD. *Diplomacy.* New York: Harcourt, Brace & World, 1933.

ROSENAU, JAMES N. ed. *International Politics and Foreign Policy.* Glencoe, Ill.: Free Press, 1964.

SPANIER, JOHN. *Games Nations Play: Analyzing International Politics.* New York: Praeger, 1972.

SPERO, JOAN. *The Politics of International Economic Relations,* 2d Ed. New York: St. Martin's Press, 1981.

STOESSINGER, JOHN. *Why Nations Go to War,* 3d Ed. New York: St. Martin's Press, 1981.

TAYLOR, CHARLES L., and DAVID A. JORDIES. *World Handbook of Political and Social Indicators,* 3d Ed. New Haven, Conn.: Yale University Press, 1982.

ULLMAN, RICHARD H., and RAYMOND TANTER. *Theory and Policy in International Relations.* Princeton, N.J.: Princeton University Press, 1972.

WALLERSTEIN, IMMANUEL. *The Capitalist World Economy.* New York: Cambridge University Press, 1979.

WALTER, KENNETH N. *Theory of International Politics.* Reading, Mass.: Addison-Wesley, 1978.

WALZER, MICHAEL. *Just and Unjust Wars.* New York: Basic Books, 1977.

Contributing Authors

Robert J. Art is Christian A. Herter Professor of International Relations at Brandeis University and Research Fellow at the Center for International Affairs at Harvard University. He is author of *The TFX Decision: McNamara and the Military* and coeditor of *The Use of Force* and *Reorganizing America's Defenses*. He has published extensively in professional journals.

Vernon V. Aspaturian is Evan Pugh Professor of Political Science and Director of the Slavic and Soviet Area Studies Center at Pennsylvania State University. He is the author of *Process and Power in Soviet Foreign Policy*, *The Soviet Union in the World Communist System*, *The Union Republics in Soviet Diplomacy*, and coauthor of *Euro-Communism Between East and West*. He has also contributed many articles to professional and scholarly journals on Soviet Politics and Foreign Policy.

Josef Joffe is foreign editor of the *Süddeutsche Zeitung*, West Germany's largest quality daily. His most recent book is *The Limited Partnership: Europe, the United States and the Burdens of Alliance* (Ballinger, 1987). He was educated at Swarthmore, Johns Hopkins, and Harvard, and he has taught international politics at the Johns Hopkins School of Advanced International Studies. Previously a senior associate of the Carnegie Endowment for International Peace in Washington, he has written extensively on German foreign and defense policy, European-American relations, strategy, and arms control in professional journals and scholarly collections.

Robert J. Lieber is Professor of Government at Georgetown University. His most recent book is *No Common Power: Understanding International Relations* (Little, Brown, 1988). He is coeditor and contributing author of *Eagle Resurgent: The Reagan Era in American Foreign Policy* (1987), of *Eagle Defiant: U.S. Foreign Policy in the 1980s* (1983), and of *Eagle Entangled: U.S. Foreign Policy in a Complex World* (1979). He is also author of *The Oil Decade* (1986); *Oil and The Mid-East War: Europe in the Energy Crisis* (1976); *Contemporary Politics: Europe* (coauthor, 1976); *Theory and World Politics* (1972); and *British Politics and European Unity* (1970).

Roy C. Macridis is Lawrence Wien Professor of International Cooperation at Brandeis University. He is author of *The De Gaulle Republic—Quest for Unity* (with Bernard E. Brown), *French Politics in Transition—The Years After De Gaulle; Contemporary Political Ideologies—Movements and Regimes*, among many other publications and articles.

Riordan Roett is Professor and Director of the Latin American Studies Program at The Johns Hopkins School of Advanced International Studies in Washington, D.C. He is the author of *Brazil: Politics in a Patrimonial Society*. He and Wolf Grabendorff coedited and coauthored *The United States, Latin America and Western Europe: A New Atlantic Triangle*. Previous books include *The Politics of Foreign Aid in the Brazilian Northeast* and *Brazil in the Seventies*.

Nadav Safran is Murray A. Albertson Professor of Middle East Studies at Harvard. His previous books include *Egypt in Search of Political Community* (Harvard, 1961); *The United States and Israel* (Harvard, 1963); *From War to War: The Arab-Israeli Confrontation 1948–1967* (Pegassus, 1969); *Israel, The Embattled Ally* (Harvard, 1978 and 1981); *Saudi Arabia, The Ceaseless Quest for Security* (Harvard, 1985 and Cornell, 1988).

Robert A. Scalapino is Robson Research Professor of Government, Director of the Institute of East Asian Studies, and Editor of *Asian Survey* at the University of California, Berkeley. In addition to numerous writings, he is also the author of *Democracy and the Party Movement in Pre-War Japan, Parties and Politics in Postwar Japan, The Japanese Communist Movement*, and editor of *The Foreign Policy of Modern Japan*.

Françoise de la Serre is Senior Research Fellow at the International Research Studies Center of the National Foundation of Political Science, University of Paris, France. She is the author of many articles on the foreign policy of the European Community and on European political cooperation and the author of *La Grande Bretagne et la Communauté Européenne*, (Presses Universitaires de France, 1987).

Bengt Sundelius is Associate Professor of Political Science and Director of the International Graduate School at the University of Stockholm. He is the author of *Managing Transnationalism in Northern Europe*, coauthor of *Internationalization and Foreign Policy Management*, and editor of *Foreign Policies of Northern Europe* and *The Neutral Democracies and the New Cold War*.

Allen S. Whiting is Professor of Political Science and Director, Center for East Asian Studies, University of Arizona. He served as Director, Office of Research and Analysis, Department of State (1962–1966) and Deputy Consul General, Hong Kong (1966–1968). He is author of *Soviet Policies Toward China: 1917–1924* (1954); *Sinkiang: Pawn or Pivot?* (coauthor, 1956), *China Crosses the Yalu* (1980); *The Chinese Calculus of Deterrence* (1975); *China's Future* (coauthor, 1977); and *Siberian Development and East Asia* (1981).

1

British Foreign Policy: the Limits of Maneuver

Robert J. Lieber

Contemporary British foreign policy is shaped by a tension between means and ends. That is, the economic, military, and even geographic basis on which Britain's power rests imposes a constraint on her traditional global objectives. As a consequence, British policymakers have repeatedly been forced to grapple with the problem of reconciling Britain's capabilities with its goals.

In recent years, this continuing tension has been evident in such issues as the debate over nuclear versus conventional defense capabilities, the decisions regarding the budget of the European Economic Community, and the allocation of foreign aid.

An analysis of British foreign policy thus begins with the contrast between that country's extraordinary international role—which appeared intact as late as the end of World War II—and the experience of declining power—which the United Kingdom has faced in the decades since 1945.

Viewed from across the Atlantic, Britain has been important to the United States because of its indelible imprint on American history, language, institutions, and culture. At the end of the Second World War, the United Kingdom stood—with the United States and the Soviet Union—as one of the Big Three world powers and victorious allies against Nazi Germany and Japan. Britain rested at the apex of an empire and a commonwealth which spread across vast reaches of the earth. Its troops were stationed around the globe, and the claim to be a major world power was unquestioned. Added to this, the United Kingdom shared a unique partnership with the United States, had played a special part in the development of the American nuclear program, and was one of the key international actors in hammering out the postwar rules and institutions which were to shape the future course of international political and economic life.

Yet departing from this powerful base, the problem for Great Britain during the past four decades has been to adapt its foreign policy to a steady decline in national economic and military power. The need for this adaptation has been caused by both a drop in the relative strength of the United Kingdom itself and by major changes in the configuration of world politics.

The first of these changes saw a shift in the balance of world power away from the European continent itself. European states had been the leading international actors for centuries, and Europe itself the focus of international attention and conflict. But after 1945—and two world wars—there began a global East-West competition in which the United States and the Soviet Union were now the principal players. Although Britain and the other countries of Western Europe remained important, they no longer retained their previous degree of centrality.

Second, strategic military decisions became increasingly based on massive nuclear forces and the capacity of continental-sized countries to muster resources and manpower on a global scale. Here too, Britain and its European neighbors lacked the national scale to deploy forces and economic resources on a level comparable to that of the United States and the USSR. Great Britain, and later France, did develop strategic nuclear weapons, but these capabilities were dwarfed by those of the superpowers.

Third, there was a growing diffusion of power. Large numbers of developing countries, which had hitherto not been significant international actors in their own right, achieved independence or much greater autonomy and importance. In a world of more numerous and widespread actors, the United Kingdom's influence was proportionately reduced.

Fourth, and finally, there was a globalization of the international economy. Here too, the United Kingdom was unable to maintain the kind of primacy which it had previously possessed. At the same time, Britain found itself pressed to compete with the other industrial democracies, whose post-war recovery and development began to challenge and then outpace its own.

Together, these changes created a post–World War II world in which Britain would face a continual problem of declining influence and power. In this environment, the United Kingdom also encountered a series of external constraints which made adaptation difficult and which reduced the country's domain of choice in foreign policy. It is these two major themes, the long-term secular decline in British power, and the constraints which the United Kingdom has faced, that provide the basis for the analysis of British foreign policy which follows.

BRITAIN'S DECLINING WORLD ROLE

While Britain's immediate postwar status eroded, the power and influence of the United States increased dramatically. Indeed, American abandonment of previous peacetime isolationism was in part caused by the need to fill a power vacuum left by the decline in Britain's world role. This is nowhere better symbolized than in the events leading to the Truman Doctrine in February 1947. Britain had been the dominant external power involved in Greece and Turkey. However, increasingly grim economic problems forced the Labour government of Prime Minister Clement Attlee to announce that it would no longer be able to sustain the economic and military aid which Britain had been providing to these two countries. It was United States concern that this British withdrawal would leave Greece and Turkey gravely exposed to internal unrest and to external pressure from the Soviet Union which caused President Truman's historic announcement of major economic and military assistance.

During the late 1940s, the long process of decolonization began. In 1947–1948, Britain granted independence to the countries of the Asian subcontinent—India, Pakistan, and Ceylon. In the decades which followed, its remaining colonies throughout Africa, Asia, and the Caribbean gained independence as well. This decolonization was accomplished with a minimum of violence. There were small conflicts prior to the granting of independence in, for example, Malaya and Kenya, but nothing comparable to the experience of France, which fought long, bloody, and traumatic wars in Indochina and Algeria.

Indeed, British prime ministers of both the major parties, Labour and Conservative, showed considerable foresight in accommodating to the process of decolonization and in seeking to prepare the colonies for independence. Thus Conservative prime minister Harold Macmillan caused a substantial stir in South Africa when he delivered a speech there in 1960 calling for recognition of the "winds of change." Efforts were also made to promote the Westminster model of parliamentary democracy and to leave behind a legacy of British institutions and culture.

Yet, if the British did not find themselves enmeshed in the major wars of the French, there was no dearth of violence after their withdrawal. Former British colonies became the scene of bitter and costly conflicts—and often within a very short interval after the Union Jack was lowered. For example, India and Pakistan experienced repeated hostility and warfare, and major conflicts were fought in Nigeria, Rhodesia (Zimbabwe), and Uganda, as well as between Israel, Egypt, and Jordan.

A watershed for Britain's world role was crossed with the Suez expedition of October 1956. After a protracted and increasingly bitter dispute, President Nasser of Egypt nationalized the Suez Canal and took control of this waterway, which had been formerly owned and operated by Britain. Alarmed by the radical nationalism of the Egyptian president, as well as by Nasser's improving relationship with the Soviet Union, and moved by the memory of Western failures to resist aggression in the 1930s, Conservative prime minister Anthony Eden agreed to a coordinated French and British military operation to retake the Suez Canal. This was launched just after the outbreak of war between Israel and Egypt in the Sinai desert.

The military operation itself proved successful—although with greater delay and difficulty than had been anticipated—but the Eden government immediately faced a grave international crisis. Although the Suez expedition received public support within Britain, despite opposition by the Labour party under Hugh Gaitskell,[1] the action touched off a storm of international criticism. The Soviet Union—itself then in the midst of crushing the Hungarian revolution—bitterly attacked the Anglo-French action and threatened the use of missiles if the British and French failed to withdraw. Much more devastating to Britain, however, was the opposition of the United States under President Eisenhower and Secretary of State John Foster Dulles. The United States joined with the Soviet Union in voting for a United Nations resolution of condemnation. The Americans also refused to come to the aid of the British in response to a growing financial crisis, involving a run on the pound sterling.

In response to political and financial pressure, the British and French were forced into a humiliating withdrawal. This episode left a major legacy of bitterness in Anglo-American relations, with the British remaining resentful at the failure of their Atlantic ally to support them in the midst of a grave crisis. More importantly, however, it marked the last time that the United Kingdom would seek to mount an independent military operation of any consequence without American support (at least until the Falklands War in 1982).

In subsequent years, Britain steadily reduced its remaining global involvement, withdrawing forces from east of Suez (the Middle East and Persian Gulf) in the late 1960s and gradually reducing its military role to modest garrisons in a handful of far-flung outposts. These mostly involved small detachments in minor possessions or former colonies, in-

---

[1]See Leon D. Epstein, *British Politics in the Suez Crisis* (London: Pall Mall Press, and Urbana. Ill.: University of Illinois Press, 1964).

cluding Belize (on the Caribbean coast of South America), Brunei, Cyprus, Gibraltar, and Hong Kong. However, Britain's principal international military commitment remained to NATO in Europe. It deployed in Germany 56,000 troops of the British Army of the Rhine (BAOR).[2]

BRITAIN'S CHOICES: THE "THREE CIRCLES"

In seeking an appropriate world role, postwar leaders such as Winston Churchill and Anthony Eden defined a special place for the United Kingdom. Although the entire country occupied a land area no greater than that of the American state of Oregon, and although its population of some 54 million people left it far smaller than the superpowers, postwar leaders conceived of Britain as possessing a unique role. This role lay at the intersection of three strategic or geopolitical groupings. Although other important countries participated in one or the other of these "three circles," Britain was unique in being the only country to play a key role in all of them.

The first of these three circles encompassed the relationship with the Empire and Commonwealth. The second circle designated the special relationship of England with the United States. The third involved Western Europe. But the problem of Britain's foreign policy adaptation is evident when we consider each of these relationships in turn.

The Commonwealth

As the evolving successor to the British Empire, the Commonwealth became a loose association of former British colonies and possessions. Its members shared a mixed legacy of British institutions, language, and culture, often retained the British monarch as symbolic head of state, included the queen's portrait on their postage stamps, and were governed by elites who themselves had ties of education, politics, or sentiment to the British Isles. For Conservatives, the emphasis here was on past imperial greatness, with a special affinity for the old "white dominions" of Australia, New Zealand, and Canada. In turn, supporters of the Labour and Liberal parties tended to stress the values of the evolving multiracial Commonwealth, with its diversity of political and economic systems and cultures.

Despite these ties, the reality was more symbolic than substantive. These far-flung countries gave increasing priority to their own development and to their regional interests and problems, rather than to links with London. Although Australia, New Zealand, and Canada retained

[2]For specific details, see International Institute for Strategic Studies, *The Military Balance*, 1987–88 (London: IISS, Autumn 1987), p. 82.

considerable affinity with the United Kingdom, the institutional and cultural ties with the newly independent states of Africa and Asia eroded rapidly, especially with the growth of nationalism.

Within the United Kingdom, advocates of a close Commonwealth attachment suggested that this could or should become the focus of Britain's world role. Economic links, in the immediate postindependence period, were often substantial, and most of these states had tied their currencies to the British-led sterling bloc. However, the reality of Britain's international economic role was one of growing trade with Europe as well as the rest of the world. During the 1950s and 1960s, the United Kingdom actually sent a declining percentage of its total exports to the Commonwealth.

Equally important for the Commonwealth countries, Britain was simply too narrow a focus for their own economic activity. By size and population the United Kingdom could not possibly absorb the massive level of exports which the ex-colonies were generating, nor were British firms necessarily the leaders in quality or price for those products or technologies which the Commonwealth countries needed to import. Above all, an early pattern of the United Kingdom as the supplier of manufactured goods in exchange for food and raw materials could no longer reflect the dynamics of economic development occurring outside Europe.

While the Commonwealth continued to exist as a forum for international contact and a modest degree of economic and political influence, it could not function as the predominant arena in which Britain's world role would be exercised.

The Special Relationship with the United States

In its immediate conception, postwar British leaders saw the Atlantic tie, based on history and intimate partnership in two world wars, as perhaps the most important of Britain's international relationships. For some, the sudden emergence of the United States to a position of global power even required that Britain exercise a guiding (or even civilizing) influence: to play "Greece" to America's "Rome." Yet the opportunities for Britain to assume a meaningful role in close partnership with the United States were distinctly limited. They hinged on special circumstances of the immediate postwar period and of the personal experience and ties of leaders such as Churchill, Eden, Macmillan, and Eisenhower.

Current analyses of Anglo-American (as well as European-American) relations usually rest on the assumption that the postwar pattern of close alliance relations, under United States leadership, is the benchmark from which any deviation must be measured. Yet, as the British experience reflects, the period which began in the late 1940s was itself an innovation. World War II had seen the development of a close association between the United States and the United Kingdom, embodied in the strong personal relationship between Roosevelt and Churchill. However, despite the appearance of parity with the United States and the USSR, Britain was poised on the edge of a precipitous decline from global and imperial power. In these circumstances, any attraction for the United States in a privileged relationship with the United Kingdom was bound to diminish.

For Britain, on the other hand, the link with the United States in many ways exerted the greatest attraction among the alternatives seemingly available. Yet well before the Suez crisis, and even at the height of British-American cooperation, there had been simultaneous friction. During World War II, for example, there were tensions over cooperative development of the atomic bomb and postwar control of atomic energy. In 1946, the United States imposed as an essential loan condition that the United Kingdom agree to the convertibility of sterling. This stipulation led to a financial fiasco when Britain attempted to implement the measure on July 15, 1947. The resulting run on the pound forced the United Kingdom to suspend convertibility only five weeks later.

Ironically, at the time of Britain's internal debate over seeking Common Market entry in 1960–1961, the United States encouraged Britain toward the European option. For both the Eisenhower and Kennedy administrations, a close relationship with the United Kingdom was more attractive if the British were to become full and active members of the European Community.

Britain and Europe

The wartime experience of having emerged as one of the victorious Big Three powers and, alone among the Western European countries, being neither defeated nor occupied during the course of World War II, left Britain resistant to early attempts at creating a unified Europe.[3] Successive British governments in the late 1940s and throughout the 1950s missed a series of historic opportunities to participate in the formation of the Common Market. Only in 1961, when it had become painfully clear that other major alternatives were unavailable, did the government of Conservative prime minister Harold Macmillan at last seek formal membership in the European Community.

Yet despite the British decision to negotiate, the actual process of gaining Common Market entry proved protracted and painful. In January 1963, French president Charles de Gaulle vetoed Britain's application on the grounds that the United Kingdom was not yet ready for membership, and because he viewed Britain as too closely aligned with the United

[3]Robert J. Lieber, *British Politics and European Unity: Parties, Elites and Pressure Groups* (Berkeley, Calif.: University of California Press, 1970).

States. Not until after de Gaulle's death in 1969 and subsequent agreement between Prime Minister Edward Heath and French president Georges Pompidou was Britain at last able to gain entry. But by the time of formal accession in 1973, much of the initial European momentum had dissipated, and Britain itself continued to experience deep internal divisions over the wisdom and terms of membership.

In 1974, a British Labour government took office with a position unsympathetic to the Common Market. After renegotiating the terms and cost of Britain's membership, it held an unprecedented national referendum. In the face of a divided Labour party, but with support from Liberals and Conservatives, the June 1975 referendum endorsed continued British participation by a margin of two to one. This temporarily resolved the internal legitimacy of Britain's participation, but successive governments continued to find themselves absorbed in struggles over the European Community budget. Indeed, as late as the general election of 1982, the opposition Labour party resorted to a position of out-right hostility toward Europe. By the time of the 1987 election, however, Labour finally accepted a commitment to remain within the Common Market.

Britain's participation in Europe did provide a wider forum for its energies and influence. Within the Common Market, the United Kingdom was one of the three leading powers (along with France and the Federal Republic of Germany) in an important grouping of international economic and political stature. This gave greater weight to British views on major international questions than if no such link existed. On the other hand, the initial enthusiasm of many British and continental leaders proved to be exaggerated. Despite its economic size and visibility, the Common Market did not provide the nascent European identity needed to redress the erosion of European and British power in the postwar world. This was nowhere more evident than in the continuing problems of military security and in the experience of the two great oil shocks of the 1970s.

THE EUROPEAN SECURITY CONSTRAINT

Any consideration of British foreign policy and bilateral Anglo-American relations is most usefully undertaken against the broader background of European security. The central question here concerns the necessity and durability of the Atlantic connection. That is, are the contemporary problems that bedevil European-American relations a phenomenon which could irreparably damage or even destroy the postwar alliance? Or are the allies experiencing inevitable tensions that stem from deep-seated historical, geographical, political, and economic sources, but which will remain a manageable fact of life and which will continue to constrain British and European room for maneuver?

The former view has been forcefully expressed by a number of observers. For example, Robert W. Tucker concludes a study of the Atlantic Alliance with a series of pessimistic observations: "The transatlantic compact has not held. The critics are largely justified in their visions of a dark future. . . . The alliance is visibly unravelling today, and the rising tempo of its disintegration can fail to impress only the most determined of optimists."[4]

If the above assessment is accurate, then consideration of the British component is mainly of interest for determining whether a significant bilateral United States–United Kingdom tie may survive the disintegration of the alliance. Yet there are compelling reasons for seeing the Atlantic connection as more durable. If these are valid, then understanding of the limits and tensions in the American-British relationship can improve our appreciation of differences which are bound to continue as long as the alliance itself exists.

In fact, the Alliance, as well as the broader array of United States–European relationships, has been characterized by internal disagreements and crises virtually since its inception.[5] The present round of Alliance problems should not cause us to forget that this has long been a "troubled partnership."[6] Disputes across the Atlantic have been common, and the early 1980s controversy aroused by the stationing of 160 American cruise missiles in Britain was by no means unique. During the late 1950s, for example, the British peace movement seemed to be leading the Labour party toward a policy of unilateral nuclear disarmament, in sharp contradiction of prevailing American-British links. The early 1960s also saw growing European-American friction over trade and monetary policy. In 1966, President de Gaulle's withdrawal of France from the NATO integrated military command seemed to shake both the political and strategic foundations of the Atlantic Alliance. The Vietnam War—to which neither Britain nor any of the European allies committed troops or political support—also caused serious political differences across the Atlantic. In August 1971, the Nixon-Connally economic measures marked a period of grave economic friction among the advanced industrial countries. And,

---

[4]Robert W. Tucker, ed., *The Atlantic Alliance and Its Critics* (New York: Praeger, 1983), p. 188. Also see Theodore Draper, "The Phantom Alliance," Ibid., pp. 1–27; and Pierre Lellouche, "Does NATO Have a Future?", Ibid., pp. 129–154.

[5]See, for example, A.W. DePorte, "The Uses of Perspective," in Tucker, *The Atlantic Alliance,* pp. 29–59.

[6]The term originates in Henry Kissinger, *The Troubled Partnership: A Reappraisal of the Atlantic Alliance* (New York: McGraw-Hill, 1965). Consider also the early and deep-seated resentment over German rearmament, culminating in the 1954 French rejection of the European Defense Community. This caused John Foster Dulles, then secretary of state, to threaten an "agonizing reappraisal" of America's links with Europe.

beginning in 1973, Britain and France found themselves at loggerheads with the United States over the Yom Kippur War, the Arab oil embargo, and subsequent problems of energy security. Even the American bombing of Libya on April 15, 1986, in retaliation for Colonel Qaddafi's sponsorship of international terrorism, caused a certain degree of friction. Whereas the U.S. action received the support of Prime Minister Thatcher, in that she allowed the use of American F-111 bombers based in Britain for the air strike, the majority of public opinion in the United Kingdom was, nevertheless, not sympathetic. In short, the list of past disputes between the United States and Europe is a long one.

Moreover, the causes of these tensions are many and deep-rooted. In the realm of defense, they include British and European anxiety over the risks of becoming a battlefield—whether nuclear or conventional—as well as concern over the credibility of American security guarantees in view of strategic nuclear parity between the United States and the USSR. In economic affairs, differences arise over Europe's greater dependence on international trade as well as its sensitivity to changes in American fiscal and monetary policies. During the early 1980s, for example, high American real interest rates and record strength in the value of the dollar—which for the first time in history saw the pound slip below $1.10 in early 1985—were seen as causes of impaired economic growth, increased costs for imported raw materials, and continued inflation. Conversely, in 1986 and 1987, as the dollar reversed course and fell more than 40 percent in value against the pound, as well as against the other major currencies of Europe and Japan, an entirely different set of financial concerns began to be expressed. Geography also continued to underlie differences of perspective, as did disagreements over regional problems in non-NATO areas.

Disputes are thus an inevitable part of Anglo-American and American-European relations. Yet despite periodic crises, a set of intrinsic needs and basic interests creates a powerful allied bond. This tie may not be impregnable—what international relationships endure in perpetuity?—but it is certainly more robust than is often assumed.

What then are the basic factors which hold the United States and Britain together? The most important of these result from the postwar division of Europe and Germany. There is little reason to anticipate any change in this bifurcation of the Continent. Nor, unfortunately, is Soviet domination of Eastern Europe likely to end in the near future, despite the perennial unrest experienced by Soviet-supported regimes and the impact of Gorbachev's policy of Glasnost. As long as these circumstances persist, and along with them the reality of Soviet military power, Britain and the other countries of Western Europe are virtually compelled to rely on the United States to guarantee their security.

In essence, both the conventional and nuclear deterrence of the ɔoviet Union, and, hence, the maintenance of a stable balance of power in Europe, require the American presence. In the words of a Conservative defense minister, Michael Heseltine, "There can be no coherent strategy to defend Europe without America. There is no more evident manifestation of American support for this view than the 500,000 American men and their families serving in Europe."[7] It would require profound change to end this division of Europe and the concomitant need for an American commitment. One such change would be removal of the Soviet threat to Western Europe as well as a waning of its imperial presence in Eastern Europe. Yet this is hardly conceivable in the absence of a profound internal change within the USSR itself. Alternatively, the Western Europeans could provide a credible defense and deterrent effort of their own, commensurate with their levels of wealth and population. Indeed, since the early 1960s, there have been repeated suggestions that the British nuclear deterrent, along with that of France, could be somehow developed into the basis for a truly European defense.

But despite periodic proposals for this defense cooperation—which constitute a recognition that there can be no real British and European international security autonomy without control of the means for their own nuclear and conventional defense—no major achievements to this end have been accomplished. Such a step would require the attainment of a far-reaching European political and institutional unity, within which Britain would play a major role. However, this development remains extremely unlikely. In addition to the obstacles to greater political development of the European Community and to a more vigorous and committed British role, the prohibition on Germany's possession of nuclear weapons also works against any major change. Hence, in the absence of Soviet withdrawal or creation of a unified Europe, only the political collapse of Western Europe or its effective neutralization could alter the present structure on which the Atlantic Alliance is based. Despite the anxieties of some observers,[8] this too is extremely improbable.

In sum, Britain and Europe need the United States, but American commitment to the security of Europe is no mere act of altruism. From the standpoint of the United States, the defense of Europe involves a vital American self-interest. A world in which the Soviet Union exercised effective domination over the territory, population, and productive resources of Western Europe would be extremely threatening to the United States and would imply a disastrous tilt in the global balance of power. Indeed, the importance of Europe exceeds that of other areas which have

---

[7]Statement to the House of Commons, 19 July 1983, "The Defense Estimates," *Policy Statements* (New York: British Information Service, July 1983).

[8]Irving Kristol, for example, holds that neither the United States nor the allies can rely on each other in case of war. "The Western Misalliance," *The Washington Quarterly,* Winter 1981.

so preoccupied American policymakers in the past decade. Thus, even the Reagan administration's secretary of defense, Caspar Weinberger, acknowledged that the maintenance of United States forces in Europe is not an act of charity.[9]

THE BRITISH NUCLEAR DETERRENT

In seeking to preserve its own strategic forces, Britain has maintained an independent nuclear deterrent. However, despite its early status in nuclear technology and development of its own atomic bomb through a program begun in 1947, the United Kingdom has relied heavily on the United States. After the termination of wartime cooperation in atomic weapons development, Britain was accorded privileged access to United States nuclear secrets during the 1950s under the MacMahon Act.

In 1960, after problems with its own Blue Streak missile program, the United Kingdom committed itself to the purchase of the American air-launched Skybolt missile. But the British government received a shock when the United States cancelled the program in 1962. As a result, at a celebrated Anglo-American summit meeting at Nassau in the Bahamas in December of that year, President John F. Kennedy agreed with Prime Minister Harold Macmillan that the United States would provide American Polaris missiles for use with British-designed nuclear warheads in British nuclear submarines. It was this Nassau Agreement, with its intensified British security reliance on the United States, that helped to trigger the de Gaulle veto of Britain's Common Market application a month later. France had pursued its own nuclear deterrent program on a costly but independent basis, and Britain's new reliance on American warheads was sharply at odds with de Gaulle's conception of European autonomy.

In the late 1970s and early 1980s, Britain faced an internal debate about how to or whether to maintain its strategic nuclear deterrent. In addition to a force of medium-range aircraft, this force was based primarily on four nuclear-powered submarines, each with sixteen Polaris missiles (with each missile carrying three nuclear warheads—though these were not independently targettable). However, the submarines were to reach the end of their life span in the mid-1990s, and Britain therefore faced a choice of whether to modernize its submarine force, to rely on some other principal means of delivery (such as land-based or sea-based cruise missiles), or to abandon its independent nuclear deterrent altogether.

---

[9]"U.S. forces are maintained in Europe directly in support of U.S. political and military interests—not as an act of charity toward our Allies." Caspar W. Weinberger, secretary of defense, *Annual Report to the Congress, Fiscal Year 1984* (Washington, D.C.: February 1, 1983), p. 187.

The decision, together with a planned deployment of American-controlled cruise missiles in Britain, touched off a major public debate. This was in part reminiscent of a controversy more than two decades earlier, when a large peace movement argued for giving up nuclear weapons altogether. During the British general election of June 1983, the opposition Labour party advocated abandoning the British nuclear deterrent.

The party had once before taken such a position, in 1959, but this had been reversed the following year under the leadership of the late Hugh Gaitskell. This time, however, although Labour remained sharply divided internally, the party reaffirmed the "unconditional" nature of the commitment at its annual party conference in October 1983. This position helped to give British voters a sense that Labour lacked a serious defense policy. Along with the inept leadership of Michael Foot, who led a bitterly divided party during the election campaign, and burdened with a highly unpopular party platform, this contributed to Labour's worst national election defeat in half a century.

Under Foot's more popular (though less experienced) successor, Neil Kinnock, the Labour party remained a significant force in British politics. Due to the British electoral system, Labour also managed to withstand the challenge of a newly created centrist alliance. The Social Democratic and Liberal parties won nearly as many votes in the 1983 election as the Labour party (25.4 percent versus 27.6 percent for Labour), but as a result of the single member district system, they gained only a handful of seats in parliament (23 as against 209 for Labour and 397 for the Conservatives).[10]

Subsequently, in the June 1987 general election, Labour again called for the unilateral nuclear disarmament of Britain as well as the ouster of American nuclear bases from the United Kingdom.[11] Although Labour's defense policy did reaffirm the British commitment to NATO, and even called for an increase in the country's nonnuclear forces, the party's defense policy was widely rejected by the electorate. The Conservative government of Prime Minister Thatcher won reelection with 43 percent of the popular vote and 376 seats in Parliament, for a 102 seat majority. Labour received 32 percent of the vote and 229 seats, while the uneasy coalition of the Social Democratic–Liberal Party Alliance slipped to 23 percent of the vote and just 22 seats.

The Conservative government of Margaret Thatcher, which initially had won office in 1979, opted to purchase Trident missiles from the United States after its 1983 reelection victory. This decision was made

[10]Data from the 1983 general election are available in *The Economist* (London), 18 June 1983, pp. 33–36.

[11]See, "Britain will win," *The Labour Party Manifesto*, British General Election Campaign of 1987 (New York: British Information Services, May 1987), 211/87.

over the opposition of the Labour party. Ultimately, this £8 billion commitment* would involve four nuclear submarines, each with sixteen American-supplied D-5 missiles, each missile carrying eight independently targettable warheads of high accuracy and long range.

This maintenance of an independent nuclear deterrent would give Britain a potentially powerful force of some 512 nuclear warheads by the late 1990s and thus a claim to a continued role in international participation and recognition among the world's great powers (the other recognized members of the "nuclear club" being the United States, the USSR, China, and France). Yet the constraints upon the United Kingdom meant that it encountered trade-offs in making this decision. The program was costly, making Britain less able to meet commitments for conventional defense forces, especially the army and navy.[12]

As the Falklands War in the spring of 1982 demonstrated, the United Kingdom now had great difficulty in deploying forces at a distance from its shores. Britain had been on the verge of selling its last major aircraft carrier—which would have left it unable to project power several thousand miles into the South Atlantic where the fighting with Argentina occurred. This reduction in forces had accompanied a decision to concentrate primarily on a European role, in which British naval forces would be used mainly in the North Atlantic, and for antisubmarine purposes in coordination with the United States and other NATO allies.

In addition, the Trident decision once more made evident Britain's close dependence on the United States in security matters. Although ties of interest, sentiment, and belief were likely in any case to insure a close Anglo-American relationship, this dependence suggested very real limits on the extent of British autonomy in future defense policy and strategy.

INTERNATIONAL ECONOMIC CONSTRAINTS

The international economic environment has played an especially compelling role in circumscribing Britain's room for maneuver in foreign policy. During the immediate postwar years, cutbacks in British overseas commitments were forced by problems of cost and of economic recovery. In later years, and especially throughout the late 1950s and much of the 1960s, Britain faced a perennial problem of maintaining the exchange rate of its currency, the pound sterling, at its then fixed value of $2.80. Britain sought to preserve the value of the pound in order to maintain

*At the exchange rate of £1 = $1.77, as of January 1988, this was equivalent to more than $14 billion.

[12]See the thoughtful analysis by Arthur Cyr, "Britain: National Defense, NATO Obligations and the Trident Decision," in Catherine M. Kelleher and Gale Mattox, eds., *Evolving European Defense Policies* (Lexington, Mass.: Lexington Books, 1987), pp. 205–222.

the international role of sterling—thought to be an important source of prestige and influence for Britain—as well as to retain a basis of economic association for many countries of the Commonwealth. Fixed exchange rates were also thought to be important for international economic stability.

The cost of this policy, however, was severe. At a time when the other advanced industrial countries were experiencing remarkably strong economic growth, Britain faced a problem. Whenever its domestic economic growth sharply increased, this would cause a major rise in imported goods, thus moving the country's international balance of payments toward a deficit. But this in turn brought the value of the pound under pressure, forcing the government to support it. One of the most damaging methods of doing so was by deflating the economy in order to reduce imports and ease pressure on the balance of payments. Directly and indirectly, by reducing growth and investment, this policy had the effect of sacrificing longer-term expansion of the British economy as well as the modernization of British industry.[13] To be sure, other factors were also involved, including problems of outmoded plants and equipment, and attitudes of both management and the trade unions.

As Table 1.1 illustrates, Britain paid a serious price in economic growth. From 1960 to 1973, gross national product increased at a real annual rate of 3.2 percent, compared with 4.8 percent in Germany, 5.7 percent in France, and 10.5 percent in Japan. This performance explains the relative decline in Britain's economic position, as the country's stand-

TABLE 1.1 Average Annual Growth of Real GDP/GNP (%)

	1960–1973*	1974–1985**	1986–1988**
Japan	10.5	3.8	3.6
France	5.7	2.2	2.8
Canada	5.4	2.9	3.0
Italy	5.2	2.2	2.6
Fed. Rep. of Germany	4.8	1.9	2.6
United States	4.2	2.3	2.7
United Kingdom	3.2	1.1	2.2

*Source: Adapted from David Calleo, *The Imperious Economy* (Cambridge, Mass.: Harvard University Press, 1982), p. 204.
**Source: Adapted from International Monetary Fund, *World Economic Outlook,* (Washington, D.C. April 1987), p. 56.

13See Stephen Blank, "Britain: The Politics of Foreign economic Policy" and "The Domestic Economy and the Problem of Pluralistic Stagnation," in Peter J. Katzenstein, ed., *Between Power and Plenty: Foreign Economic Policies of Advanced Industrial States* (Madison, Wis.: University of Wisconsin Press, 1978), pp. 89–137.

ing in per capita gross national product fell behind that of most advanced countries in Western Europe as well as Japan.

As late as 1960, Britain had a GNP per capita slightly higher than its major competitors in Europe, and almost three times that of Japan. Yet two decades later, the United Kingdom had been substantially outdistanced not only by Germany (with a figure nearly 50 percent higher than that of Britain) and France, but even by Japan. (See Table 1.2.)

Despite devaluation of the pound in 1967, which the Labour government of Harold Wilson had spent several years attempting to avoid, Britain's international economic problems continued.[14] These included the effort to maintain markets for British goods and services abroad in order to earn the foreign exchange to pay for imports of food and raw materials. With the development of North Sea oil in the late 1970s, Britain became a net oil exporter. However, while alleviating balance of payments problems, this only partially offset the country's other problems of high inflation, low productivity and investment, and lagging economic growth.

The impact of these economic constraints on British foreign policy can be illustrated by a series of disputes which affected Britain's relations with the United States. These occurred despite very considerable political congruence between successive administrations in Washington and Whitehall. Though the overlap was not wholly symmetrical, there was a consid-

TABLE 1.2 GNP Per Capita

	1960*		1980**		1985***
United States	$2817	Fed. Rep. of Germany	$13,410	United States	$16,690
Canada	2196	France	12,300	Canada	13,680
United Kingdom	1357	United States	11,540	Japan	11,300
France	1336	Canada	10,310	Germany	10,940
Fed. Rep. of Germany	1300	Japan	9,400	France	9,540
Italy	701	United Kingdom	9,080	United Kingdom	8,460
Japan	463	Italy	6,600	Italy	6,520

*Based on current prices and exchange rates. Source: U.S. Department of Commerce, *Statistical Abstract of the U.S. (1971)*, in Calleo, *The Imperious Economy*, p. 204.

**Data from national currencies at average 1980 exchange rates. Source: National Foreign Assessment Center, *Handbook of Economic Statistics, 1981.* (Washington, D.C.: November 1981), p. 14.

***World Bank, *World Development Report 1987* (Washington D.C.: The World Bank, and New York: Oxford University Press, 1987), pp. 202–3.

[14]The impact of the sterling problem on Labour governments was especially serious. See Robert J. Lieber, "Labour in Power: Problems of Political Economy," in Bernard E. Brown, ed., *Eurocommunism and Eurosocialism: The European Left Confronts Modernity* (New York: Cyrco Press, 1979), pp. 181–209.

erable parallel of leadership between Conservative prime minister Edward Heath and Republican presidents Richard Nixon and Gerald Ford, between Labour prime minister James Callaghan and Democrat Jimmy Carter, and between Conservative Margaret Thatcher and Republican Ronald Reagan—that is, a correspondence between successive governments which were center-right, center-left, and then assertedly conservative. The fact that problems occurred even during these periods of congruence suggests that the tensions are triggered by significant international constraints that impose themselves upon any British government and thus constitute underlying differences of interest.

Three distinct examples of United States–United Kingdom frictions stand out during the past decade. These include reactions to the October 1973 Yom Kippur War and the 1973–1974 oil crisis, differences over sanctions against Iran after the seizure of American hostages in November 1979, and disagreement over European purchases of Soviet natural gas and the sale of European pipeline equipment to the USSR in 1981–1982.

The successive governments of Prime Minister Margaret Thatcher pursued economic policies that differed in important respects from those of previous Labour and even Conservative governments. In reaction to a period of some three decades in which Britain's growth fell behind that of the other industrial democracies (the countries of the OECD), Prime Minister Thatcher sought to open the British economy to a greater degree of international competition and to sell off many of the nationalized industries.

At one level, the Thatcher policies were a qualified success in that Britain's rate of real economic growth did improve (relative to its competitors) during the mid-1980s. However, this growth was purchased at a price: to some extent it was reflected the unusual severity of the 1980–1981 recession in Britain, to which the Thatcher government's monetary policies contributed. Thus, despite a notable increase, manufacturing output remained lower in June 1987 than it had been in 1979. Still more important, unemployment in 1986 amounted to more than 3.2 million persons, a level unparalleled in Britain's post–World War II experience. For 1987, the U.K.'s average unemployment rate of 10.75 percent was the same as those of France and Italy.[15]

The 1973–1974 Crisis

The outbreak of the October 1973 Yom Kippur War found the United States and Britain with sharply divergent positions. Britain was unsympathetic to American support for Israel, and the Heath govern-

---

[15]Unemployment statistics from OECD, *Economic Outlook* (Paris: December 1987), no. 42, p. 28.

ment embargoed spare parts for British-supplied Israeli Centurion tanks. United States planes were not allowed to use British bases in either the resupply of Israel or in battlefield surveillance activities. Indeed, after the war, Secretary of State Henry Kissinger complained to Britain's Sir Alec Douglas-Home that the Soviet Union had been freer to use NATO airspace than the United States, since much of the Soviet airlift to Egypt and Syria overflew allied airspace without being challenged.[16]

While France, under the leadership of Gaullist president Georges Pompidou and Foreign Minister Michel Jobert, adopted a more abrasive and antagonistic posture, the Conservative British government of Edward Heath also took a number of positions that contradicted the policies favored by President Nixon and Secretary of State Kissinger. These included (briefly) a tacit willingness to observe the Arab oil embargo against the Netherlands. The United Kingdom also cooperated in the admission of five Arab foreign ministers to the EC summit meeting in Copenhagen on December 14–15, 1973,[17] thereby granting a special access which the United States had long sought without success. Ultimately the Heath government did side with the American-sponsored effort to establish cooperation among oil-consuming countries and to create what ultimately became the International Energy Agency. However, the British did so only after a series of bilateral efforts at special deals with Arab oil producers and other measures which exhibited little European—let alone Atlantic—solidarity.

Iranian Hostage Sanctions

Following the seizure of the United States Embassy in Teheran on 4 November 1979, Britain and the other Common Market countries supported American efforts to gain the hostages' release.[18] They also backed a series of measures aimed at exerting pressure on Iran. On January 13, 1980, Britain and France voted for the UN Security Council Resolution—vetoed by the Soviet Union—which would have imposed extensive sanctions on Iran.

In the spring of 1980, after a series of diplomatic efforts had failed to secure the release of the hostages, the heads of government of the European Community countries approved a sanctions policy. However, implementation of the measures required approval by the individual governments and national parliaments. At this point, the Conservative government of Prime Minister Margaret Thatcher, which had come to office in May of the previous year, began to weaken in its resolve.

---

[16]Henry Kissinger, *Years of Upheaval* (Boston: Little, Brown, 1982), p. 709.

[17]Robert J. Lieber, *Oil and the Middle East War: Europe in the Energy Crisis* (Cambridge, Mass.: Harvard Center for International Affairs, 1976), p. 18.

[18]Robert J. Lieber, *The Oil Decade: Conflict and Cooperation in the West* (Lanham, Md.: University Press of America, 1986).

The proposed EC sanctions would have applied to export contracts dating from the time of the hostage seizure. These measures were a retreat from the UN resolution, which excluded only food and medicine from the trade embargo. Yet, despite strong moral support for the Americans, the Thatcher government did not give strong backing to the sanctions when they came before Parliament. Thus, despite a substantial Conservative working majority of some forty seats, the House of Commons rejected the measures in their proposed form. Instead, the legislation was revised to take effect only from May 30, 1980, rather than from the time of the hostage seizure, and to apply only to new contracts by traders not previously involved in a given type of business with Iran. As a result, less than 10 percent of Britain's trade with Iran was at stake. Not least, the revised measures protected the Iranian contract of Britain's faltering Talbot automobile firm, and with it the jobs of Talbot's British employees.

At the same time, Britain under the Thatcher government proved to be one of the primary gainers in trade with the USSR. The Carter administration had reacted to the Soviet invasion of Afghanistan in December 1979 by restricting technology and grain exports. Thus, in 1980, total United States exports to the USSR dropped by 54 percent as compared with 1979. Yet, in the same period, British exports *increased* by 67 percent—a figure substantially higher than those enjoyed by France (35 percent), the Federal Republic of Germany (32 percent), or Japan (25 percent).[19]

The Soviet Natural Gas Pipeline and United States Sanctions

During 1981, the Reagan administration had become sharply critical of Western European plans to buy increased amounts of natural gas from the USSR, as well as to supply substantial amounts of equipment and technology to be used in construction of the pipeline. At first, this opposition was based on a concern about the possibility of Soviet energy blackmail against Western Europe. Subsequently, United States concern shifted to denying the benefits of major hard currency earnings to the Soviets.

In December 1981, reacting to the imposition of martial law in Poland and to Soviet responsibility for repression there, the Reagan administration imposed a series of sanctions measures. These were designed to impede construction of the pipeline, by preventing United States firms from exporting pipe-laying machinery and turbine rotors (used in pipeline pumping stations). However, the restrictions were also extended to three European firms which manufactured equipment in association with the American firm of General Electric. In addition to West German and

[19]U.S. Congress, Office of Technology Assessment, *Technology and Soviet Energy Availability*, (Washington, D.C.: November 1981), p. 379.

Italian companies, the British company of John Brown was affected by the measures.

Although Britain, as an exporter of petroleum and major producer of natural gas, was not a potential purchaser of Soviet gas, it was directly involved through major contracts for pipeline equipment. The issue became more sharply delineated in June 1982 when the Reagan administration intensified its sanctions, in this case applying them to foreign subsidiaries of American firms as well as to foreign companies that held United States licenses. Among those affected by this new decision were companies in France, the Federal Republic of Germany, Italy, as well as the United Kingdom.

While Prime Minister Thatcher and leading members of her government shared many of the instincts and policy preferences of the Reagan administration, especially toward the Soviet Union, the British diverged sharply over the American measures. Along with the other Western European governments affected, British leaders opposed the United States position and directed their companies (including John Brown Ltd., which held a $350 million contract) to comply with British rather than American law and to proceed with the work.

Britain's trade secretary, Lord Cockfield, described the American export embargo as "an unacceptable extension of American extraterritorial jurisdiction." He invoked the Protection of Trading Interests Act of 1980, and declared that the attempted United States controls were "damaging to the trading interests of the United Kingdom."[20] Prime Minister Thatcher even declared that Britain felt "deeply wounded" by the United States actions, and that "I feel very strongly that once you have made a deal you ought to keep it." She added that, in view of continuing American wheat sales to the USSR, the allied burden was being shared unequally. Other British government officials noted that the government was "determined to defend the United Kingdom's national interest."[21] Ultimately, the abrasive allied dispute ended when the American government abandoned its sanctions measures in November 1982.

THE ROOTS OF BRITISH-AMERICAN FRICTION

British differences with the United States during the past decade have not been limited to the three occasions considered above. Thus, to cite

[20]British Information Service, *Survey of Current Affairs*, Vol. 12, No. 8, (New York: August 1982), p. 266; *Financial Times* (London), July 1, 1982.

[21]Quotations from *New York Times*, July 2, 1982, and *Washington Post*, September 11, 1982.

more recent examples, the Thatcher government reacted sharply to the Reagan administration's imposition of quotas and tariffs on the export of European specialty steels to the United States. Prime Minister Thatcher described the action as "deplorable."[22] At the same time, the British minister for trade, Paul Channon, added a complaint about the United States Export Administration Act, which had come before Congress for renewal in July 1983. Channon criticized the extraterritoriality aspects of the act and added, "It is unacceptable to us—and I stress that this is still a dispute among friends—for the United States or anyone else to extend its laws into our country and to dictate to British companies whom they shall and shall not trade with."[23]

Although successive British governments have often stood in closer proximity to the United States position than have other European governments, the United Kingdom has often lined up with its Common Market partners when disputes pitted the Europeans against the Americans. Why?

The answer is not difficult to fathom: The pursuit of British national interests leads to periodic policy disagreements with allies. Some disputes are virtually inevitable, especially when the stakes appear to be "zero-sum," as they can be on certain economic issues. For example, export markets and jobs can pose highly visible issues of the *who-gets-what* variety. Thus British unwillingness to forgo industrial export contracts with Iran was a root cause of the Thatcher government's unwillingness or inability to secure parliamentary approval for a tougher sanctions policy in 1980. And again, during the allied dispute over the Soviet gas pipeline, the British government was unwilling to relinquish an export contract for pipeline machinery. To be sure, the latter case also involved symbolic and political components, especially in terms of opposition to a perceived intrusion of American law into European and British internal affairs.

This suggests another cause of friction in American-British (and allied) relations, that is, on some occasions, it is the perception—accurate or not—of sovereignty or of a national interest which is at stake. Symbolic British and European positions on Middle East issues, fed by anxiety over energy security, are one such example, as was United States policy over the gas pipeline. Assertive defense of British national interests in the Falkland Islands War with Argentina provides another instance. Though in this case there was support by the United States for the British position, the subsequent evolution of British defense policy had the effect of diverting some 70 percent of Britain's naval strength toward the South

[22]The U.S. Steel Import Restrictions, *Policy Statements*, (New York: British Information Service, July 8, 1983), 14/83, p. 1.

[23]Ibid., pp. 2–3.

Atlantic and consequently away from NATO—at least temporarily—to the detriment of common allied interests.

The impulses of sovereignty or of self-interest, and the specific policy choices which they engender, may or may not work to the benefit of the country involved. Whatever the case, the resultant allied frictions have been no less real. All the same, Britain's foreign policy relationship to the United States has continued to remain close. Illustratively, during the expansion of America's naval involvement in the Persian Gulf during 1987, the United Kingdom increased its own role, in cooperation with the United States, while providing political support for American efforts at the United Nations aimed at halting the Iran-Iraq War. The case of the Soviet-American INF Treaty provides another useful illustration. Throughout the lengthy period of East-West negotiations, British leaders, along with those of France, successfully insisted that their own nuclear forces could not be included in the Soviet-American arms reductions. Following the signing of the treaty in December 1987, Britain supported the arms control measure. At the same time, while also responding sympathetically to French suggestions for a stronger European pillar in the Atlantic Alliance, the British government continued to stress that this must not come at the expense of a reduced U.S. role in NATO nor to the detriment of the Anglo-American special relationship.

CONCLUSION

In recent years, reassessments of European-American relations have proliferated. The rediscovery of West-West relations as a matter for serious attention and analysis is amply justified, given the weighty agenda of problems in defense policy (both nuclear and conventional), economics, East-West strategy, and disagreements vis-à-vis non-NATO areas.

In this context, consideration of the United States-United Kingdom relationship provides valuable insights concerning the broader European-American pattern. Specifically, previous studies by this author and others have focused on the limits of national autonomy experienced by the European powers. In the case of France, for example,[24] these analyses have explored the constraints on French freedom of maneuver in foreign and defense policy, in international economic policy, and in dealing with problems of energy and the Middle East. Where the Federal Republic of

[24]See, for example, Stanley Hoffmann, *Decline or Renewal? France Since the 1930s* (New York: Viking, 1974), p. viii; Edward Morse, *Foreign Policy and Interdependence in Gaullist France* (Princeton, N.J.: Princeton University Press, 1973); Edward A. Kolodziej, *French International Policy under de Gaulle and Pompidou* (Ithaca, N.Y.: Cornell University Press, 1974); and Robert J. Lieber, *The Oil Decade*, especially chapter 5.

Germany is concerned, the familiar themes of security dependence on the United States, the weight of history (not least the horrors of Nazism and World War II), the division of Germany, the renunciation of access to nuclear weapons, the deep involvement of Germany in the international economy, and the proximity to the Soviet Union all profoundly condition and constrain the range of foreign policy choices.[25]

The British experience, however, ought to shed light on another dimension of alliance relationships. In addition to reflecting the constraints on autonomy or on freedom of maneuver, its additional value lies in illuminating the limits to the closeness of the relationship between the United States and one of its principal European allies. In short, gaining some sense of these boundaries can be as important as understanding the limits of autonomy. Great Britain, after all, has been and still is one of the closest, if not *the* closest, of United States allies. To examine the constraints on this relationship, even when the basic tie is not in real doubt, should thus suggest what degree of distance is inevitable among allies, even under the best of circumstances.

Just as there are limits to the autonomy or room for maneuver of the Western European countries, and hence to the degree to which they are free to pursue policies wholly independent of their regional partners or of the United States, so too, conversely, there are limits to the intimacy with which allied relations can be pursued. These limits affect not only transatlantic ties, but intercharge among the Europeans themselves.

As the British case suggests, there are always some differences of perspective and national interest. This does not by itself mean that the alliance is disintegrating; rather, it suggests an inevitable fact of life. Thus, within the U.K., the dominant foreign policy orientation remains essentially Atlanticist: witness the position of the reelected Thatcher government, the platform of the Liberal and Social Democratic parties, and the outlook of the moderate wing of the Labour party—battered though it may be. While inevitable differences over specific policies and initiatives exist (and these were particularly abrasive in the late 1970s and early 1980s), there remains considerable agreement on broad areas of defense and foreign policy, on the maintenance of international economic arrangements (though less so on the specific international economic policies to be pursued), and on the "rules of the game."

The implication of this analysis, therefore, is that it is premature to see Britain and Western Europe decisively pulling away from the United

25Anton W. DePorte, *Europe Between the Superpowers* (New Haven, Conn.: Yale University Press, 1979); Josef Joffe, "German Defense Policy: Novel Solutions and Enduring Dilemmas," chapter 3 in Gregory Flynn, et al., *The Internal Fabric of Western Security* (Totawa, N.J.: Allanheld, Osmun, 1981); Hans-Dietrich Genscher, "Toward an Overall Western Strategy," *Foreign Affairs*, Fall 1982, pp. 42–66.

States and having both the need and the opportunity to plot a distinctly new course for themselves.

A careful reading of the American-British relationship thus suggests an important insight. It is that while broad interests and purposes correspond, there remain other, inherent, differences of interest, perspective, and policy. These will inevitably generate disagreements and even periodic crises. Policy choices will exacerbate or alleviate these conflicts, but they will not eliminate them.

FOREIGN POLICY LANDMARKS

March 1946	Winston Churchill's speech at Fulton, Missouri warns of Soviet "Iron Curtain" descending across Europe
February 1947	Labour government of Prime Minister Clement Attlee notifies United States that it is unable to continue economic and military aid to Greece and Turkey
1947	Independence granted to India and Pakistan
1949	Establishment of NATO
1951	Refusal to participate in creation of European Coal and Steel Community or the proposed European Defense Community
1956	Refusal to participate in creation of European Common Market
October–November 1956	Anglo-French invasion of Suez and subsequent withdrawal; Soviet suppression of Hungarian Revolution
1960	Conservative Prime Minister Harold Macmillan speech in South Africa calls for recognizing "winds of change"
1961	Macmillan government seeks entry into European Common Market
1962	United States cancels Skybolt missile program
December 1962	At meeting in Nassau in the Bahamas President Kennedy promises Macmillan that Americans will cooperate with Britain in Polaris submarine missile program in lieu of Skybolt program
January 1963	French President Charles de Gaulle vetoes Britain's bid to enter Common Market
October 1967	Labour government of Prime Minister Harold Wilson devalues the pound to $2.40, after three year effort to maintain it at $2.80
January 1973	Britain enters Common Market
October 1973	Egypt and Syria attack Israel in Yom Kippur War; oil crisis begins
1981–1982	Friction with United States over British participation in Soviet natural gas pipeline project
April–June 1982	Falklands War with Argentina
June 1983	Labour party advocates abandoning British nuclear

<table>
<tr><td></td><td>deterrent; Conservative government of Prime Minister Margaret Thatcher is reelected in landslide</td></tr>
<tr><td>April 1986</td><td>Thatcher government permits use of American airbases in Britain for launching of United States F-111 aircraft participating in the bombing of Libya</td></tr>
<tr><td>June 1987</td><td>Labour party calls for unilateral nuclear disarmament and removal of American nuclear bases from Britain; Conservative government of Prime Minister Margaret Thatcher again wins reelection</td></tr>
<tr><td>December 1987</td><td>Thatcher government supports INF Treaty signed by Reagan and Gorbachev</td></tr>
</table>

SELECTED BIBLIOGRAPHY

BEER, SAMUEL H. *Britain Against Itself: The Political Contradictions of Collectivism.* New York: Norton, 1982.

BELOFF, MAX, and GILLIAN PEELE. *The Government of the United Kingdom.* 2d Ed. New York: Norton, 1984.

BIRCH, ANTHONY H. *The British System of Government.* 6th Ed. Boston: Allen & Unwin, 1983.

BRADLEY, IAN. *Breaking the Mould? The Birth and Prospects of the Social Democratic Party.* London: Martin Robinson, 1981.

BUTLER, DAVID, and GARETH BUTLER. *British Political Facts, 1900–1985.* London: Macmillan, 1986.

BUTLER, DAVID, and DENNIS KAVANAGH. *The British General Election of 1983.* London: Macmillan, 1984.

BUTLER, DAVID, and DAVID MARQUAND. *European Elections and British Politics.* New York: Longman, 1981.

COKER, CHRISTOPHER, ed. *A Nation in Retreat: Britain's Defence Commitments.* London: Brassey's/Pergammon, 1986.

COOK, CHRIS, and IAN TAYLOR, eds. *The Labour Party.* New York: Longman, 1980.

EPSTEIN, LEON D. *British Politics in the Suez Crisis.* Urbana, Ill.: University of Illinois Press, 1964.

FRANKEL, JOSEPH. *British Foreign Policy, 1945–1973.* New York: Oxford University Press, 1975.

HALL, PETER. *Governing the Economy: The Politics of State Intervention in Britain and France.* New York: Oxford University Press, 1986.

KALDOR, MARY, and STUART WEIR, eds. *A New Foreign Policy for Britain.* Oxford: Polity Press, 1986.

KAVANAGH, DENNIS A. *Thatcherism and British Politics: The End of Consensus.* New York: Oxford University Press, 1987.

KING, ANTHONY. *Britain Says Yes. The 1975 Referendum on the Common Market.* Washington, D.C.: American Enterprise Institute, 1977.

KITZINGER, UWE. *Diplomacy and Persuasion.* London: Thames and Hudson, 1973.

KRIEGER, JOEL. *Reagan, Thatcher and the Politics of Decline.* New York: Oxford University Press, 1986.

LIEBER, ROBERT J. *British Politics and European Unity: Parties, Elites and Pressure Groups.* Berkeley, Calif.: University of California Press, 1970.

LOUIS, WILLIAM ROGER, and HEDLEY BULL, eds. *The Special Relationship: Anglo-American Relations Since 1945.* Oxford: Clarendon Press, 1986.

McINNES, COLIN, *Trident: The Only Option.* London: Brassey's Defence Publishers, 1986.

NEUSTADT, RICHARD. *Alliance Politics.* New York: Columbia University Press, 1970.

NORTON, PHILIP, and ARTHUR AUGHEY. *Conservatives and Conservatism.* London: Temple Smith, 1981.

PIERRE, ANDREW. *Nuclear Politics: The British Experience with an Independent Strategic Force: 1939–1970*. New York: Oxford University Press, 1972.

POLLARD, SIDNEY. *The Wasting of the British Economy*. London: Croom Helm, 1982.

ROPER, JOHN, ed. *The Future of British Defense Policy*. New York: Cambridge University Press, 1985.

ROSE, RICHARD. *The Territorial Dimension in Government: Understanding the United Kingdom*. Chatham, N.J.: Chatham House, 1982.

SMART, IAN. *The Future of the British Nuclear Deterrent*. London: Royal Institute of International Affairs, 1977.

WALLACE, WILLIAM. *The Foreign Policy Process in Britain*. London: Allen & Unwin, 1977.

WALTZ, KENNETH N. *Foreign Policy and Democratic Politics: The American and British Experience*, Boston: Little, Brown, 1967.

2

French Foreign Policy: the Quest for Rank

Roy C. Macridis

France is the only middle-rank power that has undertaken a search to attain world rank. One of the foremost world powers until 1940, it refused to be drawn, as a subordinate, into the Atlantic Alliance, dominated by the U.S.A., and it sought independence within and outside of the Alliance. Unlike West Germany, which acquiesced to American tutelage for a long time; unlike England, which clung desperately to a "special relationship" with the U.S.A. that only underwrote its declining power; and unlike Japan, which accepted American protection in return for the American market for its products—France aspired to a restoration of its commanding position in Europe and elsewhere. How does a middle-rank power confronted by the Soviet Union and the United States and perhaps the growing power of China strive for independent status and world rank?

The available means are limited, but the guidelines to be followed are quite simple. First, an increase of one's own power basis. This can be achieved through rapid industrial and economic modernization, the increase of population, and the development of modern weapons; a power basis can also be strengthened through regional alliances that provide additional weight and resources. Second, a middle-rank power, in a world of two superpowers, should avoid an entangling and integrative alliance with either of the two—for such an alliance will inevitably subordinate it to the superpower with which the alliance is made. The looser an alliance is, the more leeway and freedom it gives to a middle-rank power. Third, a middle-rank power should exert itself to prevent the development of close collaboration between the two superpowers—such a collaboration may amount to a "condominium" of the world by the two superpowers, overshadowing all other nation-states. (In fact, one of the reasons why integrative alliances with one or the other of the two superpowers is to be avoided is precisely to give to a middle-rank power the necessary freedom to maneuver against the realization of such a condominium.) But a middle-rank power should also try to prevent any direct confrontation between the two superpowers, for invariably such a confrontation will force it to take sides and, by so doing, forfeit its freedom of action. A middle-rank power must strive constantly for a détente between the two superpowers but in such a way that détente is never translated into an entente!

The policy of France since World War II can be easily understood in terms of the basic concepts outlined above. As we shall see, France remained suspicious of both the Soviets and the Americans. It opposed all along, and continues to do so, any hegemony of the one or the other over any region of the world, and it deplored the division of Europe into two blocs. It gave support sometimes to the United States and sometimes to the Soviet Union—depending upon how its leaders estimated the balance of forces in the world and the relative strength and the intentions of the two superpowers. It attempted to strengthen the base of its power through economic modernization and rapid industrial development; and its population increased by almost 20 percent in the period since World War II. Its position and role within the European Common Market also created a regional base that could be used for political purposes, as did its influence and control in Africa. Finally the development of an independent nuclear force, planned before de Gaulle came to power in 1958, gave France a nuclear deterrent and, according to some of its strategists, genuine independence that ultimately made its withdrawal from the integrated military command of the Atlantic Alliance possible.

We shall examine the background factors that have shaped France's foreign policy—its geographic position, its economic and social development, its ideology and culture, its persistent pursuit of national interests in the past, and its foreign policy objectives, as they were reformulated in the years of the Fourth Republic (1946–1958) and, more particularly, as they have been restated in the years of the Fifth Republic under de Gaulle and under his successors—Georges Pompidou (1969–1974), Giscard d'Estaing (1974–1981), and Francois Mitterrand, heading a left-wing coalition, since 1981, and after 1986 when the conservation bloc won a slim legislative majority in the election of March 16.

BACKGROUND FACTORS

The dilemma facing France at the end of World War II may be stated in rather simple terms: France, one of the great powers in the world, found its position drastically weakened. But the aspirations of greatness and rank have persisted. These aspirations were expressed succinctly by the architect of France's post-World War II policy, General Charles de Gaulle. "I intended," he wrote in his *Memoirs,* referring to the period immediately after the defeat of Germany,

> to assure France primacy in Western Europe by preventing the rise of a new Reich that might again threaten her safety; to cooperate with the East and West and, if need be, contract the necessary alliances on one side or another without ever accepting any kind of dependency; to transform the French Union into a free association in order to avoid the as yet unspecified dangers of upheaval; to persuade the states along the Rhine, the Alps and the Pyrenees to form a political, economic and strategic bloc; to establish this organization as one of the three world powers and, should it become necessary, as the arbiter between the Soviet and the Anglo-Saxon camps.[1]

This was an ambitious scheme, and, as he admitted, the means available to his country "were poor indeed." But it was a goal widely shared by the majority of the French elites. In fact, right after the Liberation of France in 1944, while the war was still going on the French people were asked in a survey whether they thought their country was still a "great power." Eighty percent said "yes."

In 1944, after the liberation of Paris, with the return of General de Gaulle and the establishment of his provisional government on the French territory, France and her overseas possessions were in a state of dependency. Drained of manpower, with her economy seriously undermined after four years of occupation, facing urgent problems of social and economic reconstruction at home and powerful centrifugal forces in the empire, the power and even the political will to fashion the instruments that would lead to an independent course of action were lacking. France was dependent upon Britain and, primarily of course, upon the United States. In terms of Walter Lippmann's axiom that commitments in foreign policy must be commensurate with strength, it was very clear that there were few commitments that France could undertake and carry out successfully without Anglo-American support. France's liberty of action, therefore, was limited. Her aspiration to remain a top-rank power seemed to be at variance with her capabilities.

Thus the dilemma confronting France's post-World War II governments and political elites was either to accept the situation as it developed

[1]*War Memoirs*, Vol. 3, *Salvation* (New York: Simon & Schuster, 1960), p. 204.

after World War II or to continue to seek "greatness" and "rank" without the physical, military, and economic resources to implement it. It called for difficult political decisions and choices; it demanded the rapid reconsideration of some of the traditional French foreign policy patterns; and, above all, it required a meaningful debate among political leaders and elites about alternatives and choices.

Neither the political system under the Fourth Republic nor the political parties and the press managed to provide for such a debate. There was no "great debate" to redefine the French position and status in the world. Strangely enough, it was only after the return to power of General de Gaulle in 1958 and the establishment of the Fifth Republic that foreign policy themes began to be stated with enough clarity to invite debate, to elicit support, or to provoke criticism.

The Economic Foundations

The most significant feature of the French economy until World War II was its relative decline. While industrialization went forward rapidly throughout the nineteenth century in England, Germany, Japan, and the United States, and also in the Soviet Union in the twentieth century, France's economy advanced at a snail's pace.

Yet France began with a marked head start over *all* other countries. During the Napoleonic era and until the middle of the nineteenth century, France was one of the economically best developed nations of the world. From then on, despite a wealth of resources and skilled labor, its economy declined in comparison with almost all the other countries of Western Europe. France's total national income, between 1870 and 1940, rose by about 80 percent; that of Germany increased five times; that of Great Britain, three-and-a-half times. In the years between the two world wars (1918–1940), investment declined to a point below zero—that is, France was living on its capital, using its factories and equipment without replacing them in full.

The destruction wrought by World War II was an additional setback. With its industrial equipment destroyed or dilapidated and its transportation network paralyzed, France's economy was in a state of collapse.

There were many long-range factors associated with this stagnation—notably, the very slow growth of population (France's population peaked at about 40 million by the end of the nineteeth century and failed to grow until after 1945), a backward agriculture, the protectionist policies of the state, and, finally, the narrow and conservative outlook of the business and managerial groups.

Geographic Position

France's geographic position has accounted for contradictory interests and commitments. On the one hand, France has been a continental power with frontiers that include, to the east, Belgium, Germany, Switzerland, and Italy, and, to the southwest, Spain; on the other hand, it had a colonial empire (developed and consolidated by the end of the nineteenth century and after World War I) with possessions throughout Asia and Africa and in the Pacific, Indian, and Atlantic oceans.

On the Continent, the frontier with Spain and Switzerland presented no problems. The threat came from Germany—a Germany that after 1870 had been unified and after 1930, despite its defeat in 1918, confronted France once more with a population of some 65 million and an economic and industrial system far superior to that of France. The empire called for everlasting vigilance against potential marauders, particularly England, and against nationalist independence movements, so that France needed a strong army at home as well as a strong navy. This involved heavy economic sacrifices.

From whichever point of view one looks at the situation, one cannot help but realize that the French predicament was a serious one. France, more than any other country of the world, had to assume the heavy burdens both of a continental power with a strong standing army and of an empire.

Persistent Patterns

A number of patterns underlie France's foreign policy. In the nineteenth century they reflected France's strength, but they slowly crystallized into dogmas and myths that were ultimately separated from twentieth-century reality. It is, nonetheless, in terms of such myths that France's foreign policy was shaped—immediately after World War II—rather than in terms of the new factors that developed partly as a result of the war and partly as the result of a number of social, economic, and ideological forces that stirred the world. These myths continue to play an important role today.

The basic objectives of foreign policy remained (*a*) the continuation of France's imperial position, and (*b*) continental strength. The first meant, as we have seen, the maintenance of the far-flung empire with all the financial difficulties and obligations it entailed. Not for a moment was the notion of federalism and self-government for its members seriously entertained. Maintenance of the empire was conceived as a part of France's mission and as a continuous challenge to French culture and influence. The resurrection of France as a continental power was also an automatic reflex; no political leader doubted it. The end of World War II with the defeat of Germany was, in a sense, France's revenge for the German occupation. Victory, it was thought, simply reestablished the prewar balance. To implement France's continental position, the same alliances with the West and with the East were contemplated—all of them directed against a Germany that lay prostrate and divided. The fact that the Soviet Union had gained a foothold in the heart of Europe did not alter the traditional French reflexes; Germany was the enemy of France. A weak Germany and a Franco-Russian alliance remained the conditions for French security. When General de Gaulle visited Moscow and signed the Franco-Russian treaty in December 1944, he was preserving French security in the best tradition of the nineteenth century.

THE SUBSTANCE OF FOREIGN POLICY: TRENDS AND PROBLEMS

France has followed four basic foreign policy objectives ever since the eighteenth century. The first is the policy of *natural frontiers* in Europe; the second is the policy of what might be called *European status quo* or *balance of power* in Europe; the third is colonial expansion and the preservation of its colonial empire; and the fourth is the preservation of world power status.

The "natural frontiers" of France have been considered to be on the Rhine and on the Alps. They include Belgium, Holland, Luxembourg, and the German territory that lies west of the Rhine. This was interpreted to mean that France's strategic and military interests extended to those areas, and that no other power could set foot there without jeopardizing her interests. The continuity of this policy is remarkable. Danton stated in 1793, "The frontiers [of the Republic] are marked *by nature*. . . . They are the Rhine, the Alps and the Pyrenean mountains." Clemenceau affirmed in 1919, "The move towards the Rhine was the tradition of our ancestors. . . . It was the tradition to create a frontier, a *true* frontier marking the French territory." General de Gaulle, in 1944, stated, in the name of a weak and defeated country, "The Rhine *is* French security and I think the security of the whole world. But France is the principal interested party. . . . She wishes to be solidly established from one end to the other of her *natural frontier*."[2]

The policy of *status quo*, on the other hand, was based upon two assumptions:

1. No single power should gain preponderant strength in Europe.
2. France would become the protector of these small states throughout Europe and play the role of arbitrator and maintain its position of supremacy in Europe.

The immediate reaction of France after liberation in December

[2]See the excellent article by J. Raoul Girardet, "L'influence de la tradition sur la politique étrangére de la France," in *La Politique étrangére et ses Fondements*, ed. Jean-Baptiste Duroselle (Paris: Librairie Armand Colin, 1954), pp. 143–63.

1944, was to attempt to reestablish its traditional position of security in Europe and of independence as a world power. From 1944 until mid-1947, a policy was followed that for all practical purposes was identical to that of 1919. France proposed the following:

1. The dismemberment of Germany and prolonged occupation of the country.
2. Heavy reparations and tight control of German industrial output.
3. The reestablishment of French control in the area west of the Rhine by the detachment of these territories from Germany.
4. A prolonged occupation, if not annexation, of the Saar.
5. The independence of the small nations of Europe.
6. An alliance with the Soviet Union directed against a threat to French security from Germany.
7. An alliance with Great Britain.

Under the first government of General de Gaulle (1944–1946) this policy was pursued with great tenacity. After the liberation, a Treaty of Mutual Assistance was signed with the Soviet Union. The two countries agreed to take "all the necessary measures in order to eliminate any new menace coming from Germany and to take the initiative to make any new effort of aggression on her part impossible" (Article 3). Immediately after the signing of the pact, General de Gaulle declared, "Because two of the principal powers of the world—free from any conflict of interest in any part of the world—decide to unite under specific conditions, it does not mean that either the one or the other envisages to organize the world and even its security without the help of other nations."[3]

In fact, until the beginning of 1947, every effort was made by France to gain the support of *either* the Soviet Union *or* the United States (along with Great Britain) in the implementation of its German policy. Neither of the two allies, however, responded favorably, since they both hoped to see, ultimately, an economically and politically unified Germany *on their side*, something that would have meant the end of French aspirations for European security and leadership. When Soviet Foreign Minister Molotov declared himself, in July 1946, in favor of a politically unified Germany, *Année Politique* commented. "There was reason for France, which could count on the support of her ally in the East *against* the Anglo-Americans, to be disappointed."[4]

The Cold War and the Development of Western Alliances.   The Cold War, whose origin can be traced to Yalta and Potsdam, erupted in the beginning of 1947. Conferences in Moscow and London had failed to produce

[3]Quoted in *Année politique, 1944–45,* p. 89.
[4]*Année politique, 1946,* p. 400.

any kind of agreement on the problem of Germany. The lines were being drawn, and the division of Germany into two zones—Soviet and British-American—became a certainty. The conflict implied the strengthening of both zones, and hence the development of a West German Republic supported by the United States.

France managed to maintain control over the Saar, but failed in all its other claims. After June 1947, the whole of Western Europe and Great Britain received massive American aid to develop their economies. In 1948 the Brussels Pact brought together the Benelux countries, France, and Great Britain. It provided for a permanent consultative council and negotiations to promote economic development of the countries concerned, and included a military clause calling for common action against a German attack or aggression and to cope with a situation that constituted a menace to peace, no matter where it occurred or from where it came. In 1949 the creation of a large military umbrella was logically called for. Not only the Brussels signatories, but also most of the Western countries, including ultimately Greece and Turkey, participated. The United States became a permanent part of this alliance that still continues as the North Atlantic Treaty Organization (NATO). Article 5 stipulates that an attack against any one of the signatories, either in Europe or in North America, would be considered an attack against all, without providing, however, for *automatic* military assistance among the signatories. It further provides (in Article 9) for a permanent deliberative organization and the establishment of a common military command. The Federal Republic of Germany was originally excluded from NATO.

These developments determined France's position. France became a member of NATO, under the overall leadership and military direction of the United States. Such an alliance underwrote French security and, in general terms, the integrity of the empire. The exclusion of Germany continued to give France a strategic position in Western Europe, as well as the semblance, if not the reality, of national power and independence.

But the question of Germany's future had been only postponed. A military Western alliance without Germany hardly represented a solution of the problems of military defense. Furthermore, as the struggle between the East and the West not only continued but was intensified with the Berlin Blockade, with the takeover of Czechoslovakia by the Soviets, and with the Korean War, the prize of Germany became more important for the two major opponents. For the United States, the rearmament of the Federal Republic of Germany seemed the logical step in the construction of a strong defensive line against a potential Soviet attack.

The European Defense Community and Its Alternatives. It was, strangely enough, the French who came forth with the answer: the creation of a West European army, the European Defense Community (EDC), involving a genuine integration of national forces and a unified—and, if possible, a supranational—command. The United States endorsed this policy as an alternative to the rearming of West Germany within NATO.

No sooner had the European Defense Community (EDC) been announced and formulated, however, than it provoked a storm of protest in France. The political parties came out actively either for or against it. Extreme right-wing and extreme left-wing parties joined hands against the treaty, which was defended by a sharply divided center. To French public opinion, the most controversial part of the treaty was the envisaged German rearmament. A majority of the members of the National Assembly considered German rearmament, even within the EDC, a direct challenge to French sovereignty, clearly spelling the end of France's aspirations to remain a leading European nation. Since there was no genuine majority for or against the treaty,[5] it was on a procedural motion that, in August 1954, the EDC was rejected by the French National Assembly. In the meantime, all the other prospective members had honored the signature of their governments. Only the French assembly used its constitutional prerogatives and refused to ratify the treaty. The rejection climaxed four years of equivocation. It was only in December 1954, that the National Assembly, six months after defeating the EDC for fear of German rearmament, allowed Germany to become a member of NATO and eventually to rearm herself within the framework of the NATO alliance.

France and the Empire

The French Empire extended over every continent of the world. Its administration was a vestige of the Napoleonic conceptions of a highly centralized bureaucratic system—an administration in which Paris, through the colonial officials, made the ultimate decisions and legislated for the whole empire. Its cementing ideology was that of "assimilation"— the notion that ultimately every inhabitant would become a French citizen and be represented in the French Parliament—a notion at marked variance with the Anglo-Saxon conception, according to which political and cultural evolution of the colonial peoples would ultimately bring about political autonomy and self-government.

In 1944 the basic charter of colonial policy had been drafted at the Brazzaville Conference. There it was decided that "the purpose of the civilizing work accomplished by France in the colonies excludes any idea

---

[5]The division of the political system in the French Parliament and in the various coalition cabinets reflected very closely the division of public opinion: in July 1954, 36 percent of those asked were "for" or "rather for" the EDC. 31 percent were "against" or "rather against," and 33 percent did not answer.

of autonomy, any possibility of an evolution outside of the French Empire. The establishment, even in the remote future, of "self-government' in the colonies must not be considered."[6] In 1945, when a trusteeship committee was appointed within the United Nations, the French made it quite clear that they would not accept its jurisdiction. The empire was French, and hence a matter of domestic policy.

In almost every case, the French insisted upon assimilation and maintenance of French sovereignty. In 1945 France refused to withdraw its army from Syria and Lebanon. Within a year it had to give in. In 1947 it refused to enter into negotiations with Ho Chi-minh, and engaged in a war that lasted until 1954. The war in Vietnam cost France more than a billion dollars a year, retarded its internal investment policy, and paralyzed its alternate plans for an economic and social reconstruction of the North African territories. It was in part responsible for France's inability to keep pace with German economic reconstruction in Western Europe.

But the Vietnam War brought other problems to a head. In Algeria, Tunis, and Morocco, the independence movements were gaining strength. These movements, however, envisaged continued cooperation with France. In every case, the French political leaders and representatives and the various military leaders in command of the French troops reiterated the philosophy of the French vocation. Time after time, the strategic interests of France were evoked. Time after time, the representatives of the French government and army intervened. By 1956, both Morocco and Tunisia became independent. The refusal to grant self-government left only one alternative: independence.

This situation was most evident in Algeria, where there was a very strong movement in favor of self-government after the liberation of France in 1944. It gained strength after the independence of Morocco and Tunisia. Yet there were many opportunities to cope with the Algerian situation, and progress had been made in 1947, when special legislation granting considerable political autonomy to Algeria was passed, although never implemented. Claims of French sovereignty in Algeria and assertions that France "intends to stay there," made in the last years of the Fourth Republic, sounded very similar to the assertions made about Syria, Lebanon, Indochina, Tunis, and Morocco.

THE LEGACY OF THE FOURTH REPUBLIC (1946–1958)

Speaking on October 28, 1966, General de Gaulle, now back in office as president of the Fifth Republic, stated with remarkable succinctness the objectives of French foreign policy in terms that applied to the Fourth Republic (1946–1958) as well:

[6]*Année politique, 1947–45.*

In the world as it is, people sometimes feign surprise over the so-called changes and detours of France's action. And there are even those who have spoken of contradictions or Machiavellism. Well, I believe that while the circumstances are changing around us, in truth there is nothing more constant than France's policy. For this policy, throughout the extremely varied vicissitudes of our times and our world—this policy's essential goal is that France be and remain an independent nation.[7]

Despite the divisions of the political system under the Fourth Republic and the fact that they often spilled over into the area of foreign policy, there was continuity in the pursuit of basic objectives of foreign policy. The political elite, the political parties (with the exception of the Communists), and the public remained steadfast in their attachment to the traditional interests of France, in spite of rapidly changing world conditions. Discontinuities were occasionally introduced, but only to lead to decisive choices. This was the case with the termination of the Vietnam War (1954), the granting of autonomy and later independence to Morocco and Tunisia (1956), and the Paris agreements that consecrated West German sovereignty and allowed for German participation in NATO (1954). The political system remained, by and large, committed to the following objectives: (*a*) the maintenance of an Atlantic and world position that implied a weak Germany and a militarily independent France; (*b*) a European rapprochement in terms of which France could gain strength at the head of Western Europe; and (*c*) the maintenance of a top-rank world position.

What has been called *la politique du grandeur* ("the policy of greatness"), according to which France's vocation is that of a world power and therefore a partner in the development of world strategy, or—under propitious conditions—an independent force, was ever present.

The Empire: The Foundation of a New Policy.   It was only in the last two years of the Fourth Republic, between 1956 and 1958, that France's leadership decided to accept the irresistible trend of colonial emancipation rather than attempt to oppose it. In 1956, the French parliament began consideration of new legislation to put an end to the theory and practice of assimilation. A *loi-cadre* ("framework law") empowered the government to give considerable autonomy to the African republics and Madagascar. They became semi-independent republics, with their own parliaments and responsible executives. France retained jurisdiction over important areas of policy making such as defense, foreign policy, trade, and education. But the first path toward gradual political emancipation had been made, and it proved to be irreversible.

---

[7]Charles de Gaulle, *Discours et Messages,* Vol. 5 (Paris: Plon, 1970), p. 97.

Economic and Military Policy. The Fourth Republic also laid the groundwork of France's economic and military recovery. The Atomic Energy Commissariat, founded in 1945, continued in operation throughout the many years of cabinet instability, and it was endowed with adequate credits. The possession of an atom bomb in a world in which only three powers had developed nuclear weapons became associated, in the eyes of the French political leaders and public alike, with France's national independence and security.

Although favoring the Atlantic alliance, the political leaders of the Fourth Republic never agreed to play a secondary role and acquiesce in American or British-American supremacy. They did not accept any genuine integration of military command within NATO and, alleging their colonial obligations, insisted on maintaining autonomy over their military forces. They remained reluctant to permit the United States to establish stockpiles of nuclear weapons or to construct launching sites on French soil. The same fear of integration of the military forces applied to a European army, as we have seen.

A New Economic Policy. There was a clear perception among most of the political leaders of the Fourth Republic that France could not recover its prewar position without drastic economic effort. A rapid modernization of the French economy and a gradual movement toward increasing European cooperation were required. A strong France in a well integrated western European economy could become even stronger. Therefore, the Fourth Republic, after many equivocations, moved after 1956 in the direction of the European Economic Community (EEC) providing for liberalization of trade, lowering, and ultimately eliminating tariffs, and providing for free movement of capital and labor among West Germany, Italy, France, and the Benelux countries. The treaty formalizing the EEC ("Common Market") was signed in Rome in 1956 and put into effect on January 1, 1959.

THE FIFTH REPUBLIC AND GENERAL DE GAULLE— WORLDWIDE ASPIRATIONS (1958–1969)

Whatever the factors and the immediate causes associated with the military uprising of May 13, 1958, in Algeria that brought the Fourth Republic to an end, it was to General de Gaulle that most of the political groups and leaders turned. Army officers, veterans, the political parties from the Socialists to the Independents, and a great number of intellectuals turned to de Gaulle as the symbol and the person around whom this new spirit of French nationalism could find expression.

The Basic Assumptions

De Gaulle's basic assumptions—what we may call his overall philosophy—begin and end with the notion that there is one social force—the "reality of the nation" *(le fait national)*—that overshadows all others. No other force or forces—ideological, social, or economic—have succeeded in undermining the nation-state as the focal point of the ultimate loyalty of man.

From the postulate of national reality a number of inferences flow. They do not always have the logical consistency that an academician would desire; but consistency is not a necessary ingredient of statecraft. Situations change so fast in our world that the only consistency lies in the ability to adjust.[8] Consistency means, in the last analysis, realism. Yet the inferences that follow from the postulate on national reality constitute guides to action and must be spelled out.

The Reality of the Nation and the Means of Achieving Independence. The reality of the nation requires power in order fully to manifest itself. Surveying the world situation before the Allied victory in Europe, de Gaulle could not restrain his bitterness: "How dull is the sword of France at the time when the Allies are about to launch the assault of Europe."[9] Although not the only one, the basic ingredient of power is the military. In the ruins of France after the liberation, de Gaulle set himself to recreate the French army. He was haunted with the certainty that the Allies were blocking his efforts because they were unwilling to allow France to develop the military strength that would enable it to become an equal. When the matter of Germany's occupation seemed in doubt, he ordered his divisions onto German soil, suspecting, perhaps rightly, that the Allies might prevent France from participating in settling the future of Germany and remembering, also, that in war possession is nine-tenths of the law. His vision remained the same throughout the months following the liberation—to recreate the French armed forces. When there was not enough gas to heat French stoves, he established a Commission for Atomic Energy.

But there are other important factors in the equation of power. De Gaulle recognized many and used them all: alliances, diplomacy and skill in negotiations, cultural relations, spirtual influence, economic resources, and population.

A strong ingredient of power—indeed, the only valid expression of

---

[8]Almost always, for instance, de Gaulle, speaking on international issues, inserted the phrase "given the present conditions in the world," or "in the actual state of developments," or "things being as they are."

[9]*War Memoirs.* Vol. 2, *Unity* (New York: Simon & Schuster, 1959), p. 245.

a nation—is the state and its political organization. Gaullist revisionism, both before and throughout the Fourth Republic, was predicated upon de Gaulle's ideas about world relations and the role of the French nation. To play the proper role, France needed a strong state. In this state, one man, the president of the republic, should make foreign policy on behalf of the nation—the "real France"—incarnating the national interests over and above the welter of particular interests and ideological factions.

A third ingredient of power that de Gaulle evoked very frequently led him to follow policies to which he had seemed firmly opposed. This is what he called the imperative of the *grand ensembles* ("great wholes"). Nations must establish cooperative "wholes" that provide the structural bases and the resources for the economic development and defense of each one and of all. This is not contrary to his emphasis upon national uniqueness, nor did it lead him to the espousal of projects of military integration. The building of large wholes creates something that is more than an alliance and less than a federation. It is a close association and a cooperation between nation states which, by pooling some of their resources, find the strength to sustain a common purpose.

The Idea of Balance.   De Gaulle's emphasis upon the reality of the national phenomenon and its concomitant accessories—power, both military and political—led him to a theory of international relations that is often referred to as "realist." International relations comprise an arena of conflict in which every participant nation-state attempts to increase its strength at the expense of the other. Every political leadership, no matter what ideology inspires it, acts in terms of national consideration. *If so, it is only power that can check power—and the only possible international world is one in which an equilibrium of powers is reached.* This led de Gaulle to follow conclusions that directly shaped his actions and have influenced his successors.

The present balance is unnatural, precarious, and unwise— unnatural, because it involves a polarization of the world and the creation of political satellites, which are inconsistent with the secular realities and interests of nations; precarious, because both the big and small nations are continuously on the brink of war; unwise, because it gives to the two of the least qualified nation-states (the United States and the Soviet Union) full liberty to act, the independence to decide their fate and with it the fate of the world.

Both the American and the Soviet efforts are expressions of national power, in one form or another. If they are allowed free sway, they might enter upon armed conflict. If they find a temporary accommodation, it will be in order to establish a joint hegemony over the world. *Either eventuality will be to the detriment of the other nation-states* including, of course, of France and Europe as a whole. This can be avoided only by creating a balance of power consistent with the growing realities of the world, in which the economic and political development of Europe is bound to play a growing role.

General de Gaulle's conception of a balance was a permanent trait of his thinking and action. It took a number of forms. In the third volume of his Memoirs, de Gaulle pointed out that the only way to keep the Soviet Union out of the heart of Europe was to dismember Germany. Thus the threat of a new Germany would be eliminated, and the fears of the Soviet Union and the Eastern European nations alleviated. Moreover, a treaty with the Soviet Union, directed against the revival of German power, would free France to pursue her other world obligations. It was the failure of Yalta to revive the pre-World War II arrangements in Europe that also accounted for the bitter denunciations against the settlement. Although France received a number of compensations, perhaps far beyond what the French leadership had a right to expect in terms of her real power at the time, Yalta became slowly identified with a betrayal of Europe and France by the Anglo-Saxons.

As late as August of 1968 the response of de Gaulle to the Soviet invasion of Czechoslovakia was a condemnation of Yalta! He then stated that

> the armed intervention by the Soviet Union in Czechoslovakia shows that the Moscow government has not freed itself from the policy of blocs that was imposed on Europe by the effect of the Yalta Agreements, which is incompatible with the right of peoples to self-determination and which could and can only lead to international tension. . . . France, who did not take part in these Agreements and who does not adopt that policy, notes and deplores the fact that the events in Prague—besides constituting an attack on the rights and the destiny of a friendly nation—are of the kind to impede European détente, such as France herself practices and in which she urges others to engage, and that, alone, can ensure peace.[10]

De Gaulle made an open offer to Churchill in November 1944, to combine forces so that the two countries with their far-flung empires would be able to act independently of the Soviets and the Americans.

A third scheme involved an alliance with the Soviet Union, directed against German recovery and guaranteeing the status quo of Europe. Speculating before his trip to the Soviet Union in December 1944, only a few weeks after he had made his offer to Churchill, de Gaulle wrote wistfully, "Perhaps it might be possible to renew in some manner the Franco-Russian solidarity, which even if misunderstood and betrayed in the past, was nonetheless compatible with the nature of things *both with*

---

[10]Ambassade de France, Service de Presse ed d'Information, no. 1121, August 21, 1968.

regard to the German danger and the Anglo-Saxon efforts to assert their hegemony."[11]

A fourth and perhaps more persistent effort to recreate a balance is the revival of Europe as a "third force." What "Europe" meant to de Gaulle, exactly, is a difficult matter. In his *Memoirs* he spoke of an organization of the peoples of Europe from "Iceland to Istanbul and from Gibraltar to the Urals." Sometimes Russia is considered a part and sometimes it is not, although emphasis is often put on the European destiny of Russia. Sometimes it is Western Europe and sometimes the whole of Europe. Sometimes "Europe" implies a dismembered Germany, sometimes a divided Germany, and sometimes a Franco-German rapprochement without qualifications. Two things are certain: "Europe," whatever it is, is distinct from the "Anglo-Saxon powers." It is also separate from Soviet Russia, without, however, always denying the European position of Russia and hence its participation.

In the name of balance, de Gaulle envisaged in the course of less than twenty years the following alliances: (*a*) with the British, in order to create an independent bloc vis-á-vis the Soviets and the Americans; (*b*) with the Soviet Union, in order to maintain French supremacy in Europe vis-á-vis Germany; (*c*) with all against the revival of a unified, militarized, and strong Germany; and (*d*) with West Germany and the other Western European states, in order to create an independent bloc—a third force in Europe that might reestablish a new worldwide balance of power.

The Constitution of the Fifth Republic.   As we noted, one of the serious difficulties throughout the Fourth Republic was the lack of strong executive leadership to formulate and implement policy and to translate overall foreign policy goals and aspirations into effective decisions. The Constitution of the Fifth Republic provides that the cabinet "shall determine and direct the policy of the nation" and that "it will be responsible to Parliament."; in addition, "the Prime Minister is responsible for national defense" (Articles 20 and 21). The president of the republic, on the other hand, "shall be the guarantor of the national independence, of the integrity of the territory, and of the respect . . . of treaties" (Article 5). He "shall negotiate and ratify treaties" and "he shall be informed of all negotiations leading to the conclusion of an international agreement" (Article 52). All major treaties, however, must be "ratified by law" (Article 53). The president of the republic is "the head of the Armed Forces" and "presides over . . . the Committees of National Defense" (Article 15).

The differences with the constitutional arrangement of the Fourth Republic lie primarily in the conception of the role of the president. He was given both implicitly and explicitly broader powers. The president is the guarantor of the national integrity; the commander-in-chief, presid-

---

[11]Ibid., p. 54, italics supplied.

ing over the meetings of the various defense councils; and has large emergency powers. He has the power to dissolve the legislature and to ask the public, in a referendum, to endorse or reject his policy. Legislation has given him the ultimate decision on the use of nuclear weapons.

Under de Gaulle, the presidency became the coordinating office for the major decisions: military policy, foreign policy, and colonial policy. His successors endorsed this position. Cabinet meetings are simply for the execution and implementation of the decisions made by the president and his immediate advisers. The president is not simply informed of foreign policy negotiations. He negotiates directly with foreign representatives, prime ministers, and heads of state; he outlines the goals of the government—at times taking even the cabinet and the prime minister by surprise. Matters pertaining to NATO, to the ties among the members of the Common Market, to negotiations concerning suspension of atomic tests, to the advisability of a summit meeting—all are decided by the president.

THE GAULLIST YEARS

We shall discuss the Gaullist period of the Fifth Republic (1958–1969) with regard to (*a*) colonial and economic policy, (*b*) NATO, (*c*) Europe and the Common Market, (*d*) the atom bomb, and (*e*) relations with the Soviet Union.

End of Empire

In 1958, General de Gaulle pledged to all overseas territories a new political arrangement—the French Community—and, if they wished it, their independence. All of the territories, with the exception of Guinea, entered the French Community. They became republics federated with France. They were governed by the president of the French republic, who was also president of the community, with the assistance of an Executive Council which consisted of the president of the republic, a number of French ministers charged with community affairs, and the prime ministers, or their delegates, of the African republics and Madagascar. A Community Senate, with primarily consultative powers, was also established, as well as a community arbitration court, to hear and pass on controversies among the member states. In the course of 1959-1960, the community was abandoned. Speaking in Dakar, Senegal, in December 1959, de Gaulle promised to grant "international sovereignty"—that is, complete independence—to all of France's African territories. All the African republics have become independent, and all of them have become members of the United Nations as independent, individual states with the freedom to vote as they please in the United Nations General Assembly and to participate in its organs and specialized commissions.

Thus France, under de Gaulle, put an end to colonialism. In doing so, it improved its position in Africa, where it was assured of a reservoir of good will. Large subsidies to the African republics and Madagascar continue, and technical and military assistance programs have increased. Thus, politically and economically, the road was paved for better relations.

Algeria.   It was not until July 3, 1962, after a series of zigzags and equivocations (which we need not dwell on here) that Algeria was finally granted full independence. The leaders of the rebellion were released from jail. Between 1962 and 1965, almost 1 million European French citizens and a sizeable number of Algerians who had fought in the French army or in territorial units were resettled in the metropolis with substantial financial aid from the state. Thus the war in Algeria (1954–1962) that, like the war in Vietman, had sapped the energy of the country, that had provoked sharp and, at times, irreconcilable conflicts, that had seriously qualified France's freedom of action, that had gravely undermined its prestige among its former colonies, particularly in Africa, came to an end. In 1962, for the first time since World War II, French soldiers were no longer fighting anyone, anywhere.

NATO: Participation; Reform; Withdrawal.   Immediately after his return to power, de Gaulle asserted that it was not the purpose of France to limit its foreign policy "within the confines of NATO." On September 23, 1958, he addressed a memorandum to NATO's Secretary-General Paul-Henri Spaak, to Prime Minister Macmillan, and to President Eisenhower. The memorandum contained a diagnosis of the problems facing NATO and a statement of French policy. He proposed the establishment within NATO of a "directorate" of three—England, France, and the United States—with responsibility for elaboration of a common military and political strategy for the whole of the planet, for the creation of allied commands for all theaters of operation, for joint deliberations about strategy, and for joint decision on the use of atomic weapons. "The European states of the continent," he stated on April 11, 1961, ". . . must know exactly with which weapons and under what conditions their overseas allies would join them in battle."[12] NATO should accordingly revise its organization to meet joint non-European problems. There was also a threat in the memorandum: France would reconsider its NATO policy in the light of the response of England and the United States.

Although ostensibly addressing problems related to NATO, de

[12]News conference, April 11, 1961, in *Speeches and Press Conferences*, No. 162, pp. 7–8.

Gaulle was actually attempting to place France on a level to which no other continental European power in NATO could aspire. NATO was to remain a broad organization, according to his proposal, but with three of its members—France, England, and the United States (the Federal Republic of Germany was excluded)—jointly in charge of global strategy. The three great powers were to be in charge, at the NATO level, of the Atlantic Alliance problems, and jointly in charge of planetary strategy. De Gaulle remained adamant. When his suggestions were rejected, France withdrew its Mediterranean fleet from NATO command; refused to integrate its air defense with NATO; and prevented the building of launching sites and the stockpiling of atomic warheads over which it could have no control. But this stand was to bring France in conflict with the Federal Republic of Germany that wished to see a strong NATO alliance continue.

With the end of the Algerian war, there was no doubt at all as to where de Gaulle stood and what he wanted. First, European problems had better be left to the European nations. Second, European nations, notably France, had worldwide commitments that transcended the regional limits of NATO, just as did the United States. Hence the future of the national armed forces and their deployment and posture was a national matter belonging to France. Third, without ever stating it, de Gaulle seemed to infer that the presence of American troops in Europe was becoming, at least politically, a liability. Fourth, NATO and its integrative aspects were to be thrust aside and replaced by a classic alliance among individual and separate states—an alliance that was to be negotiated. The partners would be free to differ on everything that did not involve their defense against a specified foreign attack under the stipulated conditions. France would be free to move in its own way in China, in Southeast Asia, and in Latin America, as well as reconsider its relations with the Eastern European countries or the Soviet Union. De Gaulle's revisionist policy with regard to NATO was, in other words, an explicit reformulation of France's full-fledged independence to act as a world power. In three separate memorandums—on March 11, March 29, and April 22, 1966—the French government communicated its decision to withdraw its forces from NATO by July 1, 1966, and demanded the withdrawal, by April 1, 1967, of all United States armed forces and military personnel and of all NATO instrumentalities from the French soil. The only possibility was that American forces could be stationed in France, and French forces in Germany, on the basis of bilateral arrangements between France and the countries involved.

The Common Market

Under de Gaulle the economic growth and development continued. The improvement was partly due to measures, originally suggested by a "special" committee of experts, designed to eliminate inflationary tendencies and restore monetary stability. This plan aimed "to restore to France its international status" in the economic field and "to establish the nation on a foundation of truth" which alone can enable it to build its prosperity.

On January 1, 1959, France implemented, in full, the European Common Market treaty provisions for the reduction of customs duties and the liberalization of trade. De Gaulle's acceptance of the Common Market was motivated in part by economic reasons and in part by considerations favoring the development of a European "whole." The crucial reason, however, was political. This became abundantly clear after 1960. The Common Market suggested the possibility that a larger European "whole" could be placed under the leadership of France, armed with atomic weapons that were denied to Germany by virtue of the Paris accords. Britain's participation was highly desirable, provided Britain was willing to abandon the intimate Atlantic connections that underwrote the dominance of the United States, and also provided that Britain brought into a European pool—under some form of Franco-British control—her atomic and hydrogen weapons and know-how. Britain's nuclear power was to be its dowry in the contemplated marriage with the Common Market. When it became clear that England was unwilling to cut her "special" ties with the United States, de Gaulle decided to refuse entry to England. In his now famous press conference of January 14, 1963, de Gaulle, alleging economic and cultural reasons, rejected England's entry. The heart of the matter, however, was political and strategic. England, de Gaulle feared, would remain under the domination of the United States, and her entry into the Common Market would thus reinforce America's influence.

With England at least temporarily out of the picture, de Gaulle turned to the Federal Republic of Germany. A Franco-German alliance providing for frequent consultations and possibly for the elaboration of common policy on military, foreign, cultural, and economic questions, would provide the hard core for consolidating Western Europe and, given France's military superiority, safeguard French leadership at the same time. In January 1963, a Franco-German treaty, embodying the principle of consultations on matters of defense, foreign policy, and cultural affairs, was signed. However, the very logic of the treaty raised serious questions. It was again based on the assumption that West Germany would accept French, rather than American, leadership and protection. But in the light of its military and economic ties with the United States, and especially in the light of the overwhelming superiority of the United States in these areas, it was unlikely that any German political leader would acquiesce to this. Gradually, the treaty was bypassed and the policies of the two countries on military and foreign policy questions began to diverge, with Germany accepting American leadership. It was only de Gaulle, and only France, that seemed to believe that Western Europe could do without the United States; and it was only France that pressed for a European solution of the European problems at the very time when Europe's defense continued to lie across the Atlantic.

But the Common Market remained a successful economic arrangement. It had, by 1965, reached the stage when increasing commitments to supranationality were to be made, and when some decision could be made by a qualified majority of the participants. In other words, the Common Market had moved to the critical stage when it was about to assume, even to a limited degree, genuine supranationality. However, such a supranationality was, as we have seen, contrary to de Gaulle's basic assumptions. He attacked the supranational character of the Rome treaty establishing the EEC and claimed that the assumption of power by a body of "stateless" functionaries was prejudicial to the independence of the sovereign member states. The Rome treaty, he concluded, had to be revised in order to do away with all supranational clauses. In effect, he insisted that the Common Market remain a purely economic arrangement, held together by the will of sovereign and independent states, and subject to the veto power of each and all.

Nuclear Strategy

Since the Allies seemed unwilling to subordinate overall strategy and the use of atomic weapons to a "directorate," France proceeded with the explosion of her own atom bomb. A number of additional reasons were given: the uncertainty about the use of the bomb by the United States, except in self-defense; the need of a French deterrent to war; the injection of new pride and a higher morale in an army that had experienced one frustration after another; and finally, the worldwide commitments of France. As long as other powers have nuclear weapons, the only policy consistent with French interests, according to de Gaulle, was to develop nuclear weapons.

On February 13, 1960, in accord with the timetable set before de Gaulle returned to office, France exploded her first atomic device in the Sahara. There were several additional tests and nuclear devices continue to be tested in the Polynesian possessions of France in the Pacific.

The reality of French nuclear capability, even if limited, was bound to cause a reconsideration of strategic thinking. General de Gaulle himself was particularly anxious not to allow France to meet a crisis with antiquated ideas and weapons. Atomic weapons have been considered the best deterrent against war since they give to the nation possessing them the possibility of retaliating against the vital centers of the enemy's power. The acquisition of military independence, or at least of a semblance of independence, would provide freedom for France to move in one or another direction as the world situation changes. This is the heart of Gaullist doctrine, and continues to be the foundation of France's strategy today.

The Soviets: The "Opening to the East"

As we have seen, de Gaulle never accepted the arrangements made at Yalta. Yet it was quite obvious that, as long as the Soviet threat continued and Soviet power was countered by American power, the division of Europe along the lines laid down at Yalta was inevitable. With the emergence of the Sino-Soviet split, the growing preoccupation of the Soviets with many internal problems, and last, with the emerging aspirations of many Eastern European nations for independence, the time appeared propitious to reopen the Yalta settlement. This necessitated, first, a reconsideration of the problem of German reunification and, second, the assumption by Western Europe of a relative degree of independence vis-á-vis the United States. For as long as NATO remained what it was, and as long as there was direct Soviet-American confrontation in the heart of Europe, there would be no relaxation of Soviet controls in Eastern Europe.

De Gaulle's emphasis upon a "European Europe," his often-repeated statements about a Europe stretching from the Urals to the shores of the Atlantic, were designed to suggest such a relaxation. Its implementation proved to be a much harder problem. One way was to achieve a genuine Franco-German entente within the context of the Common Market, and then to begin a dialogue with the Soviet Union. This proved difficult because of the unwillingness of the Germans to substitute French protection for American, and because of the legitimate doubts of American policymakers about the advisability of such a course of action. De Gaulle then made repeated overtures in the direction of the Eastern European satellites. Cultural and economic ties were stressed; visits were exchanged, a number of leaders of Eastern European countries visiting Paris; and France refused to consider any arrangement that would give the Germans a say about nuclear arms. Thus, under de Gaulle, France was returning increasingly to the pre-World War II arrangements—in which an understanding with the Soviet Union is indispensable to the maintenance of peace in Europe, and in which Germany (preferably divided) must reenter the concert of European powers, but without the ultimate weapon. The Atlantic Alliance was considered necessary but not its integrative military arrangements. The French army was reorganized in a manner that emphasized the primacy of the nuclear weapon—with improved delivery capabilities and the development of some four nuclear submarines with missiles. France stood alone, free to deploy the weapon "against anybody." as General Ailleret announced in 1967. The "opening to the East" was calculated not only to establish better relations with the Soviet Union and make American military presence less imperative, but also to convince the Soviet Union to relinquish its hold over Eastern Europe. The Soviet invasion of Czechoslovakia in the summer of 1968 was only an indication of how illusory the Gaullist hopes were.

THE POMPIDOU YEARS (1969–1974)

When Pompidou came into office the Gaullist aspirations had not materialized. On the contrary, it seemed that the basic Gaullist design, to create an independent Europe under French leadership and protection to undermine the Soviet and American positions in Eastern and Western Europe, respectively, and to prevent a Soviet-American cooperation that he equated with a "condominium," had failed. Even the remarkable industrial growth in France and her strong economic position in the world declined dramatically in 1968 in the wake of two months of revolutionary uprisings that left the economy crippled.

We shall examine the foreign policy under Pompidou with regard to the Common Market and Europe, the Atlantic Alliance, the Franco-Soviet relations, and the evolution of French strategy.

France and the Common Market

The ultimate goal of the founders of the Common Market was political union. They expected that ultimately decisions would be made by a qualified majority vote and that a European executive—the Commission—and a European Parliament would begin gradually and in specified areas to make decisions binding upon the member states. The ultimate dream of the founders was to establish a federation of European states with common political institutions endowed with supranational powers. As a candidate for the presidency, Pompidou ran as a European, and it was widely rumored that he favored not only stronger European ties but also the inclusion of Great Britain in the Common Market. Only *in* Western Europe and *with* Western Europe, that is, the Common Market, could France again become a center of power. But what kind of Europe was it to be? And what would be the relations between such a Europe and the United States, the Soviet Union, and the rest of the world?

Pompidou's policies and objectives are clearly evidenced in the proceedings of three major European summit conferences—in Hague in 1969: in Paris in 1972; and in Copenhagen in 1973—aimed at enlarging and completing the European community. But when the Common Market partners urged the strengthening of the political integrative institution by giving more powers to the Executive Commission and to the European Assembly, Pompidou demurred. He was willing to allow for the rapid exploration of means to "develop in depth" the Common Market in the direction of a monetary union, the establishment of a common patents office, and harmonizing taxation, but he opposed any form of political integration. Throughout his presidency this remained the dominant position of the French.

The Referendum of April 23, 1972.   In January 1972 the four candidate members of England, Denmark, Ireland, and Norway were admitted into the Common Market in a treaty that had to be ratified in one form or another by the Common Market countries and also by the new member states. "Having assumed personally the responsibility for this," stated Pompidou in his press conference, "first in Hague, then in my meeting with Prime Minister Heath [in the summer of 1971] and having authorized the signature of the Treaty. I consider it both my duty and in accordance with democratic principles to ask the French people, who have elected me . . . to express themselves directly on this European policy."[13] The referendum was to be held on April 23, 1972, and was to be followed by a new European Summit meeting of all the members of the Community—including the new ones.

Opinion was divided. The Communist party had urged a "No" vote; the socialists had counseled abstention; the centrists voted "Yes," because they wanted European union and favored the entry of England even though they opposed Pompidou's lack of willingness to go beyond vague phrases about a confederation. The results were disappointing for the president. For every hundred registered voters only 37 voted "Yes"; 17 voted "No," and the rest abstained.

The Paris Conference.   The summit meeting of the nine European countries (Norway decided not to join the Common Market), represented by their top political leaders, took place October 19–20, 1972 to consecrate the entry of England, Denmark, and Ireland into the European Economic Community, but also to face up to some new and urgent monetary problems and to consider the reform of its institutional structures.

The Nine (England, France, West Germany, Italy, Belgium, Holland, Luxembourg, Denmark, and Ireland) constituted a formidable economic, trading, industrial, financial, and, potentially, military bloc. Little progress had been made, however, in the establishment of an institutional arrangement that stops short of a genuine federation but is something more than a loose confederation. It was only agreed to study the prospects "of transforming before the end of the present decade and *with the*

[13]*Année Politique,* 1972, p. 216.

fullest respect of the Treaties already signed the whole complex of relations of member states into a European Union." It was in the summit at Copenhagen in December 1973 that a declaration was adopted stressing the following:

1. The understanding that all bilateral arrangements made by the nine should take into greater consideration the common positions agreed by them.
2. The chiefs of state should meet more frequently.
3. The specific character of the European entity should be respected.
4. The institutions of the community must function fully, and rapid decisions must be made.
5. The relations among the Commission, the Council of Ministers, and the European Parliament should be improved in order to expedite decisions and to reinforce the budgetary control powers of the latter.

The Atlantic Alliance and Defense

Two basic propositions have shaped French foreign policy and defense with regard to the Atlantic Alliance: first, that the division of the world into two "blocs," under the respective control of the United States and the Soviet Union, is unacceptable; second, that in our nuclear world possession of nuclear weapons is the only corollary to national independence. Hence, no integrative alliances should be made that qualify a country's freedom to act.

These two propositions have diametrically contradictory implications when they apply to the United States—the leader of the Atlantic world—and to other states, particularly in Europe, that do not have the nuclear weapon. In the first case France's position is a call for independence from the United States; in the second it is a call for the dependence of the European states upon France for their protection and makes France (or at least so it is hoped) the leader of the Western European nations. It is this contradiction that has made European unity difficult to achieve and has also marred relations between France and the United States.

The French "revolt" against the Unites States[14]—a revolt that dates from the first exchanges between de Gaulle and Roosevelt—has taken every conceivable form: political, economic, cultural, diplomatic, and strategic. Powerfully supported by the Gaullists and the Communists (for different reasons) it was popular among the French. It led to the withdrawal of France from NATO and her unwillingness to consider perma-

[14]Stanley Hoffmann, *Decline or Renewal: France Since the 1930s* (New York: Viking Press, 1974), pp. 332–62.

nent and binding consultative relations between the Common Market and the United States.

French Defense Strategy

But it was France's concept of defense and her strategy within the Atlantic Alliance that created more serious problems. French strategists attempted to develop a theory that reconciled France's place in the Alliance with her independent nuclear force. Their arguments ran as follows: Supposing there is an aggression from the East—then the Alliance becomes operative and the NATO and French forces together engage the aggressor on the basis of the existing bilateral arrangements—presumably somewhere in Europe. If, however, during these forward operations it becomes clear to the French leaders that the aggressor is *aiming* at France's territory, that his *intent* is indeed to occupy France, or destroy it, or seriously imperil its vital interest, then France will be free to act alone, by using its nuclear forces. This point, the so-called *critical threshold of aggressiveness,* is to be determined by the French leaders. The French can and will communicate to the aggressor through appropriate but unequivocal signals their readiness to use their nuclear weapons if the aggressor fails to respond appropriately. In other words, all cooperative arrangements that may exist between France and the Alliance are set aside in favor of French unilateral action the very moment the French leaders decide that the critical threshold of aggressiveness *for France* has been reached. A nuclear retaliatory strike will presumably follow against the aggressor irrespective of what the allies do and even if they are still engaged in battle.

The French position has remained contrary to the inherent logic of the Atlantic Alliance. Why should allies agree to engage their forces in common against an aggressor while leaving one of them free to jeopardize the whole in the name of its own vital interests? Why should West Germany, for instance, act as France's first line of defense unless there is a common strategy that protects both France and the German forces and German interests? Why should the allies go along in a common effort that threatens the existence of their own forces by putting them at the mercy of one of them?

Relations with the Soviet Union

Pompidou continued to follow the guidelines laid down by de Gaulle in France's relations with the USSR. Frequent consultations between the leaders of the two states were held; however, economic arrangements were negotiated representing only a modest increase in the trade between the two countries. With the occupation of Czechoslovakia by the Russian troops in the summer of 1968 the last efforts on the part of France to provide an "opening to the East," based upon a withdrawal of Soviet political and military control there, had failed. There was little that the French could give and even less that the Russians wanted.

In the growing world of détente the French under Pompidou had even less to give. With the withdrawal of the French forces from NATO, but the continuation of the Alliance, there was little that could change the status quo. In the last year of the Pompidou presidency the remarks made by the French president and his minister of foreign affairs about a Soviet-American "condominium," and more particularly an independent European defense, were sharply criticized by the Soviet leaders. Since there was no prospect for France to trade off its Atlantic Alliance for a different one, there was very little that France could do to arouse genuine Soviet interest and support. The Gaullist strategy of using the one side against the other cannot be successful when the two superpowers manage to reach direct agreements.

GISCARD D'ESTAING (1974–1981)

Like Pompidou, Giscard d'Estaing ran in the presidential election of May 1974 as a "European." But unlike Pompidou, he seemed inclined to follow a different approach to the realization of the reconstruction of Europe. First and foremost he appeared to return to de Gaulle's realization that it is only through a firm consolidation of the relationship between France and West Germany that a European vocation can be kept alive and prosperous. The first political leader to visit him in June 1974 was his former fellow minister of finance, Chancellor Helmut Schmidt of West Germany, and he returned the visit within a few weeks. The new minister of foreign affairs, a former French ambassador to West Germany, was appointed because of the great importance the new president attributed to Franco-German relations.

In the declaration of the NATO countries in Ottawa and subsequently in Brussels in the summer of 1974 the "identity" of Europe was recognized and so was its freedom to act and negotiate with others without any binding obligation to prior consultations with its Atlantic partners, notably the United States. But such consultations were deemed to be "necessary" and "highly desirable." Thus the declaration on "European independence" sought by the Gaullists in the past and especially by Pompidou's foreign minister gave way to an assertion of an "identity" of Europe, in the context of the realities of the Atlantic Alliance.

Similarly, in matters of defense and the disagreements between France and virtually every other member of the Atlantic Alliance every effort was made to reconcile them. There was no question of a European independent defense, as the French insisted, but of a "distinct" defense.

There was a recognition of the contribution of the European (that is, French and British) nuclear deterrents to the common Atlantic defense. The general chief of staff, General François Maurin, continued to argue in favor of a French national nuclear striking force, but he conceded that it was the duty of France to foresee all possibilities, and if it were to engage in battle "in the framework of the Alliance," to determine and define in advance the procedures in terms of which France would engage its forces. Consultations for this purpose were to be undertaken with the appropriate NATO organs.

The French nuclear force was strengthened and modernized but there was never any question of France's return to the integrated military command of NATO. Yet a growing "Atlanticism" was very much in evidence. First, as we noted, the French deterrent was to be considered as a part in the global deterrence of the Alliance; second, the notion that the French force would come into play only when the vital interest—that is, the territory—of France were at stake began to give place to a broader formulation according to which the "French space" was interpreted to mean the "territories of our neighbors and allies."

France joined the NATO telecommunication system; it ceased nuclear testing in the atmosphere in 1975 and accepted, on its own accord, many of the provisions of the non-proliferation treaty. It was therefore assumed that in the context of this gradual return of France into the realities of the Atlantic Alliance relations with the U.S.A. would improve. They did, but the differences between the two countries remained.

The Summit of Paris

The most important landmark in the progress of closer cooperation among the Nine was the summit meeting of the heads of the nine governments held in Paris, December 9–10, 1974. It was decided to regularize the convening of such meetings with the participation of the foreign ministers at least three times a year and to establish an "administrative secretariat" (the term *political secretariat* was dropped) to provide minimal liaison services. More important, it was agreed to bring into these deliberations the Executive Commission of the Common Market and to coordinate diplomatic action in "all areas of international affairs which affect the interests of the Community" so that the Nine could speak through their periodically designated president with one voice. The French president stated that he would live up to the timetable to establish such a "European Union" by 1980.

As noted, special efforts were also made to accept some of the supranational provisions of the Treaty of Rome (for instance, decision making in the Council of Ministers by reinforced majorities). The main thrust, however, was in the direction of a political Europe—the European Political Cooperation arrangements, through which the Nine would be able to speak with one voice on foreign policy questions (discussed in Chapter 8).

The U.S.A. and the Soviet Union. For Giscard d'Estaing cooperation with the U.S.A. was a way to strengthen France's and Europe's political, economic, and military independence. It was a means to give an opportunity to Europe to emerge as a genuine third force and by exploiting the climate of détente and good relations with both superpowers to carve out a special area of influence and strength. The president remained particularly solicitous of the Soviet interests. He thought that his grand design—Europe—would suffer if the conditions and the climate of détente came to an end. He forcefully supported the Helsinki Accord that recognized the existing territorial arrangements in Europe after World War II, as the Soviets wished—legitimizing in effect the Soviet positions in Eastern Europe and the sovereign status of the East German Republic. When President Carter began to stress the second major part of the Helsinki Accord—human rights—Giscard d'Estaing demurred. He felt that Carter was "introducing an ideological element . . . that jeopardized détente." For the same reasons Giscard d'Estaing refused to receive Soviet dissidents, or to react strongly to the taking of the American hostages in Teheran, and above all, he did not react forcefully against the invasion of Afghanistan and to events in Poland. The fundamental reason was his fear that if détente were in fact jeopardized and there was a return to the Cold War (as in fact happened) France would be again forced to abandon its ambitions to play an independent role. It would have to return to its natural alliance with the United States and become dependent upon the dominant power within the Atlantic Alliance.

Africa. If there is one area where Giscard d'Estaing's foreign policy consolidated the Gaullist legacy, it was in French-speaking Africa. He granted independence to Djibouti, the last French possession in the continent (also the islands of the Comores became independent). But at the same time he institutionalized the economic, military, cultural, and political relations between France and the former colonies. Special military accords allow for the stationing of French troops—in Djibouti, Senegal, Gabon, Centre-Afrique, and elsewhere; they have intervened frequently to support friends and punish foes and to preempt political turmoil and revolution. Special cultural and economic aid programs tie the former colonial leaders to France; economic aid either directly by France or through the Common Market provides the needed supports to many of these African regimes and leaders. Yet at the same time Giscard d'Estaing insisted on the genuine participation of the African statesmen in the elaboration of policies, visited them repeatedly during his presidency, establishing personal contacts with most of them and convinced them, apparently, of his firm respect for the principle of self-determination and of their sovereign status. His motto remained "Africa for the Africans." France's role, he claimed, was only to help its realization. Not only incidentally did France maintain a privileged position in the procurement of raw materials and through military oversight. Yet for the French president, Africa was also a demonstration of his major thesis regarding U.S. and Soviet confrontations. If France were allowed to play an influential role in military, political, and economic terms in certain regions of the world, Soviet-American confrontations would be averted and the Cold War deferred or avoided. The logic of this position was that France, especially if supported by a united Europe, could act as a buffer between the Soviets and the Americans. But it is a logic that, if accepted, also promotes French power and independence!

In the last analysis, the role Giscard d'Estaing, wanted France to play was essentially similar to that desired by de Gaulle. He wished to reassert French independence within the European context, often interpreting détente in a manner that was to elicit Soviet approval; he felt, however, that a cooperative stance with the U.S.A. and the Atlantic Alliance was necessary not only to secure American support but also to reinforce his position vis-á-vis the Soviet Union. He assumed that the development of a European entity would be more acceptable to the Soviets than a Europe dominated by the Atlantic superpower and that, therefore, his Europeanism would be the better appreciated by the Soviet Union and beyond—by the Third World and in the Middle East. If his conciliatory gestures to the Soviets were calculated to maintain the climate of détente, none had any influence or provided for any restraint on Soviet policy moves— especially in Poland, Afghanistan, or some of the countries of the Third World, including Ethiopia, Mozambique, and Angola. Under Giscard d'Estaing, the discrepancy between ambition and power continued to be the most spectacular trait of French policy and strategy. His conciliatory and cooperative tactics, however, both vis-á-vis the U.S.A. and the Soviet Union, made the discrepancy less apparent than was the case with General de Gaulle.

A SOCIALIST PRESIDENT (1981–1988)

On May 10, 1981 François Mitterrand, who had headed the Socialist party for ten years, was elected president of the republic. His election was followed by the dissolution of the National Assembly and legislative elections in which the Socialist party won an absolute majority of 270 seats out of 492. Their allies—the Communists—with whom there was cooperation at the elections—saw their strength dwindle to a mere 16.5 percent of the national vote and to only 45 legislative seats. But the president ultimately invited them to participate in the new Socialist cabinet—where they were given four posts—and it was expected that they would continue to support the policies of the new prime minister and the new president. It was a clear left-wing victory with the Socialists in control of the government.

Two major questions regarding foreign policy were raised immediately after the election. The one regarded the constitution—would foreign policy and defense continue to be a presidential prerogative? The second regarded substance—what major changes were to be expected in the overall direction of the French foreign policy? Would it follow the Gaullist basic guidelines—independence but within the Atlantic Alliance; cooperation in the Common Market but without any overhaul of the European institutions in the direction of supranationality and an increase in the powers of the European Parliament; continuing close Franco-German ties as the basis of a European regional system; and maintenance of the French position (including military presence) in Africa, as opposed to retrenchment? Nationalism—political and cultural—were the dominant themes of the Gaullists. Would Mitterrand in the name of internationalism, which socialism embodied, stress international and regional cooperation and even integration? Finally, the Gaullists had appeared as the champions of independence and freedom—from Quebec to Central America and from the Middle East to Vietnam. Would the Socialists continue to champion it even among their many client states in Africa, and even more importantly, in their own overseas departments and territories in the Caribbean, in Reunion, and elsewhere?

The constitutional question can be easily answered. The new president, despite his previous hostility to the Gaullist constitution, assumed the full powers of the office and its prerogatives in foreign policy-making and defense. François Mitterrand continued, like his predecessors, to conduct and shape foreign policy through personal contacts (he traveled as often as his predecessors) and indirectly through his personal advisers. The new minister of foreign affairs (the title was changed to *minister of external affairs*), Claude Cheysson, gave the best account of the role of the president and, incidentally, of his own role: "With regard to foreign policy there is one policy. . . . It is defined by the president of the republic and the government." The major guidelines come from the presidency, as in the past. They are implemented through the minister of external affairs in cooperation with the minister of foreign trade, the minister of defense, and the minister of cooperation (in substance in charge of the relations between France and the Third World countries and in particular the former African colonies of France).

The second question—have there been any subjective changes in French foreign policy?—is no more difficult to answer. Only matters of emphasis seem to distinguish the Socialist president from his predecessors.

Continuity in Style and Aspirations

As did de Gaulle, Mitterrand views France as a special country—culturally and politically—devoted to the spread of civilization and freedoms. The superiority and the uniqueness of the French culture has been emphasized by Socialists: It must be sharply distinguished from the mediocrity of all others—especially American. Unwilling and unable to stress economic or military national strength and accomplishments, the Socialist fell back upon a strident cultural nationalism now clothed in Socialist colors. Thus Mitterrand said in his inaugural address: "France . . . can light the path of mankind"; "For many people on this earth turn their eyes toward France. . . . For many of them it represents hope." And not unlike de Gaulle, he opened the heart of France to all the poor and the downtrodden in Latin America in a speech in Mexico City (October 20, 1981): "To all the freedom fighters France sends a message of hope. . . . Greetings to the humiliated, exiled, refugees. . . . Greetings to the . . . persecuted, tortured and assassinated. . . . Greetings to the brutalized clergy, to imprisoned trade-unionists, to the unemployed who sell their blood in order to live, to the Indians chased in the forests, . . . to the peasants without land, to the resistants without arms. . . . To all of them France says: Courage, freedom is on the way . . ." And as with de Gaulle's "Vive le Québec libre!" Mitterrand concluded with "Long live Latin America, fraternal and sovereign!" How was France to translate the message of hope into political action, some continued to ask? And if it could, would it be extended everywhere?

The assertion of French independence is both a matter of style, and of political tactics that has been followed uninterruptedly ever since the end of World War II. Continuity here both with regard to substance and style is remarkable. With regard to style, it consists in the reiteration of the Gaullist affirmation—France will continue to drink from its own glass no matter how small it is (especially since the wine is always tastier). It will not be bound by international entanglements that impede its freedom of choice and action; within an alliance, no matter how binding, France will have a veto power or freedom to act on its own—no matter how contradictory this appears to be; under no circumstances will France subordinate its decision making to an international entity or to a regional or international political or economic regime; no agreements can bind France in which France has not directly participated and to which it has not formally given its consent. The only means for binding France is through bilateral arrangements and agreements with other individual countries. France can, however, speak on behalf of others—but none can speak on its behalf!

This style—some may call it the ideological core—that shapes perceptions and actions in foreign policy directly affects the subtance of Mitterrand's foreign policy and accounts for the striking continuity with that of his predecessors, especially with de Gaulle's foreign policy.

Independence with Regard to the Economic Policies of France. Indeed, Mitterrand's economic policies were at first clearly opposed to the prevailing patterns of austerity in England, West Germany, and the United States. It took more than one year before austerity measures were introduced. Secondly, in East-West trade, the French led the way in rejecting the efforts made by the U.S.A. to embargo materials produced with American patents for the construction of the gas pipeline that was to bring Soviet gas across Eastern Europe and Germany and into the Western European countries. As was the case with the Olympic games of 1980, and with the International Energy Commission in 1973, the French refused to accept American leadership and reacted negatively to its policies. The same was the case with the nomination of Communist ministers to the cabinet. It was not only a shrewd domestic move but a symbolic act of defiance against the United States, whose misgivings about the inclusion of Communists in the French cabinet had been made clear by Vice-President Bush, when he visited Paris. French independent action was also manifest in their retaliatory strike against the Druze positions in Lebanon for the attack against the French units of the peacekeeping force. It was undertaken even before the U.S.A. retaliated. But France refused to allow American planes to fly over its territory when they took off from England to attack Libya in May 1986.

Independent Defense Posture. Their atomic and nuclear weapons— the *force de frappe*, the French have insisted, should not be counted as a part of the allied nuclear force—irrespective of whether it relates to European deployment involving intermediary missiles, INF, or strategic talks involving intercontinental ballistic missiles. Their force is not integrated; it is independently targeted. It can come into play only when vital French interests are involved. Despite reconsideration in the direction of a "forward" strategy—to include the Federal Republic of Germany— French retaliatory weapons are located on the soil of France. Yet the French continue to be members of the Atlantic Alliance but not under its integrated military wing of NATO. They are *in* the Alliance and at the same time *out* of it. Their links to NATO or to individual countries of the Atlantic Alliance are determined by bilateral arrangements the French command makes with the NATO command or with bilateral arrangements between France and individual NATO members—the Federal Republic of Germany, for instance. Under the Socialist government the renovation of the French nuclear force has continued (with considerable increase in military spending), and the construction of a seventh nuclear submarine with missiles and independently targeted multiple warheads has been completed. All their supersonic planes have been virtually replaced by ground-to-ground missiles. As under de Gaulle, the French *force de frappe* under Mitterrand continues to remain the basis of French defense while increasing pressure is being put on them to improve and expand their *force d'action rapide* (FAR)—conventional forces capable of rapid action and deployment anywhere.

Independence within the European Community.   The French position on unanimity in the decisions of the Council of Ministers remains the same, despite the qualifications introduced by Giscard d'Estaing. It has in fact been institutionalized in the European Council (the summit meetings of the heads of the members states of the European Community), where the major guidelines for policy are set forth. The French attitude with regard to the European Parliament remains the same—the French insist on restricting the powers of the latter with regard to the allocation of Community funds and resources. In fact the European Council acts as a superexecutive for the Community in order to prevent the expansion of the powers of the Commission and the European Parliament—both endowed with some supranational powers. Similarly, many trade agreements continue to be made unilaterally by the French, thus defying the role of the Commission to act on behalf of the ten member-states. As for the role of European Political Committee to speak, with one voice, on behalf of the ten member-states on foreign policy questions, the French often act unilaterally without prior consultations with the other member-states. (See Chapter 8.) Thus the Socialist position remains by and large similar to the Gaullist one—a Europe of nation-states in which each state (and especially France) can speak with its own voice even before a common voice can be found. There has been, however, a noticeable shift in the direction of European social and economic integration.

The Franco-German Relationship Continues to Play a Primary Role.   President Mitterrand talked about a Franco-German link (not an "axis"). The meetings envisaged by the Franco-German Treaty of 1963 have continued and special celebrations accompanied the twentieth and twenty-fifth anniversary of the signing of the treaty in 1983 and 1988. For the first time French defense strategy showed signs of change—with a new understanding that the French nuclear force must "cover" their more exposed ally to the east. The "forward" strategy to defend the "vital interests" of France is being refined. Those interests are defined more broadly to include territories to the east of her borders. The Pluton missile deployed close to the Franco-German borders covered a range of only eighty to ninety miles. They were destined to hit "the enemy" *in* German territory. They are being replaced with longer-range missiles—the HADES missiles with a range of 175 miles. Yet the French accepted the deployment of the American Pershings and cruise missiles in West Germany, Italy, and England without reservations or qualifications. They strengthened the American guarantee, kept Germany under American control, provided a deterrent against the Soviets and, above all allowed France to maintain its independent strategy.

France under the Socialist Presidency Remained the "Gendarme of Africa.". Presidential trips to African capitals have been numerous; particular efforts continue to be made to promote trade and provide financial aid to the African countries both directly and through the Common Market; and the so-called North-South dialogue on economic development and modernization is being spear-headed by the French. This was to be expected under the Socialists, who committed themselves to France's African vocation on condition that the "neocolonialist" policies of the past be abandoned and emphasis be placed on economic assistance, social reforms, and development. Jean-Pierre Cot, the first minister of cooperation, insisted at first on the need for reform and economic aid, and so did Claude Cheysson, who had suggested the establishment of a "Marshall Plan" for the Third World countries.

But the cloud that previous presidents and governments had also known remained on the horizon—political instability and unrest, and with it, revolutionary upheavals often supported by hostile regimes in the name of anti-imperialism (both American and French imperialism!). Qaddafi, Castro, and Khomeini were ready to give them a willing hand, often to instigate violent and terrorist acts. Military aggression and revolutionary coups occurred in Tchad, Soudan, Zaire, Centrafrique, Niger—all of them within the French "preserve." They were all particularly disturbing to the established regimes in the whole region for whom continuing French support was often the condition of survival and who in most cases relied upon special military agreements with France and often the presence of French garrisons. Between 1961 and 1981 French troops had been used more than ten times in active or preventive combat. In 1961–1962 in the Cameroun; in 1964 in Gabon; in 1967 in Centrafrique to protect "Emperor" Bokassa; in 1968–1971 the French troops participated in operations against rebels supported by Libya; in 1977 the French provided logistical support and transport for Moroccan troops to protect President Mobutu in Zaire; in 1978, the French sent combat troops to Tchad—against the rebel forces; in 1978, two French companies were transported to Kolwezi in Zaire to repatriate Europeans and to stabilize the political situation; in 1979 French force supported David Decko against Emperor Bokassa, whose "imperial credentials" became increasingly tarnished—especially after the apparent murder of hundreds of children by his mercenaries; in 1980 reinforcements were sent to Tunisia. Would the Socialists confront similar predicaments in the same way or act otherwise? The answer was quickly forthcoming when in 1983 the rebel forces supported by Qaddafi of Libya began their attack, for the third time, on the government and the capital of Tchad. The government appealed to the French for help—an appeal that for many other African leaders would test the will and policies of the new Socialist president. He reacted like all his predecessors by dispatching French military forces that stemmed the advance of the rebels. He did so again in 1985 and 1986.

Without much publicity and with little rhetoric, France has maintained a military presence in her former colonies and especially in Equatorial and Western Africa. Small garrisons of highly mobile and well-equipped forces are scattered through her former colonies, capable of moving rapidly at short notice to help friends and punish enemies. There are 1,200 troops in Senegal, a contingent of 500 in Ivory Coast, another 500 in Gabon, 700 to 1,000 in the Republic Centrafique; 2,000 to 3,000 are on a quasi-permanent assignment in Southern Tchad, defending France's ally against Libyan incursions. There is, in addition, a strong contingent of 3,500 troops in Djibouti, close to the Persian Gulf. Military assistance agreements and arrangements with Madagascar, Mauritania, Congo, Zaire, the Commores and the Seychelles islands, Mali, Niger, and Guinea give France the needed instruments of control while their rapid intervention force—a highly mobile, well-equipped and trained force of some 60,000 based in France give substance to the existing agreements. Of all Western powers, France has been the only one to manage a continuing oversight over the former colonies in the African continent and beyond.

France Has Worldwide Interests and a Worldwide Visibility—"Presence.". The Socialist position remains the same as the Gaullist one. The French "presence," especially if France were to speak on behalf of Europe, might, it is hoped, provide both a challenge to the superpowers and a spokesperson for smaller nations. To provide both, the French presidents and their ministers of foreign affairs have been among the most assiduous travellers in contemporary diplomacy, President Mitterrand and his foreign secretaries, Claude Cheysson (1981–1984) and Ronald Dumas (1984–1986), continued with the same dedication the practice established by de Gaulle, Pompidou, and Giscard d'Estaing and their ministers. India, Israel (Mitterrand was the first French president to visit the country), Saudi Arabia, Mexico, the U.S.A., China, most of the French-speaking African states, Algeria, and Greece have all been visited—some on more than one occasion—to say nothing of the constant criss-crossing to Western European capitals. Some of these visits took place within the framework of regularly scheduled international or regional conferences and meetings; but many were individual ones. There has been but one exception—in his first three years in office Mitterand did not visit the Soviet Union, in sharp contrast to Giscard d'Estaing, who met with Brezhnev in Moscow or Paris or elsewhere eight times in a period of seven years.

The purpose of the visitations are many: trade agreements; the exchange of technology and weapons for raw materials and oil; contracts for industrial development, training programs, sales of nuclear reactors and arms, and, of course, personal diplomacy. But over and above all this—after all, most trade agreements and industrial development projects are prepared in advance by the ministries of the countries concerned and by the competent authorities in France—it is the symbolism that counts. The presence of France is confirmed and reaffirmed on every possible occasion everywhere. It attracts attention, the more so when policy statements appear to diverge from the leading power within the Atlantic Alliance—the United States.

The continuity of French foreign policy under President Mitterrand is apparent. Only a few discontinuities can be noted. The first relates to Franco-Soviet relations; the second to a different stance towards Israel. How fundamental these changes are is open to question. Some may have deep roots in the ideology of French socialism; others may be only tactical, resulting from changes in the balance of power in the international system.

Mitterrand (Who Received the Reluctant Support of the Communist Party in the Election) Appeared to Take a View of the Soviet Union Different from that of His Predecessors. In fact, Giscard d'Estaing was accused by the Socialists of "softness" and "appeasement" to the Soviet Union, failing to take the proper stand with regard both to the invasion of Afghanistan and the events in Poland. In 1980 he met Brezhnev in Warsaw in an effort to elicit only some conciliatory gestures from him—such as the promise to withdraw some of the Soviet forces from Afghanistan. In return the Soviets showed their approval of the "realistic" foreign policy of Giscard d'Estaing (as they had shown approval for de Gaulle's), against his rival in the presidential election. The Socialists in turn spoke of "the wages of Warsaw." Giscard d'Estaing had failed, according to the Socialists, to take a clear stand against the deployment of the Soviet missiles targeted at Western Europe; finally, he had vacillated before condemning the Soviet involvement in Poland and the repressive tactics used against Walesa and the Polish trade union, Solidarity.

President Mitterrand spoke openly against the Soviet military occupation of Afghanistan. Though his foreign minister admitted that there was very little that could be done in Poland, the president condemned the dissolution of Solidarity and the imposition of martial law. In both cases we are in the realm of what may be called "declaratory" or symbolic" foreign policy. What counted, however, was that the Socialist leaders seemed particularly concerned with Soviet aims in Western Europe and the deployment of the Soviet missiles. They spoke clearly and strongly in favor of the NATO decision of 1979 to deploy Pershings and cruise missiles in Western Germany and elsewhere. Mitterrand supported fully the attitude of the Christian Democrats *against* his fellow Socialists in West Germany, as the latter took a firm position against deployment. The Soviet menace appeared far worse to the French than the American

presence, and perhaps for the first time since the Cuban missile crisis in
1962 did a president of France come so close to the American strategic
concerns. In turn the French military presence in West Germany became
more important than in the past, and, as we noted, the French began to
consider a forward strategy that would reassure the West Germans of the
French position and role in the Atlantic Alliance. In one word, under
Mitterrand the French military posture became increasingly Atlanticist.

A change in Franco-Israeli Relations.   The French had refused to deliver the Mirage planes that had been ordered and paid for by Israel;
they had delivered a nuclear reactor to Iraq that was bombed and destroyed by the Israelis; they continued to promote the cause of Palestinian
independence; and they proclaimed their attachment to the UN resolution calling for the withdrawal of all Israeli forces from the areas they
held, but also for the stability and territorial integrity of all nation-states
in the region, including Israel. But when the Egyptian leader Sadat visited Jerusalem to lay the foundation of an Israeli-Egyptian dialogue that
led to peace between the two countries and the exchange of ambassadors,
the French president sent a telegram of congratulations only to Sadat! In
the meantime the French continued to have—or at least to aspire to—
close relations with the Arabs, with whom they developed trade relations,
including the massive sales of arms and planes.

French policy under Mitterrand shifted from a pro-Arab position to
a more balanced stance. The Camp David accords were endorsed, and
Mitterrand visited Israel—the first French president to do so. The invasion of Lebanon by Israel in 1982 was condemned, but the French agreed
to join England, the U.S.A. and Italy in a peacekeeping force in Lebanon,
whose real purpose was to establish a buffer—between Syria and Israel—
and keep the former from gaining a dominant position in the region.
There is no certainty—if ever there could be any in the Middle East—
about the French position in the region. But as in Western Europe and
even in the Third World, the French seemed to be aligning themselves on
the U.S. side, while they continued to proclaim that their moves are an
expression of French rather than alliance interests.

In summary, continuity has been the predominant trait of French
foreign policy under Mitterrand and the Socialists. The overall strategy
remains the same, and any changes that occur are more tactical than
fundamental. France's alliances remain the same—with a noticeable shift
in the direction of greater and more positive interaction with the U.S.A.
and a drift away from the warm relationship that existed under Giscard
d'Estaing with the Soviet Union. Franco-German relations continued to
remain pivotal for French security, especially when West Germany
seemed to be seeking its own identity, perhaps even a neutralist stance
and reunification outside NATO. (See Chapter 3.)

"COHABITATION" AND THE FOREIGN POLICY CONSENSUS

On March 16, 1986, legislative elections were held in France and the Socialists were defeated. The president, whose term was to expire in May 1988, remained in office and was faced with a majority in the National Assembly consisting of the Centrists, the Conservatives, and the extreme right-wing party, the National Front. Jacques Chirac, the leader of the Gaullist Party (Rally for the Republic) became prime minister. This was the first time in the history of the Fifth Republic when a president (a Socialist in this case) was faced by a hostile majority in the National Assembly and by a prime minister speaking on its behalf. The question, therefore, was whether the two would be able to "cohabitate" politically. It was a question raised with even greater urgency with regard to foreign policy.

As we noted, foreign policy had come under the virtually exclusive control of the president—under de Gaulle, Pompidou, Giscard d'Estaing and Mitterrand—not only because of their constitutional power but also because there was a majority in the National Assembly for the president. There could be no conflicts, therefore, between the prime minister who is, according to the Constitution, in charge "of the direction of national policy" and a president who gradually assumed the monopoly in foreign policy-making, defense, and strategy. Would there be conflicts now, and how would they be resolved?

The two years of cohabitation between a Socialist president and a conservative prime minister (March 1986–May 1988) indicated that the general agreement on the basic objectives of foreign policy that we have outlined was so great—the consensus among all political elites and parties so overwhelming—that differences between the Socialist president and a Gaullist prime minister were few and easily managed. A secretary of foreign affairs—Jean-Bernard Raimond—appointed by the prime minister with the consent of the president provided the appropriate linkage between the French Department of State—the Quai d'Orsay—the president and his immediate associates and the prime minister.

Before the legislative election of 1986 the platform of Socialists, on the one side, and the two major opposition parties—the Gaullists and the Union for French Democracy—on the other, did not differ on the fundamentals of foreign policy. No foreign policy pledges divided the two political blocs that departed from the basic foreign policy objectives that we have discussed. When the new prime minister took office, there were some frictions—mostly of a symbolic character: Who represented France, for instance, in the various international conferences and who could speak authoritatively for France with other heads of state? In most cases, they were resolved by having both prime minister and the president attend such meetings, having each one separately discuss matters with other foreign leaders.

In overall terms, the foreign policy consensus remained strong and the president and the prime minister managed to live together!

THE FOREIGN POLICY CONSENSUS AND PROSPECTS

The predominant characteristics of the present consensus are the following:

France continues to remain both inside and outside the Atlantic Alliance; it participates in consultations, but is outside the military organization, even though in case of world crisis it is expected to come to the aid of its allies. It benefits from the information NATO gathers through satellites and other devices and from bilateral technical arrangements between France and NATO. But France maintains its options—to act or not to act and to evaluate a crisis in terms of its own interests and to deploy its forces accordingly. In effect, it benefits from the Alliance and its military organization without assuming explicit obligations and burdens within the Alliance by agreeing to follow NATO's decisions. The viability of this posture depends very much on circumstances—and on the willingness of the allies to accept it.

The Gaullist legacy in Europe continues; France has agreed to the European Community and often has promoted economic and political measures favoring integration and enlargement, but its European vocation remains linked to the assumption that France can play within the Common Market institutions the leading military, political, and even economic role. The nuclear weapon and its independent strategic posture provides the military component; its vaunted know-how and astuteness in diplomacy, thanks to its excellent foreign service and the legacy of leadership throughout the nineteeth century and beyond, give it a claim to political leadership. Even if her economic growth appears to lag compared to the economies of the Federal Republic of Germany and (more recently) England, Italy, and Spain, the political and military advantages could give France a leadership role. If so "Europe" will be supported and promoted.

Can France assume a primary responsibility in the defense of Europe? With what kind of arrangements? Can it do so without the U.S.A. and if not, what binding arrangements can be envisaged with the United States?

These questions are not easily answered; yet they are more pressing than ever, especially after the agreements between the Soviet Union and the U.S.A. reached on December 8, 1987 and May 1988, to withdraw the intermediary nuclear missiles stationed in Eastern and Western Europe—the so-called INF Treaty. A number of options have been entertained and publicly discussed:

1. One is the revival of the Western European Union (WEU) signed in 1948 between England, France, the Benelux countries, and Italy and enlarged in 1954 with the addition of the Federal Republic of Germany. The Treaty provided for *automatic* military assistance by all to any of the members threatened from outside—and the signatories agreed to advance consultations and plans on how to meet such a contingency. The Treaty was, however, overshadowed by the Atlantic Alliance, but it can be revived at any time, if France took the leadership. It will not do so because the moment WEU is revived, the members will want to link it directly with the U.S.A., since they do not believe that it can provide adequate protection without their Atlantic partner—a position that France has refused to accept.

2. The same situation is exactly the case with the revival of the European Defense Community that the French refused to sign in 1954. It provided for integrative military and political arrangements among the six European countries (without England, at that time). All members wished that the European defense community should be linked with the U.S.A.—something that France rejected and continues to reject.

3. A third alternative is the full implementation of the Franco-German Treaty of 1963, and the integration of the Franco-German strategy and defense. This would involve a clear commitment on the part of France to use its nuclear deterrence to defend the Federal Republic, to proceed with the formation of Franco-German units—a matter that has been recently discussed and agreed upon in principle—and to reconsider carefully the role of the United States, especially when the American INFs have been removed.

The Common Market was founded in 1958, was enlarged with the membership of England, Denmark, and Ireland in 1972–1973, with Greece in 1981, and with Spain and Portugal in 1986. It is, as yet, to become a genuine economic and political whole and has not developed decision-making mechanisms to be made by a qualified majority. The French, despite the concessions they have made, continue along the Gaullist doctrine to insist on unanimity (that is, a veto) when vital national interests are involved (see Chapter 8). France continues to resist genuine integrative arrangements. It deplores the lack of a common political will, but does little to promote it. In the meantime 1992 is the year set for the *complete* economic integration of the European Community. Can it be accomplished without some form of political integration? What will be the position of France?

There is finally the question of France's worldwide rank and responsibilities. It is the only European country that has managed a sustained presence—administrative and military—in so many parts of the world. We noted her presence in Africa and beyond. In addition, Guadeloupe and Martinique in the Caribbean and Reunion in the Pacific remain French departments. Colonial outposts can be found in the Polynesian islands, New Caledonia, and elsewhere. Underground tests in the Polynesian archipelago are conducted annually—much to the dismay of Austra-lia and New Zealand. Almost everywhere France acts alone—continuing her imperial vocation. For how long is this posture to be sustained when powerful national movements exist—as is the case today with New Caledonia? And is it commensurate with France's resources?

■ ■ ■ ■

These assessments and the questions raised underline the French posture. The foreign policy consensus appears overwhelming, but its ambiguities remain critical. For the last two years, "cohabitation" between a Socialist president and a conservative prime minister has muted the ambiguities. Each political leader has refused to endorse policy options for fear of making a mistake that might have helped the other!

After the presidential election of April–May 1988, in which Mitterrand was reelected, and the legislative election that followed in June 1988, which failed, however, to provide a socialist majority, there is no doubt that many of the contradictions in French foreign policy consensus will come out into the open. The political system wbe tested as it was during the Fourth Republic.

FOREIGN POLICY LANDMARKS

See also Chapter 8 on European Community.

1944	Liberation of France
December 1944	Franco-Soviet Pact
1945	Potsdam Conference (France does not participate); France becomes one of the four powers "occupying" Germany; France becomes a permanent member of the Security Council of the United Nations
January 1946	de Gaulle resigns
1947	Hostilities begin in Vietnam with occupation of Hanoi by French Army. Dunkirk Pact (between England and France)
January 1947	Institutions of French Fourth Republic put in place
June 1947	Marshall Plan announced
1948	Western European Union formed; Organization of European Economic Cooperation (OEEC) formed
1949	Atlantic Alliance and NATO—France becomes a member
1951	Pleven proposes formation of European Defense Community; Coal and Steel European Community formed
1954	European Defense Community is defeated in the French Parliament; Federal Republic of Germany becomes member of NATO; end of hostilities in Vietnam and with-

	drawal of French forces; beginning of insurrection in Algeria
1956	Morocco granted independence; French African colonies are granted internal autonomy; French-British forces land in Egypt
1957	Treaty of Rome instituting the European Common Market signed; Tunisia granted independence
1958	De Gaulle returns to establish Fifth Republic European Common Market comes into effect
September 21, 1958	De Gaulle Memorandum asking for the establishment of a tripartite directory with United States and England to direct and plan global strategy
1960	Explosion of the first and the second French atomic bombs in the Sahara
1961	Rebellion of four French generals in Algeria against the Fifth Republic
1962	Algeria is granted independence; African French colonies are granted full independence
1964	France recognizes Communist China
1965	France withdraws from the integrated military wing of the Atlantic Alliance (NATO)
1966	Official trip of General de Gaulle to the Soviet Union
1968	Invasion of Czechoslovakia by Soviet Army puts de Gaulle's hopes for an "opening to the East" to an end
1969	De Gaulle resigns; Pompidou elected President
1970	Death of General de Gaulle
1973	England, Ireland, and Denmark join the Common Market
1974	Giscard d'Estaing becomes President
1981	Election of President Mitterrand
1983	Speech by Mitterrand in the German Bundestag in favor of installation of American missiles in Western European countries; France intervenes militarily in Tchad
1984	Mitterrand visits the United States, Franco-Libyan accord on the evacuation of all troops from the disputed region; Mitterrand refuses to participate in the S.D.I. project ("Star Wars")
1985	Renewed French military intervention in Tchad against Libyan-backed forces; Gorbachev visits France
1986	Legislative election produces victory of Conservatives with Jacques Chirac becoming prime minister
1987	Efforts to revive Western European Union; speech by Prime Minister Chirac stating France's committment to the Federal Republic of Germany: "There cannot be a battle of Germany and a battle of France"
1988	Celebrations of the twenty-fifth anniversary of the Franco-German Treaty
April–May 1988	Presidential election in which Mitterrand is reelected with 54 percent of the votes
June 1988	New legislative elections—failure to provide a majority; the Communists have 27 deputies, the Socialists 277, the Center-Right parties 273—total number of seats 577

SELECTED BIBLIOGRAPY

Basic Sources

Année Politique Annual survey of political and economic events and developments. Presses Universitaires de France, Paris.

DE GAULLE, CHARLES. *Discours et Messages.* This is a detailed compilation of the utterances of the General between 1940 and April 28, 1969—the day he resigned. (In five volumes; with comments and notes by Francois Goguel.) Paris: Plon, 1970–72.

———. *Memoirs of Hope: Renewal and Endeavor.* New York: Simon & Schuster, 1971. They cover the first four years of de Gaulle in office after he returned to power on June 1, 1958. Their completion was interrupted by the General's death on Nov. 9, 1970.

———. *War Memoirs*, Vol. I. *The Call to Honour.* New York: Viking Press, 1955. Vol. 2, *Unity.* New York: Simon & Schuster, 1959. Vol. 3. *Salvation.* New York: Simon & Schuster, 1960.

Politique Etrangère de la France: Textes et Documents. Published by Documentation Francaise, 29 Quai Voltaire, Paris 75007. It contains all major addresses and foreign policy documents since 1966. There are an English translation for 1966, 1967, 1968, 1969, and 1970. The volumes since 1971 are available only in French. The publications of the Institut Francais de L'Opinion Publique, 30 Rued'Aumale, Paris, 9e, and of SOFRES, 16–20 Rue Barbes, 92129 Montrouge, provide invaluable survey material on French public opinion trends including occasional in-depth surveys on foreign policy.

Books

AILLERET, CHARLES. *L'Aventure Atomique Francaise.* Paris: Grasset, 1968.

ARON, RAYMOND. *The Great Debate: Theories of Nuclear Strategy*, trans. by Ernst Pawel. New York: Doubleday, 1965.

BUCHAN, ALASTAIR. *Europe's Future, Europe's Choices: Models of Western Europe in the 1970's.* New York Columbia University Press, 1969.

CERNY, PHILIP. *The Politics of Grandeur: Ideological Aspects of de Gaulle's Foreign Policy.* Cambridge, England: Cambridge University Press, 1980.

CHARLOTT, JEAN. *Les Francais et de Gaulle.* Paris: Plon, 1971.

COHEN, SAMMY. *La Monarchie Nucleaire*, Paris: Hachette, 1988.

COUVE DE MURVILLE, MAURICE. *Une Politique Etrangère.* Paris, Plon, 1971.

DE CARMONY, GUY. *Les Politiques Etrangères de la France, 1944–46.* Paris: La Table Ronde, 1967.

DE LA GORSE, ANDRE-MARI. *de Gaulle entre Deux Mondes.* Paris: Fayard, 1964.

DEUTSCH, KARL W., LEWIS EDINGER, RON MACRIDIS, and RICHARD MERRITT. *Elite Attitudes and Western Europe.* New York: Scribner, 1966.

FREARS, J. R. *France in the Giscard Presidency.* London and Boston: Allen & Unwin, 1981.

GROSSER, ALFRED. *La Politique Extérieure de la 4ième République.* Paris: Librairie Armand Colin, 1963.

GROSSER, ALFRED. *La Politique de la France 1944–1984.* Paris: Flammarion, 1984. See also his excellent article "Sommes-nous Une Grande Puissance?" ("Are we a Great Power?") in *L'Expansion,* Octobre–Novembre 1985.

———. *French Foreign Policy under de Gaulle.* Boston: Little, Brown, 1965.

HARRISON, MICHAEL M. *The Reluctant Ally: France and Atlantic Security.* Baltimore: Johns Hopkins University Press, 1981.

HOFFMAN, STANLEY, et al. *In Search of France.* Cambridge, Mass.: Harvard University Press,1964.

———. *Decline or Renewal: French Politics since the 1930s.* New York: Viking Press, 1974. Particularly chaps. 10, 11, and 12.

Institute of International Studies. *La Politique Etrangère de la France 1936–1986.* Paris: Documentation Francaise, 1987.

JOUVE, EDMOND. *Le Général de Gaulle et la Construction de l'Europe, 1940–66.* 2 vols. Paris: Librairie Generale de Droit et de Jurisprudence, 1967.

JULY, SERGE. *Les Annés Mitterrand.* Paris: Grasset, 1986.

KOHL, WILFRED. *French Nuclear Diplomacy.* Princeton, N.J.: Princeton University Press, 1971.

KOLODZIEJ, EDWARD A. *French International Policy under de Gaulle and Pompidou.* Ithaca, N.Y.: Cornell University Press, 1974.

KULSKI, W. W. *de Gaulle and the World System.* Syracuse. N.Y.: Syracuse University Press, 1967.

MACRIDIS, ROY C. *de Gaulle—Implacable Ally.* New York: Harper & Row, 1966.

———. *French Politics in Transition: The years after de Gaulle.* Cambridge, Mass.: Winthrop, 1975.

MITTERRAND, FRANCOIS. *La Politique Etrangère de la France.* Paris: Flammarion, 1986. Contains the major speeches and addresses on foreign policy by the President.

MORSE, EDWARD L. *Foreign Policy and Introdependence in Gaullist France.* Princeton, N.J.: Princeton University Press, 1973.

NEWHOUSE, JOHN. *de Gaulle and the Anglo-Saxon.* New York: Viking Press, 1970.

PIERRE, ANDREW J. *The Global Politics of Arms Sales.* Princeton, N.J.: Princeton University Press, 1982.

Politique Internationale. No. 35. (1987), pp. 21–39, 53–64. Interview with Jean-Bernard Raimond, Minister of the Department of Foreign Affairs, and André Fontaine.

ROBIN, GABRIEL. *La Diplomatie de Mitterrand ou le Triomphe des apparences,* de la Bievre. Paris, 1986.

RUEHL, LOTHAR. *La Politique Militaire de la Ve République.* Paris: Presses de la Fondation Nationale des Sciences Politiques, 1976.

WHITE, DOROTHY S. *Seeds of Discord.* Syracuse, N.Y.: Syracuse University Press, 1964.

WILLIAMS, PHILIP. *French Politicians and Elections, 1951–1969.* Cambridge, England: Cambridge University Press, 1970.

WILLIS, ROY. *France, Germany and the New Europe, 1945–1967.* New York: Oxford University Press, 1968.

3

The Foreign Policy
of the Federal Republic
# of Germany

Josef Joffe

INTRODUCTION: THE LEGACY
OF HISTORY AND GEOGRAPHY

There are few nations whose history contains as many broken threads as
Germany's. In this century alone, Germany has undergone four radical
changes of political personality—from Wilhelm II's Empire to the
Weimar Republic, from Hitler's Reich of the Thousand Years to its two
postwar successors, the Federal Republic of Germany (FRG) and the
German Democratic Republic (GDR). Other nations, like France and Russia, have also experienced revolutionary transformations. Yet throughout
modern history, they have preserved a fairly stable geographical and
physical identity. Germany, by contrast, has not. Since the Middle Ages,
"Germany" has stood for a kaleidoscopic pattern of political entities in the
heart of Europe whose boundaries were forever changing.

From the tenth to the thirteenth century, the "Holy Roman Empire
of the German Nation" saw itself as the heir of Rome. Yet its identity was
more often than not based on a claim and a spiritual idea rather than on
the realities of political control. For centuries afterwards, until its reunification under Bismarck in 1871, Germany lacked an effective central
political authority. This absence was both unique and crucial, setting
Germany apart from the dominant historical trend in Europe. In the

wake of the Middle Ages, the nation-state became the dominant form of political organization. Its model was provided by the evolution of England and France since the thirteenth century. From a central "core area"[1] political authority was successively pushed outward through military conquest and dynastic marriage. Religious homogenization and the rise of national sentiment reinforced monarchical rule.

German "nation-building" did not resume until the eighteenth century, and then under unique historical auspices. The core area was the Kingdom of Prussia, which embarked on the road to expansion under Frederick the Great's leadership around the middle of the century. Compared to the Habsburg Empire or the established nation-states like England and France, Prussia's economic resources were as sparse as its population. Yet Prussia had thoroughly absorbed the lessons of Germany's endemic vulnerability. If insecurity was the basic condition of political life, then survival was the supreme imperative. The State would have to be strong. Prussia developed one great advantage over its neighbors: an efficient administration apparatus and a modern draft system that endowed Prussia's kings with a disproportionately large standing army.

Prussia's expansion was essentially completed in 1871 when Bismarck imposed unity on the remnants of the Holy Roman Empire outside the Habsburg dominions. German unity, however, remained as elusive as it was late to arrive. It lasted seventy-four years—from 1871 to 1945, when the victorious armies of the United States and the Soviet Union met on the Elbe river at the close of World War II.[2]

From its very beginning, the Second German Empire (1871–1918) was saddled with a triple handicap. It was a latecomer to the great-power scene, it was a latecomer to nationhood, and given the peculiar way in which unification was achieved, it remained an unfinished nation. Like Prussia, the German Reich had suddenly emerged among the established powers that for centuries had regarded the European center as proper object of domination. Its rise was inseparably tied to conquest, yet it was

[1]For the concept of the "core area" and its role in nation-building, see Karl W. Deutsch, *Nationalism and Social Communication* (Cambridge, Mass.: MIT Press, 1966).

[2]Chronological note: In 1871, Germany was unified under Bismarck (Reich Chancellor) and Emperor Wilhelm II. Since the new Reich (Empire) regarded itself as successor to the medieval "Holy Roman Empire of the German Nation," it came to be known as the Second German Empire. After the brief revolution at the end of World War I, the Reich was succeeded by the Weimar Republic. The first German Republic derived its name from the small town of Weimar where its constitution was drafted. It lasted from 1919 until 1933 when Adolf Hilter was elected Chancellor. The year 1933 marked the beginning of the dictatorial Third Reich (or Reich of the Thousand Years), which was destroyed by the Allied victory in 1945. After a four-year interregnum, the Federal Republic of Germany (FRG) and the German Democratic Republic (GDR) became the de facto successor states of the Third Reich. Both gained sovereignty in 1955. For a concise introduction to political change in Germany since Bismarck, see Guido Goldman, *The German Political System* (New York: Random House, 1974), especially chaps. 1–3.

at a stage in the evolution of the European system where such dramatic increase in power could only appear as usurpation of the established order. Indeed, Germany's unification by "blood and iron" grew directly out of the Franco-Prussian War of 1870–1871, which ended in the annexation of Alsace and Lorraine against the wills of their populations. For centuries, the swapping of territories and populations had been a legitimate instrument of diplomacy. In an age of nationalism, however, annexation ran the risk of mobilizing entire nations for the cause of *revanche*. The absorption of two French provinces saddled Germany with a legacy of permanent conflict with France. It lasted three generations and took two world wars to resolve.

After 1871, Germany may have been the strongest nation on the continent, but it was only a "semihegemonial" power.[3] It was strong enough to defeat any single comer, but not strong enough to keep them all at bay at the same time. Given its vulnerable frontiers, its strength had to be predicated on speed, the offensive, and the concentration of power. Offensive capabilities always exceeded defensive ones, and in spite of vast disparities in population and size, the Reich had inherited Prussia's vulnerability. During the Seven Years' War (1756–1763) an all-Continental coalition had almost destroyed Frederick's Prussia. The "nightmare of coalitions," as Bismarck called it, became the abiding obsession of German leaders. The nightmare sprang to life twice in two world wars.

Germany remained an unfinished nation. Unification had not been achieved under the Liberal-Democratic auspices of the crushed 1848 Revolution. Instead, it was Prussia that had unified Germany by conquering it.[4] Prussia's political system, reared in the tradition of bureaucratic absolutism and dominated by the landed *Junker* oligarchy, was superimposed on Germany as a whole. The result was a unique discrepancy between extremely rapid industrialization and political backwardness.

Bismarck fully understood Germany's precarious position in the European system. He constantly assured his neighbors that the Reich was "saturated." He avoided challenging England's supremacy at sea. He fought off domestic pressures for imperial conquest in Africa and Asia. And he remained on friendly terms with Russia, France's most likely ally.

After Bismarck's retirement in 1890, however, the Reich drifted into a collision course with the rest of Europe, aided by the ineptness of Bismarck's successors, especially of that "maniac on the throne,"[5] Kaiser Wilhelm II. But not even a second Bismarck could have managed to freeze Europe's tenuous order, let alone prop up the obsolete and

---

[3]This term has been borrowed from Ludwig Dehio, *Deutschland und die Weltpolitik im 20 Jahrhundert* (Munich: Oldenbourg, 1955), p. 15.

[4]Thus the apt heading of chapter 6, "The Conquest of Germany by Prussia," in A. J. P. Taylor's *The Course of German History* (London: Hamis Hamilton, 1945).

[5]Alexander Gerschenkron, *Bread and Democracy in Germany* (New York: Howard Fertig, 1966), p. 88.

conflict-ridden domestic system of Imperial Germany. Certainly World War I was a war nobody wanted, but pent-up conflicts had been brewing for a long time.

Germany's geographic situation has always provided an obsession as well as a temptation. The obsession was Bismarck's "nightmare of coalitions," and it seemed to have come true in 1907 when England, France, and Russia joined forces in the Triple Entente. The temptation (posed by encirclement) was to launch a lightning strike against the most threatening opponent at any one time or, worse, an all-out war for hegemony which would break the stranglehold permanently. Thus the so-called Schlieffen Plan prior to World War I foresaw a quick victory in the West as the prelude to a second strike in the East before the cumbersome Russian mobilization machinery was ready for war. A similar strategy was employed by Hitler during World War II. In both cases, it activated the coalition nightmare that it was designed to thwart once and for all.

In 1945, the seventy-four year experiment in German unity ended in cataclysmic defeat and sixfold dismemberment.[6] The Nazi Revolution had destroyed much of Germany's old social and political order. Having acted as a "modernizer," the Nazi dictatorship was in turn swept away by the Allied victory. In contrast to 1918, when defeat and short-lived revolution had barely affected the social foundations of German political life, surrender and occupation in 1945 wiped the slate almost completely clean.

THE POLITICS OF IMPOTENCE: WEST GERMANY AS A SPECIAL CASE

The study of comparative foreign policy is based on the application of yardsticks by which we compare and contrast in order to distinguish the unique from the general. By virtue of, say, its size, population, and resource base, the Federal Republic of Germany (FRG) falls into the elusive category of "middle powers" like England, France, or Italy. Yet if we look more closely at the peculiar origins and handicaps of the Federal Republic, we see that there are some conspicuous distinctions which suggest a special case.

To begin with, the very existence of the FRG represents something of a historical fluke. In 1945, when the four victorious powers assumed "supreme authority"[7] over its affairs, Germany had virtually ceased to exist as a political entity. In the aftermath of the hatreds unleashed by the

---

[6]The Federal Republic of Germany, the German Democratic Republic, East Berlin, West Berlin, and the territories incorporated by Poland and the Soviet Union.

[7]Beate Ruhm von Oppen, ed., *Documents on Germany Under Occupation, 1945–1955* (London: Oxford University Press, 1955), p. 30. This is a useful collection of documents on the first postwar decade.

Third Reich, an indefinite period of punishment and subjection appeared as Germany's most likely fate. Yet in the wake of victory, the wartime alliance between East and West disintegrated. A new conflict, the Cold War, superseded the old one. The Cold War represented an inconceivable windfall gain for Germany. A "Super-Versailles" did not materialize. Instead, in 1949, Germany suddenly found itself doubly reincarnated on either side of the Elbe river.

Thus, the very establishment of the FRG was not so much an act of choice as it was the result of Allied fiat. The Federal Republic was an offspring of bipolarity, conceived and nurtured by the strategic imperatives of the West. Yet while the Federal Republic was bound to profit from the transformation of the dominant international conflict, it was also its prostrate captive and, by virtue of partition, its starkest symbol.

For a good part of its existence, the Federal Republic has been subjected to a unique degree of dependence and external constraints. In many ways it was more of an artifact than a nation-state. Founded in 1949, it continued to lack sovereignty, the most essential attribute of a state, until 1955. Even after 1949, sovereignty was only delegated and subsumed under the Occupation Statute by which the United States, England, and France retained supreme authority. After sovereignty was devolved in 1955, the three Western powers reserved important prerogatives, notably those pertaining to Berlin and Germany as a whole, which they retain to the present day. But even on the German side, there was a deliberate refusal of complete statehood. Apart from the amputation of its eastern territories, the nation was split into two political units. Accordingly, the officially proclaimed raison d'être of the FRG was that of a *Provisorium,* a transitional polity which would liquidate itself on the day reunification came.[8]

Dependence imposed itself in many guises. First, and most crucially, the FRG suffered from a unique disjunction between diplomacy and its moral and material wherewithals. Deprived of sovereignty, armed forces, economic strength, and moral credibility, West German diplomacy was reduced to empty-handed bargaining. The main objective of policy was not the pursuit of concrete goals, but the accumulation of resources-in-being, which could be expended for political influence. Indeed, the overriding problem was to acquire the very *right* to conduct a foreign policy in the first place.[9] This predicament was aptly expressed in Konrad Adenauer's (federal chancellor from 1949 to 1963) first declaration before the *Bundestag:* "For the German people there is no other way of attaining

---

[8]There is no constitution but only a "Basic Law" which was enacted for a "transitional period" only. Its preamble explicitly charges the German people with the task of achieving reunification.

[9]Cf. Alfred Grosser, *Germany in Our Time* (New York: Praeger, 1971), p. 291.

freedom and equality of rights than . . . in concert with the Allies. There is only one path to freedom. It is the attempt to extend our liberties and prerogatives step-by-step and in harmony with the Allied High Commission."[10]

Second, instead of domestic structures affecting the FRG's foreign policy, the foreign policies of others came to shape the evolution of domestic institutions and societal orientation. On the level of society, the widespread reaction against both National Socialism and Communism served as a fertile breeding ground for the seeds planted primarily by the American occupation in form of reeducation, denazification, federalism, and free-enterprise economic development. While the constitution—the Basic Law—was not imposed on the Germans (as it was on the Japanese), it did follow the guidelines laid down by the Military Government. Yet even if direct interference was limited, it was surely no coincidence that societies and institutions in both Germanies closely resembled those of their patron powers. In the end, Stalin's famous dictum was manifestly vindicated: "This war is not as in the past. Whoever occupies a territory also imposes on it his own social system. Everyone imposes his own system as far as his army can reach. It cannot be otherwise."[11]

Third, instead of its own foreign policy affecting the Federal Republic's international milieu, the bipolar structures of postwar Europe determined West German policy and interests. There was the escape from subjection; the shattered economy that had to be rebuilt; and, as Stalin imposed ideological uniformity on Eastern Europe and made his unsuccessful bid for Berlin in the Blockade of 1948–1949, security against subversion and invasion became an intense preoccupation. As the most exposed member of the Western coalition, the Federal Republic has tended to subordinate other concerns to the demands of Alliance cohesion and readiness. On the other hand, and in spite of the reversal of alliances in the Cold War, the FRG had to guard against the nightmare of coalitions which might still be resurrected in the reassertion of Four-Power solidarity. Finally, the amputation of the eastern territories and partition mortgaged the FRG with a powerful legacy of revisionism. Although reunification was deliberately postponed to another and better day, it remained the official raison d'être of the Federal Republic. As we shall see, the contradiction between an actual policy of integration into the West and the aspiration for reunification with the East posed the dominant dilemma of West German foreign policy for a generation.

10*Verhandlungen des Deutschen Bundestages* (the official record of West German parliamentary proceedings), September 20, 1949, p. 29.

11As quoted by Milovan Djilas, *Conversations with Stalin* (New York: Harcourt Brace Jovanovich, 1962), p. 114.

THE POLITICAL STYLE: SOVEREIGNTY
THROUGH INTEGRATION

After its establishment in 1949, the FRG had to live without power and the capacity to reward or to punish. Yet it did retain one important bargaining counter: the capacity to *deny* cooperation to its would-be allies—a value that grew as a direct function of the West's determination to turn West Germany into a bulwark against the East. The repetitive gamble of West German diplomacy consisted of discovering and exacting the highest political price for voluntary collaboration. West German diplomacy confronted an all but impossible task. It had to build a tradition of trust; it had to gain recognition as a legitimate actor in the community of nations.

In his pursuit of international respectability, Adenauer consistently followed three basic principles. First, France needed reassurance that there would be no resurgence of the "German peril." Second, there was only one method of spanning the gap between Allied insistence on constraints and German aspirations for sovereignty. The West had to be persuaded to reverse Lenin's classic precept that "Trust is good, control is better." Accordingly, Adenauer's entire diplomacy was devoted to transmuting the constraints imposed unilaterally by the victors into mutual controls shared voluntarily by all. Finally, the best way to achieve both objectives was political and economic integration that would supersede the ancient logic of power politics by the new logic of community and mutual gain.

As a result, Adenauer became a compulsive joiner on the simple theory that voluntary compliance would make Allied imposition less likely, while membership in any international organization would bestow not only the trappings of equality, but also the real chance to influence the course of events. It is impossible to understand the success story of European integration without taking into account these basic facts of West Germany's postwar condition. For the FRG, integration was a low-cost, high-payoff policy. Since the Occupying Powers retained supreme authority, West Germany's integrationist virtues carried their own tangible rewards. For the Federal Republic, integration merely involved sacrificing nonexisting, potential rights in exchange for actual, partial sovereignty. Since integration was predicated on the equal subjection to common rule, self-abnegation became the condition for self-assertion. As such, Adenauer's tactics were exactly the reverse of the early Europeanists such as Jean Monnet, one of the founding fathers of European integration. They saw partial integration as an irresistibly spreading solvent of national sovereignty because each concrete integrative measure in any one area would force leaders to integrate more and more sectors. Adenauer, however, reversed the logic by using each concession of the FRG as a lever for lifting the restraints upon German statehood and freedom (that is, upon German national sovereignty).

If the West insisted on reparations and control of the iron and coal industries of the Ruhr district, Adenauer complied, but also proposed that the FRG join the International Ruhr Authority. If the French were afraid of the FRG's superior economic potential, Adenauer suggested that American reconstruction capital be channeled through France. When France moved to detach the iron-rich Saarland from West Germany, Adenauer countered with a call for complete Franco-German union.[12] In other words, the unique quality of Adenauer's style rested in his persistent attempt to transcend the normal diplomatic process which begins by haggling over each issue at hand and ends up by splitting the difference. Instead, his most elementary diplomatic technique was forever dedicated to "upgrading the common interest" and, hence, to dwarfing a particular clash of interest by enlarging the framework for its solution.

This was certainly Adenauer's basic objective in the aftermath of World War II. It is doubtful, however, whether he would have succeeded in transforming the stakes as quickly as he did without another enormous windfall gain: North Korea's attack on South Korea in the summer of 1950. To trade cooperation for emancipation was one thing; to reduce West Germany's crushing impotence was a far more formidable task. "I began to understand," Adenauer was to reminisce many years later, "that in our days influence required power. Without power, one cannot conduct policy. Without power, our words will not be heeded."[13]

Acting on Machiavelli's dictum that strong armies make for reliable allies, Adenauer had taken a calculated risk as early as the winter of 1949 when he floated his famous trial balloon on German rearmament. Against the background of the Prague Coup and the Berlin Blockade, he told an American correspondent in December of 1949 that "Germany should contribute to the defense of Europe in a European army under the command of a European headquarter."[14] Unperturbed by protests at

---

[12]This bold gamble did not work, or only to the extent that the French responded with the so-called "Schuman Plan" for the integration of West Europe's coal and steel industries, which blossomed into the European Coal and Steel Community (ECSC), the forerunner of the Common Market. With French control instincts satisfied, Adenauer succeeded in persuading the French to postpone the formalization of the Saar's autonomy. A few years later France agreed to a Saar referendum. When the population rejected autonomy, the Saar became a *Land* of the Federal Republic in 1957.

[13]As quoted by Dieter Schröder in *Süddeutsche Zeitung* January 7, 1960, p. 3.

[14]Interview with John Leacacos, *Cleveland Plain Dealer,* December 4, 1949. There is a rich literature on the story of German rearmament. On the German side, the best is Arnulf Baring's *Aussenpolitik in Adenauers Kanzlerdemokratie* (Munich: Oldenbourg, 1967). For treatments in English, see Laurence W. Martin's classic study "The American Decision to Rearm Germany" in Harold Stein, ed., *American Civil-Military Decisions* (Birmingham, Ala.: The University of Alabama Press, 1963) and the more recent analysis by Robert McGeehan, *The German Rearmament Question: American Diplomacy and European Defense After World War II* (Urbana, Ill.: University of Illinois Press, 1971).

home and abroad, he kept fishing for an Allied invitation to contribute integrated German contingents. In order to foreclose an easy way out for the West, which would have robbed him of the most crucial bargaining chip toward sovereignty, he was quick to brand the "idea of raising volunteers in Germany" as exploitation which would reduce Germany to a supplier of mercenaries.[15]

The North Korean attack succeeded where Adenauer had failed with his deflated trial balloon on German rearmament. It dramatized (if only by false analogy) the strategic and political logic inherent in the founding of NATO and the Federal Republic. By the late summer of 1950, the American decision to rearm West Germany finally delivered the vehicle on which Adenauer could coast towards sovereignty. Furthermore, it enlarged a primarily Franco-German contest over the extent of West German emancipation to a three-party game in which the United States switched from reluctant referee to tacit ally.

At first France responded with an ambitious project to supranationalize the very hard core of sovereignty (that is, defense) in a European Defense Community (EDC). The EDC and West German sovereignty were firmly linked in the settlement between the FRG and the West, concluded in 1952. Yet France could never make up its mind what was more important: the containment of the Soviet Union or the control of Germany. Thus, on August 30, 1954, the French National Assembly repudiated the entire settlement. The grandest design of European unity was sacrificed to the sturdier ideal of national sovereignty. (See Chapter 2.)

Yet the United States and Britain were now firmly committed to German rearmament. France was finally swayed by a host of new contractual and configurational constraints against the resurgence of a German threat. Among them, the most crucial guarantee was an Anglo-American commitment to maintain a substantial military presence in West Germany and Europe. In 1955 the occupation regime was terminated. With its sovereignty restored, the Federal Republic was admitted directly into NATO. Ten years after World War II and total defeat, Adenauer succeeded in purchasing respectability and security for half of the nation at the price of an unprecedented policy of self-denial and dependence for the FRG and partition for the whole.

REUNIFICATION VS. REALPOLITIK

In 1966, three years after his retirement from the chancellorship and one year before his death, Adenauer was asked: "Let us assume, though, that a reunified and neutral Germany had been possible, would you have

---

[15]Konrad Adenauer, *Erinnerungen, 1* (Stuttgart: Deutsche Verlags-Anstalt, 1965), p. 343.

wanted it?" Adenauer's answer was an emphatic "No, never."[16] As curt as this reply was, it probably contains the most concise explanation for the course of West German foreign policy in his thirteen-year tenure.

Why did Adenauer place a higher value on the Federal Republic's amalgamation into the West than on reunification? An answer must resist two facile theories which suffer from the imputation of either excessive idealism or excessive cynicism to his motives. According to the one, Adenauer reduced reunification to a second-order concern because Europe was more important to him than Germany. According to the other, he treacherously wrote off East Germany as a presumptive stronghold of the Social Democratic Party (SPD) and Protestantism and thus as a threat to his own tenure.

There probably were elements of both of these theories in his calculus. Adenauer's "Rheinocentrism" has been a source of persistent speculation. As mayor of Cologne in the 1920s, he had an ambiguous record of separatism in favor of a Rhenish Republic economically linked with Belgium and France and politically tied to a German federation.[17] If the Cologne Cathedral somehow symbolized the spiritual fount and the political center of an ancient European civilization, then the "Asian steppes"[18] began in Magdeburg, Berlin being a "heathen city."[19] Similarly, Prussia represented the very nemesis of Germany while the Social Democrats (whose electoral strength was concentrated in Protestant East Germany) were the latter-day political descendants of the power-hungry Prussian *Junker* class.[20]

Yet no foreign policy—not even the allegedly simple- and single-minded diplomacy of Adenauer—can ever be reduced to the ideology or psychology of its perpetrator. Since the problem was more complex than reunification, the explanation is also more complicated. Apart from the volitions of any German leader, reunification was an unrealistic goal. After the war, Germany was the "prize, the pivot, and the problem of European politics."[21] Accordingly, there was no way either side would voluntarily let go of *its* German half. Politically, bipolarity in Europe was strictly a zero-sum game; whichever superpower succeeded in incorporating all of Germany on its side would have scored an enormous, unacceptable gain against the other. Militarily, on the other hand, nuclear weapons

16In an interview with Golo Mann on April 18, 1966. Golo Mann, *Zwölf Versuche über die Geschichtsschreibung* (Frankfurt: S. Fischer, 1973), p. 136.

17For the record, ambiguous as it is, see the painstaking account by Karl D. Erdmann, *Adenauer in der Rheinlandpolitik nach dem ersten Weltkrieg* (Stuttgart: Klett, 1966).

18Interview with Hans-Peter Schwarz as quoted in his *Vom Reich zur Bundesrepublik* (Berlin: Luchterhand, 1966), p. 433.

19As quoted by *Gazette de Lausanne*, July 15, 1947. See also *Hannoversche Presse*, July 16, 1957.

20As quoted by Schwarz, *op. cit.*, p. 432.

21Pierre Hassner, "Europe West of the Elbe" in Robert S. Jordan, ed., *Europe and the Superpowers* (Boston: Allyn and Bacon, 1974), p. 103.

had turned Cold War politics into a non-zero-sum game with an incalculable negative payoff for both. The use of force was out of the question, for no conceivable stake was worth the cost of potential nuclear devastation.

There was one logical alternative: a reunified and neutral Germany. Yet Germany was not Austria (which was neutralized in 1955). For good reasons, the West was not interested. A neutralized Germany would have bottled up Western defenses behind the Rhine while giving the Soviet Union all the strategic and psychological advantages of proximity. More generally, neutrality raised all the uncertainties of the ancient "German problem." Germany has always been either too strong or too weak. Before unification in 1871, the problem was posed by Germany's weakness and inability to stave off domination by others. After 1871, Germany was too strong to be contained by its neighbors, yet not strong enough to impose its lasting rule on the Continent.

Given Germany's critical size, neutralization would have rolled both of these problems into one. If Germany were neutral and *disarmed*, it would raise the dual problem of keeping it disarmed and keeping others from dominating it. If Germany were neutral and *armed*, it would pose the reverse problem of keeping it neutral or keeping it from dominating Europe either alone or with another power.[22] By contrast, bipolarity and partition had paradoxically defused all of these risks in an order which was as novel as it was stable.

The Cold War alliance systems protected Germany not only against others, but also against itself. Contrary to the Bismarck Empire, Germany did not have to labor under the double burden of projecting the main threat to Europe's order *and* of managing its stability from a solitary position at the center. Unlike the Weimar Republic, it did not have to (and could not) play East against West as the condition of survival. With *two* Germanies countervailing each other and their respective patron powers, German strength was at once neutralized and harnessed. At the same time, they were not left alone, but remained anchored in two antagonistic communities which gave them shelter as well as a role.

Yet what about German interests? Why did Adenauer refuse to grasp the opportunity for reunification-cum-neutralization as fleetingly offered by Stalin's notorious notes to the West in March of 1952?[23] In the first place, Adenauer did not have a choice except to cast the FRG's lot with the West. West Germany's peculiar condition prejudged not only the style, but also the substance and direction of its diplomacy. By definition,

[22]For an interesting "internalization" of this reasoning on the part of German policymakers, see Heinrich von Brentano's address before the Bundestag. (He was foreign minister from 1955 to 1961.) *Verhandlungen des Deutschen Bundestages*, February 27, 1955, p. 3883.

[23]For the exchange of notes, see the Council on Foreign Relations, *Documents on American Foreign Relations, 1952* (New York: Harper & Row, 1953), p. 248 ff.

sovereignty could only mean its devolution from the West, while security could only mean security against the East. Any *Schaukelpolitik* (a policy of maneuver and balance) between the two blocs carried the high risk of either postponing sovereignty forever or, worse, reactivating a collusive Four-Power policy. As Adenauer put it at the time: "One false step, and we would lose the trust of the Western powers. One false step, and we would be the victim of a bargain between East and West."[24] For if there was anything worse than partition, it was precisely the kind of neutralization extended by the Soviets just prior to the conclusion of the Western settlement with the FRG in May of 1952.[25]

The real problem of West German policy transcended the antinomy between integration and reunification. If we are to believe Adenauer, the real crux was the protection against yet another "nightmare of coalitions," the abiding obsession of modern German foreign policy. This priority was articulated by Adenauer in an interview given in 1953. It bears citing at length because it captures the articles of faith (or fear) on which his entire foreign policy was based. If Bismarck's obsession had been the "nightmare of coalitions," Adenauer's horror was Potsdam:

> It is no coincidence that the Soviets keep referring to this agreement over and over again. To them it represents an eternal Morgenthau Plan imposed by the Four Powers. . . . Potsdam signifies nothing but: Let us strike a bargain at Germany's expense. . . . Bismarck spoke about his nightmare of coalitions against Germany. I have my own nightmare: its name is Potsdam. The danger of a collusive great power policy at Germany's peril has existed since 1945, and it has continued to exist even after the Federal Republic was established. The foreign policy of the Federal Government has always been aimed at escaping from this danger zone. For Germany must not fall between the grindstones. If it does, it will be lost.[26]

The settlement with the West as concluded in 1952 and amended in 1954[27] (after France had vetoed the original compact) ratified an unprecedented policy of dependence and self-denial on the part of the Federal

[24]Adenauer, *Erinnerungen*, 2, p. 88.

[25]"I considered neutrality between the two power blocs as an unrealistic position for our nation. Sooner or later, one side or the other would attempt to incorporate Germany's potential on its side. . . . We had to join either one or the other side, if we wanted to prevent being crushed by both." Adenauer, *Erinnerungen*, 1, p. 96

[26]In a broadcast interview with Ernst Friedländer on June 11, 1953. Presse- und Informationsamt der Bundesregierung, *Mitteilungen an die Presse*, No. 561/53, pp. 3–4.

[27]For the documents, see Council on Foreign Relations, *Documents on American Foreign Relations, 1952* and the volume for 1954 (New York: Harper & Row, 1953 and 1955). For a succinct analysis of the 1954 settlement, see Charles E. Planck, *The Changing Status of German Reunification in Western Diplomacy, 1955–1966* (Baltimore, Md.: Johns Hopkins Press, 1967), pp. 6–10.

Republic.[28] In exchange, the West limited its own options by a number of pledges which explicitly or implicitly precluded the wrong kind of German settlement with the Soviet Union:

1. As the only government "freely and legitimately constituted," the Federal Government was "entitled to speak for Germany as representative of the German people in international affairs." By thus underwriting the FRG's *Alleinvertretungsanspruch* (its claim to be the sole representative of Germany as a whole), this declaration bestowed the title of succession to the German Reich to the Federal Republic and, by implication, precluded Western recognition of the GDR.

2. By agreeing that the "final determination of the boundaries of Germany" must await a *freely* negotiated peace settlement, the West not only refused the legitimacy of the postwar demarcation lines (that is, the borders between the two Germanies and the Oder-Neisse line), but also reassured the FRG against a peace treaty imposed by fiat of the Four Powers.

3. By extending their security guarantee to Berlin, the former German capital now located within the territory of the GDR, the Western powers again demonstrated their refusal to recognize the finality of partition as well as their determination to preserve Four-Power responsibility in Berlin and Germany as a whole as anchor point for a reunification settlement.

4. "Pending the peace settlement, the Signatory Powers will cooperate to achieve by peaceful means their common aim of a reunified Germany enjoying a liberal democratic constitution like that of the Federal Republic and integrated within the European Community." This was theoretically the "efficient" part of the bargain. If the first three commitments were to hold open an unacceptable and presumably temporary status quo, the fourth pledge bound the West to a joint policy dedicated to its transformation.[29]

Given these terms, especially reunification under "liberal," "democratic," and "integrated" auspices, the contractual pledges of the West could not (and did not) lead to national unity. By elevating the contradic-

[28]In the first place, West German sovereignty was sharply circumscribed by the retention of Allied reserve powers relating to "Berlin and Germany as a whole." Second, the FRG bound itself to raise 500,000 troops and to integrate them *wholly* into NATO. Third, the FRG renounced the right to manufacture nuclear as well as biological and chemical weapons. Fourth, the FRG undertook by a threefold declaration of self-limitation to refrain from any action "inconsistent with the strictly defensive character of NATO," to "resolve by peaceful means" its disputes with other nations, and, most importantly, "never to have recourse to force to achieve the reunification of Germany." Lest there remain any doubt, these good-conduct pledges were reinforced by an Allied declaration which was certainly directed against the Federal Republic. Accordingly, "they will regard as threat to their own peace and safety any recourse to force which . . . threatens the integrity and unity of the Atlantic alliance . . . [and] . . . will consider the offending government as having forfeited its right to any guarantee and any military assistance. They will act . . . with a view to taking other measures which may be appropriate." *Documents on American Foreign Relations*, 1954, pp. 115–17.

[29]*See Documents on American Foreign Relations*, 1954, pp. 116, 117, 139.

tion between integration and reunification to the level of solemn codification, the compact with the West was clearly a second-best solution. At best, the West's refusal to concede the finality of the status quo would keep the *prospect* of reunification alive while undercutting the danger of a collusive settlement with the Soviet Union. Similarly, if the West continued to demonstrate its commitment to German unity in word and deed, reunification would continue to serve as a vital myth at home.

On the domestic front, Adenauer was hounded by a Social Democratic opposition which was forever hammering home the contradiction between integration and reunification. Once Adenauer had secured his bargain with the West, he had to mobilize domestic support, or at least deflate the opposition's best arguments against him. The neutralization of domestic opposition to his *Westpolitik* was outlined in a circle-squaring feat which represented the Western settlement as not only compatible with reunification, but also as its necessary precondition.[30] Rhetorically, the gap between aspiration and reality was spanned by the dominant myth of the 1950s—the "policy of strength." In its strongest version it echoed Dulles' "roll-back" policy:

> Only the sufficient strength of the West will create a real basis for peaceful negotiations. Their objective is to liberate peacefully not only the Soviet Zone but also all of enslaved Europe east of the Iron Curtain.[31]

As a political promise, the "policy of strength" required tangible proofs and tests in the years to come, but no deadlines were suggested or spelled out. When *would* the West be strong enough to warrant a dialogue with the Soviet Union? By failing to define the time horizon for an active reunification policy, the departure point was left undetermined. The "policy of strength" precluded any method of comparing rhetorics with reality. Yet it did fulfill the vital function of stabilizing the domestic base of Adenauer's foreign policy. By suggesting that reunification would require time, it was a call for patience and did help to postpone domestic frustrations and the moment of truth. Moreover, under the terms of the Western settlement, the Allies had assumed primary responsibility for reunification.

DOMESTIC SOURCES AND FOREIGN POLICY

In many ways, the Federal Republic found itself in the same situation as the Weimar Republic. Both were tenuous democratic experiments, and

[30]As Adenauer put it in 1952: "I assure you: We are convinced that this treaty is the first step toward reunification." Quoted in *Frankfurter Allgemeine Zeitung*, May 27, 1952.

[31]In a broadcast interview with Ernst Friedländer, *Bulletin*, no. 27, March 16, 1952, p. 262.

both had to live with externally imposed restrictions. Similarly, the built-in revisionism of both was totally at odds with international realities. The Weimar precedent was hardly encouraging. As the rise of Hitler had shown, national grievances could become the breeding ground for ultra-nationalist revolt and dictatorship.

Yet Bonn did not repeat the Weimar experience, and it is perhaps Adenauer's greatest achievement that he managed to turn the conditions of potential disaster into the sources of social stability and democratic evolution. The most crucial difference between Weimar and Bonn was economics. Unlike the Weimar Republic, the FRG could *enjoy* the economic consequences of peace. In the 1920s, security for France spelled reparations and indefinite economic controls on Germany. In the 1950s, however, security for the United States spelled speedy recovery and sustained prosperity for West Germany and Western Europe. Instead of a staggering reparations burden, there were massive infusions of American capital. Instead of "beggar-thy-neighbor" policies, there was free movement of goods and capital. enforced and encouraged by the United States.

Having been robbed of its East German markets, West Germany, traditionally the Reich's industrial center of gravity, found itself in the same position as export-dependent England, minus its far-flung trading network. Although Adenauer pursued European integration primarily for its political payoffs, integration and free trade were also an enormous economic boon. They provided both markets and competitive pressures. Moreover, partition produced a blessing in disguise—a massive influx of skilled labor.

About ten million people came from the territories incorporated by Poland, Czechoslovakia, and the Soviet Union. Until 1961 when the wall sealed off the Berlin refugee conduit, about 3 million came from the GDR, among them a disproportionate number of the young and highly trained. Apart from feeding a sustained expansion process, the millions of refugees exerted a downward pressure on the level of wages. The sheer numbers of the population transfer surely explained the astounding "discipline" of West German labor unions, the high rate of investment, the long-term competitiveness of West German exports, and hence, the stuff from which the "economic miracle" was made.

With the economy set on a path of sustained growth, the political institutions of the Federal Republic could draw their legitimacy from an ever-expanding base of economic performance. In contrast to Weimar, democracy was not associated with national humiliation, inflation, and large-scale unemployment. The economic miracle compensated for the lack of historically grown legitimacy normally rooted in the continuity of institutions and national identification.

Unlike the leaders of Weimar, Adenauer succeeded in divorcing territorial revisionism from economic grievances. Although long forgotten (or precisely because it is), the deliberate and speedy integration of the refugees from the East was an impressive testimony to Adenauer's political farsightedness. Its antirevisionist thrust emerges most dramatically by contrast to the Palestinian refugees of 1948 who were just as deliberately interned in camps around Israel's periphery as pawns for territorial change.

With their economic problems rapidly divorced from their political complaints, the refugees never formed that reservoir of *déracinés* (the uprooted) which was turned against the Weimar Republic. Economic co-optation soon paid off politically. The refugee party managed to poll only 5.5 percent of the total vote in 1953, the only election in which it gained entry into the Bundestag.

Nationalism, the less clamorous brother of revisionism, was similarly defused. After World War I, Germany was spared the trauma of total defeat and occupation. Defeat could therefore be transfigured through a "stab-in-the-back" legend. By contrast, the apocalyptic failure of the Third Reich's ultranationalist experiment had certainly pulled the sting of aggressive German nationalism. Whatever potential for German nationalism was still left in the wake of demoralization and apathy could be safely enveloped in the *transnational* surrogates of Europeanism and anti-Communism.

Transcending national boundaries, the twin ideology of Europeanism and anti-Communism produced multiple domestic payoffs. In the first place, they dovetailed perfectly with the dominant conflict and the direction of West German diplomacy. In addition to legitimizing the truncation of West German foreign policy, they also served to underwrite the asset of diplomatic reliability which Adenauer had brought into his partnership with the West. Second, the "European fatherland" served as a safe and constructive outlet for the affective instincts of the population. Aggressive impulses, on the other hand, could be channeled into the *communal* ideology of anti-Communism. For the first time, Germany did not stand alone. And given the lack of autonomy, Adenauer could reap the benefits of a unifying ideology and an external threat without having to pay the price of actual conflict (as did German leaders before and after World War I). External tensions—the prime source of solidarity at home—were not of German making.

Third, anti-Communism was an invaluable asset in the nation-building process and the domestic struggle for tenure. Insulated from the societal model implemented across the Elbe, nation-building could proceed under liberal-capitalist auspices toward what some commentators have called the "Adenauer Restoration."[32] In terms of domestic politics,

---

[32]"Restoration" is a suggestive but misleading description for postwar West German society. Power was certainly not "restored" to the Nazi clique or the quasi-aristocratic ruling class of Weimar. Instead, there was a great deal of upward mobility. "Restoration" should thus actually read "fractured continuity" plus "capitalist economic development" plus "expanding welfare state."

anti-Communism delivered a potent electoral weapon against the Social Democratic opposition. It did not matter that the SPD was staunchly anti-Communist. Yet its residual or reformist Marxism allowed the government to discredit the SPD as the party of crypto-Communism and ultimately national treason.

THE POLITICS OF DEPENDENCE

With the bargain struck in the 1954 agreements, the Federal Republic had acquired a certain veto power over the future course of East-West relations in Europe. At a maximum, the terms of the settlement enjoined the West to demonstrate its commitment to reunification by policy and proclamation. At a minimum, it precluded Western recognition of the German Democratic Republic and the demarcation lines drawn after World War II. Both objectives came to be embodied in the *Politik des Junktim* (policy of linkage) which constituted the linchpin of German diplomacy throughout the 1950s and most of the 1960s. By linking *any* East-West negotiations to a resolution of the German question, it operationalized the West's reunification pledge.

In theory, any kind of East-West settlement would have to be preceded or at least paralleled by progress on reunification in peace and freedom. In practical terms, this meant free elections in the GDR and freedom of alignment for a reunified Germany. Both conditions, if realized, would have delivered the German prize to the West. Hence the various quadripartite conferences of the 1950s (Berlin in 1954, Geneva in 1955 and 1959) ended in predictable stalemate. Yet in terms of West German interests, stalemate was better that the "wrong" kind of agreement. Since Soviet security proposals were always targeted on West German "revanchism" and the consecration of the status quo, *any* Four-Power conference tended to evoke the specter of Germany's discrimination and victimization. Even if it failed as an instrument for the transformation of the status quo, the *Junktim* served reasonably well in blocking its deterioration as long as the FRG managed to persuade its Western allies that *their* conflict with the Soviet Union was identical with the more special German-Soviet quarrel.

The FRG's veto power was therefore derivative. It was strength on lease, predicated on the long-run willingness of the West to subordinate its search for a modus vivendi with the Soviet Union to West Germany's quest for national unity. The ratification of the alliance system in 1955 marked the zenith of West German influence in the Western coalition. For both East and West, Bonn's integration into NATO terminated a six-year period of courting and concessions. If the FRG was now a bulwark for the West, it could always become a stumbling block towards accommodation with the East.

By the same token, the Federal Republic had lost its attraction for the Soviet Union. In the previous decade, Soviet policy had always oscillated between courting Germany's allegiance and controlling it in collusion with its wartime allies. Yet whether courtship or control, this ambivalence was at least centered on Germany as a whole, and therefore predicated on some kind of reunification. After 1955 this option vanished.

As reunification receded into a hazy future, the FRG was confronted with the hazardous dialectics of a changing nuclear balance. In 1953, the Soviet Union had acquired the hydrogen bomb, and it was only a matter of time until America's nuclear superiority, the cornerstone of the Atlantic Alliance, would give way to "peril parity." In the fall of 1957, the Soviets launched their first *Sputnik,* and the notorious "missile gap" was born. Years later, the "gap" was exposed as a sham, but in the meantime, the Soviets played their presumed technological advantage for all it was worth by gradually stepping up pressures against the West. In response, the United States sought to reassert the waning credibility of its deterrent threat by introducing medium-range ballistic missiles and tactical nuclear weapons in Europe. With NATO about to go nuclear, the FRG was faced with yet another fateful choice, like that between integration and national unity, which had already been made.

After a brief effort to resist the nuclear tide,[33] the FRG decided to acquire an atomic armory of sorts (that is, dual-purpose delivery vehicles and a stockpile of tactical warheads under American control). To the West Germans, tactical nuclear weapons appeared as panacea for all the ills which had befallen the Alliance since 1955. Adenauer had never quite trusted American pledges to abstain from its past isolationist habits. As public opinion in the West began to speculate about the merits of disengagement in Central Europe (in the wake of the Hungarian revolt), Adenauer's fears were fueled by the specter of a Soviet-American collusion whose seeds seemed to have been planted in the combined superpower pressure against the Franco-British Suez expedition in 1956. Tactical nuclear weapons for the *Bundeswehr* (Federal Forces) would forge an additional bond between the FRG and its senior American partner, forever prone to withdrawal symptoms. Second, they would strengthen the hostage function of American troops in Germany and prop up the tilting European balance. And finally, given French and English determination to develop their own independent deterrents, nuclear weapons appeared as a crucial symbol of political status. Having no say over the Alliance's nuclear strategy was seen as a retrograde fallback to an earlier role of voiceless dependence.

---

[33]Adenauer was afraid that the "New Look," that is, the Pentagon's attempt to save money by substituting nuclear firepower for conventional forces, would serve as a smoke screen for U.S. withdrawals from Europe.

The Soviet Union had minced no words in warning the FRG against a nuclear decision. Thereafter, events unfolded with inexorable necessity. In its very attempt to escape from inferiority, the FRG soon found itself entangled in even greater dependence on the West as a result of Khrushchev's Berlin Ultimatum[34] in the winter of 1958. The crisis over Berlin lasted four years until it was superseded by the new superpower crisis in Cuba. The atom bomb in German hands may have been of puny military significance (especially since the Americans clutched both the trigger and the ammunition), but it became a formidable tool in the hands of the Soviets. German revanchism, an earlier tradition of international violence, *and* German nuclear weapons presented the Soviets with a tailor-made legitimization for a *Westpolitik* that sought to rally Europe around "peaceful coexistence" and their own vision of European security. If the former required the lasting acceptance of the status quo, the latter implied security not so much for, as against, Germany.

Although ostensibly targeted on the Allied presence in the former German capital, the Berlin crisis ultimately turned into the most dramatic crisis of confidence between the FRG and the West. Berlin was clearly well chosen. The Soviets had all the advantages of geography on their side, and they could saddle the West with the psychological burden of having to fire the first and perhaps fateful shot. The Soviets were evidently trying to make the best of the Sputnik shock, knowing that the margin of Western concessions on Berlin—the prime locus and symbol of Western resistance in the Cold War—was so minute that, short of retreat or violence, they would have to offer compensation elsewhere. Hence, if the West were going to submit to the Soviet bluff, it would most likely yield on the "secondary theater" of, say, a tacit recognition of the GDR, the nuclear armament of the *Bundeswehr,* or on a European security system which, as Adenauer claimed, would reduce the FRG to a "second-class" state. In short, the Berlin Gambit was a brilliant opening bid toward a "moveable status quo,"[35] and for the time being, Khrushchev could simply sit back and wait for the payoffs which would soon come his way.

The ups and downs of the Berlin Crisis have been described at great lengths elsewhere.[36] Suffice it to say that it did not take much arm-

[34]Khrushchev's message on November 27, 1958, called on the West to recognize the abnormality of its presence in West Berlin. If after six months, West Berlin was not turned into a demilitarized Free City, the Soviets would turn the control of access over to the GDR (subsequently flanked by the threat of a separate peace treaty). Thereafter the West would have to negotiate with the GDR but face the military might of the entire Warsaw Pact if it resorted to force. Furthermore, the best way to solve the entire German problem was the withdrawal of both German states from their alliance systems while their armed forces would be limited by the needs of maintaining domestic law and order.

[35]Herbert Dinerstein, *Fifty Years of Soviet Foreign Policy* (Baltimore, Md.: Johns Hopkins Press, 1968), p. 34.

[36]See for instance Philip Windsor, *City on Leave* (London: Chatto and Windus, 1963); Jean Smith, *The Defense of Berlin* (Baltimore, Md.: Johns Hopkins Press, 1963); Hans Speier, *Divided Berlin* (New York: Praeger, 1961); and Jack M. Schick, *The Berlin Crisis, 1958–1962* (Philadelphia: University of Pennsylvania Press, 1971).

twisting before the West began to cringe and offer concessions on European security and the de facto recognition of the GDR in order to preserve its position in Berlin. As a result, the Federal Republic was confronted with a dual problem. In the short run, it was faced with the paradoxical prospect of having to pay the political price of Allied resistance in Berlin. The long-run problem was even more insidious. Like any client state, the FRG drew its derivative strength from an intimate association with its patron powers—in particular, the United States. The weak become strong if they can persuade their protectors that their interests are alike. Then a threat to the weak constitutes an obligation for the protector. And since the commitments of the strong powers are not only worldwide but also interdependent, they cannot easily retract any particular engagement for fear of damaging their credibility elsewhere. Until the Berlin Crisis exposed the heterogeneity of interests between the West and the FRG, the latter could extract leverage from impotence by identifying its own special conflict with the East with the global bipolar conflict as a whole.

The Berlin Crisis was a watershed because it began to unravel this "indivisibility of conflict."[37] Berlin was clearly a bipolar issue, and so were the security and Western ties of the Federal Republic. Yet reunification was not. As it turned out, the Geneva Conference of 1959 was the last time East and West met to discuss the reunification of Germany.

Allied policy began to draw an increasingly rigid distinction between its own and West Germany's conflict with the Soviet Union. England's temptation to compensate its decline from empire and power with a policy of splendid mediation between the blocs became a source of persistent concern for the FRG. While Bonn gained some solace in de Gaulle's refusal to negotiate under pressure, what mattered was the United States. In the 1960 presidential campaign, Kennedy had forcefully attacked the Republican administration for its military weakness and lack of will, yet in terms of West German interests, the advent of the Kennedy administration in 1961 turned into a disaster in disguise.

While demonstrating his resolution to resist Soviet pressure through well-publicized increases in defense spending and the reinforcement of the American garrison in Berlin, Kennedy was also obsessed by both powers' capability to inflict devastating nuclear damage on each other. "This had changed all the answers and all the questions."[38] Above all, the new situation required the scrupulous avoidance of confrontations and misperceptions. As a result, Kennedy placed a maximum value on superpower negotiations. Regardless of outstanding political issues, the military milieu had to be stabilized through arms control measures, such as a test

---

[37]Richard Löwenthal, *Vom kalten Krieg zur Ostpolitik* (Stuttgart: Seewald, 1974), p. 57.

[38]As quoted by Theodore C. Sorensen, *Kennedy* (New York: Bantam Books, 1966), p. 577.

ban and a non-proliferation pledge. While Alliance cohesion was important, the realization of German national aspirations could no longer be allowed to define the touchstone of the East-West relationship.

Maintaining Western rights in Berlin was one thing, but "the reunification of Germany seemed to him an unrealistic negotiating objective."[39] Kennedy drew a clear distinction between preserving the FRG's loyalties to the West and the active pursuit of reunification:

> Germany has been divided for sixteen years and will continue to stay divided. The Soviet Union is running an unnecessary risk in trying to change this from an accepted fact into a legal state. Let the Soviet Union keep Germany divided on its present basis and not try to persuade us to associate ourselves legally with that division and thus weaken our ties to West Germany and their ties to Western Europe.[40]

The Berlin Crisis marked a definite break in the evolution of West German foreign policy. In the first place, the climax of the Crisis—the erection of the Berlin Wall in August of 1961—shattered the vital myth of reunification. The wall not only sealed the status quo in the most drastic sense of the term, but also spelled the end of East Germany's accelerating depopulation, the most visible proof of the regime's failure and illegitimacy. (Prior to 1961, about 3 million East Germans had crossed over into the FRG.) By taking a high risk in Berlin, the Soviet Union had clearly demonstrated the extent of its commitment to the viability of the East German regime. Moreover, the closure of the refugee conduit foreshadowed an uninterrupted period of East German nation-building and ultimately, the slow convergence between totalitarian rule and popular consent. August 13, 1961, thus constituted the long-postponed moment of truth. Henceforth, unity could only mean reassociation and coexistence, but no longer a unification effort which would turn Germany into a larger version of the Federal Republic. As Willy Brandt, then mayor of West Berlin, put it a few months after the wall was erected: "After twelve years, we must recognize our aspirations as illusions. . . . Today, there is no visible price of reunification except for the renunciation of freedom."[41]

The Crisis eroded the fundamental premises of German foreign policy. Again, in the words of Brandt: If in the 1950s the policymakers presumably really did believe that "integration and rearmament would also achieve the unification of our divided people. . ., everybody knows today that such automatism does not exist and that it has never existed."[42]

[39]Arthur Schlesinger, *A Thousand Days* (Greenwich, Conn.: Fawcett Crest, 1967). p. 371.

[40]Kennedy in a conversation with Finland's President Kekkonen in October 1961. As quoted by Schlesinger, Ibid.

[41]Address to the Bundestag, December 6, 1961, as reprinted in Willy Brandt, *Der Wille zum Frieden* (Hamburg: Hoffmann & Campe, 1971), p. 68.

[42]"Denk ich an Deutschland. . .," address at the Evangelische Akademie, Tutzing, July 15, 1963. *Pressedienst des Landes Berlin*, no. 135, July 15, 1963.

If the West was ready to pursue détente regardless of a solution of the German question, then the FRG either had to go along or "go it alone." If the latter raised the traditional specter of isolation, the former required a fundamental transformation of policy. It required accepting the consequences of World War II which the Soviets exacted as the price for accommodation.

OSTPOLITIK: OLD AND NEW

Halfhearted Reform, 1963–1969

Two of the great postwar crises—in Berlin and Cuba—marked the most critical watershed in the evolution of West German foreign policy. The Berlin Wall, literally sealing the German status quo in concrete, demonstrated that the nation's partition was here to stay. The resolution of the Cuban Missile Crisis in the fall of 1962 opened a new chapter in Soviet-American relations, battering the traditional assumptions of West German foreign policy just as thoroughly as had the Berlin Wall. Henceforward, as the Cold War gave way to superpower détente, the previous "fit" between German interests and the general direction of Western policy was successively undone.

To the United States, the duel at the brink in Cuba drove home an enduring lesson. Superpower confrontations had to be avoided, arms control had to diminish the risk of accidental war, and diplomacy in general had to become less ambitious. In the shadow of the nuclear apocalypse, diplomacy's foremost purpose was to stabilize the military milieu, not to change the map of Europe. Such objectives were of course at odds with the basic purpose of West German foreign policy which sought, at a maxium, to transform the political status quo in Central Europe and, at a minimum, to keep it from being frozen at the expense of German interests.

In essence, superpower détente consisted not "in resolving disputes but in ignoring them."[43] The United States and the USSR were primarily interested in stabilizing their strategtic relationship at a lower level of risk and in recentralizing their alliance systems during a détente period that had awakened the forces of "polycentrism" in both Eastern and Western Europe. The main standard bearer of polycentrism in the West, de Gaulle's France, had a very different détente agenda. De Gaulle's policy was directed against the "twin hegemony" of the superpowers. Not blocs, but the *states* of Europe had to dominate the stage. With the Cold War apparently ended, the time had come for a "European Europe"—*l' Eu-*

---

[43]See Philip Windsor's excellent analysis of the 1960s, *Germany and the Management of Détente* (London: Chatto and Windus, 1971), p. 23.

rope des patries (the Europe of fatherlands)—stretching from the "Atlantic to the Urals."

The Federal Republic could obey neither vision. Following the Amerian lead would require acquiescence in the status quo and hence the acceptance of partition. Neither could Bonn join the French effort, which sought to rally the lesser states of Europe against the superpowers, hence also against the very American alliance that was the very backbone of West German security. In fact, given Bonn's long-standing principles, the FRG could hardly move at all. While everybody else could start out on the road to détente with agreements on minor issues, the FRG immediately ran up against the central questions of borders and of its relationship to the GDR. A nice example in point was one of the highlights of post-Cuba détente, the Limited Test Ban Treaty of 1963. Whereas none of the other nonnuclear powers had any problem in signing that treaty, Bonn initially balked at acceding to the treaty because the signature of *both* German states affixed to the same piece of paper could be construed as the de facto recognition of the GDR.

The very attempt at exploring détente-minded coexistence forever involved setting foot on the slippery slope of legitimizing a hateful regime. On the other hand, the FRG could no longer simply hold on to the orthodoxy laid down in the heyday of the Cold War. Though Bonn would forever remind the West of the obligations they had assumed in the grand bargain of 1954, the Federal Republic had to tread softly for fear of alienating it allies. In short, the single most important variable of the German foreign policy—the nature of the overall East-West relationship—began to take its toll. And within seven years of the Cuban Missile Crisis West German foreign policy would be transformed beyond recognition.

That septennium marked a process of painful adaptation to forces beyond the control of the Federal Republic. At first, there was sheer resistance and the affirmation of entrenched dogma. The "German question," Adenauer's successor, Chancellor Ludwig Erhard, proclaimed, "is one of the principal causes of tension in the world, and one cannot hope to eradicate these tensions if the German question remains unsolved."[44] But the traditional "linkage," according to which great power accords were always to subsume progress toward German unity, was slightly loosened to permit détente if the resolution of "peripheral" issues did not prejudice the resolution of "central" problems like the German one.[45]

---

[44]Ludwig Erhard, who had replaced Adenauer in 1963, in his inaugural address before the Bundestag. As quoted in a collection of documents issued by the Foreign Office. Auswärtiges Amt, ed., *Die Bemühungen der deutschen Reqierungen und ihrer Verbäundeten um die Einheit Deutschlands, 1955–1966* (Bonn: Bundesdruckerei, 1966), p. 461.

[45]See Foreign Minister Gerhard Schröder's address before the Parliamentary Assembly of the Western European Union, December 4, 1963. Presse- und Informationsamt der Bundesregierung, *Bulletin*, no. 214, December 4, 1963. (Hereafter cited as *Bulletin*.)

At the same time, Bonn embarked on a cautious Ostpolitik of its own which sought to circumvent rather than solve the central dilemmas of German diplomacy. Gerhard Schröder's (CDU foreign minister from 1961 to 1966) vaunted "Policy of Movement" was based on a seemingly persuasive premise.[46] Perhaps the hard-core issues like borders and recognition could simply be set aside in favor of *economic* engagement in Eastern Europe. Moscow's satellites were presumably eager to partake of Western economic plenty and to lighten the burden of Soviet dominance. Yet since the "Policy of Movement" sought to outflank both the GDR and the Soviet Union, it would soon grind to an abrupt halt.

To begin with, the underlying premise turned out to be wrong. Overestimating the power of "polycentrism," Schröder's East European foray assumed that economic rewards would loosen the ties of bloc loyalty and allow Bonn to isolate the GDR. For a while that strategy proved to be deceptively successful. Trade missions were opened in Poland, Romania, and Hungary in 1963 and in Bulgaria in 1964. Yet the limits of economic diplomacy were promptly redrawn in Czechoslovakia. Prague refused to discuss trade without any of the political downpayments toward a resolution of the "Munich legacy"[47] which Schröder had studiously sought to avoid.

Moreover, there was the vexing ambiguity of the West Germany posture, which sought to combine an opening to the East with the unyielding retention of traditional dogma. And thus, the "Hallstein Doctrine"[48] and the refusal to recognize the Oder-Neisse Line allowed Moscow and East Germany to villify the FRG as *revanchiste* and the last cold warrior. But most important, Schröder had severely misunderstood the GDR's role in the Soviet scheme of things. True, the East German regime was the most dependent satrap of the Soviet Union. But it did not follow that West German encouragement of East European "polycen-

---

[46]For an astute analysis of Schröder's policy, see Windsor, *Germany, op. cit.,* especially chap. 3.

[47]The Munich Agreement by which Czechoslovakia was forced to cede the Sudeten territory to Hitler's Germany in 1938 was a persistent source of conflict between the FRG and CSSR. After the war, the Sudetenland reverted to Prague, which proceeded to expel about 3 million Sudenten Germans. While the Erhard government renounced all claims to the Studetenland, it did not concede the invalidity of the Munich Agreement from the very beginning. The contest essentially boiled down to the question of which government was legally responsible for the property claims of the expelled Germans. For review of the legal conundra, see Lawrence L. Whetten, *Germany's Ostpolitik* (London: Oxford University Press, 1971), p. 167–71.

[48]After the establishment of diplomatic relations between the Soviet Union and the FRG in 1955, the so-called Hallstein Doctrine was formulated, which branded any diplomatic recogntion as an "unfriendly act . . . tending to deepen the division of Germany (Adenauer's declaration before the Bundestag, *Verhandlungen des Deutschen Bundestages,* September 22, 1955, p. 5647.) If the intent of that doctrine was to block the international recogntion of the GDR through the threat of severing diplomatic relations by Bonn, it also foreclosed diplomatic ties with the East European states which, having already recognized the GDR, were by definition out of bounds.

trism" would somehow weaken the GDR to the point where Bonn could dictate the terms of the relationship between the two German states and the measure of liberalization within the GDR.

As Philip Windsor has pointed out, "in reality, East Germany was the bastion of polycentrism." Precisely because the presence of a huge Soviet army in the GDR "enabled the Soviet Union . . . to encircle and contain the more independent regimes, East Germany buttressed the framework of polycentrism."[49] Rather than isolating East Berlin, the Policy of Movement accomplished the opposite: It made the GDR all the more important to the Soviet Union. The much-advertised Soviet–East German Treaty of Friendship and Mutual Assistance of June 1964 drove that point home, underlining the sterility of Schröder's strategy.

Parallel developments in the West were to underline the irony of a situation where the isolator himself became isolated. Here, too, West Germany had been caught in a painful squeeze: between the United States as indispensable guarantor of its security and de Gaulle's France as its most important ally in Western Europe. Having flung down his challenge against the "twin hegemony" of the superpowers, de Gaulle needed a Continental partner to strengthen France's hand in the contest to come. He thought that he had found one in Chancellor Adenauer who, smarting from what he saw as "betrayal" on the part of President John F. Kennedy during the Berlin Crisis, was only too eager to accept de Gaulle's embrace. (See Chapter 2.)

Yet after a spectacular beginning, the newly found partnership, culminating in the Franco-German Treaty of Friendship and Cooperation (1963), proved too strenuous for Bonn. On the one hand, Adenauer regarded his French connection as a tool, to be wielded in order to remind Washington that he was not without alternative partners. Never, however, did he dream of substituting a Franco-German "axis" for the indispensable security relationship with the United States. If dependence was an inescapable fact of German life, it was at any rate more profitable and honorable to subordinate the FRG to a remote superpower like the United States than to a political peer and economic inferior like France.

On the other hand, the Kennedy administration responded to that challenge exactly as calculated. Faced with the specter of an anti-American "Continental Couple," the administration quickly shifted from coolness to courtship. In the summer of 1963, only months after the Franco-German Treaty had been signed, Kennedy embarked on a triumphant trip to Germany, bearing with him the promise of an equal Atlantic partnership between the United States and its allies. Moreover, he held out a tempting prize to Bonn, which had signed away the right to a national nuclear deterrent in the grand bargain of 1954. Labeled "MLF"

[49]Windsor, *Germany*, pp. 62–63.

(Multilateral Force), the scheme promised the glory and power of indirect nuclear status by offering Bonn membership in a fleet of nuclear missile-carrying freighters under NATO command.[50] Flattered by American attention and alienated by de Gaulle's increasingly anti-American rhetoric, Bonn gladly returned to the American fold during the mid-1960s.

The supreme irony was that the FRG ended up with neither Franco-German friendship nor with German-American intimacy restored. Seeing his courtship bear no fruits, de Gaulle followed the ancient tenets of *realpolitik* by enacting a classic outflanking maneuver. If Bonn was content to play America's "continental sword," France would approach Russia, its traditional ally. By 1965, after seven years, de Gaulle had lost patience and returned to the most ancient roots of his German policy: "We will move toward the Russians to extent to which the Germans move away from us."[51] By early 1965, a German editorial noted the new constellation with uncomprehending frustration: There was "nothing left of the Gaullist concept that no concessions should be made to the Soviet Union as long as there is no sign of Soviet accommodation on the German problem."[52]

But as de Gaulle turned toward Moscow, so did the United States. Beset by the escalating war in Vietnam, the Johnson administration had more pressing interests to pursue than the local claims of its junior partner in Bonn. Perhaps a deal could be struck with Moscow in Vietnam. As a result American policy manifestly reordered its priorities toward "collaborative bipolarity." One dramatic signal was Lyndon B. Johnson's much-advertised "bridge-building" speech of October 7, 1966.[53] In effect, the president proposed reconciliation with the communist half of Europe while tacitly offering not to press German claims for the time being. Another augur of changing times was the speed with which Washington scuttled the Multilateral Force in favor of concluding a non-proliferation treaty with the Soviet Union.

Nothing could better dramatize the forces of "system dominance" than the fall of Chancellor Erhard in the autumn of 1966. Eager to finance the Vietnam War without recourse to higher taxes, the Johnson administration turned to West Germany, the land of the "economic miracle" for collection, as it were. There were about 200,000 American troops stationed in West Germany, and so Bonn was asked to put up full "offset payments" for their maintenance. Yet Chancellor Erhard had a recession on his hands, and so he traveled to Lyndon Johnson's Texas ranch,

---

[50]The best account of this episode is still Henry Kissinger's *The Troubled Partnership* (New York: McGraw-Hill, 1965), chap. 5.

[51]As quoted by J.R. Tournoux, *La Tragédie du Général* (Paris: Plon, 1967), p. 499.

[52]*Die Welt*, April 29, 1965.

[53]Reprinted in the *New York Times*, October 8, 1966.

hoping to soften the American terms. When he returned with empty hands, his political fate was sealed. In the fall of 1966, the Erhard government was replaced by a grand coalition between the Christian Democrats (CDU/CSU) and Willy Brandt's Social Democrats (SPD). The Grand Coalition's point of departure in a world rapidly outpacing Bonn's straggling Ostpolitik was aptly characterized by its architect and Minister for All-German Affairs, Herbert Wehner: "Until now we have lived beyond our means—as if we had been a victor power by adoption."[54]

Yet the Grand Coalition was immobilized by its very strength and even though together Christian Democrats and Social Democrats commanded over 90 percent of the Bundestag seats, Chancellor Kurt George Kiesinger (CDU) could not move very far. Its most significant departure in the East-West arena was twofold. Faced with the specter of either going along or going it alone, Bonn set out gingerly to join the general détente trend. Having traditionally defined reunification as the touchstone of détente, Bonn now reversed priorities with its avowal "not to burden the policy of détente in Europe with any preconditions" because "the problems of Europe like those of Germany cannot be settled in a Cold War atmosphere."[55]

In a second substantial departure, the Grand Coalition quietly dismantled the "Hallstein Doctrine." That principle, which had precluded diplomatic ties with any state apart from the Soviet Union and which recognized the GDR, was modified. It now permitted formal relations with the Warsaw Pact countries on the "birthmark theory," according to which the Soviet satrapies never had a genuine choice in this matter. As the first major success of this new Ostpolitik, Bonn exchanged ambassadors with Romania in early 1967.

Yet the previous distinction between the GDR and the other Warsaw Pact members remained operative. "Détente in Europe . . . must include détente in Germany," and hence, as Willy Brandt put it, "we aspire to an 'organized coexistence' in Germany."[56] Coexistence, however, did not imply formal recognition. Nor did the FRG concede the finality and legitimacy of the Oder-Neisse line, although the Kiesinger-Brandt coalition assured Eastern Europe that the FRG no longer harbored any "territorial claims."[57] In short, in its quest to unshoulder the odium of Cold War obstructionism, the Grand Coalition sought conciliation while withholding codification of the status quo. This was nicely exemplified in its attempt to envelop the hardcore territorial issues in the offer of comprehensive renunciation-of-force agreements.

[54]As quoted in *Die Welt*, February 20, 1967.

[55]Foreign Minister Willy Brandt before the Consultative Assembly of the Council of Europe, January 24, 1967. *Bulletin*, No. 8, January 26, 1967.

[56]Ibid.

[57]Willy Brandt on June 10, 1968. As quoted in *Bulletin*, no. 73, June 12, 1968.

Ambiguity, however, soon exacted its price. Given the inroads West Germany had made in Eastern Europe, the GDR was now indeed faced with the specter of isolation. Proclaiming a "Hallstein Doctrine in reverse," East Berlin now called on its allies to make diplomatic ties with the FRG contingent on the latter's recognition of the GDR. By March 1967, East German leader Walter Ulbricht had succeeded in erecting a formidable barrier against further West German advances by concluding twenty-year treaties of friendship with Czechoslovakia and Poland. The Ulbricht-forged "Iron Triangle" manifestly raised the price for Bonn's access to Eastern Europe. The price was the recognition of the GDR, the ratification of the Oder-Neisse border, the unequivocal renunciation of the Munich Agreement, and abstinence from any form of nuclear weapons sharing. Like Adenauer in the 1950s, his East-German rival Ulbricht had now acquired a veto over his bloc's policy toward the other side.

A Legacy Unshouldered: Willy Brandt's "New Ostpolitik"

By the end of the 1960s, twenty years of West German foreign policy had come to a dead halt. Its power had been derivative; its pursuit had been financed with borrowed money, as it were. The basic problem of policy had been to make the best of an impossible legacy. World War II had amputated part of the nation (by shifting territory to Poland and the Soviet Union) and divided the rest between the FRG and the GDR. In its self-perception the FRG remained a half-nation, destined to be fused with the other half on its own terms. In the meantime, Bonn would not consecrate what the war had wrought: the legitimacy of both partition and amputation. Hence the refusal to recognize the Oder-Neisse border and its East German "counterstate." That refusal embroiled the FRG in a permanent conflict with the Soviet Union.

By itself, the Federal Republic was of course far too weak to sustain that separate conflict. Hence the enduring problem of West German statecraft was the quest for derivative power. To gain it, Konrad Adenauer struck his great bargain with the West in 1954. On his part, Adenauer inserted the FRG (and what was to become Western Europe's strongest army) into the Atlantic coalition. In exchange, he obtained a series of political pledges from his new allies that defined the essence of Bonn's "borrowed" power. The West would not confer finality on the postwar status quo; it would subordinate its own policy toward the East to the claims of the Federal Republic. What Adenauer had achieved was a classic in the repertoire of small-power foreign policy. He had succeeded in persuading the United States, Britain and France that West Germany's separate conflict with the East was their own. Henceforth, their freedom of action vis-à-vis the Soviet Union and Eastern Europe was severely constrained by their pledges to Bonn. As a result, East-West diplomacy was frozen around the unresolved German question—and the West Germans had acquired a veto over their allies' Eastern policy.

That moment arose on September 28, 1969 when a twenty-year cycle of German electoral politics came to an end. On September 28, 1969, Willy Brandt's left-of-center Social Democrats (SPD) and their smaller allies, the Liberals (FDP), emerged as the victors of the national election; for the first time in West German history, the Christian Democrats were in the opposition. The campaign had been heavily dominated by foreign policy, with the SPD presenting itself as the party of long-overdue *rapprochement* with the East. As result, the outcome of the September 28 election suggested a popular mandate for unshouldering the sterile, even counterproductive, legacy of the past.

And so, the new Brandt government quickly began to signal its resolution to do what all previous Bonn governments had sought to resist: to accept the postwar status quo for what it was. The quest for reunification was reduced to a minimal policy of "prophylaxis." Accordingly, Willy Brandt did not even mention the word "reunification" in his inaugural address. Dispensing with the FRG's claim to "sole representation" of Germany as a whole, he spoke of "two German states in one nation." While a joint heritage and nationality precluded the final step of formal recognition, Brandt offered "contractually regulated cooperation" to the GDR. In renewing his predecessors' offers of reunciation-of-force agreements, he emphatically included the GDR as well as the crucial assurance that these compacts would be based on the "territorial integrity" of each signatory state.[58] Having served notice that it was ready to *unlink* and *quarantine* the German issue, the Brandt government signed the Non-Proliferation Treaty (NPT) in November of 1969. Bonn's accession was a signal as well as a turning point, since West German access to nuclear weapons had been a prime focus of the Soviet-German quarrel since 1957.

The stage was now set for an incredibly complex diplomatic exercise that amounted to a virtual settlement of World War II. Only a formal peace conference was missing. Resolution unfolded in a crisscrossing pattern of multilateral and bilateral negotiations. The vehicles of reconciliation were renunciation-of-force treaties (based on the affirmation of the territorial status quo) with Moscow and Warsaw, the "Basic Treaty" with East Berlin (regulating coexistence without formal recognition), and a quadripartite agreement on Berlin (ensuring access and the ties between the FRG and West Berlin).

It was no surprise that the prime obstacle proved to be the GDR. Like the FRG in the earlier phase of détente, the GDR mounted an all-out effort to retain its role as "guardian at the gate" between the two

---

[58]Bundesministerium für innerdeutsche Beziehunge, *Texte zur Deutschlandpolitik*, Vol. IV (Bonn: Vorwärts-Duck, 1970), pp. 11–13, 38–39.

blocs. Both had gained their identity and derivative power through their struggle against each other. Monopolizing the national heritage, they had drawn their own legitimacy from denying it to the other. Both had been able to harness their alliance to a hard-line policy against the other side by cultivating intimate links with their bloc leader. However, like the United States in the 1960s, the Soviet Union was now no longer willing to subordinate its own interests to the claims of its junior partner. Indeed, Ulbricht's quiet ouster in May of 1971 (no doubt with Soviet prodding) evoked comparison with the fate of Adenauer, whose political decline began in earnest in the wake of the Berlin Wall and the United States' passivity after 1961.

Moscow's prime aim in the entire enterprise was a West German treaty and an all-European conference that would finally ratify the territorial redistribution wrought by World War II. In its quest to escape from inferiority, the GDR had more demanding objectives. It sought not only the long-denied diplomatic recognition by the West and the FRG, but also an explicit change in the status of West Berlin, a Western enclave within East German territory whose mere existence posed a permanent challenge to the sovereignty of the GDR. But in West Berlin, where the wartime rights of the United States, Britain, and France were at stake, the interests of the three Western powers were still the same as those of the FRG. Détente, no matter how eagerly pursued, could not come at the expense of Western positions in the former capital of the Reich. With that leverage in hand, the Brandt government could outflank its hostile brother in the East by tying the Eastern treaties to a satisfactory Berlin settlement.

Although Moscow had initially balked at including Berlin in its bilateral talks with Bonn, Berlin became the touchstone of the entire détente mosaic. The three Western powers began to define a Berlin agreement as the key test of Soviet intentions, and therefore they predicated the convocation of a European security conference and the recogntion of the GDR—both at the top of the East German and the Soviet agenda—on a Berlin agreement. After years of resistance to Western détente efforts, Bonn's policy was now at last reintegrated into the larger framework of Western diplomacy. This was one of Brandt's greatest achievements. On the one hand, it helped to relieve American anxieties about the haphazard pace of German Ostpolitik, which, because of the Berlin link, was now subject to some supervision by the West. On the other hand, the Berlin link strengthened Bonn's hand vis-à-vis the East. Failure in Berlin would threaten the entire edifice of détente, and hence the Soviet Union was forced to rein in its obstreperous East German ally.

The Berlin Agreement was signed on September 3, 1971. For the first time since the War, the Soviet Union pledged to ensure "unimpeded access" to Berlin. While reaffirming that West Berlin was not a "constituent part" of the FRG, the agreement did concede the crucial point that the ties between both could be "maintained and developed."[59] The Eastern Treaties (with Poland and the USSR) were ratified on May 17, 1972. On June 3, the Berlin Agreement entered into force. Having narrowly escaped from a no-confidence vote in Bundestag, Willy Brandt called for an out-of-turn election in November of 1972. It was again heavily dominated by Ostpolitik. Its outcome, a comfortable majority for the Brandt coalition, suggested that the quasi-ratification of the status quo abroad had been accompanied by the transformation of the ideological consensus at home. Thereafter, the de facto recognition of the GDR was formalized in the Basic Treaty between both German states concluded on December 21, 1972. Although the GDR now maintains diplomatic ties with the Western world, it did not succeed in gaining *de jure* recognition from the FRG. The fine distinction between de facto and *de jure* was drawn by the fact that both states now maintain "permanent missions" rather than embassies in each other's capital.

The Continuities of West German Foreign Policy

Having surmounted the tortuous obstacle course of negotiation and ratification, Brandt's Ostpolitik spelled the end of an era in postwar German foreign policy. Yet in spite of evident differences in style and tactics between Adenauer and Brandt, both phases were linked by some profound continuities which reflect enduring givens of West German diplomacy.

In the 1970s, Willy Brandt closely followed in the footsteps of the FRG's Founding Father, Konrad Adenauer. Domestically, Brandt's Ostpolitik forged a new consensus by carefully dismantling the "vital myth" of revision and reunification; diplomatically, it reintegrated the FRG into the overall détente trend of Western diplomacy. Both Adenauer and Brandt sought to defuse the dangerous potential of German revisionism toward the East, and both were haunted by the perils of Germany's exposed position in the European center. During the ratification debates on the Eastern Treaties, Brandt again evoked the ancient nightmare of German diplomacy in defense of his Ostpolitik: "An anti-German coalition has been Bismarck's as well as Adenauer's nightmare. We, too, are faced with this problem, and we should make sure that our own policy does not turn this problem into a burden."[60]

Brandt thus heeded one of the oldest lessons of German diplomacy: don't go it alone. Britain, an offshore maritime power closely tied to the United States, could historically seek safety in a policy of "splendid isola-

[59]For the German and English texts of the Agreement, see *Europa-Archiv*, No. 19, 1971, pp. D 443–53.

[60]*Verhandlungen des Deutschen Bundestages*, May 17, 1972, p. 10897. Compare this with Adenauer's statement on June 11, 1953; see p. 83 and note 26 of this text.

tion." France could afford a policy of "splendid aggravation" that would occasionally test Alliance patience to the breaking point precisely because France remained safely ensconced behind the bulk of NATO and American forces in West Germany. And both nations had acquired the ultimate insurance of a national nuclear deterrent. For the Federal Republic, by contrast, stable relations with Western Europe and the United States virtually amount to an unwritten law of its constitution. The country's position in the heart of Europe is too precarious to allow for a solitary diplomacy between East and West. The détente of the 1960s had rent the consensus between the FRG and the West, confronting Bonn with the prospect of isolation or adaptation. As Adenauer had integrated the young German state into the Western Community, Brandt's Ostpolitik returned his country's policy into the mainstream of Western diplomacy. Indeed, in the very process of resolving the FRG's separate conflict with the East, the treaties with the Soviet Union and Poland explicitly affirmed the continued hold of previous "bilateral and multilateral" agreements concluded by the signatories.[61] In other words, these treaties underlined rather than loosened the FRG's earlier commitments to the West as formalized in the 1954 settlement, the accession to NATO, and the various treaties of the Europan Community.

OUT FROM DEPENDENCE: THE HELMUT SCHMIDT ERA, 1974–1982

West Germany Ascendant, 1974–1979

"At best you can stand on one leg, but you can't walk on it."[62] With these words, spoken during a Bundestag debate a few months after Helmut Schmidt's inauguration in May 1974, the Social Democrat's floor leader, Herbert Wehner, aptly described the underlying aspiration of Willy Brandt's Ostpolitik and the momentous changes it had already wrought. The acquisition of a "second leg," ending the artificial truncation of Bonn's policy after a quarter century of self-denial, would allow not only for mobility in the East but also relieve pressure on the Federal Republic's "Western leg." Bonn's separate conflict with the Soviet Union and its allies, centering on its refusal to accept the verdict of World War II, had translated into excruciating dependence on the West. Diplomatic dependence bred diplomatic deference. Even among allies, solidarity ex-

---

[61]Cf. *The Treaty of August 12, 1970 Between the FRG and the USSR* (Bonn: Press- und Informationsamt der Bundesregierung, 1970).

[62]Herbert Wehner, Parliamentary Leader of the Social Democrats, before the Bundestag, November 6, 1974. *Texte zur Deutschlandpolitik*, Series II, Vol. 2 (Bonn: Bundesministerium für innerdeutsche Beziehungen, 1976), p. 295.

acts its price, and to keep them in line, the Federal Republic had routinely displayed the behavior of a typical client state.

Conscious of its exposed position on the frontline, the Federal Republic bore the brunt of offset payments for American troops stationed in Germany. German concessions on the European Community's agricultural policy were heavily conditioned by the need for French diplomatic support against the East. To forestall the international recognition of the GDR, the Federal Republic practically invited blackmail by the Third World, buying their cooperation with massive doses of foreign aid.

With Helmut Schmidt, there arrived a new era.[63] "Our margin of diplomatic maneuver," the Chancellor told the Bundestag in 1975, "has been extraordinarily enlarged." First of all, the Eastern treaties "have largely . . . liberated our country from its role as a client . . . who believed almost incessasntly that he needed yet another pledge of assurance from his patron powers . . . Secondly, our treaties with Moscow, Warsaw, East Berlin and so forth, as well as the Four-Power Agreement [on Berlin] have greatly reduced the numerous reasons we had in those days to seek, and beg for, continuous reassurance."[64] The third reason for West Germany's new found self-confidence was the country's enduring "economic miracle." Thus, it was the "great success . . . of Germany's economic course and its economic policy" that had "increased our weight."[65]

Economic strength was doubly significant. Not only did it bespeak wealth and worldly success, it was also the most valuable currency of power in an international system that had apparently shifted from "high politics" to "low politics" in the wake of the 1973 oil crisis.[66] While Europe was poised on the threshold of an unprecedented era of stability, the ancient East-West conflict seemed to become eclipsed by a new contest between North and South, or more precisely, between the industrial world and the *nouveaux riches* of the OPEC oil cartel. In this world, the clash of traditional politico-strategic interests mattered less than the management of "global interdependence," a term most fondly used by Foreign Minister Hans-Dietrich Genscher. The real stakes, according to Helmut Schmidt, were no longer shaped by the quest for military security but by the "struggle for the world product."[67]

---

[63]Willy Brandt had resigned from office in May of 1974 when one of his close collaborators, Wilhelm Guillaume, was exposed as East German spy planted in the Chancellor's Office. With their majority intact, the Social Democrats and Liberals elected the SPD Defense Minister Helmut Schmidt as Chancellor.

[64]Address to the Bundestag, July 25, 1975. *Bulletin*, July 29, 1975.

[65]"Wir sind ein erstklassiger Partner," interview with *Der Spiegel*, January 1, 1975.

[66]The Organization of Petroleum Exporting Countries (OPEC) used the 1973 Yom Kippur War as an occasion to quadruple oil prices. That acted as a gigantic tax on the rest of the world, shifting income to the OPEC states and pushing the Western world into inflationary recession. In Western Europe, the FRG weathered the oil crisis better than most.

[67]Thus Helmut Schmidt in "The Struggle for the World Product," *Foreign Affairs*, April 1974.

"Our weight has grown," was a standing Schmidt phrase, whence it followed that the FRG had become "an actor whose counsel is being asked and whose voice is being heard."[68] By the end of 1975, the *Sunday Times* celebrated Helmut Schmidt as the "first West European leader of genuine world status since Charles de Gaulle."[69] Four years later, *Time Magazine* devoted a cover story to Helmut Schmidt and his country: "West Germany has finally come of age as a Continental power. More than any other postwar Chancellor since . . . the late Konrad Adenauer, Schmidt has shouldered his way into the front row of international leaders."[70]

Hardly in office, the new Chancellor served notice on the European Community (EEC) that the FRG would no longer act as the Common Market's trustiest "Euro-payer." First, the Schmidt government vetoed an EC support program for the poorest oil-importing countries of the Third World. Then, Bonn forced the EEC Commission to cut its proposed 1975 budget by 20 percent. Finally, the Chancellor personally blocked a 5 percent rise of the Community's agricultural prices. That move was a jejune way of marking a historic transition. Exactly ten years earlier, France and the FRG had squared off over the Community's grain prices, with Chancellor Erhard resisting lower prices on behalf of his high-cost grain producers. Yet within days, Erhard caved in—conscious of Bonn's need to buy French diplomatic support in West Germany's separate conflict with the East. By 1974, Ostpolitik and reconciliation with Moscow and other Eastern bloc countries had reduced such leverage to naught. Or as Schmidt's Finance Minister Hans Apel put it: "Germany's past is no longer a building block of European integration."[71] (See Chapter 8.)

The distance Bonn had traveled could be measured best in terms of its sustained revolt against the United States. After one year in office, Schmidt informed Washington in June 1975 that he would not sign a new "offset agreement" by which Bonn had in the past helped to maintain American troops on West German soil. Also in June 1975, West Germany and Brazil concluded the largest nuclear transaction in history. The $4 billion dollar deal encompassed the entire fuel cycle: reactors, enrichment facilities, and reprocessing plants. The latter two items, crucial for weapons production, were a nasty blow to American non-proliferation policy. When Jimmy Carter arrived in the White House in 1977, the administration demanded that Bonn withhold the critical equipment or place it under multinational control. But "the Germans stood firm' and all [we] received was their assurance that they would observe existing safeguards."[72]

[68]Declaration before the Bundestag, as reprinted in *Vorwärts*, April 15, 1976.

[69]Godfrey Hodgson, "The Professional: A Profile of Helmut Schmidt," *Sunday Times Supplement* (London), November 16, 1975.

[70]Leading from Strength," *Time* (European Edition), June 11, 1979.

[71]As quoted in "Wer reich ist, muss zahlen," *Der Spiegel*, September 30, 1974.

[72]Zbigniew Brzezinski (Carter's National Security Advisor), *Power and Principle* (New York: Farrar, Straus & Giroux, 1983), p. 131.

Here, too, history offered a lesson in the shifting fortunes of power. Fourteen years earlier, the United States and the Federal Republic had engaged in a similar contest of wills over the politics of trade. The stake was a contract for the export of large-diameter steel pipe to the Soviet Union. As in the Brazil case, the U.S. government intervened in force only after the contract had been signed and sealed. Yet whereas the Schmidt government insisted on the sanctity of contracts and won, Konrad Adenauer had caved in. In March 1963, Adenauer imposed an official embargo, defying for the sake of harmony with Washington a grand coalition of the German steel industry, his Liberal coalition partner, much of his own CDU party, and the SPD opposition.

Nor did Jimmy Carter succeed in pushing Bonn to assume the role of "locomotive" in the world economy. Rather than fiscal stimulation of the German economy, Jimmy Carter received endless lectures on sound economic management. According to Schmidt, American policy was "irresponsible." The Americans had "neither accepted nor even understood their leadership role in the international economy." It was "unbelievable that the strongest economic power in the world has a balance-of-payments deficit at its current high level."[73]

Back to Basics: Afghanistan, the Euromissile Crisis and "Cold War II"

In the 1970s, the FRG could afford to conduct a more "normal" and self-assertive foreign policy than in the 1950s and 1960s for three reasons. First, by shelving its "separate conflict" with the East, it had unshouldered some excruciating dependencies on the West. Or as Helmut Schmidt put it: "Ostpolitik . . . gave us a much greater freedom of action."[74] Second, overall East-West détente, launched by the Soviet-American agreement on strategic arms limitation (SALT) in 1972, had profoundly changed the political climate in Europe. The Cold War of the past—from the Berlin Blockade (1948–1949), to the Berlin Crisis (1958–1962)—had given way to the all-round acceptance of the status quo. Though the Soviet Union was still in possession of Eastern Europe, though Germany remained divided, the situation was rendered ultrastable by the conviction that, in the shadow of nuclear parity, war was no longer a rational means of politics. Third, with military force largely devalued, economic power was pushed to the fore, and here the Federal Republic's impressive resources added up to virtual super-power status.

---

[73]Address before an economics conference in Hamburg, April 28, 1978, as quoted in reports of the *New York Times*, April 29, 1978, the *Süddeutsche Zeitung*, April 29, 1978, and *Die Welt* ("Das sagte Helmut Schmidt zum deutsch-amerikanischen Verhältnis"), May 24, 1978.

[74]In an interview with the *Economist*, September 29, 1979, p. 47.

Yet this happy state was not to last. Two trends conspired to undo the détente of the 1970s, to trigger "Cold War II," circa 1979–1985, and to transform the benign setting of German foreign policy. First, détente began to unravel on the periphery—in Angola and in the Horn of Africa where the two superpowers arrayed themselves on opposite sides of local conflict. Cold War II began in earnest in the final days of 1979 when the Soviet Union marched into Afghanistan. For the Carter administration, heretofore dedicated to "world order" politics and nuclear disarmament, the invasion was tantamount to a call to arms. Jimmy Carter let the SALT II Treaty go unratified, imposed a grain embargo on the Soviet Union, and called on the rest of the world to boycott the 1980 Moscow Olympics. Ronald Reagan picked up where Carter had left off. He embarked on a massive rearmament program and summoned the allies to oppose the "evil empire" around the world.

The second trend unfolded closer to home and impinged on the Federal Republic more directly. Regardless of détente, the Soviet Union had continued to arm across the board, on the nuclear as well as conventional level. In Europe, the star player in this drama was the SS-20 missile, incapable of reaching the United States but with enough range to reach all of Western Europe. The triple-warhead SS-20 entered deployment around 1977, and about fifty of them were added year after year. In the fall of 1977, Helmut Schmidt was the first to raise a public alarm. These missiles posed a separate threat to Europe, and they were potent "instruments of pressure."[75] Worse, superpower arms control not only ignored the challenge to the "Eurostrategic" balance but also left Moscow free to intimidate Western Europe with weapons unconstrained by SALT II. In Schmidt's words: "Strategic arms limitations confined to the United States and the Soviet Union will inevitably impair the security of the West European members of the Alliance *vis-à-vis* Soviet military superiority if we do not succeed in removing the disparities of military power in Europe parallel to the SALT negotiations." The German chancellor preferred to solve the problem by arms control, but if not, "the Alliance . . . must be ready to make available the means to support its present strategy."[76] In "translation" this meant that NATO might have to counterdeploy missiles similar to the SS-20 if negotiations failed.

It was the beginning of the worst and longest crisis in East-West and German-Soviet relations since the Berlin Crisis from 1958 to 1962. The crisis was not resolved until ten years later when, in December 1987, the United States and the USSR signed the Washington Treaty, eliminating INF (intermediate-range nuclear forces) worldwide. The ten-year contest

[75]This was a recurrent leitmotiv, see for instance his "A Policy of Reliable Partnership," Foreign Affairs, Spring 1981, p. 747.

[76]"The 1977 Alastair Buchan Memorial Lecture," October 28, 1977, reprinted in *Survival*, January–February 1978, p. 3–4.

also offered a dramatic lesson in "system dominance". Suddenly, the great stakes were no longer economic but strategic ones, reminding a middle-power like the FRG of its continuing security dependence in a world where force, while partially devalued, remained the ultimate currency of power. Imposing fearful diplomatic choices on Bonn, Cold War II also triggered a protracted battle at home which polarized West German society and ultimately toppled the Schmidt government.

Initially, the Soviet Union even refused to negotiate, pretending instead that "an approximate balance" existed even as it continued to add about fifty SS-20 missiles to its Eurostrategic arsenal per year. In December 1979, NATO responded with the "Brussels Decision," also known as the "two-track" approach. The Alliance offered to negotiate for four years; if by then, the Eurostrategic balance was not restored, NATO would deploy 464 American cruise missiles in Britain, Belgium, Holland, Italy, and West Germany, and 108 Pershing II ballistic missiles in the Federal Republic alone.

Though Helmut Schmidt had been the first to thrust the Euromissile issue to the top of the Alliance agenda, he was now caught in a double squeeze. Triggered by the Afghanistan invasion, Cold War II threatened to refreeze what Ostpolitik had so painstakingly unthawed. Instead of freedom of maneuver, renewed confrontation spelled dependence on the West and diminished access to the East. West German defense minister Hans Apel cast this situation in the form of a virtual law of German foreign policy by noting "how limited the margin of movement of lesser alliance members becomes when superpower tensions increase."[77] Conscious of West German vulnerability to Soviet pressure, Helmut Schmidt could not fall in line behind Washington's post-Afghanistan policy of militant neo-containment. Ostpolitik, as he had postulated previously, could "not proceed against or around the Soviet Union."[78] Neither could the FRG afford to alienate the United States, its most important and powerful patron in the West.

The squeeze abroad was compounded by mounting pressure at home. By 1981, the clamor of a burgeoning peace movement filled the streets and squares of West German cities. Hundreds of thousand beleaguered Bonn in 1981 and 1982. For the activists, the deployment of U.S. Pershing II and cruise missiles would turn Germany into a "shooting gallery of the superpowers." The domestic debate was shot through with nationalist and anti-American code words, and for many in the outside world, especially in France, it looked as if West Germany was about to succumb to the forces of pacifist neutralism.

Though the noise was great (and amplified by key segments of the

[77]As quoted in "Die Krise infiziert Europa," *Der Spiegel,* February 2, 1980.
[78]Address before the Bundestag, May 11, 1978; *Verhandlungen des Deutschen Bundestages,* May 11, 1978.

West German media), the numbers were simply too small. At no point in the "Battle of the Euromissiles" was the peace movement even remotely strong enough to turn antinuclear moods into antinuclear majorities. The data of public opinion consistently told the same story.[79] Antinuclearism remained a minority quest; as in the first battle against nuclear weapons in the late 1950s, the issue was simply not salient enough to overturn traditional loyalties and voting patterns. The following data illustrate the point. In the fall of 1981, a West German sample was asked to respond to NATO's "two-track" approach (which foresaw negotiations with the Soviets, but counterdeployment if arms control failed). About four out of ten were favorably disposed, and about 20 percent were opposed to the dual strategy. The most striking figures emerged from the rest of the sample, revealing a solid block of ignorance and indifference. Exactly 40 percent admitted that they either "did not know" or "did not care." The next fifteen months witnessed the grand flowering of the West German peace movement. Prominent figures of moral and political authority (like former Chancellor Brandt and many Protestant theologians) added their voices to the growing chorus of protest and militancy. And in 1983, the West Germans were asked to the same question about the two-track approach, phrased the same way as in 1981. Again, the average voter responded as he had before; again four out of ten displayed either ignorance or indifference, signaling astounding immunity to the passions of the self-selected few.[80] In other words, one and a half years of militant nationwide agitation (plus Soviet pressure) had done nothing to change the attitudes of the electorate at large.

The real problem lay elsewhere—not in the populace but in Helmut Schmidt's Social Democratic Party (SPD). As the Chancellor embarked on his tightrope act between Washington and Moscow, between the imperatives of détente and those of deterrence, the balance of power in the SPD tilted inexorably to the left. There, the Chancellor faced a motley but growing coalition of the Old Guard (around Party Chairman Willy Brandt), the prophets of the New Politics (ecologism-cum-pacifism) and the New Left, the forty-year olds who had emerged from the university battles of the 1960s to pack the party caucuses of the 1970s and 1980s. The most urgent aim of the Left was not to keep control of the Government but to gain control over their own party, the SPD. Nuclear weapons, depicted as harbingers of collective victimization, offered a perfect vehicle of intraparty influence for all those who sought to wrest power from the middle-of-the roader Helmut Schmidt, who once said of himself: "The people [at large] would have been glad to see me belong to no party."[81]

[79]For an analysis, see Josef Joffe, "Peace and Populism: Why the European Anti-Nuclear Movement Failed," *International Security*, Spring 1987.

[80]For the data, see Ibid., p. 10–11.

[81]As quoted in "Schmidt plaudert aus dem Nähkästchen," *Bild-Zeitung*, May 5, 1984.

For Schmidt, there was only one way out of this double-squeeze. At a minimum, he had to protect West Germany's détente with the Soviet Union. Returning to Bismarck "as a man who understood that one had to live in peace . . . with Russia," he stressed his nineteenth century predecessor's "key idea:" to "keep both countries, the great, powerful Soviet Union and the Federal Republic of Germany permanently attached to the process of peace."[82] Yet Schmidt had to do so without incurring the charge of disloyalty to the United States and the West as a whole. Whence an improbably difficult task followed: If Bonn could neither allow the United States to drag the FRG into its global quarrels with the Soviet Union nor afford the odium of a "separate détente" with the East, then West Germany somehow had to tackle the great power conflict itself—to mute the global confrontation so as to save regional détente in Europe.

On the one hand, Bonn joined the Olympic boycott against Moscow; on the other, it refused to participate in economic sanctions. Then Helmut Schmidt took another page out of Bismarck's book by putting himself forward as "honest interpreter of Western policy." (Bismarck, in 1878, had tried to play the "honest broker" between Britain and Russia.) "We have an important role to play in [preserving the dialogue between the superpowers], both toward our friends in the United States and toward the Soviet Union."[83] The test came half a year after the invasion of Afghanistan when the Chancellor traveled to Moscow to snatch the most vital piece of détente from the jaws of the rattled giants. In addition to Afghanistan, the key issue was the Soviet SS-20 missile. If Soviet leader Leonid Bhrezhnev would relent and finally consent to arms control negotiations, relations would return to calmer waters. Just as important, West Germany would be spared the necessity of counterdeployment, and that would undercut the anti-Schmidt *fronde* within his own party.

Unfortunately, the Federal Republic was not the Bismarck Empire. While an economic giant, the FRG was a political dwarf when it came to playing in the arena dominated by the super-powers. As a nation that depended on American protection and the good will of the Soviet Union, the FRG was badly positioned to exact moderation from either. And thus, Moscow refused to negotiate while continuing to add to its SS-20 arsenal. Deployment and counterdeployment had now burst through the purely European dimensions of the problem, defining the stakes in a grand contest of wills between the two superpowers. Moreover, the Kremlin might have read too much into the antinuclear upheavals in West Germany and Western Europe. Why should the Soviet negotiate away a Eurostrategic advantage which it might keep by just waiting—and letting domestic politics claim its due?

[82]Address to the Special General Assembly of the UN, May 25, 1978; *Bulletin*, May 30, 1978.

[83]In a speech to the Federation of German Newspaper Publishers, November 10, 1981, as quoted in *Süddeutsche Zeitung*, November 11, 1981.

It was Helmut Schmidt's personal tragedy that he desperately clung to an equipoise while the times demanded choice, that he tried to play the mediator long after his own country—the pillar and prize of Europe's postwar order—had turned into the foremost stake of the Soviet-American battle. That task, forbidding from the very beginning, became even more improbable when Bonn's trustiest Continental ally, France, shifted course under its newly elected president François Mitterrand in 1981. Worried that France's glacis to the East would yield to Soviet pressures and blandishments, Mitterrand came to act as Ronald Reagan's most stolid ally. "Soviet SS-20 missiles . . . are destroying the equilibrium in Europe," he told the Germans one month after his election. "I cannot accept this, and I admit that we must arm to restore the balance."[84]

Unable to budge the Soviet Union, the FRG could not afford to defy its two most important allies, the United States and France, simultaneously. The European system, so promising at the beginning of his rule, had now hardened into all-but-implacable restraint. And so, nine months before his fall from power, Helmut Schmidt returned to first principles: "Let nobody make a mistake. We Germans are not wanderers between the worlds [of the East and the West]. Our allies can rely on us, and we can rely on them."[85]

Technically, Schmidt fell on October 1, 1982 because his Liberal (FDP) coalition partners abandoned him in the heat of budgetary battle. In a larger sense, however, he was the victim of external forces which, in the end, he could no longer control. Nor was this a unique outcome in the annals of the Bonn Republic. With one exception, all of Schmidt's predecessors had stumbled not at the polls but in the midst of their tenure, and they were pushed by events that intruded from without: Adenauer by the Berlin Wall, Erhard by Lyndon Johnson's insistence on the punctual disbursement of "tribute" that went by the name of "offset payments" for American troops, and Brandt by an East German spy lodged in the heart of his Chancellor's Office.

In Schmidt's case, the fateful link between the system and society came in the guise of nuclear weapons, the very symbol of bipolarity and West German sovereignty denied.[86] Schmidt could have easily weathered the antinuclear revolt in the streets, and so there was but one mortal threat to his rule—emanating from his own Social Democratic Party which acted as a crucial transmission belt between the international and the domestic system. On the *Land* (state), caucus after caucus voted for antimissile resolutions, and by April 1982, the Chancellor could only

---

[84]In an interview with the German mass-circulation magazine *Stern*, July 9, 1981, p. 83.

[85]Before the Bundestag on January 14, 1982; *Bulletin*, January 15, 1982.

[86]In the grand bargain with the West, by which the FRG regained sovereignty in 1954, Bonn had to foreswear the right to an independent nuclear deterrent.

avoid a fearsome test of strength at the Munich national congress by giving in on economic policy.

Here, too, the benign international setting of yesteryear had turned against the Chancellor. Worldwide recession, set off by the second oil price explosion in 1979, had finally reached the land of a seemingly permanent economic miracle. In 1981, unemployment had jumped to 5.5 percent; in 1982, the figure soared to 7.5 percent. While yielding to Schmidt on the missiles (by allowing him to postpone a predictable anti-missile vote until next year), the Party congress layed down the law on the economy, calling for a massive boost of government spending and hence of the national debt. "I simply had the stamina no longer," Schmidt recalled, "to fight yet another battle against my comrades in the arena of economic policy."[87] And so he allowed the Party to overwhelm his government's tight fiscal policy which, in turn, offered to the deployment-minded Liberals the final reason or pretext for abandoning the coalition. (Joining forces with the Christian Democrats, the Free Democrats helped to elect the CDU's Helmut Kohl as Chancellor on October 13, 1982.)

On October 26, 1982, Schmidt took leave from his party; he would no longer lead them in the 1983 election. The final humiliation came on November 22, 1983 when a huge majority of the SPD's deputies voted to reject the impending deployment of Cruise and Pershing II missiles *against* Schmidt's pleas. They did so in the presence of the former Chancellor as he vented his frustration by sailing paper airplanes into the debating chamber of the Bundestag.

CONCLUSION: THE CONTINUITIES OF GERMAN FOREIGN POLICY

A Balance Restored: The Helmut Kohl Era, 1982–1988

The Liberal-Conservative coalition, led by Chancellor Helmut Kohl (CDU) and Foreign Minister Hans-Dietrich Genscher (FDP), called for an out-of-turn election in early 1983 to have the electorate certify the new marriage. The Social Democrats, now free of Helmut Schmidt, fought the campaign largely on foreign policy and defense issues. Their key slogan was "In the German Interest", a codeword designed to rally anti-Reagan and antimissile sentiments to the Party's cause. The choice confronting the voter was clearer than in most democratic elections. While the SPD, if victorious, would seek to derail the deployment of cruise and Pershing II missiles, the coalition parties (CDU/CSU and FDP) made no bones about their determination to stick to the deployment schedule, absent an arms control agreement.

On March 6, 1983, Kohl and Genscher were returned to power with

---

[87]In a conversation with the author, Hamburg, March 3, 1985.

an impressive margin (53.4 percent) while the Social Democrats emerged with their worst showing since 1961 (37 percent). The moral of this outcome was hardly surprising, conforming to long-established patterns of democratic voting behavior. Only in exceptional times does foreign and defense policy (as opposed to "pocketbook" issues) dominate the average voter's choice. In the Federal Republic, four issues had emerged as the decisive ones prior to the 1983 election: unemployment, social security, inflation, and the national debt. Conversely, foreign policy had sunk to the bottom of the agenda.[88] In other words, nuclear missiles were simply not "salient" enough to make for a winning issue. (The same moral emerged in Britain where the vociferously antinuclear Labour Party did worse in 1983 than at any time since 1918.)

On November 22, 1983, the Bundestag confirmed the, Government's pro missile choice; on the next day, the first Pershing II and cruise missile components arrived in West Germany. In the moment of truth, then, the Federal Republic chose deterrence over détente, and alliance obligations over Ostpolitik. The new Christian Democratic chancellor, Helmut Kohl had presumably learned a lesson from the fate of his predecessor, Helmut Schmidt. Schmidt's premise had been correct: The FRG could only flourish in a permissive East-West climate. Yet his attempt to "Germanize" East-West relations during Cold War II, that is, to hold both superpowers to the détente bargain struck in the 1970s, overtaxed German power. While Bonn, emulating Bismarck, had tried to act as a bridge and a brace between East and West, it had in fact become the premier stake of the renewed superpower contest. Though acted out on the chessboard of strategy, with Euromissiles as the pawns, the real issue was, as in the Cold War of the 1940s and 1950s, the balance of power in Europe. And that issue has always boiled down to the age-old question: Who controls Germany? At that point Ostpolitik began to collide mercilessly with Westpolitik, raising the great question of détente: How much dissolution in the West for how much evolution (and access) in the East?

Conscious of Schmidt's failure and of the costs his "honest interpreter" role had exacted in the West, the Kohl coalition presented more modest answers than its predecessor. "In my view," Helmut Kohl said, "it is a hoary illusion to believe that the relationship between. . . . the GDR and the Federal Republic of Germany can really improve while the global political climate remains at subzero temperatures." And then the Chancellor cited an old peasant's saying: "A big stream carries the smaller river along with it." By which he meant to say the obvious: The conditions in the larger milieu have to be right for Ostpolitik to flourish.[89]

[88]See "Polit-Barometer," an opinion analysis broadcast by Second German Television (ZDF), December 7, 1983.

[89]Interview with Süddeutscher Rundfunk (South German Radio), December 18, 1984, as cited from mimeographed record of the Bundespresse und Informationsamt, December 19, 1984, no. II/1218–1225.

The best and most comprensive statement on Kohl's Ostpolitik was a speech by the cabinet-rank Director of the Chancellor's Office, Wolfgang Schäuble. On the one hand there were several changes in nuance that distinguished Kohl's approach from the policy of his Social Democratic predecessor. There was the stress on the "opposition freedom and bondage" that separates the two German states. The profound clash of values between East and West is not a matter of compromise." There was also a more sober assessment of West Germany's strength and the explicit recognition of the indispensable Western connection: "Any estrangement from the Atlantic Alliance would render the Federal Republic incapable of conducting a *Deutschlandpolitik* and *Ostpolitik* deserving of the name."[90]

At the same time, Schäuble stressed a more recent tradition, the legacy bequeathed by Willy Brandt and Helmut Schmidt. "The consequences of partition for [our] people" must be "rendered more tolerable." The emphasis on the value conflict between East and West must neither "sound arrogant nor provoke the GDR." There has to be "dialogue and cooperation." Finally, he paid homage to the key principle of Ostpolitik in a language that could have been Brandt's or Schmidt's: "Overcoming the partition of Germany means to overcome the partition of Europe." And then there was that critical quantum of obeisance to Soviet sensitivity and interests. The Kohl Government knew only too well that "a *Deutschlandpolitik* that would try to circumvent Moscow could not succeed."[91]

Moscow, however, was determined to punish the Federal Republic for the deployment of Pershing II and cruise missiles that had allowed the United States to carry the day in the great Cold War II contest of the early 1980s.[92] To demonstrate that the Soviet Union held the key to Bonn's relationship with the East, the Kremlin vetoed the eagerly awaited first trip to West Germany by the East German Head of State Erich Honecker, scheduled for the fall of 1984. After his accession in 1985, Soviet General-Secretary Mikhail Gorbachev demonstratively left out Bonn as he traveled to Britain and France, while meeting three times with the American president (in 1985, 1986, and 1987). Only in 1988 did a lower-level emissary—Soviet Foreign Minister Shevardnadze—visit Bonn, and then only after the larger relationship between the two superpowers had been sorted out.

Cold War II was essentially ended when Soviet leader Mikhail Gorbachev met with Ronald Reagan at the Geneva summit of 1985. Détente

[90]In German usage, *Deutschlandpolitik* refers to FRG–GDR relations, while *Ostpolitik* designates the policy toward Eastern Europe and the Soviet Union.

[91]"Die deutsche Frage im europäischen Rahmen," address before the Swedish Institute for International Relations, May 15, 1986, as published in *Europa-Archiv,* Vol. 41 (June 1986), pp. 34–48.

[92]Here was an echo of the late 1950s when the Soviet Union launched the protracted crisis over Berlin after the Federal Republic had acquired nuclear delivery vehicles for its armed forces (with warheads under American control).

II was formally declared during the Washington summit of December 1987, when the United States and the USSR concluded a treaty eliminating intermediate-range nuclear forces (INF) with a range of 500 to 5,000 kilometers worldwide. The SS-20, the Pershing II, and the cruise missiles had been at the heart of the superpower contest throughout the 1980s. Hence, the Washington treaty signaled the crucial permissive condition of Central European détente: a modicum of agreement between the two great powers. But, as in decades past, the change in the major conflict relationship forced West Germany once more to adapt to trends beyond its control. In the face of the coming INF Treaty, Bonn had launched a determined rearguard action to keep its own 72 Pershing I missiles (with a range of 700 kilometers and with American warheads) out of the grasp of the superpowers. When the Soviet Union all but predicated the INF accord on the removal of the German Pershings, the Kohl Government had to yield. It did so on August 26, 1987 when Kohl renounced the missiles, claiming: "I merely want to help the American President toward a successful conclusion of the Geneva [INF] negotiatons."[93]

As general East-West détente began to blossom again, the two German states came to enjoy a larger scope for their own *Mitteleuropa* détente. On the eve of West Germany's national election in 1987, Moscow claimed, as routinely in years past, that relations with Bonn were "poisoned." Yet on the very same day, East German Prime Minister Willy Stoph pledged that *his* country would "take particular care to secure the peace and good-neighborly relations at the dividing line between the two social systems and great military blocs in the heart of Europe."[94] That was a gesture of defiance which reflected a basic rule of German diplomacy: Small-power freedom grows as great power conflicts subside. Still, Honecker's West German trip, on ice since 1984, would have to wait until the two superpowers had formalized their new truce.

With the INF agreement in the making since the summer of 1987, it was at last safe for Honecker to launch his long-postponed foray to West Germany. His westward trip in September of 1987—arranged with all the trappings of a state visit—also symbolized the end of an era. Since their birth in 1949, the two German states had fought a seemingly endless "War of the German Succession." Who was going to be the true successor to the German Reich? Who would subvert whom? When the East and Wept German flags flew side by side in the gardens of the Chancellor's Office while the music corps of the *Bundeswehr* played both national anthems, the answer was clear for all the world to see and hear. The war was over, and yesterday's mortal enemies were now linked in a tacit Central European partnership.

[93]As quoted in "Kohl erklärt Bereitschaft zum Verzicht auf die Pershing-1-A-Raketen," *Süddeutsche Zeitung*, August 27, 1987.

[94]Quoted in "Moskau: Beziehungen zu Bonn vergiftet" and "Stoph: Um gute Nachbarschaft bemüht," *Süddeutsche Zeitung*.

German Foreign Policy: Enduring Problems

What is more important in explaining foreign policy—the "domestic sources" or the "international system," the inside or the outside? This is the basic question of all foreign policy analysis, and there is no satisfactory answer. To say that one set of factors is decisive is to ignore the other and to succumb to the deceptive plausibility of "single-cause analysis," which seeks to explain too much and ends up explaining too little. To say that *both* matter may be seemingly more sophisticated, but it runs into the problem of overdetermination, meaning the introduction of more explanatory variables than are logically necessary.

Foreign policy analysis requires a paradigm that must determine *ex ante* what is more important—the players or the international environment in which they act? How does one decide? The Federal Republic of Germany may well be a special case where geography and history—the country's location and its origins—virtually foreordain a presumption in favor of "system dominance." The FRG arose literally from the ashes, and it was conceived by fiat of the three Western powers in 1949. In the beginning, there was not a state that made foreign policy, but the foreign policy of others that created a state. Yet "system dominance" went deeper still. West German *society* was recreated in the Western image as a liberal, capitalist, and federal order. Even the economy was restructured by outside forces. Following America's cues, the FRG's economy, was transformed into a market economy, and classic trade flows were radically redirected. Prior to 1945, the main trade flows went East-West, from the industrial West of Germany to the agrarian East. With the East cut off by partition, West Germany was suddenly dependent on new markets in Western Europe and the United States; today, more than half of the FRG's exports go into the European Community.

Then there was and is geography. The FRG shares a, 1,000-mile border with the Warsaw Pact, and thus it is condemned to play the venue and victim of East-West war in Europe. This has produced a large security deficit that turned the FRG into a net importer of security *made in U.S.A.* In turn, this deficit implies special sensitivity to the wishes of the United States, as well as to the other two main powers in Europe, Britain and France. Precisely because it is so security-dependent, however, the Federal Republic cannot ignore the other superpower in Europe, the Soviet Union, which poses the main threat. To diminish that threat, the FRG must consistently pursue two opposite policies: to contain the Soviet Union with the help of others (deterrence), and to accommodate the Soviet Union on its own (détente).

This is *prima facie* evidence for the presumption of "system dominance." How can this presumption be tested? An obvious test is to look at the structure of the international system, how it changed over time, and then at German foreign policy: Does it reflect those changes, does the actor's script change in response to a rearranged stage? History reveals an impressive "fit"—and more than mere correlation. Throughout the past forty-odd years, the milieu changed first; then came the appropriate response of West German foreign policy, and finally domestic politics would respond later.

Tight bipolarity and Cold War abroad dovetailed nicely with a foreign policy that was almost exclusively Western-oriented and a domestic consensus that was highly anti-Communist. From 1949 to 1969, all Chancellors of the Federal Republic were Christian Democrats. Conversely, the Social Democrats, who opposed rearmament and NATO, were regularly beaten at the polls. Toward the end of the 1960s, bipolarity became muted along with Cold War I, and both German foreign policy and domestic politics subsequently changed *pari passu*. In 1969, a Social Democratic Chancellor, Willy Brandt, was elected for the first time in twenty years; at the same time, the FRG launched its New Ostpolitik.

The external cues, however, came first. Because the FRG's key allies embarked on détente, Bonn followed, and then only after protracted resistance (see Chapter 4). In the 1980s, the reverse process occurred. In the face of Cold War II, Helmut Schmidt tried to preserve détente in the face of renewed superpower confrontation and rearmament. It is no accident, however, that the renewed change in the external milieu brought about a change in both policy and tenure. In charge of the Federal Government throughout the détente-minded 1970s, the SPD's fortunes declined along with the gathering chill in East-West relations. Helmut Schmidt, the Social Democrat, was ousted in 1982. In the following year, Helmut Kohl, the Christian Democrat, who had campaigned on a pro-NATO and promissile platform, emerged triumphant from the 1983 national election, to be reconfirmed in 1987.

It should not come as a surprise that a country which is the very product of bipolarity should also be so uniquely beholden to the forces of that system. Why? West Germany (and its East German twin) are both the greatest profiteers and the greatest victims of the postwar system. Without Cold War I, the two Germanies could not have become what they are now: the two strongest and richest European members of their respective alliance systems. Instead of revenge and prostration in a kind of "super-Versailles," the two Germanies regained sovereignty and then found a shelter and a legitimate role as the two most important junior partners of the two superpowers.

On the other hand, the two Germanies are also the main victims of bipolarity. The postwar order was built around the partition of Germany, with each German state assuming a vanguard role in the Cold War—as pillars of their respective alliance systems and as forward bastions of mutual containment. The price has been the division of the nation, and more. In their unique role, both Germanies became uniquely dependent on their patron powers and uniquely beholden to the strictures of their milieu. Each German state must take care not to alienate its key allies. Each hosts the largest concentration of peace-time military power on its soil. And if new accoutrements of nuclear war are added, as they were in the shape of Pershing II and cruise missiles in the West and SS-12/22 missiles in the East, their bulk goes into the FRG and the GDR.

Dependence was acceptable, and even profitable, as long as both Germanies had to worry about first things first: about consolidation, respectability, economic reconstruction, and security. These purposes having been achieved, the blessings of dependence have begun to wane, while their burdens have come to chafe. Dependence, which used to be the *raison d'état* of both Germanies, now spells submission and a limited margin of diplomatic maneuver. And so both Germanies, the pillars of the *ancien régime*, have begun to rethink their peculiar roles in the bipolar order.

Once hostile brothers who used to play a vanguard role in each other's containment, the two Germanies have virtually become tacit allies. Though more strongly tied to NATO and Warsaw Pact than others, the FRG and the GDR have cautiously begun to transcend these constraints. Symbolized by the pomp and circumstances of Erich Honecker's week-long visit to the Federal Republic in the fall of 1987, that tacit partnership goes back to the beginning of the 1980s. In those days, when Cold War II threatened to engulf Central Europe, too, both Helmut Schmidt and Erich Honecker began to talk about *Verantwortungsgemein-schaft* ("community of responsibility") which is but another word for a separate, intra-German détente that must flourish independently from the ups and downs of the superpower relationship.[95] Nor is this permanent détente imperative limited to the fringes of the political system. It unites Christian Democrats and Social Democrats, Greens, and Free Democrats.

The "tacit partnership" serves both states. The GDR need no longer fear closer contacts with the FRG. Recognized abroad and tacitly accepted at home, the East German regime can live with the risks of interaction because profits of reassociation are so rich. West Germany delivers technology and billions in cash subsidies; these, plus a carefully controlled amount of westward travel, do not so much endanger as buttress regime stability and legitimacy at home. For West Germany, it is the very impossibility of reunification that strengthens the permanent détente imperative. The prize is the progressive reassociation of the two Germanies toward a relationship where the inter-German border of the future is no more forbidding than the one between Austria and the Federal Republic today.

Yet a separate inter-German détente is not enough. Because the two Germanies are so uniquely tied to their milieu, foreign policy must change the system's structure. The rationale is as simple as it is ambitious:

[95]For an elaboration, see Josef Joffe "The Tacit Alliance " in Lincoln Gordon, et al, *Eroding Empire: Western Relations With Eastern Europe* (Washington: Brookings Institution, 1987).

Less bipolarity equals less dependence equals more freedom of movement. Hence the basic purpose of German foreign policy must be necessarily the "subtle subversion" of bipolarity—where confrontation is muted, bloc-transcending cooperation is accentuated and military power loses its hold as main currency of international influence.

If the demand for security is the main source of West Germany's unique dependence, then dependence will be lessened by reducing that demand. This was the main rationale for Willy Brandt's New Ostpolitik, Helmut Schmidt's strenuous attempt to shelter German-Soviet détente against the ravages of Cold War II, and Helmut Kohl's quest to restore the Soviet link after the Euromissile crisis of early 1980s. The basic principle behind all of these policies is a classic small-power strategy. Dependence on great-power allies can be reduced by propitiating the common enemy—by reducing his reasons for threatening or pressuring the smaller adversary. There is less need to pay for insurance in the West if a reinsurance policy can be taken out in the East. A typical reinsurance policy is made up of side-payments to one's opponent—in form of conciliatory behavior or economic benefits, which are both essential components of all Ostpolitik.

Though more cautious, East German policy follows a similar rationale. If disarmament diminishes the American military presence in the West, East Berlin can legitimately ask the Soviets to lighten the burden of their military power on East German soil. If there are fewer nuclear weapons in West Germany, why have so many Soviet missiles in East Germany? East Berlin has been an avid supporter of a chemical weapons ban and of a nuclear-free corridor on either side of the Elbe because that would clearly diminish the GDR's war time risk and undercut Soviet arguments for keeping the bulk of its Warsaw Pact forces in East Germany. Moreover, the more secure détente, the larger the diplomatic freedom of Moscow's client states.

Why should this process be "subtly subversive" of bipolarity in Europe? The postwar order was built around the partition of Germany and Europe. It must logically collapse once the two Germanies no longer assume their traditional roles in that order: as pillars of their respective alliance systems and as forward bastions of mutual containment. If and when the two Germanies are closer to each other than to their own alliances, meaning that nationality has triumphed over ideology, then the *ancien régime* must perforce lose its meaning. The Soviet Union would lose the very brace of its empire in Eastern Europe; the United States would be thrown back to a rump alliance along the rim of Western Europe with dubious survival value.

How far will that process go, how far can it go? Whether it will lead to reunification is the wrong question. The dynamics of "subtle subversion" are driven precisely by the fact that the two Germanies no longer treat each other as object of eventual unification (which blocked all movement) but as tacit allies in transformation. And transformation works precisely because they no longer question each other's separate statehood.

Yet the two Germanies are not only the pillars but also the *products* of the postwar European system, based on the dominant position of the superpowers on either side of the divide. That reality, whose disappearance remains hard to conceive in our time, implies stringent limits on the freedom of the lesser powers, and on the two Germanies above all. They can experiment with all kinds of system-transcending policies, yet they are free to do so only as long as the essentials remain untouched. The contemporary system is a "stalemate system", and "dreams are [its] victims."[96] That system remains low on flexibility and choice, and it delivers few trumps and options.

The Soviet Union will not voluntarily withdraw from its pontifical and political empire in Eastern Europe. Conversely, the United States will surely retract if so told by its allies, but short of real integration, the West Europeans must still live with an enduring reality: Alone, they cannot defend themselves against the Soviet Union, and the United States remains their only natural protector. Still, nobody can imagine the permanence of an order built on the partition of an ancient continent and its domination by two outside superpowers. On the part of the Europeans there is acceptance *faute de mieux*, but little happiness—and least of all among the two Germanies who continue to pay the highest price for the enduring stability this order has produced. German foreign policy, both East and West, will thus face an enduring problem: how to change the postwar system that was built in and around Germany by the two superpowers whose hold on Europe only the two superpowers themselves can relinquish.

FOREIGN POLICY LANDMARKS

May 8, 1945	Capitulation of the Third Reich
May 23, 1949	Proclamation of the Basic Law (Constitution)
September 7, 1949	Founding of the Federal Republic of Germany (FRG); First Chancellor: Konrad Adenauer (CDU), who rules until 1963
May 5, 1955	The Federal Republic regains sovereignty and joins NATO
1957	The FRG decides to acquire dual-purpose nuclear delivery vehicles with warheads under U.S. control
November 27, 1958	The Soviet Union delivers the so-called Berlin Ultimatum
August 13, 1961	The Berlin Wall is built
October 1962	The Cuban Missile Crisis
January 22, 1963	France and the Federal Republic conclude the Treaty on Friendship and Cooperation
November 16, 1963	Ludwig Erhard (CDU) replaces Konrad Adenauer as Chancellor

[96]Stanley Hoffmann, *Gulliver's Troubles, Or, The Setting of American Foreign Policy* (New York: McGraw-Hill, 1986, pp. 52, 54.

May 12, 1965	The Federal Republic establishes diplomatic relations with Israel; in response many Arab states sever their diplomatic ties with the FRG
April 19, 1967	Adenauer dies
December 1, 1966	Grand Coalition of CDU, CSU, and SPD with Kurt Georg Kiesinger as Chancellor and Willy Brandt (SPD) as Foreign Minister
October 21, 1969	Coalition of SPD and FDP with Willy Brandt as Chancellor and Walter Scheel (FDP) as Foreign Minister
November 28, 1969	FRG signs the Non-Proliferation Treaty
March 19, 1970	First official encounter between FRG and GDR occurs when Willy Brandt meets with East German Prime Minister Willy Stopf in Erfurt, East Germany
August 12, 1970	FRG concludes treaty on normalization of relations with the Soviet Union followed by similar treaty with Poland and with Czechoslovakia; these treaties are collectively known as "Eastern Treaties"
December 21, 1972	FRG and GDR conclude the "Basic Treaty"
April 16, 1974	Helmut Schmidt (SPD) replaces Willy Brandt as Chancellor
December 1979	Soviet Union invades Afghanistan
December 12, 1979	NATO announces the so-called Brussels Decision, which provides for the deployment of 572 Pershing II and cruise missiles beginning in 1983 if arms control negotiations with the Soviet Union do not remove the Soviet SS-20 missile threat
October 10, 1981	250,000 demonstrators assemble in Bonn to protest against the missile deployment
October 1, 1982	Helmut Kohl (CDU) replaces Helmut Schmidt as Chancellor as result of no-confidence vote in the Bundestag
March 6, 1983	National election confirms Helmut Kohl in power
November 23, 1983	First Pershing II missile components arrive in the Federal Republic; in response the Soviet Union ruptures the Geneva nuclear arms talks
March 12, 1985	The United States and the Soviet Union resume nuclear arms control negotiations in Geneva
May 5, 1985	President Reagan visits German military cemetery in Bitburg. Intended as gesture of reconciliation forty years after the capitulation of the Third Reich, the ceremony was widely condemned in the United States because of the presence of Waffen-SS graves. (The Waffen-SS was the military arm of the Nazi SS which played a key role in the annihilation of European Jewry.)
October 8, 1985	Richard von Weizsäcker becomes the first president of the Federal Republic of Germany to visit Israel
November 19, 1985	First Reagan-Gorbachev summit meets in Geneva
May 16, 1986	During their national congress in Hannover, the Greens resolve to pull the FRG out of NATO
October 12, 1986	Second Reagan-Gorbachev summit held in Reykjavik, Iceland.
January 25, 1987	National elections confirm Helmut Kohl's CDU/CSU-FDP government in power; the Christian Democrats lose 4.5 percentage points while Hans-Dietrich Genscher's FDP picks up an additional 2.1 percent of the vote

June 14, 1987	Hans-Jochen Vogel replaces Willy Brandt as chairman of the SPD
August 26, 1987	Chancellor Kohl declares his readiness to scrap the FRG's seventy-two Pershing Ia missiles (with U.S. nuclear warheads) if the United States and the Soviet Union agree on the worldwide elimination of INF (intermediate-range nuclear forces, that is, Pershing II's, ground-launched cruise missilels, SS-4's, SS-20's, SS-12/22's and SS-23's)
December 8, 1987	The United States and the Soviet Union, during the third Reagan-Gorbachev summit in Washington, sign treaty on the worldwide elimination of INF
January 22, 1988	On the twenty-fifth anniversary of the Franco-German Treaty of Cooperation, the FRG and France announce the formation of a joint brigade and a joint Defense Council

SELECTED BIBLIOGRAPHY

Primary Sources and Documents

AUSWÄRTIGES AMT, ed. *Die Auswärtige Politik der Bundesrepublik Deutschland.* Cologne: Verlag Wissenschaft und Politik, 1972.

BUNDESMINISTERIUM FÜR INNERDEUTSCHE BEZIEHUNGEN, ed. *Texte zur Deutschlandpolitik* (a series of volumes containing documents and speeches on intra-German relations published in loose succession since 1969).

BUNDESMINISTER DER VERTEIDIGUNG, *Weissbuch* (a posture statement by the Defense Minister, published in irregular intervals in English and German. The latest was issued in 1983.)

DEUTSCHER BUNDESTAG. *Verhandlungen des Deutschen Bundestages* (record of parliamentary proceedings).

EMBREE, GEORGE D., ed. *The Soviet Union and the German Question, 1958–1961.* The Hague: Nijhoff, 1963.

OPPEN, BEATE RUHM VON, ed. *Documents on Germany Under Occupation, 1945–1955.* London: Oxford University Press, 1955.

Presse- und Informationsamt der Bundesregierung. *Bulletin* (a regular compilation of important speeches, documents, press conferences, etc., in a German and an English edition).

Books and Articles

ADENAUER, KONRAD. *Memoirs, 1945–1953.* Chicago: Regnery, 1966.

ARDAGH, JOHN. *Germany and the Germans: An Anatomy of Society Today.* New York: Harper & Row, 1987.

BARNETT, RICHARD J. *The Alliance.* New York: Simon and Schuster, 1983.

BIRNBAUM, KARL E. *East and West Germany: A Modus Vivendi.* Lexington, Mass.: Heath Lexington Books, 1973.

BRANDT, WILLY. *A Peace Policy for Europe.* New York: Holt, Rinehart ¢ Winston, 1969.

BULMER, SIMON and WILLIAM PATERSON. *The Federal Republic of Germany and the European Community.* London: Allen and Unwin, 1987.

CHILDS, DAVID. *From Schumacher to Brandt: The Story of German Socialism, 1945–1965.* Oxford: Pergamon Press, 1966.

CRAIG, GORDON. *From Bismarck to Adenauer: Aspects of German Statecraft.* New York: Harper & Row, 1965.

DEUTSCH, KARL W., and LEWIS J. EDINGER. *Germany Rejoins the Powers: A study of Mass Opinion, Interest Groups and Elites in Contemporary German Foreign Policy.* Stanford: Stanford University Press, 1959.

EDINGER, LEWIS J. *Kurt Schumacher: A Study in Personality and Political Behavior.* Stanford: Stanford University Press, 1965.

FELD, WERNER. *West Germany and the European Community.* New York: Praeger, 1981.

FREY, ERIC G. *Division and Detente: The Germanies And Their Alliances.* New York: Praeger, 1987.

GATZKE, HANS W. *Germany and the United States: A Special Relationship?* Cambridge: Harvard University Press, 1980.

GENSCHER, HANS-DIETRICH. *Deutsche Aussenpolitik.* Stuttgart: Bonn Aktuell, 1981.

GIMBEL, JOHN. *The American Occupation of Germany: 1945–1949.* Stanford: Stanford University Press, 1968.

GOLDMAN, GUIDO. *The German Political System.* New York: Random House, 1974.

GRIFFITH, WILLIAM E. *The Ostpolitik of the Federal Republic of Germany.* Cambridge: MIT Press, 1978.

GROSSER, ALFRED. *The Western Alliance.* New York: Seabury Press, 1980.

HANRIEDER, WOLFRAM. *The Stable Crisis: Two Decades of German Foreign Policy.* New York: Harper and Row, 1970.

———, ed. *West German Foreign Policy, 1949–79.* Boulder: Westview Press, 1980.

———, ed. *Helmut Schmidt: Perspectives on Politics.* Boulder: Westview Press, 1982 (a useful collection of speeches and interviews).

JOFFE, JOSEF. "Germany and the Atlantic Alliance: The Politics of Dependence, 1961–1968," in William Cromwell et al., *Political Problems of Atlantic Partnership.* Bruges: College of Europe, 1969.

———. "All Quiet on the Eastern Front," *Foreign Policy,* Winter 1979/80.

———. "European-American Relations: The Enduring Crisis," *Foreign Affairs,* Spring 1981.

———. "German Defense Policy: Novel Solutions and Enduring Dilemmas," in Gregory Flynn et al., *The International Fabric of Western Security.* Montclair: Allenheld, Osmun, 1981.

———. "Squaring Many Circles: German Defense Policy Between Deterrence, Detente and Alliance" in Gordon Craig et al., eds. *The Federal Republic of Germany and the United States: Political, Social and Economic Relations.* Boulder: Westview Press, 1984.

———. *The Limited Partnership: Europe, the United States and the Burdens of Alliance.* Cambridge, Mass.: Ballinger, 1987.

———. "The Tacit Alliance: West German Policy Toward Eastern Europe," in Lincoln Gordon, ed., *Eroding Empire: Western Relations With Eastern Europe.* Washington, D.C.: Brookings Institution, 1987.

KAISER, KARL. *German Foreign Policy in Transition.* London: Oxford University Press, 1968.

KISSINGER, HENRY A. *The Troubled Partnership.* New York: McGraw-Hill, 1965.

McADAMS, JAMES. *East Germany and Detente.* Cambridge: Cambridge University Press, 1985.

MERKL, PETER H. *The Origin of the West German Republic.* New York: Oxford.

———. *German Foreign Policies, West and East.* Santa Barbara, Calif.: Clio Press, 1974.

MORGAN, ROGER. *The United States and West Germany, 1945–1973: A Study in Alliance Politics.* London: Oxford University Press, 1974.

NERLICH, UWE and JAMES A. THOMSON. *The Soviet Problem in American-German Relations.* New York: Crane Russak, 1985.

NOELLE-NEUMANN, ELIZABETH, ed. *The Germans: Public Opinion Polls, 1967–1980.* Westport, Conn.: Greenwood Press, 1981.

RICHARDSON, JAMES L. *Germany and the Atlantic Alliance: The Interaction of Strategy and Politics.* Cambridge: Harvard University Press, 1966.

ROSOLOWSKY, DIANE. *West Germany's Foreign Policy: The Impact of the Social Democrats and the Greens.* New York: Greenwood Press, 1987.

SCHICK, JACK M. *The Berlin Crisis, 1958–1962.* Philadelphia: University of Pennsylvania Press, 1972.

SCHMIDT, HELMUT. *Menschen und Mächte.* Berlin: Siedler, 1987; this is the quasi-memoirs of the former chancellor.

SIMONIAN, HAIG. *The Privileged Partnership: Franco-German Relations in the European Community, 1969–1984.* Oxford: Clarendon, 1985.

STERN, FRITZ. *Dreams and Delusions: The Drama of German History.* New York: Alfred A. Knopf, 1987.

STRAUSS, FRANZ JOSEF. *Challenge and Response: A Program for Europe.* New York: Atheneum, 1970.

WILLIS, FRANK R. *France, Germany and the New Europe, 1945–1967.* London: Oxford University Press, 1968.

WINDSOR, PHILIP. *Germany and the Management of Détente.* New York: Praeger, 1971.

WINDSOR, PHILIP. Germany and the Western Alliance: Lessons from the 1980 Crises. London: International Institute for Strategic Studies, Adelphi Papers No. 181, 1983.

4

America's Foreign Policy

Robert J. Art

The age of Pax Americana is over. From 1945 until the early 1970s, the United States experienced a world preeminence that only a few nations throughout history have enjoyed. During these years America reigned as the world's foremost military and economic power. She forged a network of alliances that committed her to come to the defense of over fifty nations if they were subject to attack. When she chose to intervene somewhere with military force, she did so at will. For over twenty-five years, she maintained a military force of over a half-million men stationed overseas. Through her nuclear might she faced down her foremost adversary in their singular test of wills over Cuba in 1962. Through the sheer size and dynamism of her economy, she generated an economic presence throughout the world that left few areas untouched. She was and still remains the world's best single national market for the sale of manufactured goods and raw materials. Her multinational corporations dominated the economies of some nations and significantly affected those of many others. For hundreds of millions of non-Americans, the American standard of living was the yardstick by which to measure progress. With the exception of the Vietnam War, America's foreign policy for over thirty years, as measured by the objectives she set for herself, was mostly a string of successes, not a series of failures. The age of Pax Americana was brief but brilliant.

By the early 1970's, America had passed the zenith of her power. It was not that she was becoming weaker absolutely, but rather that others were becoming stronger in relation to her and were thereby narrowing the gap between their power and hers. By 1972 the Soviet Union had effectively closed the gap between her strategic nuclear forces and those of the United States. In signing the Strategic Arms Limitation Accords of 1972, America publicly accepted this fact and gave to the Russians something that had become central to their foreign policy objectives—official recognition by America of their coequality in nuclear armaments. Although not yet possessing conventional forces as transportable and flexible as those of the United States, the Soviet Union was rapidly developing the sea and air transport capabilities that would enable her to act, not merely as a regional, but also as a global conventional power.

While the SALT Accord of 1972 officially marked the end of America's nuclear preeminence, the devaluation of the dollar in 1971 symbolically marked the passing of America's overweening economic dominance. No longer the fixed bedrock of international economic dealings, the dollar became subject to the same types of pressures that had caused other currencies before it to be devalued. Underlying the dollar's devaluation was a host of structural changes in the noncommunist international economy, but prime among them was the revived prosperity of Western Europe and Japan. Her two erstwhile dependents, after extremely rapid growth throughout the 1960s, had become America's toughest economic competitors by the early 1970s. Reflective of America's recognition of this fact was the dual nature of the 1974 Trade Reform Act: it provided both for the lowering or virtual elimination of tariff and quota barriers *and* their reimposition should foreign competition prove too severe to American industry.

Within this context of the rise, exercise, and waning of America's singular global dominance, three central questions about post-1945 American foreign policy arise. First, what were the underlying factors responsible for producing America's overweening world power? Second, to what ends did the United States choose to utilize that power? Third, can she still afford to pursue an activist foreign policy? The remainder of the chapter will deal with these three questions.

THE HEYDAY OF CONTAINMENT, 1945–1968

Viewed in historical perspective, America's foreign policy after 1945 has been truly revolutionary. For almost 150 years, from 1800 until 1945, the United States shied away from entangling commitments. In the space of the next twenty years, she became entangled with literally most of the world. Instead of isolationism, she pursued an internationalist policy under the guise of containment, the intent of which was to prevent the spread of communism.

Although containing communism has been the consistent underpinning for post-1945 American foreign policy, containment has nonetheless gone through three distinct phases. During the first phase, from 1945 until 1950, the United States evolved a coherent policy with respect to Europe, but not toward the Far East. The major instruments of policy were political and economic, not military. Containment was mostly a European policy, certainly not a global one. The policy developed gradually, not all at once, due to the executive branch's concern over how much activism in foreign affairs the Congress and the public would tolerate. During the second phase, 1950 through 1968, the United States globalized and corrupted its containment policy. The major instruments of policy were alliances, foreign aid, and reliance on military force. The executive generally had little difficulty in obtaining from the Congress what it considered essential in order to achieve its goals. During the third phase, not yet over, from 1969 onward, containment was muted but not ended by détente with Russia and China. The instruments of policy began to shift back to greater reliance on political-economic means. The Congress began increasingly to challenge the president's predominance in foreign affairs and slowly but steadily to circumscribe the flexibility he had enjoyed for over twenty years.

During the first phase, the primary threat perceived by American decision makers was not a direct attack by Russian troops on Western Europe or in the Far East, but rather the internal decay of those nations into communism as a result of the economic disintegration and chaos that they were experiencing in the mid- and late-1940s. During the second phase, there were two prime threats. As a consequence of the Korean War, the fear of the fifties was of a direct attack by Russia on Western Europe; as a consequence of Castro's rise to power in Cuba by successful guerrilla warfare and because of Khrushchev's declaration in 1961 that such wars of national liberation were communism's strategy for the future, the fear of the 1960s became one of internal subversion in the Third World. During the third phase, the prime threat was no longer external to the United States but came from within: fear that the American public would withdraw its commitment to contain communism and lapse back into isolationism.

Throughout most of this period, then, America's pursuit of containment remained steadfast, but the means she chose in each period to implement it were tailored to the particular form the threat was perceived to have taken. Containment was simply a reactive policy designed to counter Russian initiatives. From 1945 onward, the United States became committed, first, to shoring up the 1945 status quo and then to preserving it essentially unchanged. As with all status quo powers, America's foreign policy became defensive in tone and precedent-conscious. The foreign policy elite became obsessed with the fear that if America failed to fulfill the terms of any one of her commitments, then the rest would lose their credibility, her foreign policy edifice would crumble, and her world influence would rapidly unravel. This obsession with setting and enforcing precedents created a "domino-mania": if one commitment (domino) that America made was not honored, then all the rest would lose their credibility (would fall). This obsession with precedents created a peace-is-indivisible mentality, in which any action that America took was seen as inextricably linked to every other that she had taken and would take. Foreign policy became a seamless web.

The Forging of Containment, 1945–1949

In 1945 the United States faced a world that had changed radically from that which had existed before 1941. All the traditional landmarks were gone. Europe ceased to exist as an independent actor able to exert influence beyond its borders. It became instead the object of the actions of more powerful actors. In the Far East, Japanese power was shattered; China was rent by civil war; Indochina was poised on the verge of one. The wartime policy of cooperation with Russia was dissolving. Russia was in the process of installing communist-dominated governments in Eastern Europe. Alone among the great powers, only the United States emerged unscathed from World War II; America had in fact become the stronger for having fought it. Unlike the situation in 1919 after the end of World War I, after World War II, there was not even the façade of a world order, much less a structure for it, behind which the United States could retreat.

America's European Policy.   Confronted with these circumstances, the Truman administration's prime concern lay with preserving anticommunist governments in Western Europe, not with imposing democratic governments on Eastern Europe. Some commentators have argued that the Truman administration overestimated Russia's power immediately after World War II, that it did not realize how seriously the war had weakened her, and that it was therefore too cautious in dealing with her. Others have argued the reverse: the Truman administration was well aware of Russia's weakness and tried to exploit it in order to create an American sphere of influence in Eastern Europe, thus denying Russia what was rightfully hers by virtue of the tremendous sacrifices she had made during the war. Both views are wide of the mark. With regard to the latter, the Truman administration talked long, loudly, and forcefully about the violations to the Yalta Declaration of February 1945 that Russia was committing. (The declaration promised that free elections would be held in the liberated countries of Eastern Europe.) But the Truman administration did virtually nothing other than talk, nothing that could have significantly influenced what was occurring there, such as the threat to use military force unless Stalin desisted. If the intensity of a commitment to a goal is measured by the resources devoted to attain it, then America's commitment to preserving democracy in Eastern Europe, or to keeping the door open to American capitalism there, or whatever one calls it, had to rank near the bottom of her list of priorities. All nations have desires that surpass their resources to fulfill them. How scarce resources are allocated among competing goals determines their true relative worth. Preserving the right to hold free elections in Eastern Europe was not worth much to the Truman administration, if measured by what it was willing to pay in order to get them.

With regard to the first view, the Truman administration's overestimation of Russia's power or, for that matter, her underestimation of it is relevant only if the administration was bent on wresting Eastern Europe from the Soviet Union. True, the administration could have been as vapid as it was its response to Stalin's actions there because it overestimated Russian strength. But consider the facts. Russian troops were in Eastern Europe; America had none there. Tough talk had been used and proved futile. Stalin had not desisted. The next effective step after tough talk is threats to use force. And such threats always carry with them risk that they might have to be made good. Only the issuance of such threats could have determined how strong Stalin felt he was, how firm was his resolve, and thus whether the Truman administration had over-, under-, or correctly estimated Russian power.

Harry Truman chose not to issue such threats for two reasons. First, he calculated, almost certainly correctly, that the American public would not support another war following immediately on the heels of one they had just finished fighting and one against their recent ally to boot. Immediately after the war's end, the tug of demobilization was too strong to resist, unless one wished to commit political suicide. Second, if the United States were to have any hope of reversing the evolution of political events within Eastern Europe by mere threats to resort to force, it had to act sometime before the end of 1945 at the latest. After that, Russia's position there would be so entrenched that mere threats to use force would have even less of a chance of working than they had in 1945; and, consequently, the surety of the need to resort to force would increase. In 1945, however, the administration was reluctant to issue such threats, strangely enough, out of fear of endangering the American public's support for an activist, internationalist-oriented postwar foreign policy.

The key to the apparent puzzle of how in 1945 an activist, threatening policy towards Russia over Eastern Europe could have determined the American public's support for an activist foreign policy elsewhere lies with the Truman administration's view of the political function that the

United Nations was to play *within* the United States. Well aware of the mistakes that Wilson had made in not carrying along the American public and the Senate in support of the League of Nations, Roosevelt was quite careful during the war to do everything possible to ensure the public's support for the United Nations, going to such lengths as enlisting Republican senatorial involvement in the planning for it that went on during the war. Truman continued this policy. To both presidents the United Nations was to be the guise through which a postwar internationalist foreign policy would be sold to what had historically been a profoundly isolationist public. Given the nature of the Security Council, however, with the veto power that each of the permanent members possessed, it was thought at the time that the United Nations could not function effectively without Russian-American cooperation. To have taken actions in 1945 that threatened war against Russia, such as all-out opposition to her takeover of Eastern Europe, would have meant risking such cooperation. That, in turn, would have risked discrediting the United Nations as a viable body. And, finally, that would in turn have risked the American public's support for it and by extension their backing for a nonisolationist postwar foreign policy. Thus, both the peculiar linking of events in Eastern Europe to the status of the United Nations and the special role that the United Nations was intended to play within the United States hamstrung the Truman administration in Eastern Europe.

Clearly, immediately after the war's end, it was the perceived domestic constraints on the use of force, not any estimation regarding the relative strengths of the United States and the Soviet Union, that explains why the Truman administration reasoned that it could do little more than talk tough in Eastern Europe. But would not the same domestic limits on action also apply to Western Europe? And if that was the case, would it not be cause for the gravest concern because by culture, by tradition, by economic and security interests, Western Europe was the area valued most in America's postwar calculations? The answer to the first question is not definite, but clearly if it were even a tentative "yes," then the answer to the second would be a resounding "yes." But, from 1945 until 1950, these questions, and their answers, were largely academic; therefore, a "yes" answer to each loses most of its force. "Yes" answers to these questions would have been significant only if the Truman administration had feared that Russian armies were poised in Eastern Europe, ready to march at a moment's notice straight across Western Europe to the Atlantic. The administration feared no such thing during the first phase, which suggests that it did have a good sense of Russia's capabilities even if it could not with certainty plumb her intentions. From the end of World War II until the beginning of the Korean War in June of 1950, the prime fear concerned the political leverage that the large communist parties of France and Italy could gain from the economic chaos prevailing there.

And if these two nations were "subverted" from within, then the political fate of the rest of Europe would be in doubt. During the first phase of containment, the overriding concern of policy makers was to keep Western Europe from going communist; but military means were not used because the threat was considered to be primarily political and economic.

It is only in this light that the three major actions of America toward Europe from 1945 to 1949 make sense. Each in its own way, the Truman Doctrine, the Marshall Plan, and the NATO Alliance, was designed to deal with the political-economic aspects of the situation. The Truman Doctrine was the first postwar manifestation of the domino theory. The Truman administration sent economic aid and some military arms to Greece and Turkey in order to enable the Greek monarchy to win the civil war against the communists and to bolster Turkish resistance against the political pressure that the Soviet Union was placing on her. If Greece and Turkey were allowed to fall under Russian influence, the gateway to the Middle East would be opened, with the attendant threat to the vast oil reserves there. And, so it was reasoned, if the Middle East became a fertile field for Russian penetration, then Western Europe, with its dependence on Middle East oil, would ultimately find it necessary to accommodate itself to Russia. Greece and Turkey were the first dominoes that could ultimately lead via the Middle East to the "fall" of Western Europe, to its detachment, that is, from America's influence. If the United States failed to show its mettle in Greece and Turkey, then it would be less able to persuade the noncommunist political forces in France and Italy that their fortunes lay with the United States, or that their efforts to preserve noncommunist governments had a good chance of success. The short-term strategic consequences of the "fall" of Greece and Turkey might not be severe, but the long-term political consequences for Western Europe would be. Inaction now, it was feared, could very well breed irreversible defeat later on.

The aid to Greece and Turkey embodied in the Truman Doctrine was thus aimed at influencing political developments within Western Europe. The same was true for the Marshall Plan and the NATO Alliance. The Marshall Plan was designed to bring about the economic recovery of Western Europe in order to forestall a communist electoral victory arising from the economic chaos prevailing there. In a little over four years the United States sent to Western Europe over $12 billion in grant aid in order to provide the capital required to reconstruct their war-shattered economies. Economic recovery was deemed so crucial that the United States pressured England and France to amalgamate their two occupation zones in Germany with that of the United States in order to create a West German state. The Americans argued that the economic recovery of France, Italy, and England could not occur unless Germany were also revived. Not American altruism toward her former enemy, but the need to revive Western Europe in order to prevent the emergence of parliamentary communism, was responsible for the beneficent treatment that Western Germany received from the United States.

Similarly, the NATO Alliance (The North Atlantic Treaty Organization) was designed to foster the development of strong noncommunist governments in Western Europe. In 1948 the Berlin Blockade, but more particularly the communist coup in Czechoslovakia, clearly demonstrated the political leverage that Russia could gain from mere proximity to a nation without the actual use within it of her large conventional forces. Russian troops massed on the border of Czechoslovakia intimidated the noncommunist forces within, and prevented them from resisting the bloodless coup staged by the communists. Fearful that Russia might try to repeat this in Western Europe, worried that this coup would demoralize the noncommunist forces there unless something were done, and anxious to offset the profound psychological shock that the fall of Czechoslovakia had produced, the United States formed the NATO Alliance in early 1949. With this pact the United States tied its fate to that of Europe by declaring "that an armed attack against one or more of them [the signatories] in Europe or North America shall be considered an attack against them all." The intent of NATO, however, was not to provide an effective defense against a Russian attack but to deter such an attack. Yet American policy makers rated the likelihood of such an attack as quite low. Why, then, was the need felt to deter something not thought likely to occur?

The answer lies with the larger perspective within which Western Europeans viewed what had happened in Czechoslovakia, and it illustrates the political motive the Truman administration had in entering into this alliance. Europe's historical memory was much longer than America's; it was replete with duplicity in dealing with allies. Czechoslovakia, moreover, had a special symbolism. It had been sacrificed by France and England to Hitler in order to protect themselves from war in 1938. Europeans had also not forgotten that America's commitment to them after World War I was short-lived. What the Europeans had once done to Czechoslovakia, what the Americans had once done to Europe, could happen again. In order to erase Europe's fears that America would lapse back into isolationism and sell them out once the going got tough, the Truman administration formed NATO. The essence of the alliance was political: to convince Europeans that America had "staying power." Only if they were confident of this could they be expected to throw their lot in with the United States. NATO was thus to be Europe's security blanket behind which the aid provided by the Marshall Plan would resurrect her.

America's Far Eastern Policy.   The policy toward Europe was clear and coherent. A definite distinction was made between America's interest in Western as opposed to Eastern Europe. A series of steps, mainly political and economic, were taken in order to do that which was necessary to keep Western Europe in America's camp. Unlike its European policy, however, America's Far Eastern policy had no such coherency. Instead it was marked by temporizing and expediency, with no overarching strategy of containment applied there. That did not come until after the outbreak of the Korean War, when America's policy toward the Far East as a whole finally crystallized.

There was in fact not one Far Eastern policy, but really four—one for Indochina, one for China, one for Korea, and one for Japan—with no clearcut linkages among them. The policy toward Indochina was reluctant deference to the French, who were in the process of reimposing their colonial control there. The United States was officially opposed to imperialism, but it tacitly supported the French effort because that was the price they demanded for their participation in NATO and for the creation of a West German state. America's strategy in Europe thus dictated her policy toward Indochina. Before 1950 the most the United States did there was to urge the French to give autonomy or independence to Indochina so as to be able to co-opt the cause of anti-imperialism and to weaken the political appeal of the Vietminh. It is important to stress the tacit and reluctant nature of America's political support for the French effort at this time. For while the French were in fact fighting Ho Chi-minh and the communists, the United States saw no Russian design to take over Asia; or if it did, it certainly did not get exercised about it and did not proclaim a holy war against Vietnamese communism or even communism in Asia. Thus, the Truman administration made no linkage before June of 1950 between the communists in Vietnam and those in China, but instead kept them quite distinct. By 1948, in fact, it had written off the Chinese Nationalists, had concluded that the Chinese communists would ultimately triumph, and was searching for ways to accommodate itself to a communist China. This search yielded an initial estimate that a China gone communist would not be harmful to American interests because of the calculation that the traditional hostility between Russia and China and the antagonistic force of their nationalisms would easily override any of the ties that might arise from the sharing of a common Marxist ideology. There was not even any fear that a communist China would be out to take over all of Asia.[1] Here is clear evidence that not until somewhere between July 1949 and June 1950, the year during which the Truman administration began to clarify a containment policy in the Far East and worldwide, did the United States see a monolithic communist threat, a central direction by the Soviet Union over world communism, or a Russian design to take over the world.

[1]See Tang Tsou, *America's Failure in China, 1941–1950* (Chicago: University of Chicago, Press, 1963), chap. 12.

The policy with regard to Japan was clear concerning how to deal with her domestic affairs, but not beyond that. The United States had prevented Russia from involving herself in Japan's postwar occupation and kept her as a solely American preserve. Japan was being democratized under America's tutelage, but with the collapse of Chinese power in the region, no definite plans had yet been made with regard to the role Japan might play in Far Eastern politics because the United States had no coherent policy toward the region. It did not sign a peace treaty with Japan until 1951 and did not permit her to rearm until 1955. Again, not until after the outbreak of the Korean War did America's thinking about Japan's foreign role begin to crystallize. Finally, planning towards Korea was probably the most muddled. The United States had rushed troops into Korea to accept a Japanese surrender there so that the Soviet Union could not occupy the entire peninsula. But with Russian armies in the north and American troops in the south, Korea quickly became divided. The United States pledged itself to the peaceful reunification of Korea, but by late 1947 had decided that its troops stationed there were a liability and withdrew them in 1948. Economic aid and defensive arms were sent, but there were no plans for using American troops if South Korea were attacked.

What is most remarkable about American thinking towards Korea before June of 1950, in view of the dramatic reversal in policy that occurred at the outbreak of the Korean War, is this: until South Korea was attacked, the Truman administration saw no significant linkage between a communist military conquest of the Korean peninsula and the political situation within Japan. The only potential linkage made was a military, not a political one; and because it was thought easy to deal with, the linkage was of no real concern. From 1945 until the Korean War, America's defense planning centered on a general war with Russia, not on a limited one with either her or one of her client states. If in such a war the Soviet Union occupied the entire Korean peninsula, the disadvantage which that might pose for America's defense of Japan would be tactical, not strategic, and could be handily dealt with by America's sea and air power based in Japan. Through interdiction the United States could thus quickly neutralize any Russian military threat to Japan from the mainland. Unlike Europe, where the Truman administration saw a clear linkage between the proximity of Russian military power and the evolution of political events within America's sphere of influence, it saw no such thing, or chose to discount it, in the relation of Korea to Japan. Before June of 1950, the administration did not conclude that a Korea gone communist might influence the political debate then raging in Japan over the future course that her foreign policy should take, a debate which pitted the neutralists who favored nonalignment for Japan against the conservatives who wished to throw Japan's fortunes in with the United

States. There was no calculation that a Korea having recently fallen to the communist camp might help tilt Japan towards neutralism.

The reason this calculation was not made may have been due to the gap developing between America's foreign policy commitments and the military power available to back them up. Until she began a major rearmament effort in 1950, America's military power was stretched thin. In the order of priorities, the defense of Korea loomed small. Japan was the prime concern, and because any military threat to her from Korea would occur only in the context of a general war with Russia, such a threat could be handled from Japan. Necessity may thus have fathered policy: the lack of sufficient forces to defend Korea may have led to deeming her unimportant to America's Far Eastern interests.

The Globalization of Containment, 1950–1968

By 1949, then, the United States had developed a clear containment policy for Europe but not for the Far East. In both areas the likelihood of war with Russia was deemed low, and that estimate governed the policy pursued in each. As had historically been the case, mainland Asia ran a poor second to concern for Europe. In fact, as we have seen, the only reason that the United States had backed France in Indochina was to gain her support for NATO. The same was true for the Truman administration's backing of the Chinese Nationalists after 1947. Even though it thought their defeat inevitable, the Truman administration continued to send economic and military aid to the Nationalists only because that was the price demanded by the Republicans in Congress for their support of the Democrats' European policy. In a curious way, then, events in the Far East were linked to those in Europe, but only in the sense that the exigencies of her European policy—the need to buy French and congressional support—shaped much of America's Far Eastern policy. In no way, however, were they linked in the sense that the administration was operating on the basis of a belief in the indivisibility of peace or upon a conviction about the monolithic nature of communism. Commitments were being made and honored in the Far East, but not because they were believed to reflect on American credibility in the minds of Europeans. (The administration in fact viewed the China policy it had to pursue in just the reverse manner: because resources were so scarce, aid to China detracted from its commitments to Europe.) In this regard, therefore, the Truman administration acted as if events in Europe and the Far East were discrete and disjunct.

Planning for Global Containment: July 1949 to June 1950. The Korean War soon changed that. But before its outbreak, the United States began to take tentative steps in two directions—one toward adopting a containment policy in the Far East and another towards planning for a systematic containment policy for the entire world that would relate America's global interests to her military power.

With regard to the Far East, there were two events—Mao Zedong's foreign policy pronouncement of July 1, 1949, and the Sino-Soviet Treaty of Friendship and Alliance—that pushed the Truman administration toward planning for a coherent containment policy there. Mao's speech shattered the administration's initial calculation that Sino-Soviet relations would be antagonistic rather than harmonious. In his speech Mao proclaimed essentially what Secretary of State Dulles was to say later on in the 1950s, that is, "if you're not with us, then you're against us," that neutrality in the communist-capitalist struggle was not possible, that one was forced to choose sides. Mao aligned China with the Soviet Union in the worldwide struggle against the forces of imperialism led by the United States.

This speech could have been dismissed as mere rhetoric for internal domestic consumption, but it was followed by the Sino-Soviet Treaty in which Stalin returned to China most of the territorial concessions that he had wrested earlier from the Nationalists as his price for Russia's entry into the Pacific War. Here was concrete proof that the binds of ideology between them were stronger than the repellent forces of their nationalisms. As a consequence of Mao's speech, the Truman administration began to take tentative steps towards formulating a containment policy in Asia. This policy must be termed highly tentative, however, because of the other actions that the United States was pursuing in the area. At the same time that Secretary of State Acheson was calling for a commitment to containment in Asia he was also removing South Korea from America's defense perimeter; he was failing to support the French war in Indochina in any way except verbally; he was not lifting a finger to reverse the tide of events within China; he was not proposing to interject the United States again in a military way into the Chinese civil war by defending the Nationalists from a communist attack in their redoubt on Taiwan; he was not, finally, pushing for a rapid rearmament of Japan that a containment policy could logically require. Acheson was doing, in short, what America had traditionally done in her policy towards the Far East: making commitments far in excess of what she was willing to commit in resources to back them up. Therefore, we must conclude that at this time the containment policy toward the Asian mainland and beyond was highly tentative, that it was not likely to be implemented if it proved too costly, and that before June 1950 there was in fact no real containment policy toward the Far East but only the *desire* to have one.

With regard to the second tentative step, the Truman administration began systematically to assess the relation between its security and that of the entire free world and to analyze the type of military force that such a global containment policy would require. This effort resulted in what became known as NSC-68 (National Security Council Study 68), the first high-level review since 1945 of America's evolving foreign and military policies. NSC-68 took stock of what the nation had done over the last five years and of where it should be going over the next several. The immediate catalysts for the study were the Russian explosion of an atomic bomb in August of 1949, three years before the American intelligence community predicted it would occur, the triumph of the communists on mainland China in late 1949, and Truman's uncertainty over whether the United States should begin development of a hydrogen bomb now that the Russians had the atomic one. The combined effect of these developments was to produce a belief among some, but not all, top-level decision makers that America may have been too piecemeal in her approach to containment, that a worldwide perspective which would integrate all the various parts into a coherent whole was necessary, and that recent Russian military developments required the United States to build up her military forces significantly if she were to be able to deter Russian aggression. NSC-68 was thus a call for major American rearmament because of a communist threat more potent and pervasive than had theretofore been realized. NSC-68 asked for major rearmament, in short, because it predicated the need for a global containment policy.

What must be stressed, however, is that NSC-68 *asked* and *predicted*. It was not a program the president had made his own, but rather a joint State-Defense recommendation to the president about what type of national security program he should make his own. It was a staff study, not a policy ready for implementation. NSC-68 was completed in the late spring of 1950. For that reason its exact effect on American foreign policy is difficult to assess, since the Korean War came only a few months later. Its significance, however, is clear: it demonstrates that just before the Korean War, which was the catalytic event that globalized containment, the United States government was moving toward an indivisibility-of-peace view of its security and toward a containment policy heavily laden with military overtones.

The Effects of Korea on American Foreign Policy.   The Korean War, together with the Vietnam War, are the two most important single events for shaping the general contours of post-1945 American foreign policy. The Korean War served as the catalyst that helped forge a consensus for a global containment policy; the Vietnam War was the one that helped shatter it. The Korean War had two general effects on American foreign policy. First, it undermined all the key assumptions that had governed the conduct of foreign policy in the previous five years. Second, it reinforced the predisposition, which was shared by most top-level decision makers, not to repeat in the post-1945 world the mistakes that America had made in the interwar period (1919–1939). With the outbreak of the Korean

War, therefore, a "mind-set" was crystallized that significantly influenced the next twenty years of American foreign policy.

There were three key assumptions of the 1945–1949 period that Korea helped to undermine. First, instead of viewing separate national communisms as discrete phenomena, the United States took the view that communism was monolithic, that is, that it was centrally directed and controlled by the Soviet Union. The Truman administration had already begun to think this way starting with its reassessment of the implications of a communist China in mid-1949. In early 1950, after China and Russia recognized Ho Chi-minh, the United States applied the same attitude toward Indochina and began to view the French effort not as anticolonial but as anticommunist. Korea clinched the process, but in a dramatic way that had wide public recognition and effect. The Truman administration assumed that North Korea would not have attacked South Korea had it not had Russia's orders, support, or merely encouragement to do so. Whether Russia gave such support, whether she even knew of the attack before it was launched, is still not known. But such knowledge is irrelevant to the central point: the Truman administration did not know either. The Truman administration jumped to a conclusion that was justifiable to make at the time, *even if it may have been wrong,* something which the West to this day still does not know.

Second, because the Korean attack seemed to give dramatic proof that the Soviet Union was the world control center of communism, the Truman administration concluded that the United States could no longer treat events in the Far East and Europe as if they were disconnected. The Korean War was what tied the Far East to Europe. It drove home the indivisibility-of-peace proposition in a way that no staff paper could. Such a blatant act, so reasoned the Truman administration, could not go unanswered by the United States; for if it did, America's word would have no credibility elsewhere, to friend and foe alike. Korea per se was not intrinsically important; it was the psychological effects that would be produced by not fighting there which were. Unless it responded, the Truman administration worried that the Europeans, who had just concluded a defensive pact with the United States, and the Japanese, who were in the process of deciding whether to conclude one, would have no faith in alliances with America. Korea was thus a war fought by the United States initially in order to demonstrate the credibility of its commitments to its European and prospective Japan allies.

Finally, the Korean attack demonstrated that internal subversion through economic and political chaos was not the sole or even primary threat. Direct military attack had now to be accounted for. After Russia had exploded the atomic bomb in 1949, the American intelligence community calculated that no military action would occur before Russia had built up a nuclear arsenal, which would not be before the middle 1950s.

NSC-68 had reasoned that local wars were more likely now that the Soviet Union had the security with which to wage them and now that the mutual possession of nuclear weapons decreased the chances of a direct, general war between Russia and America. But neither foresaw an attack upon Korea; neither predicted military action was inevitable. The Truman administration had unconsciously extended its view of what was the primary threat in Europe—internal subversion—to Korea when it had discounted the likelihood of a military attack there. Once Korea was attacked, the administration consciously transferred this materialized threat in the Far East back to Europe. If Russia could order a military action by a nation in which she no longer had combat troops, then she certainly could do so in those where she had large armies. Once again Korea provided what seemed to be incontrovertible proof that the threat had changed in form and, therefore, that the means to counter it had better change too. Rearmament became the order of the day. America's defense budgets throughout the 1950s achieved a level three times greater than they had been in the late 1940s, reaching $45 to $50 billion as opposed to $15 billlion. And as further illustration that Europe still counted more in America's calculations than the Far East, most of the rearmament effort during the Korean War went to build up the military forces in the United States and Europe, not in Korea.

Korea thus gave immediate proof that communism had to be viewed in a worldwide perspective, but the full force of the Korean War on American policy makers cannot be understood unless it is seen in the broader historical context that they themselves at the time placed it. For the generation of policy makers that ran America's foreign affairs for most of the post-1945 era, Korea threatened a repetition of what they had lived through in the 1930s, to wit, piecemeal aggression that was abetted by dealing with it on a piecemeal basis. For these men the lessons of the 1930s were clear. Appeasement stimulates an aggressor; it does not satiate him. Aggression is monolithic; if one aggressor gets away with it, others will be emboldened to try. Had England, France, and America only stood up to Japan in China or Mussolini in Ethiopia, so these men at the time and later argued, Hitler might well have been deterred in Europe. The appeasement of Hitler at Munich, at Czechoslovakia's expense, moreover, only emboldened him to go for Poland next and subsequently brought on World War II.

Truman was a product of the 1930s in this regard. As president, he was determined not to allow this sequence to be repeated. Aggression could only be dealt with effectively if it were met forcefully and decisively at its first showing. Truman acted in Korea because he viewed it as the test of America's willingness to assume the leadership of the free world that NSC-68 had called for.

The Korean War was thus the pivotal event in America's foreign policy from 1945 to 1965. It was not that Korea radically altered the general contours of policy as they had been evolving since 1945, but rather that Korea solidified, crystallized, and broadened them. The Truman Doctrine is often taken as the proof that the United States had quite early on decided to adopt a global containment policy. Certainly the words that Truman used in order to defend his aid request support his view: "I believe that it must be the policy of the United States to support free peoples who are resisting attempted subjugation by armed minorities or by outside pressures." But these words were rhetoric designed to obtain support from a public that had traditionally thought more in ideological than in balance-of-power terms when thinking about foreign affairs. The rhetoric used belied the policy intended. For immediately after Truman's speech to the Congress, then Under Secretary of State Acheson in his testimony to the Senate Foreign Relations Committee qualified the unlimited nature of the doctrine: "Any requests of foreign countries for aid will have to be considered according to the circumstances in each individual case."[2] Acheson's qualifiers could, of course, have been a ploy by the administration to lead Congress on, to ask piecemeal with full knowledge that the ultimate intent was to obtain a global reach. Certainly the request for the Marshall Plan a few months later could support this view. But none of the other actions do until 1950. The Truman administration limited itself primarily to Europe. It was, in fact, trying to keep down governmental spending, which a huge foreign-aid program would not have helped. It is fair to conclude, therefore, that the Truman Doctrine's rhetoric did not reflect its intent. It was the Korean War, not anything before, that marked and forged a globalized containment policy.

Deterrence and Subversion in the 1950s and 1960s.   With Korea, the main contours of American foreign policy were set until the Vietnam War challenged them and until the Nixon administration began subtly to alter them. The mind-set toward communism that Korea crystallized by no means wholly predetermined America's subsequent actions, but because it was the framework with which decision makers approached and interpreted succeeding events, it did shape the general tenor of America's response to them. Korea was one of those pivotal decisions that influences much of what follows them. What the United States did from 1950 through 1968 was not inevitable, but neither was it wholly accidental. During these years there were, of course, differences in tone, style, and substance between Democratic and Republican administrations. By comparison with Democrats, Republicans were more restrained in their activism, even if their rhetoric sounded more fearsome. Under Kennedy and

[2]Quoted in George F. Kennan, *Memoirs,* Vol. 1 (Boston: Little, Brown, 1967), pp. 321–22.

Johnson the Democrats gave more attention to fashioning effective means for military interventions than did the Republicans under Eisenhower. Europe loomed large and primary for both, but by comparison with Republicans, Democrats tended to give more nearly equal attention to the Far East. The Republicans worried mostly about direct military attack by the communists on the nations bordering on, or in close proximity to, their spheres of influence and, consequently, directed American resources to fashioning these states into strong, defensible, military bastions. The Democrats continued that policy in the 1960s, but decolonization brought an obsession with communist wars of national liberation and their concomitant counterinsurgency techniques. The differences in Democratic and Republican policies, however, are clearly overshadowed by the basic similarities. None of these administrations intervened in every area they could have, but all viewed every situation from the standpoint of how America's specific actions there would affect her general relations with the Russians. Not every adverse situation was contained, but each was scrutinized with a view as to whether not acting would cause America's general world position to deteriorate. Containment in the *conceptual approach to events,* not in omnipresent interventionism, was the essence of a global policy. The basic continuity of this approach over four different administrations shows that global containment was a bipartisan foreign policy.

There were three central hallmarks to this twenty-year global policy: a proliferation of new commitments and a strengthening of old ones; a reliance on military power and a quest for general military superiority in order to deter attack and to maintain a political offensive against communism; and a willingness to resort to military intervention where the threat of force did not suffice. The need to make new commitments and to strengthen old ones stemmed directly from Korea. America's policy toward South Korea before the attack seemed to give incontrovertible evidence that a prior commitment to defend a nation against attack was necessary in order to prevent it. By immediate hindsight, the omission of South Korea from America's defensive perimeter was viewed as directly responsible for bringing on the North Korean invasion. As a consequence, the United States proceeded to conclude a whole series of such commitments: with Japan in 1951 through the Japanese-American Security Treaty; with New Zealand and Australia in 1951 through the ANZUS Pact; with nations in the Middle East and South Asia in 1955 through CENTO; with nations in Southeast Asia in 1954 through SEATO; and over the years with a host of nations, like Spain, Thailand, and the Philippines, through numerous base rights' agreements. Most of these commitments were made in the 1950s, but all were honored during the 1960s. The Korean War thus pushed American policy makers one step beyond Munich: it was no longer sufficient to stand fast against aggression in order to deter it again; now it was necessary to commit in advance to prevent aggression. Ambiguity of intent, flexiblity in purpose, unpredictability in response—these were not viewed as diplomatic virtues during this period. As a consequence of the Korean War, the United States globalized its NATO policy; that is, it proliferated deterrent pacts around the world. In the space of little over eight years from 1949 through 1956, the United States went from having no such commitments to endorsing well over twenty-five of them.

Strengthening old commitments meant bolstering the NATO Alliance, which was only one year "old." Beginning with Korea, three successive administrations thought it necessary to take significant steps designed to enhance in European eyes the credibility of America's commitment to them. The Truman administration sent four combat divisions to Europe as tangible symbols, hostages in effect to a Russian attack, of the depth of the American commitment to defend Europe. It also worked to turn NATO into a semi-integrated multilateral military force, rather than permit it to remain merely a loose coalition of separate national military forces. In order to redress NATO's presumed inferiority in conventional forces vis-à-vis the Warsaw Pact, the Eisenhower administration sent thousands of tactical nuclear warheads to Europe (though they were to remain under American control). The troops were guarantees that America would fight if Europe were attacked; the tactical nuclear weapons were guarantees that America would use her nuclear arsenal in such an attack. But Europe wished neither to be used. It did not want another war of liberation fought on its soil, nor did it wish to have nuclear weapons devastating the very soil they were intended to defend. The NATO allies were persuaded, largely by the United States, that the troops and nuclear weapons were the means best suited to deter war.

The Kennedy administration went two steps further. In order to offset any lingering doubts that Russia had a nuclear superiority over the United States, the administration engaged in a massive missile-building program at home. The main intent was to persuade the Europeans that America had the strategic nuclear wherewithal to take care of them and thereby that they need not acquire or keep their own national nuclear forces. America's own nuclear buildup was meant to restore Europe's confidence in American power in order to discourage further proliferation of nuclear forces there. The Kennedy administration also launched a large conventional buildup at home and pushed the Europeans to do so too. The logic was that these forces would give greater credence to deterrence because they would demonstrate that NATO had a true conventional war-fighting capability. Enhancement of its conventional capability would add to its deterrent power, reasoned the administration, because if the Russians knew NATO could fight a conventional war, they would not launch one. To the Europeans, however, such a buildup only weakened nuclear deterrence, because it signaled the Russians that the Americans did not put much credence in the deterrent value of their nuclear forces; otherwise, why would they build up their conventional ones?

The second and third hallmarks of these years were integrally related to the first. In an era when prior commitment per se was not thought sufficient to hold the line against further communist expansion, the United States built a military force that would enhance the credibility of its commitments. It did not begin a major rearmament in 1950 nor significantly increase its defense budgets in the early 1960s because it feared a Russian attack was imminent. The United States created and tried to maintain through the late 1960s a marked military superiority over Russia, not for its own security, but for that of its allies. The point of having the military edge was psychological—to convince both the Soviet Union and America's allies that the United States had more than enough power to back up its commitments.

Whether the United States ever had an overall force superior to that of Russia cannot be definitively known. Only the test of their arms could have determined which was the stronger. There was a clear desire by the United States to have the appearance of superiority; and it was reflected in America's commitment to have a nuclear force "second to none." During these twenty years every administration operated under the belief that a superiority in numbers and quality of nuclear forces could be turned to America's political advantage. Belief in "the more the better" caused the Truman administration to rush development of the hydrogen bomb to stay ahead of the Russians, once they developed the atomic bomb. Three years before Russia's Sputnik launching of 1957, the Eisenhower administration committed the country to a massive intercontinental ballistic missile development program. Soon after the Kennedy administration came into office, and even after aerial intelligence indicated that the United States had a marked superiority in ICBMs, the administration nevertheless programmed a further increase in America's strategic nuclear forces. During the mid-1960s, the Johnson administration used the "greater-than-expected-threat" estimate as the basis for determining America's nuclear forces. This process estimated the outer limits of Russia's capabilities, then multiplied *that* figure by some number, which then became the basis for America's needs. Even the second Eisenhower administration, which was at the time lambasted as laggard for not countering the Russian nuclear threat dramatized by Sputnik, nevertheless proceeded with a rapid ICBM development program, shipped still more tactical nuclear weapons to Europe, and sent hundreds of intermediate range ballistic missiles there. In the era of global containment, the quest for nuclear superiority was a permanent feature of America's foreign policy.

The third hallmark of these years was a logical extension of the first two. If the commitment to use force, backed up by enough military power to make it credible, did not work, then force was used where the interests involved dictated it. From 1950 through 1968, the United States engaged in almost the whole spectrum of military interventionism. There were the overt uses of significant numbers of combat troops, as in Korea in 1950, Lebanon in 1958, the Dominican Republic in 1965, and Vietnam in 1965. There were the covert paramilitary uses of force or the severely circumscribed overt uses of force, as in Iran in 1953, Guatemala in 1954, and Cuba in 1961. There were, finally, the clearly communicated threats to intervene with force, as in Laos in 1961 and Cuba in 1962. Despite the differences in circumstances, all of these interventions shared either or both of two overriding aims: preventing communists from coming to power and/or preventing the appearance of Russia's gaining at America's expense. Military interventionism was the last resort of Cold War liberalism's attempt to preserve the status quo.

In the global containment era, Korea and Vietnam were the two most significant military interventions. Both were fought for the same reason, namely, to protect America's global commitments. Korea was fought to consolidate them; Vietnam, to keep them from eroding. In this regard, however, Korea was a plausible war. Vietnam was not. Korea came at a time when America's fidelity to Europe had yet to be demonstrated and in the midst of Japan's debate over whether to opt for neutralism or alignment with the United States. Monolithic communism was a new and reasonable proposition. Vietnam came at a time when the unity of the communist world had been proved a sham, when America had demonstrated her loyalty to her Japanese and European allies for fifteen years, and after America had repeatedly demonstrated her will to intervene militarily against communism. Yet, successive administrations saw Vietnam as the test of America's continuing determination. It was the United States alone, not Russia, China, the Vietnamese communists or noncommunists, or any of America's allies, that made Vietnam into such a symbol.

Only if viewed in America's global perspective, therefore, does the Vietnam War make even the slightest sense. Vietnam was America's imperial war. Just as the British during the Boer War once feared the effects that the loss of the South African Cape Colony might have on her other colonial holdings, so too did the Americans fear the effects of the loss of Vietnam on her other commitments. Edward Gibbon, the historian of Rome, said that one of the telltale signs of an imperial power in decline was its waging of wars far from the imperial center and with little or no tangible benefits to the empire as a whole. The imperial government, in short, did not know when it was prudent to stop fighting and when to avoid taking on new commitments. Although the parallel between Rome and America is not exact, still the Vietnam War must be viewed in the

Gibbonian sense. It was the telltale sign of America's loss of prudence and the overreaching of her power.

DÉTENTE AND RETRENCHMENT, 1969-1979

Beginning in 1969, and for eleven years after that, America retrenched. The three hallmarks of the global containment era began to erode, but were by no means totally discarded. Rather than continue to proliferate commitments, the United States began to cut back—the withdrawal from Indochina being the most significant first step. Rather than continue to rely on military superiority in order to achieve political ends, the United States, because it accepted rough nuclear parity with Russia, was forced to return to the diplomatic maneuvering reminiscent of the classical balance-of-power days, even though the world remained militarily bipolar. Rather than continue a quick and easy resort to military intervention, President Nixon, because of the 1973 War Powers Act, found his flexibility severely circumscribed. And President Ford, for example, was unable to launch B-52 strikes in Vietnam in 1975 in order to prevent a South Vietnamese collapse. Retrenchment meant consolidation and a withdrawal from positions of weakness. It did not, however, mean retreat from the goal of containing communism, but rather the search for new means in order to persevere with the old goal. Retrenchment had three key aspects: (1) détente with America's main adversaries, the Russians and the Chinese; (2) difficulties with her main allies, the West Europeans and the Japanese; and (3) a decreased willingness to bear alone the price necessary to support the free world's economic structure.

Détente with Adversaries

President Nixon's desire to insure his reelection in 1972 probably affected the timing of his trip to China and his signing of the SALT I Accord with Russia, but it had little to do with the basic decision to pursue a relaxation in tensions with America's two foremost adversaries. The détente with Russia and China was a personal triumph for Nixon's acumen and toughness and Kissinger's negotiating talents, but both of these are not sufficient to explain the fundamental shift in America's strategy towards these two countries. Rather, in order to explain the desire to mute hostilities, we must look to the basic change in the international balance of forces that occurred in the 1960s. Genius in statecraft, said the gifted French statesman, Talleyrand, is to recognize the inevitable and then exploit it. What was inevitable was something that Secretary of Defense Robert McNamara realized as far back as the early 1960s–that Russia would eventually acquire nuclear parity with the United States. It was the tremendous military power that Russia had acquired during the 1960s, when America was dissipating hers in Indochina, that made détente with Russia and China highly advantageous, if not inevitable. Nixon understood the consequences for the United States of this structural shift and tried to turn it to America's advantage.

Détente with China is easy to explain. Viewed in historical perspective, the American-Chinese hostility that prevailed from 1953 to 1972 was neither necessary nor advantageous for the larger purposes of American foreign policy. Neither was this hostility "natural." Aside from their differences over Taiwan, there were no life and death matters of conflict between them, nor any disputes that involved significant clashes of material interests. America's hostility to Communist China was an indirect by-product of America's global containment policy, not a direct result of a fundamental clash in their national interests. As a consequence of the outbreak of the Korean War, the United States had reinjected itself into the Chinese civil war by deciding to interpose the Seventh Fleet between the Communists on the mainland and the Nationalists on Taiwan. After all, it would have looked politically incongruous to fight the communists in Korea and meanwhile allow them to take Taiwan without lifting a finger to prevent it. As a consequence of its miscalculation about Chinese interests, warnings, and perceptions of American actions in Korea, the United States became embroiled in a needless war with China. Even if ill-considered and unintentional, these American actions gave good grounds for the hostility between the two nations to linger for awhile after the 1953 truce between them.

But this hostility persisted long after it made reasoned sense for the United States, largely because of the exigencies of American electoral politics. Particularly after the Sino-Soviet rift became apparent in the early 1960s, the United States was foolhardy not to attempt to consort with the Chinese Communists. Fears of the Democrats over another Republican campaign about China deterred them from making any overtures of significance. The lack of any compelling foreign policy need to open up contacts with China gave the Democrats no political incentive to take the risk and make the case to the American electorate. America's rigid nonintercourse with, and nonrecognition of, Communist China after the mid-1950s were thus ideological, reflecting Dulles' desire not to give an ounce of legitimacy to the communists where he did not have to; and electoral, reflecting the Democrats' sensitivity to the China issue. The internal deterrents to détente with China were powerful; the external "compellents" were weak. Still, the United States could have gained a degree of flexibility in her Far Eastern policy had she tried to come to terms with China sooner than she did. It would have been advantageous, but it was not essential.

By the early 1970s, however, such a rapprochement was necessary.

Just as the twenty-two years of American-Chinese hostility was a product of America's globalizing her containment policy, so too was the American-Chinese détente, from the American side, a product of America's retrenching on that global policy. And the same factor that caused the United States to become hostile to the Chinese Communists, namely the Soviet Union, also caused her to warm up to them. Certainly there was a strictly Far Eastern interest in détente with China—obtaining any assistance the Chinese could give in extricating the United States from the Vietnamese War. But this was only a contributing factor. Fundamentally, it was the need to offset the expansion of Russian military power that dictated the move. Despite Nixon-Kissinger denials at the time, the détente with China was clearly anti-Russian in motivation and purpose. No longer able to count on the political leverage that her vast military superiority over Russia had afforded her, America had to resort to other means to maintain a global posture against the Soviet Union. Operating under the old dictum that "the enemy of my enemy is my friend," Nixon moved toward China in order to be in a position once more to extract concessions from Russia.

Détente with China can therefore be understood only in the context of the change in American-Russian power relations. It was the means to preserve a flexibility for the United States vis-à-vis Russia that America's military superiority had once yielded. The achievement of military parity between the world's two foremost military powers dictated the once dominant power's switch to diplomatic tactics. The détente with China heralded in the age of "balance of maneuver" diplomacy.

There were two basic motives for seeking a détente with the Soviet Union. Both derived from the same increase in Russian power that made détente with China a logical step. Although we cannot dismiss Nixon's desire to obtain Russia's help in extricating the United States from Vietnam, nevertheless, this must, as it was with China, remain a secondary motive. Rather, it was the search for a new basis for American-Russian *security* relations and for American-Russian *global* relations, both of which were altered by the emergence of Russian-American nuclear parity, that impelled the Nixon administration towards détente.

Russia's pulling roughly even with the United States did not mean that the American-Russian nuclear arms race had come to an end, but rather that if the United States wished to continue it, then it would prove exceedingly expensive and perhaps even more dangerous than before. Russia's actions since her humiliation in the Cuban Missile Crisis had demonstrated how tenacious was her determination to have strategic nuclear forces "second to none." Within the Nixon administration, moreover, there developed a gradual acceptance of two views—that "more was not necessarily better" and that when both sides had such huge numbers of nuclear forces, superiority in numbers had no clear military or political meaning. As long as each superpower could retaliate upon the other if attacked first and cause the other to suffer extreme devastation, the military value of ever larger forces became questionable. Such increases would add to neither nation's security and only cause each to spend billions more in order to end up where they both were before.

By drawing even with the United States, Russia ended any appearance there might have been of the United States having possessed a first strike capability vis-à-vis the Soviet Union. The political value of superior forces had become increasingly tenuous. If the United States could no longer use a nuclear threat to intimidate the Russians and extract political concessions from them, as was the case with Cuba in 1962, what would be the political use of a superiority that yielded only a larger number of missiles? If there was no longer a meaningful military potential in superiority, then there could be little practical political value in it. In short, if Russia was determined to maintain parity with America, and if both nations had strategic forces that were invulnerable to a surprise attack for the foreseeable future, then America's quest for military superiority would be costly, illusory, and of no real advantage.

Nixon accepted the logic of this position. Nixon the candidate spoke of the need for continued American superiority, but Nixon the president spoke instead of sufficiency, an oblique reference to his acceptance of parity. In its military terms, the SALT I Accord had two principal features: (1) a quantitative and a qualitative freeze on antiballistic missile systems (ABMs), and (2) a quantitative freeze only on offensive ballistic missiles. By severely limiting ABMs in a treaty of unlimited duration, the SALT I Accord signified an American and Russian acceptance of MAD, or mutual assured destruction. The ABM agreement meant that each nation accepted the ability of the other to retaliate as the foundation for their security relations. In effect, both had officially guaranteed the existence of each other.

The 1974 Ford-Brezhnev statement of intent for a SALT II agreement signified a mutual desire to make permanent and equal the offensive freeze of SALT I, which was only to be a five-year agreement and which had given the Russians more missiles than the Americans. The Ford administration, despite strenuous efforts in 1975 and 1976, failed to consummate a SALT II Accord. The Jackson Amendment to the SALT I Accord of 1972 required that in a future nuclear arms accord the United States have missiles equal in number to those of the Russians. At the same time that the Ford administration was thereby bound to achieve equality in offensive missiles, it tried to deal with the "heavy" missile threat of the Russians, the SS-9s and SS-18s that were viewed as a first-strike threat against America's land based minutemen, by seeking to reduce their number. The Russians, for their part, were trying to constrain America's development and deployment of air-launched cruise missiles (ALCMs) that could drastically increase America's offensive nuclear capabilities vis-à-vis the Soviet Union. Despite intense bargaining, by 1976 the politics of a presidential election year intruded and made achievement of a SALT II Accord dead by midyear. For until midsummer, Ford was running more against Reagan for the Republican nomination than he was against Carter for the presidency. Even after he had secured the Republican nomination, Ford had to retain the loyalty of the Republican right wing in his fight against Carter. As a consequence, he was unable to conclude a compromise that would have offset Russia's heavy missiles with America's cruise missiles. Carter won the election. The Republican search for a lasting follow-on to SALT I had failed.

Even though eight years of Republican rule had failed to secure a permanent accord on offensive nuclear missiles, success in this area clearly surpassed that in the political realm. Détente between the United States and the Soviet Union had embodied not simply military but also political limitations on the two superpowers' relations with one another. The political aspect of détente was embodied in the "Statement of Principles" signed in Moscow in June of 1972 and is commonly referred to as "The Basic Political Agreement" (BPA).

The political understandings incorporated in the BPA are worth quoting because they illustrate both what Nixon and Kissinger tried to achieve and why they ultimately failed:

> First, they [the United States and the Soviet Union] will proceed from the common determination that in the nuclear age there is no alternative to conducting their mutual relations on the basis of *peaceful coexistence.*
>
> Second, the U.S.A. and the U.S.S.R. attach major importance to preventing the development of situations capable of causing a dangerous exacerbation of their relations. Therefore, they will do their utmost to avoid military confrontations and to prevent the outbreak of nuclear war. . . . Both sides recognize that efforts to obtain *unilateral advantages* at the expense of the other, directly or indirectly, are inconsistent with these objectives. . . . The prerequisites for maintaining and strengthening peaceful relations . . . are the recognition of the security interests of the parties based on the *principle of equality.* . . .
>
> Third, the U.S.A. and the U.S.S.R. . . . have a special responsibility . . . to do everything in their power so that conflicts or situations will not arise which would serve to increase international tensions.[3]

The Basic Political Agreement was a compromise document. For the Soviet Union, the BPA, together with the SALT I Accord, meant America's recognition of it as both a military *and* a political coequal. Strategic nuclear parity earned for the Soviets the right to be treated globally as political coequals. The operative words in the BPA for them were "peace-

---

[3]Quoted in Alexander George, *Managing U. S.–Soviet Rivalry: Problems of Crisis Prevention* (Boulder, Colo.: Westview Press, 1983), pp. 107–8. Italics added.

ful coexistence" and the "principle of equality." Peaceful coexistence meant that the Soviet Union could continue to support progressive or revolutionary forces in the Third World. The principle of equality meant that Soviet interests and influence would have to be taken into account in significant global settlements. SALT I and the BPA—the twin pillars of détente—thus signified for the Soviet Union its coming of age as a global power. Nuclear parity had bought political parity. Détent was a means to tame the United States so that the Soviet Union could continue to compete, but now more successfully and safely, throughout the world. As Brezhnev declared in 1973,

> We have always regarded and regard now as our inviolable duty stemming from our Communist convictions, from our Socialist morality, to render the widest possible support to the peoples fighting for the just cause of freedom. This has always been the case, this will be the case in the future as well.[4]

For the Soviets, the BPA was important because it promised to reduce the risks of competition with the United States. Détente was intended to further, not abet, their ability to compete globally by taming the United States. For the United States, it was the reverse. Détente was intended to tame, not unleash, the Soviet Union. For Nixon and Kissinger, the operative phrase in the BPA was that "both sides recognize that efforts to obtain unilateral advantages at the expense of the other . . . are inconsistent with these objectives," that is, with the objectives of their special responsibility to avoid situations that would risk confrontations between them. The Soviets saw détente as a means to break out of containment. Nixon and Kissinger saw détente as a means to continue containment.

To Nixon and Kissinger, therefore, the political or global aspect of American-Russian relations was of equal import with the military or security aspect. In fact, the two were inextricably intertwined. A détente in its deepest sense between America and Russia—that is, a genuine relaxation in tensions—could not be achieved and sustained unless their nuclear arms competition were stabilized. For two powers that continued to race intensely against one another militarily would find it difficult to experience a prolonged détente. A security accord between the two would come under severe political attack in both nations if each took advantage of it to undermine the other in their global political competition. In short, a sustained détente required a muting of the arms race; but such a muting would be short lived if each succeeded in unilaterally undercutting the other elsewhere.

The political aspect of détente began to unravel almost as soon as it

[4]Quoted in Ibid., p. 127.

had been consummated. The United States was the first to violate it (or interpret it in ways most suited to American interests). During the 1973 Middle East War, the United States gave rhetorical obeisance to the Basic Political Agreement, but it acted in such a way as to evict the Soviet Union politically from the area for nearly a decade. By preventing the Israelis from decimating the Third Egyptian Army and thus laying Cairo open to Israeli attack, by thus saving Sadat from a humiliating military defeat, and by engaging in brinkmanship in order to prevent the Soviets from sending troops to the Middle East to save Sadat, Kissinger began the process that made the United States the external political arbiter of events there. By making the United States the pivotal superpower actor, Soviet influence was reduced, essentially, to Syria.

As noted above, the Soviet Union had clearly stated at the outset of détente that none of the understandings in the BPA would restrain it from supporting socialist revolutionary forces worldwide. Thus Russian actions in Africa—in Angola in 1974 and in the Horn of Africa in 1977— followed quickly upon America's actions in the Middle East. This time it was the Soviets who gained political influence in Angola and Ethiopia at the expense of the Americans. Thus, the United States had adhered to the symbolism but not the substance of the superpowers' political accord during the Middle East War. Having noted America's actions there, the Soviet Union heeded neither in Africa in the mid-1970s.

What had happened was clearly predictable, even if not inevitable. The muting of the nuclear arms race could have led to either a genuine détente or a more intense competition. An arms accord is a necessary, but not a sufficient step for a sustained political détente. In fact, such an accord reflects an easing of tensions that has already occurred. But how far politically such an accord extends depends upon political ambitions reigning in both nations. By their actions less than two years after they had concluded the SALT I Accord, both superpowers showed that neither was prepared to curtail its global designs. It was the paradox—and curse—of the nuclear age that it is precisely because the two powers put their security relations with one another on a firmer and more predictable footing than ever before that their global relations in the process became more unpredictable and intense.

When America had an overweening nuclear superiority, and when Russia lacked a global conventional capability, the Russians, despite all their bluster, were quite restrained in their actions. Their putting offensive missiles into Cuba in 1962 is the exception that proves the rule. Once the Americans publicly announced in October of 1961 what the Russians had known since 1957, to wit, that America was far superior in nuclear strength, Khrushchev reasoned that he had to resort to his own "quick fix" in order to reduce the clear gross disparity in forces between the two nations. Khrushchev took a gamble and poured intermediate-range offensive missiles into Cuba in order to reacquire (this time, on the basis of actual capability, not bluff) the nuclear strength he believed necessary for a vigorous foreign policy. Khrushchev's actions in Cuba in 1962 and Brezhnev's since then clearly demonstrated that the Russians always understood the basis of America's global influence: a sophisticated, large, and visible nuclear force. This has been the precondition since World War II for waxing strong on the world's stage.

With the signing of SALT I, Russia clearly had such a force. Parity brought the assurance of mutual survival, no mean feat, but only a short-lived political détente. Under parity, with each nation feeling more secure about its physical survival, both were emboldened by that very sense of security to pursue their global political ambitions. Each had the nuclear shield behind which to do so. The Cold War was not over; it had merely changed its coloration.

In the first two years of his administration, President Carter began where Nixon and Ford had left off. He was more successful with China than with Russia. Carter and Zbigniew Brzezinski, the president's national security advisor, sought to revive the Chinese-American détente that had languished since 1975. Their motives were largely the same as Nixon and Kissinger's. As Brzezinski put it in his memoirs: "Indeed, such U.S.-Chinese collaboration could be valuable in helping Moscow understand the value of restraint and reciprocity."[5]

What had been advantageous for Nixon and Kissinger became crucial for Carter and Brzezinski. Russian military power had inexorably increased since 1972, with the Soviet Union enhancing its military budgets in real terms during the 1970s by 3 to 5 percent per year. During this same period, America's nominal military budgets were flat; and the real ones (inflation adjusted) actually declined. Russia had increased her conventional forces in Europe, expanded her air and sea lift capabilities, and begun to field a true "blue water navy." Having achieved nuclear parity with the United States by the end of the 1960s the Soviet Union proceeded in the 1970s to strive for a worldwide conventional parity. America's need to use China against Russia had grown in importance as America's conventional global edge over Russia had waned. On December 15, 1978, the United States normalized its relations with China. Subsequently, the two would begin to discuss military cooperation in the guise of the sale of American arms to China.

The Chinese-American relation was solidified under Carter. The American-Russian one was not. In his first three years, Carter failed to secure an arms accord with the Soviet Union that was acceptable to the United States Senate. In his last year, Carter began to rearm the United

---

[5]Zbigniew Brzezinski, *Power and Principle: Memoirs of the National Security Advisor, 1977–1981* (New York: Farrar, Straus & Giroux, 1983), p. 196.

States, to add to America's global commitments, and to press the Russians hard. The "new" Cold War was begun by Carter. Reagan simply intensified it.

Carter's first arms control approach to the Russians was naive and hurt him politically both at home and abroad. Rather than simply pick up where Ford had left off, with a proposal that adhered closely to the Vladivostok Agreement of 1974, Carter chose instead to seek deep cuts in the strategic forces of each nation. Vladivostok had envisioned strategic forces at 2,400 delivery vehicles (missiles and bombers) for both sides, with a sublimit of 1,320 on "mirved" ICBMs (those with more than one warhead per missile). The offer that Secretary of State Vance made to Brezhnev in Moscow in March of 1977 proposed aggregates of 1,800 to 2,000 delivery vehicles and 1,100 to 1,200 mirved missiles. The offer, known as the "Comprehensive Proposal," also required the Russians to reduce their heavy missiles from 308 down to 150. For its part, the United States would limit the range of its cruise missiles to 2,500 kilometers. With this proposal, the Americans were asking the Russians to reduce their strategic forces by 25 percent, to cut their heavy missiles by 50 percent, to permit the United States to exploit its lead in cruise missiles, and to require that America make only marginal reductions in its strategic forces. To this the Russians said, "no."

In April the United States followed with what became known as the "Three Tier Approach," the fundamentals of which were embodied in the SALT II Accord signed by Carter and Brezhnev in June of 1979. The aggregates were higher (2,250); so too were the "mirved" sublimits (1,200 for missiles and 1,320 for missiles and bombers combined). The ceiling on heavy missiles stood at 308 (the number the Russians had currently deployed), and the range limits on cruise missiles were 2,500 kilometers for air-launched and 600 kilometers for ground-launched. Not surprisingly, Carter's SALT II Accord of 1979 looked a lot like Ford's Vladivostok Agreement of 1974, with modifications that closely resembled those that Kissinger had proposed in January of 1976.

It took two years to obtain an agreement on strategic forces that both the United States and the Soviet Union could sign. Ratification by the United States Senate, however, was another matter. For between June and December of 1979, American intelligence discovered a Russian combat brigade in Cuba, one that had probably been there for several years; and the Soviet Union invaded Afghanistan, an action that Brezezinski had been predicting for nearly a year. Both events strengthened the resistance that had been slowly building in the Senate to ratification of the SALT II Accord. Both served as dramatic symbols that focused attention on the previous five years of Russian aggressiveness, from Angola to Afghanistan. Both called into question the merits of Carter's cooperative approach with the Soviet Union. In short, both broke détente.

Quite early in his presidency, Carter had pronounced America's inordinate fear of communism and overweening concentration on the Soviet Union to be over. For the next three years, he pursued détente with Russia, normalization with China, the fostering of human rights around the world, a comprehensive peace settlement in the Middle East, and a more accommodating stance with the South in the North-South economic relationship. But three years later, in early January of 1980, he withdrew from the Senate the SALT II Accord that he had signed with Brezhnev in June of 1979; and in late January 1980, he proclaimed the "Carter Doctrine," which committed the United States to use force against Russia should she use her newly acquired base in Afghanistan to move into the Persian Gulf oil fields. Once again, relations with the Soviet Union moved front and center in Washington's concern. Thus, Carter's seeming vacillation between a hard and soft line toward the Russians, the undeniable aggressiveness of the Soviet Union in Africa and Afghanistan, the unease with which many Senators regarded an accommodation with the Soviet Union that had seemed to work more to its advantage than to America's, and the President's political ineptness with Congress—all played their part in dooming SALT II. The seven-year search for a follow-on to SALT I and the claim that some semblance of détente still existed—both died in December of 1979.

Difficulties with Allies

During the decade of détente and retrenchment, America's relations with her major adversary improved, then worsened. Those with her major allies, Japan and Western Europe, worsened, then improved. Not surprisingly, the first had some bearing on the second. In periods of détente between America and Russia, America's major allies worry about superpower collusion at their expense. In periods of superpower hostility, they worry about either the possibility of a war into which they will be drawn or the sacrifice of their interests in superpower global disputes over which they have no control and in which they have little interest.

The first to worry about the consequences of détente for their security were the Japanese, but, ultimately, their concerns turned out to be less severe than those of the West Europeans. As for the Europeans in their relations with the United States, so, too, did the Japanese face two choices. Either the United States would not risk its own destruction for the defense of Japan, or the Soviet Union would never risk its own devastation for the conquest of Japan. But the choices for Japan are starker than for the West Europeans. Because they do not have nuclear weapons, the Japanese have no claim even to the pretensions of independence that the French and British have. For their security, their dependence on the United States is all the more complete. The Japanese have publicly said as much.

The signs of concern began to surface at the beginning of the 1970s. In early 1976, the Japanese Defense Agency calculated that in a conventional attack by Russia, if Japan received no immediate American military assistance, her air force would be knocked out in a matter of hours; her navy would cease to function after four days; and her army could hold out for no more than ten.[6] The Defense Agency assumed, moreover, that the United States could not give military assistance immediately after Japan invoked her security treaty because of the nature of the treaty. That is, the American-Japanese defense treaty pledges American aid, but only after the United States has gone through its due constitutional processes. In short, while the Congress and the Executive were consulting on what to do, Japan could not defend herself and would not receive aid in sufficient time to survive defeat or destruction. Doubt over the degree of immediacy of America's aid was thus an oblique reference to doubts over whether such aid would in fact ever be forthcoming. The conclusion the military drew was obvious: unless she rearmed, Japan's defeat was inevitable and surrender the only possible course. What makes this conclusion significant is not that it had been widely accepted within Japan, but merely that it was presented for public debate. This was the military's first comprehensive reassessment of Japan's security position in twenty-two years. And by no accident did it come after Nixon proclaimed in the Nixon Doctrine that America's allies must henceforth provide the bulk of the combat troops for their own defense.

As the 1970's progressed, these concerns waned, at least in the public debate. Rather than worry about whether the Americans would defend them, the Japanese instead worried over how to fend off American demands for more defense spending. Beginning with Melvin Laird, every American Secretary of Defense pressed the Japanese to increase their defense budget. The Americans had asked for this increase because the Russians had begun to press them with conventional forces worldwide and especially in the Far East. With North Vietnam's conquest of the south, the debt North Vietnam owed to Russia began to be paid back. With Hanoi's agreement, the Soviet Union established itself in Cam Ranh Bay and utilized the facilities the United States had built there in order to extend the reach of its naval and air power in the Far East. As a consequence, the United States began to argue that the Japanese had to spend more in order to defend by air and sea its sea lines of communications (SLOCs) 1,000 miles out from Japan.

During the 1970s, these efforts bore few results. The Japanese have obtained since 1945 "security on the cheap." The domestic impediments

[6]See the *New York Times*, March 4, 1973, p. 16. These figures could have been exaggerated, for obvious political effect, to aid the Self-Defense Forces in making a case for larger defense budgets. But even if they are exaggerated, they are still reflective of Japan's utter dependence on the United States for military protection.

to a large rearmament effort remained strong. But so too did the external ones. Japan remained a "conversion economy," one that imports most of her raw materials and exports manufactured goods. Good relations with suppliers and buyers have been the paramount concern of Japanese foreign policy, other than its relations with the United States. Japanese diplomacy since the mid-1950s has been characterized by an extremely low profile. Rather than risk dissent at home and trouble abroad, the ruling Liberal-Conservative Party chose to deflect the American demands and concentrate instead on its economy. The paramountcy of economic matters relegated military and political issues to a secondary position. America may have withdrawn from Vietnam, but her actions in South Korea, the Philippines, and Japan showed that she was in the Far East to stay. Concerns over America's reliability as a military protector waned as disputes over America's reliability as Japan's best customer came to the fore.

Relations with the West Europeans followed the reverse sequence. America's détente with the Soviet Union provoked little concern in Europe largely because the Europeans, led by the West Germans, had initiated their own détente with the Russians even earlier than had the Americans. Under Willy Brandt, the West Germans had concluded a series of treaties with the Soviet Union and Eastern Europe that ratified the post-1945 division of Europe and that stabilized relations between East and West Germany. These treaties became known as "Ostpolitik" and served in West Germany as the functional equivalent to the unification of the two Germanies. Where West Germany led, the rest of Europe followed. America's détente with Russia abetted, not thwarted, this process.

For five years after the conclusion of SALT I, America's Russian policy assuaged any concerns the West Europeans may have had about superpower collusion. SALT I helped create a climate for the Europeans that fostered trade and good relations with the East and an apparent easing of Russia's hold over its Eastern European empire. Concerns over superpower collusion at Europe's expense did not surface, not only because the foreign policies of America and Western Europe toward Russia were in harmony, but also because America's search for a SALT II Accord did not then appear to harm Europe's security. Under the terms of SALT I, though the Russians were granted more offensive missiles, the United States retained an acknowledged qualitative and warhead superiority. The West Europeans had always felt more comfortable about America's nuclear guarantee when the United States appeared to have the edge over Russia. SALT I did not threaten it. While Russia may have viewed SALT I as signifying superpower nuclear parity, the West Europeans did not.

This view began to change in 1976 and 1977. Under the impact of three events, Europe's concern over America's reliability as a military protector surfaced. First, Russia expanded and qualitatively improved her conventional forces stationed on the European central front. The conventional balance there began to turn against NATO. Second, Russia began to deploy the SS-20, an intermediate-range nuclear missile that was mobile, had three highly accurate warheads, and was aimed primarily at Western Europe. The balance of forces in theater nuclear weapons began to turn against NATO. Third, and most serious, in its quest for a SALT II Accord, the United States took measures that caused European officialdom to worry that America was seeking her security at Europe's expense. These measures revolved around America's proposed treatment of cruise missiles. They became the symbol of America's securing its own protection at Europe's expense.

In order to obtain a SALT II Accord, in February and then again in September of 1976, Kissinger had proposed to the Russians that ground-launched cruise missiles (GLCMs) would be deployed by the United States only if they had ranges not exceeding 600 kilometers (a range insufficient to hit Russia from Western Europe). After his Comprehensive Proposal failed to entice Russian interest, Carter in April of 1977 came forward with what became known as the "Three Tier Approach." One of its elements was "The Protocol," which essentially repeated Kissinger's cruise missile offer of a year earlier. Both offers offended the Europeans because they believed that the United States was giving up a military option without extracting from the Soviet Union any concessions in return. The SS-20 threat was increasingly worrying official Europe. It could be directed only against them, not the United States. But the one weapon that the United States appeared to have on hand to counter it, the GLCM, was being given away without any attempt to constrain Russian deployment of the SS-20. To make matters worse, the United States was attempting to limit the range of the newest Russian bomber, the "Backfire," to intermediate, not intercontinental ranges. To the Europeans, then, their security vis-à-vis Russia was being sacrificed for the consummation of a SALT II Accord. Apparently, the United States cared more about Russian worries over GLCMs than it did about European worries over SS-20s.

The Americans did not see matters this way. To them the Protocol was a brilliant ploy that gave the Russians a face-saving way to sign SALT II but without giving anything away to them. The Protocol provided for testing GLCMs at ranges up to 2,500 kilometers (a range sufficient to strike into the Soviet Union from Western Europe), and for deploying them at ranges up to 600 kilometers. In addition, the Protocol was to last only three years. The United States pointed out that these two features protected European interests in the cruise missile. Not only were the ground-launched versions not yet available (so that the range constraint on deployment was meaningless), but when they did become available for deployment in roughly three years, the Protocol would have expired. Furthermore, during the next three years when cruise missiles would be in the development stage, they could be tested at their full ranges. Thus, argued the Americans, the Protocol would enable the Soviet Union to take the position that the cruise missile threat had been dealt with and sign SALT II; while, at the same time, it protected a military option that was of interest to Europe.

Unfortunately, what the Americans saw as a throwaway to the Russians, the Europeans saw as a giveaway. They were concerned that in the negotiations that would follow for a SALT III Accord, in which they expected intermediate-range nuclear forces to be taken up, the Soviet Union would press to make the Protocol limits permanent. The European view was that once you conceded a point to the Russians, it becomes nearly impossible to take it back. What therefore seemed temporary to the Americans looked permanent to the Europeans.

Who was correct in this dispute is irrelevant. What mattered was that cruise missiles had become to Europeans the symbol of superpower collusion at their expense. Five years after the first superpower nuclear arms accord, superpower negotiations over their security relations finally began to have their predictable effects on America's European allies.

Helmut Schmidt, chancellor of West Germany, gave these concerns public expression in October of 1977 when he spoke of the need for the United States to take Europe's security interests into account in the SALT II negotiations. Six months earlier, at the NATO heads of state meeting in London, he had spoken of the "neutralization aspect of strategic parity." By that he meant that once the two superpowers had strategic nuclear forces of roughly equal capability, the only thing they were good for was to deter each other's use of them. If each side's strategic nuclear forces cancelled one another out, then the conventional and theater nuclear balances in Europe became of prime concern. If America were to deal only with intercontinental weapons and neglect the intermediate threat to Europe, then the Europeans could become political hostage to Russia's expanding conventional and theater nuclear military power on the Continent. It was not direct military attack but indirect political blackmail that worried Schmidt. Cruise missiles had thus merged with SS-20s and conventional forces. With strategic parity, the theater balance of power became all important. By 1977, the West Europeans too had entered the era of parity and accepted the view that five years earlier only the Russians had taken of SALT I.

The concerns expressed publicly by Schmidt and privately by other European officials in 1977 resulted in NATO's "dual track decision" of 1979. At its December heads of state meeting, NATO collectively agreed to deploy a new generation of theater nuclear forces in Europe capable of striking into the Soviet Union (Pershing II ballistic missiles and GLCMs) *and* to conduct negotiations with the Soviet Union on limiting both sides' deployment of their new generation of intermediate-range theater weapons. As with most of NATO's decisions, this one was a compromise. The Americans, who were initially dubious about the need to deploy new weapons in Europe, stressed deployment more than negotiations. The Europeans, who initially asked for the weapons, stressed negotiations more than deployment as the time for deployment drew near. Finally, in the midst of all of this, NATO had agreed in 1978 to increase each of its members defense budgets by 3 percent annually in order to counter what all agreed was a dangerous momentum in Russia's conventional military expansion in Europe. The Russian buildup that had at the beginning of the decade produced détente was by the end of the decade destroying it.

Economic Retrenchment

The third hallmark of the decade of détente and retrenchment was a weakening of America's economy and a concomitant decline in its willingness to bear the costs of supporting the free world's economic structure. At the end of World War II, the United States had created a set of institutions that provided for a relatively open economic order among the nations of the free world. The World Bank, the International Monetary Fund (IMF), and the General Agreement on Trade and Tariffs (GATT)—all three were American initiatives dedicated to creating a postwar structure that avoided the pitfalls of the interwar period. Goods would be traded freely. Currencies could not be easily devalued against one another. And capital would be lent for reconstruction and development. As the preeminent economic power at the time, these measures obviously benefited the United States. But so too would they aid the rest of the world because they would foster economic growth that, in turn, would promote peace. The lesson of the 1930s was that economic nationalism bred war. The task for the postwar world was to create a structure of economic internationalism that would keep the peace.

By the late 1940s, the institutions of economic internationalism—the World Bank, the IMF, and the GATT—were in place. But, by then, the Cold War with the Soviets had begun in earnest. In support of its global containment policy against the Soviet Union, America accepted departures from its vision of economic internationalism. For nearly a decade after the initiation of the Marshall Plan, the United States tolerated a Western Europe relatively closed to America's economic influence. For nearly twenty years into the postwar era, the United States tolerated an economically nationalist Japan. Economic nationalism in both Western Europe and Japan were accepted so that each area could build itself up economically in order ultimately to share part of the burden of containing Soviet power. Well into the 1960s, the United States accepted departures from its vision of an open economic order in the name of containment. America's economic principles had taken second place to her political and security interests. Economic internationalism was a casuality, not a cause, of the Cold War.

The overweening economic power that the United States possessed at the end of World War II made its support for the institutions of economic internationalism relatively painless. World War II had stimulated, not destroyed, its economy. America's manufacturing prowess was unsurpassed, and she could undersell all. Her capital was bountiful and her technology second to none. Her trade with Western Europe and Japan flourished even in spite of the restrictions that did exist. Throughout the 1950s and 1960s, international trade increased at a rate of 9 percent annually, roughly double the rate of annual economic growth in the United States and Western Europe. International trade had become an important source of growth for both Western Europe and Japan.

By the late 1960s, however, support for economic internationalism was becoming increasingly costly to the United States. With American aid, Western Europe and Japan had rebuilt themselves and had become America's foremost economic competitors in world markets. Japan had an access to America's market that Japan denied to the United States. Management of the dollar to pay for the increases in world trade increasingly conflicted with management of the dollar for the health of the American economy. The surpluses in the trade account that the United States had regularly experienced since the 1890s diminished in size in the 1960s and became negative in the early 1970s. The closing of the gold window, the devaluation of the dollar, and the institution of floating rather than fixed exchange rates—all reflected the fact that America's economic power had peaked. The costs of management of the world's economic order had to be shared with others.

Although the United States did not resort to pure economic nationalism in the 1970s, it did begin to assert its own economic interests more aggressively than it had earlier. But it also remained committed to an open world order and to protection of its allies. The need to reconcile these divergent interests created both ambivalences in America's foreign economic policy and conflicts with its allies.

The oil crisis was a case in point. Actions that the United States took to protect the overall shared interest, Europe and Japan saw as a further entrenchment of America in her still dominant position. In an attempt to lessen the dependence of Europe, Japan, and itself on OPEC oil, the United States pushed its allies to set a floor price under oil. The intent was to encourage the development of alternate energy supplies by guaranteeing their competitiveness with oil. A floor price for oil would insure that the OPEC nations could not manipulate the price of oil in order to drive alternative energy sources out of the market. Becasuse Europe as a whole was poor in natural energy sources compared to America, Europe viewed America's proposal with suspicion, no matter how sound was its economic logic. The Europeans saw the United States as trying to get them to underwrite the costs of America's acquisition of energy self-sufficiency, something Europe could probably never achieve. The United States would end up with diversified and protected energy sources, while the Europeans would be left only with a higher price for imported oil. Whether the United States intended this is irrelevant; the point was that it could be viewed as a logical outcome of its policy.

Similarly, at the Toyoko Round negotiations of the General Agreement on Trade and Tariffs concluded in the late 1970s, the United States pushed for a lowering of barriers to trade in services among countries. At earlier negotiating rounds, the barriers to the movement of capital and goods had been significantly reduced. Services were the one remaining area where significant restrictions remained. A lowering of restrictions on the exchange of services made good economic sense for the free world nations because their economies were becoming less manufacturing and more service oriented. If the logic of comparative advantage had worked for trade in goods, it would do so for trade in services too. But such a policy also made economic sense for the United States, not only because its economy had led the way in becoming more service oriented, but also because the United States held a significant edge in this area. In the realm of services, then, the United States was following a pattern at the end of the 1970s that it had followed at the end of World War II: the encouragement of a more open economic order that would also benefit its economy. As America's economic edge began to shift from heavy manufacturing to the services and high technology sectors, the focus of its free trade efforts similarly shifted. Understandably, the Japanese and West Europeans viewed this shift with mixed feelings.

Finally, in its management of the value of the dollar internationally, the United States tried to reconcile its domestic needs with its international commitments, the problem that Robert Gilpin has referred to as "Keynes at home and Smith abroad."[7] By force of its dominant economic position at the end of World War II, the dollar became the world's reserve currency. Its value was pegged to gold at the rate of $35 per ounce, and the values of other currencies were tied to that of the dollar. Not only did the dollar become the free world's unit of account, it also became the vehicle by which the large annual increases in the free world's trade were carried out. By the early 1960s, the movement of dollars overseas had become so great that the United States could not back them with gold.

[7]See his *The Political Economy of International Relations* (Princeton, N.J.: Princeton University Press, 1987). The task of reconciling the commitment to a full-employment economy at home (Keynesianism) with that of economic internationalism abroad (Smith) is a theme that runs through this brilliant book.

That is, if other nations chose to exchange the dollars they held for the gold the United States possessed, a provision that the Bretton Woods Agreement of 1944 had stipulated, foreigners' claims on dollars would quickly exhaust American's supply of gold. In the 1960s, America's "gold window" was effectively, even if not officially, closed. Because the dollar had become the world's reserve currency, other nations could not turn them in for gold. If they did, the value of the dollar would collapse and so too would the world's trade for want of a currency to finance it.

This overhang of dollars made the Europeans and to a lesser extent the Japanese heavily dependent on the vagaries of the American economy. Funded by the printing of dollars, inflation in America was quickly transmitted abroad. Foreign nations had two choices, neither of which was especially palatable. Either they could accept more dollars, thereby create more currency at home, and fuel their own inflation; or they could revalue their currencies upward, make the price of their exports more expensive to others, and thereby contract their economies. Because they were more dependent on foreign trade than America, they usually opted for inflation over contraction.

The closing of the gold window in 1971 and the institution of floating exchange rates, both done unilaterally by the United States, were designed to deal with this overhang of dollars by passing from the United States to other nations more of the costs of managing the international value of the dollar. Although these measures lessened the burden of management for the United States, they did not reduce the vulnerabilities of the West Europeans and the Japanese to the fluctuations in the dollar's value. In fact, because the price of oil in the 1970s increased by a factor of nearly ten, the economies of others became even more vulnerable. For not only was the price of oil set in terms of dollars, but also the OPEC nations demanded payment in dollars for their oil. Consequently, when America experienced inflation, the dollar's value declined. Foreigners could get dollars more cheaply with their currencies on hand and thereby pay less for their oil. But this came at a delayed cost. For as the dollar depreciated, the costs of the goods of other countries (exports) to Americans increased; and the amount of goods bought by Americans from abroad decreased. The net effect for the West Europeans and the Japanese was that America bought fewer of their goods. That translated into a decline in their exports. But when the value of the dollar increased, the ability of other countries to buy dollars with their currencies decreased; and the price of oil to them thereby increased. Both inflation and "disinflation" in the United States hurt the Europeans and Japanese, either in the price they had to pay for imported oil or in the level of their economies' activity. Not surprisingly, they criticized the United States when its inflation rates were going up or down.

If the vulnerability of others to the state of both the dollar and

America's economy increased from the 1960s to the 1970s, so too did the stake that America held in foreign economic activity. In the 1960s, and historically for the previous hundred years, exports as a percentage of America's GNP averaged only 5 percent. By the end of the 1970s, this figure had nearly doubled. Moreover, nearly one-third of America's agricultural and one-fifth of its manufacturing output was sold abroad. If not as dependent as others on trade, nevertheless, America's stake had increased significantly. In a fundamental sense, what had happened was that the United States itself began to experience the results of the relatively open economic structure that it had created thirty years earlier. Committed to openness, the United States instituted and persevered with measures that ultimately made the American economy more dependent than it had been on foreign economic activity. The irony for the United States was that this greater stake had come precisely at the time that its economic edge internationally began to wane. The costs of openness to the United States had increased because its competitiveness had declined. Both the difficulties that the American economy experienced in the 1970s and the ambivalences in its policies—continued pursuit of openness combined with a sensitivity to the costs of such openness at home—resulted from these two underlying trends.

RESURGENCE AND REVERSAL, 1980–1987

The "New" Cold War

The United States entered the decade of the 1980s by reversing the policies of détente and retrenchment pursued in the 1970s. During that decade, it had retrenched, first, by permitting its defense spending to decline in real terms; second, by making clear that in any future conflicts in the Third World it would provide financial aid and arms but would look to those directly involved to provide the bulk of the combat troops necessary (the Nixon Doctrine); and, third, generally, by eschewing new and extensive commitments. It had pursued détente, first, by signing a nuclear arms control accord with the Soviet Union, and, second, by trying to implement a political accord to govern superpower competition. The rub, however, was that, despite détente and retrenchment, the United States had never given up its goal of containing the expansion of Russian influence. In retrospect, containment conflicted with détente and retrenchment.

The Basic Political Agreement of 1972 had stipulated that neither superpower was to utilize any situation in order to obtain a unilateral advantage. But as long as the Soviet Union was bent on expanding its global influence, and the United States on containing if not diminishing it, the political accord could remain only a piece of paper. Throughout the 1970s, each superpower had sought unilateral advantage at the expense of the other. In 1979 Cuba and Afghanistan finally discredited détente in the United States, but the seeds of its destruction were sown earlier in the decade and were inherent in the nature of the rivalry into which both powers were locked. What had changed in the 1970s was, not the fact of the rivalry, but simply the terms on which it would be waged. The 1970s saw the Soviet Union emerge as a true global superpower, not simply a powerful regional one as it had been in the 1950s and 1960s. No piece of paper could change that fact.

Thus, containment of Russian expansion *had* to conflict with détente and retrenchment. At bottom, as was seen, America's conception of the political changes permitted by the BPA was anti-Soviet. The Soviet Union had sensed this at the outset of détente and had refused to accept the "rules of engagement" between the superpowers as envisioned by the United States. Retrenchment was a necessary adjustment to the political conditions prevailing in the United States in the early and mid-1970s. Detente was an attempt to make a virtue out of necessity. Neither, however, could long serve a policy of containing Soviet expansion if in fact the Soviet Union sought to exploit its new found nuclear parity and its emerging global conventional capability. In the 1970s, the two superpowers had achieved only an unstable equilibrium in their competition for global preeminence. Neither was prepared to opt out of the struggle. Once awareness of this fact had sunk in, the United States would cast aside the larger expectations about détente that had taken political root in the country. In essence, that was the meaning of Afghanistan for America.

In 1980, then, the United States quickly shed its policies of the 1970s. It sought significant increases in its defense budgets. It shelved the SALT II Accord. It foresook détente. And it began to expand its worldwide commitments beginning with the enunciation of the Carter Doctrine and the formation of a global interventionist military force (the RDF or Rapid Deployment Force). The "New" Cold War was marked by a return to the pattern of the 1950s and 1960s—to an escalation in aggressive rhetoric between the United States and the Soviet Union, to a greater reliance on military means, and to a grim determination to offset Soviet influence whenever and wherever necessary.

Resurgence under Reagan

The policies of the Reagan administration differed in intensity, but not in the basic direction that Carter had set in his last year in office. The "New Cold War" dates, not with Reagan's assumption of the presidency in 1981, but with Carter's disillusionment over Soviet actions in late 1979. Four aspects of Reagan's policies are worth noting: first, the expansion of America's military power; second, the pursuit of a tough arms control policy; third, the holding of the Russians as strictly accountable for their actions worldwide; and, fourth, the strain of unilateralism inherent in America's political and military resurgence.

First, in only three years, President Reagan increased the real size of America's defense budget by over 40 percent. He began an ambitious modernization program in both her nuclear and conventional forces. He committed America to building a capability to fight a "protracted" nuclear war and to erecting a shield over the United States, the Strategic Defense Initiative (SDI), to protect its population against ballistic missile attack. And he enhanced the readiness and sustainabilty of her standing conventional military forces.

Second, this rearmament effort went hand in hand with a tough nuclear arms control policy, one that initially required large concessions from the Soviet Union without corresponding ones from the United States. President Reagan renamed the SALT talks the START talks (the Strategic Arms Reduction Talks) and sought large reductions in Russia's heavy missiles, those that could threaten America's Minuteman force. But for nearly two years he refused to offer in return a curtailment either on deployment of America's new heavy bombers (the B-1 and Stealth bombers) or on the placing of nuclear-tipped, air-launched cruise missiles (ALCMs) on her bombers. For over a year, in what were renamed the INF talks (intermediate nuclear forces), he offered no negotiating proposals on the theater nuclear weapons—the GLCMs and Pershing IIs—destined for Europe, other than to cancel America's planned deployment if the Soviet Union would dismantle and destroy all its SS-20s. This was the famous "zero" option that Reagan enunciated in November of 1981, put forward less because he wanted it than because he believed the Soviet Union would not accept it.

President Reagan continued to pursue a vigorous research and development policy for his SDI and subsequently enunciated what was termed the "broad" interpretation of the Anti-Ballistic Missile Treaty (ABM) of 1972. Signed by both superpowers in 1972 and amended by them in 1974, the ABM Treaty had committed each nation not to develop, test, or deploy mobile land-based, sea-based, air-based, or space-based anti-ballistic missile systems. The Treaty also proscribed development, testing, or deployment of systems based on new or exotic technologies, like lasers or X-ray pumped, space-based weapons. By insisting that the "broad" rather than the traditional (or "strict") interpretation was the correct reading of the Treaty, the Reagan administration was trying to lay the groundwork for subsequent deployment of an anti-ballistic missile system based on the exotic technologies that it was developing in its SDI program.[8] Finally, he continued to insist that the Soviet

---

[8]Most informed observers argued that the broad interpretation violated not only the terms of the 1972 Treaty but also the basis upon which the Senate had ratified it. Senator Sam Nunn, no softliner on defense matters, was among them. See his, "Interpretation of the ABM Treaty," March 13, 1987, mimeograph.

Union accept large cuts in the number of its strategic nuclear warheads (which would be matched by American cuts), but only if it would agree to a revision of the ABM Treaty to permit deployment of the strategic defenses that America was seeking to develop. In other words, President Reagan continued to ask the Soviet Union to cut its strategic missile force in half and then allow the United States to erect a defense shield against what remained. Because of this position and because of Soviet intransigence, no visible progress took place in either set of negotiations until the spring of 1987.

Third, the Reagan Administration escalated the hostility of the rhetoric in American-Russian relations by calling the Soviet Union the "focus and source of evil" in the world. Not simply in rhetoric, however, but also in policy did the Reagan administration seek to hold the Russians accountable. Carter had tried to turn away from a single-minded focus on the Soviet Union and be more attuned to the local causes of regional rivalries. Afghanistan shattered that attempt. Reagan intensified the theme to which Carter was forced to return.

The conflicts in Central America were a case in point. Prevailing in El Salvador and reversing the course of the Sandinista revolution in Nicaragua were deemed crucial to America's worldwide credibility in its competition with the Soviet Union. Reagan put military backing of the El Salvadoran government above political pressure on El Salvador to follow through with its land reform policy and to reign in its right-wing "death squads." He sought not simply an end to the Sandinista's military support of the guerrillas in El Salvador but also a fundamental change in the nature of the Nicaraguan government, in effect calling for the dismantling of the Sandinista government and the institution of democratic rule in Nicaragua. Under the Reagan administration, legitimate concerns about the establishment of a Soviet military base in Nicaragua or about Sandinista export of its revolution were lost in its support of the "freedom fighters" (the "Contras") who were trying to overthrow the Sandinista government. Out of a concern for perceived Russian gains, America's sensitivity to the local causes of the troubles in Central America diminished. Holding the Soviet Union accountable meant both interdicting its support of left-wing forces and preventing them from winning and ruling.

Fourth, in its reassertion of American power and purpose, the Reagan administration exhibited a strain of unilateralism that was first evident in its relations with the West Europeans. Détente had worked for the Europeans. It had meant greater trade with the communist bloc, a lessening in political tensions with the Soviet Union, the hope of a secular evolution towards greater freedom in Eastern Europe, and tangible humanitarian benefits for both West and East Germans. As the United States turned away from détente, the Europeans tried to insulate them-

selves from the hardening in American-Russian relations. They continued to pursue policies that seemed of benefit to them, such as their
financing of, and provision of equipment for, the trans-Siberian gas pipeline. In doing so, they found themselves at odds with the United States,
which unilaterally imposed sanctions on European-based American firms
that were engaged in this deal. Although the United States soon lifted its
sanctions, the residue of ill will remained. In pursuing their own interests, the Europeans were trying to distance themselves from an America
that seemed to them to have an increasingly unilateral, if not unpredictable, character.

Unilateralism in American policies was also exhibited in her actions
towards Libya and the Middle East. Having come into office determined
to take an aggressive stance against terrorism, early on the Reagan administration fixed on the Qaddafi regime as a financial and military
supporter of terrorists of all brands. Qaddafi's genuine support of terrorists, his attempts to destabilize Egypt and the Sudan, his continuing military intervention in Chad, his extremist stance in the Arab-Israeli dispute,
and his generally quixotic and bizarre behavior—all gave legitimacy to
American claims that Qaddafi ran a "renegrade regime." Disciplining
Qaddafi soon became the symbol for Reagan's tough stance against terrorism. The need to act against terrorists became even more pressing
after the U.S. Marine debacle in Lebanon (largely seen as a terrorist
attack against America's peacekeeping forces there) and after the terrorists bombings of December 27, 1985 against the airports in Vienna and
Rome, the most dramatic of the continuing terrorist attacks in Europe.
After it had failed to persuade its European allies to go along with its
economic sanctions imposed against Libya in January 1986, and after it
claimed to have irrefutable proof that the Libyans were behind the April
5, 1986 terrorist bombing of a West Berlin discotheque, the administration
decided to act. On April 15, 1986, eighteen American warplanes attacked
Tripoli, with some asserting that one of the primary purposes for the raid
was to kill Qaddafi.[9]

Except for the British, who permitted American F-111B bombers to
fly from England, the West Europeans gave no assistance to the American
action and publicly, at least, distanced themselves from it. Having stated
that he would take action against the sources of terrorism when they
could be identified and having identified Libya as the source of terrorism
in the West Berlin attack, Reagan had to act or else lose credibility. In
fact, the evidence is strong that, almost from the outset of the Reagan
administration, extensive planning for covert actions against Qaddafi had
taken place. Whether the evidence for Libyan involvement in the April 5

[9]See Seymour M. Hersh, "Target Qaddafi," *The New York Times Magazine*, February 22,
1987, pp. 17 ff.

bombing was ironclad, good enough, or only circumstantial may never be known. What is clear is that the administration had been looking for a pretext to act and did so in April, with almost no support from the very allies who were suffering most from the terrorists attacks.

By its actions against Libya, the Reagan administration showed that it was prepared to act militarily when it thought the case compelling, without the support of its allies or even against their wishes. But such actions were undertaken against small powers and in situations where the likelikhood of failure was quite low, the costs of action also quite low, and the benefits of success quite high. Although two American bombers were shot down during the Tripoli raid, Qaddafi did not have the military reach to retaliate against the United States. Qaddafi's subsequent support of terrorist activity seemed to have waned, though some of that could be attributed to the grave reversal that he suffered in 1987 in his military intervention in Chad.

The final military intervention undertaken by Reagan during this period was a much higher stake, higher risk affair. In the spring of 1987, the administration began to convoy through the Persian Gulf Kuwaiti oil tankers that had switched their registry to the American flag. In the process, with the large naval armada that it sent to the region, the United States became militarily entangled in the war between Iran and Iraq that had been raging on land and in the Gulf without resolution since the Iranian revolution of 1979.

Three reasons stand out to explain why the United States undertook what was widely seen as the most significant military intervention of the Reagan presidency. First was the need to restore the credibility that the United States had lost in the region when its secret arms sales to Iran became public in the fall of 1986, an affair that quickly became known as "Irangate."[10] Second was the desire to forestall any expansion of Soviet influence in the Persian Gulf, a concern that was triggered in early 1987 when Kuwait asked *both* superpowers to protect its shipping against Iranian attacks. Third was the necessity to provide some tangible military security to Kuwait as a symbol of America's military commitment to the Arab states of the Persian Gulf, to make, that is, a visible downpayment on the Carter Doctrine enunciated seven years earlier. Although the third factor was important, it was clearly of secondary significance in explaining the timing and the reason for the American intervention. After all, Kuwaiti tankers, just like those of many other nations, had been subject to Iranian attacks for several years. Even though Iran had recently stepped up its attacks on Kuwaiti and other national tankers and even though some disruption of oil shipping had occurred, Iraq too had been

[10]The two best sources to read on "Irangate" are *The Tower Commission Report*, issued as a paperback (New York: Bantam Books, 1987); and the *Report of the Congressional Committees Investigating the Iran-Contra Affair*, 100th Congress, First Session, November 13, 1987.

attacking tankers in the Gulf; and neither the Iraqi nor Iranian attacks had cut significantly the supply of oil through the Gulf. Insurance rates on tankers went up somewhat, but the supply of oil exiting the Persian Gulf did not go down significantly, in part because by 1987 nearly half of Gulf oil was shipped by pipelines over land to the Red Sea and the Mediterranean. It was only after the American arms sales to Iran became known and when Soviet naval intervention looked possible that America's military intervention in the eyes of the Reagan administration became imperative.

Irangate was a complex affair. The Reagan administration had taken a tough public stance against dealing with terrorists. In private, it turned out, it had sold arms to Iran either in the hope of establishing relations with the more "moderate" elements there in a post Khomeini regime or for the exchange of American hostages held in Lebanon. Iranian specialists argued that the former was counterproductive because any elements within Iran that dealt with the United States would immediately lose credibility once their dealings became known. Moreover, over the longer term, the Soviet threat to Iran and the Iranian fundamentalist Moslem hostility to communism would act in America's favor. Simple geopolitical analysis showed that Iran would need the United States as an offset against the Soviets and would seek to establish more normal relations with it in due course. Events quickly proved that the arms-for-hostages trade was futile because terrorists groups in Lebanon simply took new hostages to replace the ones that Iran had used its influence to get released. Both actions were taken against the adamant advice of Secretary of State Schultz and Secretary of Defense Weinberger. Both actions were closely held and run within the White House by the National Security Council, probably with the knowledge, if not full assistance, of CIA Director William Casey. Both actions were reflective of the Reagan administration's penchant for covert actions designed in such a way as to elude congressional oversight previously legislated by the Congress.[11]

Whatever were the reasons for the sale of arms to Iran, the effects on America's relations with her European and Persian Gulf allies were disastrous. In the eyes of the Europeans, Irangate tended to discredit the administration's vigorous antiterrorist policy and called into question the efficacy of actions like the Tripoli bombing. In the eyes of its Persian Gulf

[11]The full story of the Reagan administration's covert action policy is still to come. The sales to Iran and the fianancing of arms to the Contras with profits from the Iranian arms sales were both parts of a larger covert program established in the National Security Council as early as 1982. This was the hidden side of "Project Democracy," the Reagan administration's program to fund deomocratic institutions as part of what became known as the "Reagan Doctrine," the active encouragement of democracy abroad. The best journalistic accounts of the covert aspects of Project Democracy appear in stories by Joel Brinkley in the *New York Times*, February 15, 1987, p. 1; Kurt M. Campbell, the *Boston Globe*, p. 15; and Seymour Hersch, as cited in note 9.

clients, Irangate tended to discredit America's word and thereby called into question her commitment to their security. For both military and ideological reasons, Iran presented a far greater threat to the Persian Gulf sheikdoms than did Iraq. Iran is the local superpower of the region, and Iran's revolutionary brand of Shiite fundamentalism presented a grave challenge to the stability of the Sunni governments there. It was for these reasons that the Kuwaitis and the Saudis had been underwriting Iraq's war effort to the tune of many billions of dollars per year. By sending, covertly at that, arms to Iran—arms that were of real utility against Iraqi tanks and planes —the Reagan administration enhanced, not diminished, the possible triumph of Iran over Iraq.

Even the loss of credibility produced by Irangate, however, was not enough to cause the administration to move. It was only when Kuwait forced his hand that Reagan acted. The story is succinctly told by Karen Elliott House, the *Wall Street Journal's* foreign editor:

> Kuwait . . . found late last year [1986] that its tankers were under growing pressure from Iran because of Kuwait's support for Iraq in the seven-year-old Iran-Iraq War. So, Kuwait went privately to both the U.S. and the U.S.S.R. seeking protection for its 22 tankers. The Reagan administration dallied, answering that reflagging was complicated and time-consuming and besides, Kuwaiti tankers might not meet U.S. standards. Moscow promptly offered to allow three Kuwaiti ships to fly the Soviet flag. The Reagan administration then hastily reversed course and agreed in early March to reflag 11 other Kuwaiti tankers rather than run the risk that Moscow would do so.[12]

The Persian Gulf action was undertaken without fully consulting either the West Europeans or the Japanese. They were presented more or less with a *fait accompli,* and initially both distanced themselves from it. Each was concerned about the escalatory risks and about whether the United States would see the matter through if things escalated. Irangate had created doubts about American consistency; the withdrawal of the U.S. Marines from Lebanon had created doubts about American staying power. Only after it had begun the escort service and only after Congress then began to question the merits of a policy undertaken to protect Persian Gulf oil used mainly by the Europeans and Japanese, neither of whom were supporting the action, did the administration then begin to exert pressure on its allies for assistance. Ultimately, both came along. The Europeans sent their own ships to the area, especially much needed minesweepers, and the Japanese began talking of ways to help defer the

---

[12]*Wall Street Journal,* June 25, 1987, p. 24. See also the report by Stephen Engelberg and Bernard E. Trainor, *New York Times,* August 23, 1987, pp. 1 and 12. They report that Regan's approval of the reflagging and escort policy "was primarily based on this perceived need to counter Soviet influence in the region."

estimated $300 million annual cost of the American naval task force. To protect their access to oil and to protect themselves against congressional charges of free riding, the Europeans and the Japanese joined with America in an action that benefited them more than it did her. Even the Persian Gulf sheikdoms, always reluctant to cooperate overtly with the United States, began to do so. In this case, although America at first led, her allies, from their own interests, soon followed.

Nuclear Politics and Détente Again?

The Persian Gulf intervention will likely be seen as the most significant, large-scale, anti-Soviet military action of the Reagan administration. And yet, at about the very time when this was taking place, the five-year logjam in nuclear arms control negotiations between the two superpowers began to break up. The turning point came at the first summit meeting between Reagan and Gorbachev, held at Geneva in November 1985. At that meeting, both leaders agreed to seek a 50 percent reduction in their strategic nuclear forces and an interim agreement on intermediate nuclear forces (INF) that would leave each with low but equal levels of forces deployed in Europe.

What then followed was a ten-month exchange of letters between the two that resembled in key respects a combination of a poker game, in which each raised the ante and tried to outbid the other, and a sparring match, in which each circled the other and occasionally probed to determine the strength of his opponent's defenses.[13] Gorbachev opened the bidding in January of 1986 by proposing the complete elimination of all nuclear weapons by the year 2000. Reagan responded in late February with a proposal to eliminate all intermediate nuclear forces worldwide within three years. Gorbachev then replied in June that he would be willing to compromise on the INF forces, but he did not give any specific proposals. Furthermore he asked that the United States agree to the latest Soviet proposals made at Geneva in the late spring of 1986. There Soviet negotiators had proposed a 30 percent reduction in strategic forces, but tied that offer to two other agreements—an accord by both superpowers permitting research, development, and testing of SDI in the laboratory only—and an accord agreeing not to withdraw from the ABM Treaty for fifteen to twenty years. Reagan responded in late July 1986 with the following offer: an agreement for reductions of less than 50 percent in strategic forces, an agreement to permit either side to deploy strategic

---

[13]The best discussion of this period, as well as the account of American preparations for, and actions at, the Reykjavik Summit, to be discussed below, appears in *The Reikjavik Process: Preparation for and Conduct of the Iceland Summit and Its Implications for Arms Control Policy,* Report of the Defense Policy Panel, Committee on Armed Services, U.S. House of Representatives, Ninety-ninth Congress, Second Session, January, 1987.

defenses within seven-and-one-half years within the framework of a modified ABM Treaty, and a proposal to eliminate completely all offensive ballistic missiles. Foreign Minister Shevarnadze visited Washington in September and delivered Gorbachev's reply to Reagan's proposals of July. Gorbachev proposed the retention of a token force of INF missiles in Europe, insisted on a fifteen year nonwithdrawal from the ABM Treaty, and suggested that the two leaders get together in either London or Iceland to prepare plans for the next summit meeting that they had both agreed to at Geneva in 1985.

This was the background for the pivotal Reagan-Gorbachev meeting that occurred on October 10–11, 1986 at Reykjavik, Iceland. Reykjavik was significant, not only because it led to subsequent progress in nuclear arms negotiations between the superpowers, but also because it affected deleteriously America's relations with her European allies. At Reykjavik, Gorbachev proposed a 50 percent cut in strategic missiles, the complete elimination of both superpowers' INF forces in Europe, no withdrawal from the ABM Treaty, and a strengthening of the Treaty's language on testing ABM components. Gorbachev's overriding goal at Reykjavik was the same as that which he had been pursuing since late 1985: preventing the United States from deploying strategic defenses. In order to obtain that at the Reykjavik negotiations, he was offering to accept two of Reagan's previously proffered proposals: the zero option in Europe (complete elimination of INF forces) and the 50 percent cut in strategic forces. To sweeten the pot even more, he added a third inducement: after the completion of an INF Treaty, there would be subsequent negotiations to reduce both superpower's short-range nuclear missile forces in Europe, an area in which the Soviets had a commanding lead. At Reykjavik, Gorbachev in effect made Reagan an offer that the president could not refuse: he accepted the zero option that Reagan had proposed back in November of 1981. Reagan had no choice but to accept. The basic outlines of a treaty on intermediate nuclear forces had been set at Reykjavik.

Similar progress, however, was not made on strategic or intercontinental weapons. The stumbling block in this area came with Reagan's insistence on pursuing his strategic defense initiative unfettered by any mutually agreed upon restrictions, or even by the 1972 ABM Treaty itself. Since March of 1983, when he had announced his "star wars" or SDI program, Reagan had been consistently committed to reducing, if not eliminating, the threat of nuclear weapons. He saw ballistic missiles as especially destabilizing because, once fired, they could not be recalled and because, once unleashed, they could reach their targets quickly. Ballistic missiles had come to be viewed by Reagan as "hair trigger" weapons. At Reykjavik, therefore, Reagan refused to budge on his SDI program and countered with an offer that both superpowers eliminate all ballistic missiles within ten years. If the threat of ballistic missiles could not be eliminated by deploying a defense against them, then it could be removed by totally eliminating them. The offer made at Reykjavik was the first time that the United States had proposed elimination of ballistic missiles *with a specified time period affixed to it.* Previously, because Reagan's proposal for their elimination had no time limit, it was widely seen by national security bureaucracies in both America and Europe as more an expression of Reagan's wish to denuclearize the world than as a serious negotiating proposal. Reagan at Reykjavik, however, showed that what he had first proposed in July was for him no idle wish but instead a deadly serious goal.

Because the United States had an overwhelming lead in bombers and in air- and sea-launched cruise missiles, the Soviet's acceptance of the zero ballistic missile proposal would have left them at a serious disadvantage. Ever-mindful of world public opinion, Gorbachev therefore countered instead with a proposal to eliminate all nuclear weapons within ten years. Reagan is reputed to have agreed with this goal of total elimination, but still insisted on pursuing his SDI program. Gorbachev refused to compromise on SDI testing and finally stated that any other agreements, including his acceptance of the zero INF option, were in abeyance until the SDI issue could be resolved. The meeting broke up with this exchange:

Gorbachev: I think we can still deal.
Reagan: I don't think you really wanted a deal. I don't know when we'll see each other again.
Gorbachev: I don't know what else I could have done.
Reagan: You could have said yes.[14]

Publicly, after Reykjavik, the administration argued that it had not agreed to the total elimination of all nuclear weapons; but it left standing its offer for the ten-year elimination of all ballistic missiles. Reykjavik culminated the ten-month "bidding war" in which the two leaders had been engaged. With each trying to outdo the other, both had ended up by agreeing in principle to the complete elimination of all nuclear weapons within ten years. What had thus begun as an arms control minuet ended up as a mutual embrace of complete nuclear disarmament.

The tentative zero INF accord bothered European governments because they had invested much prestige with their publics in deploying the GLCMs and Pershing II missiles and because they had come to believe in the rationale for deployment. But, as the zero proposal was official NATO policy, they reluctantly accepted it. The zero ballistic missile proposal and the complete elimination of all nuclear weapons, how-

[14]Ibid., p. 12.

ever, drove them nearly into a frenzy. With one (or two) fell swoops, Reagan was threatening to undermine the entire strategy of the NATO alliance and hence Western Europe's security vis-à-vis the Soviet Union.

To the Europeans, nuclear deterrence was the heart of NATO's defense posture; and ballistic missiles were the keystone of the American nuclear umbrella. To the British and the French, moreover, whose nuclear forces consisted primarily of ballistic missiles, the zero ballistic missile proposal would mean the end of their independent deterrents. To all officialdom in Europe, Reagan's proposal to eliminate ballistic missiles, combined with a zero INF accord, threatened the denuclearization of the NATO alliance, which was, of course, seen by them as a long standing Soviet goal. To the Europeans, Reagan's actions at Reykjavik looked naive at best; at worst, he looked duped by Gorbachev. To the Europeans, finally, the ultimate irony was that a Soviet-American deal to eliminate all nuclear weapons failed of consummation because of Reagan's stubborn insistence on pursuing his SDI program, a vision that the Europeans had never been enthusiastic about in the first place. Reagan's commitment to a defense that would neutralize ballistic missiles, that is, saved them from the possibility that they might be eliminated!

Whether the Soviets would have accepted the zero ballistic missile proposal had the SDI issue been resolved is problematical. What bothered the Europeans was not only that Reagan had proposed it in the first place, but also that he had done so without consulting them. As a consequence, after consultations with Chancellor Kohl and President Mitterand, Prime Minister Thatcher made a trip to Camp David to present Europe's concerns over what had transpired at Reykjavik. The result of her message was that the zero ballistic missile proposal was dropped from the American position and in its place was substituted the 50 percent cut in strategic forces. Sweeping but not zero reductions in INF forces were also replaced for the zero option. Consultation after the fact had redressed what lack of consultation before the fact had produced.

Nevertheless, the zero INF proposal was now on the negotiating table, put there by Reagan and provisionally accepted by Gorbachev. So, too, was Gorbachev's proposal to begin discussions on the reduction of shorter-range missiles based in Europe. An agreement on limiting missiles in Europe was easier to achieve than one on strategic forces. The interest of both political leaders in some type of arms control accord was strong. Gorbachev needed a respite from the arms race and hoped that an INF accord would pave the way to one on strategic weapons. Reagan became concerned about his place in history and did not want to go out of office as the only president since Eisenhower who had failed to achieve some significant arms accord with the Soviet Union. The result of the proposals floated at Reykjavik and of the political interests of the two leaders was the INF Treaty signed in Washington in early December, 1987. With this accord, which became known as the "double zero" accord, the two superpowers agreed to remove and dismantle from Europe (and Asia) all nuclear missiles with ranges between 500 and 5,500 kilometers over a three year period. What would be left were short-range missiles (those with ranges under 500 kilometers), nuclear bombs on aircrafts, and battlefiled nuclear weapons. Finally, intrusive verification provisions were written into the treaty to make certain that both nations abided by its terms.

Even with the reductions it mandated, the INF Treaty would leave NATO with approximately 4,000 tactical nuclear weapons remaining in Europe. By early 1988, nevertheless, fears about the denuclearization of Europe were in the air. Concern that Gorbachev would next propose the elimination of all nuclear missiles and battlefield nuclear weapons too, and that European governments would be under considerable pressure from their publics to accept these proposals—those were the worries of the West European governments. Suspicious of Gorbachev's long-term motives and fearful that NATO had landed on the slippery slope of denuclearization, the Europeans once again became concerned about the consequences of superpower arms accords for their security. In 1979, it was this fear that had caused them to accept the deployment of GLCMs and Pershing II missiles in the first place. Now, ironically, in 1988, this same fear arose again when agreement was reached to take them out.

Did the INF Treaty in late 1987 presage a détente between the United States and the Soviet Union, just as the SALT I Treaty had in 1972? In the early 1970s, both the United States and the Soviet Union had powerful economic incentives to mute their competition. The same was true for the late 1980s. Then, as now, the Soviet Union confronted an economy less and less able to generate the resources necessary to meet both consumer and military needs. Both Brezhnev and Gorbachev turned to the West for the credits and technology necessary to modernize the Soviet economy. By accompanying his turn to the West with *perestroika*—economic restructuring at home—Gorbachev both promised more than Brezhnev had and encountered more resistance to his plans. His need, consequently, for a relaxation in tensions with the United States was all the greater. Reagan, just like Nixon before him, faced a Congress hostile to increases in defense spending, but the economic problems of the United States in the late 1980s were much more severe than they were in the early 1970s. Consequently, the need for the United States to lessen its military burdens so as to address its economic problems at home was all the greater. For both superpowers, peace abroad was necessary for success at home.

During the three-day December summit, Reagan said that he believed the Soviets no longer wanted to conquer the world. Rather, they want "to prove that we can live in the world together at peace."[15] Gorbachev expressed similar hopes about the future of American-Soviet relations. Will economic incentives, powerful as they are, and genuine efforts to reduce tensions be sufficient to bring about détente? The answer is not clear. But what can be said is this: the United States and the Soviet Union will remain competitors for the forseeable future. Each is the greatest military threat to the other. Neither, however, can attempt conquest of the other without devastating itself in the process. Nor can either significantly weaken the other because the sources of strength for each are largely indigenous. Both are therefore doomed to compete and yet to find some minimum basis for coexistence. The threat that each provides to the other will make both wary. The competition for global influence will undercut the possiblity of a long-run harmony between them. But the possibility of mutual devastation through miscalculation will force both to meliorate periodically the intensity of their competition. The cycle of intense hostility and then relaxation of tension, with all that implies for other nations, will continue. Only Gorbachev's staying power and the next American president's policies will tell whether the two have entered, once again, into détente.

THE FUTURE OF CONTAINMENT

After four decades of America's pursuit of containment, there are three questions about it that need to be addressed. First, did containment work? Second, is the need for it now over? Third, if the need for containment remains, can the United States still afford it? Because the answers to the second and third questions hinge on what type of response is given to the first, how containment is evaluated is crucial.

As expressed in his famous "X" article forty years ago, George F. Kennan, then political advisor in the American embassy in Moscow, set forth two tasks for containment.[16] The first was to prevent the geographical expansion of Soviet control; the second was to produce, through the vigilant containment and, hence, frustration of Soviet expansion, a mellowing in its aggressiveness. Kennan saw the sources of Soviet expansion as internally not externally generated. Because the fruits of communism

---

[15]Quoted in *The New Republic,* January 4 and 11, 1988, p. 17.

[16]The "X" article orginally appeared in *Foreign Affairs* in 1947 under the title "The Sources of Soviet Conduct" and was a reworking of a long telegram that Kennan sent to Washington from Moscow. Its effect was profound on official thinking because it both explained the recent pattern of Soviet actions and laid out a path for dealing with them. The "X" article appears in Kennan's *American Diplomacy, 1900–1950* (New York: Mentor Books, 1962), pp. 89–106.

had not been realized at home, the Soviet rulers needed to portray the world external to the Soviet Union as hostile in order to justify their continued dictatorial rule at home. Kennan gave no rationale as to why containment of Soviet expansion would lead to a dimunition in its agressiveness. It was more a hope stated than an argument spelled out. In his later writings, Kennan tried to distinguish between the spread of communism and the expansion of Soviet control. He was a firm believer in the potency of nationalism and, therefore, did not equate the former with the latter. He believed that over the long term the centrifugal forces of nationalism would overwhelm the centripetal forces of communistic ideology. He applied this perspective to Chinese-Soviet relations and correctly predicted the Sino-Soviet split.

In his emphasis on containment, he did not call for an open-ended commitment but rather took a geopolitical perspective that emphasized keeping the world's major power centers free of Soviet control. Finally, in arguing for the necessity of containment, Kennan warned of the dangers of an overreliance on military means and stressed the importance of economic and political measures.

If containment is judged by Kennan's first test (preventing the expansion of Soviet geographical control), then surely it has succeeded. Apart from the United States and the Soviet Union, there are three other power centers in the world, repositories, that is, of great economic and/or military power. They are Western Europe, Japan, and the Persian Gulf. They are as free of Soviet control today as they were in 1945. If China is counted as an additional power center, it is today less under the influence of the Soviet Union than it was in 1949. This is not to say that the Soviet Union has less influence worldwide today than it had forty years ago. Clearly, that is not the case. But apart from Cuba, Yemen, and perhaps Ethiopia, the record of sustained Soviet success in the Third World is unimpressive. At the beginning of 1988, moreover, the Soviet Union appeared poised to withdraw from a war in Afghanistan that it could not win after eight years of heavy commitment, and it was not even making the establishment of a regime friendly to it after its withdrawal a condition of leaving. Influence must be distinguished from control. The only area of the world that the Soviet Union controls today remains the same area as that in 1945, namely, Eastern Europe. Since the outset of containment, Soviet influence worldwide may have expanded somewhat, but not the Soviet empire.

If measured by Kennan's second test (the dimunition of Soviet aggressiveness), the ultimate answer cannot yet be clear. Certainly the Soviet Union did not see détente in the 1970s worth the forgoing of the expansion of its global influence. Whether Gorbachev's desire for a relaxation in tensions with the United States represents a genuine mellowing of Soviet expansionist urges, or whether it is merely a tactical retreat designed to buy time for the system to regroup, to strengthen itself, and to turn outward again with greater force, will not be known for several years. Those who see *perestroika* as a significant change in the Soviet system of control incline toward the former view; those who see it as a change that will not threaten the ultimate control of the Communist party incline toward the latter view. It may very well be that Gorbachev's restructuring campaign is akin to Lenin's "New Economic Policy" of the 1920s and Brezhnev's détente of the 1970s. Both were designed with the ultimate purpose of saving the system, not changing it.

We cannot be certain now which is the case. But even if we were sure that the Soviet system is now in the process of fundamental change, that would not obviate the need for some type of containment strategy. There is no offset to Soviet power worldwide, save that of the United States. Containment in some form or other must continue because the United States cannot allow the resources of Japan, Western Europe, and the Persian Gulf to come under Soviet control. Were the Soviet system to change radically, it would still possess great power. Even were the Soviet Union to become in its actions a totally benign power, the necessity of a contingent containment policy would remain if only to guard against the possibility that Soviet intentions could alter and become bellicose once again. Good intentions do not check power; only power checks power.

Because this is the case, the issue, finally, becomes this: if containment must continue, what form should it take and how should it be pursued? No answer to those questions, in turn, can be given without some assessment of the costs to the United States of its forty year containment effort. Soviet actions, whatever form they will take, are only half the story; America's resources to sustain the effort are the other half.

Here the assessment must be more pessimistic. As was argued earlier, the United States created an internationalist economic order, both for its own benefit and for that of its major allies. But by the early 1980s, it was facing fierce economic competition from the West Europeans, the Japanese, and the newly industrializing countries (the NICs). It had neglected the modernization of its industrial base and had suffered a decline in its economic competitiveness. With the exception of the West Europeans, who have since the late 1960s born a defense burden heavier than most realize, it has been the United States that has provided the military power requisite to underwrite economic internationalism and the American economy that has served as the engine of world growth and the market of last resort. Just as structural changes in the world balance of military power in the late 1960s made America's turn to détente desirable, so too have structural changes in the world economy made some retrenchment in America's commitments necessary.

Under Reagan, however, the United States chose not to retrench but to expand; and it did so with a vengeance. The Reagan administration's economic and defense policies made what was already a bad problem worse. By the late 1980s, it was suffering huge budgetary and trade deficits that were running on the order of $200 and $170 billion, respectively. In 1987, the United States switched from being a creditor to a debtor nation and was borrowing close to $120 billion a year to finance its budgetary and trade deficits. By 1987 the United States had become the world's largest debtor nation, dwarfing the huge sums that Brazil and Mexico, currently the world's largest debtors, owe. It came to rely heavily, first on the West Germans, then on the Saudis, and finally on the Japanese to support its twin economic hemorrhages. The Japanese in particular were lending the United States the money necessary to purchase their goods and were buying up American companies and real estate with the huge surpluses that their favorable trade balance with America generated. By 1986, America's net assets abroad were zero; those of the Japanese, British, and West Germans were, repectively, $130, $90, and $50 billion. So bad had things become that one analyst termed this state of affairs "the Japanese subsidization of American hegemony."[17]

By definition, all great powers suffer an imbalance between their commitments and their resources. For them the issue has always been how to keep that imbalance within manageable proportions. Now into the fifth decade of containment, this is the overriding task for the United States. It must narrow the gap between its global responsibilities and its declining resource base. It must tend to its economy. It must discriminate more wisely in the challenges that it takes up. It must be more efficient in its generation of military power and more skillful in its application. And it must ask more from its major allies, the West Europeans and the Japanese. After all, America's assistance in restoring Western Europe and Japan to economic health was predicated in part on their assuming a share of the burden in containing the Soviet Union.

No matter what form containment shall take in the future, the United States will need to restore its economic prowess and to rely on others more than it has thus far. Unless it does so, it could in time risk its position as the world's preeminent power.

FOREIGN POLICY LANDMARKS

1947	The Truman Doctrine is promulgated; the Marshall Plan is announced
1950	The Korean War begins
1953	Eisenhower's "New Look" is announced; Korean War armistice is signed
1956	Eisenhower opposes the Suez invasion
1961	The Bay of Pigs invasion of Cuba fails
1962	The Cuban Missile Crisis occurs
1965	United States sends 100,000 troops to Vietnam

[17]See Robert Gilpin, *The Political Economy of International Relations*, pp. 328–336.

1972	SALT I Accord with Soviet Union is signed; détente with China begins
1973	United States goes on nuclear alert against Soviet Union; Arab oil embargo against United States is declared
1975	United States withdraws from Vietnam
1979	United States and Soviet Union reach agreement on SALT II Accord; Soviet Union invades Afghanistan
1980	Carter announces "Carter Doctrine" and withdraws SALT II Accord from Senate
1983	United States begins deployment of new nuclear weapons to Europe
1984	United States invades Grenada; United States withdraws marines from Lebanon
1986	United States bombs Libya
1987	United States begins convoys in Persian Gulf; United States and Soviet Union sign INF Treaty

SELECTED BIBLIOGRAPHY

ADLER, SELIG. *The Isolationist Impulse.* New York: Collier Books, 1961.

BEARD, CHARLES. *The Idea of the National Interest.* Chicago: Quadrangle Books, 1966.

BEMIS, SAMUEL FLAGG. *A Diplomatic History of the United States.* 5th Ed. New York: Holt, Rinehart & Winston, 1965.

BROWN, SEYOM. *The Faces of Power.* New York: Columbia University Press, 1983.

BREZINSKI, ZBIGNIEW. *Power and Principle: Memories of the National Security Adviser 1977–1981.* New York: Farrar, Straus & Giroux, 1983.

CALLEO, DAVID P., and BENJAMIN M. ROWLAND. *America and the World Political Economy.* Bloomington, Ind.: Indiana University Press, 1973.

GADDIS, JOHN LEWIS. *The United States and the Origins of the Cold War, 1941–1947.* New York: Columbia University Press, 1972.

———. *Strategies of Containment.* New York: Oxford University Press, 1982.

KENNAN, GEORGE F. *American Diplomacy, 1900–1950.* Chicago: University of Chicago Press, 1951.

KISSINGER, HENRY A. *White House Years.* Boston: Little Brown, 1979.

———. *Years of Upheaval.* Boston: Little Brown, 1982.

KOLKO, GABRIEL. *The Politics of War.* New York: Random House, 1968.

KOLKO, JOYCE, and GABRIEL KOLKO. *The Limits of Power.* New York: Harper & Row, 1972.

MAY, ERNEST R. *"Lessons" of the Past.* New York: Oxford University Press, 1973.

OSGOOD, ROBERT E. *NATO: The Entangling Alliance.* Chicago: University of Chicago Press, 1962.

PERKINS, DEXTER. *The American Approach to Foreign Policy.* Cambridge, Mass.: Harvard University Press, 1952.

SCHLESINGER, ARTHUR M., JR. *The Imperial Presidency.* Boston: Houghton Mifflin, 1973.

STEINBRUNER, JOHN D. and LEON V. SIGAL, eds., *Alliance Security: NATO and the No-First Use Question.* Washington, D.C.: Brookings Institute, 1983.

TUCKER, ROBERT W. *Nation or Empire?* Baltimore, Md.: Johns Hopkins Press, 1968.

ULAM, ADAM B. *The Rivals.* New York: Viking Press, 1971.

WALTZ, KENNETH N. *Foreign Policy and Democratic Politics.* Boston: Little, Brown, 1967.

WILLIAMS, WILLIAM APPLEMAN. *The Tragedy of American Diplomacy.* New York: Dell, 1962.

5

Soviet Foreign Policy

Vernon V. Aspaturian

INTRODUCTION: THE BREZHNEV LEGACY AND THE GORBACHEV VISION

The death of Leonid Brezhnev in November 1982, after eighteen long years of leadership, ended one of the longest periods of leadership and political stability in the history of the Soviet Union, and marked the end of one era and the prelude for a new potentially long period of leadership under Mikhall S. Gorbachev, who became Brezhnev's definitive successor in April 1985. During the long period of the Brezhnev era, the United States entered into an extraordinary period of fractured and interrupted leadership as Brezhnev was forced to deal with no less than five different American presidents during this period. With the inauguration of President Ronald Reagan in 1981 and the death of Brezhnev in the following year, the leadership situation was dramatically reversed, as President Reagan was compelled to deal with no less than four Soviet leaders (Brezhnev, Andropov, Chemenko, and Gorbachev) during a relatively short period of time as the Soviet leadership entered into a debilitating interregnum and a prolonged power struggle, which has yet to run its course, although Gorbachev has demonstrated extraordinary ability in consolidating his power in the face of strong resistance and even opposition to his far-reaching program.

There is no doubt that Brezhnev's death marked the end of a definite era in the evolution of the Soviet state and its role and status in the international system. Furthermore, he left a distinctive legacy, although the last years of his incumbency were marred by stagnation and immobility and tainted by internal corruption because of his infirmities and failing physical powers. The Brezhnev legacy is a mixture of achievements and failures in both domestic and foreign policy, with the failures accumulating towards the end of his incumbency. Thus, Brezhnev's death marks the beginning of a new era because of the unfinished goals, frustrations, and serious chronic problems that were left to his successors, who in turn were confronted by a new American president determined to reverse the course of Soviet-American relations and to blunt the growth and expansion of Soviet power and influence.

Brezhnev's achievements, particularly in foreign and military policy were impressive and extensive, but questionably durable or sustainable. Soviet foreign policy is shaped by many variables, but among the most important and difficult to calculate, is the Soviet perception of risks, opportunities, and costs in pursuing objectives, whatever they might be at any given time. When risk and cost perceptions are low and opportunity perceptions are high, Soviet leaders are inclined to pursue their foreign policy goals more vigorously and exploit opportunities with greater alacrity, even at the expense of resolving serious domestic problems. When risk and cost perceptions are high, Soviet leaders are likely to behave more cautiously and prudently, consolidating and retrenching rather than expanding their power, and they are likely to concentrate on the solution of pressing internal problems rather than risk confrontation abroad. During the decade of the 1970s, as a result of the Vietnam debacle, Watergate, and the consequent general U.S. disillusionment and demoralization, the Brezhnev leadership perceived the risks and costs of acting more vigorously in foreign policy to be low. In fact, the low risk environment came as a welcome surprise, since initially Moscow envisioned an essentially long period of standoff between the USSR and the U.S.A. after the SALT I agreements signed in 1972. But, soon after Nixon's reelection, when Watergate overwhelmed him and he was forced to resign, the United States appeared to enter a period of self-paralysis and incapacity to behave assertively in foreign policy, which was viewed by many Soviet leaders as the beginning of a long period of irreversible decline for the United States. Brezhnev decided to mortgage the immediate Soviet domestic future by investing in expanding Soviet power abroad.

It was during this period that Brezhnev's achievements manifested themselves as the Soviet Union (1) achieved status and recognition as a global power, with global interests and presence; (2) achieved and gained recognition as the political and military equal of the United States; (3)

established an extended empire of dependent and client states beyond the Soviet periphery in South and Southeast Asia, the Middle East, Africa, and the Caribbean; and (4) shifted the overall world or strategic balance of power or "correlation of forces" to immense Soviet advantage.

His accomplishments were not achieved without a serious price. Soviet successes in foreign policy generated an inevitable serious counter-response from the United States and its allies, which in turn undercut and threatened to nullify many of Brezhnevs' successes. The Soviet leadership mistakenly perceived a temporary reversible U.S. debility for a secular, irreversible decline and were thus ill-prepared to deal with a reassertive United States under a new president, and its foreign policy floundered and foundered during the decade of the 1980s, aggravated by the interrupted succession process. Under Brezhnev, the Soviet Union seriously overextended itself by overestimating its own capabilities and underestimating the recuperative capabilities of the United States. Its invasion of Afghanistan bogged down into a prolonged, inclusive, and debilitating guerrilla war, and Gorbachev has set high on his agenda an extrication of Soviet involvement in Afghanistan, even if it risks the overthrow of a client regime by anti-Soviet insurgents. Neither the situation in Ethiopia or Angola, two of its most important client states in the Third World, has been terminally resolved, and Moscow may be forced to retreat and retrench here as well, in order to eliminate the serious economic burden of sustaining these regimes, including the expense of supporting some 40,000 Cuban troops in Africa. There were additional signs of Soviet disenchantment and disillusionment with its empire of client states in the Third World, which have become a potentially serious, endless drain upon Soviet resources and efforts. This may also prompt a limited retrenchment from its overextended positions in Central America and the Caribbean. In summary, the expansion of Soviet power and influence has now resulted in the familiar "burdens of empire," without the compensating yield of economic benefit for the Soviet Union.

Furthermore, the challenge of Solidarity to the Communist regime in Poland, the growing autonomy of East European states, and the failure to resolve its prolonged deterioration of relations with Communist China required that Moscow pay more attention to "consolidating the positions of world socialism" at the expense of supporting "wars of national liberation," two of the foreign policy goals enumerated in the Soviet Constitution.

The most serious and crippling price which the Soviet Union paid for its immense military growth and globalist ambitions was the dislocation of the Soviet economy, which entered into a period of stagnation and decline, threatening to leave the Soviet Union and its East European client states far behind the United States, Western Europe, and Japan.

The stagnation of the Soviet economy had manifold domestic reverberations. The standard of living grew at an ominously slow pace, as both workers and managers accustomed themselves to low productivity and inefficiency, and a series of shortfalls in agricultural production created serious food problems for the country. As the non-Russian nationalities, particularly the Moslems of Central Asia, grew at a rapid pace while the Russian and Slavic population neared zero-population growth, this asymmetrical demographic growth threatened not only the integrity of the labor force, but the Soviet military as well. The less educated and skilled Moslem youths, whose knowledge of Russian is poor or nonexistent, contribute an ever growing proportion of both the labor force and military recruits. Furthermore as the ethnic balance tilts in favor of the non-Slavic population, the demand and competition for relatively diminished scarce resources and wealth among the various nationalities and republics becomes sharper and more aggravated. Similar problems were generated in the Soviet Bloc as a whole, as the Stalinist socioeconomic model exhausted its potential for further constructive development. These accumulated domestic problems, of course, seriously compromised the capacity of the Soviet Union to advance its globalist ambitions abroad, which became painfully evident as the decade of the 1980s unfolded.

With the advent of the Reagan Administration and its more assertive, even belligerent rhetoric, and the promise of corresponding behavior, Moscow was compelled to enter into a new phase in its competition with the U.S.A. Squeezed between the war in Afghanistan and the political turmoil in Poland, burdened with insistent and expensive demands by its Third World clients for greater military and economic assistance as they faced increasing guerrilla opposition supported by the United States, successive Soviet leaders were loathe to risk confrontation with the Reagan Administration and engage it in a new and higher level of arms competition in the age of high technology. Moscow gradually entered into a defensive and retrenchist mode as the new Reagan Administration signalled that the years of low-risk easy pickings for Moscow were over, as the U.S. pressure on Cuba and Nicaragua increased, the regime in Grenada was forcibly overthrown, the military assistance to the Afghan guerrillas and others was escalated, and the intermediate-range nuclear missiles were deployed in Western Europe, to counter the Soviet deployment of SS-20s missiles. The prolonged leadership uncertainty, the serious domestic problems, and American reassertiveness all congealed to compel a fundamental reexamination of the Soviet agenda and its priorities in foreign and domestic policy.

There is little question but that Gorbachev has repudiated the Brezhnev legacy for the most part, and to this end has embarked upon an at least partial rehabilitation not only of Brezhnev's predecessor, Khrushchev, but of Nicolai Bukharin as well, who was executed by Stalin in 1938. Some Gorbachev supporters link Gorbachev's reform program to both the ideas of Bukharin and the reforms introduced by Khrushchev, which were arrested and reversed in part by Brezhnev.

Recognizing that Brezhnev's inattention to accumulating domestic problems had crippled its capacity to keep up with or benefit from the main currents of development in science and technology, and that the USSR was seriously lagging behind the United States, Western Europe, and Japan in these areas, Gorbachev has proposed an ambitious, radical, and extensive program of reforming and revitalizing the Soviet system. In Gorbachev's view, unless the situation is reversed quickly and effectively, the Soviet Union would be left behind as a second-rate, semideveloped giant floundering in economic and social stagnation and in political and military decline.

Gorbachev's vast and ambitious program for reforming the Soviet system has received considerable publicity outside the Soviet Union and in many quarters he is more popular outside the country than inside. The new Soviet leader has an excellent "public relations" sense and his program has achieved considerable attention and support because of the way he has packaged and presented it, creating and inventing new catchwords and slogans, some of which have become virtually a part of an international vocabulary. The overall architectonic catchword for his reform program is *perestroika,* the Russian world for restructuring. *Perestroika* is conceived to pervade all aspects and sectors of Soviet society, but generally it is interpreted as meaning the massive reorganization of the economic system and the replenishment of its bureaucracy with younger, more vigorous, and more competent personnel as the holdovers are eased out or purged. But as Gorbachev and his supporters have asserted, *perestroika,* or restructuring, must also be applied to the government, to the military, to the police, to the health system, to culture and education, to journalism, and last but not least to foreign policy.

Although *perestroika* is the key, central concept, a close runner up is the concept of *glasnost,* that is, publicity or "make known" (incorrectly translated as "openness"). *Glasnost* has also caught the Western imagination and although it has resulted in an unprecedented display of hitherto taboo expressions of opinion or even revelations of truths and falsehoods in virtually all walks of Soviet life, it does not mean "freedom of expression" in the Western sense. What it does mean is greater tolerance for differing views and opinions, greater discussion of hitherto taboo subjects, whether in the Soviet past or present, and in general, acceptance of the notion "that whatever is not prohibited is permissible," rather than the hitherto prevailing principle that whatever is not explicitly permissible is implicitly prohibited. As a result of *glasnost,* Soviet journalists have allowed their pages to be used for a wide range of critical views, including letters from readers. Not only past Soviet history has been subjected to reexamination, but subjects like unemployment, prostitution, drug addiction, organized crime, official falsehoods, elite privileges, the war in Afghanistan, and nationality relations (including the rise of Russian and non-Russian nationalisms and inter-nationality antagonisms, many of which were supposedly nonexistent social phenomena) have been given considerable attention. Journalists openly discuss whether or not *glasnost* is "for real" or whether it will last. Indeed, in many ways, it has been the element in Gorbachev's program which has drawn the greatest fire from his detractors. Both Secret Police Chief Chebrikov and the Second Secretary, Yegor Ligachev, have called for more restraints on freedom of expression, and even Gorbachev, after the so-called Yeltsin Affair in the Fall of 1987, has appeared to call for more prudence in exercising *glasnost,* emphasizing that it does not mean the total absence of restraint and that it must be exercised to advance the cause of socialism, not to engage in antisocialist or anti-Soviet expression of opinion. Perhaps, even more ominously for Gorbachev, his own hand-picked Minister of Defense, Marshal Yazov, has sharply criticized *glasnost* for allowing the press to publish views that tarnish the military, undermine patriotism, and encourage young people to evade the military service. These three members of the Politburo represent the three most important strategic elites or power structures in the Soviet system: the Party Apparatus, the Secret Police, and the Armed Forces.

Perhaps nothing has forced the emergence of polarization in the post-Brezhnev leadership more than the concept, practice, and more importantly, the public expectation of *glasnost.* It is the element of Gorbachev's program that has attracted the most visible and explicit criticism from within the leadership; with Chebrikov, Ligachev, and Yazov being the most conspicuous and audible. In many ways *perestroika* and *glasnost* are contradictory, and although both are viewed by their detractors and the cautious as being socially and politically destabilizing, *perestroika* is viewed as essentially a potentially constructive and positive force which can provide a more durable stability if successful, whereas *glasnost* is viewed as inherently destabilizing, an impetus to infinite and inexhaustible criticism of the Soviet system, and ultimately demoralizing and subversive. Thus, while all of Gorbachev's colleagues on the Politburo subscribe to *perestroika,* they are not persuaded with respect to *glasnost.*

Another controversial component of his reform program is called *demokratizatsiya* (democratization), which means instituting more extensive and intensive participation by the citizenry in Soviet decision making and public discussion. Although the participation called for is mild and modest by Western standards, it has caused considerable apprehension among conservatives and has been misinterpreted by some reformers as a call for authentic democratization, including even the possibility of a multiparty system. Gorbachev's initial intentions in this regard, however, are limited to increasing participation within the existing single-party system. He has called for multiple candidacy and authentic secret elections at the lowest levels of the party and Soviet organizations as well as in economic and social enterprises. The results, so far, have been exceedingly modest and where implemented has engendered disorientation since many Soviet citizens find it difficult to choose between supposedly equally acceptable nominees offered by the party. One unintended consequence of *demokratizatsiya*, however, has been the spontaneous generation of thousands of "unofficial" organizations of various kinds, including ultranationalist Russian organizations, as well as environmental groups, and various other kinds of social and political groupings, all outside the framework and control of the party and government. Only a few years ago all of these organizations would have been crushed and its members punished. Even organizations interested in arms control, foreign policy, and related issues have gingerly made their appearance. Eventually, however, this may be repressed once again.

And, finally, there is the component known as "the new political thinking," which is a euphemism for ideological restructuring. The "new political thinking" is designed to provide coherence and theoretical guideposts to *perestroika, glasnost,* and *demokratizatsiya,* and to properly relate them to one another. The "new political thinking" calls for a radical psychological and cognitive reorientation of Soviet thought processes, to purge oneself of old obsolete, ossified "truths" and falsehoods and to assume a more critical and honest evaluation of events. It, in effect, calls for the shedding of the "false consciousness" that pervades Soviet thinking and behavior (the idea that there is always only a single truth), and instead it calls for the perception of problems and issues in terms of not a single, absolute truth or course of action, but in terms of various acceptable or tolerable alternative approaches to the solution or management of problems. An important subcategory of the "new political thinking" is a "new foreign policy philosophy," which will be discussed in greater detail subsequently.

THE SOVIET UNION AS AN ACTOR IN THE INTERNATIONAL SYSTEM

At one time it was fashionable to emphasize the enigmatic aspects of Soviet foreign policy behavior, to accentuate its remarkable capacity for evoking the most variegated and contradictory responses to its diplomacy. Edward Crankshaw could write that while "in its distant objectives, the foreign policy of the Soviet Union is less obscure and more coherent than that of any other country," its immediate intentions and the motivations behind its day-to-day diplomacy often appeared incoherent, capricious, and almost always enigmatic.[1] As the Soviet state crosses its seventieth anniversary, we might observe that its distant objectives have become less clear-cut, more ambivalent, and infinitely more complex, while its immediate purposes and goals in foreign policy have become less obscure, even though they are still no less capricious and contradictory than its previous behavior.

To understand Soviet foreign policy it is necessary to properly define the Soviet Union as an actor in the international system. This is by no means a simple task. The Soviet Union increasingly betrays many characteristics similar to those of other actors, particularly the United States, which has increasingly, although not always consciously or advertently, served as a model for the Soviet Union. This stems from the fact that during the past two decades the United States has stood at the apex of the international system, and the Soviet Union has been its principal rival and challenger for that status.

The many characteristics which the Soviet Union shares with the United States as a global power or with China, however, should not obscure the significant characteristics of the Soviet Union that makes it unique. Indeed, the two sets of characteristics the Soviet Union shares with the United States and China—global power and revolutionary ideology respectively—emerge as only one source of confusion about Soviet foreign policy behavior. The duality of the Soviet Union as the center of a revolutionary movement, defined as its party role, and as a state among states in the international system, has long been recognized. Yet the perception of the Soviet Union as a dual entity is an oversimplification of a more complicated existence. The Soviet Union is more than a dualistic entity. It is a mulitple one, whose components have both contradictory and competing constituencies with intersecting, conflicting, and harmonious interests, inspired by a variety of motives. The Soviet Union as the successor to the historical Russian national state, its current manifestation as legal-constitutional multinational federal-confederal state representing the interests of its component nations individually in the international community, and its position as a commonwealth of nations representing their interests collectively, provide the content and substance for three additional Soviet roles.

The USSR is endowed with multiple identities in international affairs, influenced by a wide spectrum of elements that intersect to fundamentally impinge on the contours of Soviet behavior. Currently the Soviet Union is the only authentic multiple actor in international affairs. It reveals itself as an aggregate of five distinct but interrelated institutionalized personalities. These are (1) state, (2) party, (3) Russian nation, (4) non-Russian nation (variable), and (5) multinational commonwealth.

---

[1]*New York Times Book Review,* July 3, 1949, p. 4.

All the identities developed in the periods of evolution in the Soviet system are not equally significant in assessing the behavior of the Soviet Union. Their relative importance varies not only with the changing goals of the leadership, but also with the changing alignment of internal forces, the corresponding demands and pressures of its various constituencies, and the opportunities and risks that manifest themselves in the international environment.

As a *state*, the Soviet Union functions in its broadest dimension, operating in four of the five environments to which it must respond. As a state, the Soviet Union plays no formal or overt role in the world Communist movement. In its capacity as a state, the Soviet Union must articulate the interests of social constitutencies within the sociopolitical system in accordance with a shifting structure of power and priorities. These, in turn, must be coordinated with the demands of the nationalities within the Soviet multinational order, and harmonized with the interests of other Communist states in the interstate subsystem, before it acts within the general interstate system.

In the general interstate system, the Soviet Union functions as one of the two global powers. In this capacity, it must accept minimum obligations in return for corresponding rights and privileges. The increasing importance of the Soviet Union as an actor in the international system has impressed itself on the consciousness of the Soviet leaders, imparting to Soviet behavior a measure of maturity, responsibility, and prudence that has, at the same time, served to erode its responsibilities as the center of a revolutionary movement.

In its capacity as a state, the Soviet Union is charged with defending and advancing the interests of the Soviet Union and its domestic constituencies against those of other states in the international community. The foreign policy outputs of the Soviet state are formulated internally in accordance with a changing spectrum of priorities arrived at in response to the constituencies that can influence the process. These constituencies can be nationalities, institutions, bureaucratic structures, sociofunctional elites and social classes, and subgroups within them. The foreign policy of the Soviet state may assume the patterns of self-perpetuation (security and maintenance), self-extension (aggrandizement), or self-fulfillment (development, prestige, and status), either for the state as a whole or constituencies, individually and collectively.

The credentials of the Soviet state as a global power rest upon its powerful economic-technological foundations and the possession of advanced technological weapons systems, including thermonuclear warheads and ICBM delivery systems. The Soviet Union is thereby able to assert unilaterally an interest anywhere and take corresponding action, including intervention. As a global power, the Soviet Union has intervened successfully in the Caribbean and the Middle East, leading to the creation of allied states in both regions, and in recent years has successfully established itself on the Horn of Africa and in southern Africa. It has successfully maintained a presence in South Asia and Southeast Asia, where its rivalry is increasingly with China, rather than the United States. The Soviet Union has supplemented its military prowess with diplomatic initatives, economic assistance programs, and political support of selected states in an endeavor to shift its international influence from a military foundation to a more durable foundation of prestige, but with less success.

The Soviet role as a global power is further enhanced by being the leader of an ideological-military coalition (institutionalized as the Warsaw Treaty Organization) that reigns supreme in its own region, Eastern Europe, in which the USSR tolerates no external intrusion. Beginning in 1971, the United States and West Germany through a series of treaties have informally recognized Eastern Europe as a Soviet sphere of influence. The simultaneous immunity of the Soviet regional sphere from external intervention and the formalization of an exclusive Soviet right to intervene in Eastern Europe was consecrated in the enunciation of the so-called Brezhnev or Socialist Commonwealth Doctrine in 1968 after the military intervention and occupation of Czechoslovakia by the military forces of the Soviet Union, Poland, East Germany, Hungary, and Bulgaria.

Before the advent of the Soviet state there existed the Communist (Bolshevik) party. It inspired and created the Soviet state in response to the values of its ideology, Marxism-Leninism. One of its important goals was to facilitate and encourage the communization of the world, allegedly in consonance with the imperatives of inexorable historical laws of development. Originally, the Soviet state was conceived as an instrument of the party in its mission of communizing the world. The Soviet socialist order, the world Communist movement, and the Communist interstate subsystem were creations of the Soviet Union in its capacity as a revolutionary party in furtherance of this aim. Thus, the party fashioned the very environments within which it functions, but the feedback effects of these creations have in turn influenced the changing roles and functions of the party.

In its capacity as a revolutionary party, the Soviet Union performs the following roles and functions: (1) the ideological guardian of the existing Soviet sociopolitical order (socialist society) and the initiator and architect of its future development (Communist society); (2) the ideological and organizational leader of the ruling Communist parties; and (3) the ideological leader and source of inspirational and material support of the universe of Communist parties, made up of both ruling and nonruling Communist parties. As a party, the Soviet Union functions in the three environments of the Soviet sociopolitical order, the Communist interstate subsystem, and the world Communist parties.

In recent decades, the prominence of the party has waned as that of the Soviet Union as a state has waxed. Since Stalin's death in 1953, the Soviet grip on the interstate subsystem and the world Communist movement has loosened. China has emerged as a rival of the Soviet Union in Communist environments as well as the general interstate system, while the East European states have achieved degrees of autonomy in domestic affairs (within parameters decreed by the Soviet Union). Under Khrushchev, Moscow unilaterally renounced its position as the leader of the world Communist movement, fragmented and divided since 1960, although the Soviet Union simply retrograded itself to be the leader of a truncated movement, of which China and Albania and a number of other parties are not formal members. While China is not the leader of a rival world Communist movement, it remains a rival of the Soviet Union within the world of Communist states and parties.

These trends will probably continue during the Gorbachev era as this attempt to promote his reform program in Eastern Europe meets with varying responses, ranging from all out rejection in Romania to a cautious and prudent welcome in Poland and Hungary. In any event, East European states are likely to assume greater leverage in dealing with Moscow and greater autonomy in charting their own directions in both internal and external policy.

In addition to these two major identities of the Soviet Union in international affairs, a brief word is in order with respect to one other identity: the Russian national state, which has contributed to the confusion about Soviet foreign policy. The Soviet Union includes within its domain the entire Great Russian Nation and is territorially and demographically indistinguishable from the Russian Empire that preceded it as a Russian national state. Its constituency is thus the entire Great Russian Nation. In this role, the Soviet state manipulates patriotic symbols, commemorates national glories, venerates historic heroes (mostly tsars and generals), worships at national shrines, extols Russian culture and language, and celebrates the lofty goals and achievements of Holy Mother Russia, while rationalizing and downplaying the more negative features of the Russian tradition.

The powerful role of the Soviet Union as a Russian national state, however, should not be interpreted as meaning that the USSR does not play a meaningful role in its representation of the interests of the non-Russian nationalities. The Soviet Union is an authentic multinational state. It is the state embodiment of more than a dozen major nations and scores of smaller ones who have no role in the international community other than their representation through the Soviet State. Two major

Soviet Union Republics, the Ukraine and Byelorussia, have partial separate representation in the interstate system as members of the United Nations and affiliated agencies, but the remaining Soviet nations are bereft of such recognition.

ANALYZING SOVIET FOREIGN POLICY BEHAVIOR

During the decade of the 1970s, as Soviet military capabilities developed and the United States reduced its international commitments in the wake of the Vietnam War, appearing immobilized by the wounds of the Vietnam defeat and the Watergate scandal that resulted in a series of fractured presidencies, Soviet ideological goals appeared to reassert themselves with greater force in Soviet foreign policy behavior. The resurgence of ideological imperatives was accompanied by the increasing prominence of Brezhnev in his capacity as Secretary-General of the party in Soviet foreign policy and foreign affairs.

As the Soviet Union expanded its global activities and reached into the remote regions of Asia, Africa, and Latin America to lend military support and assistance to friendly revolutionary movements and regimes, ideology was increasingly invoked to legitimize its behavior. The apparent re-ideologization of Soviet foreign policy found explicit expression in the new Brezhnev Constitution of 1977. In an entirely new and juridically unprecedented Chapter on Foreign Policy, Article 28 in effect converted ideological commitments into state obligations by defining the goals of Soviet foreign policy as follows:

> The foreign policy of the USSR is aimed at ensuring international conditions favorable for building communism in the USSR, safeguarding the state interests of the Soviet Union, consolidating the positions of world socialism, supporting the struggle of peoples for national liberation and social progress, preventing wars of aggression, achieving universal and complete disarmament, and consistently implementing the principle of peaceful co-existence of states with different social systems.

It would be reasonable to assume that the seven distinct goals of Soviet foreign policy as enumerated above are listed in order of priority and precedence, in which case, "consolidating the positions of world socialism" (3) and "supporting the struggle . . . for national liberation" (4) have a conspicuously higher priority than either arms control and disarmament (6) or "peaceful coexistence of states with different social systems" (7), which brings up the rear.

The new constitution's Chapter on Foreign Policy thus reflected the goals and ambitions of an ideological global power, sufficiently confident and self-assured to pronounce its ideological goals in foreign policy more openly and militantly. Earlier, ideological goals in foreign policy were clearly separated from official state policy because their inclusion aroused strong counterreactions and responses from the outside world and could endanger the security and survival of the Soviet state. The advent of the Reagan Administration in the United States in 1981 with its own ideological bent in foreign policy would seem to reconfirm that, whenever Moscow is perceived as pursuing ideological goals in foreign policy, a strong counterideological response is stimulated in other countries, and state relations become entangled in ideological conflict, rendering the diplomatic settlement of outstanding issues much more difficult.

With the appearance of an assertive American administration, which has injected a strong dose of ideology into U.S. foreign policy, the new Soviet leader, Gorbachev, was impelled to call for a moratorium in the ideological conflict at the interstate level, since Moscow is at a disadvantage at this level of ideological confrontation. "Removing the ideological edge conflict from interstate relations,"[2] as Gorbachev has expressed, would mean that formal Soviet diplomatic behavior would be stripped of its ideological color and the ideological conflict would then be sustained only at the nonstate level, where the Soviet Union has the advantage. Since Brezhnev, in the new Soviet Constitution of 1977, formally and constitutionally invested the Soviet state with ideological commitments in the prosecution of its foreign policy, it may be difficult for the Soviet Union to persuasively shed its ideological edge in interstate behavior. For example, the Soviet military presence in Afghanistan is described as the fulfillment of its "internationalist duty," which is essentially a self-declared and self-assumed ideological obligation. A Soviet decision to withdraw its troops from Afghanistan would be an important indication that Gorbachev is serious about removing the "ideological edge" from Soviet state behavior abroad.

CONTINUITY AND CHANGE IN RUSSIAN FOREIGN POLICY

In order to draw a proper appraisal of Soviet diplomacy, the voluntaristic aspects of Soviet foreign policy must always be measured against its power to overcome international objective reality. Thus, although the Soviet Union can plan the calculated growth of the economic and military foundations of its power, it cannot "plan" foreign policy. This fact was eloquently stated by Maxim Litvinov to the Central Executive Committee in 1929:

> Unlike other Commissariats, the Commissariat for Foreign Affairs cannot, unfortunately, put forward a five-year plan of work, a plan for the

[2]M. S. Gorbachev, *Perestroika* (New York: Harper & Row, 1987), p. 221.

development of foreign policy. . . . In . . . drawing up the plan of economic development we start from our own aspirations and wishes, from a calculation of our own potentialities, and from the firm principles of our entire policy, but in examining the development of foreign policy we have to deal with a number of factors that are scarcely subject to calculation, with a number of elements outside our control and the scope of our action. International affairs are composed not only of our own aspirations and actions, but of those of a large number of countries . . . pursuing other aims than ours, and using other means to achieve those aims that we allow.[3]

In the initial stages of the Bolshevik Republic, its foreign policy was virtually at the mercy of external forces over which it could exercise little control, and Soviet diplomacy assumed the characteristic contours of a weak power struggling for survival under onerous conditions. As its economic and military position improved, it gradually assumed the characteristics of a great power and, given its geographical and cultural context, it took on the distinctive features of its tsarist predecessors and the impulse to subjugate its immediate neighbors.

The Geographic and Historical Inheritance

"Marxism," according to a Soviet specialist on diplomacy, "teaches that economic factors determine the foreign policy and diplomacy of a state only in the long run, and that politics and diplomacy are, in a certain sense, conditioned by the concrete historical period and by many other elements (not excluding even, for instance, the geographical situation of a given country).[4] Geography is the most permanent conditioning factor in a country's foreign policy; for location, topography, and natural resources are significant—and often decisive—determinants of a country's economic and military power.

The Soviet Union, like tsarist Russia before it, is the largest single continuous intercontinental empire in the world. Embracing fully half of two continents, the Soviet Union has the world's longest and most exposed frontier, which is at once both its greatest potential hazard and one of its prime assets in international politics. As a part of both Europe and Asia, and embracing more than 150 ethnic and linguistic groups ranging from the most sophisticated nations to the most primitive, the USSR achieves a unique microcosmic character denied any other country, including the United States with its ethnically variegated but linguistically assimilated population. Russia's serpentine frontier is both a consequence of the indefensibility of the central Russian plain and, at the same time,

---

[3]*Protokoly Zasedani Tsentralnovo Ispolnitelnovo Komiteta Sovetov*, Bulletin 14 (Moscow, 1930), p. 1.

[4]I. Kozhevnikov, "Engels on Nineteenth Century Russian Diplomacy," *Sovetskoye Gosudarstv ii Pravo*, no. 12 (December 1950) pp. 18–34.

an important conditioning factor in the further evolution and execution of its foreign policy. For a weak Russia, such a frontier affords maximum exposure to attack, but for a powerful Russian state, this extended frontier, bordering on nearly a dozen states, offers an enviable and limitless choice for the exertion of diplomatic pressure. Since 1939, the Soviet Union has annexed four of its former neighbors, seized territory from seven more, and has made territorial demands upon two others; most of this territory had been previously lost by a weak Russia. Of all her bordering states, only Afghanistan had not been imposed on to cede territory to the Soviet Union, an uncharacteristic anomaly that was rectified in December 1979 when the Soviet Union invaded Afghanistan with over one hundred thousand troops.

In the past, Russia's geographical position has exposed her to continuous depredations and subjugation from all directions—an inevitable consequence of political disunity in a geographically indefensible community. But if geography simplified the conquest of a divided Russia, it also facilitated the expansion of a united and powerful Russian state, which pushed out in all directions until it was arrested by superior force.

In the absence of more obvious geographical obstacles to her enemies, Russia's physical security became irrevocably attached to land space, while her psychological security became inseparable from political centralization. This conviction was confirmed by Stalin, himself, on the occasion of Moscow's eight hundreth anniversary in 1947:

> Moscow's service consists first and foremost in the fact that it became the foundation for the unification of a disunited Russia into a single state with a single government, a single leadership. No country in the world that has not been able to free itself of feudal disunity and wrangling among princes can hope to preserve its independence or score substantial economic and cultural progress. Only a country united in a single centralized state can count on being able to make substantial cultural-economic progress and assert its independence.[5]

It is a persisting fact of Russian history that this dual quest for physical and psychological security has produced in Russian foreign policy a unique pattern. A divided Russia invites attack, but a united Russia stimulates expansion in all directions. The revolutions in 1917, and the terrible purges of the 1930s when Stalin undertook to enforce unity at home, exposed Russia's internal schisms to the world and stimulated foreign intervention. In each crisis, after surviving the initial assault from without, she embarked on a campaign designed to carry her beyond her self-declared national frontiers. The campaign failed in 1921, but she

[5]*Pravda*, September 11, 1947.

succeeded after World War II, bringing all of Eastern Europe under her hegemony.

The Bolsheviks fell heir not only to Russia's geography and natural resources, but also to the bulk of her population, her language, and the Russian historical and cultural legacy. Marxism gave Russia new goals and aspirations, but once the decision was taken to survive as a national state, even on a temporary and instrumental basis, the Soviet Union could not evade assuming the contours of a Russian state and falling heir to the assets and liabilities of its predecessors. Foreign attitudes remained remarkably constant; fears and suspicions, sympathies and attachments, were reinforced more than erased. Designs on Soviet territory still came from the same quarter, exposure to attack remained in the same places, and the economic and commercial lifelines of the tsars became no less indispensable to the new regime. In short, even if the Soviet Union refused to remain Russia, Japan remained Japan, Poland remained Poland, and the U.S.A. remained the U.S.A. Moscow eagerly laid claim to all the advantages of historic Russia, and the outside world just as assiduously refused to permit her to evade the liabilities and vulnerabilities of the Russian past. Thus, partly by choice and partly by necessity, the foreign policy of the Soviet Union could not but assume some of the contours of its predecessors.

The impact of a voluntaristic doctrine like Marxism on the geographical facts of Russia and her messianic traditions not only reinforced the psychological obsession for security, but provided an ideological rationale for assuming the implacable hostility of the outside world and sanctified Russian expansion with the ethical mission of liberating the downtrodden masses of the world from their oppressors. The hostile West of the Slavophils became the hostility of capitalism and imperialism; instead of the parochial messianism of the pan-Slav enthusiasts, Marxism provided Russia with a mission of universal transcendence—transforming the outside world into her own image, in fulfillment of her historic destiny and as the only permanent guarantee of absolute security. Up until the Twentieth Party Congress in 1956, the Leninist-Stalinist thesis that "the destruction of capitalist encirclement and the destruction of the danger of capitalist intervention are possible only as a result of the victory of the proletarian revolution, at least in several large countries,"[6] continued to be accepted; "capitalist encirclement" was declared ended by Stalin's successors.

Since the enormous power of the Soviet Union and its status as a global power undermined the credibility of the traditional Russian-Soviet invocation of security as a justification for intervention in the domestic life of its neighbors, Soviet spokespersons now justify Soviet behavior not

[6]*Kommunist*, January 1953, no. 2, p. 15.

so much in terms of security, but as an imperative of Moscow's global power credentials and credibility. In the words of Alexander Bovin, an influential foreign policy adviser, the crackdown in Poland gave an ominous and concrete meaning to the words, "consolidating the positions of world socialism," which appear in the new Soviet constitution:

> It is not a matter of our physical security . . . it is a matter of relations between a great power and smaller states that are socialist states. Not only security is at stake but ideology as well. For example, if Lech Walesa became leader of Poland, Poland would leave the Warsaw Pact. That would not be a threat to our physical security, but it would be a terrible loss of prestige. It would be like what happened to you in Iran. When the United States was thrown out of Iran, the United States lost prestige everywhere.[7]

Whereas in the past, when the Soviet Union was weak, indiscriminate emphasis on the revolutionary aspects of its foreign policy tended to undermine its basic instinct to survive, now its military reflexes tend to subvert not only its continuing leadership of world Communism, and the eventual success of the movement itself, but also to impart to Soviet behavior an imperial cast.

SOVIET IDEOLOGY AND FOREIGN POLICY

The relationship between Soviet ideology and foreign policy has been subject to great controversy, ranging from the view that it is substantially irrelevant to the conviction that foreign policy is rigidly dictated by ideology. The precise role that ideology plays in Soviet foreign policy is also subject to periodic and episodic controversy inside the Soviet Union as well, with each new leader or set of leaders often redefining and reshaping ideology in reference to Soviet foreign policy. Every Soviet leader from Lenin to Gorbachev has made major emendations in Soviet ideology in terms of its relevance for foreign policy. Since Soviet ideology is not a unidimensional or monofunctional entity, various dimensions of Soviet ideology have been "restructured" periodically, to use Gorbachev's favorite term, at different times and in differing degrees. The function of Soviet ideology in setting and defining ultimate, often transcendental goals, which has been described previously, is the best and most widely known, but sometimes thought to be its only function. Actually, Soviet ideology performs five additional distinct, interrelated, but separable, functions in Soviet behavior, as follows:

1. As a system of knowledge, and as an analytical prism, it reflects an image of the existing social order and the distinctive analytical instruments

[7]Joseph Kraft, "Letter From Moscow," *The New Yorker*, January 31, 1983.

(dialectical laws, and categories like the "class struggle," "historical stages," and so on) for its diagnosis and prognosis);

2. As an action strategy with which to accelerate the transformation of the existing social order into the communist millenium;
3. As a system of communication, unifying and coordinating the activities of its adherents;
4. As a system of higher rationalization to justify, obscure, or conceal the chasms that may develop between theory and practice;
5. As a symbol of continuity and legitimacy.

Under Gorbachev, Soviet ideology in general, but in terms of its application to foreign policy in particular, is in the middle of a major restructuring process, in which all of its functional dimensions are subject to radical review and change, perhaps more far-reaching than in previous periods. It should be emphasized, however, that the process is only in its beginning and discussion stage; what the ultimate consequence will be, both in terms of restructuring and its relevance for foreign policy, at this point remains unknown. "The new political thinking," as the restructuring of ideology is called, and the "new foreign policy philosophy," as the subcomponent relating to foreign policy is dubbed, for the first time promises a radical reexamination and overhaul of Soviet ideology's analytical and epistemological dimension. Previously, the goal orienting and action strategy components have been the most conspicuously tampered with, whereas the epistemological-analytical dimension has suffered relatively little change. Both Stalin and Khrushchev. made substantial and critical emendations with respect to the "inevitability of war" analytical thesis and the nature of the ideological polarization and confrontation between socialism and capitalism, but their principal innovations were in the realm of strategy and approach, rather than epistemology and cognitive analysis.

The Changing Soviet Image of the World

The Soviet ideological prism has traditionally reflected an image of the world that is virtually unrecognizable to a non-Communist, yet it is on this image that Soviet foreign policy has been based. It reflects a world of incessant conflict and change, in which institutions, loyalties, and philosophies arise and decay in accordance with the convulsive rhythm of the dialectic, which implacably propels it on a predetermined arc to a preordained future—world Communism. This image has been accepted as the real world by Soviet leaders. Their foreign policy rested upon the conviction that Marxism-Leninism is a scientific system that has uncovered and revealed the fundamental and implacable laws of social evolution, and, hence, afforded its adherents the unique advantage of prediction and partial control of events. This conviction has imparted to Soviet diplomacy an air of supreme confidence and dogmatic self-righteousness:

> Soviet diplomacy . . . wields a weapon possessed by none of its rivals or opponents. Soviet diplomacy is fortified by a scientific theory of Marxism-Leninism. This doctrine lays down the unshakeable laws of social development. By revealing these norms, it gives the possibility not only of understanding the current tendencies of international life, but also of permitting the desirable collaboration with the march of events. Such are the special advantages held by Soviet diplomacy. They give it a special position in international life and explain its outstanding successes.[8]

The history of Soviet diplomacy, however, is by no means a uniform record of success, although "errors" in foreign policy are ascribed not to the doctrine, but to the improper apprehension and application of these infallible laws. Failure to apply these laws properly, according to the Soviet view, divorces foreign policy from international realities. Although it is true that "the record of Soviet diplomacy shows an inability to distinguish between the real and the imaginary, a series of false calculations about the capabilities and intentions of foreign countries, and a record of clumsy coordination between diplomacy and propaganda,"[9] still, Marxism-Leninism, on the whole, has furnished a system of analysis that has yielded a sufficiently utilitarian comprehension of power. The dogmatic reliance on techniques and methods that have proven successful under other conditions and the frequent refusal to jettison concepts that either have outlived their usefulness or consistently produce dismal results in terms of foreign policy aims, and the concentration of all decision-making authority in one man or in a tight oligarchy—these practices at times tend to convert Marxism-Leninism from a unique asset for Soviet diplomacy into a straitjacket. And this is precisely what Gorbachev has recognized and is determined to rectify.

Soviet ideology is not self-executing; that is, it does not interpret itself automatically and does not reflect images of reality that can be unambiguously perceived, but rather it is based upon an authoritative interpretation of changing events by the Soviet leaders, who must choose from among a variety of possible interpretations, only one of which could be tested at a time for truth in the crucible of action. As long as Stalin was alive, interpretation of doctrine was a monopoly reserved for him alone: it was his interpretation.

[8]V. P. Potemkin, ed. *Istoriya Diplomatii* (Moscow, 1954), 3:763–64.

[9]Max Beloff, *Foreign Policy and the Democratic Process* (Baltimore, Md.: Johns Hopkins Press, 1955), p. 98. See also Vernon V. Aspaturian, "Diplomacy in the Mirror of Soviet Scholarship," in *Contemporary History in the Soviet Mirror*, J. Keep, ed. (New York: Praeger, 1964), pp. 243–74.

The Two-camp Image. Stalin's image of the world after the Russian Revolution was one of forced "coexistence" between a single socialist state and a hostile capitalist world surrounding it—a coexistence imposed on both antagonists by objective historical conditions. Neither side being sufficiently powerful to end the existence of the other, they were fated to exist together temporarily on the basis of an unstable and constantly shifting balance of power. The contradiction between the socialist and capitalist camps was considered by Stalin the most fundamental and decisive, but it was not to be aggravated so long as the Soviet Union was in a weakened condition. War between the two camps was viewed as inevitable; however, it could be temporarily avoided and delayed by astute maneuvering within the conflicts raging in the capitalist world.

Stalin's postwar policy initially appeared to be predicated on an inevitable conflict with the West, organized by the United States. The organization of the Cominform and the forced unity of the Communist orbit, the expulsion of Tito from the Communist fraternity, the extraction of public statements of loyalty from Communist leaders in all countries, the urgency with which Stalin sought to eliminate all possible power vacuums between the two blocs along the periphery of the Communist world, all were preparatory measures based on the false assumption that the American ruling class was betraying anxiety at the growth of Soviet power and was preparing to launch Armageddon. At the founding convention of the Cominform in 1947 the late Andrei Zhdanov revealed the authoritative Soviet interpretation of the emerging bipolarization of power:

> The fundamental changes caused by the war on the international scene and in the position of individual countries have entirely changed the political landscape of the world. A new alignment of political forces has arisen. The more the war recedes into the past, the more distinct become two major trends in postwar international policy, corresponding to the division of the political forces operating on the international arena into two major camps; the imperialist and antidemocratic camp, on the one hand, and the anti-imperialist and democratic camp, on the other. The principal driving force of the imperialist camp is the U.S.A. . . . The cardinal purpose of the imperialist camp is to strengthen imperialism, to hatch a new imperialist war, to combat Socialism.[10]

During the Korean War and just prior to the Nineteenth Party Congress in 1952, a "great debate" had apparently taken place in the Politburo concerning the validity of the expectation of imminent war between the two camps. Two divergent views were discussed by Stalin in

---

[10]Full text reprinted in *Strategy and Tactics of World Communism* (Washington, D.C.: Government Printing Office, 1948), pp. 216–17.

his *Economic Problems of Socialism*: (1) that wars between capitalist countries had ceased to be inevitable and hence war between the two camps was imminent, the view that was then current; and (2) that wars between capitalist states remained inevitable, but that imminent war between the two camps was unlikely. Although the first view was the basis of Soviet postwar policy, Stalin ascribed it to "mistaken comrades," and elevated the second to doctrinal significance.[11]

Stalin's only modification of his two-camp image was thus to concede that war between the two blocs was no longer imminent, but might be preceded by a series of wars among the capitalist powers themselves— between the United States and its satellite allies, France and Britain, on the one hand, and its temporary vassals, Germany and Japan, on the other. The Soviet Union would remain outside the conflict, which would automatically seal the doom of world capitalism.

The Post-Stalin Image. At the Twentieth Party Congress (February 1956) Stalin's image of the world was considerably modified in an attempt to bring it into closer focus with the realities of international politics. These modifications were made to eliminate the threatening schisms in the Communist camp, to break up the unity of the non-Soviet world and dismantle anti-Soviet instruments like NATO, to head off the impending nuclear war that Stalin's doctrines and policies were unwittingly encouraging, and to enhance the flexibility of Soviet diplomacy in exploiting the contradictions of the capitalist world.

In place of Stalin's fatalistic image of a polarized world, Khrushchev at the Twentieth Party Congress drew a more optimistic, and, in many respects, a mellower picture:

1. "Capitalist encirclement" was officially declared terminated, as major speakers like Molotov echoed the Titoist doctrine that "the period when the Soviet Union was . . . encircled by hostile capitalism now belongs to the past."The permanent insecurity of the Soviet Union, pending the worldwide victory of Communism, as visualized by Stalin, was replaced with the image of a permanently secured Soviet Union, surrounded by friendly Communist states in Europe and Asia, embracing nearly one-third of the world, with imperialism in an irrevocable state of advanced decay.

2. In place of Stalin's fixed vision of coexistence between two irreconcilable camps poised in temporary balance, which was declared obsolete and inapplicable to the postwar world, his successors recognized a third, "anti-imperialist" but nonsocialist, group of powers, carved out of decaying colonial empires, which had separated from the capitalist camp but had not yet joined the Communist. Stalin's inflexible two-camp

11J. V. Stalin, *Economic Problems of Socialism* (New York: International Publishers, 1952), pp. 27–30.

image needlessly alienated these new states and tended to force them into the capitalist orbit. This belt of neutralist states—a concept which Stalin refused to recognize—insulated the entire Communist orbit from the capitalist world and, together with the socialist states, was viewed as constituting an "extensive 'zone of peace,' including both socialist and nonsocialist peaceloving states of Europe and Asia inhabited by nearly 1.5 billion people, or the majority of the population of the planet."

3. Stalin's doctrine of the "fatal inevitability" of wars was pronounced antiquated, since its emphasis on coercive and violent instruments of diplomacy tended to render the Soviet peace campaign hypocritical, accelerated the formation of anti-Soviet coalitions, and, in a era of nuclear weapons, appeared to doom both worlds to a war of mutual annihilation.

4. Stalin's five main contradictions were retained as valid and persistent, but the radical shift in the equilibrium of class forces in the world dictated a change of emphasis and the reordering of priorities. Stalin stressed the conflicts among the major capitalist countries as the main object of Soviet diplomacy, relegating other contradictions to minor roles, but his successors saw the main contradiction of the current historical stage to be that between the anticolonial and the imperialist forces. In short, the world has moved out of the stage of the "capitalist encirclement" of the Soviet Union and, during the current phase of coexistence, is moving into the stage of the "socialist encirclement" of the United States, as a prelude to the final victory of Communism.[12]

The new image of the world drawn by Khrushchev at the Twentieth Party Congress was by no means the consequence of a unanimous decision. Foreign Minister Molotov and the so-called Anti-Party Group bitterly resisted the demolition of the Stalin myth and the entire de-Stalinization program, and they systematically sabotaged the foreign policy decisions of the Twentieth Party Congress, which they had publicly accepted. After a bitter struggle, involving an attempt to oust Khrushchev, Molotov and the Anti-Party Group were defeated and expelled from the leadership.

"Molotov," Khrushchev bluntly stated in a later speech, "found more convenient a policy of tightening all screws, which contradicts the wise Leninist policy of peaceful coexistence."[13] Thus, it can be assumed that Molotov advocated a continuation of the basic foreign policies of the Stalinist era, based on a perpetuation of the two-camp image. It was Molotov's contention that Soviet policy could reap its greatest dividends by maintaining international tensions at a high pitch and running the risks of nuclear war on the assumption that an uncompromising, cold-blooded policy would force Western political leaders, through lack of

[12]Full text broadcast by Moscow Radio, February 18, 1956. See also the "Mikoyan report," *New York Times*, February 19, 1956.

[13]*New York Times*, July 7, 1957.

nerve and under pressure of public opinion, to continually retreat in the face of Soviet provocation, for fear of triggering a war of mutual extinction. It appears that he considered as un-Marxist the idea that the ex-colonial countries could be regarded as having deserted the capitalist camp and as constituting an "extensive zone of peace" together with the Soviet bloc. Rather, he believed that their behavior in international politics was motivated purely by considerations of opportunism and expediency. The main arena of rivalry for Molotov remained in Western Europe and the Atlantic area—the bastions of capitalism—and not in Asia or Africa. He continued to view the new countries of Asia and Africa with hostility and suspicion as appendages to the capitalist camp.

THE NEW POLITICAL THINKING AND GORBACHEV'S IMAGE OF THE WORLD

The "new political thinking" includes a substantially revised image of the outside world from that of the Stalinist era, and builds upon and extrapolates upon the image which emerged during the Khrushchev period. This new image of the world can be found in its various stages of evolution in Gorbachev's speeches and statements and in the speeches of his advisers and supporters, especially people like Secretariat and Politburo member Alexander Yakovlev, Evgeny Primakov, Alexander Bovin, and others. Its most straightforward and clearest exposition is to be found in Gorbachev's book, *Perestroika*, especially in the chapter entitled, "How We see the World of Today.[14] This chapter summarizes in simple, clear language the basic outlines of Gorbachev's image of the world, but since the book is designed primarily for external audiences, many of the harsher edges of Soviet ideology have been burnished away, and the result is essentially a propagandistic variant of the Gorbachev vision. Particularly missing are the harsh and bitter comments about capitalism, the United States and the West in general, which are still to be found in his speeches and reports delivered at home. He emphasizes the "positive," avoids the negative and focuses on areas of common concern. Many of the ideas in the new political thinking may be new to Soviet ears and eyes, but not to Western, since in many respects they simply represent ideas, concepts, and themes developed in the West, co-opted by Gorbachev and his supporters, and given a Soviet twist. Ideas such as interdependence, mutual security, concern for ecology, environmental problems, depletion of natural resources, the unity of mankind, irrationality of nuclear war, and so

[14]All of the unannotated quotations below are taken from M. S. Gorbachev, *Perestroika* (New York: Harper & Row, 1987), pp. 135–170.

forth, have long achieved platitudinal status in the West and are new only to the Soviet political agenda.

It should be emphasized that the description of the new political thinking that follows is still tentative, exploratory, and not definitive, since it is still in the process of evolution and definition. Furthermore, the rhetoric of the new political thinking is notably absent from the speeches and statements of Ligachev, Chebrikov, and other high Soviet leaders, with the conspicuous exception of Yakovlev, who appears to be one of the principal architects of the new political thinking. Thus, these views do not represent as yet a consensus of the Soviet leadership, and many aspects of the new political thinking in the writings of Gorbachev's supporters may go beyond what Gorbachev himself may ultimately accept when and if he does definitely consolidate his power and lay down his imprint.

Only residual elements of the old two-camp image of the world are to be found in the Gorbachev outlook, just barely enough to retain a continuity in the Soviet perspective. Gorbachev still subscribes to the notion of two radically divergent dominant ideologies and social systems, seeking to extend their reach into the developing Third World, which subscribes to neither of the two dominant ideologies but is ambivalently and episodically pulled in one direction or another. What is extraordinarily new in the Gorbachev view, for a Soviet position, is the idea that the world constitutes a material and civilizational unity, integrated and interdependent, in spite of its contradictory, diverse, and tension-laden character, whose survival has a higher priority than the expansion of *either* of the two ideologies or social systems:

> The time is ripe for abandoning views on foreign policy which are influenced by an imperial viewpoint. Neither the Soviet Union nor the United States is able to force its will on others. It is possible to suppress, compel, bribe, break or blast, but only for a certain period. From the point of view of long-term, big-time politics, no one will be able to subordinate others . . . the fundamental principle of the new political outlook is very simple: nuclear war cannot be a means of achieving political, economic, ideological or any other goals. . . . Nuclear war is senseless; it is irrational. There would be neither winners nor losers in a global nuclear conflict: world civilization would inevitably perish.

The revolutionary character of Gorbachev's view, from the standpoint of a Soviet leader, is that it explicitly repudiates the conviction that the worldwide victory of socialism is inevitable under any and all conditions, and thus implicitly subverts the scientific credentials of Marxism-Leninism, which was hitherto based upon the inescapable inevitability of the demise of capitalism and the universal triumph of socialism. The real possibility of nuclear war renders universal socialism only a highly likely possibility, but not a certainty. Furthermore, in order to emphasize his point, Gorbachev explicitly disavows General von Clausewitz's famous dictum as being obsolete and invalid under modern conditions, because resorting to even nonnuclear war could have the same catastrophic result:

> But military technology has developed to such an extent that even a non-nuclear war would now be comparable with a nuclear war in its destructive effect. . . . Clausewitz's dictum that war is the continuation of policy only by different means, which was classical in his time, has grown hopelessly out of date. It now belongs in the libraries. For the first time in history, basing international politics on moral and ethical norms that are common to all humankind, as well as humanizing interstate relations, has become a vital requirement.

Noting that "no one can close down the world of capitalism . . . or the world of developed socialism," Gorbachev asserts that "the new political outlook calls for the recognition of one more simple axiom: security is indivisible."

> Universal security in our time rests upon the recognition of the rights of every nation to choose its own path of social development. . . . A nation may choose either capitalism or socialism. This is its sovereign right. Nations cannot and should not pattern their life either after the United States or the Soviet Union. Hence, political positions should be devoid of ideological intolerance.

Since the new political thinking explicitly contradicts some fundamental and seminal elements of Marxist-Leninist principles, Gorbachev must reconcile his new views with traditional Marxist-Leninist notions concerning dialectics, the class struggle, and class analysis in general. Gorbachev goes beyond simply stating that ideological conflict should not be reflected at the interstate level, a standard strategy often invoked by his predecessors, but demands that foreign policies should no longer be shaped by ideological differences:

> Ideological differences should not be transferred to the sphere of interstate relations nor should foreign policy be subordinate to them, for ideologies may be poles apart, whereas the interest of survival and prevention of war stand universal and supreme.

If this view prevails, it will represent a monumental step in the repudiation of Marxism-Leninism itself, for it is an explicit admission that, first, ideological differences are a source of tension and conflict, second, that they pose a barrier to the solution of world problems, and third, that survival and prevention of war take priority over the promotion of ideological positions.

Apparently, Gorbachev is cognizant of the fact that his views are remarkably un-Marxist in nature, since they invoke supraclass concepts, based upon the premise that interests exist that rise above classes and are beyond the reach of the class struggle. Recognizing that he may be charged with the resurrection of bourgeois concepts like "eternal truths" and "universal interests," Gorbachev implicitly admits to intellectual improvisation and the restructuring of Lenin's ideas:

> A new way of thinking is not an improvisation, nor a mental exercise. . . . We draw inspiration from Lenin. Turning to him, and 'reading' his works each time in a new way . . . to see the most intricate dialectics of world processes. . . . More than once he spoke about the priority of interests common to all humanity over class interests. . . . It is they that are feeding our philosophy of international relations, and the new way of thinking. One may argue that philosophers and theologists throughout history have dealt with the ideas of 'eternal' human values. True, this is so, but then these were 'scholastic speculations' doomed to be a utopian dream. In the 1980's . . . mankind should acknowledge the vital necessity of human values and their priority.

Where does this leave the "class struggle," the elemental foundation of Soviet cognitive analysis? Gorbachev comes close to repudiating the class struggle, although he concedes its past validity and its current partial and residual validity, but clearly he recognizes that reliance upon the concept of the "class struggle" as the basis of political analysis is not only a barrier to peace but may in fact promote war and destruction:

> Since time immemorial, class interests were the cornerstone of both foreign and domestic policies. . . . Marxists . . . are convinced that in the final analysis the policy of any state or alliance of states is determined by the interests of prevailing sociopolitical forces. Acute clashes of these interests in the international arena have led to armed conflicts and wars throughout history. . . . Today this tradition is leading directly into the nuclear abyss. . . . The backbone of the new way of thinking is the recognition of the priority of human values, or to be more precise, of humankind's survival.

And, then in a remarkable series of statements, Gorbachev in his book, all but concedes that dogmatic and rigid adherence to ideological orthodoxy by Soviet leaders in the past had inadvertently promoted tension and courted disaster:

> It may seem strange to some people that communists should place such strong emphasis on human interests and values. Indeed a class-motivated approach to all phenomena of social life is the ABC of Marxism. . . . Humanitarian notions were viewed as a function and the end result of the struggle of the working class—the last class which, ridding itself, rids the entire society of class antagonisms. But, now with the emergence of weapons of mass, that is, universal destruction, there appeared an objective

limit for class confrontation in the international arena: the threat of universal destruction. For the first time ever there emerged a real, not speculative and remote, common human interest—to save humanity from disaster.

The new realities impelled a revision of the Party Program in a number of important particulars, which again recognized the Soviet contribution to the generation of international tension and conflict. At the Twenty-seventh Party Congress, he writes, "we deemed it no longer possible to retain in it the definition of peaceful coexistence of states with different social systems as 'a specific form of class struggle.' " Thus, the concept of "peaceful coexistence," invented by Stalin as a "tactic" in relations with the capitalist world, and which was converted by Khrushchev into a long-term "strategy" in dealing with the external world, has now been transformed into a "principle" governing relations with the external world, that is, it becomes a concept defining a condition rather than a process.

Furthermore, according to Gorbachev, the old Marxist-Leninist ideas concerning war and revolution, particularly the idea of war as the midwife of revolution, has become not only obsolete but dangerous and must be repudiated:

> We have taken a new look at the interdependence of war and revolution. In the past, war often served to detonate revolution. . . . The First World War provoked . . . the October Revolution in our country. The Second World War evoked . . . revolutions in Eastern Europe and Asia, as well as a powerful anti-colonial revolution. All this served to re-enforce the Marxist-Leninist logic that imperialism inevitably generates major armed confrontations, while the latter naturally creates a 'critical mass' of social discontent and a revolutionary situation in a number of countries. Hence a forecast which was long adhered to in our country: a Third World War, if unleashed by imperialism, would lead to new social upheavals which would finish off the capitalist system for good, and this would spell global peace. But when the conditions radically changed so that the only result of nuclear war could be universal destruction, we drew a conclusion about the disappearance of the cause-and-effect relationship between war and revolution.

In order to underline the profundity of the Soviet change of view on the genesis, nature, and likelihood of war and revolution, Gorbachev wrote the following:

> At the 27th CPSU Party Congress we clearly 'divorced' the revolution and war themes, excluding from the new edition of the Party Program the following two phrases: 'Should the imperialist aggressors nevertheless venture to start a new world war, the peoples will no longer tolerate a system which drags them into devastating wars. They will sweep imperialism away and bury it.' This provision, admitting in theory, the

possibility of a new world war was removed as not corresponding to the realities of the nuclear era.

In other words, the earlier assurances and certitudes that even in the event of a nuclear war, the world would suffer immensely, but capitalism would perish while socialism would nevertheless survive, has been repudiated. There is not a shred of optimism left about the inevitability of the victory of socialism as long as nuclear war is possible. Gorbachev, after his recital of the new image of the world projected by the new political thinking, asks himself the logical and rhetorical question, which not only the outside world, but his own colleagues in the Communist world must be contemplating:

> Does this imply that we have given up the class analysis of the causes of the nuclear threat and of other global problems? No.

Class analysis as a basis for understanding the behavior of the capitalist world is still valid, but as a basis for concluding that nuclear war will be the inevitable result, it is not. The differences and incompatibilities between socialism and capitalism remain, but they need not eventuate in war:

> Economic, political and ideological competition between capitalist and socialist countries is inevitable. However, it can be and must be kept within the framework of a peaceful competition which necessarily envisages cooperation. It is up to history to judge the merits of each particular system. It will sort out everything. Let every nation decide which system and which ideology is better. Let this be decided by peaceful competition, let each system prove its ability to meet man's needs and interests. The states and peoples of the Earth are very different, and it is actually good that they are so. This is an incentive for competition. This understanding, of a dialectical unity of opposites, fits into the concept of peaceful coexistence.

After acknowledging that past Soviet positions on ideology were substantially contributory to the genesis and sustenance of international tensions because of its emphasis on inevitability of war, Gorbachev asks the world to ignore and forget past Soviet statements, mentioning in particular Khrushchev's infamous boast that "we will bury you," which he called "probably the most hackneyed statement by a Soviet leader in the West." This statement, he said, was not to be taken literally, and then, deceptively or in ignorance, asserted that it was simply a vulgarization of an old debating style during the 1920s and 1930s between farm experts about "who will bury whom," ignoring the fact that this question was originally posed by Lenin as the question of questions with respect to the inevitable conflict between capitalism and socialism. "People in the West," writes Gorbachev, "must stop exploiting those few words by one who is no longer among the living, and must not present them as our position." Even less convincing is Gorbachev's assertion that neither Marx, Lenin, or any of the Soviet leaders ever had intentions of "imposing communism throughout the world" or "plans for subduing the whole of Europe." Any attempt to assert the contrary, he writes, "are the fruit of crude falsification or at best ignorance." Gorbachev's revision of the Soviet image of the world is profound and far-reaching, but whether it becomes the definitive basis for Soviet foreign policy still depends upon its acceptance by the total Soviet leadership or Gorbachev's undisputed consolidation of political power.

THE EVOLUTION OF THE SOVIET
DECISION-MAKING SYSTEM

The Stalin era was essentially a period of one-man dictatorship and it came to an end in march 1953 with his death. In the post-Stalin era, Soviet decision-making procedures have moved away from one-man rule in the direction of a limited pluralistic system in which increasing increments of participation have taken place.

During this entire period, however, diversity of opinion and participation in decision making tended to spill out of the Politburo and Secretariat into the larger Central Committee. The sharp and close factional divisions in the Politburo revived the prominence and activity of the moribund Central Committee. Factional differences and other dissident views were increasingly displayed before plenums of the Central Committee (held at least twice a year) where the actions of the Politburo could be appealed or reviewed. In this relatively large body, discussion of the views current in the Politburo was still more ritualized than free, with each view in the Politburo supported by its own retainers in the Central Committee. Voting was conditioned not only by divisions in the Politburo, but also by considerations of political survival and opportunism, with members being extremely sensitive to the course that the struggle assumed in the higher body.

The Central Committee assumed increasing importance during the Khrushchev era. Khrushchev was almost fanatical in his zeal to enshrine the Central Committee as the ultimate institutional repository of legitimacy in the Soviet system. The body was enlarged and convened regularly by Khrushchev, and all changes in personnel and major pronouncements of policy were either confirmed by or announced at Central Committee plenums.

Differences in the Politburo arise as a result of both personal ambitions for power and fundamental conflict over doctrine and policy. Both factors are so intricately interwoven that attempts to draw fine distinctions between personal and policy conflicts are apt to be an idle exercise. Although Soviet ideology neither recognizes the legitimacy of factional groupings in the party nor tolerates the doctrinal schisms that are their ideological expression, the party, throughout its history, has been constantly threatened with the eruption of both. After Stalin's death, the rival cliques he permitted—and may even have encouraged—to form among his subordinates developed into factions, each with its own aspirations and opinions. Since no single faction was sufficiently powerful to annihilate the others, necessity was converted into virtue and the balance of terror in the Politburo was ideologically sanctified as "collective leadership."

The Central Committee thus began emerging as the most important political organ of power and authority in the Soviet system. The growing power of the Central Committee reflected the increasingly pluralistic character of the Soviet social order. This body is composed of representatives from the most powerful and influential elite groups in Soviet society. It includes the entire membership of the Politburo and the Secretariat; the most important ministers of the government; the first secretaries of the several republics' party organizations and of important regional party organizations; the most important officials of the Soviet Union's republics; the marshals, generals, and admirals of the armed forces and the police; the important ambassadors; the trade union officials; cultural and scientific celebrities and leaders; the leading party ideologists; and the top Komsomol officials. Increasingly, these representatives perceive attitudes reflecting their institutional or functional roles and status in Soviet society, and this provides the social basis for the political factions which now characterize the Soviet system.

Thus, the Khrushchev decade emerges as a transition from Stalinist, one-man rule to a quasi-pluralistic, consensus type of political behavior established during the eighteen years of the Brezhnev era. Factional polarization and stabilized factional dominance made up the characteristic leadership style of Khrushchev, whereas, under Brezhnev, a dynamic consensus pattern was established in which Brezhnev managed to organize a different coalition across various issues rather than rely upon a permanent, stabilized factional majority. The brief Andropov period betrayed the characteristics of a factional coalition whereby the dominant group in the Politburo represented neither a single majority faction nor a moving consensus, but a coalition of factions representing institutional interests. The Andropov coalition was made up essentially of the secret police, the military, and the foreign policy establishment, with Andropov, Defense Minister Ustinov, and Foreign Affairs Minister Gromyko as the governing troika. The Party Apparatus, represented by Andropov's putative rival and Brezhnev's preferred successor, Chernenko, and the state/ economic apparatus represented by Premier Tikhonov were the major components of the minority coalition of factional and institutional interests.

The death of Andropov altered the equilibrium of factions in the Soviet leadership somewhat. The KGB-military-foreign policy coalition lost its clear predominance, whereas the party and government apparatuses gained in power, so that power was more equally divided between the two principal coalitions. But no important personnel or institutional changes were made in the immediate wake of Andropov's departure, and the Soviet leadership appeared stalled at dead center as it awaited the next episode in the evolution of the Soviet leadership, that is, the impending death of Chernenko, which took place a year later, and the accession of Mikhail Gorbachev.

Leadership Changes under Gorbachev

During the past decade, nay even during the past five years, the Soviet system has experienced an unprecedented upheaval in turnover in its leadership, comparable only to the dramatic turnovers during the mid-1930s, but without the tragedy of the purges. This, in turn, has created unprecedented opportunities for various personalities and groups to enhance their power and influence in the Soviet political system and to even successfully challenge the Party Apparatus as the dominant political elite in the Soviet Union. Three ailing and aging top leaders of the Soviet Union (Brezhnev, Andropov, and Chernenko) have died in rapid succession, creating an unprecedented vacuum in the Soviet leadership, which has yet to be completely and definitively filled.

The Twenty-seventh Soviet Communist Party Congress convened on February 27, 1986 to confirm leadership changes already made, to announce new changes in the personnel of leading party organs, to establish the line for political, economic and social policy and development not only for the next five years, but also for the next fifteen (that is, preparing the Soviet Union for entry into the twenty-first century), and to adopt a new Communist Party Program to replace the ambitious, yet unrealistic and disorienting, program introduced by Khrushchev in 1961.

Of the twenty-two full members and candidate members of the Politburo elected at the Twenty-sixth Party Congress in 1981, only four full members (Gorbachev, Gromyko, Kunayev, and Shcherbitsky) and four candidate members (Demichev, Solomentsev, Shevardnadze, and Aliyev) survived removals and deaths to be reelected in 1986 at the Twenty-seventh Party Congress. A similar turnover has taken place in the

High Command of the Armed Forces and an even more dramatic turnover has occurred in the party Secretariat, particularly among the senior secretaries. Of the five senior secretaries in 1980, only Gorbachev has survived. The smaller Council for Defense has been similarly ravaged during the same period, with only Gromyko surviving of the six full members in 1979.

Since Gorbachev's election as General Secretary, Romanov, Grishin, and Kunayev have been clearly purged and disgraced, Tikhonov was retired with praise and honor, Aliyev, who may have vacillated on Gorbachev's election, has also since been dropped from the Politburo, whereas Shcherbitsky has been under constant attack by Gorbachev. Vorotnikov and Solomentsev have faded into the background as new appointees like Ligachev, Chebrikov, Ryzhkov, and Yakovlev have assumed greater prominence. By the beginning of 1988, no less than eight of the thirteen full members of the Politburo and three of the five candidate members were elected or promoted since Gorbachev's advent to the helm.

The Secretariat has experienced an even greater turnover in personnel. Of the five senior secretaries in 1980, only Gorbachev has survived. The remaining four senior secretaries (Yegor Ligachev, Viktor Nikonov, Nikolai Slyunkov, and Aleksander Yakovlev) are all newcomers to the leadership. Senior secretaries are secretaries who are simultaneously full Politburo members. Five of the six junior secretaries are Gorbachev appointees. Thus nine of the ten secretaries (excluding Gorbachev) have been elected to this body since Gorbachev's elevation to General Secretary. This represents an unprecedented turnover in the Soviet leadership and is a tribute to Gorbachev's remarkable abilities as a politician. Nevertheless, the unrepresentative character of the new leadership suggests that the changes were due more to objective power-political processes rather than calculated planning. This is suggested by the equally unprecedented insensitivity to the nationality factor that has manifested itself in the personnel changes. The top leadership is more intensively Russian and Slavic than any previous leadership, although the Russian and Slavic proportion of the population has been diminishing. Not a single representative of the Moslem nationalities remains in the party leadership with the removal of Kunayev and Aliyev. The only non-Slav is Eduard Shevardnadze, a Georgian, who is a full member of the Politburo and Foreign Minister, whereas Slyunkov and Shcherbitsky, a Byelorussian and Ukrainian respectively, are the only other non-Russians on the Politburo. Of the eleven-member Secretariat, the only non-Russian is the Byelorussian, Slyunkov, although this body includes among its junior sectetaries, A. P. Biryukova, the second woman to reach this level of leadership in the entire seventy year history of the Soviet Union.

Since the membership of the Council for Defense is essentially *ex officio*, its change in personnel has been equally traumatic. Gromyko is the only holdover from the previous decade, whereas Gorbachev did not become a member until 1984 and has served as Chairman of this body since 1985. In other upper reaches of the Soviet system, 60 percent of the Ministers of the USSR, 70 percent of the Heads of Central Committee departments, 46 percent of the *obkom* and *kraikom* first secretaries, and about 50 percent of the republic first secretaries have been replaced under Gorbachev. In the Central Committee itself, 60 percent of the 1981 full members and 44 percent of the candidate members were re-elected in 1986, which falls short of giving Gorbachev undisputed control. Indeed, it appears that Gorbachev's obstacles to reform begins with the Central Committee itself, which is the informal representative body of the powerful functional and territorial power substructures that make up the strategic sociopolitical elites in Soviet society.

Although Mikhail Gorbachev is clearly the most conspicuous personality in the Soviet leadership, he has not yet established his undisputed authority. In spite of the extensive personnel changes made in the higher reaches of the party and state since Gorbachev's election as General Secretary, it is by no means clear that all of the new appointees are beholden to the new leader or that they are his supine and obedient subordinates. The top leadership clearly reflects at least three distinctive groupings: (1) Brezhnev holdovers; (2) Gorbachev partisans; and (3) Gorbachev coalition allies. It is important to distinguish between the two latter groups, since they are often collapsed together as Gorbachev partisans simply because they represent the post-Brezhnev generaiton of leaders. Political alliances and coalitions are frequently opportunistic and allies often betray a tendency to displace their partners and change alignments accordingly. Gorbachev's allies are by no means immune from these tendencies, and the challenge to Gorbachev's leadership is likely to come from among his allies rather than from the Brezhnev holdovers, whose aging and ailing condition severely limit their opportunities.

Party Leadership and Strategic Elites

These turnovers at the apex of the Soviet system reflect the more fundamental social transformations that have been taking place in Soviet society as a whole and in particular among the universe of professional and strategic elites, from which the circle of decision makers is recruited. Originally, during simpler times, the party constituted the one and only elite, with little or no room for sub-elites of any substantial magnitude. But the concept of the party as a coherent and distinctive elite structure is no longer appropriate. It is no longer an elite, or even a power structure, but more an arena, in which the Party Apparatus (often confused with the party as a whole) coexists alongside other elite structures such as the armed forces, the police, the state and economic bureaucracies, and the scientific-technological elites. All of these elites, particularly their leaders, are members of the party and occupy important positions within it in addition to performing their professional functional roles. What is more accurately meant by the term "party" in correction with formulations like party-military relations is the permanent core of party officials and functionaries, the Party Apparatus.

The military, in particular, because of its functional capabilities, its popular image among the Russian people, and its obvious symbolism as a structure of patriotism, was viewed by Stalin as a potential challenger to the Party Apparatus for leadership of the country. Furthermore, during this period, the military was viewed not so much as an alternative to the Party Apparatus but as an alternative to the party itself, since its assimilation of party values and philosophy was incomplete and suspect.

During the war, the role, status and prestige of the professional military was nevertheless enhanced, while state institutions also experienced an enhancement that imparted to the state credentials of legitimacy which could challenge the authority of the Party Apparatus. By investing himself with all of the key state and military posts in the Soviet political system during and after the war, Stalin transferred the enormous personal authority and prestige that accompanied his presence from party bodies to state bodies, and the Party Apparatus became just another power string to Stalin's bow rather than his principal instrument. Given the prestige attached to the state and the military, an arm of the state, and Stalin's position within these two institutions, the Party Apparatus became less important and its organs suffered a substantial atrophy as the principal organs of decision.

Not only the state and military, but other structures, notably the scientific, technological, and economic elites, also experienced an enhancement of their prestige because of their services during the war. The role of the Party Apparatus increasingly was perceived more as a hindrance than as a contribution to the war effort. This was further reenforced by the downplaying of ideological themes during the war and the manipulation of traditional patriotic symbols of historic and traditional Russia, symbols and traditions more in tune and in accordance with the functions of the state and the military than the party or Party Apparatus.

As the Soviet Union developed during the postwar period and expanded into Eastern Europe and East Asia to establish a regional sphere of influence, the role and importance of the military as an instrument of Soviet power grew, but there was no corresponding growth of military influence in the Soviet political system. In fact, Stalin's prophylactic measures probably envisioned the possibility that, as the importance of the military grew in the foreign policy calculations of the Soviet Union, there would be a commensurate tendency for the military to enhance its position as a political actor within the Soviet political system. But the relative importance of the military in the domestic political process was bound to grow in any event because, as the Soviet Union developed economically, its social order became more intricately differentiated and structured in terms of sociopolitical specialization. As the system became more complex and complicated, the capacity of the Party Apparatus to maintain itself as the preeminent elite within the system was gradually diminished. With the growth of other elites in numbers and their acquisition of arcane and specialized skills indispensable for a modern society but beyond the ken of the Party Apparatus, their co-optation into the central organs of the party converted them in effect into party leaders as well as leaders of their functional organizations.

The emergence and growth of these strategic elites, previously lumped together as the "technocratic elites" within the party but outside the Party Apparatus, have eroded the preeminence of the Party Apparatus and created the conditions for challenging its traditional control of the party as a whole. Those structures combining specialization and expertise with a monopoly on the instruments of force, the KGB and the military, are the sectors of the "technocratic elites" that appear to have the best prospects for a successful challenge that will force the Party Apparatus to share control over the party, but will not necessarily displace it completely.

The party can no longer be viewed as a cohesive organizational entity, unlike the Party Apparatus which is, but more akin to an ideological arena within which Soviet elites contend and cooperate with one another over control of the party turf and the symbols of legitimacy it provides. The Party Apparatus, the KGB, and the military are three of these elites which compete for organizational predominance or autonomy, while at the same time sharing substantially identical political, ideological, cognitive, and epistemological values and outlooks. The Party Apparatus continues to insist that its elite interests are those of the party and it is this idea which the military and other institutional structures challenge. These Soviet elites share common ideological values associated with the party, but exhibit differences, divergences and even conflicts of interests with one another as elites.

All elites are members of the party and their highest representatives consider themselves to be simultaneously leaders of their institutions and sectors as well as leaders of the party, which is common property. Membership in the Politburo and Central Committee, the leading organs of the party, translates into leadership of the party.

It is true that a leading organ, the Secretariat, which is the *sanctum sanctorum* of the Party Apparatus, is difficult to penetrate by other elites (Andropov's reassignment to the Secretariat after Suslov's death is an ambiguous case because of Andropov's unusual career profile) and the Party Apparatus tends to confuse itself with the party leadership and its elite interests with party interests, whereas other elites consider the Party Apparatus to be simply the permanent administrative and logistical infrastructure of the party. After all, it is the Politburo and not the Secretariat which is the central and leading organ of the party. And yet, the situation continues to be muddled because the General Secretary, who is acknowledged to be the single most important party leader, is almost always recruited from the Secretariat, which he continues to head, whereas he is theoretically only *primus inter pares* in the Politburo, which has neither a chairman nor an institutionalized presiding officer.

Internal Politics and Soviet Foreign Policy: Interest Groups and Factional Polarization on Foreign Policy Issues

As the Soviet System matures and becomes identified with the interests of its various privileged elites, the decision makers must give greater consideration, in the calculation of foreign policy, to factors affecting the internal stability of the regime; and they will show greater sensitivity to the effects of decisions on the vested interests of the various elites in Soviet society. The rise of powerful social and economic elites in the Soviet Union, and their insistent pressure for participation in the exercise of political power, could only introduce stresses, strains, conflicts, and hence new restraints into Soviet diplomacy.

Within the context of an ideology that imposes a single interest representing society as a whole, each interest group will tend to distort ideology and policy in an endeavor to give them the contours of its own interests; the next step is to elevate these to transcendental significance. Under these conditions, Soviet ideology may constantly be threatened with a series of fundamental convulsions if one interest group—or coalition groups—displaces another in the struggle for the control of the party machinery. Hence, a rational system of accommodating conflicting interests appears to be evolving. As the vested stake of each major group becomes rooted in the Soviet system, the contours of Soviet diplomacy and national interest will inexorably tend to be shaped more by the rapidly moving equilibrium or accommodation of interests that develop internally than by abstract ideological imperatives.

Although, ideologically, the basic purpose of external security and state survival was to develop into a power center for the purpose of implementing ideological goals in foreign policy (world Communism), increasingly the purpose becomes to protect and preserve the existing social order in the interests of the social groups which dominate and benefit from it.

The foreign policy and defense posture of the Soviet state establish a certain configuration of priorities in the allocation of effort and scarce resources. Various individuals and groups develop a vested interest in a particular foreign policy or defense posture because of the role and status it confers upon them. Correspondingly, other individuals and groups in Soviet society perceive themselves as deprived in status and rewards because of existing allocation of expenditures and resources and, hence, they might initiate proposals which might alter existing foreign policy and defense postures or support proposals submitted by other groups or individuals.

The same is true of groups to which are assigned limited or arrested functions in society, except that these develop a vested interest in expanding their role, dignifying it with greater prestige, and demanding greater rewards. Consequently, it is extremely difficult to distill from Soviet factional positions those aspects of thought and behavior that express conflicting perceptions of self-interest on the part of various individuals, factions, and groups as opposed to authentic "objective" considerations of a broader interest, whether national or ideological, since they are so inextricably intertwined and interdependent.

All that we can assert at this point is that certain individuals and socioinstitutional functional groups seem to thrive and others to to be relatively deprived in their development under conditions of exacerbated international tensions, while the situation is reversed when a relaxation of international tensions takes place. Therefore, it might be assumed that groups that are favored by a particular policy or situation have a greater inclination to perceive objective reality in terms of their self-interest. Groups that are objectively favored by heightened international tension might have a greater propensity to perceive external threats and a corresponding disinclination to recognize that the nature of a threat has been altered or eliminated, thus requiring new policies which might adversely affect them. On the other hand, groups that are objectively favored by relaxation of international tensions or a peacetime economy might be more prone to perceive a premature alteration of an external threat and a corresponding tendency to be skeptical about external threats which arise if they would result in a radical rise in defense expenditures and a reallocation of resources and social rewards.

The groups in Soviet society which appear to benefit from a militant foreign policy and the maintenance of international tensions are (1) the traditional sectors of the armed forces; (2) the heavy industry managers; (3) professional conservative party *apparatchiki* and ideologues; and (4) the secret police. By no means do all individuals or sub-elites and cliques within these groups see eye to eye on foreign policy issues. Some individuals and sub-elites, for opportunistic reasons or functional adaptability, are able to adjust to a relaxation of tensions by preserving or even improving their role and status. The significant point is that the impetus for an aggressive policy and the chief opposition to a relaxation of tensions find their social and functional foundations within these four sociofunctional or socioinstitutional groups, whose common perception of interests results in an informal "military-industrial-apparatus complex." Their attitudes stem almost entirely from the role they play in Soviet society and rewards in terms of prestige and power which are derived from these functions in time of high international tensions as opposed to détente.

The professional military, on the whole, has a natural interest in a large and modern military establishment and a high priority on budget and resources; the heavy industry managerial groups have a vested stake in preserving the primacy of their sector of the economy; and the Party Apparatus traditionally has had a vested interest in ideological conformity and the social controls which they have rationalized, ensuring the primacy of the Party Apparatus over all other social forces in the Soviet system. All of these functional roles are served best under conditions of international tension. Consequently, this group, wittingly or unwittingly, has developed an interest in either maintaining international tensions or creating the illusion of insecurity and external danger. To the degree that individuals or sub-elites within these groups are able to socially retool their functions and adapt them to peacetime or purely internal functions, then do they correspondingly lose interest in an aggressive or tension-preserving policy.

For purposes of analytical convenience, those social groups which would seem to benefit from a relaxation of international tensions can be classified into four general categories: (1) the state bureaucracy, in the central governmental institutions as well as in the republics and localities; (2) light industry interests, consumers goods and services interests, and agricultural interests; (3) the cultural, professional, and scientific groups, whose role and influence seem to flourish under conditions of relaxation both at home and abroad; and (4) the Soviet "consumer," who will ultimately benefit from a policy which concentrates on raising the standard of living. The technical-scientific branches of the professional military, including the nuclear missile specialists, also appear to benefit during periods of relaxed international tensions, when the main reliance for national security is on them and the traditional forces are subject to severe budget reductions.

While the contradiction between Soviet security interests and ideological goals in foreign policy has long been recognized by observers of the Soviet scene, a new variable in Soviet policy is the contradiction between enhancing economic property at home and fulfilling international ideological obligations. Under Khrushchev, this emerged as a contradiction between the requirements of "building Communism" and the costs and risks of remaining faithful to the principle of "proletarian internationalism," whereas under Gorbachev, it has been redefined as striking a more rational balance between the imperatives of a fundamental restructuring of Soviet society and a more manageable global policy externally.

The Fragmentation of the Decision-Making Process

Under Stalin, policy formulation and decision making were tightly centralized in Stalin's person: thought and action were coordinated by a single personality. Under his successors, however, the inconclusive struggle for power has resulted in the fragmentation of the decision-making structure, distributing power among various individuals and factions, each in command of parallel institutional power structures.

All of these tendencies have intensified since the death of Brezhnev and continue under Gorbachev because the radical nature of his restructuring program threatens so many powerful vested interests, who may be provoked to retaliate and defend their positions with whatever instruments they may be able to employ. This erratic pattern was reflected particularly in the Soviet leadership's responses to the Reagan Administration's arms-control proposals, as successive "inflexible" positions replaced one another on issues involving the INF Treaty, the SDI, strategic missiles, and so forth, culminating finally in three summit meetings at Geneva, Reykjavik, and Washington, and the signing of a "zero-zero" INF Treaty in Washington in December 1987, which was a modified version of President Reagan's original INF arms reduction proposal.

Although polarization of interests along foreign policy issues has not yet been discussed in the Soviet press, even under the policy of *glasnost*, polarization between those who have a vested interest in the Soviet status quo and those whose interests will improve with restructuring are now freely discussed. Thus a leading Soviet sociologist, Tatyana Zaslavskaya, who is now an important academic advisor to Gorbachev, and who concedes "that in former times my views must have been considered 'seditious,' " frames the polarization and confrontation as follows:

> The structure of society is made up of a great many groups whose statuses differ and which have different (sometimes opposing) interests and goals for which they struggle. . . . Restructuring is being carried out in the interests of . . . the majority of the people, but it has a very serious effect on the interests of the minority, which is by no means inclined to surrender.[15]

Another Gorbachev supporter, the economist G. Popov, spells out the polarization over restructuring even more bluntly:

[15]*Izvestia*, April 20, 1987.

Employees of various economic bodies who stand to lose their jobs as a result of restructuring are a principal retarding factor. . . . Restructuring is also being retarded by employees and agencies whose jobs and existence are not threatened, but whose status and role are being changed. . . . The situation is compounded by the fact that the retarding factors in the management system receive indirect support from the position of certain executives of local Party bodies. . . . The shift to economic methods, the development of self-management, and the creation of elective management positions sometimes strike Party functionaries as all but a deathblow to their former skills and experience. . . . There are workers and employees who, in their hearts, still do not want restructuring—who prefer today's small bird in the hand to tomorrow's large bird in the bush. Certain enterprise executives are entirely satisfied with the present system, which exempts them from accountability and risk-taking. And passivity in the basic production unit is the base that allows even management personnel who outright retard restructuring to hold onto their jobs. Who does want changes? It's the far-sighted political leaders and management personnel and the outstanding people in science and the cultural sphere. They understand that in the twenty-first century the present variant of development will be dangerous for the country. Further, it's the leading contingent of the working class and of collective farmers, engineers and technicians who are striving to improve their lives and who want to earn more, but to earn it by their own labor, without any finagling. And it's the segment of the intelligentsia that is interested in scientific and technical progress.[16]

THE CENTRAL POLICY-MAKING AND DECISION-MAKING ORGANS

The three most important decision-making organs in the areas of national security and foreign policy are the Politburo, the Secretariat, and the Council for Defense. These three bodies represent the most intense concentration of top decision makers undiluted with political ciphers, as is the case with other institutions, particularly those of the state. Furthermore, all of the important state decision makers are to be found within these three organs. Of the three, the Politburo still remains the most important since both the Secretariat and the Council for Defense are subordinate to the Politburo.

The Politburo: How it Functions

According to Brezhnev and other Politburo members who have commented on the workings of the Politburo, the Politburo meets regularly on Thursday afternoons for about three to six hours, depending upon the agenda and the contentiousness of the issues. Between the Twenty-fourth and Twenty-fifth Party Congresses (1971–1976), accord-

[16]*Pravda*, January 21, 1987.

ing to Brezhnev, the Politburo had 215 sessions, an average of 45 per year, and between 1976 and 1981, it met 236 times.[17] Foreign policy issues are always high on the agenda, both short-term and long-range. Special sessions of the Politburo are also convened during crisis periods or to deal with extraordinary issues or occasions. During the SALT I negotiations in May 1972 in Moscow, for example, the Politburo was convened four times to discuss issues and respond to proposals made by President Nixon and Henry Kissinger, which means that it was in virtually continuous session during this period.[18] Again, according to Brezhnev, agreement is reached after discussion and debate without a formal vote 99.9 percent of the time. If no consensus is reached, according to the late General Secretary, the issue is submitted for resolution to a Politburo committee composed of members whose responsibilities bear on the issue. If a vote is required, only full members are entitled to vote. It is not known whether formal permanent Politburo subcommittees exist on various issues, as under Stalin, or whether Politburo subcomittees are essentially *ad hoc*. At the Twenty-sixth Party Congress (1981), Brezhnev revealed that *ad hoc* subcommittees or task forces continued to be created by the Politburo to facilitate its work:

> In certain circumstances the Politburo sets up special committees for comprehensive investigation and generalization of specific problems and also for the purpose of efficiently resolving the relevant practical undertakings.[19]

Arkady Shevchenko provides the most detailed description of how the Politburo exercises its functions in recent years. According to Shevchenko, his work as Gromyko's adviser brought him into direct contact with the Politburo and other key leaders. In Shevchenko's words:

> Soviet leaders are able to conceal their policy-making processes primarily because of an extraordinary concentration of power in the hands of about two dozen men at the apex, supported by the most influential regional Party bosses. . . . Another essential element on which policy-making in the Kremlin is based is complete secrecy. . . . Within the Politburo there is a core that can be called the "Politburo" of the Politburo. Fundamentally, this group consists of Moscow-based members. Those from various Republics and districts of the Soviet Union play a less important role and often are not privy to precisely how certain decisions on domestic or foreign policy are arrived at. . . . Non-Moscow members do not attend all the regular Thursday Politburo meetings. In addition . . . there are also non-scheduled ones. [There are] . . . no verbatim records. Occasionally, however, segments of Politburo discussions have been recorded, and, of course, full texts of all

[17]*Pravda*, February 25, 1976 and February 24, 1981.
[18]Henry Kissinger, *White House Years* (Boston: Little, Brown, 1979), pp. 1202–1257.
[19]*Pravda*, February 24, 1981.

decisions are kept in the Central Committee archives. These decisions are forwarded to those responsible for their implementation.[20]

On March 21, 1986, in publishing the weekly report on the meetings of the Politburo after the Twenty-seventh Party Congress, *Pravda* provided a rare public glimpse of how the Politburo carries out its architectonic responsibilities:

> The Politburo of the Central Committee advised the USSR Council of Ministers, executives of the USSR State Planning Committee, of the USSR State Committee for Material and Technical Supply and of the relevant ministries and departments of the CPSU Central Committee to arrange in the near future for the preparation of a number of legal acts on questions of carrying out Congress directives. The Secretariat of the Central Committee was charged with monitoring the progress of this work.[21]

Shevchenko goes on to state:

> Because of this cumbersome practice and the absence of verbatim records, non-attending members are often unaware of nuances or conditions related to many of the decisions made. Moreover, the Politburo has no established rule of procedure. The conduct of the work is left primarily to the leader of the Party and otherwise determined by tradition.[22]

In this way, according to Shevchenko, the inner core of the Politburo actually makes the most important decisions because of its location and its control over the procedures of the Politburo and the lack of written records. This leaves ample room for rumor, intrigue, and misinformation.

National security issues and related foreign policy issues are probably screened beforehand by the Council for Defense or referred to it by the Politburo. Although this body, whose composition and functions are discussed below, is a state institution rather than a party organ, it appears to be a de facto Politburo subcommittee. Since Brezhnev simultaneously served as (1) chairman of the Presidium, the formal state organ responsible for creating the Council, (2) presiding officer and "head" of the Politburo, to which it was de facto subordinate, (3) chairman of the council itself, and (4) General Secretary and head of the Secretariat, all bases were covered and no legal or political gaps existed. Since both Andropov and Chernenko succeeded to the four key positions described above, the situation remained unchanged after Brezhnev's death. Now that Gorbachev does not occupy the first of these key positions, the potential for confusion, conflict, and paralysis is omnipresent.

[20]Arkady Shevchenko, *Breaking with Moscow* (New York: Knopf, 1985), pp. 175–176.
[21]*Pravda*, March 21, 1986.
[22]Shevchenko, *Breaking with Moscow*, p. 176.

Although the General Secretary normally presides at Politburo meetings, in his absence the chair passes to the de facto Second Secretary or another Senior Secretary (Suslov and Kirilenko under Brezhnev; Chernenko under Andropov; Gorbachev under Chernenko; and Ligachev under Gorbachev). The agenda of the Politburo is prepared by the staff of the General Department of the Central Committee, whose long-time chief was Brezhnev's loyal satrap, Chernenko. The reorganization of the International Department of the Central Committee staff, with Anatoly Dobrynin at its head, suggests strongly that foreign policy and national security issues will be processed and coordinated here rather than in the General Department.

The General Secretary as presiding head of the Secretariat thus in fact indirectly prepares the agenda of the Politburo, and as presiding member of the Politburo is in a position to raise, frame, and define issues to his maximum advantage. If the presiding member wishes to freeze out the opinions of the candidate members who may oppose him, he can call for a formal vote and thus both cut off the debate and silence the candidate members on particular issues. Or, he can frame questions or determine their timing in such a way as to isolate individual members of the Politburo. Since all Politburo members have administrative responsibilities in either the government or party, they must rely on their professional and technical staffs to control the flow of information and problems that reach them from the lower levels of the state and party. Each Politburo member has a small staff of aides and assistants to handle administrative logistics. Furthermore, Politburo members who are not residents of Moscow often are not involved in early stages of deliberation during crisis situations.

Once the Politburo decides, the decision flows back through channels to the appropriate party or government agency for implementation and administration. The presence of the Ministers of Defense and Foreign Policy, Secret Police Chief, and party secretaries dealing with foreign communist parties on the Politburo has served to simplify and clarify administrative flows.

The Party Secretariat and the Central Committee Staff

Although the formal authority to make policy is vested in the Politburo, this power is clearly shared with the Secretariat, which at times tends to overshadow the Politburo. Whenever the dominant Soviet leader holds no formal executive position within the government, the role of the Secretariat increases, whereas it tends to diminish once the dominant leader assumes the top government post. This was the pattern established by Stalin, continued by Khrushchev, and reconfirmed by Brezhnev. During the period 1964–1977, when Brezhnev held no formal executive position in the state apparatus, the role of the Secretariat in the foreign policy process was considerably enhanced, as Brezhnev increasingly gathered the various strands of Soviet and foreign and national security policy in his hands and employed the Secretariat and its Central Committee staff as his chief implementing agencies. Under Brezhnev's direction, the Secretariat not only performed its traditional audit, monitoring, and supervising functions, but became more intimately involved in the operational side of foreign policy as well.

The Secretariat, through the practice of *nomenklatura*, must sanction or approve all high appointments to the Foreign Ministry and the diplomatic service. This body usually meets once a week, a day or two before regular Politburo sessions, and functions through its General Department as the staff of the Politburo, and prepares the agenda. Aside from the General Department, the Secretariat's participation in the foreign policy process is also effected through five Central Committee departments.

1. *Cadres Abroad.* Under the direction of Central Committee member S. V. Chervonenko, who has also served in diplomatic and other party posts, and supervised by new Party Secretary, G. Razumovsky, the functions of this department are somewhat uncertain and obscure. It probably participates in the selection of personnel to serve abroad in diplomatic and other overseas assignments and carries out the *nomenklatura* functions of the Secretariat with respect to lower ranking officials on the *nomenklatura* list.

2. *The International Department.* This department, under the long-time direction and supervision of Party Secretary and candidate Politburo member, B. M. Ponomarev, maintains contact and communications with Communist and Marxist-Leninist parties in non-Communist countries, and with national liberation movements and regimes in the Third World. With the appointment of Dobrynin to replace Ponomarev, its functions and responsibilities will probably expand. (This will be discussed further subsequently.)

3. *The Department for Liaison with Communist and Worker's Parties of Socialist Countries.* Formerly directed by Party Secretary, K. V. Rusakov, and now by V. Medvedev, this department maintains contact and communication with Communist parties in Communist countries.

4. *International Information Department.* Formerly directed by L. M. Zamyatin, but apparently abolished and absorbed by the Propaganda Department described below, under the direction of new Party Secretary and full Politburo member, A. Yakovlev. This department functioned as the press office for the General Secretary and provided information, analysis, and data to the General Secretary. Zamyatin, who is now ambassador to Great Britain, often served as the General Secretary's official spokesman.

5. *The Propaganda Department.* Directed by new Party Secretary, A. Yakovlev, this department, whose main functions are domestic, is involved in the foreign policy process through its supervision of Soviet journalists abroad, the Novosti press agency, and the contacts and exchanges with foreign countries made by the numerous Soviet nongovernmental societies, associations, organizations, and institutions involved in such

activities. These Departments also apparently work closely with relevant sections of the KGB in the filtering and analyses of information and intelligence.

Of these five Departments, the International Department has been the most actively involved in foreign policy, often competing with the Foreign Ministry itself as a center of foreign policy determination. Created after the dissolution of the Comintern in 1943 in order to maintain contact with foreign Communist parties, after the war, with the creation of a separate department dealing with ruling Communist parties, the International Department's primary function was to maintain relations with nonruling Communist parties. Somewhat later, its responsibilities were expanded to include contacts with various national liberation movements and radical national regimes in the Third World.

According to Shevchenko and other reports, Gromyko paid minimum attention to Ponomarev and his Department, which he viewed as a rival to the Foreign Ministry, and relations between the two were cool. With the surprise appointment of Ambassador Anatoly Dobrynin to the Secretariat, replacing Ponomarev, and the appointment of G. Korniyenko (erstwhile First Deputy Foreign Minister) as his First Deputy, the character and functions of this Department are likely to change. First of all, there is the curious irony that the International Department that long sought to subordinate the Foreign Ministry to its influence has now been captured by career Foreign Ministry officials. Furthermore, both Dobrynin and Korniyenko are Americanists and Gromyko protégés, as is Foreign Minister Shevardnadze's new First Deputy, Vorontsov.

Meanwhile, the Foreign Ministry is presided over by a Foreign Minister, who was a career police and Party Apparatus functionary and whose entire professional career was spent in the Republic of Georgia. He knows little about foreign policy and his previous foreign affairs experience was nil. He did not even have administrative experience on an all-union scale and his appointment remains a mystery, although speculation abounds. Furthermore, Shevardnadze, himself, is isolated in the Foreign Ministry, since he brought no high subalterns to the Ministry with him, and the Ministry is still larded with the diplomatic service fashioned by Gromyko. Although Gromyko told Shevchenko that two foreign policy centers were to be avoided, it appears that the career diplomats are in charge of both centers, which is the most best thing if two could not be avoided.

The General Secretary

Under Brezhnev, the role and power of the General Secretary as an institution developed enormously, particularly in the realm of foreign and national security policy.

TABLE 5.1 Interlocking of Government and Party Institutions and Personnel in the Soviet Political System, 1988

	PARTY				STATE				
	OTHER	REPUBLIC SECRETARIES	SECRETARIAT	POLITBURO	COUNCIL OF MINISTERS	PRESIDIUM OF SUPREME SOVIET	DEFENSE COUNCIL	REPUBLIC PREMIERS	OTHER
			Gorbachev (General Secretary)	Gorbachev		Gorbachev	Gorbachev (Chairman)		
				Gromyko		Gromyko (Chairman)	Gromyko		
				Ryzhkov	Ryzhkov (Chairman)		Ryzhkov		
			Ligachev	Ligachev			Ligachev		Ligachev[2]
				Chebrikov	Chebrikov (KGB)		Chebrikov		
				Shevardnadze	Shevardnadze (Foreign Affairs)		Shevardnadze		
			Yakovlev Nikonov Slyunkov	Yakovlev Nikonov Slyunkov					
		Shcherbitsky (Ukraine)		Shcherbitsky		Shcherbitsky			
	Zaikov[1] Solomentsev[3]			Zaikov Solomentsev Vorotnikov				Vorotnikov (R.S.F.S.R.)	
				Demichev		Demichev (First Vice Chairman)			

Full Members

Politburo

226

Candidates	Soloveyev[6]	Dolgikh	Dolgikh Yazov	Yazov (Defense)	Yazov
Junior Secretaries		Dobrynin Medvedev Razumovsky Lukyanov Biryukova	Soloveyev Talyzin	Talyzin[5]	Dobrynin[4]

[1]Moscow Party Secretary
[2]Chairman, Foreign Affairs Commission, Council of Union
[3]Chairman, Party Control Commission
[4]Chairman, Foreign Affairs Commission, Council of Nationalities
[5]Chairman, State Planning Commission
[6]Leningrad Party Secretary

227

In 1966, Brezhnev reinstituted the title of General Secretary and this position was considerably strengthened in 1971 when he was reappointed to this position. At the outset of the Brezhnev-Kosygin regime, a scrupulous regard was maintained for diplomatic protocol. Kosygin, as head of the government, and Podgorny, as head of state, conspicuously and jealously preserved their diplomatic and official prerogatives. Gradually, however, Brezhnev intruded more and more into official diplomacy, initially restricting himself to Communist states, then extending his activities to Third World countries, and then to Western Europe and the United States.

As Brezhnev's responsibilities and visibility increased, new institutions and procedures were correspondingly developed. The General Secretary's personal staff, as distinct from the Secretariat's apparatus, was enlarged. Several aides and formal "assistants to the General Secretary" were appointed who combined high party appointments and diplomatic experience to aid Brezhnev in the conduct of Soviet foreign policy and, in effect, became a third, if lesser, center for foreign policy. These assistants became highly visible and extremely important as they prepared speeches, provided data and analyses, and coordinated the various strands of national security and foreign policy for the General Secretary who, as a plenipotentiary of the Soviet government, insisted upon and was given the ceremonial and protocol trappings of a chief of state by foreign countries. The SALT I Agreement and the Helsinki Document were among the important international documents signed by Brezhnev in his sole capacity as General Secretary.

The Council for Defense

Although the Council for Defense is a constitutional body and theoretically an organ of the state, it will be discussed in this section because it is, in fact, directed by the Politburo rather than state organs.

On April 27, 1973, Andropov as head of the KGB, Grechko as Minister of Defense, and Gromyko as Minister of Foreign Affairs, were all simultaneously appointed full members of the Politburo. For Andropov, it was a promotion from candidate status, but for the other two, it was clearly an institutional and *ex officio* appointment. Apparently, in the same year, the Council for Defense was created by secret statute or decree with Brezhnev as Chairman. Public mention of the Council for Defense, which was the immediate successor to the Higher Military Council, was first made in 1974. In 1976, when Brezhnev was invested with the military rank of Marshal of the Soviet Union, it was also revealed that he was chairman of this body. In 1977, Brezhnev displaced Podgorny as President of the Soviet Union while retaining his post of General Secretary, and in the new Brezhnev Constitution of 1977 the Council for Defense was converted from a statutory body into a constitutional organ whose creation and composition were determined by the Presidium of the Supreme Soviet of which Brezhnev was now Chairman.

During the past decade all of the principal decision-making organs of the Soviet system have been subjected to rapid and repeated changes in composition. The Council for Defense remains much of a mystery in terms of its origins, functions, power, procedures, and even composition. Aside from it existence and the episodic identification of its chairman, little else is known for certain. Until Gromyko's appointment as a First Deputy Chairman of the Council of Ministers in 1983, the Chairman of the Council of Ministers was the only member of that body's Presidium who sat on the Council for Defense. This further strongly suggests that the Council of Ministers no longer had any jurisdiction over national security and foreign policy matters or the Council for Defense, which emerged as a de facto inner core of the Politburo and under its effective jurisdiction. This is further suggested by the fact that Brezhnev, in his capacity as General Secretary, was Chairman of the Council for Defense without being a responsible official of the government, and hence was not accountable to the Council of Ministers or its Chairman, a situation which finds itself repeated under Gorbachev.

The Council for Defense was transformed into a constitutionally mandated body with the adoption of the Constitution of 1977. Article 121(14) states that the Presidium shall "form the Council for Defense of the USSR and confirm its composition." Note that the constitution does not invest the Presidium with the power to appoint its composition, but to confirm it. On the other hand the same article gives the Presidium the authority to "appoint and dismiss the high command of the Armed Forces of the USSR." No other law or decree or Soviet publication has provided additional information on this body. A military journal dated October 1977 further revealed that Brezhnev was also Supreme Commander in Chief of the Soviet Armed Forces, thus suggesting that this post can be separate and distinct as well as united with the position of Chairman of the Council for Defense. General Secretary, Chairman of the Presidium, Chairman of the Council for Defense, and Supreme Commander in Chief are four distinct posts, and while Brezhnev, Andropov and Chernenko united all of them in their person, it is juridically possible for the four positions to be held by four separate individuals. It took Andropov nearly nine months to gather all of these positions into his hands, although Chernenko gathered them over a shorter period of time. As noted earlier, although Gorbachev is Chairman of the Council for Defense, he was not elected President.

FULL MEMBERS

*General Secretary
*Chairman, Presidium of the Supreme Soviet

Second Secretary
Chairman, Council of Ministers
Minister of Defense
Chairman, KGB
Minister of Foreign Affairs

ADVISORY MEMBERS

Chairman, Military-Industrial Commission
Chief of the General Staff, Armed Forces
Commander-in-Chief, Warsaw Pact Forces
First Deputy Defense Minister, without portfolio
Director, Main Political Administration

*If these posts are held by one person, he represents both positions.

No public disclosure of a Council for Defense meeting has ever been made, and it is unknown how often and for what purpose it meets, although the general surmise is that it serves as either an inner national security core of the Politburo or a Politburo subcommittee dealing with matters related to national security and defense. It is unknown whether the Council for Defense has a staff or an infrastructure.

From these scattered accounts, it appears that the Council for Defense is not simply a command group, but engages in broad military policy and development in peace time, establishing military doctrine, perhaps making threat assessments, measuring internal needs against external demands, balancing military capabilities with foreign policy goals, and providing the necessary coordination and mobilization of human and material resources. It is probably the single most important forum where top Party Apparatus and government officials meet and interact with the professional military. It provides an arena where individual political figures can make alliances with military professionals and where the military can exert its demands and make its influences felt. One can reasonably surmise that in the Council for Defense Andropov successfully forged the national security coalition which managed to win out over Brezhnev's preferred successor, Chernenko. Since his succession, Gorbachev has mentioned several times that he serves as Chairman of this body.

THE ADMINISTRATION AND EXECUTION OF SOVIET FOREIGN POLICY

Party Policy and State Administration

Gorbachev's concept of *perestroika* as applied to Soviet foreign policy involves three separate but intimately intertwined components: (1) reconceptualization of foreign policy goals and national security requirements so that the latter more sharply determine the former, even if it subverts ideological imperatives; (2) redirection of Soviet foreign policy goals in accordance with a more rational structure of foreign policy priorities and a redefinition of the proper balance between the foreign policy agenda and the domestic agenda; and (3) the reorganization and restructuring of the foreign policy decision-making apparatus, in terms of personnel, institutions, and processes, in order to effectuate the first two components in terms of policy-making, implementation, and execution.

Each Soviet leader attempts to resolve constitutional issues that relate to policy-making in his own unique way. Just as Brezhnev introduced a new constitution in 1977 to establish himself as a full unimpaired chief executive of the Soviet political system, Gorbachev unveiled his plans for restructuring the apexes of the two structures and to fuse them in his person. Gorbachev convened an extraordinary Party Conference (19th) in July 1988, to circumvent the entrenched opponents of his reforms, and gained its approval to fundamentally revamp the top side of the central institutions of the State to his satisfaction. Although he did not call for a new constitution, his proposals will require extensive amendments to the existing document.

Gorbachev's proposals envisage the replacement of the existing Supreme Soviet in favor of an extraordinarily cumbersome system of a legislature within a legislature, reminiscent of the system which prevailed under the 1924 constitution. Voters would elect a large body, called the Congress of People's Deputies, consisting of 2,250 members, which would meet annually for a brief session to elect first a small, compact Supreme Soviet of 300 members, divided into two chambers, that would sit more or less continuously during the entire year. It would also elect a President of the Supreme Soviet, who would have the full power of both a Chief of State and Chief Executive Officer. According to Gorbachev's prescription, the General Secretary of the Party would be the sole nominee for this new powerful Presidency. The Council of Ministers and its chairman would be retained, but they would be under the jurisdiction of the new President. Although not clearly spelled out in detail, the new President, who would also be the General Secrtary of the Party, would have the full status and authority of a Chief of State and function also as the ceremonial head of the U.S.S.R. in foreign affairs, much like that of the President of the United States.

If everything proceeds on schedule, these changes will be made in time for Gorbachev to be elected to the new Presidency in April 1989. These measures are also designed to clearly circumvent the powerful Party Central Committee and the Party Apparatus in general. Although as General Secretary, Gorbachev presides over the Central Committee and the Party Apparatus, many of his most determined opponents are entrenched there. The new Supreme Soviet is designed to strip the Central Committee of its de facto legislative power and re-locate it in the Supreme Soviet. Similarly, the new Congress of People's Deputies will assume many of these constitutive functions of the Party Congress. The Party, under Gorbachev's new design, will be stripped of its existing de facto administrative power and be relegated to the background as the "vanguard" of society, setting guidelines as the ultimate custodian of the spirit of the revolution.

As long as Gorbachev functions solely from his position as General Secretary, the initial steps in the restructuring of the foreign policy apparatus will be improvisional rather than definitive. In the Soviet political system, the party proposes but the state disposes, that is, whereas policy formulation and decision making are executed through party organs, the execution, implementation, and administration of policy is through state organs and personnel. Given Gorbachev's lack of an executive constitutional position in the Soviet political order, he becomes, in effect, an incomplete Soviet executive, who presides and controls essentially the policy-making machinery. The juridical machinery is presided over by Andrei Gromyko in his capacity as Chairman of the Presidium of the Supreme Court, that is, the juridical head of state, whereas the administrative machinery, which includes the Foreign Ministry, is headed by Ryzhkov in his capacity as Chairman of the Council of Ministers, that is, head of government.

Gorbachev's only official positions in the Soviet political order, with one exception, are relatively modest and essentially token in character. Like Stalin before 1941 and Khrushchev and Brezhnev before they assumed formal official state executive positions, Gorbachev's serves as an ordinary member of the Presidium and as an ordinary deputy to the Supreme Soviet. Gorbachev, however, serves also as Chairman of the Council for Defense. But unlike his predecessors as General Secretary, Gorbachev also functions openly as the de facto head of state and government, represents and commits the Soviet state, meets with diplomatic representatives and heads of state and government, signs official state documents, including international treaties, and does so almost to the total exclusion of both the formal head of state and government in these activities. As noted earlier, when Khrushchev modestly, and Brezhnev more overtly and actively, asserted themselves in diplomacy in their capacity as party leader, they found the situation uncomfortable and eventually assumed a formal state executive position.

Hence the restructuring of the foreign policy apparatus under Gorbachev is designed to accommodate itself to this unprecedented situation, whereby the General Secretary functions virtually as the sole responsible spokesman and actor for the Soviet Union in the international arena.

Another important difference between the current situation and the Stalin period, is that state organs and institutions have since 1941 become far more important in size, complexity, and professional competence. All of the implementing and administrative machinery of foreign policy are located in state and government institutions, over which Gorbachev exercises no direct or juridical control. Rather, Gorbachev must function through Politburo colleagues, whose relationship to Gorbachev is far different from counterpart officials to Stalin, and who preside over and exercise formal executive control over these administrative departments. Thus, in order to bridge this gap between real and formal authority and enable him to manage the foreign policy machinery, Gorbachev has enhanced the size, power, and professional competence of the relevant Departments of the Central Committee (especially the International Department) and has accordingly reorganized the Departments of the Foreign Ministry to correspond with the expanded role of Central Committee Departments in managing the foreign policy machinery.

Under Anatoli Dobrynin, long-time Soviet Ambassador to the United States, who has been appointed a junior Secretary in the Secretariat (but not yet to the Politburo), the International Department has been reorganized, with the old Party functionaries replaced with experienced diplomatic specialists reassigned from the Foreign Ministry. Dobrynin, in turn, works very closely with Aleksander Yakovlev, another former diplomat, who serves as a Senior Secretary and full member of the Politburo, and is a principal architect of Gorbachev's new political thinking. Dobrynin and Yakovlev emerge as Gorbachev's chief professional advisers on foreign policy, whereas Eduard Shevardnadze, who replaced Gromyko as Foreign Minister and is a close *political* confidante and friend of the General Secretary, functions essentially as Gorbachev's *alter ego* in his capacity as the General Secretary's principal representative to the outside world.

Shevardnadze has little experience in foreign affairs, but is a shrewd politician and has a good public relations sense. His professional background was largely in the party Apparatus and police apparatus, and he presides over a Foreign Ministry, whose personnel are among the most experienced and competent diplomats in the world. Thus, Gorbachev and Shevardnadze, two career party functionaries, must manage two apparati that are filled almost exclusively with professional diplomats recruited during Gromyko's twenty-eight years of incumbency as Foreign Minister. The restructuring of Central Committee departments and reshuffling of diplomatic departments becomes, in effect, a surrogate for replacing personnel which neither Gorbachev nor Shevardnadze are in a position to do because they have no reserve of potential or ready replacements. The restructuring of the foreign policy apparatus was broadly explained and justified by Gorbachev as follows:

> At present, a restructuring of the work of the Ministry of Foreign Affairs is underway and a reorganization of the structure of its central apparatus and foreign institutions is being carried out. This leadership is being renewed.

This line must be pursued consistently, increasing the efficiency of the activity of the diplomatic service and *striving* to have it correspond fully to the vigorous international activity of the CPSU and the Soviet State.[23]

The Ministry of Foreign Affairs

In over seventy years of Soviet diplomacy, there have been only eight foreign ministers: Leon Trotsky (November 1917–April 1918); Georgi Chicherin (1918–1929); Maxim Litvinov (1929–1939); Vyacheslav Molotov (1939–1949 and 1953–1956); Andrei Vyshinsky (1949–1953); Dimitri Shepilov (during 1956); Andrei Gromyko (1957–1985); and Eduard Shevardnadze (1985–present). The typical tenure of a Soviet foreign minister is ten years. Over sixty years of Soviet diplomacy, foreign affairs have been directed by only four individuals, thus giving Soviet diplomacy an enviable continuity.

With Gromyko's replacement as foreign minister by the Gorbachev confidante, Shevardnadze, it was expected that the Foreign Ministry would be restructured and replenished to correspond with Gorbachev's political style and foreign policy ideas. But given the fact that the Soviet Union's most experienced foreign policy personnel are located in the Foreign Ministry, the new Soviet leader had little choice but to simply rearrange chairs and departments. Personnel changes have been many since the advent of Shevardnadze, but virtually all have been promotions and reassignments from within. There has been no infusion of personnel from the KGB, the Party Apparatus, or other agencies into the Foreign Ministry and Shevardnadze remains surrounded by diplomats raised in the Gromyko mold. On the contrary, experienced Foreign Ministry officials have been reassigned to important positions in other Soviet ministries and in the central Party Apparatus. This relative immunity to purges and personnel infusion from the outside is in stark contrast to the massive turnovers at the topside of the Soviet political structure: the Politburo, Secretariat, Council for Defense, Central Committee apparatus, and so forth. This means that the Foreign Ministry remains among the most stable of agencies in the Soviet system in terms of personnel and is a remarkable tribute to its high competence and professionalism.

Shevardnadze's reorganized Foreign Ministry, at the top, consists of two First Deputy Foreign Ministers, appointed in 1986, and nine Deputy Foreign Ministers, seven of which were appointed since Shevardnadze assumed control, of which only the deputy in charge of personnel is drawn from the Party Apparatus. The Minister, First Deputies and Deputies, together with eleven others, mainly important department heads, made up the Collegium, the highest collective body in the Foreign Ministry. All top officials of the Foreign Ministry have personal aides, and some

[23]*Pravda*, January 28, 1987.

ten experienced diplomats are designated as ambassadors-at-large and may also participate in Collegium meetings on an ad hoc basis. In recent years, the number of administrative units in the Foreign Ministry have proliferated enormously as the Soviet Union has expanded and assumed a greater role in international affairs. The organizational structure consists of about fifteen functional administrations, fourteen geographical departments, two new ideogeographical administrations, and seven nongeographical departments. New heads have been appointed to eight of the fourteen geographical departments, both of the ideogeographical departments, and to a majority of the functional administrations and departments. Furthermore, the basic administrations and departments have generated a large number of subunits and subdepartments.

The Soviet Union maintains diplomatic relations with about 135 countries and its missions abroad are among the largest in the world. In addition the Soviet Foreign Ministry is responsible for supplying personnel for innumerable international, regional, and multilateral organizations, including those affiliated with the United Nations, and these missions also employ substantial numbers of people. But its principal function is still to supply personnel for Soviet embassies to individual countries and to staff the geographical and country desks in the Foreign Ministry itself. In the recent reorganization of the Foreign Ministry, the number of functional administrations and departments have been increased to account for new areas of concern and expansion of activities, whereas the number of geographical departments have been reduced from eighteen to fourteen departments and two new administrations.

The Foreign Ministry maintains its own training and research institutes, although, of course, it also relies upon universities, research institutes of the Academy of Sciences, the party Central Committee academies and research institutes, the KGB, and other government and party agencies for both information and personnel.

The Foreign Ministry also provides general supervision for the "foreign ministers" of the fifteen Soviet national republics, most of which have only peripheral involvement in Soviet foreign policy, but two of which (Ukraine and Byelorussia) have separate membership in the United Nations and must therefore maintain a substantial professional staff to supply their missions and delegations to the various international and multinational organizations affiliated with the United Nations and its agencies. Republican "foreign ministries" are in fact simply geographically dispersed sections of the Central Foreign Ministry.

The Foreign Ministry's Relations with the Defense Ministry, the KGB, and other Ministries and Party Agencies in the Execution of Soviet Foreign Policy.

No analysis of the Soviet foreign policy process would be complete without devoting some attention to the role of various ministries and departments in the process. Although the Ministry of Foreign Affairs is charged with responsibility for the administration and implementation of Soviet foreign policy, Soviet activities abroad have become too multiform and diverse to be monopolized by a single ministry. Hence, although the Foreign Ministry is the mainline diplomatic and foreign policy instrument of the Soviet Union, other government ministries, agencies, and party agencies are increasingly involved in the operation and implementation of Soviet policy abroad. Other ministries which play a substantial role in this regard are the following:

1. *The Ministry of Defense,* with its bases and installations deployed around the globe, its military assistance and interventionist personnel in many countries, its separate intelligence agency (GRU), and its numerous attachés serving in Soviet diplomatic missions.
2. *The State Committee for State Security* (KGB) or Secret Police, with its numerous agents installed undercover as Soviet diplomats in missions abroad and in international organizations, and its ramified intelligence, sabotage, espionage, terrorist, subversive, disinformation, and assassination missions operating legally and illegally.
3. *The Ministry of Foreign Trade,* which handles all foreign commercial transactions with state-owned and privately owned enterprise in foreign countries. Soviet foreign trade is a state monopoly and its activities have always been closely coordinated with those of the Foreign Ministry. Soviet foreign trade organizations also often serve as a cover for KGB operatives and other Soviet illegal operations in foreign countries.
4. *State Committee for Foreign Economic Relations,* which negotiates and administers foreign economic and technical assistance programs in the Third World countries.
5. *Ministry of Culture,* whose responsibilities are largely domestic, but which also supervises cultural contacts and exchanges with foreign countries.
6. *State Committee for Foreign Tourism,* whose functions are self-evident.

Aside from the fact that many other Soviet ministries and state committees have a Foreign Relations Administration Department to handle contacts and exchanges abroad with appropriate foreign counterparts, there are a myriad of so-called public, nongovernmental associations, societies, organizations, and committees, which are essentially propaganda instruments whose associational titles usually define their missions, for example, the Soviet Committee for the Defense of Peace; Soviet Committee for Solidarity with Asian and African countries; and the Union of Soviet Societies for Foreign and Cultural Relations with Foreign Countries.

And finally, mention must be made of the Soviet propaganda, press, communications, and media operations. Information flow is tightly controlled by the Soviet state; all newspapers, magazines, journals, books, and so forth are published only by authorized official agencies and are subject to state censorship. Journalists abroad are essentially officials of the Soviet state and report only the official Soviet line and propagate a support of Soviet policy without deviation. The same is true of the Soviet press agencies, TASS and NOVOSTI. Most Soviet journalists abroad are connected with the Soviet Secret Police and function as gatherers of open intelligence information. Many high-level journalists also assume more direct roles in the administration of Soviet foreign policy by serving as diplomats or as functionaries in the press, information, and propaganda departments of various party and state agencies. This, however, appears to be changing. Apparently many honest journalists are now speaking out under *glasnost* and demanding a more independent status. Thus, one Soviet journalist has simultaneously complained about the subservient and servile character of the Soviet press in the past and his hopes for the future:

> Restructuring has made journalists who write on international topics take a sober look at the fruits of their labor. . . . The journalist's basic law—reportorial honesty and devotion to principle, plus truthfulness of information—was broken. . . . The main thing . . . is not the truthful coverage of events but an interpretation of them that corresponds to the departmental line of the day. It is probably for this reason that we—and "they"—are used to thinking that the opinion of a Soviet journalist, in essence, only repeats or explains the viewpoint of official circles. And, no matter how ardently we contend in debates with our ideological opponents that we are expressing our own viewpoint, in most cases, unfortunately, that is in fact not the case.[24]

There appears to be little in the way of interagency committees or even contacts between intermediate administrative units of the various ministries and agencies dealing in foreign matters, and rather rigid and severe compartmentalization and specialization of functions are the result. Coordination is virtually the exclusive domain of those at the top, in the Politburo, Secretariat, and Council of Defense. Interagency contact and cooperation between the Defense Ministry and the civilian ministries, in particular, appear to be meager, with the military jealously guarding its special and highly secret knowledge concerning weapons, defense, security strategy, and planning. About the only interaction between the military and the Foreign Ministry is at the level of arms control negotiations with the United States and elsewhere (in contrast to planning and preparing for negotiations, which remains largely parallel, separate, and compartmentalized). Foreign Ministry officials have little access to sensitive military information and play little or no role in defense and military planning. Other areas of Foreign Ministry and Defense Ministry contact

[24]Boris Asoyan, in *Literatunaya Gazeta*, October 7, 1987, p. 14.

are, of course, the presence of Soviet military attachés in all Soviet diplomatic missions abroad, although they report back through separate channels to the Defense Ministry. The Foreign Ministry is also involved when Soviet military installations and assistance programs abroad are being negotiated and maintained.

Interaction between career foreign service officials and career party officials is somewhat more extensive, but essentially a one-way operation. The Soviet foreign service has been used for many years as a soft exile for wounded party officials who lost out in the factional struggle or whose patron lost out. Immediately after Stalin's death, in particular, defeated party bureaucrats found themselves farmed out as ambassadors and ministers abroad or as Foreign Ministry officials. This practice has been unnecessary in recent years, although a handful of former high party and state officials are still to be found in comfortable exile abroad. A few lesser provincial and republican party officials are still to be found sprinkled around Soviet Third World embassies in remote areas, which would not seem to suggest reward for outstanding or faithful service.

Another tradition of party penetration into the diplomatic service represents a different and opposing pattern—the stationing of high party officials, usually Central Committee members, as ambassadors to friendly communist countries. These ambassadors should be distinguished from veteran career ambassadors posted to important Western countries and given high party rank, usually membership in the Central Committee, which represents a reward for outstanding high-level diplomatic service. They are ambassadors with high party rank in contrast to party officials who hold high diplomatic rank.

Whereas party officialdom restricts itself largely to quasi-diplomatic activities with foreign Communist states, nonruling Communist parties in foreign countries, and ideologically kindred political and revolutionary movements, its formal participation in the implementation of Soviet foreign policy becomes more direct in Soviet relations with Communist states. All Communist states, with some exceptions, receive as Soviet ambassadors high Soviet party officials, invariably full members of the Central committee who also have a history of service in the Party Apparatus. These ambassadors serve simultaneously as Soviet party representatives to the Communist party of the host country and thus report back through two channels, reflecting their dual role. They report to the Central Committee Department for Liaison with Communist and Workers' Parties of Socialist Countries in their party role and to the appropriate geographical department in the Foreign Ministry. With the elevation of Gromyko to full membership in the Politburo and membership in the Council of Defense, the problems of coordination and confusion had been considerably reduced. With Gromyko sitting at the apex of the system, no ambassador was likely to send contradictory reports through his two channels of communication, which apparently was a problem in the past when many Soviet ambassadors enjoyed higher party rank than the foreign minister. The creation of the two new socialist countries administrations in the Foreign Ministry is designed to eliminate whatever confusion of lines of responsibility existed in the past because of the dual character of Soviet ambassadors to communist countries.

At the apex of the Soviet system, the Secret Police have a powerful input into the formulation and execution of Soviet foreign policy. This was particularly the case under former Secret Police Chief Andropov. Yuri Andropov represented in his person and professional career the interaction of the diplomatic service, the Party Apparatus, and the Secret Police.

There is substantial evidence that suggests considerable rivalry, competition, and disagreement between Foreign Ministry personnel outlooks on world affairs and those of other government and party agencies. Parallel structures and functions automatically create competing and often opposing outlooks reflecting the interests and ambitions of institutions as well as those of individuals. This is not only true of divergent perspectives held by civilian and military officials, but even among civilian agencies as well. The Soviet Foreign Ministry jealously guards its domain while gingerly attempting to intrude into the domain of the diplomats. Even among civilian agencies, the Foreign Ministry is particularly on the alert for competing attempts by specialized think tanks, like the Institute on the U.S.A. and Canada, to substitute its views on policy to policymakers for the policy of the Foreign Ministry. Specialists on various regions, countries, and other aspects of international relations are to be found in think tanks maintained by the party Central Committee, the Academy of Sciences, the universities, and other government ministries aside from those maintained in the Foreign Ministry.

FUTURE DIRECTIONS IN SOVIET FOREIGN POLICY

The balance sheet of Soviet foreign policy over the past seventy years shows an impressive range of accomplishments. An outlaw state in 1917, governed by a pariah regime, beset on all sides by powerful enemies, racked internally by social convulsions, civil war, fragmentation, and foreign occupation, the Soviet Union, whose chances for survival then were extremely poor, stands today as a modernized global power, second only to the United States.

Throughout much of its history, Soviet foreign policy has operated within a self-defined framework of a two-camp or bipolar world with two basic players, Communism (the Soviet Union) and capitalism (everybody else), so that all losses in the capitalist world were automatic gains for the

Soviet Union. For nearly two decades the Cold War was pursued within this framework, as the bipolarization of power around Moscow and Washington increasingly assumed the objective character of a zero-sum game. The disintegration of the European colonial empires, the advent of weapons of instantaneous and universal destruction, the progressive dissolution of the Soviet Bloc, the erosion of the NATO alliance, and the eruption of the fratricidal Sino-Soviet conflict, however, have all but destroyed the bipolarized international community in which gains and losses could be registered with zero-sum gamelike simplicity.

The Soviet Union's current status and position in the world community represents a blend of success and failure. The Soviet Union has been a resounding success when its achievements are measured against the traditional yardstick of power politics, but a conspicuous failure when measured against its initial ideological inspiration and purpose. Instead of transforming the world, it is the Soviet Union that has been transformed. From a self-anointed center of world revolution dedicated to the destruction of the existing social and political status quo, it has been objectively transformed into a mature global power whose interest in stabilizing the status quo matches its professed dedication to revolution. Finally, its ideology has been transformed from a vehicle legitimizing world revolution into one legitimizing Communist rule in Russia; instead of raising the standard of revolution abroad, Moscow emphasized raising the standard of living at home in the name of ideology; instead of justifying further social changes in the Soviet system, it rationalized the social status quo.

If we employ the traditional criteria of success in foreign policy (power, influence, and prestige), it is indisputable that the Soviet Union has been more successful than any other state in the past fifty years, save the United States. The most significant factor in the simultaneous rise of Soviet power and decline of the power of other states was the Second World War. Germany was dismembered and occupied; Japan was squeezed back into her main islands and disarmed; Italy was shorn of her colonial empire, while a weakened France, Great Britain, and Netherlands progressively relinquished theirs. During the same time period, the Soviet Union annexed 250,000 square miles of territory in Europe and Asia, established vassal states in East Asia and Eastern Europe, displacing Japan and Germany respectively as the dominant powers in those two regions. It supported a successful Communist takeover in China; sponsored the growth and proliferation of Communist parties abroad, which it manipulated as instruments of its foreign policy; continued to maintain the largest military establishment in the world; and poised to move into new vacuums which might be created by the convulsions and agonies of colonial empires in dissolution and by the internal turmoil that swept Western Europe in the postwar period.

Although the Soviet Union has certainly failed in its original ideological mission of communizing the world, its half-century attempt has left a lasting imprint upon the physiognomy of the globe. It has fundamentally restructured the social, political, economic, and ideological configurations of one-third of the world and reoriented the direction in which the rest is moving. As a consequence of its endeavors, an international subsystem of fourteen Communist states has been established. These states not only share a common ideology, but a common socioeconomic system with a distinctive set of property relationships, giving rise to a shared social structure, governed and regulated by highly similar political institutions and processes. Nevertheless, this failed to guarantee solidarity and unity of behavior.

Furthermore, Communist parties are to be found in some one-hundred additional countries on every continent, ranging from minuscule, furtive and illegal conspiratorial groups to large mass parties, such as those in France, Italy, and India. All these parties are inspired by variants of a common ideology, Marxism-Leninism, and are thus derivative emanations from the Bolshevik Revolution of 1917, but many of the important Western Communist parties have moved away from Soviet orthodoxy, and others have charted exotic paths.

As the Soviet Union approaches the year 2000, the definite contours of the Soviet state in foreign policy appear to be taken shape. A multinational state, dominated by Great Russians, and controlling its immediate periphery, with strong revolutionary reflexes, functioning as a global power, with global interests and ambitions—these are the contours of the future Soviet state. Given the nature of its multinational composition, with nearly a score of historic nationalities denied independent statehood to satisfy historic Russian security requirements and Communist ideological imperatives, given its domination over more than a half-dozen adjacent Communist states, whose internal and external sovereignty is severely infringed, and given the appearance of nearly a score of client states called "socialist-oriented regimes" scattered across the Third World, the Soviet Union has all of the earmarks of an imperial system, and will be burdened with both its benefits and disadvantages.

The Soviet extended empire is a direct result of its growing military power during the past decades as the Soviet Union finally achieved equality with the United States in one important dimension—the military. Hence global expansion rather than internal development assumed highest priority in Soviet calculations because of its asymmetrical capabilities. Military power gives the Soviet Union its role, status, and credentials as a global power in the international community, but also enhances the role of the military in the Soviet political process. It is this combination of a Soviet state with powerful military and military-industrial production capabilities together with a deficient civilian economy which posed both a danger and a challenge to the new generation of Soviet leaders and the outside world alike. Will the new Soviet leaders, armed with sufficient nuclear capability to destroy the globe unilaterally, continue to compete in the areas where they are most competitive and successful, and seek to extend their global empire and influence, or will they consolidate their gains, retrench abroad, and devote greater attention and effort to remedying the deficiencies of their economy, raising the Soviet standard of living, and solving the difficult and harsh social and demographic problems which have been accumulating and now confront them?

The first years of the Gorbachev regime suggests very strongly that the new leadership has opted for the last alternative, to consolidate and retrench abroad and to reform and upgrade at home. Gorbachev's agenda, for the most part, is still a "wish list," which arouses considerable resistance from entrenched power centers in the Soviet system, and may ultimately prove to be too ambitious and utopian. When one analyzes Gorbachev's agenda, first and foremost of his objectives is to retain and consolidate power. The second item on his agenda is implementing his ambitious program designed to reform, renovate, and revitalize not only the Soviet economic system, but Soviet society as a whole. The first and second items on the agenda are, to some degree, inherently contradictory. Since his restructuring program still encounters strong resistance from entrenched bureaucracies, which constitute a potential source of political leverage for possible contenders in the leadership, Gorbachev may have to compromise and modify his program in order to retain and consolidate power. How much of his program may survive is still in question, even as he succeeds in retaining power. Over and above this is the still debatable issue of the feasibility of his program. Prior to restructuring comes dismantling of existing structures, and many in the Soviet Union remain dubious as to whether a successful transition can be made from a known structure being dismantled to the erection of new structures, whose promised performance characteristics are largely untested and hypothetical.

The third item on Gorbachev's agenda finally is about foreign policy, and here, the restructuring of Soviet-American relations assumes highest priority. The achievement of the first two items on his agenda requires the existence of a stable and predictable international environment, which would ensure the absence of confrontation, surprise, and diversion of effort and resources, particularly in dealing with issues that involve the United States. The Soviet Union, during its restructuring, will enter a prolonged period of vulnerability as it dismantles and restructures, and Gorbachev wants to minimize the possibility of the United States taking possible advantage of periods of vulnerability. Hence amicable relations with the United States are an indispensable prerequisite for the success of his domestic agenda.

Defusing tensions between Moscow and Washington and reducing the possibilities of confrontation will allow Gorbachev to consolidate and retrench in other areas of foreign policy with minimum damage and risk: withdrawing Soviet troops from Afghanistan, drawing back from overextended commitments to remote, vulnerable, and difficult areas, like Central America, Southern Africa, and Southeast Asia. Brezhnev's overseas empire has exhausted its symbolic value and the material and psychic burdens of this Empire are becoming more evident.

Disillusionment and disappointment with the failure of events to coincide with Soviet prognostications, based upon falsified information, has impelled Gorbachev to reassess the costs and benefits of Soviet policy in the Third World. Therefore, it should not be surprising to witness the Soviet Union not only arresting its expansion into the Third World (to avoid becoming ensnared in its problems), but also trimming back its commitments and obligations in marginal areas of the world.

A renewed Soviet-American détente, to use a badly abused but still appropriate concept, will also allow Gorbachev to trim the Soviet military budget, to shift allocations and resources away from the military side of the economy to the nonmilitary sector, and to reduce the swollen size of the Armed Forces, and to release perhaps a million workers to participate in the labor force. There is little doubt that this shift in allocations, as in the past, will cause alienation among the professional military and strong resistance to Gorbachev from that direction.

The fourth item on Gorbachev's agenda is the restructuring of relations with Eastern Europe, encouraging change, renovation, and modernization in an area which has also been floundering in stagnation and decline. Gorbachev has called, in effect, for greater political autonomy for Eastern Europe in return for closer economic, scientific, and technological integration. Eastern Europe, as a military asset, has been steadily eroding, and its main value to Moscow is as a symbolic ideological asset—that is, an ideological extension of the Soviet system, which serves to preserve the universalist credentials of Soviet ideology—and a potential economic asset. As subservient political clients, the East European countries have become deformed economic entities, with demoralized and sulking anti-Soviet populations for the most part. As an incentive to revitalize and renovate themselves, Gorbachev is offering the countries of Eastern Europe a greater participation in determining their own destiny, hoping that this will benefit not only Eastern Europe but the Soviet Union as well. The objective is to transform nonviable societies governed by dependable regimes into viable societies, whose regimes will associate themselves with Moscow out of self-interest rather than fear. Whether this is possible remains to be seen, for not only resistance from various directions, but also actual turmoil and confusion is omnipresent since Gorbachev's programs of *perestroika, glasnost,* and *demokratizatsiya* are inherently destabilizing. But for the first time the winds of reform are coming from the East, and resistance in Eastern Europe comes from the Brezhnevit East European leaders, who cherish the status quo. Whereas, *perestroika, glasnost,* and *demokratizatsiya* aid Gorbachev in his consolidation of power, they would undermine the power of most East European leaders.

Gorbachev has also called for a normalization of relations with China and may withdraw more Soviet troops from the Sino-Soviet frontier, but so far the Chinese have not responded to his proposals. As the Soviet Union retrenches, it will come to rely on other forces and institutions in the international system as instruments of its foreign policy. This serves to explain Gorbachev's sudden interest in a broader and more responsible role for the United Nations and its institutions in dealing with world problems. Moscow has also evinced interest in joining international financial and economic organizations, which it has spurned in the past, again largely for the same purpose. Thus, the Soviet Union appears to be inching away from unilateralism towards multilateralism in accordance with Gorbachev's reinvention of the concept "interdependence."

The Soviet Union in the past has gone through alternative periods of expansion and consolidation and retrenchment in foreign policy, and corresponding intensified internal development. What is happening under Gorbachev may be just another episode in this recurring cycle, to be superceded by another change in direction after the turn of the millennium, depending upon what happens in the 1990s. Risks and opportunities, self-confidence and vulnerability also run in cycles, and a period of self-perceived vulnerability and lessened opportunity is by no means necessarily permanent. Indeed, some observers of the Soviet scene interpret Gorbachev's reform program as simply a phase in which the Soviet Union plays "catch up" with the West, so that it might resume its expansionist pace with greater vigor and effectiveness in the next few decades of the coming century.

Hence, during the coming decade, barring any slippage of the United States into confusion and irresolution, the Soviet Union is likely to be preoccupied with internal development and renovation. We have it on no less an authority than Gorbachev himself that the chief impetus to Moscow's change of direction has been Gorbachev's assessment of the Soviet Union's inability to compete successfully in the modern world and to participate fully in the ongoing scientific-technological revolution, to say nothing of being a part of its cutting edge.

One of the great disillusionments and unpleasant surprises for the Soviet leadership has been the continuing vitality of capitalism in the United States, Western Europe, and Japan. Gorbachev, in his assessments, feels almost betrayed by Marxist-Leninist historicism which misled Soviet leaders into believing that both the United States and capitalism were on their last legs. In his report to the Twenty-seventh Party Congress in 1986, Gorbachev referred to capitalism's inability "to cope with the acute problems of the declining phase of capitalism's development," but he almost ruefully complained that not only did capitalism refuse to die, but was demonstrating unexpected resilience and strength:

> True, the present stage of the general crisis does not rule out the possibilities for economic growth, and the mastering of new scientific and technical fields. The stage "allows for" sustaining concrete economic, military, political, and other positions, and in some areas even the possibility for social revenge, for regaining what had been lost before.[25]

Far from being exhausted capitalism has exhibited extraordinary inventiveness, creativity, and productivity, in contrast to the "epoch of the decline and decay" under Brezhnev. It is as if Marxism-Leninism yielded upside-down predictions in that; instead of socialism being the "cutting edge" of science and technology it is capitalism, and instead of capitalism in decay, it is socialism. History has seemingly played a cruel joke on the Soviet Union. And the entire Soviet establishment shuddered in response to President Reagan's characterization of the Soviet Union as an "evil empire" destined for the "ashbins of history," a formulation which Marxism-Leninism reserved for capitalism. This idea was still to find its echo in Gorbachev's Report, when he condemned capitalism for "becoming the ugliest and most dangerous monster of the twentieth century," and it was clear that he meant, first and foremost, American capitalism.[26]

Gorbachev's closest academic and journalistic foreign policy advisers are even more graphic in exhibiting their profound psychological disillusionment and sense of historical betrayal, when they concede that the Soviet model of socialism was stagnated and was failing:

> Imperialist ideologues are rushing to interpret what is happening as a historic defeat for socialism. . . . The history of socialism is filled with unexpected twists. . . . Socialism survived and prevailed but had to pay a high socio-political price. . . . Was the model of socialism we built the only possible one. . .? Under the form of socialism that took shape . . . socialism's principal economic task—overtaking capitalism in labor productivity and per-capita output—was not solved. We had not created a society that in every respect was capable of serving as an example, as a model for imitation, and as a stimulus in the struggle for the socialist transformation of the world. . . . Apathy and social passivity grew . . . the management system . . . had completely exhausted its capabilities. Retaining it was causing economic stagnation, bringing our society to the brink of a crisis, and weakening the Soviet Union's prestige and influence in the international arena.[27]

[25]Milkhail Gorbachev, *Toward A Better World* (New York: Richardson and Steirman, 1987), pp. 95–96.
[26]*Ibid.*, p. 91.
[27]Aleksander Bovin, *Izvestia*, January 11, 1987.

Consequently, socialism lost its appeal to the developed world, and instead was being adopted by unstable Third World countries. Capitalism, in contrast, demonstrated remarkable strength in its competition with socialism:

> At the same time, we must admit that capitalism's ability to adapt to the new historical environment has exceeded our expectations. The prospect of socialist transformations in developed capitalist countries has been put off to the indefinite future. In a number of countries that are socialist in orientation, the situation remains unstable and fraught with the possibility of backsliding; communist parties in the capitalist countries and the Third World, with few exceptions, have not been able . . . to gain the support of the majority of the working class and the working people. There are a number of reasons for this, and the failures, contradictions, crises phenomena and stagnation phenomena in the development of the Soviet Union, the socialist countries, and the world socialism in general doubtless figure among them.[28]

The sense of pessimism reflected in the views of Gorbachev and many of his supporters are not new, but not since the darkest days of the German invasion of the Soviet Union has so much doom and gloom pervaded Soviet society, except that now it is reflected in the Soviet media. Socialism's failure to extinguish capitalism, however, should not be confused with the imminent extinction of the Soviet Union as a state or the nullification of the power it can still muster and demonstrate. Soviet leaders and writers are only now beginning to realize that coexistence with capitalism is not a sequential process, whereby socialism eventually "overtakes" and "supercedes" capitalism, but rather coexistence is a parallel process in which each system evolves and develops in accordance with its own values and norms. It becomes unnecessary for one to prevail in order to justify its own existence and validate its historical credentials. Gorbachev's new political thinking goes a long was in restructuring the foundations of Soviet legitimacy, shifting it away from success in transforming the external world to success in developing Soviet society. Cheap gains in the Third World proved to be an expensive and inadequate surrogate for an exhausted and impoverished ideology. A new basis for legitimacy is needed, a legitimacy founded upon effective performance and acceptability rather than upon abstract propositions. The new political thinking goes a long way in repudiating the notion that Soviet legitimacy can only be validated by the demise of capitalism, a proposition that appears not only increasingly unattainable but also one that Gorbachev recognizes can only promise to generate further international tension and conflict between the Soviet Union and the Western world. The new political thinking takes a big step in the direction of replacing the sequential

[28]*Ibid.*

concept of coexistence with a parallel concept, and dissipating the Soviet conviction that only the destruction of capitalism can historically validate the Bolshevik Revolution and the Soviet system.

FOREIGN POLICY LANDMARKS

February 9, 1946	Stalin preelection speech warning Soviet people of new war being hatched by the capitalist world
March 12, 1947	Truman Doctrine proclaimed to protect Turkey and Greece
September 1947	Cominform established to control Eastern European states; "Two-Camp" Doctrine proclaimed
June 1948	Yugoslavia expelled from Cominform and Soviet Bloc; Berlin blockaded by Soviet force
January 1949	Council for Economic Mutual Assistance (Molotov Plan) established to control and coordinate Eastern European economies
March 1949	Berlin Blockade ended
February 1950	Mao Zedong in Moscow; Sino-Soviet treaties signed subordinating China to the USSR
October 1952	Nineteenth Communist Party Congress meets
January 1953	Kremlin "Jewish-Doctors" are alleged to have plotted to poison Soviet leaders; Kremlin doctors arrested
March 5, 1953	Stalin dies; collective rule established with Malenkov as Stalin's successor
August 8, 1953	Malenkov announces "new course" emphasizing consumer goods and "peaceful coexistence"
October 1954	Khrushchev heads Soviet delegation to China; Soviet bases and economic enterprises in China given up; Mao Zedong makes territorial demands upon Moscow
February 1955	Malenkov forced to resign and replaced by Bulganin; Khrushchev emerges as top Soviet leader in his capacity as First Secretary
May 1955	Warsaw Treaty Organization (Warsaw Pact) established to counter NATO
July 1955	Khrushchev-Bulganin summit with Eisenhower in Geneva; "Spirit of Geneva" proclaimed
February 1956	Twentieth Party Congress meets. Khrushchev denounces Stalin and "inevitability of war" thesis
April 17, 1956	Cominform abolished
May–June 1956	Molotov resigns as Foreign Minister; Tito visits Moscow
November 1956	Hungarian uprising put down by Soviet invasion

June 1957	Anti-Party group led by Molotov fails to oust Khrushchev; Molotov is expelled from leadership
October 4, 1957	Soviet Union places first man-made satellite in orbit (Sputnik)
March 27, 1958	Khrushchev replaces Bulganin as Premier, while retaining position as First Secretary
September 15–17, 1958	Eisenhower-Khrushchev "Camp David" summit meeting; Khrushchev tours United States
January 1960	Khrushchev announces new Soviet military doctrine, emphasizing rocket forces; navy and air force declared obsolete, and ground forces reduced by more than 1 million
May 1960	American U-2 spy plane shot down over Soviet territory; Paris summit aborted as Eisenhower refuses Khrushchev's demand for apology over U-2 incident
June 3–4, 1961	Kennedy-Khrushchev summit meeting in Vienna; Berlin crisis revived by Khrushchev
October 1961	Twenty-second Party Congress meets; new party program and statutes adopted; U.S. economy to be surpassed by 1970 and communist society to be built by 1980
October 1962	Cuban Missile Crisis
July 25, 1963	Limited test-ban treaty signed
October 15, 1964	Khrushchev ousted from power; Brezhnev and Kosygin succeed as First Secretary and Prime Minister respectively
March–April 1966	Twenty-third Party Congress meets; Brezhnev emerges as top man and General Secretary with restoration of Politburo
June 1967	Arab-Israeli war; Moscow breaks diplomatic relations with Israel
July 1967	Johnson-Kosygin summit meeting at Glassboro, New Jersey
August 21, 1968	Soviet invasion of Czechoslovakia; "Brezhnev Doctrine" proclaimed
March 1969	Soviet-Chinese military clashes on Ussuri River border
March–April 1971	Twenty-fourth Party Congress meets; Brezhnev consolidates power
May 1972	President Nixon visits Moscow; SALT I Treaty signed; detente inaugurated
July 1972	Sadat expels Soviet military advisors from Egypt
June 1973	Brezhnev visits U.S.A.
June 1974	Nixon visits USSR
November 1974	Ford-Brezhnev summit meeting at Vladivostok; Soviet-Cuban intervention in Angola
July 1975	Helsinki Agreement signed; human rights organizations spring up in USSR and are repressed
February 1976	Twenty-fifth Party Congress meets
March–April 1976	Sadat renounces Soviet-Egyptian treaty of friendship and cooperation; Soviet naval point facilities in Egypt closed down
October 1977	New Brezhnev constitution replaces 1936 Stalin constitution
June 1979	SALT II Treaty signed at Carter-Brezhnev summit meeting in Vienna
December 1979	Military dictatorship established in Poland under General Jaruzelski; Solidarity banned
November 1982	Brezhnev dies; Andropov succeeds as General Secretary
September 1983	Soviet aircraft shoot down Korean airliner

February 1984	Andropov dies; Chernenko succeeds as General Secretary
March 10, 1985	Chernenko dies; Gorbachev succeeds as General Secretary
July 2, 1985	Shevardnadze appointed Foreign Minister; Gromyko becomes President of the USSR
September 27, 1985	Ryzhkov replaces Tikhonov as Premier
November 19–21, 1985	Reagan-Gorbachev summit meeting in Geneva
February 25, 1986	Twenty-seventh Party Congress convenes; Gorbachev consolidates position
April 1986	Chernobyl nuclear reactor explodes
October 11–12, 1986	Reagan-Gorbachev summit meeting in Reykjavik
December 1987	Reagan-Gorbachev summit meeting in Washington, D.C.; Intermediate Nuclear Forces Treaty signed, banning all intermediate-range nuclear missiles worldwide; President Reagan to visit Moscow in 1988
February 1988	Gorbachev announces that Soviet troop withdrawal from Afghanistan will begin in May
May 1988	First Soviet withdrawal from Afghanistan
May 1988	Reagan visits the Soviet Union
July 1988	19th Party Conference convenes and approves restructuring of central state institutions and creation of new powerful presidency to be occupied by Gorbachev in early 1989.

SELECTED BIBLIOGRAPHY

ARBATOV, G., and W. OLTMANS. *The Soviet Viewpoint*. New York: Dodd, Mead, 1983.

ASPATURIAN, VERNON V. *The Union Republics in Soviet Diplomacy*. Paris: Libraire Droz, 1960.

———. *The Soviet Union in the International Communist System*. Stanford, Calif.: Hoover Institution Studies, 1966.

———. *Process and Power in Soviet Foreign Policy*. Boston: Little, Brown, 1971.

ASPATURIAN, VERNON V., et al, eds. *Eurocommunism Between East and West*. Bloomington, Ind.: Indiana University Press, 1981.

BIALER, SEWERYN. *Stalin's Successors*. Cambridge: Cambridge University Press, 1980.

———, ed. *The Domestic Context of Soviet Foreign Policy*. Boulder, Colo.: Westview Press, 1981.

BIALER, SEWERYN. *The Soviet Paradox*. New York: Knopf, 1986.

BRZEZINSKI, ZBIGNIEW K. *The Soviet Bloc*. rev. ed. Cambridge, Mass.: Harvard University Press, 1971.

COLTON, TIMOTHY. *Commissars, Commanders and Civilian Authority*. Cambridge, Mass.: Harvard University Press, 1979.

DALLIN, ALEXANDER, ed. *Soviet Conduct in World Affairs*. New York: Columbia University Press, 1960.

DINERSTEIN, HERBERT. *War and the Soviet Union*. 2d Ed. New York: Praeger, 1963.

GADDIS, JOHN L. *Russia, the Soviet Union and the United States*. New York: Oxford University Press, 1978.

———. *Strategies of Containment*. New York: Oxford University Press, 1982.

GARTHOFF, RAYMOND. *Detente and Confrontation*. Washington, D.C.: The Brookings Institution, 1985.

GATI, CHARLES. *Hungary and the Soviet Bloc*. Durham, N.C.: Duke University Press, 1986.

GEORGE, ALEXANDER. *Managing U.S.-Soviet Rivalry*. Boulder, Colo.: Westview Press, 1979.

GITTINGS, JOHN. *Survey of the Sino-Soviet Dispute*. New York: Oxford University Press, 1968.

GORBACHEV, MIKHAIL. *Perestroika*. New York: Harper & Row, 1987.

GROMYKO, A. A., and B. N. PONOMAREV, eds. *Soviet Foreign Policy 1917–1980*. 4th Ed. Moscow: Progress Publishers, 1981. 2 vols.

HILGER, G., and A. C. MEYER. *The Incompatible Allies*. New York: Macmillan, 1953.

HOLLOWAY, DAVID. *The Soviet Union and the Arms Race*. New Haven, Conn.: Yale University Press, 1983.

HORELICK, ARNOLD, and MYRON RUSH. *Strategic Power and Soviet Foreign Policy*. Chicago: Chicago University Press, 1966.

KEEP, JOHN, ed. *Contemporary History in the Soviet Mirror*. New York: Praeger, 1965.

LAIRD, R., and E. HOFFMANN, eds. *Soviet Foreign Policy In A Changing World*. New York: Aldine, 1986.

LEITES, NATHAN. *A Study of Bolshevism*. New York: Free Press, 1953.

MARX, KARL, and FRIEDRICH ENGELS. *The Russian Menace to Europe*. New York: Free Press, 1952.

McCGWIRE, MICHAEL. *Military Objectives in Soviet Foreign Policy*. Washington, D.C.: Brookings Institutions, 1987.

————. *Stalin, Hitler and Europe, 1939–1941*. Cleveland, Ohio: World Publishing, 1970.

Nazi–Soviet Relations, 1937–1941. Washington, D.C.: Government Printing Office, 1948. Selected documents from the German archives.

SCHWARTZ, MORTON. *Soviet Perceptions of the United States*. Berkeley, Calif.: University of California Press, 1978.

SCOTT, H. F., and W. F. SCOTT. *The Armed Forces of the USSR*. 2d. Ed. Boulder, Colo.: Westview Press, 1981.

SHEVCHENKO, ARKADY. *Breaking With Moscow*. New York: Knopf, 1985.

SOKOLOVSKY, V. D. *Soviet Military Strategy*. 3rd Ed. London: MacDonald and Janes, 1975.

TALBOT, STROBE. *Endgame, the Inside Story of SALT II*. New York: Harper & Row, 1979.

————. *Deadly Gambits*. New York: Knopf, 1984.

ULAM, ADAM B. *Expansion and Coexistence*. 2d Ed. New York: Praeger, 1974.

————. *Dangerous Relations*. New York: Oxford University Press, 1983.

U. S. Defense Department. *Soviet Military Power*. Washington, D.C.: U.S. Government Printing Office. See latest edition.

USSR Ministry of Defense. *Whence the Threat to Peace?* Moscow: See latest edition.

VALENTA, JIRI. *Soviet Intervention in Czechoslovakia*. Baltimore, Md.: Johns Hopkins Press, 1979.

VALENTA, JIRI, and WILLIAM POTTER, eds. *Soviet Decision-Making for National Security*. London: Allen & Urwin, 1984.

WOLFE, THOMAS W. *Soviet Power and Europe, 1945–1970*. Baltimore, Md.: Johns Hopkins Press, 1970.

————. *The Salt Experience*. Cambridge, Mass.: Ballinger, 1979.

6

Foreign Policy
of China

Allen S. Whiting

CONCEPTUAL FRAMEWORK

China is the world's oldest continuous civilization but our analysis of Chinese foreign policy must be largely inferential. Little primary research in Chinese archival materials has been completed to provide us with an evidential base for understanding the perceptual framework, the organizational interaction, and the political determinants which combine to make foreign policy. Too few detailed case studies exist of specific interactive situations involving the People's Republic of China (PRC) to lay a foundation for systematic generalization about behavior. Even the conventional historical record provides relatively little help. Although its political systems date back more than 2,000 years, China is a relative newcomer to contemporary foreign relations. For centuries, its relations with the outside world remained tributary in nature. No concept of sovereignty or equality interfered with domination by the Middle Kingdom

Nomenclature Note:
    Most Chinese names are rendered in the new transliteration system adopted by the State Council of the People's Republic of China in 1978. This phonetic spelling differs from that generally used abroad, the equivalent version of which is listed at the end of this chapter. Source citations in footnotes remain in the original spelling to facilitate locating them in a standard card catalog.

over dependencies such as Tibet and Mongolia, or vassal states such as Korea and Annam.

The collapse of the Manchu empire and the birth, in 1912, of the Republic of China failed to produce a united nation entering the world community on equal terms. Foreign governments continued to post their own troops and police in enclaves of extraterritoriality, enjoying foreign law and privilege on Chinese soil. Civil war rent China apart during the decade 1918–1928, as a northern government at Beijing, dominated by shifting military factions, vied for power with a southern government at Canton, headed by Sun Yat-sen and his Guomindang cohorts. Officially, Beijing enjoyed recognition as the legal voice of China until its final defeat by the Nationalist (Guomindang) army in 1928. Its actual power, however, extended through only a small section of the country. During the turbulent 1920's, most of South China, Tibet, Xinjiang, Mongolia, and the northeast (Manchuria) lay beyond control of the capital. No sooner was the new government of Chiang Kai-shek established at Najiing in 1928, however, than Soviet troops fought to protect Soviet interests in Manchuria against the local warlord. In 1931 Japan overran this rich industrial area to create the puppet state of Manchukuo. Then, at the opposite end of China, Soviet authorities gave military and economic assistance to the local governor of Xinjiang, concluding formal agreements without reference to Nanjing and informally extending influence over its policy and army. Warlord autonomy, Japanese invasion, and growing Chinese Communist dissidence combined to deprive Chiang of control over more than a dozen provinces throughout most of the period 1931–1945. Meanwhile, each of these uncontrolled areas enjoyed varying degrees of independence in its relations with foreign powers.

In fact, not until 1949 and establishment of the People's Republic of China did the world's most populous nation achieve sufficient sovereignty and unity throughout its vast domain to enjoy a monopoly of full control over foreign relations in the central government. This provides a natural starting point for our analysis. Unlike its immediate predecessor, however, the People's Republic was not formally admitted to "the family of nations" for many years, lacking diplomatic recognition from most countries outside the Soviet bloc, and denied participation in the United Nations until the 1970s. Thus, on the one hand, we have historical evidence of foreign policy conducted by a somewhat fictitious central government, ruling largely in name only from 1911 to 1928, followed by a highly fragmented regime from 1928 to 1949. This approximates forty years of seemingly "normal" international relations for a weak and divided China, formally allied with the victorious powers in two world wars and a member of the League of Nations. On the other hand, our principle object of interest, the PRC, had more than two decades of semi-isolation from much of the international system, including the United Nations and such traditional great powers as the United States and Japan.

Finally the People's Republic itself offers two distinct phases of policy, both in process and in substance. The first, from 1949 to 1976, is dominated by the personality of Mao Zedong as the founding father and ideological godhead of "New China." His premier and chief foreign affairs figure, Zhou Enlai, was China's preeminent statesman throughout this period. Both men died in 1976. Their successors, initially dominated by Deng Xiaoping, totally transformed domestic and foreign policy, *inter alia* involving China in the world economy to an unprecedented degree. Their abandonment of Mao's ideological rhetoric, if not its tenets, poured new wine into old bottles. The record of Mao's domestic rule has already been rewritten by his successors to preclude a return to his catastrophic final years of the so-called Cultural Revolution. It may be that various aspects of his foreign policy will also be denounced as contrary to China's interests. In the meantime, however, we must base our analysis mainly on the evidence available, which preponderantly comes from the pre-1980s, while drawing attention to the changes that have since occurred and the factors that may give them some degree of permanence.

These historical anomalies obviate the standard approach of focusing on the nation-state as actor. Despite appearances, foreign governments were not dealing with a highly stable and continuous regime prior to 1949. To be sure, the entity "China" was an obvious empirical referent for whatever group assumed authority at whatever point in the society. Treaties were negotiated, commerce carried out (albeit through foreign-controlled customs until the 1930s), and wars fought in the name of China. However, our inquiry will concern itself primarily with the perceptions and behavior of Chinese elites, particularly the communist, which have tried to manage China's foreign relations over the past century. It is their values and views, rather than the inheritance of tradition or the bureaucratic inertia of continuing organizational entities within government that have shaped the ends, means, and style of Chinese foreign policy.

Our general conceptual framework begins with the physical environment, both real and perceived, into which these elites moved as international actors. In addition to actual size and geography, policy is shaped by perceptions of spatial relationships. Borders may be seen as secure or threatened, as inviolate or penetrable, as indisputable or contentious and negotiable. Space may be conceived as providing isolation or inviting attack. Size may be held an asset of strength or a liability for defense. Perceptions, in turn, are in part a function of received experience, of history as it is transmitted within a culture or political system. Received experience provides "lessons" from the past whose "truth" may be reinforced through the "real experience" of the present. Just as there are objective inputs of wars and diplomacy, as in the physical attributes of geography, to shape perception and behavior, so too there is the subjective element of anticipation, which may create a "self-fulfilling prophecy" effect whereby expected hostility from an outside power is prepared for in such a way as to cause or increase hostility. Alternatively, "selective perception" focuses only on evidence of behavior which conforms with expectation and dismisses that which does not fit anticipation. These inputs of geography, history, and psychology combine to constitute what we shall call the *Chinese components* of foreign policy.

In addition, we must consider ideology or the *communist component* of policy. Ideology is not unique to elites and cultures which articulate it in the highly formalized and conscious manner of communist systems, but its explicitness and omnipresence in their political communications make it even more of a determinant than in less ideologically structured systems. From Marx to Mao, a corpus of literature provides definitions of goals and prescriptions of means that shape the view of the world from Beijing.

These basic factors in the Chinese and communist components do not explain everything. They will be differentially affected by specific organizational roles and responsibilities such as defense, trade, diplomacy, and revolutionary activity abroad. Moreover, they will have an idiosyncratic impact upon policy as filtered through the different "operational codes" of such individuals as Mao Zedong and Deng Xiaoping. The sum of these internal interactions constitutes the decision-making process, but this in turn must interact externally for the dynamic of international relations to be complete. Foreign policy does not operate in a vacuum, nor is it the exclusive initiative of one country, least of all China over the past century. Unfortunately, however, in the absence of any concrete data on the effect of organization and personality in Chinese foreign policy, we must remain content with a larger, looser inferential framework that deals primarily with the factors we have subsumed under the Chinese and communist components. Moreover, in the space at our disposal we cannot hope to do justice to interaction analysis except for selective illustrative purposes. Within these limits, nevertheless, we can appreciate the goals of recent Chinese foreign policy and assess the means available and likely to be adopted by present and future elites in pursuit of these goals.

Physical Factors—Real and Perceived

We cannot look at any map of the world, regardless of its projection, and not be awed by the proportion encompassed by China. So extensive is its reach from north to south and from east to west as to conjure up images of supracontinental domination "overshadowing" Southeast Asia and India while "menacing" the Soviet Far East and Japan. Coupled with emphasis on China's population of over 1 billion, "expansionism" seems the perceived threat confronting China's neighbors.

These images receive reinforcement from Chinese official statements. Although the days of the Chinese empire are long past, modern Chinese leaders continue to pay obeisance to the memory of vanished glory in their delineation of China's territorial goals. Chiang Kai-shek, borrowing Adolf Hitler's concept of *Lebensraum* ("living space"), laid claim to past holdings on the basis of population pressure as well as of historical possession:

> In regard to the living space essential for the nation's existence, the territory of the Chinese state is determined by the requirements for national survival and by the limits of Chinese cultural bonds. Thus, in the territory of China a hundred years ago [that is, circa 1840], comprising more than ten million square kilometers, there was not a single district that was not essential to the survival of the Chinese nation, and none that was not permeated by our culture. The breaking up of this territory meant the undermining of the nation's security as well as the decline of the nation's culture. Thus, the people as a whole must regard this as a national humiliation, and not until all lost territories have been recovered can we relax our efforts to wipe out this humiliation and save ourselves from destruction.[1]

Nor do communist leaders remain indifferent to China's past holdings, although they temper their immediate claims according to time and place. Thus, Mao Zedong staked out his future realm in an interview more than fifty years ago:

> It is the immediate task of China to regain all our lost territories. . . . We do not, however, include Korea, formerly a Chinese colony, but when we have reestablished the independence of the lost territories of China, and if the Koreans wish to break away from the chains of Japanese imperialism, we will extend them our enthusiastic help in their struggle for independence. The same thing applies for Formosa. . . . The Outer Mongolian republic will automatically become a part of the Chinese federation, at their own will. The Mohammedan and Tibetan peoples, likewise, will form autonomous republics attached to the Chinese federation.[2]

True to his word, at least in part, Mao, despite Indian protests, sent the People's Liberation Army (PLA) into Tibet after the establishment of the People's Republic of China in 1949. His implicit definition of Korea as within China's sphere of interest received implementation when Chinese armies hurled back United Nations troops from the Yalu River to the 38th parallel during 1950–1951. Xinjiang which is presumably the region referred to above as "the Mohammedan people" (because of its predomi-

---

[1]Chiang Kai-shek. *China's Destiny* (New York: Roy Publishers, 1947), p. 34.

[2]Quoted in Edgar Snow, *Red Star over China* (New York: Random House, 1944), p. 96. Interviews with Mao Zedong in 1936.

nantly Moslem population), became an autonomous region in 1955 after considerable pacification by the PLA garrison. Only Taiwan ("Formosa"), the Nationalist refuge, and Outer Mongolia, recognized as independent by the Treaty of Friendship and Alliance concluded between the Nationalist government and Moscow in 1945 and adhered to in this particular by Beijing, remained beyond Mao's control.

Similarly, both Nationalist and Communist maps place China's borders far down in the South China Sea, off the shores of Borneo. Both could agree with statements in the official Nationalist handbook:

> Both the southernmost and westernmost borders remain to be defined. The Pamirs in the west constitute a contested area among China, the USSR, and Afghanistan. The sovereignty of the Tuansha Islands [Coral Islands] in the south is sought by China, the Republic of the Philippines, and Indo-China.[3]

At least some of these are more than mere verbal aspirations. In the past two decades Chinese Communist troops have fought over disputed border areas. The movement of Beijing's forces into Indian-claimed check-points along the Himalayas following the Tibetan revolt of 1959 triggered small clashes with Indian border guards that year. Subsequent Indian efforts in 1962 to recoup claimed land, long unoccupied until the advent of Chinese road building and patrols in 1958–1961, ignited a smoldering confrontation which finally exploded that fall in a massive Chinese offensive at both ends of the 1,500-mile frontier. While larger strategic considerations than the border itself underlay the Chinese attack, the tenacity with which Beijing bargained—and finally fought—with New Delhi over marginal land of little economic or political value illustrates the persistence of "lost territories" in shaping perceptions and goals of foreign policy.

An even more dramatic example of this phenomenon came in March 1969, when Chinese border troops fought Soviet armored units over unoccupied islands in the Ussuri River along China's northeast frontier. These incidents, while far smaller in scope and briefer than the 1962 war with India, had far more threatening implications for China's security, since they involved the much more powerful Soviet military capabilities, potentially including nuclear weapons. Again, as with India, more was perceived to be at stake than the islands themselves. Nonetheless, the role the border played throughout 1969, both here and in Xinjiang, reminded the world that Chinese sensibilities and sensitivities can hearken back to times past to a degree unique among the major powers on the world scene today.

---

[3]*China Handbook, 1955–56* (Taipei, Taiwan, 1955), p. 15. Although this was modified in later editions, continued Nationalist claims to the Paracel Islands 150 miles south of Hainan were forcefully implemented by the PLA in January 1974 when its navy ousted South Vietnamese units from the area.

Does this necessarily mean that irredentism—the drive to recover "lost territories"—literally impels Chinese leaders to restore control over thousands of square miles ruled by Russia and the Soviet Union for a century or more?

The border problem is both less and more than the question of "lost territory" per se. It is less so in terms of the amount of land actually at issue as compared with that carried on maps and tables as the maximal extent of past Chinese rule. The problem involves more than the land, however, insofar as it involves the principles of politics, both domestic and foreign, which impinge on the posture adopted by Chinese leaders vis-à-vis questions of "unequal treaties" and "lost territory." One such principle is the traditional Chinese definition of a government possessing the "Mandate of Heaven" as capable of defending the frontiers against barbarian incursions while maintaining the peace against domestic insurrection. Thus, so remote and undesirable an area as Outer Mongolia became the subject of political controversy in 1912, when young Nationalists agitated against Beijing's concessions to Mongolian demands for autonomy under Russian protection, using the issue as a political weapon against the regime of Yuan Shikai. In 1950 Chinese Nationalist propagandists sought to embarrass the new Communist regime in Beijing in a similar manner. They charged it with "selling out" Chinese soil to the Soviet Union by accepting Mongolian independence despite alleged Soviet violations of the 1945 agreements. In these agreements, Chiang Kai-shek had promised to abide by a "plebiscite" there, knowing it would confirm the area's self-proclaimed independence under Soviet domination but hoping thereby to woo Stalin away from supporting the Chinese Communists. Seen in this perspective Mongolia is primarily a political issue to be exploited in domestic or foreign politics according to expediency, not a compulsive constraint on Chinese policy.

Individual leaders may not believe in the importance of a particular border section or the literal necessity of recovering "lost territory," but the manipulative use of such an issue in internal politics may constrain their position, thereby posing foreign policy goals which exacerbate relations abroad. Two instances illustrate the complexity of this problem. Mongolia would seem strategically irretrievable without Soviet acquiescence. Yet authoritative Japanese and Soviet sources attributed statements to Mao which seemed to reflect a lingering aspiration to replace Soviet influence there, including an official Soviet claim that Mao raised the issue with Nikita Khrushchev as early as 1954. Were these statements merely an effort to press Soviet influence back, or also to advance Chinese influence? Was it Mao's personal *idée fixe* or a shared objective within the elite? While Beijing's propaganda publicly lamented Moscow's alleged transformation of the Mongolian People's Republic into a "colony" in 1969–1970, Soviet radio broadcasts accused Beijing of harboring "chauvinist" ambitions over this vast land of desert and steppe, inhabited by a million or so nomads and herdsmen. Logic may strengthen one or another explanation, but evidence is lacking to provide any definitive answer.

A second instance concerns Taiwan. Since the founding of the PRC in 1949, its leadership has ritualistically and repeatedly sworn to "recover China's province, Taiwan." Yet after imposition of the U.S. Seventh Fleet in the Taiwan Strait in 1950 and the Mutual Assistance Treaty concluded between Taipei and Washington in 1954, no serious effort from the mainland sought to recover Taiwan by force or subversion. Is this an issue of genuine irredentism which inevitably must result in reunion with the mainland by one means or another? Is it a political matter linked to the continuing presence on Taiwan of a defeated civil-war enemy, the Chinese Nationalists, who still lay claim to representation of and rule over all China? Is it a whipping-boy for attacking "U.S. imperialism," and if so, are the implications primarily for mobilizing unity? Or is there a changing mixture of motivations, varying according to the changing perceptions and priorities of the leadership in Beijing?

Suggesting these various instrumental uses of the question is not to deny objective factors which, from the perspective of those responsible for Chinese security, make China's size a defensive liability and China's borders a vulnerable point of contention. First, vague territorial claims, Chinese or otherwise, based on concepts of suzerainty and tributary relations or on disputed treaties, are an inadequate basis for determining international boundaries. Chinese Communists and Nationalists alike agree that the use of force against Tibetan leaders, whether in 1950 or 1959, is an internal affair, and does not constitute legal "aggression." Even New Delhi acquiesced, albeit reluctantly, in the earlier instance. But where runs the legal boundary resultant from a line drawn on an inadequate map by a British official before World War I and never surveyed, much less formally ratified by the government in Beijing?

Second, even where such boundaries are fixed with rough approximation, precise definition is impeded by the absence of natural lines of demarcation. Except for the coast and the Amur-Yalu river complex in the northeast, none of China's frontiers can be readily identified topographically. Instead, they twist tortuously through jungle, mountain, and desert, according to the temporary dictates of local need and the relative power available to interested parties. The absence of natural demarcation is paralleled by an absence of natural barriers against migration or invasion, complicating the responsibilities facing the central government responsible for its citizens' welfare and defense.

Thus, the ability in 1959 of 80,000 Tibetan refugees to flee through Himalayan passes, in some cases claimed and ostensibly guarded by Indian patrols, raised the possibility of these refugees returning with foreign arms and training to carry on subversion and sabotage, if not actual guerrilla war. Indeed, precisely such clandestine activities followed the exodus, described by foreign participants and correspondents from bases in the sub-Himalayan area. Again, in 1962, the flight of up to 100,000 Uygur, Kazakh, and Kirghiz refugees across the Xinjiang border to ethnically related areas in adjacent Soviet central Asia raised Chinese fears of their eventual return as instruments of Soviet subversion in a province long known for anti-Chinese revolts among its predominantly Turki-speaking Moslem peoples. Small wonder that under these circumstances the Indian and Soviet borders appear so sensitive to decision makers in Beijing.

Few lines of communication traverse the great distances from China's traditional power centers to its remote border provinces, whereas these provinces lie relatively close to rival centers of power. Not until well after establishment of the PRC did a railroad link Mongolia with northern China, although it was circled on the north by the Trans-Siberian Railroad. Only rough roads linked Tibet with China proper until the late 1950s, while Lhasa lay within striking distance of determined troops, traders, and travelers approaching from the Indian subcontinent, as evidenced by British expeditions at the turn of the century. Nor did Beijing push a railroad into Xinjiang until the mid-1950s, despite its strategic and economic importance proximate to the highly developed transportation network across the Soviet border. Even today, land communications to most points along China's southern and western boundaries are scarce and subject to the hazards of interruption by recurring natural phenomena as well as to interdiction by potential dissidents. This combination of arduous terrain and traditionally hostile non-Chinese local populaces mocks the image of size and strength projected by simple unidimensional maps of China.

China's traditional attraction for invaders was food and wealth, luring from the interior nomadic groups against whom the Great Wall was originally designed. Modern invaders came after markets (Great Britian), raw materials (Japan), or imperial prestige (Germany). Regardless of the size and distance of the predatory power, during the nineteenth and twentieth centuries China grappled with problems of defense against external pressure to a degree unique among the countries under survey in this volume. Virtually no point along the 12,600 miles of its perimeter has been safe from one or another of these pressures during the last three hundred years. At the turn of the century, many wondered whether China would become the "sick man of Asia," to be carved up by other countries as was the "sick man of Europe," the Ottoman empire.

These physical factors have combined with the behavior of other powers to make defense a major preoccupation of Chinese foreign policy elites, be they Manchu, Nationalist, or Communist. We have dwelt at length on the border problem because it looms large in the foreign policy perspective of Beijing—not because of Communist "expansionism" or "paranoia," but rather as an outgrowth of China's remembered past. Thus, thousands of PLA troops, ostensibly engaged in roadbuilding, occupied two northern provinces of Laos adjacent to China from 1962 into the 1970s. This was not only in response to an agreement with the Royal Laotian government, but to secure a buffer against possible penetration of China by American CIA-trained Meo hillsmen or by former Chinese Nationalist soldiers living in exile in nearby Thailand. Nor can we understand recurring tensions in the Taiwan Strait around the offshore islands of Jinmen and Mazu in 1954–1955, 1958, and 1962 without an appreciation of the recurring raids against the mainland launched from these islands by Chinese Nationalist teams trained and backed by the United States. Indeed, China's only major military actions—in Korea (1950) and on its borders with India (1962) and the USSR (1969)—in the first two decades of the PRC came about in large part because of anxiety over the potential penetration by hostile powers over vulnerable borders, at times when internal tensions, economic and political, heightened fears of invasion and subversion.

Historical Factors

China's defensive attitudes intermittently explode into xenophobia. The subjective evaluation of events during the past century convinced Chinese Nationalist and Communist alike that many, if not all, of China's ills came from contact with the "foreign devil," now castigated as "Western imperialism." Two hundred years ago, Li Shiyao, viceroy of Guangdong and Guangxi, memorialized the throne on regulations for the control of foreigners, warning:

> It is my most humble opinion that when uncultured barbarians, who live far beyond the borders of China, come to our country to trade, they should establish no contact with the population, except for business purposes.[4]

Chiang Kai-shek blamed the chaotic years of interregnum following the collapse of the Manchu dynasty on "secret activities of the imperialists, . . . the chief cause of civil wars among the warlords."[5] Indeed, he attributed the empire's disintegration to the so-called unequal treaties which "completely destroyed our nationhood, and our sense of honor and shame was lost. . . . The traditional structure of the family, the village, and the community was disrupted. The virtue of mutual help was

---

[4]Quoted in Hu Sheng, *Imperialism and Chinese Politics* (Peking, 1981), p. 4.
[5]Chiang Kai-shek, *China's Destiny*, p. 78.

replaced by competition and jealousy. Public planning was neglected and no one took an interest in public affairs."[6]

This simplistic explanation errs in attributing cause and effect where coincidence is the phenomenon. Western pressures hastened the collapse of the empire and its Confucian traditions, but they came after the process of disintegration had begun. The ability of Japanese society to respond to the combined impact of feudal decline and Western influence by adapting the old content to new forms demonstrates the distortion of history in Chiang's analysis.

However, it is not the facts of history that condition political behavior, but the way in which people view those facts. Hence, the similarity of an early communist analysis to those preceding it is highly suggestive of xenophobia as a recurring component of Chinese policy:

> [The imperialists] will not only send their running-dogs to bore inside China to carry out disruptive work and to cause trouble. They will not only use the Chiang Kai-shek bandit remnants to blockade our coastal ports, but they will send their totally hopeless adventurist elements and troops to raid and to cause trouble along our borders. They seek by every means and at all times to restore their position in China. They use every means to plot the destruction of China's independence, freedom, and territorial integrity and to restore their private interests in China. We must exercise the highest vigilance. . . . They cannot possibly be true friends of the Chinese people. They are the deadly enemies of the Chinese people's liberation movement.[7]

Thus, the Chinese Communist devil-theory of imperialism coincided with the popular mythology that evil is inherent in foreign contacts, and produced suspicion and hostility at various levels. The popular mythology derives from experiencing the rape and pillage by Western troops during the nineteenth century.

Injustice was also encountered at higher levels of diplomatic relations. Chinese experience in the international arena gave good reason for bitter resentment at being cast in the role of "a melon to be carved up by the powers." Throughout the nineteenth century, gunboat diplomacy forced China to abdicate her customary rights of sovereignty without reciprocal privileges. Extraterritorial law, economic concessions, and the stationing of foreign troops in Chinese cities were sanctified by treaty but won by force. Punitive expeditions, in 1860 and 1900, delivered the supreme insult of foreign military occupation of the venerated capital of Beijing.

[6]Ibid., pp. 79, 88.

[7]K'o Pa-nien, "Hsin min chu chu yi te wai chiao tse" [The foreign policy of the new people's democracy] *Hsüeh Hsi* [Study] 1, no. 2 (October 1949):13–15.

The twentieth century brought little relief. Japan fought Russia on Chinese soil for control of the rich provinces of Manchuria. China's own allies in World War I swept aside her protests at Versailles, and awarded to Japan concessions in China held by defeated Germany. During World War II, the Yalta Conference of 1945 rewarded the Soviet Union with important military, economic, and political privileges in China, all without consultation with Chiang Kai-shek. Although President Roosevelt reminded Premier Stalin that those inducements for Soviet entry into the war against Japan would have to be affirmed by Chiang, Allied pressure left China no alternative but capitulation.

In sum, China was the object of international relations but seldom the agent. Acted on by others, she was unable to act in her own right. Long the primary power in Asia, she has been cut deeply, during the past century, by an induced feeling of inferiority. Her fear of Japan followed a defeat caused by material inferiority. Her resentment against the West followed a capitulation caused by military inferiority and a humiliation caused by sensed political and ideological inferiority. Beijing's assertive stand on Hong Kong and Taiwan strikes a responsive chord among wide sectors of the populace. At long last, a determined elite has managed to restore China's place in the sun.

To be sure, irredentist claims to lost territories, denunciation of unequal treaties, and the playing off of power against power are all standard techniques of foreign policy. The difference in their use by the Chinese lies in the psychological convictions behind these techniques. Among Western states, the exploitation of grievances is an accepted stratagem among assumed equals who are struggling for limited gains and for the coveted position "first among equals." Between China and the rest of the world, however, the bitter remembrance of things past heightens the assertive aspects of foreign policy.

The communist emphasis on imperialist aggression fitted into the objective and subjective factors conditioning Chinese views of world politics. The resulting xenophobia ultimately worked even to the Soviet Union's disadvantage. Whereas originally it was exploited by Soviet leaders against the West, eventually it exploded again over such real and sensed grievances as Soviet looting in Manchuria after World War II, the resentment against dependence on Soviet economic assistance, and suspected Soviet subversion in Xinjiang. In the decade 1949–1959, official affirmations of the "monolithic unity of Sino-Soviet friendship" sought to repress the hostility with which many Chinese viewed the Sino-Soviet alliance. When Mao challenged Khrushchev for primacy in the communist world, however, such protestations of friendship disappeared in a wave of anti-Soviet invective which probably won enthusiastic support among the majority of the populace always ready to believe the worst of any foreigner in his dealing with China.

THE PROCESS OF POLICY: THE COMMUNIST COMPONENT

Ideological Content: Marxism-Leninism-Mao Zedong Thought

In addition to those aspects of continuity in policy which we ascribe to the Chinese component, there are differences in degree and substance that stem from the dedication of the present Chinese leaders to communism. As Mao declared in 1945, "From the very beginning, our party has based itself on the theories of Marxism-Leninism, because Marxism-Leninism is the crystallization of the most correct and most revolutionary scientific thought of the world proletariat."[8] More than forty years later, the constitution of the PRC adopted at the fifth National People's Congress on December 4, 1982, committed its preamble to "the guidance of Marxism-Leninism and Mao Zedong Thought."

Ideological commitment is not unique to communists. General protestations of fidelity to Christianity, international law, and human rights appear throughout statements of Western political figures. Rarely do these protestations enable us to determine the ends and means of these leaders, especially in foreign policy. Marxism-Leninism, however, carries with it a construct of goals and ways of seeking those goals that imparts form to ideology and insititutions to a degree unknown in the noncommunist world.

At the same time it is not a static ideology bound up in a few volumes and rigidly adhered to over time. Instead it has been reinterpreted and revised according to the dictates of a changing world by successive leaders in the Soviet Union, China, and elsewhere. This evolution has been no less dramatic between the regimes of Mao and Deng Xiaoping in China than it was between the regimes of Stalin and Khrushchev in Russia; in both countries the evolution of communism cautioned against a mechanistic citation of texts from one era to analyze and forecast communist policy in another era.

For example, the foremost component of classical Marxism was its goal of world communism as a necessary and inevitable successor to capitalism, to be realized through world revolution and a final war. The postponement of this goal under Lenin and Stalin resulted from a realistic assessment of Soviet weakness and capitalistic strength, but its ultimate achievement through class struggle and international conflict remained an unquestioned assumption.

Then in 1956 Nikita Khrushchev declared that peaceful coexistence and the non-inevitability of war between communism and capitalism followed from the emergence of nuclear weapons which threatened the

[8]Mao Zedong, "On Coalition Government," *Selected Works of Mao Zedong* (Beijing: Foreign Languages Press, 1965), vol. III, p. 314.

destruction of mankind. Mao railed at this, terming it "revisionism" and declaring that the final war would result in world communism. He argued that just as World War I had given birth to the Soviet Union and World War II to the People's Republic of China, so on the ashes of a nuclear conflict a still "higher" civilization would arise.

Mao based his analysis on the Marxist premise that conflict is omnipresent in human relations, whether between classes or between nations, in the most serious cases leading to war. Mao also followed Lenin's analysis of imperialism as "the highest form of capitalism" wherein conflict among the imperialist powers would accompany capitalist efforts to eliminate communism. In 1940 he reformulated the classic Chinese dictum of "using barbarian against barbarian" in Marxist-Leninist terms, "Our tactical principle remains one of exploiting the contradictions among . . . [the imperialists] in order to win over the majority, oppose the minority, and crush the enemies separately."[9] This article was reissued in 1971 to explain Mao's sudden switch from decades of attacking "U.S. imperialism" to welcoming President Richard Nixon for Sino-American détente. In his words, the Soviet Union had become "the major enemy" and the United States the "secondary enemy," thereby justifying a united front with the latter against the former.

Mao's postulates were reinforced by the attitudes and actions of the noncommunist world. In part this resulted from Chinese Communist statements and behavior that resulted in self-fulfilling prophecy. Various incidents involving American officials and property in 1948–1949 complicated efforts by those in Washington who wanted to prepare the way for recognition of Mao's regime once it displaced that of Chiang Kai-shek.

Then in June 1949, Mao declared, "All Chinese without exception must lean either to the side of imperialism or to the side of socialism. Sitting on the fence will not do. . . . Internationally, we belong to the aide of the anti-imperialist front headed by the Soviet Union, and so we can turn only to this side for genuine and friendly help, not to the side of the imperialist front."[10] Implementation of this principle followed on February 14, 1950 with the Treaty of Friendship, Alliance, and Mutual Aid between the PRC and the USSR. Mao and Stalin agreed that "in the event of one of the Contracting Parties being attacked by Japan or any state allied with her and thus being involved in a state of war, the other Contracting Party shall immediately render military and other assistance by all means at its disposal."

Mao's "lean to one side" policy aroused an image abroad of a monolithic communist bloc spanning the Eurasian land mass under control of

---

[9]"On Policy" (December 25, 1940), as translated in *Selected Works of Mao Zedong* (Bombay, 1954), vol. III, p. 218.

[10]"On the People's Democratic Dictatorship," Ibid., vol. IV, pp. 415–17.

the Kremlin and threatening all nations on its periphery with subversion, revolution, and possibly aggression. The monolithic image was wrong as became evident when Sino-Soviet friction eventually led to open differences in 1959–1960. However perceptions condition policy. The result was heightened American opposition to the new Chinese regime, thereby "proving" Mao's assumptions of implacable capitalist hostility to be "correct."

The interaction of antagonistic ideological predispositions and perceptions exploded in the first major Sino-American conflict when China intervened in the Korean War, inflicting a humiliating defeat on United States–United Nations forces in November–December 1950. This ended all prospects of normal relations between Beijing and Washington for twenty-one years. The United States thereupon enforced a total embargo on trade with China. It implemented this embargo worldwide for strategic goods and items with American-licensed components. Washington overtly shielded Chiang's regime on Taiwan from communist attack, forestalling an end to the civil war by creating an island redoubt through massive economic and military aid. Covertly it helped Chiang's agents conduct raids for espionage and sabotage on the mainland, especially in Tibet. Equally frustrating from Beijing's standpoint, the United States blocked it from taking China's seat in the United Nations until 1971.

Mao's "lean to one side" policy, both in its public definition and its political implementation, contributed to a total confrontation between China and the United States at the very start and through the 1950s. His posture went well beyond the traditional policy of playing off one country against another, demonstrating the importance of the communist component of Chinese foreign policy.

But not all aspects of that component were immutably chiseled on the Great Wall forever more. Mao's insistence on the inevitablity of war between capitalism and communism disappeared with his death in 1976. Shortly thereafter Deng Xiaoping declared that war could be "postponed" indefinitely as the "forces for peace" struggled against the "hegemonic competition of the superpowers." Thus Deng brought China's position more or less into line with that of Khrushchev twenty-five years earlier. This major modification of Mao's stance paralleled Khrushchev's change of Stalin's orthodoxy, albeit within the continued commitment to Marxism-Leninism as a universal scientific truth.

So far, we have been discussing aspects of policy that stem from the communist component as developed in Marxism-Leninism. Assumptions of conflict, antagonism against capitalism, and promoting revolution were all compatible with the ideological concepts dominant in the Soviet Union, at least until the death of Stalin in 1953. Within this framework, however, divergent strategies emerged with the rise of the Chinese Communist party (CCP). As early as 1946, Liu Shaoqi told an American correspondent, "Mao Zedong has created a Chinese or Asiatic form of Marxism. His great accomplishment has been to change Marxism from its European to its Asiatic form. He is the first who has succeeded in doing so."[11] At that time, the principal Chinese innovation appeared to be Mao's building a communist party on a peasant guerrilla army based in the countryside, as opposed to the classical Marxist method of a workers' movement which seizes power in the cities. Beneath this question of strategy, of course, lay the deeper question of historical "stages" whereby Marx posited socialism as "naturally" emerging out of advanced capitalism, in contrast with Mao's effort to move directly from China's "semi-feudal" state into socialism.

Subsequent to winning power, however, new ideological differences pitted Mao's vision of the "good society" against that manifest in the Soviet Union. At issue was nothing less than the fundamental goals of revolution, not merely as manifested in the century-old slogans of Marx and Engels, but in the present practices and future values of the new society. Mao's primary aim in carrying out a revolution in China was to transform the society's ethos from a hierarchical, elitist, authoritarian culture to an egalitarian, mass-oriented, and eventually mass-directed culture. For him, this domestic revolution conditioned other goals, such as modernization of the economy and building up national military power.

This appreciation of Mao's goals did not emerge fully until his Cultural Revolution of 1966–1968. In retrospect, however, it provides a clue to the intensity with which Mao waged his attack against "revisionism" as early as 1958, initially masked as "Yugoslav" revisionism and later revealed explicitly as "Soviet" when the polemic became public in the 1960s.

The important linkage between internal Soviet policy and Chinese foreign policy lay in Mao's recognition that national boundaries and governmental relations provide an inadequate frame of reference for understanding important levels of transnational interaction. Just as the missionaries and businessmen of the nineteenth century provided alternative models for emulation in China and transmitted values antithetical to the Confucian ethic, so the Soviet Union threatened to shape the new Chinese society in its own image. Such Soviet "leadership" was a compulsive dictate of Stalin's era whereby emulation of all things Russian seemed mandatory for "membership in the socialist camp," meaning Soviet military and economic support. Even after death removed Stalin's personal tyranny, Soviet methods and motivational values dominated allied regimes through the continuing ascendance of the Soviet model, transmitted by translated texts and articles, technical assistance teams, training in

---

[11]Quoted in Anna Louise Strong, *Dawn Out of China* (Bombay: People's Publishing House, 1948), p. 29.

Soviet institutes and research centers, and varying degrees of integration and standardization of technical systems, especially military.

The Sino-Soviet alliance promised to keep China permanently dependent—psychologically if not in fact— on the Soviet Union, since Beijing could hardly hope ever to "catch up" with Moscow's technical and material superiority, especially given China's tremendous imbalance between an enormous, largely untrained population and scarce resources of capital and food. Ideologically, the alliance confronted Mao with a model that stressed material incentives and unequal rewards of power and status for political authority and acquired skill. These values, national interest conflicts apart, threatened his twin goals of developing a China "standing on its own feet" and eliminating the hierarchical Confucian culture.

Thus, in addition to specific foreign policy conflicts which raised Sino-Soviet tensions in 1958–1959, the ideological conflict eroded the alliance because Mao was willing to risk the loss of Soviet military and economic support in order to shield China from Soviet "revisionism." Another ideological dimension, dominant in the polemic at the time, concerned the strategy and tactics best suited for advancing world revolution. Each side tended to caricature the other in this debate, the Chinese accusing the Soviets of "abandoning" the revolution to "peaceful coexistence with imperialism" while sacrificing local communists through insistence on the "parliamentary path to power," which could only end in frustration or suppression. The Soviets responded by claiming Mao to be a "nuclear madman" who would risk World War III to advance Chinese "chauvinistic, expansionistic" interests while he sacrificed local communists to bloody "people's wars" which might escalate to global proportions.

Accordingly, China's foreign policy carried a far more militant, strident tone of support for "people's wars" than did that of the Soviet Union. Mao's dictum held that "power grows out of the barrel of a gun" and that "armed struggle in the countryside" is the most reliable path to power. Moreover, his confrontation with Moscow compelled Beijing to champion communist causes throughout the world. Most important, however, was the root involvement of Mao's domestic ideological concerns which fueled his struggle with Khrushchev, thereby splitting the "socialist camp" and ultimately the "world revolutionary movement."

Mao's concerns were not without foundation. For instance, the transformation of China's military establishment from a backward army developed in guerrilla warfare against the Japanese into a modern, multiservice force moving toward a nuclear capability resulted wholly from Soviet assistance, both material and human. In Mao's eyes, however, the army was not merely for passive defense and exclusively military in function, but as in the guerrilla years of World War II, it was intimately associated with civilian political and economic activities, serving both as a model of selfless behavior and as a direct participant in mass campaigns of flood control, reforestation, and agriculture. For him it was no coincidence that opposition to his "Great Leap Forward" experiment of 1958–1959 with its mass communes and "backyard furnaces" was spearheaded by top PLA officials whose position paralleled that of Moscow. While Soviet criticism of the communes was accompanied by the cancellation of promised assistance in developing China's atomic weapons, PLA leaders attacked Mao's experiment as endangering the economy. To be sure, their argument was shared by civilian officials. But to the extent it appeared to reflect Soviet priorities of technical efficiency and technological leadership, as well as self-defined (rather than Mao-defined) roles and relationships between the military and civilian systems, the interplay between Khrushchev's "revisionism" and domestic Chinese developments fueled Mao's determination to push the Sino-Soviet dispute.

What of the external ideological goals of world revolution? How did they weigh in the scales of priority for Beijing? Despite their salience in the Sino-Soviet dispute, the goals of revolution were of lower priority than other ends of foreign policy, such as national security and international prestige. Mao excluded serious support for such foreign ventures, neither affording them success nor saving them from failure by significant contributions of Chinese assistance. In part, this was ideologically determined by the concept that "revolution is not for export" but must be indigenous to a country's problems and won by that country's revolutionary leadership. However, this was not the only constraint which limited Chinese material help to communist parties abroad. An amalgam of prudence and Sinocentrism reduced Beijing's contribution to considerably less than might be inferred from its polemic with Moscow or from its propagandistic pledges of "support" to various insurgencies.

In light of the above, the role of ideology in positing goals which require verbal, if not full, commitment should not be overlooked in understanding the factors which condition choice in Beijing. However tempting might seem the gains of disavowing world revolution for purposes of improving diplomatic, economic, or military relations the leadership can move only so far in this direction without betraying its own sense of obligation as ritualistically reiterated.

We have drawn extensively on Mao's statements and actions despite his death in 1976 and the subsequent denunciation of his domestic policies, beginning with the "Great Leap Forward" and culminating in the Cultural Revolution. Three factors justify our focus. First, Mao's strictures on foreign policy prevailed from 1949 to 1977. They shaped the thinking and writing of several generations whose perceptions of world affairs are heavily influenced thereby. Second, they have not been criticized since his death to the same degree or in the same detail as his domestic policies. While many changes have occurred in Chinese foreign policy, few have explicitly repudiated Mao's precepts.

Third and most important, no theoretical formulations have emerged from the post-Mao leadership to provide an alternative framework for foreign policy. The *Selected Works of Deng Xiaoping* constitute the most authoritative assemblage of policy statements but contain little on foreign affairs. Published speeches by officials touch on current foreign policy issues in passing but basically concentrate on domestic economic and political problems. While these problems may impact on foreign policy they do not affect the ideological framework in any direct way.

It is true that the relevance of ideology has markedly lessened, if it has not been specifically altered. By 1980 the Soviet Union was no longer vilified as "revisionist" but instead was condemned as "hegemonist." This shifted the basis of Beijing's attack from Moscow's domestic political system to its external power projection. Similarly China's professed identification with the Third World emphasized a common interest in confronting the two superpowers and in economic development obstructed by the North-South inequity. Meanwhile Beijing muted its support for Communist insurgents abroad and "national liberation struggles" except where they faced suppression by "superpower hegemonists," the United States and the USSR.

As the Marxist-Maoist aspects of ideology faded in both domestic and foreign policy the Chinese component reasserted itself in the latter domain during the early 1980s. An assertive nationalism keynoted Beijing's handling of such matters as the recovery of Taiwan and Hong Kong, pithily summarized in Deng's declaration, "No foreign country can expect China to be its vassal or expect it to swallow any bitter fruit detrimental to its own interests."[12] Hu Yoabang, then Chinese Communist Party General Secretary, likewise warned, "The Chinese people will never again allow themselves to be humiliated as they were before."[13]

In October 1983, the Propaganda Department of the Communist party of China (CPC) issued a "study outline" on "The Practice of Communism and Education in Communist Ideology" which explained the need to promote patriotism as a means of winning support for communism. The article frankly admitted thirty-four years after the founding of the PRC that the formal theories of Marxism-Leninism and the application of Mao Zedong Thought had failed to win the majority of Chinese. It thereby linked domestic mobilization with mass attitudes on foreign affairs:

> We should fully realize that those staunch Communists who have dedicated themselves to the highest ideal of communism for life are in the minority, while patriots, including Communists and those who uphold socialism, are in the overwhelming majority. . . . We must proceed from education in

12*Beijing Review*, September 6, 1982, p. 5.
13Ibid., September 13, 1982, p. 33.

patriotism, whip up the people's patriotic fervor, and raise the level of their patriotic awareness. At the same time, we must link this kind of fervor with their specific practice in building socialism, and gradually help them raise their consciousness for communism."[14]

The "Study Outline" explicitly rejected the extreme isolationist policy of "self-reliance" advocated during the Cultural Revolution, arguing that "China needs to understand the world while the world needs to understand China," and citing Deng's speech to the Twelfth National CPC Congress: "Both in our revolution and construction, we should also learn from foreign countries and draw on their experience." However, while "opening China to the outside world," the outline warned, "we are influenced by the international environment and the various trends of thought at home." An echo of Li Shiyao's and Chiang Kai-shek's xenophobic strictures could be detected in the extended injunction against "bourgeois influence" through foreign penetration:

> Since the implementation of the policy of opening to the outside world, decadent ideas and lifestyle of foreign bourgeoisie have again surged into our country. More and more people are going abroad and are being exposed to the capitalist world of sensual pleasures; cases of people worshipping foreign things, fawning on foreigners, acting in an obsequious manner and bringing shame on their country and themselves have occurred time and again. There are many serious criminal offenses in the economic, political, ideological and cultural fields and in social life. This is a concentrated manifestation of the corrosive influence of the decadent ideas of the exploiting classes at home and abroad.[15]

Instead of quoting Mao's "lean to one side" with "no third road" speech, the study outline drew the same theme from Lenin:

> Lenin said: "The question *can only be this*—either the bourgeois ideological system or the socialist ideological system. There is nothing in between (because mankind has not created any 'third kind' of ideological system. . . .) Therefore, any looking down on and *departure from* the socialist ideological system signifies a strengthening of the bourgeois ideological system."[16]

In sum, the Chinese and communist components of policy converge in reinforcing a basic suspicion of the outside world which is historically rooted in the experience of all regimes, whether imperial, Nationalist, or

---

[14] "The Practice of Communism and Education in Communist Ideology (Study Outline)," by CPC Central Committee Propaganda Department, Shanghai *Jiefang Ribao*, in Foreign Broadcast Information Service (FBIS), China, October 21, 1983, p. K41.

[15] Ibid., p. K44.

[16] Ibid., p. K43, emphasis in original.

Communist, in world affairs. Underlying this experience, moreover, is the fundamental felt need to fashion a sociocultural ethos that is distinctively Chinese, traditionally superior to and contemporarily distinct from the values and behavior of foreign societies. Mao's assertion of such an achievement for "New China" raised Chinese self-esteem while it rankled Moscow. Unfortunately his manic miscalculations not only undid much of what had initially been achieved but worse, embarassed China before the entire world.

This, in turn, posed new problems for the post-Mao leadership in addition to those inherited from "a century of shame and humiliation." The "study outline" represented one approach to the problem, calling on "the spirit to integrate patriotism with internationalism" while warning against the poison allegedly inherent in "foreign bourgeois" ways. Communist acceptance of the dialectic with omnipresent contradictions theoretically justifies the tension manifest in such formulations. However, their practical implications complicate foreign relations, particularly in their day-to-day implementation at the interpersonal as well as the intergovernmental level. This tension is likely to persist, given its historical, cultural, and psychological roots, reinforced through its ideological reiteration.

Institutional Structure of Decision Making: The Party

We have focused primarily on aggregate concepts such as "China" and "the Chinese," and on individual personalities such as Mao Zedong and Deng Xiaoping. Moving from these extreme opposite levels of analysis to the intermediate ground of governmental decision making is essential if we are to project a model of behavior compatible with other large bureaucracies. Rarely, if ever, does foreign policy result from an abstract concept of a monolithic "national interest," and never is it the product of a reified nation-state, in this case "China," behaving as an individual. Only under unique circumstances is policy the dictate of a single official acting wholly on his own initiative. Instead, specific interests and responsibilities shape the perceptions, information intake, and policy output of organized groups inside and outside the government. It is their complex interaction that defines policy in specific situations.

Unfortunately these commonplace observations cannot be confirmed for the Chinese policy process for much of the recent past because we lack solid evidence on which to accept, modify, or reject them. A few illuminating glimpses into bureaucratic relationships emerged in the turmoil and polemics of the Cultural Revolution. Personal interviews elicit responses that purportedly describe the policy process at one point or another. But in the absence of documentation, we must acknowledge that our knowledge is fragmentary and speculative at best for the first forty years of the PRC.

The available evidence, however, suggests that contrary to the normal bureaucratic model, major foreign policy decisions during the Maoist era were made by the Chairman personally. Informed colleagues later claimed that Mao often acted without consulting any relevant departments but simply ordered them to act. The role of Zhou Enlai as his close colleague and implementer of foreign policy is impossible to determine without further evidence. But at least in the bombardment of offshore islands in 1958 Mao personally assumed responsibility in admitting that he miscalculated the American response which stymied the attack. Finally there is little doubt that Mao determined China's probe for and response to the Nixon-Kissinger interest in détente against the known inclination of his Cultural Revolution cohorts.

This personalization of policy did not wholly end with Mao's death. Deng Xiaoping's visible behavior and the perception of lesser figures during his direction of post-Mao politics suggested that while he did not dictate decisions to the same degree, he dominated them at key moments. Support for this analysis came when Deng personally claimed credit for the 1984 Sino-British agreement on Hong Kong with the formula of "one country, two systems," and the designation of fourteen coastal cities as special foreign investment sites the same year.

At that time, Professor A. Doak Barnett won a unique series of interviews with top officials in Beijing, providing the best description to date of the foreign policy process.[17] While such information is essentially a snapshot of the moment as seen through a particular set of lenses, a view of China's foreign policy emerged as the post-Mao regime became increasingly immersed in the international economic and political network. The resultant picture challenges the conventional concentration on the party and state constitutions for discerning institutional responsibility. Instead Barnett's account accords with the traditional Chinese pattern of personalized politics, wherein informal groups and factions or cliques prevail over formalized channels of authority.

Thus instead of major decisions being made by the CCP Politburo, or its smaller surrogate, the Standing Committee, Barnett's sources attributed them to close interaction between the CCP Secretariat and the State Council, led by the then heads of these bodies, Hu Yaobang and Zhao Ziyang. Implicitly these two men, together with Deng as the most powerful elder statesman, formed a decision making nucleus which expanded to include other Standing Committee members on an ad hoc basis as the politics of the situation required. Formal meetings of the Standing Committee and the Politburo were not regularly convened although they could be called by the Secretariat and individual Standing Committee

17A. Doak Barnett, *The Making of Foreign Policy in China: Structure and Process*, (Boulder, Colo.: Westview Press, 1985). The following section draws largely from this work.

members respectively. Whether these gatherings ever overrode decisions advanced by the Deng-Hu-Zhao triumvirate or merely debated and modestly modified them could not be ascertained. However in the case study of special economic zones examined by Barnett, the Politburo seemed to ratify the plan already designed by the triumvirate.

On the one hand, this process significantly enlarged foreign policy participation from that of Mao Zedong's ascendancy, assuming that Hu and Zhao were free to differ with Deng's views and to propose policy on their own. On the other hand, it sharply reduced the number and nature of participants from that posited in the party rules. This point was persuasively justified by Zhao who noted that "most of the members of the Politburo are aged." At that time their average age was seventy-four, whereas the Secretariat and State Council averaged eight years less.

The Thirteenth Congress of the CCP, meeting in October 1987, retained only ten Politburo members, adding seven news ones, with an overall average age of sixty-five. Deng Xiaoping's resignation forced the hand of his older colleagues, thereby ending an historic era of party leadership. Reducing the membership from twenty to seventeen further streamlined the Politburo as a decision-making group. These developments enhanced the likelihood that Zhao's account of the policy process in 1984 will not apply in the future.

Significant changes in the CCP constitution were instituted that further aimed at regularizing the powers of the Politburo and its Standing Committee in contrast to the earlier role of the Secretariat and the informal triumvirate led by Deng. At that time, Zhao told Barnett, "all organizations concerned with foreign affairs participate in the Foreign Affairs Small Group" under the Secretariat. Chaired by the then PRC president, it included the premier, first vice-premier, the state councillor for foreign policy coordination, the foreign minister, and the minister of foreign economic relations and trade. Meeting more or less weekly, the Foreign Affairs Small Group had its own research staff, supplemented by invited specialists from other foreign affairs institutes in Beijing.

Under the new party rules however, the locus of authority shifted. Whereas previously "The Secretariat attends to the day-to-day work of the Central Committee under the direction of the Political Bureau and its Standing Committee," now "The Secretariat is the working office" of the Politbureau and its Standing Committee. Instead of being elected by the Central Committee, the Secretariat is nominated by the Standing Committee and approved by the Central Committee. These carefully worded changes reflect the move toward greater institutionalization of the political process as Deng prepared to leave the scene altogether. The party

---

[18]Harold K. Jacobson and Michel Oksenberg, *China and the Keystone International Economic Organizations* (draft, 1987).

spokesman described the constitutional changes more bluntly, "From now on decision-making involved in day-to-day affairs will fall into the realm of the Standing Committee of the Political Bureau and such decisions by the Standing Committee will be based on the decisions of the Political Bureau itself."

Consensus and collective decision making are necessary to accommodate competing bureaucracies. Complex foreign policy issues involve a process of investigation, argumentation, and negotiation before a final decision. A pioneer study of China's entry into the International Monetary Fund and the World Bank traces this process in detail.[18] Yet this does not exclude the possibility of one or more top officials exercising inordinate influence or arbitrarily adopting a posture that preempts collegial participation. A long-standing tradition in Chinese and communist politics of one individual exercising preeminent authority argues against a collectivity of equals making decisions in all instances. As Deng neared the end of his life, Chinese as well as foreigners focused on who would succeed him and with what authority, projecting factional struggles as likely to dominate formal arrangements. Thus, although the dominant mode of foreign policy decision making resembles that of other large state systems, the role of a few key individuals cannot be excluded in advance.

Basically, however, the process involves two sets of organizations, party and government. This raises a critical question, namely the relative weight of the party versus the governmental bureaucracy. This question has plagued communist systems from the start. Lenin envisioned the party's role as that of a pilot charting a ship's course through the channel, while the captain steers the vessel's actual movement. The pilot never touches the wheel. However, repeated efforts in the Soviet Union and China to lessen political party interference with professional management of the system have failed to resolve the issue. The result is excessive political involvement in practical matters to the detriment of expertise and efficiency.

This dilemma is rooted in official doctrine. The "General Programme" or preamble to the 1982 party constitution asserts that "the party . . . must see to it that the legislative, judicial and administrative organs of the state and the economic, cultural and people's organizations work actively and with initiative, independently, responsibly, and in harmony." Article 3 obligates individual members to "execute the party's decisions perseveringly, accept any job and fulfil actively any task assigned to them by the party, [and] conscientiously observe party discipline and the laws of the state." Article 10 spells out the hierarchy of authority which submits each member to rule from above, culminating in the Central Committee, in practice meaning the Politburo.

However as part of Deng's political reform program, a key provision enveloping government in the party network was revised at the thirteenth CCP Congress. Article 46 had stipulated that "A leading party members' group shall be formed in the leading body of a central or local state organ. . . . The main tasks of such a group are: to see to it that the party's principles and policies are implemented, to unite with the nonparty cadres and masses in fulfilling the tasks assigned by the party and the state, and to guide the work of the party organization of the unit." This group "must accept the leadership of the party committee that approves its establishment." Article 48 added, "the Central Committee of the party shall determine specifically the functions, powers, and tasks of the leading party members' groups in those government departments which need to exercise highly centralized and unified leadership over subordinate units; it shall also determine whether such groups should be replaced by party committees."

The new Article 46 deleted all reference to "central or local state organ," instead limiting the party group to "the elected leading body of a central or local people's congress, mass organization, or other non-party organization." Further Article 48 was reduced to the Central Committee determining whether "a party committee should be set up" in government departments, such action not being mandatory.

These changes won specific attention in Zhao Ziyang's address to the Congress. Attacking "the lack of distinction between the functions of the Party and those of the government and the substitution of the Party for the government," Zhao declared, "The key to reforming the political structure is the separation of Party and government."[19] The problem of dual authority had been exacerbated by the fact that after Mao's death the party was predominantly composed of old revolutionary veterans and young Cultural Revolution recruits. Neither group had the education or experience required to cope with economic modernization. Yet such modernization was imperative if China were to achieve self-reliance in national security and raise its standard of living.

Whether this reform can actually be accomplished, given the vested interest of party secretaries in maintaining their power and privileges, remains to be seen. Zhao acknowledged that the reforms "should gradually become institutionalized." The official spokesman for the party congress specifically noted that "the question of political restructuring is a very complicated one . . . it will be a gradual abolition of the leading party's groups in the central organs as well as in the ministries and commissions of the State Council." Another question concerns retired senior party officials who are elevated to the Central Advisory Commit-

---

[19]Zhao Ziyang, "Advance Along the Road of Socialism With Chinese Characteristics," Report to 13th National Congress of the Chinese Communist Party, October 25, 1987 in *Beijing Review,* November 9–15, 1987, p. 38.

tee, presumably with prestige but without power. They are loathe to disengage completely from politics. They seek to influence policy through long-established networks and personal intervention. For these reasons, until there is convincing evidence to the contrary, it is safe to assume that the main locus of decision making in foreign as well as domestic policy will be in the CCP Standing Committee and Politburo.

Institutional Structure: The Government

In China, as in all large complex organizations, rarely does one decision determine everything that follows. Decisions are usually incremental in nature and implementation is always organizational in practice. This is a particularly important aspect of foreign policy where success or failure often depends on perceptions abroad which in turn are based on what is said and done by individuals and organizations far removed from the initial decision makers. Thus whatever weight may be given to individuals or party organs in initiating policy, a critical role remains for governmental bodies in day to day operations.

Seen in this perspective, the cabinet or State Council is a logical point of departure, comprising the premier, vice-premiers, state councillors, and more than forty heads of ministries and commissions. Barnett's informants described a much smaller group of fifteen key officials as actually supervising governmental operations, meeting twice a week under the premier's chairmanship. In addition to officials responsible for general foreign policy management, this "inner cabinet" includes those in charge of economic policy abroad, national defense, and organizations involved in or affected by China's growing participation in the world community. In other words it is the nexus of PRC foreign policy management.

However within this fifteen person nexus, a subgroup of three further centralized the coordination of foreign policy and the consideration of policy problems. According to Zhao Ziyang, then premier, the ministers for foreign affairs and foreign trade, together with an experienced state councillor "meet frequently to discuss foreign affairs and communicate among themselves. When there are problems they cannot solve, they raise them with the State Council.[20] Barnett noted the omission of the defense minister in contrast with the usual practice in Washington. Zhao's comment illustrates the degree to which policy responsibility can devolve to a small, highly personalized group without formal authorization or public visibility.

Yet it would be wrong to exaggerate the degree of control and coordination in China's vast bureaucracy that extends throughout provincial and municipal offices that deal with foreign business, tourism, and

[20]Barnett, *The Making of Foreign Policy in China*, p. 67.

journalism. Multiple and conflicting interests coexist in time and may be acted on simultaneously without central direction from the capital.

It is natural to fix on the Ministry of Foreign Affairs together with the Ministry of Foreign Economic Relations and Trade as central in foreign policy, while it is seldom realized that the latter is by far the larger entity. But a broader vision must encompass those organizations whose information inputs and policy outputs directly or indirectly relate to China's foreign relations. Some, such as the Ministry of Defense, are highly visible and resemble their counterparts abroad in function and operation, although foreign military sales remain secret in scope and content. Others, such as those involved with intelligence or support for "national liberation struggles," are completely covert. Still others, such as the Ministry of Finance and the People's Bank, have primary domestic responsibilities that are affected by how China manages its external economic relations, and therefore they are engaged in foreign policy discussions.

For example, the aforementioned study of China's entry into the World Bank found the following institutions involved, in addition to the more obvious ones already named: the Chinese Academy of Social Science, the Ministry of Education, the State Economic Commission, the State Education Commission, the State Planning Commission, the State Statistical Bureau, and the Shanghai Institute of International Economic Management.[21] To envisage that entry as simply following a single decision made at the top would caricature the long, complex, and elaborate process of winning agreement to its implementation so as to satisfy both China and the World Bank.

China's extensive people-to-people bureaucracy also plays an important part in shaping the PRC image abroad, in introducing foreign techniques and concepts at home, and in forging links that supplement standard diplomatic channels. The Ministry of Culture, the State Scientific and Technological Commission, the Chinese People's Institute of Foreign Affairs, and the Chinese People's Association for Friendship with Foreign Countries are active in this regard. Indeed, as Barnett notes, the latter two organizations "are headed by senior retired diplomats and staffed in large part by personnel from the Foreign Ministry and other government foreign affairs organizations." Research institutes also play a role through their hosting of foreign scholars and their visits to foreign "think tanks," *inter alia* promoting image and policy while eliciting information to be incorporated in their policy research studies. Primary in this regard are the Institute of International Studies directly under the Foreign Ministry, the Institute of Contemporary International Relations, and the Beijing Institute for International Strategic Studies.

Just as China's participation in the global community is still evolving

---

[21] Jacobson and Oksenberg, op cit.

so too are its governmental policy processes in flux. Beijing's exclusion from most international organizations down to 1971 was made worse by the Cultural Revolution self-imposed isolation, which suppressed institutions as well as individuals that had previously had experience with foreign affairs. Not until Deng's ascendancy and his proclamation of the "open door" doctrine in December 1978 did the PRC begin a rapid expansion of political involvement and economic interdependence with the global system.

The brief span of a decade hardly suffices to establish an entire bureaucratic system for managing relations between a developing society of more than a billion people and a vast international network that itself is undergoing rapid transformation, especially in the economic realm. As a final point, the People's Republic existed under a uniquely dominant Mao Zedong from 1949 to 1976 and an ascendant Deng Xiaoping thereafter, each having distinctly different political styles and power. Therefore decision making at the top as well as the bureaucratic structure and process below will inevitably evolve well beyond presently perceptible patterns. This requires continuing research and analysis to test past propositions and new hypotheses, remembering that China has maintained the oldest continuous civilization by adapting to change forced on it by internal as well as external circumstances. Nevertheless, its bureaucracy has survived through the millenia as a highly complex system, whether the regime was imperial, republican, or communist. It is likely to remain a major conditioning force on policy, both domestic and foreign.

THE SUBSTANCE OF POLICY

Ends and Means

The People's Republic has radically changed its foreign policy rhetoric at home and abroad over the past forty years. Mao's world revolutionary fervor of the 1950s, carried to an extreme in the 1960s, stands in complete contrast with Deng's global integrative and interdependent stance in the 1980s. It is impossible to exaggerate the difference in tone and substance as between Beijing's pronouncements of 1949–1954 or 1966–1968 and 1985–1987.

Yet contradictory rhetoric notwithstanding, a fundamental continuity characterized the ends of policy, not only during the relatively short history of the PRC but going back to its republican and imperial predecessors. Security from foreign attack was traditionally a primary concern and, as our earlier analysis showed, a preoccupation through the first half of this century. This preoccupation did not end with Mao and it concerned Deng until the early 1980s. Meeting domestic needs sufficient to avoid rebellion was also a constant regime worry as a growing population pressed against scarce resources of food, shelter, and employment. This problem also plagued Qing, Nationalist, and Communist policymakers alike.

Mao acknowledged these practical priorities, although he mismanaged them and at times neglected them for ideological postulates of self-reliance and his own vision of communism. He recognized the linkage between external prestige and internal strength measured in economic rather than military terms. In 1961, at the depth of a prolonged economic crisis worsened by the sudden withdrawal of Soviet technical assistance, Mao declared, "Nations which are big or rich despise nations which are small or poor. . . . At present, China still finds itself in a position of being despised. There is a reason people despise us. It is because we have not progressed enough. So big a country and we have so little steel and so many illiterates. But it is good if people despise us because it forces us to strive harder and forces us to advance."[22]

Mao's remarks reflect a national sensitivity to China's inferior position of power and status after a millenium of superiority vis-à-vis the world as it existed in Chinese perceptions and experience, at least in Asia. This historical heritage of former greatness and contemporary weakness affects both the ends and means of foreign policy alternatives implicit in current approaches to Chinese nationalism. Professor Michel Oksenberg differentiates four such variants.[23] The most extreme is "strident, xenophobic, and isolationist . . . seeks to eradicate foreign influence." Advanced by the Boxers in 1900 and Red Guards in the Cultural Revolution, this approach has the least support at present. A second variant is "self-pitying, self-righteous, and aggrieved . . . blames China's ills on the transgressions of the outside world." Although similar to nationalism in other developing countries, its strength derives from a sense of China's past grandeur juxtaposed against its recent "century of shame and humiliation." Oksenberg describes the resulting ambivalent attitude as one of "scorn and admiration, resentment and appreciation" toward the outside world. A third "militant, rigid, assertive, and occasionally muscular nationalism" characterized Mao's assault on Khrushchev and Deng's attempt to "teach Vietnam a lesson." More recently this approach accepts "a limited and cautious involvement in world affairs to terminate vulnerabilities and humiliations." How it will be manifested once China acquires sufficient military strength to pursue its unsettled territorial claims on land and at sea remains to be seen.

Oksenberg finds the fourth variant dominant since the mid-1980s,

22"Notes on the Soviet Union Textbook 'Political Economy,'"*Mao Zedong sixiang wansui*, 1969, p. 392.

23Michel Oksenberg, "China's Confident Nationalism," *Foreign Affairs*, vol. 65, no. 3, (1987).

namely, "a patient and moderate nationalism rooted in confidence that China can regain its former greatness through economic growth, based on the import of foreign technology and ideas." But it partakes of the third variant in being "a determined and resolute nationalism . . . deeply committed to the preservation of national independence, the reunification of China (including Hong Kong, Macao, Taiwan, and disputed islands in the South and East China Seas) and the attainment of national wealth and power." His list could also have included disputed borders with the Soviet Union, India, and Vietnam.

This categorization captures the continuing linkage between domestic and foreign policy. Economic development as an internal goal links with the twin external goals of national security and self-defined territorial integrity. The categorization also reveals domestic differences over how to attain these goals. Neither the linkage nor the goals are uniquely Chinese. However, during most of Mao's rule the degree to which they were misperceived abroad and the way in which they were pursued at home set China apart from other major powers.

Therefore, Deng Xiaoping moved to reorder and clarify goals in foreign perception and domestic priority. On the one hand, he articulated nationalism in blunt terms as we noted earlier, vowing that China will not "swallow any bitter fruit detrimental to its own interests." On the other hand, he insisted that China "must open to the outside world" in order to progress toward modernization. Deng also translated these general concepts into medium and long-term goals for the 1990s and beyond. For the next decade he targeted the doubling of gross national product (GNP) per capita, the unification of the PRC with Hong Kong and possibly Taiwan, and the striving to "combat hegemonism and safeguard world peace." He further declared that Hong Kong's existing socioeconomic system would last "fifty years more" while the peaceful unification of Taiwan might take a hundred years.

Of the three goals, Deng repeatedly made economic growth and modernization top priority. Meanwhile "safeguarding peace" was a means as well as an end. Only by achieving a peaceful international environment could China concentrate scarce human and capital resources on the civilian economy, postponing the acquisition of modern weapons until they could be produced at home rather than purchased abroad. Thus national security no longer outranked other objectives.

More specifically, by changing the Soviet relationship from confrontation to détente, Deng could reduce the PLA by a million men and defer indefinitely the wholesale upgrading of conventional weaponry. Similarly postponing the long sought unification with Taiwan would safeguard relations with the United States and Japan as major sources of capital, technology, and markets. In short, domestic priorities determined foreign policy insofar as it was susceptible to Chinese management.

Opposition to Deng's "open door" policy came from some of the nationalistic variants mentioned by Oksenberg, but Deng met them head on. In an assertive speech he rebuked the isolationist xenophobes on the record of their predecessors, "Any country that closes its door to the outside world cannot achieve progress. We underwent this bitter experience and so did our forefathers. . . . China closed the country to international intercourse for more than three centuries from the middle of the Ming Dynasty to the Opium War, or for nearly two centuries from emperors Kangxi and Qianlong. Hence the country became impoverished, backward, and ignorant."[24] His last reference also implicitly rebutted the aggrieved nationalists who blamed all of China's ills on the foreign powers.

Speaking to the party's Central Advisory Committee, Deng reassured his more ideological veteran colleagues, "Some of our comrades are afraid that evil practices may be introduced into the country . . . of seeing capitalism suddenly looming up after having worked all their lives for socialism and communism . . . [but] nothing will be affected. It may bring some negative factors. But it will not be difficult to overcome such factors if we are aware of them."[25]

Such reassurance seemed challenged in December 1986 when student demonstrations demanding freedom and democracy broke out in Shanghai and other cities. The resulting counterattack against "bourgeois liberalization" linked domestic dissent with foreign influences, in the process toppling Hu Yaobang as General Secretary of the CCP, one of Deng's two chosen successors. However Deng responded shrewdly. On the one hand he expelled a few prominent liberals from the party and cracked down on student demonstrations with the threat of force. On the other hand he steadfastly insisted that the open door would never be closed, regardless of the "flies and mosquitoes" that might come in.

Actually the door opened outward as well as inward. By 1987 more than 17,000 Chinese were studying in the United States with thousands more in Europe and Japan. Beginning in 1979, dozens of Chinese delegations toured the world to observe military and civilian installations, factories, and training centers. Hundreds of specialists accepted invitations to attend international conferences and workshops or to give individual lectures at research centers. Reciprocally foreign experts, especially overseas Chinese, poured into the country to offer information and advice, conduct joint research, and assess problems. Almost every subject from archeology to zoology became the province of joint study between Chinese and foreigners at home and abroad. Several hundred

[24]Deng Xiaoping to Third Plenary Session of Central Advisory Commission, October 22, 1984, *Renmin Ribao,* January 1, 1985.
[25]Ibid.

thousand foreign books and journals replenished the vacant libraries left desolate by the Cultural Revolution and provided starter sets for new research centers. The massive translation of scientific materials expanded their potential use pending adequate training in foreign languages.

Information alone was not enough. China needed advanced technology and the capital to acquire it. In 1980 Beijing moved to join the major international financial organizations: the International Monetary Fund, the International Bank for Reconstruction and Development—better known as the World Bank, and its affiliated agencies, the International Development Association and the International Finance Corporation. Previously these agencies had been attacked as exploitive instruments of capitalist control over Third World economies. Beijing had also protested Taiwan's occupying the China seat in them, at the same time championing PRC "self-reliance." As another deterrent to joining these institutions they required opening the economy to detailed examination and statistical reporting. Such practices ran counter to the communist proclivity for secrecy and the Chinese sensitivity over revealing weakness.

However in the eyes of Deng and his modernizing cohorts the potential gain clearly outweighed the costs. After forcing Taiwan out, they came in, quietly abandoning the Maoist strictures on alleged North-South confrontation and calls for a New Economic Order. Instead they maneuvered to strengthen China's position over that of India so as to maximize their opportunity to influence decisions and win loans. By 1988 World Bank approved loans to China approximated $5.5 billion with an anticipated annual rate of $2 billion by 1990.

In addition to money, the World Bank provided invaluable planning assistance through its comprehensive surveys of the Chinese economy, the first, as of 1981, issued in three closely written volumes and the second, as of 1984, in six volumes. The Bank also did feasibility studies of more than four dozen projects financed by its loans, focusing on agriculture, energy, education, public health, transportation, and science.[26] Thus the World Bank impact went well beyond the provision of funds, in effect transforming the decision-making as well as the productive processes. For example, "China in the Year 2000" is no longer a rhetorical reference for political exhortation, but a systematic research effort modeled on similar studies abroad and undertaken in cooperation with the World Bank. Centered in the State Council's Technical Economics Research Center, its responsibilities include feasibility studies of major construction projects, studying the long-term comprehensive and strategic development of the economy, and assessing major economic policies already under way.

---

[26]In addition to Jacobson and Oksenberg, op. cit., this section draws on an unpublished paper by Samuel S. Kim kindly made available to the author.

This close interaction between China and the World Bank is only one instance whereby post-Mao policy links domestic development with foreign policy. With foreign trade in excess of $70 billion by 1986, Japan's share of Chinese foreign trade ranked first with more than a quarter of the total. Japan also occupied first place in China's foreign borrowing with $3.5 billion in low-interest loans committed since 1979. Acceptance of Japan, a former enemy, as the principal source of trade, technology, and credit came hard after a half century of aggression, annexation, and invasion. Reversing the traditional roles of teacher and student further exacerbated the situation for the older generation in particular.

To overcome this deep-seated antipathy, in 1983 Beijing joined with Tokyo in sponsoring the Commission for Sino-Japanese Friendship in the Twenty-first Century. Its promotion by the highest officials on both sides contrasted with the militant anti-Japanese imagery propagated by the Chinese media down to 1971 and briefly revived during a dispute over Japanese textbook revisions in 1982. Nevertheless resistance to such "friendship" prompted anti-Japanese student demonstrations on September 17, 1985, the anniversary of the Japanese seizure of Manchuria in 1931. The protests were an immediate reaction to the fortieth anniversary of Japan's surrender in World War II and its provocative commemoration in Tokyo. However student slogans also attacked "the second invasion" and "Japan's economic invasion." Yet despite this domestic opposition, PRC officials persisted in promoting the Japanese tie, explicitly justifying it as necessary for economic modernization.

In similar fashion Sino-American relations have been driven in part by domestic economic goals, thereby relegating the Taiwan issue to the background. Détente between Beijing and Washington began for security goals in 1969–1971 amid Chinese apprehension over a tripling of Soviet military forces across the border in 1965–1970, with actual clashes in 1969. The security aspect reopened in 1979 when China attacked Vietnam, allied with the Soviet Union, in a three-week long limited war.

While the security question did not wholly disappear, its significance lessened in the 1980s as Beijing became more confident of Moscow's intentions and problems elsewhere. Meanwhile the economic potential in Sino-American relationships loomed steadily larger as Washington loosened controls on technology transfer, particularly as regards technology with dual-use potential for military as well as civilian use. A $500 million avionics package for jet fighters to acquire all-weather capability won congressional approval, as did the sale of nuclear power generation technology, should Beijing want to purchase these goods. A sizeable investment in off-shore oil exploration failed to bring American corporations much profit or China much oil. Yet the continuation of oil exploration held out hope of an eventual strike that could ease China's domestic oil needs and perhaps earn additional foreign exchange from Asian neighbors, first and foremost Japan, with whom China's trade imbalance reached $6 billion in 1986.

Under these circumstances, Deng's decision to stop pressing the United States to halt arms sales to Taiwan in 1982 and, instead, to accept an ambiguously worded commitment to decrease them over time made economic sense. Likewise Beijing protested in words, but not actions, after a unanimous congressional resolution condemned the Chinese suppression of Tibetan demonstrations in 1987. This once again reflected the primacy of domestic economics in foreign policy.

Last but not least in this brief review of major relationships affected by domestic priorities is Beijing's response to Moscow's repeated bids for détente, beginning in 1981 and accelerating through 1987. We have already cited the security aspect whereby downgrading the threat of Soviet attack, both real and perceived, permitted the reduction of PLA forces and the concomitant drop in the defense share of the budget, officially stated as 10 percent in 1985 as against 15 percent in 1983. In addition, the economic modernization program enjoys relatively small but worthwhile gains through improved relations between China and the Soviet bloc. Upgrading Soviet and East European equipment of the 1950s can be more economical and feasible than replacing it wholesale with machinery from other countries. Soviet equipment is also easier to pay for on a barter basis since this does not require drawing down foreign exchange reserves. Finally cross-border trade can be important locally for the northeast and far west of China where there is a limited complementarity between the two economies. While total trade remains far below that of Japan and the United States, its tenfold growth in ten years to an expected $3 billion by 1990 makes sense to Beijing as well as Moscow.

This partly explains why Deng muted Mao's strident anti-Soviet polemics, particularly with respect to Moscow's domestic policies. To be sure, it became difficult to attack Soviet policies as "revisionist" when China's economic experiments soon surpassed them by abandoning much collective enterprise for limited private and family initiatives in the rural and urban economies. But equally important was the reintroduction of Soviet participation in economic development, where such participation might be more relevant for China's technological level than the highly advanced ways and means of Japan, the United States, and Western Europe.

Unlike Japan and the United States, however, the Soviet Union won no real respite from Chinese pressure on major foreign issues in dispute between the two countries. Beijing persisted in its support for the guerrillas fighting Soviet occupation forces in Afghanistan; and it opposed Vietnamese forces in Cambodia or Kampuchea that are backed by Moscow. It demanded a Soviet withdrawal from both situations and mobilized others to support this demand. The provision of arms in both instances, especially for the Khmer Rouge forces operating out of Thailand, showed that Beijing is willing to back its words with deeds, improved bilateral relations with Moscow notwithstanding.

Beijing's repeated declaration of an "independent" policy with no "strategic alignment or alliance" with either superpower was manifest in its public denunciation of American policy in Central America, South Africa, and the Middle East. However, nowhere did Chinese actions substantively intervene against American interests, although arms sales to Iran remained contentious in 1987. Chinese denials ducked the issue, as had previously occurred with respect to the question of China's assisting Pakistan in the clandestine development of nuclear weapons. But neither case approximated the indirect confrontation with Moscow in Afghanistan and Indochina.

A less important but symbolically more sensitive instance of economics superceding politics came with the 1984 Sino-British agreement on Hong Kong's reversion to Chinese control in 1997. The year 1997 ends Britain's ninety-nine year lease to the New Territories, adjoining the original Hong Kong territory ceded "in perpetuity" after the Opium War. Both concessions resulted from "unequal treaties." Yet Beijing permitted their termination to be settled through prolonged and intensive negotiation with London. The foregone conclusion was garbed in legalistic language bereft of anti-imperialist rhetoric. Much remained to be clarified concerning the actual manner in which Hong Kong would eventually be administered, but the basic agreement pledged continuation of its existing economic system.

As with our other cases, political considerations played a part in policy. The principle of "one country, two systems" anticipated a positive response from Taiwan, where Hong Kong might provide an attractive example for negotiating union with the mainland. Specific reference to this objective by Deng and his associates failed to bring Taiwan to the table, at least in the short run. Nevertheless Beijing hoped over time to make Hong Kong a positive precedent for Taipei.

In the interim, economic incentives dictated a soft, compromising stance on the British crown colony. Hong Kong provides between one fourth and one third of China's foreign exchange earnings. This comes through a combination of direct sales to Hong Kong, transshipment through the world's second largest port, Chinese investment in Hong Kong, and overseas Chinese remittances transmitted through its facilities. Reciprocally Hong Kong investment in China soared with the opening of Shenzhen, the first special economic zone, literally on its border. Neighboring Guangdong province and its capital of Guangzhou (Canton) likewise profited through burgeoning trade and investment from the colony. In fact, Hong Kong capital and capitalists sparked local modernization to the extent that some observers wondered, only partly in jest, whether it

was a question of Hong Kong "taking over China" rather than the reverse.

Moving more broadly, China's virtual abandonment of revolutionary
rhetoric and activity in Southeast Asia clearly stems from Deng's desire to
improve relations with ASEAN, the Association of Southeast Asian Nations. Initially he aimed at isolating Vietnam and obstructing its occupation of Kampuchea. Then economic objectives became important as
Beijing wooed investors and sought markets. Both goals required a muting of support for indigenous communists, most of whom had enjoyed
Beijing's help in insurgency at some point in the past three decades.

Little remains of Mao's once touted "three worlds" approach to
global economic relations. Instead of belaboring North-South problems
to be solved exclusively by the northern tier of industrial states, China has
hosted South-South conferences which emphasize mutual help among the
southern tier developing economies. In practical terms this often means
self-help. Beijing's representatives in the World Bank and its affiliates
work within existing norms for their own interests, not those of other
developing countries in particular. This pattern is expected to hold when
the PRC enters GATT (General Agreement on Trade and Tariffs), having made application for membership in 1986, although several years of
negotiation are anticipated to work out the details.

Thus the 1970s cry for a New Economic Order disappeared from
Chinese statements in the 1980s. Instead Beijing promoted themes of
peace, disarmament, and development in its presentations to interna-
tional bodies where its participation grew rapidly under Deng's aegis.
From 1977 to 1984 PRC membership in non-governmental organizations
(NGOs) jumped from 71 to 355, while it still remained apart from the
two major Third World groups, the Non-Aligned Movement and
OPEC.[27] China joined considerably fewer International Governmental
Organizations (IGOs) during this time, moving from 21 memberships in
IGOs to 29. Professor Samuel S. Kim speculates that hesitancy in the
latter category stems in part from limited diplomatic personnel, with
priority going to the United Nations and its specialized agencies. Therefore he foresees a gradual growth to roughly 50 IGO memberships in the
next decade.

Parallel with its expanded organizational participation was the PRC
adherence to multilateral treaties. From 1949 to 1970 it signed a total of
six, adding another sixteen before Mao's death. But between 1977 and
1985 Beijing joined ninety-one multilateral agreements.[28] Still another
indicator of China's reentry into the world community as a normal member came with high-level visits abroad, reciprocating a steady flow of

[27]Kim, op. cit.
[28]Ibid.

government leaders to China. Mao only left the country twice, both times to visit Moscow. Liu Shaoqi, head of state from 1958 to 1967, made brief tours of Southeast Asia in addition to visiting the USSR. Otherwise only Zhou Enlai as premier, and sometimes as foreign minister, travelled extensively to Eastern Europe, Africa, and Asia.

Within a few years of Mao's death, however, Deng made unprecedented trips to Western Europe, Japan, and the United States. Premiers Hua Guofeng and Zhao Ziyang expanded on Zhou Enlai's itinerary, including Western Europe and Australasia. In 1985 President Li Xiannian visited Washington, the highest Chinese official in history to do so, having been preceded by presidents Nixon, Ford, and Reagan going to Beijing.

Hu Yaobang as CCP General Secretary also travelled widely before his ouster in 1987. Gone was the so-called Mao jacket and the support for radical splinter groups in Europe and elsewhere as "true Marxist-Leninists" confronting Moscow's orthodox adherents. China's worldwide offensive against "revisionism and social imperialism" had reduced its state cohorts to Albania and North Korea and its party contacts to nonentities. This policy ended with Mao's death. Ironically the first state leader to view Mao's body in the newly erected mausoleum in Tienanmen Square was Yugoslavia's Brosip Tito, Mao's initial revisionist target of twenty years ago. By the late 1980s the CCP had not only restored relations with virtually all its major counterparts, excepting the Soviet party, but had broadened relations with socialist and left-wing parties in many countries.

As might be expected, the last and least important means of policy in the past decade has been the use of force. Except for the three week limited invasion of Vietnam in February–March 1979, the PLA has remained behind China's borders since Mao's death. Prior to that its use in defensively motivated actions had engaged United States–United Nations forces in Korea (1950–1953), Indian border troops in the Himalayas (1962), U.S. aircraft over North Vietnam (1965–1968), and Soviet border units along the Amur-Ussuri river complex and the Xinjiang border (1969). The PLA also seized the Xisha (Paracel) Islands from South Vietnam forces in 1974. Pursuing the civil war it engaged Chinese Nationalist air and sea units in the Taiwan Strait throughout the 1950s and 1960s, with concentrated attacks on offshore islands in 1954–1955 and 1958, having had limited success with only the first attack.

Beijing's perception of threat was clearly much higher during Mao's regime than subsequently, in part because its sense of vulnerability was much greater. To a considerable extent, however, miscalculation by China's opponents, most notably Washington and New Delhi, aroused this threat perception. Learning on both sides, albeit costly, ushered in a more stable and peaceful situation wholly apart from Deng's determination to minimize military expenditures by reducing tensions on all fronts. Thus in the spring of 1987 mutual accusations of military buildup by Beijing and New Delhi raised tensions in the disputed border area, but no fighting occurred. Similarly minor incidents on the Sino-Soviet border were also contained to private diplomatic exchanges. Only the Vietnam border continued to flare up periodically, with each side accusing the other of initiating mortar and artillery bombardments and occasional ground action up to battalion level.

During this decade of general military stand down and claimed reductions in defense spending, China has nevertheless continued to improve its nuclear capability. The growing inventory of missiles includes medium-range (660 miles), intermediate range (1,400–1,900 miles), extended intermediate-range (2,880–3,330 miles), and intercontinental-range (7,800 miles). In 1983 China tested its first ballistic missile submarine, firing an extended intermediate-range weapon. The airborne delivery of fission and fusion weapons is made possible by approximately a hundred bombers with a radius of up to 1,800 miles, although they are very vulnerable to Soviet defenses.

All but the intercontinental missiles were liquid fuelled as of the mid-1980s, virtually precluding a surprise attack because of the lengthy firing process. This made credible China's vow never to launch a first strike. However they served as a potential second strike deterrent to the extent that dispersal, hardening, and concealment or camouflage preclude their total destruction by an enemy. The most likely threat being Soviet, this second strike capability becomes meaningful when targetted against any of the three major Far East Soviet cities: Irkutsk, Khabarovsk, and Vladivostok. The first two sit astride the Trans-Siberian railroad, just across the border. Their destruction would cut Moscow's main communications route to its Pacific bases of which Vladivostok is the primary one, equally vulnerable to missile attack.

These considerations may have contributed to Chinese confidence that Moscow would not start a war once the crisis of 1969–1970 ebbed, in addition to the Sino-American détente with hints from Washington that it would not remain passive in a Sino-Soviet conflict. However such confidence could not be absolute, thereby justifying Beijing's continued research and development of nuclear weapons, most recently including MIRV (multiple independent targeted reentry vehicle) warheads.

FUTURE PROSPECTS

This profile of foreign policy ends and means is likely to hold for the near future. Deng's departure will not convulse the leadership in a serious succession struggle, although some jockeying for power is inevitable, during which time conflicting signals may emanate as to various aspects of domestic and foreign policy. However Deng's avowal that the "open door" will remain open is credible. China has gone too far in its interdependence on foreign trade, credits, training, and technology transfer, all essential to modernization, for another Cultural Revolution retreat into xenophobic isolation. The tragic costs of that catastrophe are vividly recalled by its survivors who are determined never to permit its recurrence.

In place of Mao's uniquely powerful and ideologically driven personal control, Deng's decade of rule has established a broad coalition of vested interests extending across economic sectors, geographic regions, and generational cohorts. Not only has this coalition already enjoyed rewards of power and profit, but also it can foresee even greater power and privileges by continuing Deng's reforms. Nor do opponents scattered throughout the system have a credible alternative policy for mobilizing sufficent strength to reverse the reforms.

This does not mean that everything will remain the same. Various problems confront the open door policy, both within China and abroad. An unfinished agenda for action, deferred for the present, faces Deng's successors.

As a final caution against complacently assuming constancy, it should be remembered that few foreign analysts anticipated the Great Leap Forward in 1958, the virulent attack on Khrushchev in 1960, and the Cultural Revolution in 1966. On the positive side, few forecast the extent of Deng's initiatives when he reemerged in 1978 from the exile of political purge. The recent changes of direction may have been the product of a revolutionary regime that, with its initial leader's death, is in the process of rationalizing its processes and policies. In any event, it is prudent to consider some of the variables that may affect China's future foreign policy, regardless of regime preference.

Annexing Taiwan has been on Beijing's agenda since 1949, although its priority has changed as has the means for acquiring it. In the 1950s millions of Chinese vowed its "liberation" in mass rallies, while leadership statements ritualistically committed the regime to this goal. By the 1980s the goal had become "reunification" through "peaceful means as a fundamental policy." Beijing refused to foreswear the use of force as its sovereign right but in deference to American policy, reiterated by every administration, it virtually abandoned any reference to this option.

The PRC made credible its peaceful policy, drawing down the military forces opposite Taiwan and opening the coastal area to foreign investment and tourism. Deng elaborated on his "one country, two systems" concept in interviews which declared that Taiwan would be even more autonomous than Hong Kong because it could keep its own armed forces and acquire weapons abroad "so long as they do not threaten the mainland." Deng pledged "not to send a single official" to the island,

asking only that Taipei abandon its flag and nomenclature so as to acknowledge its subordinate status as a province in the People's Republic.

Pending negotiations Beijing proposed that trade, travel, family reunion, and mail cross the Taiwan Strait be initiated. It invited Taiwan to
participate in international conferences, organizations, and sporting
events under the name, "China, Taiwan" or "China, Taipei," depending
on the circumstances. For its part the Taiwan regime formally refused to
sanction any direct mainland contact, but during the 1980s it closed an
eye to trade via Hong Kong that was estimated near $2 billion in 1988. It
also took no action against travel via third countries, which rose steadily,
totaling 100,000 by mainland estimates. Most visible and dramatic, however, was its participation in the 1984 Los Angeles Olympics as "China,
Taiwan" with neither its own flag or anthem.

In 1987 Taiwan formalized some of these developments without,
however, agreeing to any negotiations. It lifted all restrictions on travel to
Hong Kong, thereby opening the gate for onward movement to the
mainland. It then moved to permit certain categories of mainland travel
associated with family reunion. It also legitimized the publication of
mainland scholarly works, provided that they were not political and were
reprinted in standard Chinese characters instead of the simplified script
of the PRC.

Internally the Taiwan regime introduced major reforms. It lifted
martial law, retaining most of the necessary power through emergency
legislation, but assuring civilian trials. It permitted opposition parties to
contest Kuomintang candidates. It permitted political demonstrations
without police interference. It loosened restrictions on the press. Long
held political prisoners received amnesty. The public responded with
alacrity, proliferating demonstrations on a wide range of subjects and
supporting opposition rallies against the ruling group.

Beijing proved ambivalent on these developments. Increased contact
with the mainland was applauded as strengthening ties toward eventual
unification. But increased political freedom on the island was attacked
when it hinted at Taiwan independence under the opposition party's call
for self-determination. President Chiang Ching-kuo died in January
1988. He was the last in the symbolic lineage of Sun Yat-sen and Chiang
Kai-shek. No one appeared to combine his commitment to Taiwan's identification as the legitimate China with his political clout as a local leader.

Chiang was succeeded by Lee Teng-Kui, a Taiwanese, as both head
of the Nationalist party. In addition, the cabinet and the party's key
standing committee were replaced with Taiwanese, the majority in both
organs, as against those of mainlander origin.

This raises one key variable in China's future policy: Will Taiwan
come under a leadership that declares its independence and if so how will
Beijing respond? Deng repeatedly warned that this would necessitate the

use of force. He did not spell out how force might be applied. Logically it might begin with a closure of Taiwan's ports through proclamation and perhaps blockade, thereby cutting the island's lifeline to economic prosperity, which is dependent on exports. This action would risk economic sanctions against the PRC from the United States and perhaps Japan as well. Yet political passions aroused by decades of commitment to territorial unification could override practical economic considerations.

Admittedly this is a highly unlikely scenario. Taiwan is recognized by less than two dozen states, none major, under the rubric of the Republic of China. As an independent Taiwan it could not hope to gain international legitimation in the United Nations or through diplomatic recognition, least of all from the United States. Fear of provoking PRC reaction will deter either development. Nor can Taiwan count on American military protection should the PRC react to independence with force or the threat thereof. Presumably these calculations will compel Chiang Ching-kuo's successors to stop short of that final step while continuing to maneuver so as to remain separate of mainland control. However, human behavior is not wholly predictable. The possibility remains of Taiwan being forced to the top of Beijing's agenda through developments over which it has no control, with far-reaching implications for China's relations throughout East Asia and particularly with the United States.

The alternative prospect of Taiwan negotiating mainland union is only slightly more likely, at least so long as it enjoys its present prosperity, remains far above mainland living standards, and perceives PRC politics as both unstable and stultifying when compared with the island's ambience. These are all variables subject to change. In particular, the international economic environment can turn sour for Taiwan. Monetary disarray and protectionism could shrink its export markets, whereas the mainland offers an alternative outlet with abundant natural resources to meet Taiwan's needs. These practical considerations might coincide with the continued erosion of emphasis on Marxist-Leninist ideology and the limited liberalization of mainland life, particularly in intellectual and media activities.

Yet possible as these changes are in theory, in actuality they seem far removed from realization in combination, although they may occur separately. As of 1988 Taiwan's foreign exchange reserves were among the largest in the world, approximating $75 billion, with a steady trade surplus, in contrast with the mainland's nagging trade deficit. PRC living standards and the quality of life approximated that on Taiwan of the 1960s for urban areas and the 1950s in much of the countryside. Finally, Beijing's brutal suppression of Tibetan demonstrations and its thirty-year dispute with the Dalai Lama in exile underscored the limits of autonomy that Taiwan might face once union with the mainland was achieved.

Beijing's constant reminder to Washington that "Taiwan is a major obstacle in our relationship" need not be actionable in itself, as more than a decade of reiteration demonstrates. The subject is not foremost in public consciousness, judging from extended travel and conversations at various levels. The majority of mainland family ties with Taiwan are in the coastal provinces of Zhejiang and Fujian. Thus the leadership does not face the prospect of spontaneous demonstrations on this issue as it experienced in the case of Japan in 1985. This situation, together with the aforementioned economic risks in using force, argues against the PRC initiating action on its own.

Yet should the status quo continue to frustrate a future Beijing regime with an internal component challenging the leadership's inaction, testing Taiwan through increased pressure cannot be ruled out. This issue combines the most sensitive nationalistic questions of territorial integrity and national sovereignty, explicitly challenged by Taiwan's declaring itself to be the legitimate China. Moreover American arms sales and congressional actions place Washington in an intervening role, perceived in Beijing as responsible for Taiwan's refusal to negotiate. The resulting combination of frustrated nationalism and foreign intervention touches deep-seated sensitivities in Chinese memory and politics. A weak or divided leadership invites exploitation of such sensitivities by opportunistic or genuinely committed opponents. The possibility of such circumstances cautions against assuming that the present calculus of costs and benefits will prevail forever in Beijing with respect to the Taiwan problem.

Other territorial issues also exist although with much less potential volatility. Beijing's claims in the South China sea are symbolically represented on its maps by markings delimiting the entire area as within PRC sovereignty. We have already noted how Beijing made good its claim to the northern islands in 1974 by seizing the Xishas or Paracels from South Vietnam before it fell to Hanoi's forces in 1975. In 1987 Beijing conducted military exercises in the South China Sea for the first time, flexing its newly acquired air and sea capabilities and evoking a warning protest from Hanoi. In March 1988 Beijing responded by forcefully reasserting its right to the southern islands, the Nansha or the Spratleys. In a separate action, the PRC had previously pressed Malaysia to negotiate disputed ownership over a minor area, conceding it to Kuala Lumpor after having established the principle of a Chinese claim.

Unlike Taiwan, there is no clear and irrefutable basis for Beijing's position on its territorial claims, which are argued on various contentious grounds of archeological finds, historical presence, maps, and past statements by itself or its present opponents. Instead a final resolution on each claim will depend on the balance of power in each particular case at such time as Beijing chooses to bring the issue to a head. That power need not be exclusively military. Should offshore oil be discovered in the immediate vicinity, the need to acquire foreign investment and technology for its exploitation could persuade Beijing to compromise its position through peaceful negotiations. Force or the threat thereof would probably cause Western firms, mainly American, to withdraw their effort, which has persisted despite years of uneconomic discoveries, mainly of natural gas.

However the Vietnamese aspect adds a political motivation that might prevail in the absence of significant oil reserves being proven. Beijing's confrontation with Hanoi partakes of emotional feelings which, as with Taiwan, can be exploited in domestic politics or, alternatively, may drive confrontation to conflict. Here the Soviet factor could become significant to the extent that Moscow equips Hanoi to defend its claims or feels compelled to assist Hanoi in deterring a Chinese use of force. As with Taiwan, third party considerations are likely to inhibit Beijing's actions but do not necessarily preclude them.

China's other main offshore claim extends to the coast of Korea and to the Japanese held Senkaku Islands or Daiyutai. The claim also includes the continental shelf extending from the mainland to a depth of 250 meters under the Yellow and East China seas. PRC protests in the early 1970s warned the Republic of Korea and Japan against joint exploration of areas in their vicinity for offshore oil, and minor incidents have arisen in subsequent years involving foreign survey vessels elsewhere.

More pointedly, in 1978 more than a hundred Chinese fishing boats circled the Senkakus with signs claiming they belonged to the PRC. This proved embarrassing to Tokyo, which was in the final stage of negotiating a treaty of peace and friendship with Beijing. When Deng Xiaoping visited the capital of Japan that fall to celebrate signature of the treaty, he ducked a press question on the dispute by saying it might be better settled by future generations. The issue thereupon disappeared from public view but remained a potentially contentious issue.

Beijing could adopt a general principle of international law which holds that where a continental shelf adjoins neighboring countries the boundary delineating ownership can be drawn along the median line dividing the shelf. Alternatively it could insist on total ownership, which would also be in conformance with international law. Its inaction thus far most probably results from the failure of any major oil reserves to be discovered and the desire for a peaceful environment, particularly where economic relations with Japan are paramount.

As in our other instances, these problems are not foreseen as actionable in the near future, nor are they likely to become serious in this century, all other things being equal. Much depends on the success, both real and perceived, of economic modernization as a justification for the open door to foreign trade, investment, and credits. Success can justify tacit or explicit compromises with communist ideology in general, and with Japan and the United States in particular. Yet economic modernization is a long process, in the course of which major economic and political problems will inevitably confront the regime. Many of these had already surfaced in the mid-1980s, such as bureaucratic obstructionism, corruption, and mismanagement, together with inflation, bottlenecks in infrastructure and energy, and growing inequities of income and living standards. Protectionism by the United States against the PRC was threatened by congressional bills, albeit vetoed or argued down by President Reagan. Japan's rising yen burdened the payment of imports and repayment of loans. Meanwhile the global monetary and trading environment remained uncertain in the face of a soaring American debt and a falling American dollar, with no effective solution in sight.

China is no longer an isolated or autarkic economy avowing "self-reliance." Circumstances abroad and the International Monetary Fund forced devaluation of the currency by 15 percent in 1986, and further devaluation was expected to follow. A Chinese official calculated that exports constituted 12 percent of national income in 1986, compared with only 5.6 percent in 1978.[29] Interdependence is real and growing, thus far to Beijing's benefit, but not necessarily so in the future.

Fortunately China's membership in key international economic organizations provides it with advance warning, detailed information, and participation in addressing many of these problems. Once it joins GATT, the PRC will have a major voice on trade issues. Its economists are well trained in modeling and statistical methods, and the rapidly expanding use of computers adds another strength to their analysis. Objectively the PRC is well positioned to confront these problems as they arise.

Subjectively, however, the situation may be less easily handled. Because of China's exclusion from world councils until 1971 and the Cultural Revolution closure of all universities, a wide generation gap exists between senior officials nearing retirement who were trained abroad prior to 1949 and very junior cadres recently returning from study overseas. Middle-age people of forty to fifty years of age lack the necessary background to understand the outside world, especially its economic ramifications. Nor does their bureaucratic security, inherent in socialism, induce them to catch up on what they missed in earlier years. This poses a potential management crisis in the foreseeable future.

Economic mismanagement and miscalculation are inevitable in all systems. They are especially likely to occur in a society as vast as that of China, where socialist planning and control combines with experiments in decentralized and private initiative among a populace which often responds excessively to governmental stimuli yet lacks experience in running its own business.

---

[29]Jacobsen and Oksenberg, *op. cit.*, citing Liu Guoguang in an address at the University of Michigan, September 15, 1987.

This combination of external and internal factors could coalesce negatively to slow economic growth and frustrate expectations. The response could be a severe and sudden change of posture, if not of policy. In 1985–1986 Beijing peremptorily suspended or cancelled contracts with Japanese and other manufacturers and traders when it discovered that decentralized access to foreign exchange had contributed to a fall in reserves from $17 billion to $11 billion in one year. This action paralleled the earlier PRC cancellation of huge contracts for the Baoshan steel plant in 1979–1980. Both cases illustrated a willingness to act unilaterally without regard for foreign reaction.

Such behavior has not been typical, but its very occurrence suggests its possible repetition. Much will depend on the stability and orientation of leadership as well as on how the international environment, both political and economic, impacts on China and is perceived there. The People's Republic is clearly in transition as it moves out of the Maoist heritage and beyond Deng's reformist regime. Foreign policy is always subject to domestic developments in addition to developments abroad. A challenge therefore faces Beijing and other capitals as the world's largest population engages the global community so as to increase its security and raise its standard of living, while defining its rightful role in world affairs.

CHINESE NAME SPELLINGS

OLD	NEW
PERSONS	
Chou En-lai	Zhou Enlai
Li Shih-yao	Li Shiyao
Liu Shao-ch'i	Liu Shaoqi
Mao Tse-tung	Mao Zedong
Teng Hsiao-p'ing	Deng Xiaoping
Yuan Shih-k'ai	Yuan Shikai
PLACES	
Kwangsi	Guangxi
Kwangtung	Guangdong
Matsu	Mazu
Nanking	Nanjing
Quemoy	Jinmen
OTHER	
Ch'ing (dynasty)	Qing
Uighur (people)	Uygur

FOREIGN POLICY LANDMARKS

October 1949	People's Republic of China established
February 1950	Sino-Soviet Treaty of Alliance signed
June 1950	North Korea invades South Korea United States intervenes
October 1950	China intervenes in Korean war, drives U.N.–U.S. forces from North Korea
July 1953	Korean War ends
July 1954	Geneva Conference ends Indochina War
September 1954	PRC bombards offshore islands of Nationalist China
December 1954	United States–Republic of China Mutual Security Treaty
April 1955	Bandung Conference; PRC proposes ambassadorial talks with United States
November 1957	Mao Zedong to Moscow, wins nuclear weapons aid
September 1958	PRC bombards offshore islands of Nationalist China
March 1959	Tibetan revolt
September 1959	Border guards clash on Sino-Indian frontier
June 1960	Soviet advisers leave China, aid stops
October 1962	Sino-Indian War
October 1964	First Chinese atomic bomb exploded
September 1965	PRC ground forces enter North Vietnam
August 1966	Cultural Revolution begins
August 1968	Violent phase of Cultural Revolution ends
March 1969	Sino-Soviet border clashes begin on Ussuri River
September 1969	Zhou-Kosygin meet in Beijing; clashes end
July 1971	Henry Kissinger secretly visits Beijing
October 1971	PRC takes U.N. seat
February 1972	President Nixon visits PRC, Shanghai Communiqué
September 1976	Mao Zedong dies
December 1978	President Carter recognizes PRC, ends treaty with Republic of China
February 1979	PRC invades Vietnam, withdraws in three weeks
September 1984	PRC signs treaty with United Kingdom on transfer of Hong Kong in 1997

SELECTED BIBLIOGRAPHY
Books

ARMSTRONG, J. D. *Revolutionary Diplomacy: Chinese Foreign Policy and the United Front Doctrine.* Berkeley, Calif.: University of California Press, 1977.

BARNETT, A. DOAK. *China and the Major Powers in East Asia.* Washington, D.C.: Brookings Institution, 1977.

———. *The Making of Foreign Policy in China.* Boulder, Colo.: Westview Press, 1985.

CAMILLERI, JOSEPH. *Chinese Foreign Policy.* Seattle, Wash.: University of Washington Press, 1980.

CLUBB, O. EDMUND. *China and Russia: The "Great Game."* New York: Columbia University Press, 1971.

DOOLIN, DENNIS J. *Territorial Claims in the Sino-Soviet Conflict: Documents and Analysis.* Stanford, Calif.: Hoover Institute, 1965.

ELLISON, HERBERT, ed. *The Sino-Soviet Conflict.* Seattle, Wash.: University of Washington Press, 1981.

FAIRBANK, JOHN KING, ed. *The Chinese World Order: Traditional China's Foreign Relations.* Cambridge, Mass.: Harvard University Press, 1968.
GITTINGS, JOHN. *Survey of the Sino-Soviet Dispute.* New York: Oxford University Press, 1978.
GODWIN, PAUL H.B., ed. *The Chinese Defense Establishment: Continuity and Change in the 1980s.* Boulder, Colo.: Westview Press, 1983.
GURTOV, MELVIN. *China and Southeast Asia: The Politics of Survival.* Lexington, Mass.: Heath Lexington Books, 1971.
HARDING, HARRY, ed. *China's Foreign Relations in the 1980s.* New Haven, Conn.: Yale University Press, 1984.
HARRIS, LILLIAN, *China's Foreign Policy Toward the Third World.* New York: Praeger, 1986.
HO, SAMUEL P.S., and RALPH W. HUENEMANN. *China's Open Door Policy: The Quest for Technology and Capital.* Vancouver, B.C.: University of British Columbia Press, 1984.
HUTCHINSON, ALAN. *China's African Revolution.* Boulder, Colo.: Westview Press, 1976.
KALICKI, JAN. *The Patterns of Sino-American Crises.* Cambridge, Mass.: Cambridge University Press, 1975.
KIM, SAMUEL S., ed. *China and the World: Foreign Policy in the Post-Mao Era.* 2d Ed. Boulder, Colo.: Westview Press, 1989.
LIAO, KUANG-SHENG. *Antiforeignism and Modernization in China, 1860–1980.* New York: St. Martin's Press, 1986.
MULLER, DAVID G., Jr. *China as a Maritime Power.* Boulder, Colo.: Westview Press, 1983.
QUESTED, R. K. I. *Sino-Russian Relations.* Winchester, Mass.: Allen & Unwin, 1984.
SAMUELS, MARWYN S. *Contest for the South China Sea.* New York: Methuen, 1982.
SEGAL, GERALD, and WILLIAM T. TOW, eds. *Chinese Defense Policy.* Urbana, Ill.: University of Illinois Press, 1984.
SUTTER, ROBERT G. *China Watch: Toward Sino-American Reconciliation.* Baltimore, Md.: John Hopkins University Press, 1978.
SUTTER, ROBERT. *Chinese Foreign Policy: Developments After Mao.* New York: Praeger, 1986.
TAYLOR, JAY. *China and Southeast Asia: Peking's Relations With Revolutionary Movements.* 2d Ed. New York: Praeger, 1976.
TAYLOR, ROBERT. *The Sino-Japanese Axis: A New Force in Asia?* London: Athlone Press, 1985.
VAN NESS, PETER. *Revolution and Chinese Foreign Policy.* Berkeley, Calif.: University of California Press, 1970.
VERTZBERGER, YAACOV. *China's Southwestern Strategy: Encirclement and Counterencirclement.* New York: Praeger, 1985.
WHITING, ALLEN S. *The Chinese Calculus of Deterrence: India and Indochina.* Ann Arbor, Mich.: University of Michigan Press, 1975.
———. *China Crosses the Yalu: The Decision to Enter the Korean War.* Stanford, Calif.: Stanford University Press, 1968.
———. *China Eyes Japan.* Berkely, Calif.: University of California Press, 1989.

Periodicals

Asian Survey (Berkeley, Calif.).
China Business Review (Washington, D.C.).
China Quarterly (London).
Far Eastern Economic Review (Hong Kong).
Foreign Affairs (New York).
Journal of Asian Studies (Ann Arbor, Mich.), with annual bibliography.
Journal of Northeast Asian Studies (Washington, D.C.).
Pacific Affairs (Vancouver, B.C.).
Beijing Review (Beijing).
Problems of Communism (Washington, D.C.).

7

The Foreign Policy
of Japan

Robert A. Scalapino

THE BACKGROUND OF JAPANESE FOREIGN POLICY

In geopolitical terms, there are some obvious reasons for making a rough comparison between Japan and Great Britain. Both are island societies lying within the Temperate Zone and close to a great continental mass. From earliest times, cultural interaction with the continent has been vital in shaping the character of each society; each has definitely been a part of the larger cultural orbit centering upon the continent. The sea however, has been both a lane and a barrier. It has prevented recent invasions, enabling the development of a relatively homogeneous people who, despite many foreign adaptations, have retained a strong quality of uniqueness. Thus the encircling sea has been important to culture as well as to livelihood and defense. It has also been central to the historic dilemma over isolation versus external involvement. This has been the basic foreign policy issue of both societies throughout their existence. And in recent eras, the interaction between internal and external pressures has been such as to present essentially the same answer to this question in both Japan and Great Britain. The growth of foreign pressures and the needs flowing from modernization—the scarcity of certain domestic resources combined with the rise of unused power—these and other factors led to regional and then global commitment. When the costs of that commitment proved too great, and the power of these societies relative to others declined, a substantial withdrawal took place. Now, in the case of Japan, renewed commitments are being undertaken, reflective of the extraordinary advances made by that nation during the last three decades. To appreciate the new trend, let us turn first to the background against which it emerges.

The Tokugawa Era

The diplomatic history of modern Japan opened in the mid-nineteenth century on a decidedly reluctant and confused note. Prior to Perry's arrival in 1853, the Japanese government had pursued a rigorous policy of isolation from the outside world for over two hundred years. It abandoned that policy only under strong pressure and with many misgivings. Isolation had first been imposed as a means of maintaining internal stability. When the Tokugawa family came to power in Japan in 1606, the West had already been represented in the country for fifty years. Missionaries and traders had come in a steady stream, first from Portugal and Spain, then from the Netherlands and England. In the first years of the Tokugawa era, however, abuses were regularly reported to the government. Christian converts among the provincial nobility sought Western arms or alliances to fortify their position against the central regime. Western trade also became a means of augmenting local power, especially in the Kyushu area. Between 1616 and 1641, therefore, the Tokugawa government applied a series of anti-Christian and antitrade edicts, leading up to a policy of almost total exclusion of the West. As is well known, only the Dutch were allowed to trade, very restrictedly, at Nagasaki. This, together with some limited relations with China and Korea, constituted Japanese foreign relations until the middle of the nineteenth century.

Even before the arrival of Perry, a small group of Japanese intellectuals had begun to question the policy of rigid isolation. Out of "Dutch learning" had come exciting ideas; and there grew, in some minds, the desirability of leading the commercial revolution rather than fighting it, and of using foreign trade to develop power. How else could the intriguing slogan, "a rich country; a powerful soldiery," be made a reality? How else could Japan defend herself against Western imperialism? But this group was a small minority in the early period. Even the Tokugawa government supported the opening of the country only as a temporary expedient until force could be garnered to throw out the West. In accepting Perry's demands, it decided to accede rather than risk war, but it gave as little ground as possible. With the initial step taken, however, it was impossible to retreat. The first U.S. envoy, Townsend Harris, secured major liberalization of the Perry treaty in 1858, and similar rights were soon granted to other Western powers. From this date, Japan was truly opened up to Western commerce, and shortly the Tokugawa regime was even to seek assistance in developing arsenals and shipyards. "Support the government" and "open the country" seemed to be slogans indissolubly linked.

Yet basically, Tokugawa policy remained more a product of pressure than of purpose, and this fact worked against the effectiveness of the policy. Beset by many problems, the regime grew steadily weaker; its capacity to act vigorously in any direction diminished. It satisfied neither the West, which complained of its inability to control unruly elements, nor the provincial samurai, who regarded the central government as arch-appeasers. As so often happens in history, the regime in power found, by tortuous means, the only feasible policy for national survival—in this case, the policy of opening the country—but in the course of reaching that policy it was itself fatally weakened, so that the actual execution and fulfillment of the policy had to pass to other hands.

Meiji Foreign Policy

In 1867, the Tokugawa regime was finally overthrown and the young emperor Meiji was "restored" to the position of ruler, a position which the nationalists claimed the Tokugawa family had stolen. But real power in Meiji Japan gravitated into the hands of a small group of court officials and young leaders of the former military class. Their first major objective in foreign policy became that of removing the blemish of the unequal treaties, thereby attaining "complete independence" and equity with the Western powers. This task proved more difficult than they had expected; to accomplish it took nearly three decades. The Western powers, and particularly Great Britain, saw no reason to revise the treaties until Japanese standards came close to Western norms. The Japanese discovered that treaty revision was closely connected with basic reform in such fields as law and commerce. Thus the Iwakura mission, which left for the West so hopefully, in 1871, to persuade the powers to abandon the fixed tariffs and extraterritoriality, came home realizing that many internal developments had first to be undertaken.

Through the years, "modernization" progressed by means of German, French, British, and American models. Japanese economic and military power showed remarkable gains. Law and order prevailed despite occasional domestic crises. Finally, in 1894, after repeated failures, the first great objective of Japanese foreign policy was obtained: agreements on basic treaty revisions were concluded with the West, all of which went into effect by 1899. As the nineteenth century ended, Japan had become the first nation of Asia to attain nearly complete parity with the West in legal terms. She had done so, in part, by satisfying the West that she was prepared to abide by the general rules of Western conduct, in part by the obvious facts of her internal progress and stability, and in part by her persistence and by certain clear signs that inequity toward Japan had reached a point of diminishing returns.

In the long struggle for treaty revision, latent elements of antiforeignism occasionally came to the surface in various forms. Officials deemed obsequious to foreign powers, too pro-Western in their personal habits, or disrespectful of Japanese tradition ran grave risks. The history of these years is filled with records of assassination plots, some successful, against more moderate leaders. This was one price to be paid for cultivating a nationalist movement so assiduously, while scarcely daring to admit its excesses. But quite apart from its extremists, Japanese society as a whole tended to react in pendulumlike fashion to the West. In many respects, this was most natural. Periods of intensive borrowing and adaptation at both individual and group levels would be followed by noticeable retreats, with the primary targets being those excesses and absurdities most easily discernible, but with secondary attacks ranging over as broad a front as conditions would permit. On the one hand, Japan wanted to catch up with the West, be accepted as a "progressive" and "civilized" nation, and match the West in the areas of its own talents; in addition, a very genuine fondness for things Western was entertained by many Japanese, great and small. But on the other hand, in this period of intensive nationalist indoctrination, and when the old anti-foreign traditions were not yet completely dead, the periodic cry of "excessive Europeanization!" or "un-Japanese practices!" could have telling effect. Moreover, if selected aspects of Westernism appealed to almost everyone, there was no widespread desire to abandon the mainstream of Japanese culture or customs. These factors are not completely absent from contemporary Japan.

During the early Meiji era, there were strong overtones of defensiveness in Japanese policy and psychology. But the climate was also ripe for the rise of expansionism. Northeast Asia was largely a vacuum of power, tended haphazardly by the "sick man of Asia," China, on the one hand, and the somewhat stronger but essentially unstable and over committed tsarist forces, on the other. The Japanese mission seemed even clearer when it could be posed against the prospects of continuous Korean turmoil and the increasing threat of Western imperialism in this entire area. The theme of "Asia for the Asians" was first applied here, and ofttimes by sincere men who had a vision of liberating other Asians from backwardness and Western domination, sharing with them the fruits of the new era in Japan. Private societies like the *Genyosha* (Black Current Society) and the *Kokuryukai* (Amur River Society) emerged, to exercise a great influence on Japanese foreign policy as influential pressure groups on behalf of a forceful continental policy with some such objectives in mind.

The ideology of expansionism was complex, and it knew no single form of expression. Groups like the *Kokuryukai* represented the past: they held firm to Japanese Confucianism, exalted the primitive mythology that surrounded the emperor-centered state, and were composed of ultranationalists of a peculiarly medieval type. Yet, from another point of view, these same men were radicals associated with the new era. Wherever Asian nationalism took root, they were willing to give it nourishment, even when its ideological bases were greatly different from their own. To movements as widely disparate as those of Aguinaldo and Sun Yat-sen their assistance was given freely, and in this they often went beyond what the Japanese government was willing or prepared to do. Moreover, there was an element of radicalism in their approach to internal affairs as well, even though its source might be largely traditional. Decrying the corruption, materialism, and excessive wealth of the new order, they demanded stringent internal reforms, some of which could be considered socialist in character. Thus were connected the themes of internal reform and external expansion as twins that were to have recurrent echoes throughout modern Japanese history.

The expansionists made their first major advance in the extraordinary decade between 1895 and 1905. Prior to that time, Japan had already added the Ryukyu Islands and the Bonins to her domain, and made more secure her northern outpost, Hokkaido, by extensive colonization, but these were not spectacular ventures. By 1894, however, Japanese leadership was ready to challenge China, the weakest of her rivals, for influence on the Korean peninsula. For Japan, the war was unexpectedly short and easy, the first of a series of wars that "paid." The Western-style training and the nationalist indoctrination of her conscript military forces stood the initial test with flying colors. For China, defeat at the hands of a foe long regarded with some contempt, and treated at best as a pupil, was a profound shock. Demands for fundamental reform were now renewed, especially by younger intellectuals, and China was pushed toward accelerated change and revolution despite Manchu resistance.

In Japan, the implications of victory were fourfold. The beginnings of the Japanese empire were laid, and the first tentative steps as a modern continental power were taken; China ceded Formosa, the Pescadores, and, for a time, the Liaotung Peninsula, until the intervention of Russia, France, and Germany forced its return. And China was eliminated as a serious competitor in the Korean contest. Second, the war served as a further stimulus to industrial growth and general economic development. In an atmosphere of patriotic fervor, industrial investment and expansion were undertaken, with an emphasis upon heavy industry. The war boom brought prosperity; and afterward, Japan received both indemnities and new China markets. Third, Japan enjoyed a sharp rise in prestige; most of the West looked on approvingly as their most apt pupil demonstrated her progress and valor, and it was in the aftermath of this victory that Japan began to be received in Western circles with some semblance of equality. Finally, these factors naturally accrued to the credit of the nationalist movement and to the prestige of the military-class. The professional soldier, his samurai traditions now supplemented by Western science and by a new sense of mission not present in the Tokugawa era, promised to play a vital role in determining the future of his society.

In the aftermath of the Sino-Japanese War, a crucial decision had to be made. Japan was dedicated to increasing her ties with other Asian societies and providing leadership for them when possible. But to obtain these objectives and to have any basic security for herself, she needed a major alliance with a non-Asian power. This was still the world of the nineteenth century, when Europe collectively exercised a global influence, and when the unfolding of European power politics had a direct and immediate effect upon the non-European world. With the United States, Japan needed only to achieve some general agreement that would serve to neutralize potential conflict; indeed, she could expect no more, since American commitments toward the Pacific were still very limited, even after the annexation of the Philippines. The major powers in Asia were Great Britain and Russia, and the choice had to be made between these two.

Initially, top political circles in Japan were divided. Men like Ito and Inoue hoped for an agreement with Russia that would establish long-term peace in northeastern Asia on the basis of satisfying mutual interests. Had such an agreement been reached, Japanese expansion might have been directed southward at a much earlier point. An alliance with Great Britain, on the other hand, was recognized as a step toward stabilization in the south and fluidity in the northeast. Not merely in this respect, however, but in every respect, Japanese foreign policy was affected for nearly two decades by the Anglo-Japanese Alliance of 1902. This pact was widely heralded as insuring the peace of Asia. Within certain limits, perhaps it did contribute to that end. England, now finished with isolation, needed global alliances to protect her global interests. In exchange, Japanese "special interests" in northeastern Asia were given recognition by the leading power of the world. Under such conditions, Japan could scarcely afford not to advance those interests.

Thus, the first fruit of the Anglo-Japanese Alliance was not peace, but war. The question of Japanese or Russian hegemony over northeastern Asia, having its antecedents back as far as the seventeenth century, was now given over to military decision. As is well known, Japanese victory against a weary and distracted foe was swift. From the Portsmouth Treaty, Japan emerged in control of much of northeastern Asia, and became the first Asian world power. The fruits of defeat and victory were similar to those of the Sino-Japanese War: for the defeated, soul-searching, unrest, and revolution; for the victor, a new gain of territory and fame. Clear title was obtained to the Kuriles, and southern Saghalien was added to the empire; control over Korea could no longer be challenged, although outright annexation did not come until 1910; the Manchurian-Mongolian area also fell under the shadow of expanding Japanese power, a situation placing new pressure upon China. Again, Japanese industry had enjoyed great expansion as a part of the war effort, with some support from British and American loans. And once more Japanese nationalism had risen to the test. Only a handful of intellectual pacifists and radicals denounced the war; the great majority of the people had been deeply loyal to the cause of a greater Japan.

Some of the costs of victory could also be tabulated. One lay on the surface. Nationalist propaganda had been carried so far during the war that many patriots assumed that the peace would be dictated in Moscow, not realizing that a long war of attrition might be dangerous for a smaller country. Consequently, ugly riots broke out over the Portsmouth settlement, and the government had difficulty in restoring order. There were also deeper costs to be tallied. At home, militarism had grown stronger; the nonconformist had little protection, either in law or by the customs of his society. Abroad, Japan was moving into a new orbit of power and influence; but as a result, she was now the object of new suspicions and fears, some of them coming from such traditional supporters as the United States and Great Britain. Already it seemed likely that the critical test might be China.

In partial recompense, immediately ahead lay an era of unprecedented influence for Japan throughout Asia. It was an influence, moreover, derived from much more than mere military prowess. There is no doubt that most of the Asian world experienced a thrill at the Japanese victory over Russia, because it gave hope that the West could be beaten at its own game. But in the broader sense, Japan had become the symbol of the new Asia, a society that had successfully made the transition toward modernization by a process of synthesizing new ideas with its indigenous culture. Western science and progress had come alive within the Japanese context, and from this experience the rest of Asia had much to learn. The success of Japanese nationalism was also a tremendous stimulus, even though its precise ideological forms might not be acceptable elsewhere. Thus, as this era unfolded, Japan embarked upon an extensive career as model, tutor, and leader to eager Asians everywhere. Thousands of students flocked to Tokyo and other Japanese centers of learning and industry. The majority came from China, but every section of Asia was represented in some degree. Likewise, Asian nationalist movements found in Japan a haven and source of support. Their leaders in exile wrote polemics, collected funds, and sometimes obtained official encouragement. Tokyo became a revolutionary center for the Far East. Japan was riding the crest tide of the developing "Asia for the Asians" movement.

Already, however, the central problem of Japanese foreign policy was becoming that of distinguishing the thin line between acceptable leadership in Asia and unwelcome domination.

The Rise of Japan as a World Power

World War I was the third conflict within a generation to pay handsome and immediate dividends to the cause of Japanese prestige. It is not difficult to understand why later glorification of war by Japanese militarists produced such weak rebuttals from the society as a whole. Against the true desires of her ally, Japan entered the war "to fulfill her obligations under the Anglo-Japanese Alliance." She proceeded to capture, without difficulty, the German holdings on the Chinese Shantung peninsula and in certain other parts of the Pacific. With this mission accomplished, she directed her energies to supplying the Asian markets cut off from their normal European contacts, and to providing her Western allies with the materials of war. These tasks required enormous industrial expansion. Indeed, it was at the close of this period that industrial productivity overtook agrarian productivity in yen value, and Japan could thereby claim to have moved into the ranks of industrial societies.

These trends, and complemental factors elsewhere, stimulated the drive for a more intensive policy toward China. The Manchu dynasty had fallen in the revolution of 1911, but that revolution had failed in its major objectives. The Chinese scene was now marked by deep political cleavages, with rival factions striving desperately for both internal and external support. With Europe fully engaged in a bloody "civil war" and the United States prepared to go no further than a policy of moral suasion, Japan was soon heavily involved in Chinese politics. In 1915, the Japanese government demanded an extensive list of concessions from the Yuan Shih-k'ai regime, known as the "Twenty-one Demands." These were bitterly resisted by China, with some success. Japanese influence moved steadily forward by means of loans, advisers, and technical assistance, yet Japan soon acquired a new image in China—that of the chief threat to Chinese nationalism. This era was climaxed by the historic May Fourth Movement, now widely heralded by the Chinese Communists as their point of origin, a fervent demonstration against Versailles and against Japanese imperialism, spearheaded by Peking students and spreading throughout China in May 1919.

At the close of the World War I, however, there could be no question that Japan had become a world power. She was the one major nation besides the United States to emerge from that war in a stronger position. Her preeminence in eastern Asia could not be doubted, despite the uncertain new force of Bolshevism. What were the ingredients of this power as the third decade of the twentieth century began?

One source of Japan's new power clearly was her evolving economic capacities. Perhaps the full secret of the Japanese industrial revolution still escapes us. However, in its essence, it seems to have involved the capacity of Japanese society to utilize selected elements of Western technique and experience, adapting these to its own culture and timing, without duplicating either the historical context of Western development or the precise set of Western drives, impulses, and incentives. Toward this process were contributed both the conscious purposes of state and the remarkable talents of a people who could display creativeness through integration and discipline. By 1920, Japan was already becoming the workshop of Asia. Her large factories, equipped in many cases with the most modern machinery, contributed such basic products as textiles in great volume; at the same time, an infinite variety of cheap manufactured items flowed out of the thousands of small and medium-sized plants that formed the base of the pyramidal Japanese industrial structure. Sharing with management the credit for such productivity was the new Japanese labor force, abundant in numbers, cheap in costs, malleable (within limits) to its new task, moving out of the paddy fields into the factories, and acquiring sufficient know-how to give Japan an industrial character of which their parents could not have dreamed.

But if manpower was a strength, it was also a problem—and one that now began to have an overt influence upon policy. Shortly after World War I the Japanese population reached 60 million, more than double the figure at the beginning of the Meiji era. In many respects, the facilities existing within Japan to accommodate this great mass already seemed seriously strained, yet no leveling off was in sight. Increasing talk of *lebensraum* was inevitable. And if the population explosion had produced an abundance of cheap labor, by the same token it had placed certain limits on their consumption of goods, by throwing increased emphasis on foreign trade.

To revert to our discussion of the sources of Japanese power, the military and political ingredients certainly cannot be overlooked. The Japanese navy had become the third largest in the world. Her army, in size, equipment, and training, dwarfed other forces readily available in this part of the world. There was no foreign force that seemed prepared to challenge a Japanese force that was fully committed in its own territories or in any part of eastern Asia. The size and equipment of the Japanese military was a testament to the lavish yearly budgetary contributions of the people; the morale of that force was a tribute to intensive indoctrination, sustained by the realities of great political power and prestige within the society.

Politics, in its broader reaches, was also a wellspring of power. For a society without totalitarian restraints (albeit one strongly paternal and authoritarian in character), Japan presented a picture of remarkable stability up to this point. Besides a handful of intellectual radicals, there were few who would dare (or think) to question *Kokutai*—"the national polity" or, more vaguely, "the Japanese way of life." Thus, decisions of state, especially in the realm of foreign policy, could be taken on the assumption that they would be accepted with a maximum of conformity. The oracles of national interest could speak without fear of discordant responses, at least so long as they spoke within a consistently nationalist framework. What leadership group has not found some advantage in this?

Yet, as the postwar era began, there were indications that Japanese politics might be drastically affected by the democratic tide. The influence of Western liberalism, crowned by the global idealism of Woodrow Wilson, was strongly felt in Japanese intellectual and urban circles. Party government had assumed new importance, the office of premier was held for the first time by a commoner, and the movement for universal suffrage was receiving widespread support. Japan's liberal era was opening, bringing with it some serious efforts to establish parliamentary and civilian supremacy in Japanese politics. Temporarily, at least, the long-entrenched bureaucrats and even the military had to move to the defensive. For the latter, the Siberian expedition was the first clearly unrewarding venture abroad. And however strong the attempt to shift the blame to political timidity and lack of resolution at home, the army could not prevent some questions from arising in the public mind.

Hence, moderation in foreign policy was possible during this period. At the Washington Armament Conference of 1921, Japan accepted the famous 5:5:3 naval ratio with the United States and Great Britain, despite the bitter protests of her naval authorities. She agreed to the return of the Shantung concessions. Withdrawal from Siberia was slowly and cautiously undertaken. One cabinet even had the audacity to cut the military budget sharply, and there were some discussions (although no action) on a permanent reduction in the institutional power of the military in Japanese government. During this era, no figure symbolized moderation in foreign policy more than Kijuro Shidehara, foreign minister under the Minseito cabinets. Shidehara was a conservative, a nationalist, and a loyal servant of the emperor. He believed that Japan had special interests in northeastern Asia and a special responsibility toward China. But he wanted to avoid a "get-tough" policy which would only provoke boycotts, anti-Japanese hostility, and possibly war. Rather, he hoped Japanese influence could be exerted through trade, financial agreements, and political negotiation.

Militarism and Defeat

The liberal era was short-lived. With its collapse went much of the hope for moderation, either at home or abroad. This is not the place to spell out the story of democratic failure in prewar Japan, but its more immediate causes are familiar: economic crisis and depression; political confusion and corruption; and the consequent rise of opponents from left and right. The repercussions were felt almost immediately in Japanese foreign policy. In 1928, under the Tanaka cabinet, there was a sharp turn toward a more militant nationalism in both the economic and political fields. State support to home industry was combined with a more "positive" program of support for Japanese interests abroad, especially in China. Overtures from Chiang Kai-shek—who had just broken with the Communists—were rejected, partly because of fear that his successful northern expedition would jeopardize the future Japanese position in Manchuria and northern China. Ironically, while the Tanaka China policy was provoking sharp Chinese reaction because of its strengths, it was under simultaneous attack by Japanese military extremists because of its weaknesses. Some of these elements, working through the Kwantung army in Manchuria, engineered the murder of Chang Tso-lin in June 1928, hoping to force a decisive Japanese move in this area. The Japanese government was posed with the first of a series of direct military challenges to civilian control, challenges which went unmet.

Japanese foreign policy, in the fifteen years between 1930 and 1945, represented the natural culmination of these new trends. To be sure, not all the old themes were reversed, particularly those that could be read with different inflections. Stress continued to be placed upon Sino-Japanese cooperation, and on the need for a stable, friendly China, purged of communist and anti-Japanese elements. But action continually interfered with words. As the Japanese militarists gained control of the strategic heights of policy, especially in the field, any cooperation had to be strained through the tightening net of aggression, fanatical patriotism, and individual, sometimes mass, acts of brutality. Through these field actions, and as a result of a contrived incident, war came to Manchuria in September, 1931. The weaker Chinese forces were quickly defeated, but Manchukuo remained, to the great body of the Chinese, an unacceptable symbol of Japanese aggression.

With the Manchurian region at last under complete Japanese control, the militarists could not avoid spreading outward toward Mongolia and northern China. Thus the Second China Incident erupted, in 1937, and led eventually to total war and defeat. Throughout this entire period, Japan could always find some Chinese allies, whether as a result of the acrid internal rivalries for power in China, sheer opportunism, or some genuine hopes that this route might lead to a new and better Asia, freed from Western control. Indeed, the allies garnered from all of these sources were not inconsiderable either in number or in influence. In Wang Ch'ing-wei, Japan finally found an able if embittered leader. But, as against these facts, Japanese policy achieved what had always been feared most: a union of the dominant wing of the Kuomintang with the Communists and many independents into a nationalist popular front that was bitterly anti-Japanese. Although it had as one of its supreme goals the salvation of Asia from communism, Japanese policy, in the end, contributed more than any other single factor to communist success.

To concentrate solely in China, however, would be to examine only the weakest link of a general Asian policy which, for all its militant, aggressive qualities, had elements of real power and appeal. Building from the old "Asia for the Asians" theme, Japanese policy moved, in the 1930s, toward the concept of a Greater East Asia Co-Prosperity Sphere. The economic background for this policy lay in the rapid strides made by Japanese trade throughout Asia. By means of general deflation, changes in currency valuation, industrial rationalization, and extensive state support, Japanese trade came to enjoy highly favorable competitive conditions in eastern Asia by the mid-1930s. Western Europe complained vigorously about the practice of "social dumping" onto the colonial markets. Japan retorted with charges of economic discrimination and attempted monopoly. The fact remained, however, that Japanese penetration of the Asian market, during this period, was substantial. The basis was thus provided for later proposals of greater economic integration of an Asian region led by Japan and divorced from Western control.

The center of the Japanese appeal to greater Asia, however, remained in the sphere of political nationalism. As Japan drifted toward the Fascist bloc, Western imperialism in Asia could be attacked with less inhibition than in the past. These attacks were particularly effective in areas where nationalism was still treated as subversive by Western governors, and where Japanese policies could not yet be tested. Once again, an attempt was made to develop an expanded program of cultural relations and technical assistance. Students flocked to Japan from all parts of Asia; cultural missions were exchanged on an increasing scale; Japanese technicians went forth; and, as the Pacific war approached, the Japanese government provided underground assistance to various Asian nationalist movements in the form of funds, political advice, and even the training and equipping of military forces.

As a corollary to her new Asian policy, Japan naturally developed a new policy with respect to the West. Nearly a decade earlier, at the time of the Washington conference of 1921, Japan had reluctantly given up the Anglo-Japanese alliance, her shield and support for twenty years. In its place were substituted the more general agreements among the major powers. This concept of collective agreement (not, it should be emphasized, collective security) was especially attuned to the American position. The United States wanted an end to exclusive alliances, but it was prepared to undertake only the most limited of commitments, and it still wished to rely essentially upon moral suasion for policy enforcement.

The great symbol of this hope and this era was the famous Kellogg-Briand Pact, outlawing war.

Thus, the decline of Japanese liberalism at home was complemented by the absence of effective external checks or controls. The old system of alliances, and the type of checks they imposed upon unilateral action, had been declared obsolete in the Pacific, but no effective international order had replaced them. Consequently, in the name of her national interests, Japan could successfully defy the Nine-Power Agreement and the League of Nations, with no single nation or group making an effective stand against her. Inevitably, as she challenged the status quo powers, Japan gravitated toward Germany and Italy, the dissidents of Europe. The Anti-Comintern Pact sealed an alliance of mutual interest, though not one of great intimacy.

But the real decision that confronted Japan as the Pacific war approached had a familiar ring: Was she to seek a stabilization of her northern or her southern flanks? Who was to be engaged, the Soviet Union or the Western allies? The decision was not an easy one. In the late 1930s, Japan had participated in large-scale clashes with Soviet forces in the Mongolian region, and her historic rivalry was augmented by her hatred of communism. In the final analysis, however, she decided to count on a German victory on the steppes of Russia, and she turned to the south, whose resources had to be unlocked and whose Western masters had to be overthrown if the Japanese vision of the future were to be attained. Possibilities for agreement with the West to avoid this fateful step were explored, as all the moderates desired, but hopes were broken on the rock of China. Too much had been invested in blood and treasure to concede to Chiang Kai-shek, and so, infinitely more was to be invested—and all in vain.

THE FORMULATION OF FOREIGN POLICY IN PREWAR JAPAN

In the Tokyo trials of major war criminals that followed the Japanese surrender, the Allied prosecutors repeatedly sought the answer to one central question: Who bears the responsibility for leading Japan toward aggression and war? If they did not obtain a completely satisfactory answer, no blame should be assigned. Few questions involve greater difficulties. The problem has taken on universal dimensions as the modern state has grown in complexity and as foreign policy has developed into the composite, uncertain product of a myriad of technicians, men rigidly compartmentalized, skilled and jealous of these skills, but almost always frustrated by the limits of their power; an indeterminate number of free-roaming generalists, yet not so free, being bound by the limits of the single mind, the niceties of group decision, and the pressures—subtle or direct—of subalterns; and, finally the larger, vaguer public, varying in size but never comprising the whole of its society nor the sum of its parts—alternately indifferent and excited, overwhelmed by the complexities and focusing on some vital issue, ignored and watched with anxiety, molded and breaking out of molds.

Japan was a modern state. In the narrow sense, Japan appeared as a society of great personal absolutism. In both the family and the nation, the head was invested with absolute powers. Inferiors owed complete and unswerving obedience. There seemed no measure of egalitarianism or individualism to alleviate the rigidities of a hierarchical system which, through primogeniture and an emperor-centered mythology, found its apex in a single source. But in fact, the essence of power in Japanese society has not been that of personal absolutism. The vital center of decision making has uniformly lain in its collective or group character, and in its extensive reliance on consensus as the primary technique. It is critical to understand that, despite all superficial signs to the contrary, the basic nature of Japanese society can only be approached by a thorough appreciation of the intricate refinements of small group interaction, the great importance of induced voluntarism, and the generally eclectic quality of final agreements.

In all likelihood, it is only because these things were true that the outward signs of rigid hierarchy and absolutism were so well maintained into the modern era. Elaborate methods had already been developed to integrate theory and appearance with the needs of a dynamic society. Just as the system of adopted sons had long preserved the necessary flexibility in the Japanese family, so the institutions of senior councillor, adviser, and go-between had each, in its own way, facilitated the making of group decisions. That process, giving extraordinary attention to form and status, was often wearisome and prolonged, but every care had to be taken to make concessions and consensus possible, with a minimum of violence to the position and prestige of those involved. Necessarily, equals were wary of confronting each other in person until the formula for consensus seemed assured; and inferiors developed, to a fine art, all forms of subtle pressures and persuasive devices, so that successful superiors paid silent homage to these in the course of final action.

Not all these conditions sound strange to Western ears, although the aggregate process might seem foreign or extreme. In any case, how were such basic factors in Japanese social relations translated into politics and the making of foreign policy? In theory, the Meiji Constitution of 1889 paid its highest tribute to imperial absolutism but, for successful practice, it demanded a unity or consensus of its disparate working parts. The weakest of these, the two-house Diet, its lower house elected, had at least the power to withhold its consent from basic policies. The administrative bureaucracy, culminating in such executives as the prime minister, and the members of the cabinet and the Privy Council, had a vast range of powers and had legal responsibility only to the emperor, but it could not be effective alone. The military also drew their power from the emperor and had direct access to him; in practice, moreover, this branch acquired a potent weapon in that the ministers of war and navy had to come from its ranks, which served to limit sharply the independent power of the Japanese cabinet. The military, however, could operate effectively only in conjunction with the other major branches.

There was never any serious thought of having these forces coordinated by the emperor personally, despite the awesome nature of his stipulated powers. Instead, that task was handled, for some thirty years, by a small oligarchy of Meiji restoration leaders who acted in the name of the emperor as his "chief advisers." Ultimately, this group came to be known as the *genro* or "senior councillors," an institution without a vestige of legal recognition or responsibility, but central to the process of Japanese politics. Every basic policy decision was placed before the *genro,* and their approval was a prerequisite to action. Even the daily affairs of state frequently engaged their attention. With protégés in every branch of government, and with their own vast accumulation of experience, these men were at once the source of integration, the court of final appeal, and the summit of power. To be sure, agreement among them was not always easy; there were deep personal and political cleavages in this, as in other Japanese groups. Timed withdrawals and temporary concessions, however, enabled a consensus to operate with a minimum of crises. Until the close of the World War I, with rare exceptions, the fountainhead of Japanese foreign policy was this group.

With the postwar era, however, basic changes in government began to emerge, paralleling those in society. The members of the *genro* became old, and their ranks were not refilled. No group came forth to undertake the integrative role. Instead, Japanese politics was marked by an increasing struggle for supremacy and control among the parties, the bureaucracy, and the military. It is interesting to note that, at the outset of this era, an attempt was made to establish a liaison council under the aegis of the prime minister for the development of a unified foreign policy. It was intended to include major party, official, and military representation, but it was never accepted by the major opposition party, and it ultimately faded away.

Without a supreme coordinator such as the *genro,* Japanese constitutionalism, in both its written and unwritten aspects, revealed serious flaws. In the hectic party era, foreign policy decisions taken in cabinet or government party circles were subject not only to legitimate attacks in the Diet, but also to extensive sabotage by the ranks of the subordinate bureaucracy, and to angry challenges by the military groups. The parties never attained more than a quasi-supremacy and, as they faded, the military moved from verbal challenge to open defiance. Japanese society, in the period after 1928, was a classic example of a government divided against itself. Important segments of the military operated, both in the field and at home, in such a manner as to scorn the government. They received substantial support from within the bureaucracy, and from certain party figures as well. Every branch of government was riddled with dissension. Within the Ministry of Foreign Affairs, various cliques maneuvered for position—the militarist clique, the Anglo-American clique, and numerous others. For a time, consensus was impossible, and conditions close to anarchy prevailed.

Gradually, however, greater stability was achieved. Making full use of traditional procedures, top court officials surrounding the emperor involved themselves in unending conferences with representatives of all major groups; innumerable go-betweens explored the possible bases of compromise; certain voluntary withdrawals, strategic retreats, and silent acquiescences were effected. Slowly, a new basis for interaction developed, one which gave due recognition to military superiority but still was broad enough to include essential elements of the civil bureaucracy, court officials, and important pressure groups. Once again, the basic decisions were reached by consensus, but with somewhat greater cognizance of the realities of power. In this period, a new group of senior councillors, the *jushin*, was organized. Although lacking the influence of the *genro*, it was fashioned after that model, indicating the continuing search for an integrative center. That search was destined never to be completely successful. Another experiment was conducted in a liaison council, the purpose being to pool military and civilian policy with particular reference to the foreign scene. Ultimately, the imperial conference, with the emperor himself presiding over a small group of top military and administrative officials, became the final decision-making body. Indeed, it was this group that determined the Japanese surrender, the emperor personally settling this great issue. Perhaps this was the only basis left for the organic unity envisaged by the Meiji Constitution.

Meanwhile, a process of accommodation had been taking place between conservative militarists and the industrial and commercial world of Japan. In the initial stages of the military revolt against liberalism and a weak-kneed foreign policy, the strong notes of a radical, anticapitalist theme were heard; the historic cry of "internal reform, external expansion" once again sounded forth. However, after the February Twenty-sixth Incident, in 1936, when army units in Tokyo under radical command rebelled, this type of revolutionary activity was suppressed. Although some liberal business elements were regarded with suspicion, and certain onerous controls were sharply protested by entrepreneurs, still the necessary compromises were made, and all of Japanese industry rose to the war effort.

Japanese labor reacted in the same way. Its radical and liberal elements had long since been silenced, and the great masses worked with patriotic fervor. It was from the rural areas, however, that the bedrock of Japanese conservatism derived. The alliance between peasant and soldier now held more meaning than at any time since the Meiji restoration. As is so frequently the case, rural provincialism bred its own type of ultranationalism. The Japanese common people played a role in the formulation of foreign policy in their own way: they posed no obstacles to expansionism, their complete loyalty was assured, and no sacrifice would be too great if it contributed to the nationalist cause.

JAPAN SINCE 1945: OCCUPATION AND ITS AFTERMATH

When Japan surrendered in August 1945, both her leaders and her people were forced to reconcile themselves to being a vanquished nation. By the terms of the Yalta and Potsdam agreements, the Japanese empire was to be dissolved and Japan reduced in size to the approximate boundaries of the restoration era. The homeland was to be occupied for an indefinite period by foreign forces. For the first time in recorded history, Japanese sovereignty was to be superseded by foreign rule. Some of the broad objectives of this rule had already been stipulated: action was to be taken to insure that Japan never again would become a world menace, or a world power. Total disarmament was to be carried out, and those responsible for past aggression were to be punished; even the fate of the emperor was unclear, although Japanese leaders sought desperately to gain assurances on this point during the surrender negotiations. Along with these essentially negative tasks, the occupation was also to encourage Japanese democratic forces and movements, so that Japan could eventually take her place in a peaceful world. Thus was inaugurated, in September 1945, a radically new era for Japan, one that might well be labeled "the era of the American Revolution."

If the contemporary processes and substance of Japanese foreign policy are to be discussed meaningfully, certain pertinent aspects of this period must be set forth. In the first place, the American occupation and its aftermath can easily be divided into three broad phases: (*a*) the early revolutionary era, when the emphasis was upon punishment and reform; (*b*) the era of reconstruction, when the stress was shifted to stabilization and economic recovery; and (*c*) the era of proffered alliance, which is continuing at present. Each of these eras, in its own way, has contributed to the current nature and problems of Japanese society.

The Revolutionary Era

The American Revolution in Japan was that of 1932, not that of 1776, although some of the spirit of the latter, as it applied to basic democratic values, was certainly present. The New Deal had new opportunities along the bombed-out Ginza and in the rice fields. But first, the old order had to be eradicated. Japanese military forces were totally disbanded in a remarkably short time; before the end of 1947, some 6 million Japanese troops and civilians had been returned from overseas, demobilized, and poured into the homeland. The military forces within Japan proper had also been completely dissolved. The ministries of war and navy were abolished. And, in an effort to seal these actions with the stamp of permanency, the now-famous Article 9 was written into the new Japanese constitution:

> Aspiring sincerely to an international peace based on justice and order, the Japanese people forever renounce war as a sovereign right of the nation and the threat or use of force as means of settling international disputes.
>
> In order to accomplish the aim of the preceding paragraph, land, sea, and air forces, as well as other war potential, will never be maintained. The right of belligerency of the state will not be recognized.

The American vision for Japan during this period became widely associated with the phrase, "the Switzerland of the Far East," although, in this case, pacifism was added to neutralization. It was a vision that had a powerful appeal to many Japanese who lived amidst rubble, without adequate food or warmth, and with vivid memories of lost ones, fire raids, and the final holocaust of the atom bomb. For most thoughtful Japanese, the early postwar era was a period of deep reflection. Its dominant theme was trenchant criticism of past leaders and institutions. Once more, there was a Japanese surge toward new ideas and ways; MacArthur, no less than Perry, symbolized the beginning of a new order, and a war-weary people turned hopefully to *demokurashi* without being precisely sure of its contents. These sentiments, widespread as they were, aided the revolution that was getting under way.

Among the various SCAP[1] actions, none had more long-range implications than those which affected the nature and position of Japanese pressure groups. As we have noted, for more than a decade the most powerful group in Japanese society had been the military. Suddenly it was entirely liquidated, and it has not yet reappeared as a significant political force. Liquidation was not merely demobilization, but also the

---

[1]SCAP is the commonly used abbreviation for "Supreme Commander of the Allied Powers." It is used to designate General MacArthur personally, and the American occupation force collectively.

purge that barred all professional military officers from future political activity, and the war crimes trials, after which the top military men of the nation were executed or sentenced to prison. Although many of these actions were subsequently modified or rescinded, their total effect, combined with other circumstances, has thus far been sufficient to render postwar militarism in Japan weak.

Through the purge and other measures, SCAP ate still further into prewar conservative ranks. For the old guard it seemed like the reign of terror, although without violence or brutality. Most professional politicians of the old conservative parties had to step aside because they had belonged to some ultranationalist group or had been endorsed by the Tojo government in the elections of 1942. Conservative leadership was hastily thrust into the hands of the one group that could be cleared: the so-called Anglo-American group from within the Foreign Ministry. Kijuro Shidehara, Shigeru Yoshida, and Hisashi Ashida, all from this group, became the top conservative leaders of Japan for nearly a decade. Even the commercial and industrial world felt the shock of reform. Beset by purges, a program to break down the *zaibatsu* ("big combines"), and the general toll of wartime ravage and postwar inflation, most business elements sought merely to survive, as if seeking shelter during a gale.

Meanwhile, with American encouragement, the labor union movement attained a massive size; within a brief period it numbered some 6 million workers, whereas, in the prewar period, bona fide union membership had never exceeded one-half million. These postwar figures masked many divisions and weaknesses, but there could be no doubt that Japanese organized labor was a new force with which to reckon on the economic and political scene. And in the rural areas, the "American Revolution" was operating in the most forceful fashion. Under a far-reaching program of land reform, absentee landlordism was almost completely abolished, tenancy was reduced to less than 10 percent of total agrarian families, and land holdings were equalized beyond the wildest imagination of prewar advocates of land reform. Basically, this program was dedicated to the creation of a huge independent yeomanry. The political repercussions in the rural areas, especially among younger age groups, have only recently become measurable.

To recite these various efforts in such bald fashion may lead to the supposition that a total social revolution took place in Japan during the first years after 1945. Any such impression would be false. Conservatism, both in the form of certain dominant classes and in the form of certain traditions that operated in every class, was a sturdy force. Moreover, as might be surmised, not all SCAP experiments were successful and, by the end of 1947, in any case, the era emphasizing reform was drawing to a close. In its ripest forms, it had lasted only about two years. The conservatives definitely survived. Indeed, conservative dominance has been the hallmark of Japanese politics for the past three decades, giving Japan a degree of political stability unequaled by any other advanced industrial society during this era.

It would be equally misleading, however, to underestimate the changes that took place during the occupation, whether because of SCAP reforms or as a result of the total complex of postwar circumstances. Some of these changes should be regarded as part of the continuum inherited from prewar days. Others were largely the product of foreign intervention or the new conditions prevailing as a result of military defeat. In any case, the changes which developed during this period had a direct influence on the processes and substance of Japanese foreign policy. Most important have been the altered composition of Japanese pressure groups and the accelerated movement toward a mass society.

The nature of Japanese conservatism has been strongly affected by the demise of the military, the dramatic changes in both the size and the nature of the agrarian sector, and the exploding technological revolution that has engulfed Japanese industry and commerce. Yet through all of the changes, the Japanese bureaucracy has maintained its power. In alliance with the Liberal Democrats, Japan's dominant political party, and interacting with the business community in a supportive manner, the civil bureaucracy has played a critical role in post-1945 governance. Thus, Japanese democracy, while bolstered by widespread political freedom, competitive elections, and the legal supremacy of the Diet, in the final analysis, coexists with a powerful bureaucratic state. Only recently has the influence of private interest groups, especially within the business sector, begun to challenge bureaucratic authority—a trend to be watched.

Stabilization

Before we turn to the current status of foreign policy, some brief consideration should be given to the second and third phases of the occupation and the gradual emergence, once again, of an independent Japan. The shift of emphasis in occupation policy, from punishment and reform to economic stabilization and recovery, began as early as 1947. The change was motivated by many problems. Certain earlier American premises about the postwar world now seemed unjustified. The prospects for a China that would be friendly and democratic by American definition were dim; the honeymoon with the Soviet Union was clearly over and the Cold War was beginning; the threat of communism throughout Europe and Asia, as a result of postwar chaos and economic misery, was a matter of profound concern. In Japan itself, the close relation between economic recovery and the prospects for democratic success could no longer be slighted or ignored. In addition, the expenses of occupation and relief constituted a heavy burden for the American taxpayer; at its peak, the cost ran close to one-half billion dollars a year.

The new emphasis brought many changes. Increasingly, the supreme test to which any policy could be put was: Does it advance productivity and economic stabilization? An assessment was made of the primary obstacles—war damage, inflation, the lack of raw materials, and low industrial morale. SCAP began to interest itself in Japanese productive efficiency, and moved from merely keeping Japan alive to furnishing her with raw materials and acquainting her entrepreneurs with the most advanced machinery and techniques. The complex problem of inflation was finally faced. Under the Dodge Nine-Point Stabilization Program, stringent reforms were put into effect. These were unpopular in many quarters, but the inflationary tide was at last turned.

Meanwhile, other disruptions to production were dealt with. The deconcentration program was relaxed and gradually abandoned, after initial attempts to reduce certain large *zaibatsu* families and cartels. The United States also progressively receded from its early severity on the issue of reparations. By the end of this era, the American government had indicated its acceptance of the thesis that the Japanese ability to repay war damages was strictly limited, that large reparations would indirectly become a responsibility to the United States, and that the heavy industry on which the Japanese future was so dependent could not be used for these purposes. Finally, SCAP took a sterner attitude toward the labor movement, amending its earlier generous legislation on unionism to give the employer, and especially the government, a stronger position.

The net effect of these actions, accompanied by certain broader trends at home and abroad, was to stimulate rapid economic recovery. Japanese society could build on an industrial revolution already well advanced, and on a legacy of technical know-how. Deflation and internal readjustments were followed by new opportunities for industrial expansion. The Korean War and the great prosperity of the free world were of major assistance. Beginning in 1950, therefore, Japan entered a period of amazing economic development. For the next twenty years, the average annual rise in gross national product was approximately 10 percent, one of the most spectacular rates of growth in the world.

This second phase of the occupation, which triggered the economic surge, was not without internal political reverberations. In the revolutionary era, American actions had been an anathema to the conservatives; now, the conservatives became the new allies. The Left, which had cheered in the early days, was filled with dismay and resentment at many actions of which it did not approve but from which it had no recourse. Japanese democracy was still under the tutelage of American military rule, and criticism and opposition were strictly limited by that fact. Inevitably, however, the United States and its policies became the central issue in Japanese politics, paving the way for the sharp divergencies that came into the open later. For every political group, moreover, this second era was one of reflection and reconsideration of Western values. There was an unmistakable tendency, at all levels, to emphasize synthesis and adjustment rather than uncritical acceptance of foreign concepts. The pendulum had begun to swing back.

As can be seen, the beginnings of postwar Japanese foreign policy were established in this era, albeit under American direction. These beginnings followed a course that Japanese leadership itself might well have taken and even labeled "in the national interest," had it been an independent agent. Indeed, on issues like reparations and trade, the United States was widely accused of being excessively pro-Japanese. One policy which was emphasized was that of rehabilitating Japanese heavy industry and encouraging its orientation toward the needs and markets of the external world. With American encouragement, an export-focused strategy was developed, taking advantage of cheap energy and raw materials, the new prosperity of the advanced West, and increasing access to ex-colonial markets. As a concomitant to this policy, the United States also sought to adjust Japanese political relations with erstwhile enemies. Like a benevolent warden convinced of the successful rehabilitation of his charge, the United States pressed for Japanese re-entry into the world community.

With the second phase of the occupation, there thus began an intimate and largely new relationship between Japan and the United States, a relationship founded on a rising tempo of economic, cultural, and political interaction. This relation was far from an equal one. The United States was central to virtually every aspect of Japanese life, whereas Japan was only one of many concerns and influences to Americans. In power as well, the disparities were great, whatever measure was used. Yet the new ties were increasingly meaningful to both societies.

The Era of Alliance

Within these trends lay the seeds of the third era, that of alliance proferred by the United States to Japan. By 1949, American authorities realized, on the one hand, that the occupation was reaching a point of diminishing returns, and, on the other, that continuing economic and political ties between the two countries were a mutual necessity. The explorations which led to the San Francisco Peace Treaty of 1951 involved a series of decisions that shaped the new Japanese foreign policy and provoked heated political debate.

The critical issue pertained to the question of Japanese defense. Two broad alternatives seemed to exist. One was Japanese pacifism, which involved seeking universal agreements guaranteeing the sanctity of Japanese territory and backing these with pledges of protection by the United Nations, and possibly by the United States, separately. The alternative was to acknowledge the Japanese need for, and right to, military defense, and to underwrite Japanese rearmament with American power. Obviously, the choice between these two broad courses would affect and shape many other aspects of Japanese foreign policy.

The Yoshida government did not hesitate to support the second alternative, that of political, military, and economic alliance with the United States, as the only course compatible with world conditions and Japanese needs. To adopt a policy of neutralism, the conservatives argued, would make Japan dependent on the mercurial policies of the communist world. It would provide neither security nor prosperity. They insisted that both the economic and the political interests of Japan were best served by alignment with the free world, particularly the United States.

Official independence for Japan finally came on April 28, 1952, the day on which the San Francisco treaty came into effect. Accompanying the main treaty was a bilateral Mutual Security Treaty with the United States providing for the continuance of American military bases in Japan until adequate defenses were prepared by the Japanese government. At least as early as 1949, the creation of a Japanese defense force was being urged in some American and Japanese circles, and Japanese rearmament was first started in the summer of 1950, shortly after the outbreak of the Korean War. The National Police Reserve was activated in August of that year with an authorized component of 75,000 men. With the coming of Japanese independence, this number was increased to 110,000 and a small Maritime Safety Force was established, in May 1952. In August, these were brought together under the National Safety Agency. Two years later, on July 1, 1954, the name was changed to the Defense Agency, and the armed forces were brought directly under the office of the prime minister, who was authorized to add a small Air Self-Defense Force. The slow buildup of Japanese defense forces continued. By the end of 1955, there were about 200,000 men in the total defense force.

Twenty-eight years later, in 1983, the force numbered some 240,000 men in all branches. Numerically, this was the smallest military establishment in northeast Asia, dwarfed by the forces of the People's Republic of China and the Soviet Union as well as those of the two Koreas and Taiwan. The goal was a small but highly modernized, defensively oriented force, but controversy continued to swirl around even this objective, both within Japan and elsewhere.

Meanwhile, economic relations between the United States and Japan have grown to gigantic proportions. By the end of 1983, total Japanese trade was some $255 billion, and of this amount, trade with the United States was approximately $60 billion, with the balance greatly favoring Japan. Two critical facts immediately become clear: first, Japanese-American economic relations provide the foundation for the alliance, being of vital importance to both nations; second, economic relations now present serious problems, with no quick or simple solutions in sight.

THE FORMULATION OF FOREIGN POLICY IN POSTWAR JAPAN

Before exploring the basic issues and alternatives currently involved in Japanese foreign policy, let us look briefly at the way in which decision and administrative processes in this field operate. The post-1945 state inherited a troubled, complex record. In the critical Meiji era (between 1867 and 1910), as we have indicated, the apex of the decision making process lay with a small group of elder statesmen, the *genro*. The political genius of Japan has always lain in oligarchy and a consensus process involving intricate negotiations and compromises. After World War I, however, centripetal forces multiplied, with the *genro* institution fading away. For more than two decades thereafter, the problems of coordination mounted, with various parts of the political-economic-military elite increasingly in conflict.

In this period, the role of the bureaucracy was naturally of primary importance. In theory, this bureaucracy was an instrument of the emperor, not the Diet. Institutional limitations combined with socioeconomic realities to reduce the independent role of the political parties. The parties were significant only as they were linked with one or another faction of the bureaucracy and its senior officialdom. Public opinion was of very limited significance. Divisions within the bureaucracy, however, were serious, and tended to grow deeper with the passage of time. It has been customary to see these divisions largely as reflecting a cleavage between civilian and military. In fact, however, they were much more complex, with many competitive, conflicting civilian-military alliances. As our knowledge of decision making in the foreign policy field for the 1920–1945 era grows, the problems of coordination, the depth of policy conflicts, and the instances of open or subtle insubordination on the part of junior officials in various branches of the government have come into sharp focus. The series of crises preceding Pearl Harbor were built out of deep fissures within the conservative-radical nationalist elites that in some measure shared power during those tumultuous years.

Has the decision-making process been more coordinated in the post-war era? The new Japanese constitution of 1947 did much to clarify the ultimate responsibility for policy, domestic and foreign. Patterned almost wholly after Anglo-American institutions, it drastically altered the old system. Under its provisions, the emperor's functions became ceremonial and symbolic. Sovereignty was assigned to the people, to be exercised by their elected representatives. A parliamentary system modeled after that of Great Britain was established, with certain modifications of a distinctly American flavor.

The Diet, instead of being peripheral to the political process, is now its legal center, and both houses are elective. The upper house, the House of Councillors, is constructed in a complicated fashion, with both nation-wide and prefectural constituencies; the lower house, the House of Representatives, is based on medium-sized election districts (three to five members chosen from each district, depending upon its size). Executive responsibility to the Diet is clearly stipulated. The prime minister must be approved by the Diet or, if the houses disagree, by the lower house. In case of a vote of no confidence, the government must either dissolve the lower house and call for new elections, or resign.

A new law pertaining to the Diet was enacted to accompany the constitution of 1947. Among other things, it provided for a system of standing committees—in contrast to the prewar, British-style, ad hoc committees. Thus, each house of the Diet now has a Foreign Affairs Committee. After agreement among the parties on the allocation of committee seats, members are selected by each party on the basis of training, experience, and political connections. The standing committees exist to hold hearings on government legislation or any policy matters within their general jurisdiction. Special ad hoc committees, however, are still used extensively in the Japanese Diet, sometimes on issues involving foreign policy.

Despite these institutional changes, the Japanese Diet committee system, as it currently operates, does not give either to the Diet as a whole or to individual Diet members the degree of power possessed in the United States Congress. Party or, more accurately, factional discipline interacts with the traditions of Japanese parliamentarism to make this true. Initiative and power in foreign policy continue to lie overwhelmingly with the executive branch of government—in concrete terms, currently with the key leaders of the Liberal Democratic party. In certain respects, of course, party supremacy has been strengthened by the new institutional structure. Under a Western-style parliamentary system, major party leaders constitute the apex of authority. The emperor no longer serves as an independent and legally omnipotent channel of power. The military branch of government is no longer a separate and competitive source of influence. And even the civil bureaucracy is now clearly subordinated in law to a political administration that must be consonant with a majority of the popularly elected members of the House of Representatives.

This is the law. What are the realities? How does Japanese governance, in fact, operate? Some observers argue that given the great power and continuity of the bureaucracy, together with the fact that Japan has not in recent decades had a change of government through national elections, the Japanese system should be denominated an authoritarian corporate state, with the supremacy of state officials extensively ruling controlling or "guiding" the private sector. Foreign as well as domestic policy, it is asserted, is essentially a bureaucratic product, not the result of the electorate's desires as expressed through the Diet. While this thesis has some validity, it is both too stark and too static to convey the complexities of current Japanese politics.

The Japanese state has been and remains strong, and its application of neo-mercantilist policies has been a central factor in the extraordinary economic successes of the post-1945 (and pre-1945) eras. Respect for authority has been deeply engrained in Japanese culture, and careers as officials, especially in the most prestigious ministries such as the Ministry of Finance, have long been coveted by the brightest young Japanese. Thus, officialdom has had an abundance of talent, accompanied by a combination of efficiency and self-assurance. Centralization of power, moreover, has a lengthy history in Japan, with prefectural and local governments strongly dependent in financial and in other respects.

The picture is made more complex, however, by the fact that many leaders of Japan's dominant party, the Liberal Democratic Party, have come from the bureaucracy, and thus, have been able to use their ties to officialdom to shape key policies in the direction they favored. Yoshida Shigeru, prime minister at the time the Allied Occupation ended, was a striking example. Yoshida, a former Foreign Office man, guided foreign policies with such a firm hand that he was charged with "one man diplomacy." By the time of the Kishi era (Kishi became prime minister in February 1957), bureau chiefs in the Ministry of Foreign Affairs and other ministries had begun to maintain close contacts with party leaders. Many of these contacts were with the pertinent committees of the Liberal Democratic Party: the Research Committee on Foreign Relations, the Policy Research Council, and the General Affairs Board. These committees, particularly the General Affairs Board, officially determine the foreign policy of the party. In his tenure as prime minister, Nakasone went beyond previous practices in appointing special advisory task forces to recommend basic policies, making certain that the appointees reflected his policy preferences. This and many other developments testify to the rise of the professional politician, as opposed to the career official, in the Japanese polity.

Taking into account the growing complexities of Japanese governance, certain observers have advanced a different argument than that of the authoritarian state thesis; namely, that the power of the center is strictly limited. They assert that despite constitutional guarantees providing for a more coherent authority structure, the national government lacks the power to establish or enforce policies, foreign or domestic, being at the mercy of disparate, often conflicting groups, both in the bureaucracy and in the private sector. Like its opposite, this thesis, while containing some elements of truth, is overdrawn. Similar to all governments operating in advanced, industrial societies, the central political authority must contend with the power wielded by the permanent bureaucracy, as we have noted. It is also true that turf battles are endemic, abetted by the intense loyalty to one's inner group, so deeply engrained in Japanese culture. And the Ministry of Foreign Affairs has frequently exercised less power in connection with critical foreign policy issues than the Ministry of Finance or the Ministry of International Trade and Industry.

Japanese pressure groups, public opinion as revealed in the polls, and a frequently hostile media add to the complexities. The number, diversity and influence of Japanese pressure groups have increased significantly, and their influence on foreign policy can be substantial, as noted. On several occasions, for example, and notably with respect to textile trade regulations, the evidence suggests that the prime minister was not able to prevail over a powerful internal interest group. As in the prewar era, the commercial and industrial groups have the greatest single influence on the Liberal Democratic Party (LDP). These speak through the Japan Employers Association and many similar organizations. It would be a mistake, however, to assume that the Japanese business and industrial world speaks with a single voice. On such an issue as China policy, for example, it was far from unanimous, and that has also applied to certain economic policies. Still the broad outlines of Japanese foreign policy at present are deeply influenced by the interests and views of leading industrial and commercial groups. These groups remain the chief financial support for the LDP, and the memberships of the groups include the most intimate confidants of conservative politicians. Hence, these groups are the most powerful unofficial influence on public policy, domestic and foreign.

Logically, the pressures emanating from rural Japan should have decreased in recent years. While the farmer has long been an important element in the conservative coalition, he and his family have progressively become a smaller fraction of the Japanese electorate and normally, even among farm families, income comes partly from additional sources, such as industrial labor or commercial activities. However, the reluctance with which LDP administrations have tackled the problem of agricultural protectionism in its many forms speaks to the continued strength of the farm lobby, both in the party and in the bureaucracy. This is partly due to the gross overrepresentation of rural areas in the allocation of Diet constituencies. There are growing indications, however, that a combination of domestic and foreign pressures have at long last forced the Japanese government to consider significant revisions in protectionism, subsidies, and taxation policy pertaining to agriculture.

Organized labor has made less of a mark on governmental policies since its past commitments have been to the opposition parties (in contrast to the normal voting patterns of blue-collar workers). *Sohyo*, the General Council of Trade Unions, claiming 4.1 million workers, has been a mainstay of the Japan Socialist Party (JSP). *Domei*, the Japanese Confederation of Labor, has been closely affiliated with the Democratic Socialist Party. On November 20, 1987, Domei united with *Churitsu Roren*, the Federation of Independent Unions, to form *Rengo*, the Japanese Private Sector Trade Union Confederation. Rengo, claiming a membership of 5.5 million or over 40 percent of all trade unionists, pledged that it would work with each of the opposition parties in fashioning policies oriented toward the interests of industrial workers. It hopes to offer a stronger alternative to the staunchly leftist position of Sohyo that has so greatly influenced JSP policies. Sohyo itself has said that in three years it will merge with Rengo, time being necessary for policy and organizational adjustments. Yet it remains to be seen whether the voice of organized labor can be strengthened in an era when the internationalization of Japanese industry is progressing at an accelerated pace.

Single-issue interest groups of the type represented by the environmentalists have only recently come into view in Japan, and generally, they have limited political influence, at least on the national scene, unless affiliated with more powerful forces. One other element in Japanese society warrants attention, namely, the mass media. The Japanese press has long pursued advocacy journalism, and despite some exceptions, generally with a tilt against those in power. Thus, *Asahi*, Japan's most prestigious newspaper, like several others of national coverage, sharply attacks many LDP policies and couples with this a stance that is both nationalist and against augmented defense, one often anti-American in tone. Despite government control of the leading media outlet, moreover, Japanese TV increasingly approaches international as well as domestic news with the sensationalism to which American audiences have become accustomed. The impact of this situation upon public opinion cannot be easily measured, but, at a minimum, any Japanese administration is forced to be aware of a greater diversity of pressures operating upon and against it now than at any time in the past.

The increasing impact of public opinion deserves special attention. As a recent example shows, the strongly adverse public reaction to Nakasone's proposed sales tax in 1987 was a major factor in the measure being dropped. In recent years, polling has been extensive, with the most widely respected polls done as professionally as in the United States, and taken seriously by most political leaders, whether accepted as guidance or not. The views of the Japanese public are thus known on a wide range of matters. With respect to broad alignments, a large majority of the Japanese public continues to favor the closest relations with the United States, but a steadily rising percentage, especially among younger generations, see future United States–Japan relations as likely to be confrontational. The Soviet Union continues to garner very limited support, with China faring much better. The Japanese prejudice against Koreans is also clearly manifested in the polls, with minimal support for intimate ties with the Republic of Korea despite Japan's extensive economic interests there. Notwithstanding the buffeting taken in recent years, Japanese continue to look toward the advanced industrial West, and they consider themselves a part of that world despite the geographic and cultural ties with Asia. Only recently has the Japanese public shown a greater interest in areas like Southeast Asia.

Opinions on security matters are also revealing. The Japanese public believe that a strategic equilibrium between the United States and the Soviet Union has been reached, and they strongly favor agreements on arms limitations between the two superpowers. As the Soviet Union increased its military forces in East Asia and fortified two of the four northern islands off the shores of Hokkaido, the perception of a Russian threat to Japan's security increased. But a majority think that it is unlikely that the Soviet Union will attack Japan directly. Public opinion has been closely divided over whether the United States would defend Japan in the event of attack, despite treaty pledges to do so. Yet a large majority of Japanese favor keeping defense expenditures—and the size of the National Defense Force—at its present levels, with much smaller percentages favoring either an escalation or a reduction of military funds. In addition, support for Japan's three nonnuclear principles (no manufacture, no possession, and no permission for such weapons being on Japanese soil) remains strong.

On economic issues, the polls are equally interesting. Despite the fact that Japan weathered the global recession of the early 1980s better than all other advanced industrial societies and now continues to adjust to a rapidly changing global economic environment extremely well, and has the highest per capita gross national product (GNP) in the world, the citizenry are voicing a mounting number of complaints relating to the quality of life. Housing, the strain of an urban existence, and education are among the issues of growing concern to the Japanese public, nearly 90 percent of whom now consider themselves members of the middle class. On the international front, the public is well aware of the economic friction with other nations, especially the United States. Understandably, they see trade as a life and death matter for Japan, and the American connection as vital. A majority of the Japanese public also places primary responsibility upon the United States for trade and other economic problems in the bilateral relationship. Public support for dismantling the Japanese protectionist structure has been lukewarm. There has been strong support, however, for increasing economic assistance to the Third World, especially Asia.

As indicated, Japanese public opinion is having an increasing influence upon policymakers. When public opinion is demonstrated to be strongly for or against a given option, leaders take note. At a minimum, caution is exercised, the timing of policy enactment is affected, or an intensive public relations campaign unfolds. In some cases, as we have indicated, policies negatively received are abandoned, at least for the time being. Prime Minister Nakasone elected not to push for constitutional revision or a greatly accelerated security program, despite his personal preferences, partly because of the strong opposition revealed in all polls. Public opinion can also be used. The United States on occasion has been advised not to push too fast, too hard, on economic or security issues, given adverse public reaction. And in pursuing firm policies toward the USSR, especially on the territorial issue, the LDP leaders know that the public is with them. In Japan as elsewhere, domestic issues generally overshadow those relating to foreign policy. Moreover, LDP leaders conceive it their duty to educate the Japanese public and set about that task with varying results. Yet they have generally been careful not to flagrantly disregard the polls. The Japanese parties of the Left, on the other hand, often ignore public opinion if it conflicts with their ideological commitments, one reason for their poor electoral showing.

In sum, notwithstanding the divisions and conflicts within the Japanese political structure, the remarkable aspect of Japanese foreign policy up to date has been its continuity, and the consensus that has underwritten that continuity. If the top political leadership cannot disregard key interest groups or the force of public opinion when forcefully expressed, it can and does act in defense of what successive governments have defined as "the national interest," in general harmony with the electorate. It must be remembered that Japan, more than any other industrial nation, has had remarkable political stability in the past thirty years. Elsewhere, I have referred to Japan as having a one and one-half party system, with one party knowing only how to govern, all others only how to oppose. Admittedly, Japanese foreign policy has been the product of the Liberal Democratic Party. Consensus has not extended to either the Socialists or the Communists, although increasingly the two centerist parties, the *Komeito* and the Democratic Socialists, have moved toward key LDP foreign policy positions.

Given this background, there are two critical questions to be asked. First, will the Liberal Democratic Party remain in power in the course of the years ahead, providing the same stability as in the past? This question is highly pertinent because if the Japan Socialist Party, alone or in coalition, were to come to power as presently constructed, one might expect significant policy changes despite the efforts of recent JSP leaders to modify hard-line leftist policies reflective of the dominant faction's Marxist past.

A more uncertain, complex question is whether the Liberal Democrats, in partnership with the bureaucracy, so successful in their policies in recent decades, can sustain their record in a period when changes, some of them structural in nature and of major proportions, are essential. Indeed, certain far-reaching economic changes are already underway, with or without governmental initiatives. The issue, moreover, is not only whether the necessary alterations will take place, many of them requiring political initiatives, but whether the timing will be such as to provide the climate for improved relations with nations important to Japan, notably the United States. The answer to this question cannot be presently determined, but it is crucial, both to the future of the Liberal Democratic Party and to the course of Japanese foreign policy.

CONTEMPORARY ISSUES IN JAPANESE FOREIGN POLICY

At present, economic issues dominate the Japanese political scene, taking priority in both domestic and foreign policy. Japanese economic growth continues to approach 4 percent per year, with inflation modest and unemployment apparently stabilized and slightly declining after having risen to 3 percent, using a measurement that is more conservative than that employed in the West. In sum, the Japanese economy is healthy despite the pressures upon it. Today, Japan has the second largest economy in the world according to most estimates. Meanwhile, Japanese industry is being internationalized at an ever more intensive pace, with even small and medium plants being moved overseas, following the major industries that pioneered in foreign investment and joint ventures some years ago. The search is for cheaper costs of production and a shelter against foreign protectionist policies.

Within Asia, heightened interest is being shown in the countries composing ASEAN (the Association of Southeast Asian Nations) as production costs in South Korea and Taiwan, traditional investment targets, increase. India is also attractive to some Japanese entrepreneurs. Interest in China has fluctuated, due to the mercurial character of Chinese policies. There can be little doubt, however, that various Japanese enterprises see China as having strong long-term potential, with preparations being made accordingly. The prime source for Japanese investment, however, remains the United States, despite the uncertainties of the American economy. By the end of 1987, over 600 Japanese companies employed some 160,000 American workers in plants widely distributed in the United States, with vast holdings in real estate also being acquired.

Despite this process of internationalization, Japan faces problems with each of its trading partners, none more grave than those with the United States. Nearly 40 percent of all Japanese exports went to the United States in 1987, and a huge trade imbalance in favor of Japan existed, amounting to approximately $55 billion. Neither voluntary quotas nor promises to expand the Japanese domestic market have had any appreciable effect upon the trade balance up to date. Even the depreciation of the dollar, which reached a rate-of-exchange low of 122 yen to the dollar by the end of 1987, had not altered the picture, whatever the future potential. To a lesser, but still to a substantial degree, Japanese trade surpluses existed in 1987 with virtually all other nations with which it has traded, except its oil suppliers. Thus, its foreign exchange mounted, and was reinvested, much of it funding the mounting U.S. budget deficit.

Some Japanese industries such as iron and steel, shipbuilding, and other traditional labor-intensive operations like textiles are declining in the face of intensive competition from Korea, Taiwan, and other lower-cost producers. Extensive automation has commenced, with evidence provided by the United States that certain traditional industries can be saved via this route. The broad direction, however, is to take advantage of Japan's very high savings ratio and the state and private sector commitment to research and development so as to capture the commanding heights of high technology fields. Concentration upon electronics, communications, and such fields as biotechnology is well underway. This increases the competition with the United States, signaling the contests of the future. At the same time, the process of United States–Japanese economic interdependence—indeed, integration—moves forward inexorably.

The central charge against Japan is that despite its various promises and efforts, its markets remain extensively closed even when foreign products could compete handily in quality and price with domestic goods. The charge is leveled by virtually every major Japanese trading partner. The reasons are complex, relating only in the most limited degree to formal tariffs current in effect. By means of various regulatory devices and a multitude of rules tailored to favor Japanese producers, the system remains difficult—and, in some instances, impossible—to penetrate. Factors deeply imbedded in Japanese culture such as the highly personalized structure that undergirds business relations, the tightness of the in-group, and even the highly antiquated distribution system abet practices that have had widespread official support. In sum, Japan has made maximum use of its backward sectors as well as its modern portions in protecting its system against external penetration.

Under great pressure, the old order is gradually giving way. One challenge confronting Japanese policymakers is to give substance to the Maekawa Report commissioned by Nakasone. A central recommendation of that report was that in order to accept more imports, Japan should launch a sustained program to expand the domestic market. One formidable obstacle to this goal is the extraordinary cost of housing due to the sky-high price of land, especially in the vicinity of Japan's metropolitan centers. While it is very late, a second land reform program—quite different from that sponsored by the American Occupation—is necessary, one which among other things, would tax agricultural land in accordance with its true worth. This, together with the abandonment of the heavy protection given select agricultural products, would be of great benefit to the Japanese citizen as well as to the international community. Policies encouraging the decentralization of population are also essential. Social services must be expanded, especially since the median age of Japanese population will rapidly increase in the coming decades.

However, an expansion of the domestic market in itself, even if it meets current hopes, will not suffice to produce a major change in trade patterns. Other measures are essential. Financial as well as other markets are now being opened, with the probability that Japan will become one of the world's major international financial centers in the near future. Meanwhile, from various sources, foreign and domestic, calls have come for a Japanese-style Marshall Plan that would stimulate development in the Third World, and especially in Asia. Starting with Prime Minister Fukuda, assistance programs have been proffered. In the Nakasone era, Japan offered to recycle $20 billion of its massive current account surplus, making it available to developing nations. The idea has yet to be made operational. The most recent overture came in December 1987, when Prime Minister Noburo Takeshita visited the ASEAN heads of state meeting in Manila. He offered a $20 billion "bonus" package consisting of three parts: additional official development assistance from the Overseas Economic Cooperation Fund, Japan's aid-dispensing agency; untied loans from the Export-Import Bank of Japan; and an ASEAN investment fund made up largely of private capital.

There are numerous problems, however, with the aid program as it is currently conceived and operating. Countries that borrowed from Japan when the yen was low must now repay in the greatly strengthened yen and at interest rates higher than the average rates charged by other industrial nations. And only a very small part of the funds are to be in the form of gifts. The bulk of the loans are to be dispensed as loans via the international lending agencies. Moreover, developing countries are likely to use a sizable amount of such assistance funds to purchase Japanese-made parts and components, thereby worsening their trade imbalance with Japan. In addition, if this assistance program, coupled with the overseas migration of Japanese industries, serves to increase Japan's "round-about" trade with countries like the United States, it will produce additional friction.

In sum, there are no easy answers to the economic issues confronting Japanese foreign policy. Japan has its own complaints, with ample validity in many cases. The United States has badly mismanaged its economy for several decades, Japanese officials believe, with the resulting budget and trade deficits of the present. It is acknowledged that these deficits cannot long be sustained, and Japan, like other nations, has looked with disappointment upon the rather modest budget reductions effected in 1987. It regards American industry and labor as having belatedly tackled the critical problems of quality, productivity, and other aspects of international competitiveness. It watches with apprehension as the dollar is devalued against the yen, now dropping to levels that were earlier regarded as near-disastrous to the Japanese economy, but which that economy has assimilated thus far without serious consequences. It see U.S. protectionism as the looming threat, with Japan the principal target, and regards this as a substitute for those measures that would require current sacrifices on the part of the American people on behalf of a long-term strengthening of their economy.

American sources are not loath to list their grievances against Japan, again, with considerable validity. Numerous American officials and politicians continue to urge Japan to open its markets more fully, citing cases where American firms are excluded from bidding on public works projects or frozen out of the domestic market in diverse ways, despite their proven competitiveness in other foreign settings. Japanese saturation of the American market, and the employment of illegal practices such as "dumping" are additional complaints. Almost always, the changes taking place under extreme pressure are regarded as too little, too late.

In United States–Japan economic relations there is sufficient blame to be shared by both sides, and that signals the direction that each should take in the broadest sense. It is incumbent upon the United States to tackle the budget deficit promptly, with the least damage possible to itself and the global economy. Some combination of spending reduction and revenue enhancement must be employed. Meanwhile, the need to encourage savings, to advance research and development, to cut production costs, to stay abreast of the high technology frontiers, and to continue the internationalization of American industry are all essential steps if the

American economy is to enjoy health in the midst of a tumultuous global industrial revolution.

The supreme challenge confronting Japan is the need to move more rapidly away from the protectionist, exclusivist, inward-looking past and to develop truly internationalist attitudes and policies. This requires more than the structural changes taking place in the Japanese economy and the policy overtures thus far undertaken. It requires a change in Japanese culture. Hence, it will be difficult, painful, and too slow to prevent trauma in Japan's relations with others in the coming years. Yet speaking of the most important such relation, that with the United States, the odds favor the continuance of a troubled marriage rather than a divorce. The factors of interdependence and integration outweigh those of conflict and separation.

Japan will make a continuous effort to diversify its trade and investment, to be sure, encouraging the private sector to explore every avenue, including the socialist nations. Neither the private sector nor the majority of officials have substantial political or ideological scruples when it comes to economic matters. The key issue is economic benefit. When required by international trade agreements and regulations, the government (if not the private sector) will seek to abide by the rules in all cases. And when pressure is applied by nations associated with Japan to put a premium upon political considerations, such as the ASEAN stance with respect to economic assistance to Vietnam after its invasion of Cambodia, Japan will modify its policies. Like many Western Europeans, most Japanese believe that in general, economic intercourse with diverse states is beneficial to regional and global stability as well as to Japan. Thus, they are disposed to separate economics and politics. Nevertheless, in increasing measure the Japanese government in recent years has employed economic assistance in a political manner, especially in regions like East Asia and the Middle East.

Security Issues in Japanese Foreign Policy

In 1987, the Japanese Self-Defense Force consisted of the following units: 156,000 army personnel, with advanced type artillery, armored vehicles, antitank weapons, and air defense, including surface-to-air missiles; 45,000 naval and naval air personnel, with 15 submarines, 36 destroyers, 18 frigates, and various fast patrol boats, as well as 84 combat aircraft; 45,000 Air Self-Defense personnel with 389 combat aircraft. Japan had 90 F-15J airplanes, improved HAWK missiles, and additional sophisticated weapons. While small in quantity, Japanese forces are among the most modern in the world. Those who want to emphasize Japan's military growth point out that this force is now sixth or seventh globally in overall power and that annual Japanese military expenditures exceed those of twenty other Asian nations. The other side of the story is that Japanese military forces are almost wholly defensive in construction, and that against its most probable foe, the USSR, Japanese defenses could only survive a very short time without massive external support. Alone among major states, moreover, Japan spends only 1 percent of its admittedly high GNP on defense. West Europe and the United States spend 3 percent to 7 percent, with the latter nation bearing treaty responsibility for Japanese defense in case of attack.

Japanese leaders have taken significant steps to expand the nation's defense responsibilities in recent years. Prime Minister Suzuki, in the course of his visit to Washington in May 1981, agreed in principle that Japan would conduct surveillance by air for several hundred miles, and by sea, for approximately 1,000 nautical miles to the south and east. Such a commitment has been reiterated by his successors. Indeed, in his initial months in office, Prime Minister Nakasone spoke more firmly about Japan's security obligations than any of his predecessors. Acknowledging that Japan should share a greater portion of the defense burden with the United States, Nakasone described Japan as a vast aircraft carrier, and suggested that in the event of hostilities, the Japanese mission would be to bottle up the North Pacific Soviet fleet, helping to block the straits through which that fleet would have to move. Despite the Soviet threats and domestic criticism that followed these remarks, responsible leaders have periodically reiterated Nakasone's comments. The Japanese also made the decisions to share military technology with the United States and to participate in the Space Defense Inititive (SDI) research program.

Yet Japan's security commitments remain constrained by a number of factors. A constitutional amendment that would widen the scope of Japan's military options has been set aside by its advocates due to strongly adverse Diet and public opinion. The legality of the Self-Defense Force, resting upon the thesis that all nations have an inherent right to defend themselves, was upheld by the Japanese Supreme Court in 1959, but the Japanese goverment has placed itself under various prohibitions: no offensive weapons, no overseas use of military forces, no collective security agreements, and no conscription. In 1976, the Miki government declared that for the time being, defense expenditures would be limited to 1 percent of GNP, and not until 1987 was that principle breached when the Nakasone government presented a budget in which defense expenditures amounted to 1.004 percent of the total budget. The care with which Japan approaches this issue can be seen in the pronouncements of the Takeshita government that Japan will continue to abide by "the spirit of the 1 percent commitment," with a 1987–1988 expenditure of 1.013 percent of the estimated GNP, or over $30 billion. Meanwhile, the three nonnuclear principles remain formally in effect, but an overwhelming majority of the Japanese public as well as their leaders know that American ships carrying nuclear weapons enter Japanese waters.

More importantly, Japan has been moving very cautiously toward a soft regionalism, various inhibitions notwithstanding. Joint exercises with American forces are now conducted regularly and joint planning for various military contingencies is taking place. The commitment to regional air and sea surveillance (and potentially, defense) is coupled with some exchange of intelligence information with both South Korea and China. Despite the insistence of Japanese authorities that the $4 billion economic assistance agreement with the Republic of Korea should not be coupled with security issues, an indirect security relationship with South Korea surely exists.

Yet the fear of some observers that Japan is on route to rapid militarization seems unwarranted. Even with a staunch defense advocate like Nakasone at the helm, the gap between rhetoric and reality was substantial. It is not clear whether Japan can fulfill its current commitments with respect to air and sea surveillance by the early 1990s, given the present budgetary allocations. All of the old barriers remain to enhanced military capabilities: the 1946 constitution; the strong, continuing antimilitary sentiments of the Japanese public; the deep divisions as to whether Japan faces any imminent external threat; and an awareness of the rising concern among other Asian nations regarding Japanese rearmament. For these reasons, the term *comprehensive security* has enjoyed popularity in Japan, because this phrase is generally used to connote the principle that Japan's approach to security must encompass, indeed, lay primary emphasis upon economic policies.

In the future, Japan is most likely to move incrementally toward an acceptance of increased security responsibilities, with the principal emphasis upon economic measures. The Persian Gulf crisis, which unfolded in 1987, provides a good example. Despite its heavy dependence upon Gulf oil, Tokyo rejected any direct involvement in the Gulf, opting instead for furnishing an advanced navigational detection system to enable better guidance of ships through routes cleared of mines. In addition, it announced the commitment of low interest loans to Oman and Jordan. The Takeshita government has also signaled that it will increase the funds furnished for the upkeep of American forces stationed in Japan and has pledged that it will seek to fulfill earlier commitments with respect to surveillance. Against the opposition of a growing Japanese defense industry, the government finally decided to purchase a new fighter-bomber, the FSX, based on the F-16 from the United States. Pressure will increase within the Japanese defense industry for permission to export weapons, indicating a struggle that lies ahead.

When various factors and alternatives are weighed, the probabilities remain high that Japan will not become a major military force operating independently of American policy and power. Such regional security responsibilities as are accepted by Japan will be related to incremental adjustments in the balance of burdens under the umbrella of the United States–Japan Mutual Assistance Treaty.

Relations with Major States and the Quest for a Japanese Role in World Affairs

For reasons set forth earlier, the close ties between Japan and the United States are likely to endure despite ongoing tensions. As testimony to Japan's global economic power, moreover, that nation has become a member of the Group of Seven, the states that meet regularly to consult on a wide range of matters. In this and in other respects, Japan has been drawn into the Western world, albeit with some discomfort, given the cultural disparities. Its relations with Western Europe, similar to those with the United States, are characterized by economic friction that is offset in some degree by a steady growth of economic interconnections. While Japan may put an increased priority upon Asia in the years ahead, it can never again separate itself from the advanced industrial nations with which it shares political and security interests, as well as economic interests.

Meanwhile, relations with the two big Communist states have occupied increasing attention of Japan in the past decade, especially relations with China. Japan has long had an ambivalent attitude toward China. On the one hand, throughout history, it was attracted to China's high culture, and in more recent times, to the economic potentialities of this vast, populous land. On the other hand, now as in the past, many Japanese have doubts as to whether China can get its act together, at least in the foreseeable future. Thus, the private sector approaches technology transfer and investment with some hesitation, especially after the frequent policy changes emanating from Beijing in recent years.

One cannot dismiss the importance of various psychological factors in discussing Japan's China policy. Not without reason, the Japanese believe that they understand China better than other foreigners, since they share some cultural attributes and have had a long history of intercourse with their continental neighbor. And as has been widely publicized, many Japanese in authority have had a guilt complex in regard to China due to the Japanese wartime atrocities committed in that land. Yet this does not prevent hardheaded approaches to the economic aspects of Sino-Japanese relations. Even as they lay the groundwork for extensive long-term economic ties, Japanese entrepreneurs exhibit great caution for the present, awaiting a clearer indication of the policies that flow from China's reform efforts. And among Japanese policymakers, there is a strong, if private, desire that China make progress *slowly*. Japan does not want a chaotic China, but neither does it want a rapidly and spectacularly successful China, thereby providing conditions under which the Chinese nationalist tides might overflow into other parts of Asia or where economic competition might crest too quickly to be absorbed.

Chinese leaders have their own desires and reservations regarding Japan. They recognize that Japan can and should play a major role in assisting China's rapid modernization. In recent times, Japan has accounted for approximately one-fourth of all Chinese trade. But there has been disappointment in Japanese reluctance to transfer technology and pursue joint ventures.

Apart from economic issues, the PRC has been increasingly critical of Japan on two counts, Taiwan and "Japanese militarism." Various incidents have convinced the Chinese that Japan is following a "One China, One Taiwan" policy—which in fact is true. As in the case of the United States, this irks Beijing, although it has no painless means of counteracting such a policy except that of remonstrance. Meanwhile, as the Chinese fear of a Soviet attack has declined, PRC leaders have altered their position on Japanese rearmament. Whereas once they supported these efforts as a legitimate move by Japan to defend itself against a northern enemy, in recent times the Chinese have taken a dim view of such policies as going beyond the 1 percent of GNP limit for defense expenditures and they have called attention to various actions by Japanese leaders and others that to them betoken the rise of Japanese militarism. The prime minister's visit to the Yasukuni Shrine, which honors Japanese war dead, the revision of textbooks to soften accounts of Japan's actions during the 1937–1945 Sino-Japanese War, and various activities of Japanese ultra-rightists are cited as danger signs.

Relations between Japan and China are destined to be complex. It is recognized on both sides that these two nations can be of significant aid to each other—Japan as the engine that helps to fuel the Chinese industrial revolution and China as the market for Japanese products. In addition, both perceive a long-term security problem with respect to the Soviet Union, irrespective of current trends. Since development and security constitute the principal goals of each nation's foreign policies, there is ample reason for cooperation. At the same time, both sides have mutual doubts and suspicions, as we have seen, and certain of these have a foundation in fact. Moreover, Japan has become a global power, at least in the economic sense, whereas China is at most a regional power. The very different stages of development characterizing these two societies would dictate policies differently fashioned, even if a significant ideological-political gulf did not add further complications.

Japanese relations with the Soviet Union pose a different set of issues. It can be said without fear of contradiction that the chemistry between these two countries has been exceedingly bad for more than one hundred years. In the twentieth century, they have engaged in two declared wars and numerous incidents. Until recently at least, the Soviet Union followed an unremittingly harsh policy toward Japan, based on the premise that "one must treat the Japanese tough." In response, the Japanese have shown little inclination to concede to Soviet views, and public opinion polls verify what an observer can instinctively feel, namely, the Japanese—whether common man or official—have a strong aversion to the Soviet state and people as foreign, hostile, and unyielding. These feelings, moreover, are reciprocated by most Russians.

Thus, Japan-USSR relations have been relatively minimal, and a peace treaty formally ending World War II has yet to be signed. At the same time, it should be noted that Japanese trade with the USSR has been expanding, and is expected to average around $4.5 to $5 billion during the next few years, with the export of whole Japanese installations such as chemical plants playing an important role in the Soviet quest for modernization. Once again, Japan is prepared to separate economics and politics. The Gorbachev era, moreover, may offer opportunities for broader improvements in relations. Thus far, Soviet overtures have come primarily in the form of higher-level visits with more skillful diplomats assigned to Japan. As yet, there is no sign that Soviet leaders are prepared to give major ground on the issue of the four northern islands off Hokkaido currently occupied and (in the case of two of the islands) fortified by the Russians. The indications are that the Soviets will combine a close-in military presence (to convince the Japanese of the dangers of alignment with the United States) and expanded economic opportunities in an effort to alter Japanese policies. In the short term at least, this has a limited chance of weakening Japan–United States ties. The course of United States–Soviet, relations however, is also a variable of importance. Should a new era of détente ensue, the Japanese would feel safer in advancing economic relations with Moscow at a more rapid rate, and possibly searching for compromises on security issues.

As relations with all of the major states and regions are discussed and debated in Japan, an overweening issue haunts the Japanese people and government. As the twenty-first century approaches, what should be Japan's role in the world? Once again, this issue cannot be analyzed, without turning to certain psychological factors that operate in the Japanese scene. Any individual living outside the Japanese cultural orbit seeks to define trends with respect to such psychological factors with trepidation. The Japanese observers themselves are by no means in agreement as to the importance of these factors. However, we are witnessing a shift away from the mood that dominated the generation of Japanese deeply scarred by World War II. Many in that generation harbored intense feelings of inferiority and guilt, and showed a proclivity for dependency and withdrawal. This proclivity was naturally abetted by the harsh economic conditions that prevailed.

How substantial have the changes in Japanese psychology been? While Japan as a nation is moving rapidly toward an internationalist policy, with rare exceptions, the Japanese as a people do not yet have an internationalist outlook. Insularity and parochialism, together with a strong adherence to class and generational distinctions, have been too long and too deeply imbedded in Japanese culture to disappear in a few decades. The Japanese remain a very private people, introverted, and most comfortable in familiar surroundings with long-established reference groups.

At the same time, a new mood has been emerging in Japan, reflective of the extraordinary socioeconomic revolution through which this society is passing. Recent Japanese generations are more confident of themselves and their society, quite willing to stand comparisons with others, both Asian and Western, and increasingly less inhibited in personal and group relations. Condescension or arrogance are more commonly displayed when speaking of societies that are regarded as backward or decadent. In these tendencies, one sees the new Japanese nationalism. With good reason, a growing number of Japanese are proud of their accomplishments in the past thirty years, and they are proud of the hybrid culture that has evolved from the merging of traditional and modern ways.

It is in this context that Japan's global role is debated. The word currently in vogue is "internationalization." Virtually every commentator and politician asserts that Japan must assume a greater responsibility for world order. Yet there is a continuing uncertainty as to how that role is to be played, and what price should be paid. It does not pass unnoticed that virtually every other major state is currently seeking a lower-cost, lower-risk foreign policy so as to concentrate upon pressing domestic problems. Japan alone is being pressed to take on heavier global responsibilities, given its previous low posture and newly acquired wealth.

Two broad options have been largely discarded, at least in their purer forms. The neutralist-pacifist route has long been championed by the Japan Socialist party, but even it has recently moved to modify somewhat its traditional stance. Soviet military power remains formidable and in close proximity to Japan, and Soviet interests—some of them in conflict with those of Japan—will continue to be advanced. The Korean peninsula, so vital to Japan's interest, remains unpredictable, but most unlikely to be responsive to the appeals of a weak, isolated neighbor. And in the foreseeable future and long run, China is also a nation with which to reckon; a nation that even now exhibits a strong nationalism and views pacifism contemptuously. Unless Japan is prepared to hand over the determination of its vital interests to others, the neutralist-pacifist route is most unpromising, and the overwhelming majority of Japanese people recognize that fact.

Is an opposite course a viable option, namely a foreign policy characterized by a relatively high posture, assertive and independent, defining Japan's national interests apart from those of others? Such a policy, which we may label "Gaullist," has an appeal to a small band of ultranationalists, but under present or foreseeable circumstances, it has no chance of being adopted as the foundation of Japanese foreign policy. The backlash from Asia, already feeling threatened by the relatively modest Japanese security commitments, would be immense. Japan's economic relations in Asia and elsewhere would be undermined. The repercussions at home would also be severe, with consensus breaking down on many fronts. And irrespective of its sacrifices, Japan could not hope to balance the military power of the United States or the Soviet Union. Gaullism did not work in France, and there is no reason to believe that it would work for Japan. And once again, this view is shared by the great majority of the Japanese people and policymakers.

The remaining option is one that builds from the past, enlarging the Japanese role in diverse ways, while retaining the basic linkages that currently exist. The foundation of Japanese foreign policy will continue to be the alliance with the United States, as we have indicated. Yet within that alliance, as within all other alliances of this period, the quotients of equality and independence on the part of both partners will increase. Further differentiation of policies will take place, greater reciprocity will be necessary, and continuous consultation will be required.

Within this option, moreover, two significant variants are possible. One found expression in an earlier phrase, *omnidirectional foreign policy*. Such a course, while retaining close ties with the United States, would seek to place primary emphasis upon international economic relations. Japan would continue to turn outward, crossing ideological boundaries in seeking to play an ever growing role in the economic growth and modernization of the world, while continuing to pursue a relatively low political and military posture, counting upon American leadership, but feeling free to diverge from the United States when national interests appeared to dictate that need, and accepting only low risks in the strategic arena.

Combining as it does some elements of Gaullism and nonalignment, and yet seeking the protection—and benefits—of the American connection, such a policy understandably has great attraction. While playing from current Japanese strength and aimed at maximizing Japanese interests, it involves relatively minimal costs and risks. And in some considerable measure, it is the policy that Japan has sought to pursue since it was released from American tutelage.

The other variant is that most recently espoused by Prime Minister

Nakasone, namely, a policy of accepting greater political and military responsibilities, acknowledging that Japan must gradually assume the role of a major power with a growing stake in global affairs. Such a course does not relegate economic policies to an inferior position, but it adds additional political and security elements to a foreign policy that has been defined by some as strictly a "market policy," thereby raising Japan's voice in the international community. It also presumes a close, continuing consultative relationship with the United States, although it does not preclude a separate stance on some issues. In this policy too, there is an element of Gaullism, a reassertion of Japanese nationalism.

Japanese public opinion remains divided over which variant is preferable, a division also reflected within elite groups. Japan's future course will probably involve some mixture of the two, with the debate continuing and the given course at any one time influenced by the international climate at least as much as by internal considerations. Yet whatever precise form Japanese foreign policy takes, a policy of minimal involvement is ruled out by the incontrovertable fact that no nation is more dependent upon trends in the wider world than Japan.

FOREIGN POLICY LANDMARKS

September 8, 1945	General MacArthur accepts the surrender of Japan on the battleship Missouri
November 3, 1946	Promulgation of the new Japanese Constitution, to go into effect six months later
April 28, 1952	Effective date of the treaties of peace and security restoring Japan's independence and alliance with the United States
July 1, 1954	Transformation of the National Safety Force to the present Self-Defense Force
November 1955	The merger of the Liberal and Democratic parties to form the Liberal Democratic Party
October 19, 1956	Joint Soviet-Japan Declaration reestablishing diplomatic relations
May–June, 1960	Strikes and demonstrations protesting the revised United States–Japan Security Treaty
December 8, 1965	The establishment of diplomatic relations between Japan and the Republic of Korea
September 29, 1972	Japan–People Republic of China joint statement inaugurating diplomatic relations
September 1980	Establishment of the Pacific Economic Cooperation Conference
1981	The pledge by the Japanese government to develop capabilities to conduct defense surveillance up to 1,000 nautical miles south and east of Japan and several hundred miles by air

1981	The ground forces of Japan begin joint exercises with U.S. military forces
January 1985	The launching of Market-Oriented, Sector-Specific (MOSS) talks aimed at resolving United States–Japan trade problems
January 1985	USSR Foreign Minister Eduard Shevardnadze visits Tokyo
April 1986	The submission of the Maekawa Report to Prime Minister Nakasone
July 1986	A historic victory for the Liberal Democratic Party in national Diet elections
April 17, 1987	United States imposition of penalties on Japan in connection with the semiconductor dispute
1987	The Defense Agency budget exceeds 1 percent by 0.004 percent
December 1987	U.S. dollar reaches low point of 121 yen to 1 dollar

SELECTED BIBLIOGRAPHY

Although English-language materials are still far too limited, the last fifteen years have seen an increasing number of worthy articles, monographs, and general studies, many of which deal in some fashion with Japanese foreign policy.

To start with the historical background of Japanese international relations, one might mention the older work of R. H. Akagi, *Japan's Foreign Relations, 1542–1936* (Argus, 1936); but the historical writings of Sir George Sansom provide an excellent introduction to this subject as well as to other facets of traditional Japan: *Japan—A Short Cultural History,* rev. ed. (Englewood Cliffs, N.J.: Prentice-Hall, 1962); *A History of Japan to 1334* (Stanford, Calif.: Stanford University Press 1958), A *History of Japan, 1334–1615* (Stanford, Calif.: Stanford University Press, 1960), and *The Western World and Japan* (New York: Knopf, 1950). See also Herschel Webb, *The Japanese Imperial Institution in the Tokugawa Period* (New York: Columbia University Press, 1968).

To these should be added C. R. Boxer's *Christian Century in Japan* (Berkeley, Calif.: University of California Press, 1951) for a careful exposition of initial Western contacts.

For the modern period, a few general works include materials on Japanese foreign policy. One might select W. G. Beasley, *The Modern History of Japan,* 2d Ed. (London: Weidenfeld and Nicolson, 1973); Hugh Borton, *Japan's Modern Century* (New York: Ronald Press, 1955); and Richard Storry, *A History of Modern Japan,* rev. ed., (London: Penguin, 1982) as works of this type.

The Taisho period (1912–1926) is rather sparsely covered as yet. Masamichi Royama has written one work in English, *The Foreign Policy of Japan, 1914—1939* (Tokyo, 1941); the older work by T. Takeuchi, *War and Diplomacy in the Japanese Empire* (Garden City, N.Y.: Doubleday, 1935), may still have some utility.

The books by A. M. Young, especially his *Japan in Recent Times, 1912–1926* (New York: William Morrow, 1928), are of interest as contemporary accounts, and the Young newspaper, the *Kobe* (later *Japan*) *Chronicle,* is a most important source for many events of the entire period between the mid-Meiji and prewar Showa eras.

For most readers, the Showa Period is likely to be of greatest interest. For the militarist era of the 1930s, the most important materials are contained in two memoirs: the so-called *Harada-Saionji Memoirs* and the *Kido Diary*; neither of these has been published in English, but both are available at certain leading libraries in the United States in mimeographed form, in whole or in part.

Perhaps no single English source is as valuable as the voluminous *War Crimes Trial Documents,* running into thousands of pages, which were translated for the famous Tokyo trials. These also can be obtained; a complete set exists, for instance, at the University of California, Berkeley library.

Among existing Western memoirs, special mention should be made of J. C. Grew, *Ten Years in Japan* (New York: Simon & Schuster, 1944), and Sir R. Craigie, *Behind the Japanese Mask* (London: Hutchinson, 1946). From the Japanese side, see Mamoru Shigemitsu, *Japan and Her Destiny* (New York: Dutton, 1958).

We have a general account of this wartime period in F. C. Jones, *Japan's New Order in East Asia: Its Rise and Fall, 1937–1945* (London: Oxford University Press, 1954).

A growing number of monographs dealing with this general period are available. Yale Maxon explores the problems involved in formulating Japanese foreign policy, in his *Control of Japanese Foreign Policy: A Study of Civil-Military Rivalry, 1930–1945* (Berkeley, Calif.: University of California Press, 1957).

Japanese accounts of the war are available in Saburo Hayashi, in collaboration with Alvin D. Cox, *Kogun: The Japanese Army in the Pacific War* (Marine Corps Association, 1959) and Nobutaka Ike, trans. and ed. *Japan's Decision for War* (Stanford, Calif.: Stanford University Press, 1967); T. Kase. *Journey to the Missouri* (New Haven, Conn.: Yale University Press, 1950); M. Kato, *The Lost War* (New York: Knopf, 1946); and Mamoru Shigemitsu. *Japan and Her Destiny* (New York: Dutton, 1958).

Various aspects of the postwar period are covered in certain general books: Ardath Burks, *Japan: Profile of a Postindustrial Power* (Boulder, Colo.: Westview Press, 1983); Tadashi Fukutake, *Japanese Society Today* (Tokyo: Tokyo University Press, 1982): Frank Gibney, *Japan: The Fragile Superpower*, rev. ed., (New York: Meridian Books, 1982); Nobutaka Ike, *A Theory of Japanese Democracy* (Boulder, Colo.: Westview Press, 1978); Rei Shiratori, ed., *Japan in the 1980s* (Tokyo: Kodansha, 1983); Edwin O. Reischauer, *The Japanese*, rev. ed., (Cambridge, Mass.: Belknap Press, 1983); J. A. A. Stockwin. *Japan: Divided Politics in a Growth Economy* (New York: Norton, 1975); Robert E. Ward, ed., *Political Development in Modern Japan* (Princeton, N.J.: Princeton University Press, 1968); and Joji Watanuki, *Politics in Postwar Japanese Society* (Tokyo: University of Tokyo Press, 1977). See also *Parties and Politics in Contemporary Japan* by Robert A. Scalapino and Junnosuke Masumi (Berkeley, Calif.: University of California Press, 1962).

Recent works revealing aspects of Japanese society that provide one type of insight into Japanese attitudes and policies in international affairs include Robert Christopher, *The Japanese Mind: The Goliath Explained* (New York: Simon and Schuster, 1983); Tadashi Fukutake, *The Japanese Social Structure: Its Evolution in the Modern Century*, (trans. by Ronald Dore) (Tokyo: Tokyo University Press, 1982); Takeshi Ishida, *Japanese Society* (New York: Random House, 1971); Robert J. Lifton, et al., *Six Lives, Six Deaths: Portraits from Modern Japan* (New Haven, Conn.: Yale University Press, 1979); and Ezra F. Vogel, *Modern Japanese Organization and Decision Making* (Berkeley, Calif.: University of California Press, 1975).

A few general studies of Japanese foreign policy exist in English. See Michael Blaker, *Japanese International Negotiating Style* (New York: Columbia University Press, 1977); Donald C. Hellmann, *Japan and East Asia: The New International Order* (New York: Praeger, 1972); Frank Langdon, *Japan's Foreign Policy* (Berkeley, Calif.: University of California Press, 1973); and Robert A. Scalapino, ed., *The Foreign Policy of Modern Japan* (Berkeley, Calif.: University of California Press, 1977).

For studies emphasizing the economic aspects of Japanese foreign policy, see James Abegglen and George Stalk, Jr., *Kaisha, The Japanese Corporation* (New York: Basic Books, 1985); Robert E. Cole, *Work, Mobility and Participation: A Comparative Study of American and Japanese Industry* (Berkeley, Calif.: University of California Press, 1979); I. M. Destler and Hideo Sato, eds. *Coping with U.S.–Japanese Conflicts* (Lexington, Mass.: Lexington Books, 1982); Leon Hollerman, ed., *Japan and the United States: Economic and Political Adversaries* (Boulder, Colo.: Westview Press, 1980); Chalmers A. Johnson, *MITI and the Japanese Miracle: The Growth of Industrial Policy, 1925—1975* (Stanford, Calif.: Stanford University Press, 1982); and *Japan's Public Policy Companies* (Washington, D.C.: American Enterprise Institute, 1978); Hiroshi Mannari and Harumi Befu, *The Challenge of Japan's Internationalization and Culture* (Tokyo: Kwansei Gakuin University and Kodansha International, 1983); Yasusuke Murakami and Yutaka Kosai, eds., *Japan in the Global Community* (Tokyo: University of Tokyo Press, 1986); Daniel I. Okimoto, *Japan's Economy: Coping with Change in the International Environment* (Boulder, Colo.: Westview Press, 1982); Hugh Patrick and Henry Rosovsky, eds., *Asia's New Giant* (Washington, D.C.: Brookings Institution, 1976); Fred H. Sanderson, *Japan's Food Prospects and Policies* (Washington, D.C.: Brookings Institution, 1978); and Jimmy W. Wheeler, Merit E. Janow, and Thomas Pepper, *Japanese Industrial Development Policies in the 1980s* (Croton-on-Hudson, N. Y.: Hudson Institute, 1982).

For works concentrating primarily upon security issues, see Claude A. Buss, *National Security Interests in the Pacific Basin* (Stanford, Calif.: Hoover Institution, 1985); Reinhard Drifte, *Arms Production in Japan* (Boulder, Colo.: Westview Press, 1986); Ryukichi Imai and Henry S. Rowen, *Nuclear Energy and Nuclear Proliferation: Japanese and American Views*, Boulder, Colo.: Westview Press, 1977); Young W. Kihl and Lawrence Grinter, eds., *Asian-Pacific Security: Emerging Challenges and Responses* (Boulder, Colo.: Lynne Rienner, 1986); Hisahiko Okazaki, *A Japanese View of Detente* (Lexington, Mass.: D.C. Heath, 1974); Masashi Nishihara, "Prospects for Japan's Defense Strength and International Security Role," in Douglas Stuart, ed., *Security within the Pacific Rim* (Gower Publishing Company, 1987); Yukio Satoh, *The Evolution of Japanese Security Policy* (London: Adelphi Papers, No. 178, International Institute for Strategic Studies, 1982); Robert A. Scalapino, Seizaburo Sato, and Jusuf Wanandi, eds., *Internal and External Security Issues in Asia* (Berkeley, Calif.: Institute of East Asian Studies, University of California, 1986); Richard Sneider, *U.S.–Japanese Security Relations* (New York: East Asian Institute, Columbia University, 1982); Richard H. Solomon and Masataka Kosaka, eds., *The Soviet Far East Military Buildup* (Dover, Mass.: Auburn House, 1986); *U.S.–Japan Relations in the 1980s: Towards Burden Sharing* (Cambridge, Mass.: Cambridge Center for International Affairs, Harvard University Press, 1982); Martin E. Weinstein, *Japan's Postwar Defense Policy, 1947–1968* (New York: Columbia University Press, 1970); Martin E. Weinstein, ed., *Northeast Asian Security After Vietnam* (Champaign, Ill.: University of Illinois Press, 1982); and the yearly reports entitled *Defense of Japan* issued by the Japan Defense Agency, as well as the yearly surveys entitled *Asian Security* published by the Research Institute for Peace and Security, Tokyo.

Naturally, the American reader will tend to have a special interest in American-Japanese relations. A substantial number of books have been written on this subject. Among the older works, those of Payson J. Treat are well known: *Japan and the United States*, rev. ed. (Stanford, Calif.: Stanford University Press, 1928), and *Diplomatic Relations between the United States and Japan*, 3 vols. (Stanford, Calif.: Stanford University Press, 1932, 1938). See also Foster Rhea Dulles, *Forty Years of American-Japanese Relations* (New York: Appleton-Century-Crofts, 1937).

A broad cultural account is to be found in T. Dennett, *Americans in Eastern Asia* (New York: Macmillan, 1922). More recently, such an approach has been effectively used by Robert Schwantes in his *Japanese and Americans: A Century of Cultural Relations* (New York: Harper & Row, 1955).

For recent American-Japanese relations in addition to works cited, see *Challenges and Opportunities in U.S.–Japan Relations*, a report of the U.S.–Japan Advisory Commission, Washington, D.C., 1984; Ellen L. Frost, *For Richer, For Poorer: The New U.S.–Japan Relationship* (New York: Council on Foreign Relations, 1987); Institute of East Asian Studies, *Japanese Challenge and the American Response: A Symposium* (Berkeley, Calif.: Institute of East Asian Studies, University of California, 1982); Chae-Jin Lee and Hideo Sato, *U.S. Policy Toward Japan and Korea: A Changing Influence Relationship* (New York: Praeger, 1982); Hugh T. Patrick and Ryuichiro Tachi, *Japan and the United States Today* (Montpelier, Vt.: Capital City Press, 1986); Edwin O. Reischauer, *The United States and Japan*, rev. ed. (Cambridge, Mass.: Harvard University Press, 1976); Gaston J. Sigur and Young C. Kim, eds., *Japanese and U.S. Policy in Asia* (New York: Praeger, 1982); and *The United States and Japan in 1986: Can the Partnership Work?* (School of Advanced International Studies, Johns Hopkins University, Washington, D.C., 1986).

Official publications from the U.S. State Department, such as the series *Foreign Relations of the United States and Japan*, contain useful major documents. See also various congressional hearings, both those of the Senate Committee on Foreign Relations and the Subcommittee on Asian and Pacific Affairs, House Foreign Affairs Committee.

No serious study of Japanese foreign policy should be undertaken, of course, without reference to the periodical literature. Among the English-language journals, those carrying articles of significance at rather regular intervals include *Contemporary Japan, Japan Quarterly* (formerly *Far Eastern Quarterly*), *Foreign Affairs, Pacific Affairs*, and *Asian Survey*.

Some reference should also be made to the increasing number of English-language materials being published by the Japanese government, including valuable items, pertaining to foreign policy problems and policies, from the Ministry of Finance, the Ministry of Trade and Commerce, and the Foreign Office. In reference to contemporary issues, it will be helpful to consult the translations of the vernacular press and of selected articles from Japanese vernacular magazines that are put out by the American embassy, if one can obtain access to these.

Such newspapers as the *Japan Times* (formerly *Nippon Times*), the *Osaka Mainichi* (English-language edition), and the *Asahi Evening News* should also be examined. Naturally, many of the above materials will contain further leads and much fuller biographies.

8

Foreign Policy
of the European Community

Françoise de La Serre

In less than three decades the European Community[1] has progressively grown and has become an important actor in the international system. It has asserted itself as a "political entity" with its own institutions and policies, able to play a role in the international field. To be sure, when speaking of "foreign policy," a certain clarification must be made in reference to the European Community. Two structures coexist in this domain: the European Community proper, whose powers, internal and external, are exclusively economic; and the European Political Cooperation (EPC) consisting of the same member states who, since 1970, have undertaken a voluntary harmonization of their foreign policies. This duality of structures and functions—which is not always clearly perceived outside of Europe—explains the multiform nature of Europe's presence in the world.

[1]Strictly speaking, there is not one but three European communities: The European Coal and Steel Community (ECSC) created by the Treaty of Paris in 1951, and the European Economic Community (EEC) and European Atomic Energy Community (Euratom) set up by the Treaty of Rome in 1957. But it has become common usage to refer to them as the European Community—EC. The original signatories of the three treaties—France, the Federal Republic of Germany, Italy, Belgium, the Netherlands, and Luxembourg—were joined in 1973 by the United Kingdom, Ireland, and Denmark, in 1981 by Greece, and in 1986 by Spain and Portugal. In 1967 the previously separate institutions (Councils and Commissions) of the three Communities merged into one.

With the signature of the Single European Act in 1986 one must, however, note that the member-states attempted to reduce this dual approach. While reaffirming that European Union remains their final objective, the Twelve member states declared their willingness "to implement this European Union on the basis, first of the Community operating in accordance with its own rules, and, secondly, of European cooperation by the signatory states in the sphere of foreign policy."

BACKGROUND FACTORS

The Basic Features

It is not really surprising that the European Community has progressively asserted itself in the international system. World War II led to the effacement of a divided Europe, to its loss of power and influence and to its economic decline. This situation inspired the founders of the Community with a political project based on close economic cooperation. The project was to guarantee peace in Europe, through Franco-German reconciliation, and to preserve it by promoting intra-European solidarity.

The first effort was the European Coal and Steel Community (1951)—whose aim was to integrate the production and transportation of coal and steel. Its preamble linked economic development and integration with political union.

> "Recognising that Europe can be built only through practical achievements which will first of all create real solidarity, and through the establishment of common bases for economic development. . . .
>
> "Resolved to substitute for age-old rivalries the merging of their essential interests; to create, by establishing an economic community, the basis for a broader and deeper community among peoples long divided by bloody conflicts; and to lay the foundations for institutions which will give direction to a destiny henceforward shared. . . .
>
> ". . . have decided to create a European Coal and Steel Community."

The same concerns led to the signing of the Treaty of Rome that established the European Economic Community—EEC—while continuing to affirm in its preamble the will "to lay the foundations of an ever-closer union among the peoples of Europe." The purpose this time was, however, to extend to all economic activities the provisions set forth with regard to coal and steel. The ultimate purpose, based on the formulation of common policies and a specific timetable, was to establish not only a customs union but economic integration. New institutions, different from the institutions of the traditional international organizations, were envisaged.

The most important outcome of this unification was the constitution of a *security community* in K. Deutsch's terms eliminating the recourse to force between partners.[2] This aspect is forgotten today since it is taken for granted.

The other outcome was the economic success of the Common Market. This success was based on free trade, free movement of persons, and on common policies: external commercial policy and policies complementing the Customs Union; Common Agricultural Policy (CAP), currency reform, a community budget, and so forth. Since 1971, this budget has its own resources (customs duties, agricultural levies, and a share in each member country's value-added tax). Sixty-six percent of the budget presently finances the CAP. It has become both an instrument of financial solidarity between the member states and a symbol of the Community's autonomy.

In other areas, integration has not attained all the objectives fixed by the treaties or envisaged by the member states. In the monetary field, for instance, successive and often ambitious plans fell short of their intended results. The creation of the European Monetary System, in 1979, contributed to the stability of European exchange rates and increased monetary cooperation between central banks. But it did not lead to a common policy towards the dollar or the yen, nor did it contribute decisively to the reform of the international monetary system.

The EC's external relations, however, benefited from the dynamics of integration given by the Treaty of Rome. This text established that at the end of the period of transition a Common Commercial Policy would complete the Customs Union (Article 113) and that the member-states would concert their actions in international organizations of an economic nature (Article 116). It also provided for the possibility of concluding association agreements (Article 238). In addition, Articles 131 and 136 regarding overseas territories opened the way to what later became the Community's development policy. These provisions rapidly established the EC as an international actor, be it in the trade negotiations of the Kennedy Round (1963–1967), in Greece's and Turkey's association with the Community (1962–1963), in the association of former colonies (Yaoundé Convention, 1963, agreements with Morocco and Tunisia, 1969), and in numerous worldwide commercial agreements. In addition, the European Court of Justice's jurisprudence ruled in favor of the "externalization" of the Community's internal powers, "when such action was necessary to attain the Community's objectives." It thus established, for example, that if the EC has the power to issue regulations on fishing policy, it is *ipso facto* in its power to conclude fishing agreements with third parties.

[2]Deutsch, K. W. et al., *Political Community in the North Atlantic Area: International Organization in the Field of Historical Experience* (Princeton, N.J.: Princeton University Press, 1957), p. 5.

TABLE 8.1 CEE = USA = JAPAN = Comparison (1985)

	POPULATION IN MILLIONS	GDP AT CURRENT PRICES		GDP PER CAPITA AT CURRENT PRICES	UNEMPLOYMENT (IN PERCENTAGES)
In Billions of Dollars (Approx.)					
CEE	321.1	3,230.7	2,406.5	12,168	12
USA	240.0	6,171.9	3865	19,562	7.2
JAPAN	120.7	1,754.4	1307	13,881	2.6

Sources: OCDE
         Eurostat

With this organization—incomplete as it may be—the EC, with its population of 322 million, constitutes one of the world's large, prosperous zones.[3] With 18.5 percent of world trade (not including intra-Community trade), the Community is the world's first commercial power, even if for the past few years, and because of the economic crisis, the growth of the Community's external trade has been slightly lower than that of total world trade. Some of the Community's share of that trade (22 percent in 1958) has been lost to its competitors. Nevertheless external trade still represents a much greater proportion of the gross national product for the Community than for example for the United States.[4]

This indicates the Community's extreme dependence on the outside world from which it imports 90 percent of its raw materials. It also accounts for the EC's extraordinary network of commercial and cooperation agreements. Thanks to this network, Europe constitutes a privileged partner for the other industrialized countries as well as for the Third World, and to a lesser degree for the Communist bloc. It should be noted that, unlike China, which has shown great interest in developing relations with the Community, the USSR has until now refused to recognize the EC *de jure* for political reasons, preferring to conclude "cooperation agreements" with each member-state.

For its part the Community has not shown great readiness to create links with an organization as dominated by the Soviet Union as the COMECON. But the present evolution could lead to mutual recognition and subsequently to the conclusion of commercial accords between certain Eastern countries (who so desire) and the EEC.

The Community has also adjusted its policies to the requirements of

[3]See Table 8.1 for figures concerning the comparative weight of the EC, the US, and Japan.

[4]See Figure 8.1 for trade figures and diagrams.

External trade as a percentage of GDP (1985, estimated)

	Imports	Exports	Average of imports and exports
EEC (external) *	12.6	11.7	
United States	9.3	5.8	
Japan	9.8	13.2	

* Not including trade between member countries.

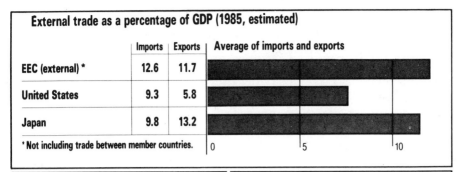

Regional spread (percentages) of world trade in 1985

	Imports	Exports
EEC (external)	18.2	18.5
EFTA	6.5	7.0
United States	21.3	13.8
Japan	7.7	11.3
Other industrialized countries	7.5	8.3
Eastern bloc	12.9	12.8
OPEC	7.2	10.1
Other Third World countries	18.7	18.2

Average of imports and exports

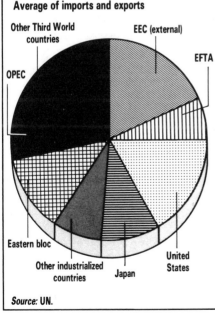

Source: UN.

Development of world and Community trade (in millions of dollars)

━━━ World exports*
── ── EEC imports (external)
••••• EEC exports (external)

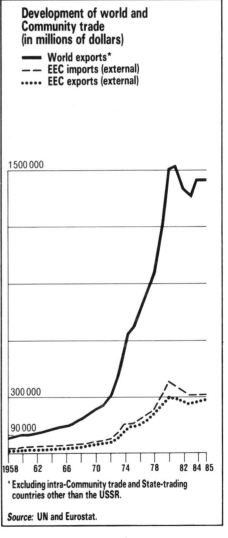

* Excluding intra-Community trade and State-trading countries other than the USSR.

Source: UN and Eurostat.

FIGURE 8.1 EEC Trade Figures.

greater cooperation with the less developed countries and to the need to contribute to stable international economic development. Thus, in recent years it has taken part in the major East-West (CSCE) and North-South (New International Economic Order) negotiations. These negotiations required consultations between Europe and its partners of the Western bloc, the United States, and Japan.

The Logic of Integration

In its present form the Community's external policy is the result of two frequently conflicting trends that have marked the development of European unification since the early 1950s: the logic of integration and that of state sovereignty.

It is true that the EC, created by the Treaty of Rome, was a less ambitious political design than the ECSC, the European Defence Community (EDC), and the Political Community that were to have accompanied it. After the French Parliament rejected the EDC treaty in 1954,[5] the EC skirted the formation of a true supranational political union and was limited to economic matters. Nevertheless, the treaty's preamble continued to stress the political goals of the undertaking—"of an ever closer union among the peoples of Europe." In addition, the institutional system as well as the decision-making process, which were to lead to common policies, illustrated the persistence of an integrationist trend.

The European Federalists—along with some neofunctionalist theoreticians—expected economic links and supranational institutions to lead, almost automatically, by means of functional processes, to some type of political integration.[6] By analogy with the American experience they expected this process to culminate in the constitution of a federation, with decision-making powers for foreign affairs. Accordingly, the EC Commission was the "embryo" of a future European government. The initial development of the Common Market, the realization of the Customs Union more rapidly than expected, the common agricultural policy, and the relatively smooth functioning of the institutions supported this view for a time.

On the other hand, other political scientists, such as Stanley Hoffmann, expressed doubts that economic integration would lead to political union. If some economic or social sectors could be easily integrated, others belonging to "high politics" would offer strong resistance. Foreign policy divergences among member-states concerning relations with the

---

[5]Macridis, Roy, ed. *Foreign Policy in World Politics*, 6th Ed. (Englewood Cliffs, N.J.: Prentice-Hall, 1976), pp. 83–84.

[6]Haas, E. *The Uniting of Europe Political, Social and Economic Forces, 1950–1957* (Stanford, Calif.: Stanford University Press, 1968), pp. XI–552. E. Haas has subsequently revised his initial theories. See "The study of regional integration: reflections on the joy and anguish of pretheorizing," *International Organization* XXIV, 4 (1970), pp. 607–646.

superpowers, the United States in particular, were also likely to impede the spillover from economic to political integration.[7]

The Logic of State Sovereignty

Charles de Gaulle as president of the French republic (1958–1969) applied himself to the task of thwarting a supranational economic integration which would reinforce the power of the Community institutions to the detriment of the member-states. This policy led to the crisis of June 1965.[8] By pursuing an "empty chair" policy within the Council of Ministers of the Common Market, France ensured that the Community remained a purely economic arrangement. De Gaulle also insisted on the unanimous consent of the member-states (the so-called Luxembourg arrangement of January 1966) before a decision was made, thus giving a veto power to each of the member-states.

However, this blow dealt to the supranational development of the Common Market was not a total victory for French diplomacy. De Gaulle did not actually succeed in substituting with the European Community the intergovernmental cooperation he had proposed in the early 1960s. In its various versions the Fouchet Plan presented to the European partners in 1961 and 1962 proposed a "Union of States." Such a union was to be founded upon cooperation between states; it was to include foreign relations and defense within its scope and retained the EC only as a technical body subordinate to the governments.

Two major objections were raised by France's partners. On the one hand the Benelux countries stressed their commitment to the existing institutions and to the supranationality which protected them from Franco-German domination. Only the participation of their traditional ally—Great Britain—could have lessened their hostility but at that time de Gaulle was not disposed to include Britain in the proposed "union." On the other hand all France's partners, Germany in particular, believed that the inclusion of defense among the union's goals might weaken the Atlantic Alliance as well as their links with the United States. Then again, British participation would have guaranteed that the union would not take an anti-American turn.

The Benelux countries took the initiative in breaking off the negotiations that had revealed such divergences in the areas of foreign policy and defense. In their eyes it was impossible to dissociate Europe's defense from the United States. The 1963 Franco-German Treaty and the special relationship that it created between the two countries was the alternative

[7]Hoffmann, S. "Discord in Community the North Atlantic area as a partial international system." *International Organization* 17, 2 (Spring 1963), p. 529.

[8]La Serre, F. de, "The EEC and the 1965 crisis" in Roy Willis, ed., *European Integration.* (New York: Franklin Watts, 1975), pp. 130–154.

conceived by de Gaulle: "It was to provide the hard core for consolidating Western Europe and given France's military superiority, safeguard French leadership at the same time."[9]

RECENT TRENDS AND NEW INSTRUMENTS

The failure of the Fouchet Plan and French opposition to the Community's supranational evolution influenced European unification long after de Gaulle left office in 1969. In the face of a challenging international situation the *two logics* (the one favoring interstate relations and the other "political intergration") continue to develop, and are particularly evident in the field of external relations. Since the 1970s, various factors, some due to the enlargement of the EC and others to the evolution of the international system, have made the Community a more outward-looking organisation.

Enlargements and the International Context

The original six members of the EC were France, Italy, West Germany, Belgium, Holland, and Luxembourg. The enlargement of the Community to include Great Britain, Ireland, and Denmark took effect on January 1, 1973, but its prospect influenced the Community's "foreign policy" even before. Britain's membership, which France finally accepted under Pompidou's presidency, significantly expanded the EC's position in the world, thanks to the scope of British international trade and ties. At the Paris summit of October 1972 present and future EC members envisaged the impact of enlargement on the Community's international role in the following terms:

> Now that the tasks of the Community are growing and fresh responsibilities are being laid upon it, the time has come for Europe to recognize clearly the unity of its interests, the extent of its capacities and the magnitude of its duties. Europe must be able to make its voice heard in world affairs and to make an original contribution commensurate with its human, intellectual and material resources. It must affirm its own views in international relations as befits its mission to be open to the world for progress, peace and cooperation.

The Community's foreign relations were thus broadened and transformed by the enlargement. In order to conform to the GATT (General Agreement on Tariff and Trade) rules, the Nine undertook new multilateral negotiations (the Kennedy Round) and adapted their commercial

---

[9]Macridis, Roy, *Foreign Policy in World Politics*, chap. 3. See Chapter 3 in this volume.

agreements to new economic trends. In addition, development and cooperation policy was profoundly transformed by the obligation to take African, Caribbean, and Pacific anglophone countries (ACP) into account. This led to the Lomè Convention of 1975. Enlargement was also expected to lead to an "overall and balanced" economic policy in the Mediterranean.

After having expanded towards the North, the European Community also expanded to include its neighbors to the South, who upon their return to democracy, applied for membership. Greece became a member on January 1, 1981. It was followed after lenghty negotiations by Spain and Portugal in 1986. By virtue of the historic relations of these two countries with Latin America and Africa, these enlargements increased Community ties throughout the world. They also reinforced Community interest in the Mediterranean and in the conflicts of this region since these conflicts could also affect the security of European supplies—oil in particular—and aggravate the political instability of the region. It is evident that, on an economic level, these successive enlargements have had major consequences both on commercial relations between the Twelve and the United States and on the global Mediterranean policy developed by the Community since 1975 with the eastern and southern Mediterranean states.

Following the first enlargement several factors—détente, the emergence of the Third World, the weight of economic considerations in the sphere of politics—accounted for the end of the postwar order based on bipolarization and on the Bretton Woods system. In the 1980s the Ten, then the Twelve, were confronted by an international economic situation dominated by recession and shaken by the crisis of détente and local conflicts.

European Political Cooperation (EPC)

The need to meet external challenges and the intent of the member-states to make Europe a new power center have inspired the search for a common foreign policy. Under France's and Britain's influence, they emphasized an intergovernmental approach: political cooperation. It went through several stages; the initiative was launched at the December 1969 European summit of the Hague when the foreign ministers were instructed "to study the best way of achieving progress in the matter of political unification."

In the Luxembourg Report of June 1970 the ministers proposed "to cooperate in the sphere of foreign policy" and to create appropriate instruments to this end. It was in such a manner that the EPC was born. "Concertation" in the field of foreign policy is thus the most recent embodiment of the attempts to unify Europe politically.

The Luxembourg (or Davigon) Report proposes "to ensure, through regular exchanges of information and consultations, a better mutual, understanding of the great international problems; to strengthen their solidarity by promoting the harmonization of their views, the coordination of their positions and, when it appears possible and desirable, common actions."

In fifteen years of European summits and reports on Political Cooperation (the Copenhagen Report, July 1973; the Paris Summit, December 1974; the London Report, October 1981; and the Stuttgart Solemn Declaration on European Union, June 1983) one witnesses the maintenance of the principles upon which the EPC was founded, the broadening of its ambitions, and the improvement of its structures.

In 1986, the Single European Act (SEA), with a chapter concerning the EPC, constitutes the last landmark in this evolution. It reaffirms the 1970 orientations. EPC remains a voluntary cooperation between member-states of the Community in the field of foreign policy and is pledged to seek consensus through consultation and exchange of information before each member-state decides on its final position. This need for the European States to consult each other prior to any national reaction or initiative was, since the Copenhagen Report, the most constraining EPC commitment. The SEA confirms this commitment and adds that member-states "shall endeavour to avoid any action or position which impairs their effectiveness as a cohesive force in international relations or within international organizations" (Article 30, paragraph 2).

It is also evident that the ambitions of EPC have progressively broadened. Limited to a few issues at the beginning of the 1970s it now deals with all areas of the world and almost all the problems facing national diplomacies. This is recognized in the SEA when it indicates that the European states "shall endeavour to formulate and implement a *European foreign policy*" (Article 30, paragraph 1).

Nevertheless vital defense issues remain the exclusive domain of national foreign policies, even though the SEA states that the political and economic aspects of European security can be dealt with within the framework of EPC. Furthermore, the political and strategic dimensions of Euro-American relations do not fall within the EPC's scope.

As far as the institutions are concerned, the specific structures created by the Luxembourg and Copenhagen reports reflect the EPC's purely intergovernmental character: the meeting of the foreign ministers (at least four times a year, but in fact a great deal more frequently) is the regular body; the political committee, composed of the foreign ministers' political directors provides initiatives and coordination; the working groups, composed of experts; and the European correspondents, who serve as the liaison between foreign ministries. Progressively the country presiding the Community has been charged with the management of

TABLE 8.2   The Institutions of the European Community

THE COUNCIL OF MINISTERS

Functions:
The Community's decision-making body.
Each government acts as President of the Council for six months in rotation.

Composition:
The government of each nation in the Community has a seat on the Council. The foreign minister is usually a country's main representative, but a government is free to send any of its ministers to Council meetings. Since 1975, three times a year, government heads meet in the European Council to discuss Community questions and Political Cooperation.

How decisions are made:
For some particularly important decisions by the Council, unanimous agreement is necessary, but in principle most decisions can be taken by a "qualified majority." For this the votes of members are weighted according to population. France, Germany, Italy, and the United Kingdom have 10 votes each. Spain 8 votes, Belgium, Greece, the Netherlands, and Portugal 5 votes each, Denmark and Ireland 3 votes each, and Luxembourg 2 votes. A total of 54 votes is needed for a proposal to be passed. However, the Council never imposes a decision on a member in a matter that a member considers to be of vital national interest.

THE COMMISSION

Functions:
The Commission is the guardian of the treaties setting up the European Community and is responsible for seeing that the treaties are implemented. The Commission therefore:
  1. Proposes Community policy
  2. Is responsible for the administration of the Community

Composition:
The Commission has 17 members chosen by agreement of the Community governments. Commissioners are obliged to act in the Community's interests and not in the interests of the country from which they come. Commissioners are appointed for 4 years and can only be removed during their term of office by a vote of censure from the European Parliament.

How policies are formulated:
Each Commissioner heads a department with special responsibilities for one area of Community policy, such as economic affairs, agriculture, the environment, transport, and so on. Regular discussions are held between a Commissioner's department and interested parties. As a result of these discussions the Commissioner formulates draft proposals that he believes will help to improve the quality of life of Community citizens. The draft proposal is discussed by all the Commissioners who then decide on the nature of the final proposal.

(continued)

TABLE 8.2 Cont.

THE EUROPEAN PARLIAMENT

Functions:

1. Advises the Council of Ministers on Commission proposals
2. With the Council of Ministers, determines the budget for the Community
3. Exerts some political control over the Council and Commission

Composition:

The European Parliament has 518 members who represent the citizens of the Community. Members have been directly elected since 1979 and serve for a period of 5 years. The citizens of France, Germany, Italy, and the United Kingdom are each represented by 81 members, Spain by 60, the Netherlands by 25, Belgium by 24, Portugal by 24, Greece by 24, Denmark by 16, Ireland by 15, and Luxembourg by 6. The members do not sit in Parliament in national groups, but in political party groups.

How the European Parliament works:

The European Parliament meets on average, once a month, for sessions which last up to a week. The Parliament has 18 standing committees, which discuss proposals made by the Commission. The committees present reports on these proposals for debate by the full Parliament. Decisions made by Parliament are influential on the Council of Ministers, but are not binding. The Parliament has the right to question members of the Commission and Council and is therefore able to monitor the work of these institutions. It has the power to dismiss the Commission by a two-thirds majority vote. It verifies that the budget was properly executed, and it also has the power to reject the Council's proposals for the Community budget.

THE COURT OF JUSTICE

Settles legal disputes involving Community laws.

Composition:

The Court has 13 judges, one from each Community country, assisted by 6 advocates general. Each judge is appointed for 6 years by mutual consent of the member states.

The powers of the Court:

Community institutions, governments of Community countries, companies, and individual Community citizens can all ask the Court to make judgements on matters involving Community laws. Judgements of the Court are binding in each member country.

EPC, particularly relations with all other countries, and this constitutes a heavy burden, especially for the small EEC countries. Under the authority of the Presidency, the SEA created a small administrative secretariat based in Brussels, which will assist the Presidency in preparing and implementing the activities of EPC.[10]

[10]On EPC see Philippe de Schoutheete, *La coopération politique européene*, 2d Ed. (Bruxelles: Labor, 1986).

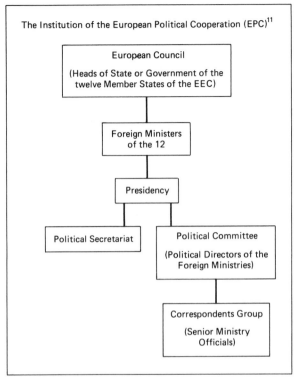

The Institution of the European Political Cooperation (EPC)11

Two Types of Actors in a Hybrid System

This "long march" towards a European foreign policy reveals two types of actors: the member-states in concert in the EPC, and the institutions created by the Treaty of Rome: the Council of Ministers and the Commission. In this latter case, the identification of the actors presents an additional difficulty. For the most part, the Council of Ministers and the Commission act in common within the framework of their respective powers. In the domain of external commercial negotiations, however, and according to the treaty, the EC is represented by the Commission alone. Thus it is the Commission acting on the Community's behalf which negotiates at the GATT and makes contacts with the COMECON, the Warsaw Pact trading bloc.

Who has the right to speak for Europe, and on what occasion, has frequently led to argument over competences. In areas of shared competence a compromise procedure was agreed upon. It allows the Commission to present and defend the agreed Community position, but it entitles

11The European Commission and the European Parliament have become progressively associated to EPC. The Parliament is kept informed of EPC activities. The Commission attends EPC meetings but plays no role in the decision-making process.

the president of the Council (the presidency rotates every six months) to supplement this on behalf of the twelve member-governments. A kind of dual spokespersonship has thus emerged in many "grey areas" of international negotiations.

One must remark that this duality in structures, procedures, and actors, has been lessened by the creation of a new institution at the Paris summit in December 1974: the European Council. It is composed of the heads of state and governments and one of its main functions is to give the existing system a minimum degree of coherence. In order to ensure consistency between Community and EPC activities it was decided that the European Council would meet "three times a year, and whenever necessary, in the Council of the Community and in the context of political cooperation." It thus became the supreme body of Europe. The European Council, and its numerous statements on international problems for the past fifteen years or so, have unquestionably enhanced the Community's external action. Nevertheless this "interstate" entity which plays a role in world affairs constitutes an oddity in the international system. This oddity and the complexity of the foreign-policy process seems to have blurred the original model in terms of which European integration was viewed. Today the EC is no longer viewed as a transitional system whose failures would delay the attainment of an ideal model of integration but rather as a hybrid system.

In order to describe such a reality, which is "complex and messy," S. Hoffmann has recently suggested we look at the EEC as an "international regime" as defined by J. Nye and R. Koehane: a set of norms of behavior and of rules and policies covering a broad range of issues dealing with both procedure and substance and facilitating agreements between members. But he also specifies the uniqueness of the EEC regime: first, the cooperation thus established on a voluntary basis has no parallel elsewhere in the world; second, "this cooperation varies from one policy area to the other usually depending on whether members-states feel that the benefits derived from joint action . . . outweigh the costs implied in any additional constraints on their independence of action.[12]

ACHIEVEMENTS AND PROBLEMS

What are the effects of the EC's presence in the world? It is beyond the scope of this chapter exhaustively to analyze Europe's multifaceted international activity. Emphasis will be placed on certain aspects so as to be able to conclude whether or not it effectively makes foreign policy.

[12]Hoffmann, S. "Reflections on the nation-state in Western Europe today," in L. Tsoukalis, ed., *The European Community, Past, Present and Future* (Oxford: Basil Blackwell, 1983), p. 33.

"To Speak With One Voice?"

The Declaration on European Identity adopted in Copenhagen in 1973, when the Arab-Israeli conflict had made Europe aware of its vulnerability, effectively sums up the Nine's foreign policy ambitions: "International developments and the growing concentration of power and responsibility in the hands of a very small number of great powers mean that Europe must speak increasingly with one voice if it wants to make itself heard and play its proper role in the world."

Fifteen years later a rapid appraisal of EPC shows that the Nine—and now the Twelve—stated their position on numerous subjects, reacted on specific issues (human rights in South Africa, Turkey, Latin and Central America, the problem of refugees in Southeast Asia) and to various events (the situation in Portugal in 1975, the taking of American hostages in Iran, the Soviet invasion of Afghanistan, the imposition of martial law in Poland, the Falkland Islands crisis, and so forth). But their major goal was to elaborate a genuine common policy in two important areas: East-West relations (particularly within the framework of the Conference on Security and Cooperation in Europe) and the Middle East conflict.[13]

Concerning East-West relations, the Nine concentrated their activity on defining a concerted approach to problems raised within the framework of the CSCE and attempted to elaborate an *Ostpolitik*. Benefiting from the relative American disengagement in the first stage of the talks (Helsinki and Geneva conferences), they were able to assert the specificity of European interests in the face of the two superpowers. The EC thus obtained the *recognition of European unification* and of its goals by the USSR in exchange for the recognition of the status quo in Eastern Europe that the USSR wanted to see confirmed once and for all.

With the support of several neutral and nonaligned countries, the Nine have also been able to impose certain "confidence-building measures" as well as measures favouring the free movement of persons and ideas between East and West.

The follow-up conferences (in Belgrade and in Madrid) and the Stockholm conference on disarmament in Europe (1984–1986) were further occasions of European cooperation. The goal pursued by the Europeans was, and remains, to strike a balance between confidence-building measures in the military field and the protection of human rights, particularly the free circulation of persons and ideas between East and West. In spite of this relative success at the CSCE one must admit, however, that the major crises provoked by the Soviet invasion of Afghanistan and the imposition of martial law in Poland produced no rapid and unambiguous European response. In the first case, more than three weeks were neces-

---

[13]Allen, D., R. Rummel, and W. Wessels, *European Political Cooperation* (London: Butterworth, 1982), p. 184.

sary to put an end to the hesitations caused by a series of separate national declarations made in scattered order. Even more time was required to propose the plan for the neutralization of Afghanistan, a plan that the USSR later rejected. The Ten were equally unable to harmonize their positions regarding their participation in the Moscow Olympic Games of 1980.

In the second case, the range of European responses to events in Poland also prevented a rapid common response. Here too a long delay occurred before the Ten were able collectively to express their "utter disapproval" of the situation in Poland. In addition, their position regarding possible sanctions was sufficiently vague so as to allow for future compromises.

The position of the EC concerning the Middle East conflict has become much more coordinated since 1973. At the outbreak of the conflict, Europe was still hampered by the various postures adopted in 1967, but from the lowest common denominator, which characterized the statement of November 6, 1973, it has moved forward to a policy intended to be no longer reactive but anticipatory. Community members have gradually reached agreement on the principles governing a settlement in the Middle East; namely, the inadmissibility of territorial acquisition by force; the need for Israel to evacuate territories occupied since 1967; respect for the sovereignty and territorial integrity and independence of all states in the region and their right to live in peace within secure and recognized boundaries; and the necessity of taking into account the right of the Palestinian people to a homeland in a just and lasting peace settlement. The Community saw these principles as a necessary basis to a peace settlement and, despite its acknowledgement of the Camp David peace negotiation, believed that such a settlement must be a global one. The nine members at the time also declared themselves ready to participate in the search for a solution and to underwrite international guarantees. The European Council held in Venice on June 12 and 13, 1980, added two new elements to the stand previously adopted: on the one hand, the explicit mention not only of Palestinian people but also of the PLO which "with all other interested parties should be involved in the negotiations"; and on the other hand, the notable decision to "make the necessary contacts with all the parties concerned. The objectives of these contacts would be to ascertain the position of the various parties with respect to the principles set out in this declaration and in the light of the results of these consultations to determine the form which such an initiative on their part could take."

In fact subsequent developments in that region, particularly in Lebanon, led to a further series of declarations of principles rather than to proper "European initiatives." Collectively the Twelve continue to adhere to the principles of the Venice Declaration and they never failed to condemn foreign interventions in Lebanon or to condemn Israel's policy in the occupied territories. Nevertheless only France, Great Britain, and Italy have participated along with the United States, in the multinational force in Beirut as they had previously participated in 1981 in the Sinai peacekeeping force. In February 1987, the Twelve called for the holding of an international peace conference under the sponsorship of the United Nations that would convene all the parties concerned about a settlement to the conflict.

As far as the other major conflict of the region is concerned, that is, the Iran-Iraq war, and its threat to free circulation in the Gulf, the position of the Twelve combines the individual initiatives of member-states (dispatching of warships) and a collective support of the United Nations peace efforts. They thus supported, in 1987, Security Council resolution 598 calling for a cease-fire and providing for eventual sanctions against the belligerents.

Thanks to the EPC, the EC member-states succeeded in creating at the UN the impression of being a united, coherent, and efficient group. Since 1973 they have coordinated their actions at the General Assembly of the United Nations by means of close and frequent consultations. From 1975 onwards, the acting president of the Community has presented the Community's position on the problems under discussion. One must admit, however, that their voting behavior has not always lived up to their declared ambitions. On the whole the percentage of resolutions voted unanimously by the Nine rose from 36 percent in 1973 to 57 percent in 1979. It then decreased after 1981 (notably because of Greece's diverging position) and rose again to about 41.5 percent in 1985. One must also note that the questions dividing the Europeans are often of greater significance than the questions leading to a common attitude. Such is the case in votes regarding decolonization, apartheid, the question of Palestine, and the banning of nuclear tests. Nevertheless progress has been made. Since 1977, no member-state voted in favor of a resolution openly criticizing one of its European partners.

The previous discussion demonstrates the progress as well as the limits of the Twelve's role on the international scene. Europe has succeeded in complementing its economic weight with a relative political presence, but it does so through a mainly "declaratory" diplomacy. But even this policy has its limits. Since they are not compelled by any binding rule to reach an agreement, which would entail the acceptance of majority views by the minority, the Europeans, instead of speaking with one voice, are sometimes without any voice at all!

Development Policy: From Regionalism to Globalism?

In the domain of cooperation and development, the EC is generally given credit for its positive achievements. For the past fifteen years Europe (the Community plus the member-states) has been the largest provider of official development aid: In 1986, 0.51 percent of its GNP, while the U.S. and Japan have granted only 0.29 percent and 0.23 percent of their GNP. In addition, by obtaining the status of observer at the UN in 1975 and in several specialized institutions, the United Nations Conference on Trade and Development (UNCTAD), for example, the EC became more directly involved in the search for a new international economic order, which is of particular concern to it.

Having an open and dependent economy, the Community became aware of its extreme vulnerability in 1973 as a result of the oil crisis and the solidarity established between OPEC and the Third World. Thereafter it systematically tried to avoid the confrontation between industrialized and developing countries.

The EC did not start from scratch in this search for a "new order." Geography and a colonial past have woven close ties between Europe and its natural zone of influence: the Mediterranean and Africa. As far as the Community was concerned these ties began to materialize in the 1960s: Yaoundé conventions with the Francophone African countries, first accords with Israel, the Maghreb countries, and so forth. From 1973 onward, the agreements became more numerous and diverse and broadened their scope so as to include trade provisions as well as new aids to development. The Community's first enlargement in 1973 led its member-states to seek a "global and balanced" Mediterranean policy for two reasons. On the one hand, the EC wanted to harmonize the mosaic of existing relations so as to avoid the Mediterranean partners' attempt to outbid each other. On the other hand, the Nine attempted to contribute to the peace and stability of the region by facilitating its economic development and offering the different parties a privileged relationship with the EC.

This policy was proposed to the Mediterranean countries plus Portugal and Jordan. It aimed at progressively creating a free trade area between each of them and the EC and also provided for some financial and technical cooperation. A series of accords has been concluded since 1974; Libya and Albania are the only countries to have declined the Community's proposals. The accords are not identical. Turkey is excluded from the global approach because of its status of *associate* and of its intention of joining the EC in the future (as Greece did). The other Mediterranean countries are linked to the Community by preferential agreements which in the case of Cyprus and Malta could lead to full customs union.

The entry of Spain and Portugal into the EC led the Community to revise existing accords so as to take into account the new conditions created by this enlargement and to assure that traditional exchanges would be upheld. Negotiated accords (or those currently under negotiations) provide Mediterranean countries free access, that is, without customs duties, for their industrial products into the market of the Twelve, customs concessions in the agricultural sector, and financial aid in the form of grants (1.618 million ECU for 1987–1990) and of loans from the European Investment Bank.[14]

It is, however, the Lomé Convention that constitutes the most complete and elaborate form of the EC's development policy. Britain's entry broadened the scope of the European development policy, which has been extended to ACP countries (African, Caribbean, and Pacific).

A first convention covering the period from 1975 to 1980 was followed by a second one. A third one, still in force, and covering the period from 1985 to 1990 links sixty-six countries to the Community. The Lomé system is based on three essential provisions: free access to the Community market for 99.5 percent of the ACP exports, a scheme of export earnings stabilization for agricultural products (and to a lesser degree for mineral resources) and significant financial aid (8.5 million ECU). Mechanisms of industrial and technical cooperation are also provided.[15]

In the case of countries depending on the exports of only one or a few commodities, the commercial dispositions alone, as positive as they may be, had to be complemented. The convention thus provides a mechanism—*Stabex*—to deal with wide fluctuations of world prices or natural disasters. A similar though less ambitious system is also applied to mineral resources: *Sysmin*. In addition one of Lomé's original features is to give preferential treatment to the poorest ACP countries: twenty-two of the thirty-one least developed countries according to UN standards benefit from the convention.

This system has been criticized. The ACP countries have complained that aid is insufficient compared to their needs and that the amounts allocated to Stabex are too small. It should be noted, however, that, in constant value, the EC has maintained the level of its transfers to the ACP countries while other official aid development donors have reduced their contributions. Other critics consider that this kind of cooperation prevents the genuine take-off of the ACP countries by perpetuating an unfair international division of labor. Conversely, the Lomé Agreement has also been accused of attempting to reproduce a Western model of development while neglecting the satisfaction of basic needs.

Nevertheless, the merits of the system that has been established are not negligible. First of all, this cooperation has got rid of its remaining colonial features since the Community no longer requires reciprocal pref-

[14]ECU = Monetary European Unit. In January 1986, $1 US = 1.13 ECU; in January 1987, 0.932 ECU; in late December 1987, 0.771 ECU.

[15]Boardman, R., T. Shaw, and P. Soldatos, eds., *Europe Africa and Lomé III* (Lanham, Md.: University Press of America, 1985).

erences. Secondly, by respecting the diversity of the regimes and ideologies at hand, it has emphasized a much appreciated nonaligned perspective. Lastly, the Lomé Conventions must be evaluated in terms of their contributions to the search for a new economic order. In spite of all its shortcomings, they can be considered if not as a model, at least as something concrete in the North-South dialogue, at a time when this is more the subject of diagnosis and resolutions than of contractual engagements. It should also be noted that the priority given to the poorest countries follows the recommendations of the UN and of its specialized institutions. While developing special relations with the ACP countries the Community has also enlarged its aid for development to include other groups of countries. Although limited, if compared with the Lomá provisions, this aid has steadily grown and has even doubled in ten years. Countries of Latin America have been the main beneficiaries of this relative deployment. There is no doubt that the Community per se cannot resolve the major problem of these countries, their external debt. But the EEC has taken steps to facilitate their exports as well as to increase its financial aid. It has thus developed both its network of nonpreferential agreements with various countries (Brazil, Mexico, Argentina, and Uruguay) and its relations with regional groupings. For example, in 1983, a framework agreement was signed on commercial and economic cooperation with the Andean Pact (Bolivia, Colombia, Ecuador, Peru, and Venezuela). This agreement aims to promote, diversify and improve trade and to stimulate industrial and scientific cooperation. In 1985, a cooperation agreement was also concluded between the EC and the countries that had signed the General Treaty on Central American Economic Integration (Costa Rica, Guatemala, Honduras, Nicaragua, and El Salvador) plus the additional country of Panama.

Most of the EC's financial aid to Latin American goes through the channels provided by these agreements. In 1985, the volume of Community aid to Latin America was more than 147 million ECU,* 60 million of which was for South America and 88 million for Central America.

In Asia, nonpreferential agreements have been concluded with the countries of the Indian subcontinent (Bangladesh, India, Pakistan, and Sri Lanka) as well as with China and ASEAN. Some financial aid has also been given to the poorest countries. As with Latin America a variety of sectorial agreements cover trade in textiles and craft goods.

Finally it should also be noted that since July 1971 all developing countries export industrial goods to the EC on a customs-free basis through the Generalized Preferences Scheme.

The Transatlantic Misunderstandings

The United States encouraged European integration from the beginning but with a particular type of Europe in mind. They have precise

---

*The exchange rate of the ECU varies. In 1988 it was worth about $1.18.

ideas as to the policies that it should implement, as to its international role and as to its ties with the United States. It was precisely this vision of an "Atlantic Community" that de Gaulle adamantly opposed. After the failure of Kennedy's grand design of a proposed partnership, the United States witnessed the strengthening of European unity with mixed feelings. The EC has effectively become an economic competitor as well as an international actor whose initiatives sometimes thwart American aspirations to Western leadership.

Recurrent crises have marked Euro-American relations for the past fifteen years.

Once the Nixon administration came to power, the tolerance shown towards European policies, in the name of acceptance of wider objectives of European unification, yielded to a harder attitude. The latter, however, was still confined, at first, to obtaining concessions from what was considered to be a formidable economic competitor. In the context of the Nixon Round, sharp criticism was turned against the Common Agricultural Policy, and also in particular against the policy and association that the Community extended to African and Mediterranean countries.

The mistrust caused by the first results of the political cooperation of the Nine was added to these grievances. A noticeable cohesion between the members of the EEC did indeed become apparent. That cohesion took the form of reservations voiced in connection with the new "*Atlantic Charter*" project proposed by Mr. Kissinger to establish new and more comprehensive relations between the U.S.A. and Europe. The display of independence exhibited by the Europeans in the conduct of their Middle Eastern policy aggravated this situation. The refusal to facilitate the routing of American military supplies to Israel, the ambition to play a role in the settlement of the conflict, the adoption in this context of a declaration on European identity, and finally the opening of a Euro-Arab dialogue spurred Washington to harden its attitude.

Europe's vulnerability in the fields of energy and security enabled the United States to limit European aspirations for independence. On the one hand the Europeans obtained, in February 1974, the setting up of a sort of cartel of consumers which was to give birth to the International Energy Agency. On the other hand, given divergences among European partners on the desirability to resist American pressure, the U.S. government obtained the assurance that the United States would be informed prior to any international initiative taken by the Europeans. It is true that President Nixon had, in a letter to the President of the Community, alluded to the consequences for America's defence of Europe a refusal could bring. When the Euro-Arab dialogue finally took place, in 1975, it fell short of the Europeans' expectations to deal with the oil supply and the issues in the region.

Thereafter the Europeans showed little enthusiasm for the Camp David agreement which, in their views, left the Palestinian problem unsolved. Under Jimmy Carter's presidency this played a role in the efforts towards a Middle East settlement, demonstrated by the Venice Declaration, and caused friction and mutual irritation. Europe's weak support of America during the hostage-taking incident in Iran did not improve matters.

Under the Reagan administration and up to a recent date, the crises of détente (Afghanistan and Poland) and the hardening of American policy towards the USSR also affected Euro-American relations. In this context economic relations with the Soviet bloc were another matter of dispute between the United States and Europe after the worsening of East-West relations following events in Poland. On June 18, 1982, Ronald Reagan decided to extend the embargo on pipeline equipment destined to the USSR to include materials produced under American license abroad. This was done without prior consultation of his allies. The reasons invoked ranged from the fear of excessive European dependence on Soviet energy (because of the gas contracts signed with the USSR) to the will to react to the imposition of martial law in Poland. Given the European countries' refusal to comply, the embargo was finally lifted in mid-November. Nevertheless, this incident illustrates the fundamental differences between the United States and Europe on East-West relations and on Europe's degree of autonomy. Interests and perceptions differed on the situation in Europe as well as on events outside the Alliance. While the United States primarily emphasized the need for a global effort to contain Soviet expansionism, the Europeans contest that all conflicts (in Latin America or in the Middle East for example) were part of the global East-West confrontation. In the light of their own interests, and of Germany's particular situation, they strove at preserving détente as much as they could. As a result they refused to use trade as a political arm against the Soviet Union—even after events in Afghanistan and Poland—and tried to pursue cooperation with the East. They also advocated a greater understanding towards the Third World and the local conflicts in Central America. In this case the Twelve's support of the Contadora peace initiative illustrates the difference of approach between Europeans and Americans.

In the economic field, in spite of all the negotiations and procedures which deal with the international economic crisis (Western summits, GATT, OECD, IMF, and so forth) strong tensions persist in the relations between the EC and the United States, particularly as far as trade is concerned. The Community is America's first commercial partner. In 1985, 22 percent of its exports were destined to the United States and 17 percent of its imports came from the United States. But these figures must not be misinterpreted. The positive balance in a sector where the EEC usually showed a deficit only appeared in 1984 and was essentially due to the high rate of the dollar, which has declined recently.

In spite of the fact that the Community has one of the lowest external tariffs in the world this evolution has led to mounting American criticism. The Common Agricultural Policy is the main American target. The United States claims that the Community subsidies create unfair competition for American food exports. The EC's unfailing reply is that European food exports are sold at world prices and that the cost of subsidizing farmers is less in the Community than in the United States. The Europeans also recall that the EC is the largest importer of agricultural goods in the world (20 percent of world imports), that it comes second to the United States for export on the world market (11 percent for Europe versus 15 percent for the United States) and that the United States sells four times more foodstuffs to Europe than it buys.

A certain number of skirmishes during the past ten years attest to American aggressiveness: a policy of ever increasing subsidies (the export enhancement program), protectionist practices (duties quotas), and the insistence that agriculture be included in the next GATT round. Given the near monopoly of the United States on the Spanish and Portuguese cereal markets, it was the entry of these two countries into the Common Market that provoked the gravest difficulties. Washington took the offensive and threatened Europe with 200 percent import duties on cognac, gin, wines, and cheese, if its privileged position were to be challenged by the enlargement. For its part, the Community prepared retaliatory measures against several American products. Commercial war was avoided, at the last moment, by an agreement concluded in early 1987 and providing for a fifty-fifty share of the Iberian market between the EC and other competitors, including the United States.

In the industrial sector, the American commercial deficit revived U.S. protectionist tendencies because many sectors had suffered from foreign competition due to the high level of the dollar. For example, under pressure from its steel industry, the United States sought to reduce European steel imports. After the Community agreed, in August 1982, to voluntarily restrain its exports in order to avoid a severe import duty, a new offensive was launched against European exports of special steels. In January 1985, as a result of a new self-limitation agreement regarding steel tubes, the European share of the American market dropped from 14 percent in 1984 to 7.6 percent. Washington also launched an offensive against the European Airbus plane accused of receiving European governments' subsidies.

New tensions have recently appeared in transatlantic relations. Given the asymmetrical interdependence resulting from the U.S. preponderance both in security (the American nuclear guarantee) and in monetary affairs (the predominance of the dollar), Europe discovered its vulnerability to sudden changes coming from the other side of the Atlantic. In the economic and monetary domain, which is of capital importance to the Community, the excessive variations of the American currency—

either its rise or its decline—posed serious problems to the European countries. Some years ago, the high interest rates designed to curb inflation and which led the dollar to rise, weighed upon European economies and, by increasing their energy bill, provoked a worsening of the EEC trade deficit. Today the structural causes of the crisis confronting Europe—the American trade and budgetary deficits—are not new but have caused sharp market fluctuations.

In addition to the risk of recession after the collapse of the financial market the dramatic fall of the dollar provoked tensions within the European monetary system due to the sharp rise of the mark. To European recriminations against the variations of the dollar, the United States respond by denouncing Europe's permanent dissatisfaction with the rate of the American currency and by emphasizing the responsibility of countries with large commercial surpluses like the Federal Republic of Germany.

Such misunderstandings, on both sides of the Atlantic, have also been heightened by the evolution of the American strategic doctrine and by a certain decline of Europe's confidence in American strategy.[16] A certain malaise was caused by President Reagan's light handed reference to a nuclear war limited to Europe and by uncertainties concerning the American nuclear guarantee. Both the Nunn Amendment (1984) proposing to cut the level of American troops in Europe and the Strategic Defense Initiative, for all the subsequent changes it implies, have deepened this malaise. In spite of their official approval, the recent U.S.–USSR accord for the dismantling of intermediary missiles in Europe (INF) is seen by many Europeans as objectively weakening the Euro-American defense "coupling" and as proof of the increasing divergence of strategic interests between Europe and the United States in important security areas.

CONCLUSION

It is difficult to answer clearly the question we raised: Does the EC truly have its own foreign policy? Several points should be considered.

Europe's "presence" on the international scene remains questionable. The Twelve have not yet developed a sufficiently coherent approach in their external activity. In spite of the proclaimed will to bridge the gap, two types of activities prevail: an essentially "declaratory" diplomacy occasionally supported by Community policies on the one hand, and a network of individual policies on the other. It is true that progress to-

---

[16]*The European Community: Progress or Decline?* Joint Report of the directors of five European Institutes of international relations. English Ed. (London: Chatham House, 1983), p. 29.

wards greater coherence has been made and that this objective is reaffirmed in the Single European Act. A frequent reproach addressed to European policy is that it consists only of declarations and reactions to events. Nevertheless on many occasions Europe adopted an operational position, undertook missions, or displayed common initiatives in international organizations. In addition, common policies often implemented the decision adopted within the framework of Political Cooperation. In April 1974, confronted by the erratic character of the first stages of the Portuguese revolution, the EC contributed to the reestablishment of democracy by declaring that it could only accord financial aid to a pluralist democracy. When Great Britain's nine partners took her side in 1982 in the quarrel with Argentina over the Falklands, they imposed an embargo on imports from Argentina. Similarly the adoption, in 1985, of sanctions against South Africa strenghtened the Twelve's antiapartheid stand. One could also cite the freeze of the financial Protocol with Israel (in 1984) following its invasion of Lebanon, or, conversely, the simultaneous increase in the financial aid to Latin America and encouragement of the Contadora peace initiative.

Even though the Single European Act affirms the objective of a European foreign policy, several obstacles remain before the Twelve's foreign policy can be transformed into a true common foreign policy. The impossibility in the present state of European integration of imposing a majority-based decision-making process on states with old diplomatic traditions and sometimes divergent interests constitutes a first obstacle. In many cases what can be achieved by means of consensus, in the framework of EPC, has evident limits. Furthermore, the absence of legal constraints in the harmonization of foreign policies accounts for the fact that individual countries can ultimately prevent the adoption of a common position. During recent years the Greek government has for example often demurred—notably on East-West relations—from the policy adopted in the EPC.

Above all, one of the EPC's most evident limits is that it does not deal with particularly sensitive or fundamental issues. For example it does not include the elaboration of a concerted policy towards the United States or the problems of defense.

It has become common place to affirm that the principal obstacle to a genuine European foreign policy is the absence of joint European defense capabilities. A twofold difference exists between the members of the Community. On the one hand, only two of them—France and Great Britain—have nuclear arms. On the other hand, there are disparities with regard to existing defense organizations. Ireland, with its neutral status, belongs neither to the Western European Union (WEU) nor to the Atlantic Alliance. Spain, Portugal, Denmark, and Greece do not belong to WEU. While remaining members of the Alliance, France and Greece have opted out of NATO's integrated structure. As a result of the 1986 referendum approving its joining the Atlantic Alliance, Spain made the same choice. Because of postwar constraints and the vigilance of the USSR, the Federal Republic of Germany cannot become a nuclear power.

But these structural difficulties are not the only ones and a common European defense clearly requires a convergence of interests and analyses among the different partners. In this regard it must be noted that times have changed. In particular, the nature of relations to be established between Europe and the United States no longer causes France to oppose its EC partners, as was the case until some years ago. The perception of a nonidentity of interests with the United States in numerous domains, including security, is now widely shared. The near conclusion of an accord in Reykjavik in 1986 on the elimination of intermediate nuclear forces in Europe sparked an evolution that will be accelerated by the Treaty signed in Washington in December 1987, all the more so since this latter also provides for the elimination of short range missiles (SRINF). It would seem that European countries, often supported by their public opinions, are now more conscious of the necessity to assume responsibility for the organization of their security and to reinforce the European pillar of the Atlantic Alliance.

Several initiatives attest to this fact. For example, the development of bilateral cooperation of several kinds—between France and Great Britain, the two nuclear powers; between Mediterranean countries (Italy, France, and Spain); and above all between France and the Federal Republic of Germany. The 1963 Treaty provided for such cooperation, but this cooperation was hampered, up to a recent date, by uncertainties concerning the exact degree of solidarity that France would show towards Germany should Germany be attacked. These doubts should be dissipated after the French government declared that France's military commitment would be "immediate and without any reservation" if Germany was to be the victim of an agression, and that "separate battles of Germany or France were not conceivable."[17]

The reactivation of the West European Union is another sign of this European revival.[18] In October 1987, the member-states of this organization adopted a "platform on European security interests" in which they stated the determination "to pursue European integration including security and defence". This text is significant because it is the first time, since

---

17Speech by the French Prime Minister J. Chirac, to the Institut des Hautes Etudes de Défense Nationale, Dec. 12, 1987.

18The fundamental obligation of the WEU Treaty (Article 5) is to "provide all the military and other aid and assistance in our power, in the event of armed attack on any one of us."

the rejection in 1954 of the European Defence Community Treaty, that Europe has renewed the idea of a European defence and places it within the integration process already under way. It also confirms Europe's attachment to the Atlantic Alliance, which remains the foundation of European security and affirms that European defence strategy "must continue to be based on an adequate mix of appropriate nuclear and conventional forces."

The future will tell if this was merely a declaration of intent or the first step towards a European defense, a prerequisite of a true European foreign policy.

FOREIGN POLICY LANDMARKS

April 18, 1951	Treaty of Paris establishing the European Coal and Steel Community; Pleven proposes the formation of a European Defense Community (EDC)
August 30, 1954	The proposal for the EDC is defeated in the French National Assembly
March 25, 1957	The Treaty of Rome establishes the European Economic Community and the European Atomic Energy Community
January 1, 1958	The Treaty of Rome comes into effect
July 7, 1961	Signature in Athens of an "Agreement of Association" between Greece and the European Community.
January 14, 1963	De Gaulle rejects the entry of Great Britain into the Community
July 20, 1963	The convention of Yaoundé associates seventeen African states, Madagascar, and the Community
September 12, 1963	Signature of an "association agreement" between Turkey and the European Community.
July 29, 1969	The convention of Yaoundé with eighteen African states
October 27, 1969	First Report of the Foreign Ministers to the Heads of State and Government on European Political Cooperation (Luxembourg Report)
January 1, 1973	England, Ireland, and Denmark become members of the European Community
July 23, 1973	Second Report of the Foreign Ministers on European Political Cooperation (Copenhagen Report)
December 14, 1973	Document on the "European Identity" published by the foreign ministers
December 9–10, 1974	Conference of the Heads of State in Paris decides to institutionalize meeting of Heads of States, formation of "European Council"
February 29, 1975	Signature of the first Lomé convention between the European Economic Community and forty-six Third World countries (African, Pacific, and Caribbean)
March 10, 1979	Creation of the European Monetary System

June 7–10, 1979	First election of the European Assembly by direct universal election (410 members)
October 31, 1979	Signature of the convention Lomé II between the European Community and fifty-eight Third World countries.
June 12–13, 1980	Declaration by the European Council, in Venice, on the situation in the Middle-East
January 1, 1981	Greece becomes a member of the European Community
October 13, 1981	London Report on European Political Cooperation
April 2, 1982	After the invasion by Argentina of the Falklands, the Ten express their support for England
June 19, 1983	Solemn Declaration on European Union by the European Council in Stuttgart
June 14–17, 1984	Second election of the European Parliament (434 members)
December 8, 1984	Signature of the Convention Lomé III between the European Community and sixty-six Third World countries
January 1, 1986	Spain and Portugal become members of the European Economic Community
April 14, 1987	Demand of Turkey to become a member of the European Economic Community
July 1, 1987	The Single European Act is adopted

SELECTED BIBLIOGRAPHY

Background Documentation

Bulletin of the European Community (monthly), EEC Information Office, Brussels; *Agence Europe* (daily in English), Brussels.

Books

ALLEN, D., R. RUMMEL and W. WESSELS eds. *European Political Cooperation.* London: Butterworth, 1982.

BOURRINET, J. *Le Dialogue Euro-Arabe.* Paris: Economica, 1979.

BURROWS, B. and G. EDWARDS. *The Defence of Western Europe.* London: Butterworth, 1982.

FELD, W. *Western Europe's Global Reach: Regional Cooperation and Worldwide Aspirations.* New York: Pergamon Press, 1980.

GROSSER, A., ed. *Les Politiques Extérieures Européennes Dans la Crise.* Paris: Presses de la Fondation Nationale des Sciences Politiques, 1976.

GROSSER, A., ed. *The Western alliance: European-American Relations since 1945.* New York: Vintage Books, 1982.

HANRIEDER, W., ed. *The United States and Western Europe: Political, Economic and Strategic Perspectives.* Cambridge, Mass.: Winthrop, 1974.

HILL, C., ed. *National Foreign Policies and European Political Cooperation.* London: RIIA and Allen & Unwin, 1983.

KAISER, K. *L'Europe et les Etats-Unis.* Paris: R. Laffont, 1973.

KAISER, K., C. MERLINI, T. de MONTBRIAL, E. WELLENSTEIN, and W. WALLACE. *The European Community: Progress or Decline?* London: Chatham House Royal Institute of International Affairs, 1983.

MOREAU-DEFARGES, P. *L'Europe et Son Identité dans le Monde.* Paris: Editions Sciences et Techniques Humaines, 1983.

MORGAN, R. *High Politics, Low Politics: Toward a Foreign Policy for Western Europe.* Washington Papers, II, Beverly Hills, Calif. and London: Sage, 1973.

PALMER, J. *Europe without America? The Crisis in Atlantic Relations.* Oxford: Oxford University Press, 1987.

SCHOUTHEETE, P. *La Coopération Politique Européenne.* Brussels: Labor, 1986.

SHONFIELD, A. *Europe: Journey to an Unknown Destination.* London: Penguin Books, 1973.

SJOSTEDT, G. *The External Role of the European Community.* Farnborough, England: Saxon House, 1977.

TAYLOR, P. *The Limits of European Integration.* New York: Columbia University Press, 1983.

TSOUKALIS, L. *Europe, America and the World Economy.* Oxford: Basil Blackwell, 1986.

WALLACE, H., W. WALLACE, and C. WEBB, eds. *Policy Making in the European Community,* 2d Ed. London: Wiley, 1983.

Reviews

Special issue of the *Etudes Internationales,* No. 1, March 1978, "Les relations extérieures de la Communauté Européenne," Centre Québécois des Relations Internationales, Université Laval, Québec.

Special issue of the *Journal of Common Market Studies,* "The European Community, Past, Present and Future," Vol. XXI, No. 1 and 2, September–December 1982.

9

Dimensions of the
Middle East Problem

Nadav Safran

INTRODUCTION

The Middle East problem is often mistakenly equated with the Arab-Israeli conflict. Actually, notwithstanding the eruption of half-a-dozen Arab-Israeli wars in thirty-five years, that conflict is only one manifestation of a more complex problem, the roots of which go back at least two centuries to the time when the Ottoman and Persian rulers could no longer defend their empires. The essence of what was then called "the Eastern Question" was the same as that of the present Middle East problem: the weakness of the area and its importance for rival outside powers. The organization of the area has since changed, as the Ottoman and Persian empires gave way to a multitude of independent states; the meaning of "weakness" altered, as the use of military power for imperial expansion became constrained; the identity of the rival outside powers competing in the region has shifted several times; and the interests of even the latest set of rival powers have evolved over the years. Yet, the combination of the factors of regional weakness, the importance of the area, and intervention by rival outside powers has remained constant.

    In the configuration it has assumed since World War II, the Middle East problem may be viewed as consisting of four distinct but interacting problems, or as a problem with four dimensions: (1) the domestic dimension, relating to internal weaknesses of the countries of the area; (2) the regional dimension, referring to problems in the relations among countries of the area apart from the Arab-Israeli conflict; (3) the Arab-Israeli conflict; and (4) the Great Powers involvement.

Each of these four dimensions has had its own particular dynamic and has also been influenced by developments in the other dimensions. Further, complicating the picture, the new issue of oil has become intertwined with each component. At various times in recent history, one or another dimension of the problem has tended to occupy the center of attention; but in all instances all four dimensions were in varying degrees relevant to understanding the problem in its totality.

The purpose of this chapter is to set out briefly, almost in outline form, a "Political map" of the Middle East problem, to sketch out the particular dynamic of each component and its relationship with the other dimensions, and to conclude with a brief assessment of the configuration they have together assumed in recent months. The tangled web to be weaved may not necessarily point to a solution for the Middle East problem; but it will hopefully serve as a guide to realistic thinking about it and enhance attempts to manage it now and in the future.

THE DOMESTIC DIMENSION

While each Middle Eastern state faces its own particular domestic problems, which will be discussed below, all of the states of the region are experiencing the problem of transition from a traditional to a modern societal order. There are many versions of just what that problem is, specifically; from our point of view it is not important which formulation one chooses. The relevant point is that they all spell domestic instability arising from social cleavages and a lack of consensus on political structures and values. Stated bluntly, social transition is a difficult and dislocative process, accompanied by tension, conflict, and violence.

In the case of Middle Eastern societies, there are special circumstances which make the problem of transition particularly acute. First, the traditional social order of these societies (except Israel) rested on an Islamic belief system which was particularly resistant to adaptive change. In order to preserve the most absolute unity, omnipotence, and omniscience for God, Islamic doctrine eliminated the idea of causation from the universe and from history, and utterly subsumed reason to revelation. There was thus no room for any notion of natural law or philosophy of history, empirical sciences or progress through human agency. Knowledge and virtue were seen as specifically defined in the divinely revealed law; conformity to that law provided the only assurance of the good society and the good man.

Second, the change that ushered in the transition period in the Middle East was not autonomously generated; it was not as in the West the result of internal processes that departed from the traditional order and pressed for its revision from within. Rather, the change that set the transition stage in motion was imposed by the rulers from above in response to military challenges from the outside.

In order to protect their realms against Western pressures, the Ottoman sultans and autonomous local leaders like Muhammad Ali in Egypt tried to emulate those features of Western society believed to be the source of its military prowess. They began by adopting Western military technology and methods of administration, and went on with economic and legal reforms which undermined without destroying the system based upon Islamic tradition, still considered valid and strong by the great bulk of its adherents. There was thus created a legitimacy gap between rulers and ruled, with no indigenously generated middle class whose interests and occupations disposed it to strive for a new world outlook, and designated it to be the agent of social transformation. The modernizing lawyers, military officers, bureaucrats, and intellectuals whom the reforms from above called forth did not form such a class. They were an extension of the state, which they sometimes took over by means of the armed forces. They carried further the process of borrowing from outside, and thus further widened the gap between the rulers and the ruled. As a result there have often arisen fundamentalist movements based on visions of a utopian Islamic polity which in fact never existed. Today's Iran is only the most recent, and most politically successful, manifestation of this phenomenon.

Third, geography and history have combined to make particularly difficult the integration of Middle Eastern societies on the basis of the nation-state principle. Throughout history, the political units of the area were organized on the basis of religion, rather than on territory or any political principle. Even the Greeks and Romans, when they controlled the area, had to adapt their customs to utilize the religious principle of organization. The reason is that the area from the Atlantic Ocean to the Persian Gulf is extremely cut up, consisting basically of a vast desert and mountainous regions interspersed with oases and strips of fertile land. All the current states in the region (with the exception of Iran, Egypt, and perhaps Tunisia) have therefore had no previous political existence in the territory they now occupy; they were largely created by Western imperialism. Consequently, during most of their political independence, their legitimacy has often been questioned by unintegrated groups within their borders, and by Arab nationalists seeking Arab political unity. (Though with the passage of time there is evidence of growing acceptance of the legitimacy of the states as they now exist.)

Finally, if one takes the region as a whole, one notices that the problem of transition is manifested in greatly varying degrees, with societies standing at widely separated positions on the continuum between tradition and modernity. This is a consequence of the geographical discontinuities of the region, which also led to different degrees of exposure of these societies to outside threats, and to their coming under the rule of different colonial powers. Thus, at one end of the continuum Egypt has been coping with the transition process for nearly two hundred years, while at the other end Saudi Arabia has been doing so for barely twenty.

These problems are common to all Middle Eastern states, save Israel. Yet each also has major specific problems which blend with the general ones and exacerbate the difficulties of achieving a stable domestic order.

Very briefly, here are the problems facing the individual countries at present and their recent internal record:

Egypt. A very poor population-to-resources ratio. Tremendous pressure of unchecked population growth and a continuing migration from the countryside to already bursting cities. An agricultural base which is contracting rather than expanding. An industrialization program choked by a bureaucratic incubus, which has not kept pace with the demands for employment.

Internal record since 1945: liberal democracy destroyed; monarchy overthrown; massive riots (three instances); coups and coup attempts (three instances); leaders assassinated (three instances).

Syria. Regionally fragmented by history and geography with resultant instability. Since 1970, ruled by a small group of military officers from the minority Alawite sect (about 15 percent of the total Syrian population). Increasing opposition from the majority Sunni Moslem community, spearheaded by the fundamentalist Muslim Brotherhood.

Internal record since 1945: liberal-democratic republic destroyed; union with Egypt and secession; popular revolts (three instances); coups and coup attempts (twenty instances?); leaders assassinated (twelve instances?).

Lebanon. Extreme sectarian fragmentation that has prevented any form of social cohesion save uneasy compromise among the autonomous groups. Recent intrusion of the Palestinian and Arab-Israeli issues into the country, fracturing the tenuous social compromise and leading to the civil war which began in 1975 and continues today.

Internal record since 1945: civil war (two instances); leaders assassinated (countless instances).

Iraq. Problem of political integration in a state which lacks any historical political tradition. Compounded by the extreme ethnic-sectarian fragmentation of the population (approxirnately 50 percent Shi'ite Muslims concentrated in the south; 30 percent Sunni Moslems, who now rule, in the center and northwest; and 20 percent Kurds in the northeast).

Internal record since 1945: liberal democracy destroyed; monarchy overthrown; revolts (two instances); Kurdish war (fourteen years); coups and coup attempts (a dozen instances); leaders assassinated (countless instances).

Saudi Arabia.   Underpopulated state with far-flung frontiers in an environment which has been historically inhospitable to centralized rule. Strains of rapid development on a traditional social and political system. Special problems include the presence of large numbers of foreign workers, strains within the modern state structure (traditional elements versus new bureaucracy, Army versus National Guard), and the possibility of dissension in the large royal family.

Internal record since 1945: one king deposed, one assassinated; revolts (at least two instances); attempted coups (four known instances).

Libya.   Vast, underpopulated, yet oil-rich state, lacking any historical political tradition or contemporary sense of national identity. Headed by a maverick leader possessed by a sense of mission (a blend of Arabism and Islam) who is prepared to use all means to advance his cause.

Internal record since 1945: Monarchy overthrown; attempted coups (several instances); leaders assassinated (countless instances).

Jordan.   Typical artifical creation of Western imperialism. Poor resource-to-population ratio. Depends upon, and makes good use of, extensive Western and Saudi help. Tension between Palestinian and native Jordanian elements, potentially ignitable by outside Palestinian and other elements. Jordan neither can solve nor can avoid involvement in the Arab-Israeli conflict. Problem of control over West Bank of the Jordan River.

Internal record since 1945: king assassinated; civil war; massive riots; leaders assassinated (three instances).

Iran.   Traditional empire historically governed by strong military ruler through compromise with local influentials. Shah's suppression of local elements left him to face alone an alienated population and revolution. Need to reconstruct a legitimate political order and viable economic base out of the turmoil of the revolution.

Internal record since 1945: monarch overthrown, restored, overthrown; total revolution; mass riots; revolts; assassination of leaders (countless instances).

Israel. Formerly fragmented political system becoming largely polarized along communal lines (European-origin versus oriental Jews). Sharp differences between two major parties over destiny of the country and future of occupied territories blends with communal problem. Explosive issue of relation between state and religion unresolved. Increasing economic dependence on the U.S.; massive inflation. Potentially troublesome Arab minority problem.

Internal record since 1948: local riots on religious or ethnic grounds (a dozen instances?); resort to anti-Arab terror by extremists.

THE REGIONAL DIMENSION

In the summer of 1982, the Middle East region was the scene of two wars, one in Lebanon involving Israel against Syria and the PLO, and the other at the head of the Persian Gulf, between Iran and Iraq. The latter war had been going on for nearly two years entirely independently of the hostilities in Lebanon and of the Arab-Israeli conflict. Moreover, with Iran's invasion of Iraq after expelling its forces from Iranian territory, the Gulf war appeared to hold potential international consequences at least as momentous as any arising out of the Arab-Israeli problem.

Yet the Gulf war is only the most recent illustration of regional conflicts apart from the Arab-Israeli issue. For much of the period since the end of foreign rule after World War II, the Middle East was raked by conflicts and strains among the Arab countries, centering on the issue of pan-Arabism. While that issue has often been intertwined with the Arab-Israeli conflict, it has had its own roots and dynamics, which have often interacted with the politics of the big powers to produce strains and crises independently of the Israeli factor. These strains and crises are illustrated by the following summary record of actions taken in the last three decades by the Arab countries under discussion in the name of pan-Arabism:

Egypt at one time or another attempted to instigate or support revolution in Syria, Lebanon, Iraq, Jordan, Saudi Arabia, Yemen, and Libya. It deployed troops against Arab opponents in Syria, Iraq, Kuwait, the Sudan, Yemen, and Algeria. Its armed forces engaged in hostilities against the Yemeni royalists, Saudi Arabia, and Libya.

Syria attempted to instigate rebellion in Iraq, Jordan, Lebanon, and North Yemen. It deployed troops against Arab opponents in all those countries, and engaged in hostilities against Jordan, the Yemeni royalists, and the leftist-PLO forces in Lebanon as well as their rightist-Christian opponents.

Iraq attempted to instigate rebellion in Jordan, Syria, the Gulf emirates, Saudi Arabia, and North Yemen. It deployed forces against Jordan, Syria, and Kuwait, and used force against the latter.

Jordan deployed forces against Iraq (in Kuwait), Syria, and the Yemeni republicans, and used its armed forces against the PLO and Syria.

Saudi Arabia attempted to instigate rebellion and political assassination in Syria, Jordan, Egypt, North Yemen, and South Yemen. It deployed troops against Arab opponents in Jordan and Kuwait, and engaged in hostilities by proxy against the Egyptians in Yemen, and by proxy as well as directly against South Yemen.

Libya attempted to instigate rebellion and political assassination in practically every Arab country, deployed forces against Egypt and Tunisia, and used proxy forces against the latter.

Pan-Arabism may be empirically described as an idea and a movement that recognize a close affinity among the Arab peoples and seek to give that affinity a meaningful political expression. In an immediate sense, the problem of pan-Arabism has been twofold. First, Arab governments and politically relevant groups have differed sharply as to the significance of that affinity and the form of the political expression into which it should be translated. Ideas on the subject have ranged all the way from conceptions which sought to achieve voluntary cooperation among sovereign states on particular shared interests to notions which viewed the Arab peoples from the Atlantic Ocean to the Persian Gulf (or rather the Arab Gulf) as constituting one nation, and sought to bring about their integral political unification.

Second, even within the framework of one conception, there have been sharp rivalries and conflicts over particular issues of policy and tactics and over leadership of the movement. In the 1940s and 1950s, for instance, when the notion of pan-Arabism as voluntary cooperation prevailed, there were clashes between state groupings centered on Cairo and Baghdad. When the more comprehensive notion of pan-Arabism gained ascendancy in the 1950s and 1960s, there were no less sharp clashes between, for example, Nasser and Qassem, Nasser and the Ba'th, the Syrian and the Iraqi Ba'th, and Qaddafi and sundry others.

From a broader perspective, however, the problem of pan-Arabism has been rooted in the balance between the real impulses that have driven it and the obstacles that have obstructed it. That balance has generated a force that was strong enough to raise aspirations beyond the level of cooperation, yet not sufficently strong to support integral unity, giving rise to a situation wherein various parties have felt entitled to meddle in the affairs of the others in the name of Arab unity, without any of them being able to enforce such unity on the others.

The real impulses for unity have included the following:

1. The absence of a heritage of distinct political identity among all but one or two of the twenty-two countries which are members of the Arab League (the exceptions being Egypt and possibly Tunisia). This disposed the peoples of those countries to receptivity to the notion of an all-embracing Arab identity.

2. Unity of religion, and a tradition, already alluded to, of viewing religious affiliation, rather than territory or anything else, as the principle of political organization.

3. A certain degree of unity of language. Not the spoken Arabic, which is fragmented into various regional dialects, which in some instances defy intercommunication, but the classical language, whose uniformity has been preserved thanks to the Qoran and the classics, and increasingly the modern literate Arabic promoted by the media.

4. A certain sense of unity of historical experience and of aspiration. Not a concrete, specific common history, and shared particular objectives—today's Arab states and peoples have had very different histories for many centuries and there is little agreement among them on particular ideologies, the nature of the state, and the ideal social order. There is, rather, a common psychological experience of certain major historic moments and a common psychological urge derived from them. One of these is the sense that Muhammad's mission, marking the birth of Islam among the Arabs and its rapid spread through their conquests, constituted a related set of events of cosmic importance—a *kairos*. Another is a sense of shock—a *trauma*—caused by the subjugation of the Arab and Muslim lands by infidels, contrary to the right order of things. Related to the preceding is a shared urge to heal that trauma and achieve a purgation of the emotions—a *catharsis*—by reasserting Arab-Muslim power against the infidel oppressor.

These impulses have provided a very strong but rather inchoate sense of unity, lacking both a focus on a particular, commonly desired end and a shared view of means. On the other hand, the obstacles in the way of unity, most of which have already been mentioned or alluded to, have been hard and concrete. They include the following:

1. Geographical discontinuities despite territorial contiguity, and even, in one critical instance caused by the presence of Israel, a lack of territorial contiguity between the western and eastern halves of the Arab world.

2. Different particular histories which, together with the geographical discontinuities, have led to different patterns of development in government, law, education, economic systems, social stratification, military systems, and bureaucracies.

3. Unstable governments unable to commit their constituencies to unity, compounded by the existence of substantial regional, ethnic, and sectarian minorities opposed to being swallowed by a large, inevitably Sunni Muslim Arab state.

4. The development of strong vested interests in and around existing state structures. These interests include the current regimes and groups which benefit from association with them. There has been no matching growth of countervailing groups with vested interests in unity and the ability to sustain abstract emotional-ideological commitment.

Historically, the interplay between impulses and obstacles, and the impact of events, produced a dialectical evolution in the concept of pan-Arabism. In the early 1950s, the dominant concept was voluntary cooperation. Within that framework, Egypt and Saudi Arabia tried to oppose Iraq's endeavor to join what came to be known as the Baghdad Pact and bring Jordan and Syria along. Egypt and Saudi Arabia were prompted by national or regime interests of their own, but they fought the Iraqi proposal in the name of collective Arab interests. When Iraq persisted, Nasser broke new ground in inter-Arab relations by appealing, over the heads of their governments, to the Arab publics concerned in the name of Arab solidarity. His conclusion of an arms deal with the Soviet Union as part of his campaign against the Western-sponsored Baghdad Pact put him in the Arab limelight and started a chain of events which led to his nationalization of the Suez Canal, and his political victory in the 1956 Anglo-Franco-Israeli war against him. By then he was cast in the role of an all-Arab hero, and when, in the following year, Syrian leaders, trapped in an internal political imbroglio, turned to him with a proposal for unity, he could not turn them down. The formation of the United Arab Republic in February 1958 marked the emergence of pan-Arabism as integral unity in opposition to pan-Arabism as mere voluntary cooperation.

Pan-Arabism as integral unity became the dominant concept in the next decade, even though in practice it made no further progress but, rather, suffered several setbacks, including the dissolution of the United Arab Republic in 1961. The setbacks merely led to an intensification of inter-Arab struggles as Nasser simultaneously clashed with rival Iraqi and Syrian proponents of integral unity, and escalated his struggle against opponents of the concept of unity who upheld a more limited concept of cooperation. The latter struggle manifested itself in a bitter war in Yemen between Egypt and a client republican regime on one side, and royalist and tribal forces supported by Saudi Arabia on the other. The war lasted for nearly five years and the hostilities spilled into the border areas of Saudi Arabia and threatened to engulf that country altogether. The conflict ended only when a sudden eruption of the Arab-Israeli conflict brought war, and total defeat, to Egypt and its Syrian and Jordanian allies in June 1967. That war was also a turning point in the evolution of the concept of pan-Arabism.

From 1967 to the present, the concept of pan-Arabism as cooperation regained its dominance; however, its previous clash with the concept of pan-Arabism as unity had endowed it with a new meaning. The principle of respect for sovereignty was restored, but cooperation among the sovereign entities came to be viewed more as an obligation than as a matter of discretion. Moreover, the substance of cooperation was expanded greatly from politics to economics and other spheres, and reached down from the governmental level to embrace people of all classes. This evolution began hesitantly during Nasser's remaining years, as he was caught between the desire to recover his standing as leader of Arab nationalism, and the necessity to accommodate other Arab countries and leaders in order to secure their assistance in recovering Egyptian national and other Arab territories lost in the war. It picked up after Nasser's death as Egypt and, coincidentally, Syria came under the leadership of men whose commitment to cooperation was more credible than Nasser's. The evolution reached its highest point in the 1973 war and its aftermath, as the oil-rich countries led by Saudi Arabia used the "oil weapon" to support the confrontation countries politically, and employed their vastly increased oil-derived wealth to assist them economically. Moreover, the massive expansion of development projects undertaken by the generally underpopulated oil-rich countries created employment opportunities for masses of migrant or guest workers from the poorer Arab countries. A symbiosis of interests thus emerged which, for the first time, provided the basis for enduring cooperation.

The triumph of a higher concept of cooperation subdued but did not obliterate altogether the ideal of integral unity, which Qaddafi has continued to promote and to which Syria and Iraq have paid occasional obeisance. It did not mean the end of inter-Arab conflicts as a major dimension of the Middle East problem. This was clearly demonstrated by the clashes between Sadat and Assad after the former signed the Sinai II agreement with Israel;, by the proxy civil war which many Arab parties fought in Lebanon in 1975–1976; by the breach between Egypt and most of the Arab countries over Egypt's 1979 peace with Israel; by the opposite positions taken by various Arab countries in connection with the Iran-Iraq war; and, most recently, by the mutual accusations in connection with the Lebanon war. The triumph of pan-Arabism as cooperation has merely removed a general, diffuse ground for inter-Arab conflict in the form of the ideal of integral unity, leaving ample room for conflict and for reconciliation on grounds of particular interests and policies.

THE ARAB-ISRAELI DIMENSION

Discussions of the Arab-Israeli conflict are replete with interpretations that attempt to explain it as a moral, psychological, legal, or political "case" abstracted from history. According to these interpretations, the conflict involves two sets of incompatible claims, attitudes, and points of view. On the Arab side, there is the prescriptive right to a land inhabited for more than a thousand years, the right of self-determination, the shock to the dignity of a once-great people seeking to make its place in the modern world, the fear of Israeli expansionism, and the plight of more than one million refugees. On the Israeli side, there is the indissoluble bond to the land that had been the cradle of the Jewish heritage, the urge of Jews barred from the nations of Europe to reconstruct a national life of their own in the land of their ancestors, their internationally recognized right to a share of Palestine, and their struggle for survival as a political entity and a culture.

This abstract approach to the Arab-Israeli conflict may be of some use in suggesting the reservoir of motives from which the parties draw. It is of little use, however, and tends in fact to mislead, in any attempt to understand the concrete unfolding of the problem. It fixes on feelings and emotions to the neglect of changing realities and facts which interact with them and greatly affect their practical implications. It assumes a single set of issues throughout the time in which the problem has existed when in fact these issues have changed and the conflict has evolved through a number of identifiable, critically different stages.

The following outline discussion will center on four such distinct stages: (1) pre-1948; (2) 1948 to 1967; (3) 1967 to 1979; and (4) 1979 to the present. The first three stages, in turn, may be seen in terms of two phases each.

1. The roots of the Arab-Israeli conflict lie in a struggle between the Jewish and Arab communities of Palestine going back some three decades prior to 1948. At issue in that struggle was the validity and meaning of the League of Nations mandate over Palestine which was given to Britain, and which incorporated an earlier promise given by the British government to the Zionist movement in the 1917 Balfour Declaration to support the creation of a Jewish "national home" in Palestine.

(a) The Arabs protested from the outset the terms of the mandate, but their resistance to it was initially weak. It manifested itself in sporadic, local outbursts of violence which the British treated as specific incidents and to which they applied specific remedies. Opposition to the mandate was in fact muted because, until the early 1930s, the threat of the projected Jewish homeland did not seem to be so imminent. Jewish settlers had established many proto-national institutions, but their numbers had grown far more slowly than the Zionist movement had hoped and the Arabs had feared. From the end of World War I through 1932, Jewish immigration averaged about 10,000 a year, bringing the total Jewish population of Palestine to 175,000 at the end of that year. The Arab population at the time was 800,000.

(b) However, Hitler's rise to power the following year and the beginning of Nazi persecution of the Jews released a flood of immigration adding up to some 200,000 in five years, which brought the total number of the Jewish population to 400,000 in 1937. This influx converted the threat of the national home into a clear and present danger and triggered Arab resistance on a national scale for the first time, in the form of a general strike launched and maintained in 1936. In 1937, the British appointed a royal commission to inquire into the entire problem of the mandate and make recommendations. Its report recognized for the first time that what was at issue was a conflict between two national communities contesting the same territory, and indicated partition as the only solution. The British government espoused the proposal after the Jews had intimated their acceptance; but the Arabs rejected partition and from 1937 to 1939 launched a wholesale campaign of sabotage and terror against the British and Jews to resist its application. In response to this violence and in order to placate the Arabs in the face of impending world war, the British tried to promote an agreed settlement at a conference in London that brought together Jewish leaders and leaders of several Arab countries. When the conference failed, the British unilaterally proclaimed their policy in the 1939 White Paper. This imposed severe restrictions on Jewish immigration and land purchases during a ten-year transition period, which would be followed by the establishment of one Palestinian state, controlled by the Arab majority, with constitutional protection for the Jewish minority.

It was now the Zionists' turn to resist. During the first years of World War II, the resistance was confined to promoting "illegal" immigration and settlement; but as the war receded from the Middle East, that resistance assumed, in addition, the form of violent rebellion. By 1947, the combination of Jewish resistance, British exhaustion, world sympathy for the Jews in the wake of the Holocaust, and American pressure led London to hand the Palestine question over to the United Nations. A UN Special Committee on Palestine comprising of representatives of small, disinterested countries, recommended, as the British royal commission a decade before, that Palestine be partitioned into Jewish and Arab states. Once again, the Jews accepted the recommendation and the Arabs rejected it. When the UN General Assembly adopted the proposal in November 1947, the Arabs resorted to force to prevent its application and the Jews responded with force for the opposite end. In the all-out intercommunal war that ensued, the Arabs initially had the upper hand, to such an extent that in March 1948, the United States proposed the shelving of partition and the imposition of a UN trusteeship instead. However, the tide of the war shifted shortly thereafter, and on May 15, 1948, Israel declared its independence. The same day, Egypt, Jordan, Syria, Lebanon, and Iraq marched their armies against the fledgling Jewish state.

2.(a) The improvised army of Israel won the war against the inexperienced, disunited, poorly led, and uninspired Arab armies. The result was a far-reaching modification of the UN partition plan. Israel ended up in control of more territory than had been allocated to it by the plan. The remainder of the territory fell under the control of Jordan (what became known as the West Bank) and Egypt (the Gaza strip). No Palestinian state emerged. Some 700,000 Palestinians fled or were expelled from the Israeli-controlled areas in the course of the fighting and became refugees. After a series of armistice agreements formally ended the war, these issues became the subject of disputes between Israel and its neighbors (as well as among those neighbors themselves). They ostensibly precluded the conclusion of peace treaties to end what had become an international, rather than an intercommunal, conflict.

The failure to resolve the issues left by the 1948 war was not so much due to their inherent intractability as it was due to the lack of any real incentive for the Arabs to make peace. In exchange for the minor border modifications and the return to Palestine of some refugees that peace would have given them, the Arab governments would have had to admit the loss of the war and close the issue of Israel's existence. This would have had severe domestic consequences (both the Egyptian and the Lebanese prime ministers were assassinated for agreeing to sign the armistice agreements). Moreover, the potentially overwhelming Arab military superiority over Israel seduced the Arab leaders into thinking that, in a few years time, they could marshal their forces and reverse the results of 1948. At the same time, those leaders quickly realized that their refusal to conclude formal peace was highly unlikely to bring upon them further military sanctions, because of the external constraints on Israeli actions provided by the UN and the Great Powers. With little to gain and much to lose from peace, and no fear of a resumption of war, a no-peace, no-war situation appeared to the Arab governments to be by far the best option.

The only dissenter among the Arab leaders was King Abdallah of the newly renamed Hashemite Kingdom of Jordan. Peace with Israel would confirm his West Bank gains, legitimize his position in Arab Jerusalem, and bring in vast amounts in compensation payment for the refugees. Abdallah, therefore, entered into secret negotiations with Israel which yielded the core of a Jordanian-Israeli agreement. However, the king was assassinated in 1951 by Palestinian opponents before he felt able to implement the proposed treaty.

In the years after 1948, the Arab governments emphasized to their populations the theme of "continuing conflict" with Israel, and gave it credibility by imposing a total boycott of Israel, encouraging Palestinian incursions, and barring Jews from the Holy Places in Jordanian-controlled East Jerusalem. This atmosphere of hostility lent particular significance to the 1955 Soviet-Egyptian arms deal. Israel took the Arab states at their word, and saw the arms deal as giving them the means to carry out their promise to destroy Israel. Thus Israel participated in the 1956 Suez campaign against Egypt as a preemptive move to change the strategic situation before Egypt could absorb its new arms. To most Arabs, however, 1956 confirmed their suspicions that Israel was a tool of imperialism and an aggressive state seeking to expand its borders. In the Arab-Israeli conflict, the passage of time, which sometimes heals wounds, led only to their festering.

(b) Up to 1958, while the dispute had been bitter and bloody, the issues over which it was formally contested were the residues of the 1948 war: border modifications and the Palestinian refugee problem. However, with Nasser's espousal of the movement for integral Arab unity, the conflict escalated to a "clash of destinies." Israel's existence violated the integrity of the Arab homeland and drove a wedge between its western and eastern halves; removal of that entity became a "necessity" for the realization of Arab nationalism under Egypt's leadership. Paradoxically, however, the 1958–1967 period, during which the issues at stake in the Arab-Israeli conflict assumed these fateful proportions, was also the quietest period in the history of the conflict. Not a shot was fired in anger between Egypt and Israel, and even the Syrian front remained relatively peaceful until the Jadid government came to power in 1966. In part, this was the result of Nasser's absorption with the problems presented by the union with Syria in 1958, its secession in 1961, and his involvement in the Yemen War since 1962, which diverted much of Egypt's military strength to that arena. However, this calm was also an indication of a shift in thinking from the impulsive to the strategic. Seriously seeking the destruction of Israel, Nasser sought to choose the most propitious time for a showdown and to avoid provoking Israel prematurely. But in fact, provoking Israel is what he ended up doing, in May 1967.

On May 14, 1967, Nasser, at Soviet instigation, mobilized and deployed his forces in Sinai to deter an alleged Israeli plan to invade Syria. On the 18th he asked the UN Secretary General to remove the UN forces which had held key positions in Sinai and the Gulf of Aqaba since the end of the 1956 war. On May 22 he proclaimed the Straits of Tiran closed to traffic bound to the Israeli port of Eilat, despite repeated previous warnings by Israel that such an act would be a *casus belli*. On May 29 he declared before the Egyptian National Assembly that the issue in this crisis was not the straits but the "aggression against Palestine" that took place in 1948, and the "complete rights" of the Palestinians. By that time, Nasser had secured the agreement of Jordan to join the Egyptian-Syrian military coalition and to put its forces under the supreme Egyptian command. Other Arab countries, notably Iraq, promised to contribute forces, too, and the Arab oil-producing countries resolved to deny oil to nations that would support Israel.

All available evidence suggests that when Nasser made his first move on May 14 he had not intended to go to war. Yet two weeks later, he was practically begging for it. In that brief span of time, he had convinced himself that all the factors that he deemed necessary for a successful military operation had fallen into place. Israel appeared weaker than he had previously estimated, precisely because it did not respond vigorously to his remilitarization of the Sinai and the closing of the Straits of Tiran. The forces at his command, on the other hand, appeared much stronger as Jordan and other Arab parties rallied to his banner. The United States had toned down its initial strong reaction to the closing of the Straits, indicating that Israel might be isolated from its possible supporter. On the other hand, the Soviets, by encouraging his first moves and then supporting the blockade after the fact, had indicated to him that they either did not fear American reactions or felt capable of neutralizing them.

By the beginning of June 1967, Nasser was ready to absorb an Israeli first strike and then fight the decisive battle. He did not want to forfeit world opinion by acting as the aggressor, or draw the United States in with a blatant attack on Israel. However, the decisive battle proved to be the first strike itself, and in six days the armies of Egypt, Jordan, and Syria were defeated on all fronts.

3.(a) The 1967 war was a turning point in the Arab-Israeli conflict in several respects. First, contrary to many contemporary comments, the Arabs, though decisively defeated, were *not* rendered helpless, as the Soviets quickly rearmed them and increased their own military presence in Egypt. Nevertheless, Nasser's defeat meant the end of the movement for Arab unity under Egyptian leadership and thus resolved the "clash of destinies" in Israel's favor. Second, the capture by Israel of the Sinai, the Golan, and the West Bank injected a new element into the conflict. From 1948 to 1958, the Arab countries had clashed with Israel over the residues of the 1948 War on behalf of the Palestinians; from 1958 to 1967, their rationale for conflict was pan-Arabism. In either phase, they had nothing to gain from peace. Now, Egypt, Syria, and Jordan had something to gain: the recovery of national territories they had lost in the war. This meant that, at least in principle, a bargaining situation emerged for the first time in the Arab-Israeli conflict, and that the conflict became more akin to other international disputes.

A third consequence of the war was the resurgence of the Palestinians as actors in their own right, contesting Palestinian territory against Israel. For a while, this did not alter much the previous picture; but before long the Palestinians, organized in the PLO under new leadership, were to become a major complicating factor, obstructing the conclusion of any actual bargain between Arab states and Israel while being unable to agree among themselves on a position that would permit their being dealt a negotiating hand.

Despite the emergence of a bargaining situation in 1967, no specific deal was struck during the next six years because of lack of symmetry in the parties' assessment of their relative positions at various times. Right after the war, for instance, Israel, confident in its superior military power, was prepared to trade off all of Sinai for a peace treaty with Egypt. Nasser, however, unable to give up entirely his pan-Arab dreams, and hoping to rebuild a military option with Soviet help, did not agree to either a formal peace or a separate deal. The most he was prepared to contemplate was a "political settlement" involving return of all the territories in exchange for arrangements regarding specific issues such as navigation, demilitarization, etc. Jordan was prepared to make peace in exchange for the territory it lost in the war, but Israel was unwilling to relinquish Arab Jerusalem and bits of the West Bank. Syria was opposed to any deal with Israel—the loss of the Golan being not too burdensome immediately—and was primarily interested in preventing Egypt and Jordan from making a separate deal. In these circumstances, UN-sponsored efforts to promote a settlement drifted, and fighting was resumed in the form of a "war of attrition" proclaimed by Nasser in March 1969.

Nasser's strategy was to take advantage of Egypt's numerical superiority in standing forces to put pressure on Israel, while relying on Soviet warnings to deter Israel from mobilizing and launching an all-out assault across the Suez Canal. His aim was to compel Israel to yield to his terms by inflicting on it unbearable losses or by driving a wedge between it and the United States, capitalizing on the latter's concern for its interests in Saudi Arabia and other Arab countries and its desire to avoid confrontation with the Soviets. Israel, however, reacted by successfully using its air power to counter Nasser's advantage in ground forces, and, after sixteen months of grinding and costly fighting, it was Nasser who was forced to relent without attaining his objectives, and it was the Egyptian-Soviet alliance that began to crack.

Nasser died heartbroken in September 1970, one month after he had agreed to an American-mediated cease-fire. Five months later, his successor, Anwar Sadat, formally indicated to UN Ambassador Jarring his willingness to sign a peace agreement with Israel in exchange for the return of all of Sinai. By then, however, Israel, having just come out of a grueling war with a rebuilt Egyptian army, flatly rejected such a deal and insisted on retaining parts of Sinai for security reasons. Secretary of State Rogers, anxious about American interests in Saudi Arabia and elsewhere, and eager to follow up on his success in mediating the end of the war of attrition, tried to put pressure on Israel to negotiate on the basis of Sadat's offer; but President Nixon and National Security Adviser Kissinger held him back. In September 1970, the latter two had engineered with Israel a concerted operation that had saved Jordan from a Soviet-supported Syrian intervention on the side of the PLO. The success of that operation, coming after Israel had foiled Nasser's Soviet-supported war of attrition, had convinced them that a powerful Israel was the most effective check against Soviet encroachment and the best protection for friendly Arab countries. In the absence of military or diplomatic pressure on Israel to move toward Egypt, and with Sadat unable to renounce Egyptian territory, a stalemate set in. To break that stalemate Sadat engineered the 1973 Yom Kippur War.

(b) The 1973 war did finally break the logjam. Thanks to the achievement of an "inconceivable" strategic surprise, the standing and ready forces of Egypt and Syria achieved impressive initial gains against the vastly out-numbered regular and conscript Israeli forces, and disrupted the mobilization of the reserves and the prepared battle plans. Although the Israeli forces were eventually able to reverse the tide and put themselves in a position to win decisively, the losses they suffered in the process were very heavy for Israeli sensitivities. Moreover, because of the way the war opened, it was prolonged beyond anyone's expectations, and this led to the intervention of the Soviet Union and the United States, first to resupply their respective clients through competing airlifts, and then to jointly sponsor a cease-fire order and bring about the end of the fighting before Israel could consummate the total victory that was within its reach. Another critical consequence of the way the war unfolded was that Saudi Arabia and other Arab oil producers brought the "oil weapon" into play two weeks into the war, including the imposition of a total embargo on the United States. All of this created suitable conditions for striking actual deals out of the bargaining situation that originally arose in 1967. The Arabs regained their dignity and no longer feared to negotiate as an inferior, defeated party. Israel was war-weary and less certain that strategic territory was preferable to peace as a means of national security. The United States had an immediate as well as a long-term interest in advancing peace, and had established a measure of credibility as a mediator with Egypt—by saving it from total defeat—and an enhanced credit with Israel—by airlifting supplies to it in its most difficult moment.

The process of working out specific deals proved to be slow and tortuous, and its outcome was incomplete and problematic, yet its effect on the Arab-Israeli conflict was decisive. Before the process could begin, the cease-fire had to be solidified and the entangled forces in the battlefields had to be disentangled. Secretary Kissinger took on this task, and the first Egyptian-Israeli agreement he mediated suggested to him "step-by-step" diplomacy as the way to advance toward comprehensive settlement involving all the parties. This approach produced one disengagement agreement between Israel and Egypt and another between Israel and Syria in 1974, but ominously, because of Israeli resistance, failed to produce one with Jordan concerning the West Bank. A second round in 1975 produced, with greater difficulty, and only after a crisis in American-Israeli relations, a second agreement on Sinai between Egypt and Israel, but the same could not be attempted with Syria. Because of lack of space in the Golan, Israel insisted on a comprehensive settlement or nothing, and the Syrians not only refused to make a separate peace, but strongly attacked Egypt for making a separate limited agreement with Israel. The dispute among the Arab parties became exacerbated by their getting entangled in a civil war that had broken out in Lebanon, which absorbed their attention for a whole year in 1975–1976, until a new administration took over in the United States and adopted a new approach to peace.

The Carter administration began with a strong commitment to achieve a comprehensive peace involving all parties through a general peace conference in Geneva. However, the efforts to convene the conference were ultimately stymied by disagreement among the Arabs over the question of Palestinian representation at the conference. After tense and laborious negotiations, the United States and Israel—which was now led by a government, headed by Menachem Begin, with a strong ideological commitment to retain the West Bank (which it called Judea and Samaria)—had agreed to a formula which, among other points, barred "known" PLO members from participating in a Jordanian-Palestinian component of an all-Arab delegation. Egypt was prepared to go along but Syria and the PLO refused, bringing the project to a halt. In order to cut through a stalemate he could not bear, Sadat made another fateful move by undertaking his dramatic trip to Jerusalem in November 1977, starting a peace process that bypassed Geneva altogether.

In Jerusalem, Sadat, and Begin vowed that they intended to pursue a comprehensive peace, not a separate treaty between Egypt and Israel, and the United States chimed in. However, as other Arab parties boycotted the negotiations that ensued, the two inevitably gravitated toward a separate agreement. The Camp David Accords, concluded in September 1978, and the Egyptian-Israeli peace treaty, signed in March 1979, were accompanied by an agreement on a "framework" for settling the West Bank question and the "Palestinian problem in all its aspects." However, the two pacts were independent of each other legally, in substance, and in the timing of their application; and, indeed, while realization of the Egyptian-Israeli peace proceeded smoothly, the negotiations for the application of the framework to the Palestinian question treaded water and then stopped altogether.

4. The 1979 Egyptian-Israeli peace treaty marked the most important turning point in the more than thirty-year-long Arab-Israeli conflict. Not only did it break the "spell" by bringing together an Arab country and Israel for the first time, but, by removing Egypt from the ranks of the confrontation states, it fundamentally altered the military and political balance in the Arab-Israeli arena. Syria tried to compensate for the "defection" of Egypt by creating an "eastern front," and to that end attempted to conciliate the hated Iraqi regime and bring it into the coalition along with Jordan and the PLO. However, the attempt foundered and, before long, Syrian forces were confronting Jordan over alleged involvement in Syrian internal troubles, and Syria was assisting Iran

in its war against Iraq. Assad also tried to draw closer to the Soviet Union for protection, but Begin was so little impressed that he gratuitously annexed the Golan in December 1981.

More important, Begin, having given back all of Sinai in order to gain a free hand in Judea and Samaria, now proceeded to accelerate the process of creeping annexation of that area. He did not repudiate the Camp David "framework," but rather used it and the stalled autonomy negotiations as a screen in order to "establish facts" that would foreclose the determination of the "final status" of the area—such as settlements and formal absorption of Arab Jerusalem into the "single, undivided, eternal capital of Israel." Egypt, which had taken the road to peace because it believed that the Arabs collectively had no military option against Israel and because it had despaired of Soviet help, was not inclined to react in a manner that risked the treaty with Israel, especially after it had thrown in its lot entirely with the United States and been ostracized and penalized by the other Arab countries.

The latest manifestation of the changed Arab-Israeli balance was seen in the Israeli invasion of Lebanon, starting in June 1982. Partly in order to secure Israel's northern settlements against PLO shelling, partly to remove the obstacle which the PLO presented to his creeping annexation of the West Bank and limited autonomy plans, Begin ordered the Israeli army to move in on the PLO forces and, if necessary, the Syrian forces, in Lebanon. The full political consequences of that war were not fully apparent at the time of writing; but two things have stood out with striking clarity: the awesome military power displayed by Israel, and the utter military and political paralysis of the remainder of the Arab camp during the longest Arab-Israeli war since 1948.

THE GREAT POWERS DIMENSION

As has been indicated, the interplay between the weakness of the area and the involvement of rival outside powers has been at the heart of the Middle East problem (whatever the name given to it) for some two centuries. During the period, the specific geographic focus of the problem often shifted, the particular configurations of domestic and regional weakness changed, the identity of the rival outside powers and the nature of their interests altered, but the matrix that made up the problem remained constant. It always involved the extension into the Middle East arena of big-power struggles involving external interests and wider power configurations.

The importance of the Middle East to outside powers is reflected in the fact that all the principal belligerents in World War II except Japan were involved in military operations in most of the region. All the countries of North Africa, from Egypt to Morocco, were major battlefields; Iraq, Syria, Lebanon, and Iran were the scenes of substantial military campaigns; and Palestine and other countries served as important staging areas.

Right after the war, Britain briefly emerged as the chief, almost the exclusive outside power in an area stretching from Russia's southern borders to the eastern border of Tunisia, with treaties and bases in half-a-dozen countries and major influence in all the others. However, the burden of holding on to these positions proved to be beyond Britain's exhausted postwar resources, and in the course of the next ten years it was compelled, under the pressure of other outside powers and local nationalisms, to retreat from most of them.

Thus, in 1947, Britain passed on to the United States the responsibility for defending Greece and Turkey against ongoing Soviet pressures. In 1948 it was forced to give up the Mandate over Palestine. In 1955, it gave in to Egyptian nationalist pressure and American prodding and agreed to leave its Suez Canal base. The following year Britain invaded Egypt together with France and Israel in an attempt to overthrow Nasser, who had previously nationalized the Suez Canal and engaged in subverting Britain's remaining Middle East positions; but the endeavor was frustrated by active American opposition coupled with Soviet threats. After the 1956 fiasco, Britain held on to its positions on the rim of the Arabian Peninsula and retained some influence in Iraq for two more years, while France cultivated a position in Israel which lasted a while longer. However, the reality, underscored by the 1956 fiasco, was that the United States and the Soviet Union had become the principal rival powers in the Middle East.

The specific interests of the United States and the Soviet Union in the Middle East and the policies they adopted in pursuit of them have shifted over the years as a function of the strategic balance between them globally and of developments in the area itself. In addition, since 1973 access to oil has become a major specific focus of American interest and policy, connected to but transcending the strategic rivalry with the Soviet Union. The course of American-Soviet rivalry in the Middle East and its interaction with other dimensions of the Middle East problem may be delineated in terms of the following seven stages.

1. Right after World War II, the northern tier of the Middle East was the scene of some of the first postwar encounters between the United States and its erstwhile Soviet ally. In 1946, the United States successfully exerted political pressure on the Soviets to evacuate their forces from Iran in accordance with the wartime Teheran agreement, and thus helped the Iranian government reassert its authority over the secessionist Soviet puppet regime in the Azerbaijan province. Since the end of the war, the Soviets had been putting pressure on Turkey for a favored

position on the Bosphorus and Dardanelles and had been supporting communist rebels in Greece. In 1947, after the British notified the United States of their intent to end the support they had hitherto been providing to Greece and Turkey, the United States responded by proclaiming the Truman Doctrine. The doctrine not only promised aid to Greece and Turkey, but also committed the United States to resist "communist aggression" everywhere. It was in fact a herald of the Cold War and a harbinger of the formation of NATO and the adoption of the containment strategy which came shortly thereafter.

In its initial version, containment called for buttressing weak countries and regions around the periphery of the Soviet bloc to stem communist expansion. The Middle East heartland, with its weak regimes, regional conflicts, and nationalist agitation, appeared as a prime area in need of such measures. Accordingly, the United States joined with Britain and France in issuing the 1950 Tripartite Declaration, which sought to deter the use of force in the Arab-Israeli conflict and pledged to regulate the flow of arms to the parties so as to prevent an arms race and prepare them to take their part in collective security arrangements. The following year, the same powers invited Egypt to participate in the creation of a Middle East Defense Organization which, among other things, would take over the British bases in the Suez Canal zone and thus settle the threatening dispute between Britain and Egypt. The project failed when Egypt rejected it on nationalist grounds and because of neutralist inclinations and unwillingness to be associated with Israel.

2. The United States had gone to war in Korea as part of its containment strategy. That costly and unsatisfactory exercise undermined the value of containment even as it induced a buildup of the United States' nuclear arsenal. Starting from these factual premises, the new administration of President Eisenhower adopted the New Look strategy, which threatened nuclear "massive retaliation" against communist encroachments anywhere, at times and places of America's own choosing.

Unlike containment, the New Look strategy did not, in itself, require any comprehensive regional association of Middle Eastern countries, or substantial indigenous military contributions. All that was needed was a few well-placed allies around the Soviet periphery who were willing to provide bases from which nuclear-armed bombers could reach various parts of the Soviet Union. Accordingly, Secretary of State John Foster Dulles came forward in 1953 with a proposal for a new alliance between the West and Middle Eastern countries of the northern tier—Turkey, Iran, and Pakistan—which had shown sensitivity to the communist threat and willingness to cooperate with the West.

Secretary Dulles's proposal had the merit of bypassing the countries of the Middle East heartland and their regional problems. However, the British, whose presence in Iraq was under nationalist pressure, sought to solve that problem by urging the Iraqi government of friendly Prime Minister Nuri al Sai'd to join the proposed pact. Nuri not only agreed, but sought to draw other Arab countries in—Jordan, Syria, and Lebanon—as a way of serving Iraq's seff-aggrandizement schemes. This aroused the apprehensions of the Saudis, ever fearful of the Hashemite rulers of Iraq and Jordan, and the jealousy of Egypt, which considered itself the natural leader of the Arab countries and sought to use Arab solidarity to advance its own national cause against the British. In opposing Iraq's intent, the Egyptians and the Saudis accused it among other things of deserting the Arab coalition against Israel, while Iraq defended itself by arguing that its project would gain access to Western arms which would strengthen the Arabs against Israel. Thus what came to be known as the Baghdad Pact got tangled from the outset with local nationalist quarrels with Britain, pan-Arabism, inter-Arab rivalries, and the Arab-Israeli conflict. The consequences were momentous.

The Soviets had viewed with alarm the American strategy based on massive retaliation and were, naturally, most anxious to deny to the United States the bases on their periphery that were essential for it. The hostility of Nasser to the Baghdad Pact created a shared interest which led to the conclusion of a major Soviet-Egyptian arms deal in 1955. In the perspective of the multibillion dollar arms contracts of the 1970s and 1980s, the $100 million deal of 1955 appears a modest affair. However, on the scale of the time it was large enough to threaten to overturn the local balances of power. Most important, the deal broke the monopoly of the Western powers in the supply of arms to the area, which they had used to try to stabilize the Arab-Israeli conflict and lure Iraq and others into the Baghdad Pact. It also opened the way for Soviet influence in the Middle East heartland for the first time, giving them a chance to outflank and undermine the northern tier.

The United States, stunned by the move, reacted to it in a piece-meal, inconsistent manner which ultimately contributed to the destruction of British and French positions in the region and left it with the sole responsibility for the defense of the region. Secretary of State Dulles first tried to counter the new Soviet influence by promising to help Egypt build a mammoth dam at Aswan and by turning a deaf ear to Israel's pleas for American arms to counter Nasser's Soviet arms. Next, he relented partly on the question of arms to Israel by supporting Canadian and French moves to supply some from inventory assigned to NATO, and then he reacted to minor Egyptian provocations by withdrawing the Aswan dam offer. This led Nasser to retaliate by nationalizing the French- and British-owned Suez Canal Company. The British and French governments threatened forceful action to compel Nasser to yield control of the vital waterway and Secretary of State Dulles initially supported their cause. However, he subsequently subordinated the issue of recovering control over the canal to the aim of preventing his allies from resorting to force, for fear of inflaming Arab anti-Western feelings and playing into the hands of the Soviets. When Britain and France finally took matters into their own hands and, in collusion with Israel, invaded Egypt, the United States condemned its allies and took actions, ironically parallel to Soviet endeavors, which utterly frustrated their design.

3. The failure of the British-French expedition thoroughly undermined the historic role of these countries as Middle Eastern powers, enhanced tremendously Nasser's stature as leader of Arab nationalism, and greatly strengthened the position of the Soviets as his proven friends in time of need. The United States, fearing that a continuation of Nasser's Soviet-supported Arab nationalist drive could overrun the remaining Western positions in the area, sought to rally as many Middle Eastern countries as possible under the banner of the Eisenhower Doctrine, which promised American assistance to any country requesting help to resist aggression by international communism. The practical expression of this latest, purely American attempt to organize part of the region in the Western camp was a concerted overt and covert campaign to stem and roll back the Nasserist drive. After scoring one success in Jordan, where the United States helped King Hussein overthrow his own pro-Nasser government, the campaign got bogged down in Syria and then backfired. Syria, split from within and threatened from without, threw itself into Nasser's arms and merged with Egypt to form the United Arab Republic. Next, the Arab nationalist enthusiasm generated by that union helped polarize Lebanon's delicate political system and plunged the country into civil war. Then, in July 1958, Iraqi troops which had been ordered to advance to the Syrian border turned on the regime in Baghdad, overthrew it, took the country out of the Baghdad Pact, and turned to the Soviet Union for support.

The United States reacted by sending the marines into Lebanon and the British assisted by sending paratroopers to Jordan, while the Soviets tried to convey an impression of willingness to support forcefully the Arab nationalist cause by holding major military maneuvers in the Caucasus. By the time the crisis was defused a few weeks later, the American and British interventions had managed to save Lebanon and Jordan from being swept by the Soviet-supported Nasserist tide, but Iraq had been lost to the West and had joined Egypt and Syria as a protégé of the Soviet Union. Other Arab countries had openly dissociated themselves from the Eisenhower Doctrine.

4. Hitherto, each time the Soviets had scored a gain in the Middle East heartland—after the 1955 arms deal, the 1956 war, the 1957 Syrian crisis—they had proposed a big-power conference to neutralize the Middle East. That is to say, they offered to give up their positions in the heartland in exchange for the West's giving up its positions in the north-

ern tier. Since the latter were an essential part of the Western strategic deterrent, the United States had naturally refused. After the 1958 Iraqi revolution, the Soviets repeated their offer, but when the United States at last showed a willingness to agree, the Soviets retracted it. The change in the attitudes of the two superpowers reflected the beginning of a change in the nature of the global strategic balance between them as well as the shift that had taken place in their relative positions in the Middle East region itself.

Soviet advances in nuclear technology and delivery capability, dramatized by the launching of Sputnik, had made massive retaliation an untenable strategy as the United States itself became a potential target for a Soviet second strike. The United States, for its part, had begun to develop its own second strike capability based on ICBMs and Polaris-carrying submarines in addition to manned bombers. As a balance of terror resting on invulnerable, independent deterrents emerged, the rivalry between the superpowers took on the form of "peaceful competition." Under the influence of Mao Zedong's "rural strategy" and his view of the unindustrialized countries as the "countryside of the industrialized world," peaceful competition meant striving for positions and influence in the Third World, caught in the throes of accelerated decolonization. In that context, the Middle East region, although no longer critical to the nuclear balance, remained a prime arena for competition because of its nodal geographic position between Europe, Asia, and Africa, its oil resources, the fact that both superpowers already held some positions in it, and the opportunities that its multiple problems seemed to present to each to score against the other.

In the actual competition that unfolded in the late 1950s and early 1960s, the United States fared better than the Soviets, mainly because the latter were now the ones who got caught in the midst of feuding clients and domestic upheavals. In 1959, Nasser's Arab nationalist drive stalled as Iraq's new ruler, General Kassem, resisted it and offered his own rival plan for unity, and in 1961 it suffered a disastrous setback when Syria seceded from the United Arab Republic. Nasser's attempt to revive the drive by intervening militarily in Yemen to support a republican coup miscarried and left him in a morass from which he could not extricate himself for five years. Two almost simultaneous Ba'thist-led coups in Iraq and Syria in 1963 briefly revived the hopes of union between these countries and Egypt only to dash them and leave behind three rival centers contending for leadership of the Arab nationalist movement. The Soviets, who had started out in 1958 as the patron power of Cairo, Damascus, and Baghdad, inevitably got caught in the midst of these crosscurrents and suffered severe damage, the most serious of which being the loss of their image as the unselfish champion of Arab unity. In contrast, the United States' position during those years resting on Turkey and Iran in the northern tier, and Israel, Jordan, and Saudi Arabia in the heartland, remained secure. The first three, being non-Arab, not only were inured to the unrest of Arab nationalism, but also provided a counterpoise to the Arab nationalist countries, which helped protect Saudi Arabia and Jordan against assaults from those directions.

Having found the vehicle of Arab nationalism troublesome, the Soviets began at the end of 1964 to seek to consolidate their position by promoting cooperation among their clients in hostility toward Israel—a dangerous tack they had hitherto avoided. The occasion for their taking this approach was the completion by Israel of a project to divert the Jordan River. Initially frustrated by continuing inter-Arab disputes, the Soviets came back to the charge in 1966, after a new regime had come to power in Syria that they particularly favored because it took communists into the government for the first time. This time they were able to mediate a mutual defense agreement between Syria and Egypt. The following year, as tension and border clashes between Syria and Israel escalated, the Soviets prodded Nasser to activate the Sinai front in order to deter Israeli action against Syria. Nasser responded, but was led by the momentum of his actions and the enthusiasm they aroused in the Arab world to raise the issue at stake again and again until he left Israel with no choice but capitulation or war. Israel chose war, and the results of its decision have dominated the configurations of the Middle East problem from that time until the eruption of the Persian Gulf in 1979.

5. In the wake of the 1967 war, the contest between the United States and the Soviet Union came to center almost entirely on the Arab-Israeli conflict. It took the form of two opposed alignments, one between the United States and Israel, the other between the Soviet Union and Egypt. The contest was complicated by the interplay of two sets of factors: first, an evolving situation in the leadership of some of the parties involved and in the global climate of American-Soviet relations and, second, the fact that the interests of each superpower and its respective client overlapped a great deal but did not entirely coincide. Thus, as events unfolded, the contest assumed the character of a double struggle: one between the two alignments, and one within each of the two alignments.

The interests of the United States were closely identified with those of Israel. Both wanted to use Israel's war gains to liquidate the Arab-Israeli conflict through comprehensive peace—Israel for obvious reasons, the United States in order to end the exploitation of the conflict by Nasser and the Soviets to its own detriment and consolidate its position in the area. The Soviets' interests, likewise, were closely linked to those of Egypt, and at one remove from Syria's. Both Nasser and the Soviets wanted to "liquidate the consequences of the war," i.e., to recover the lost territories and eliminate Israel's military predominance, without liquidating the conflict juridicially—Nasser on personal, domestic, and pan-Arab grounds, the Soviets in order to restore their position, endangered by their failure to save their clients from defeat.

On the other hand, the United States for itself was only interested in peace and was rather indifferent to terms and procedure, whereas Israel insisted on direct negotiations and certain unspecified but substantial territorial modifications. American support for Israel's specific position involved the risk of prolonging the confrontation unnecessarily and alienating friendly Arab countries in which the United States had additional and very substantial interest. The Soviet Union, for its part, while interested in the same ends as its principal client, disagreed over the means to be used in pursuit of them. Nasser (and Syria, too) had asked the Soviets to join with their forces in an all-out war to achieve their goals; however, the Soviets not only balked at the idea for fear of confrontation with the United States, but became wary lest their clients use their assistance to start a general war on their own. The Soviets feared that such a war might force on them the choice of either becoming involved, or seeing their clients suffer another, possibly final, disaster.

The struggles between and within the two alignments unfolded in three stages over the following seven years: from June 1967 to March 1969; March 1969 to August 1970; and August 1970 to October 1973.

The first stage saw the formation of the alignments and assertion of positions. As the Soviets' assistance in rearming and retraining the Arabs reached a level that threatened Israel's military supremacy, the United States committed fifty Phantom fighter-bombers to its ally in the last days of the Johnson administration.

The second stage was dominated by the war of attrition and alternating strains within the two alignments. The new Nixon administration, worried about friendly Arab countries and anxious to gain Soviet cooperation on Vietnam, engaged the Soviets in talks aimed at helping to resolve the conflict. Six months into the war of attrition, which was going well for Nasser, the talks produced agreement on an outline for a settlement based on peace in exchange for all the conquered territory. In preliminary explorations, both Egypt and Israel rejected the proposals. However, whereas the Soviets retracted their support for the proposals, the United States, worried about the effect of the continuing war on friendly Arab countries, developed and presented them publicly as its own plan, dubbed the Rogers Plan. The American-Israeli alignment was strained as the United States thus deliberately distanced itself from its client.

Starting in January 1970, Israel turned the tables on Nasser in the war of attrition through a campaign of sustained bombing of Egypt's interior. Nasser went to Moscow and asked for advanced missiles and fighter planes and Soviet personnel to man them. The Soviets, fearing to be implicated, were reluctant. However, when Nasser indicated that he might otherwise be unable to remain in power, they agreed, but extracted from him in exchange a promise to seek a political solution once the military position was restored.

In July Soviet-Egyptian missile crews were able to penetrate the combat zone and managed to bring down several Israeli aircraft. Kissinger charged the Soviets with seeking to achieve predominance in the Mediterranean and let out that the United States was out to "expel" them. Nixon announced acceleration of arms deliveries to Israel, while Secretary of State Rogers proposed a cease-fire and negotiations. Soviet-manned aircraft challenged Israeli fighters over the combat zone, and the Israelis shot down five of them. Nasser went to Moscow to urge the Soviets to continue the military pressure on Israel. The Soviets refused adamantly. Nasser went back and accepted the American cease-fire proposal in August 1970.

Insofar as the cease-fire represented the failure of the Egyptian-Soviet alignment to change the status quo by force, it was a victory for the Israeli-American alignment. The latter went on to score yet another victory at the outset of the next stage, when American-Israeli action, this time concerted jointly and deliberately, helped defeat the Soviet-supported Syrian military intervention in Jordan on the side of the PLO in September 1970. These successes paved the way for important changes in American policy. The concern to keep some distance from Israel was dropped and the Rogers Plan was quietly shelved even after President Sadat departed from his predecessor's position and agreed, in February 1971, to the idea of a formal peace in exchange for all the territories. Instead, the United States adopted the policy advocated by Kissinger which called for unequivocal political support for Israel and help to enable it maintain absolute military superiority. These steps were seen as the best means to achieve America's objectives, which were to deter war, undermine the Soviet position, press Egypt to further modify its stance to make possible fruitful negotiations, and at the same time indirectly protect friendly Arab countries.

The revised policy was brilliantly vindicated in one respect. In July 1972, Sadat expelled the Soviet advisers and military personnel from Egypt after mounting frictions between the erstwhile partners over arms supply and policy. The Soviets had refused to provide Sadat with the weapons he wanted to maintain a war option because they feared another Arab defeat and the prospect of greater involvement on their part, and because they did not want to jeopardize an incipient détente with the United States, which had taken on critical importance for them after the American opening to China. However, the break with the Soviet Union only led Egypt to revise its strategy, not its position regarding a settlement with Israel. Rather than make concessions, Sadat decided to gamble on a surprise war with a view to achieving some limited military gains and upsetting the status quo, and thus forcing negotiations under more favorable circumstances.

6. The 1973 war profoundly altered the positions and interests of the two superpowers. During the war, they both talked détente yet mounted massive resupply operations in support of their respective clients, involving themselves for the first time in an Arab-Israeli war. Next, they jointly sponsored a cease-fire to end the fighting, and then engaged in one of their most serious confrontations over the issue of enforcing the cease-fire: the Soviets threatened to send troops to Egypt to do it, and the United States called a global alert to deter them.

After the war, the two superpowers, still talking détente, jointly sponsored a project to convene a general Arab-Israeli peace conference, yet each tried to use the results of the war to undercut the other. Although the united Arab confrontation with the United States in the form of the oil embargo seemed to put the Soviets in an advantageous position, in fact the American leverage with Israel—which underlay the embargo—proved to be far more effective in causing the Arabs to turn to the United States in quest of an acceptable settlement.

While America's relationship with Israel gave it the leverage with the Arabs that enabled it to push the Soviets aside, it also placed before it a new dilemma. The Arab oil embargo had demonstrated the fallacy implicit in prewar American policy which had separated oil and Arab-Israeli questions. At the same time, the devastating effect of the embargo on Western solidarity and the rocketing of prices it caused made access to oil—uninterrupted flow at "bearable" prices—a vital goal for the United States. The dilemma was how to accommodate those requirements with the continuing American interest in Israel. Kissinger's "step-by-step" diplomacy temporized by dealing with the issue on a piecemeal basis; but after that diplomacy ran its course, the problem came back to haunt American policy in unexpected forms.

The Carter administration tried a radical solution to the problem by seeking to promote a comprehensive Arab-Israeli settlement. However, after the endeavor to get the parties to Geneva bogged down because of inter-Arab disagreements, it threw its weight fully behind Sadat's initiative and embarked on the path to peace opened by his trip to Jerusalem. That effort eventually resulted in a peace treaty between Egypt and Israel; however, that breakthrough, crucial as it was in other respects, resulted in the isolation of Egypt from the Arab world and the oil-producing countries, and an intensification rather than a resolution of the dilemma confronting the United States. A reflection of the added trouble was seen in the oil policy pursued by the Saudis after the conclusion of the peace treaty in 1979, which resulted in a doubling of the already high oil prices within a short period.

7. The signing of the Egyptian-Israeli treaty coincided with the final

collapse of the Shah's regime and the triumph of Khomeini's Islamic fundamentalist revolution. This development added several new dimensions to the problem of access to oil. The most obvious, namely the control of Iranian oil by a government bitterly hostile to the United States, was the least serious in the short run because of the glut in the world oil market. A second problem was the loss of the insurance which the Shah's regime provided in the event of internal upheavals in Saudi Arabia or other Gulf countries which could threaten the flow of oil.

A third problem was the impact of Iran's revolution on the internal stability of Saudi Arabia and other oil producers, which manifested itself partly in the seizure of the Mecca Mosque by Islamic fundamentalists and the mutiny of Saudi Arabia's Shi'ite minority in Hasa in late 1979. A fourth problem was the collapse of the balance of power in the Persian Gulf region and the effect of the resultant instability on the potential flow of oil and on superpower relations. That problem manifested itself in the Soviet invasion of Afghanistan in December 1979, and even more clearly in Iraq's invasion of Iran in September 1980, starting a war that is still going on at time of writing. The disruption of Iraqi and Iranian oil production has not caused severe problems because of the state of the oil market; but a spillover of the hostilities to other regional producers, especially Saudi Arabia, could have disastrous consequences.

The intertwining of the Gulf and Arab-Israeli arenas manifested itself in another way, rather beneficial from the point of view of the United States. Partly because of the role that the United States played in protecting the Gulf countries despite their reticence to cooperate more fully with it, the United States was not made the target of attacks, let alone sanctions, by those countries in connection with Israel's invasion of Lebanon. However, the Lebanon war created pressures on the United States to address the Palestinian problem in a basic way, which led the president to enunciate the "Reagan Plan" in September 1982, and this ultimately placed the United States in a cross fire between its Israeli ally and Arab friends.

THE CONFIGURATION IN THE FALL OF 1987

By the fall of 1987 a major reconfiguration of the Middle East problem had taken place as the focus of the problem shifted from the Arab-Israeli to the Persian Gulf arena. The shift had been in the making for some time, but it became apparent in the course of the summer of 1987, when over one hundred Soviet, American, and West European warships converged on the Persian Gulf in response to developments in the Iran-Iraq war. And the shift was fully acknowledged in the deliberations and resolutions of the Arab Summit held at Amman in November 1987, which, for the first time in the twenty-five-year history of that institution, gave priority to the Gulf War over the Arab-Israeli conflict.

As with previous historic mutations of the Middle East problem, this reconfiguration, too, was the result of developments that took place along all the dimensions of the problem; but the main thrust for the change was provided by two processes that unfolded at the regional level: (1) the eruption and subsidence of the strategic and political upheaval that followed the conclusion of the 1979 Egyptian-Israeli peace, and (2) the suspension and then eruption of the strategic and political turmoil that had been latent in the simultaneous triumph of Iran's Islamic revolution. Cutting across both processes was the development of a persistent glut in the world oil market and its ramifications.

Eruption and Subsidence in the Arab-Israeli Arena

The conclusion of the 1979 Egyptian-Israeli peace treaty had profoundly altered the balance of power in the Arab-Israeli arena. Egypt's exit from the Arab-Israeli conflict (and the concurrent confirmation of its switch from the Soviet to the American camp) eased Israel's concern about its southern flank and left it with a vast amount of "disposable" power. This development raised two crucial questions: How would Israel use its greatly enhanced power vis á vis its remaining opponents—Syria, the PLO, and, to a lesser extent, Jordan? And how would the opponents react as they confronted an Israel made much stronger?

It turned out that Israel under the leadership of Prime Minister Begin and Defense Minister Sharon tried to use its military superiority to start a war in Lebanon in an attempt to impose on its remaining opponents a settlement to its liking. Its endeavor proved to be a costly failure and a lesson in the limitations of military power. Syria, Egypt's erstwhile ally in the 1973 war, and the foremost advocate of "steadfastness and confrontation," tried to build a new "strategic balance" in order to deter Israel, regain a war option, and be able to force negotiations from a position of strength. Its effort met with considerable success but was exhausted well short of its ultimate goal. The net result of Israel's and Syria's endeavors was the emergence of a strategic stalemate that discourages war but also provides little pressure for movement toward peace. This evolution, coupled with the eruption of the Persian Gulf arena, relegated the Arab-Israeli conflict to the sidelines of the Middle East problem.

The Lebanon War. Begin, freshly reelected for a second term in June 1981, and Sharon, recently appointed as defense minister, used Israel's disposable power to launch what everyone agreed was a "war of choice" to advance particular policy goals, in contrast to a "war of necessity," imposed or clearly made inevitable by the enemy. The goals of operation

"Peace for Galilee" approved by the cabinet and proclaimed to the world were relatively modest and arguably defensive: to destroy the PLO forces in southern Lebanon and secure a forty kilometer buffer zone that would put Israel's northern settlements beyond the reach of long-range artillery. Sharon and Begin, however, had in mind far more ambitious objectives, for which they hoped to secure the necessary political support on a piecemeal basis as the campaign unfolded under their direction.

They sought to destroy the PLO presence in Lebanon altogether in a concerted action with the forces of the Christian Lebanese Front led by Bechir Gemayel, to force the Syrian army out of the country, and to establish an effective central government headed by Gemayel that would conclude a formal peace and a formal or informal alliance with Israel. Moreover, the elimination of the PLO and the weakening of Syria would make it possible, in their view, for Israel to consolidate its rule in Judea and Samaria. These achievements would allow Israel, for instance, to resume, with better chances of success, plans to establish unilaterally a regime of limited autonomy in those areas and in Gaza, which had hitherto been obstucted by PLO intimidation of Palestinians who were willing to collaborate. Sharon estimated that the military campaign would be completed in a few days, before any international intervention could galvanize, and that a reduced Israeli military presence would be required for three months thereafter to secure the establishment of the new order in Lebanon.

In fact, the Lebanon war proved to be the longest of Israel's half dozen wars, and the costliest in casualties next to the 1948 War of Independence. Moreover, despite the awesome military power deployed by Israel, the final results of the war were worse than nil. A complete analysis of the events of that venture would require a separate volume, but the highlights are as follows: The Israeli forces attacked in three more or less parallel prongs, and in the first five days the campaign proceeded auspiciously from Sharon's point of view. The western and central prongs overcame or surrounded PLO positions and advanced steadily in the general direction of Beirut. The eastern prong advanced toward the Syrian-held positions and then halted, while the central prong advanced so far on the flank of the Syrians as to place them in a position where they had either to withdraw or to fight. As they chose to fight, the Israeli air force successfully attacked Syrian SAM batteries. A battle for control of the skies developed which Israel won handily. In less than three days, starting June 9, its air force shot down nearly one hundred Syrian combat aircraft while losing none of its own. The Syrian ground forces, which in the meantime had come under attack by Israeli armor from the front and the flank, were now doomed to destruction. They were saved by a UN cease-fire injunction, which Israel obeyed on June 11 at the behest of the United States, who had in turn chosen to heed a mildly threatening

Soviet note. Begin and Sharon may have comforted themselves with the thought that the Syrian forces were neutralized and remained hostage to Israel's power. However, although the Syrian army gave no further military trouble, its continuing presence in Lebanon was to prove quite troublesome, indeed, to Begin and Sharon's plans.

On the PLO front, too, things began to go awry after the first few days. As the Israeli army approached Beirut, the Christian Lebanese Front forces failed to march against the PLO and its allies in West Beirut as they were supposed to do, and they contented themselves with helping to close the ring around the city. Even Sharon was not prepared to risk the high casualties that would be involved in storming a vast built-up area, and consequently he and Begin had to modify their aim and tactics. Instead of the destruction of the PLO, they now sought its removal from Beirut, and they hoped to achieve that by means of a siege and intense bombardment designed to turn the Beirut people against the PLO. They assumed that the operation would not take long, but events beyond their control decreed otherwise.

U.S. Secretary of State Haig had made halfhearted attempts to restrain Israel from going to war, but once the war broke out he saw it as an opportunity to score major gains in Lebanon and advance a settlement of the Palestinian question through a Jordanian-Israeli peace. His concept on the latter question was diametrically opposed to Begin and Sharon's, but his thinking regarding Lebanon coincided almost entirely with theirs. He enunciated United States policy as seeking the withdrawal of Israel "in the context" of the removal of all foreign forces from Lebanon and, after the Israeli Army reached Beirut, had President Reagan offer the services of Special Envoy Philip Habib to mediate the withdrawal of the PLO from the city. Haig, like Begin and Sharon, saw the acceptance of Habib's mission by the Arab side as a sign that it would succeed quickly; however, before that happened, Haig became involved in a dispute over policy management within the administration which led to his resignation. George Shultz replaced him. The division in the U.S. government and the fall of "pro-Israel" Haig gave heart to the beleaguered PLO and its supporters, and it ended the prospect of a successful short siege.

Habib's negotiations dragged on inconclusively for nearly a whole month, during which public opinion in the world and in Israel itself was aroused against the continuing siege. However, in the last week of July, Begin and Sharon submitted parts of the city to savage relentless bombing and bombardment in order to force a decision, and eventually succeeded. On August 6, the PLO agreed to leave Beirut, and its evacuation was completed on August 30 under the supervision of an international peacekeeping force comprising U.S. Marines and French and British contingents.

Shortly before the evacuation of the PLO the Lebanese Parliament had elected Bechir Gemayel to be president. The two events seemed to place Begin and Sharon at last within reach of their goal for Lebanon; but that only begat new, worse troubles. On September 1, 1982, the United States, seeking to capitalize on Israel's successes, enunciated what was dubbed the Reagan Plan to settle the Palestinian question on the basis of Palestinian autonomy in the West Bank and Gaza in association with Jordan. The plan ran counter to one of the main reasons for Begin's going to war in Lebanon, and his prompt and categorical rejection of it revealed a wide rift between the United States and Israel, which was exploited by Syria and the Soviet Union. Begin had not recovered from that blow when Bechir Gemayel was killed in an explosion in his headquarters on September 14. That same night Begin authorized Sharon to send the Israeli army into West Beirut in an endeavor to gain leverage over the choice of Gemayel's successor. Sharon advanced his troops the next day, but enlisted elements of the Christian Lebanese Front to enter the large Palestinian refugee camps of Sabra and Shatila and flush out PLO fighters who, Sharon believed, had hidden among the population. The Christian Lebanese Front fighters used the occasion to avenge their "martyred" leader and massacred hundreds of innocent Palestinians regardless of sex or age.

The massacres stirred an international uproar and triggered huge demonstrations in Israel itself that demanded, and obtained, the appointment of a judicial commission to investigate possible responsibilities of Israeli officials in the tragedy. In the meantime, the United States demanded the withdrawal of Israeli forces from Beirut and sent back a contingent of U.S. Marines, subsequently joined by other elements of the International Peacekeeping Force, to take over. More important, the United States now sought to distance itself from Israel even further and took direct charge of pursuing its goals in Lebanon, starting with successful lobbying to elect Amin Gemayel to succeed his brother Bechir over other candidates favored by Israel. That only added to the friction between the American and Israeli governments and contributed to defeating the purposes of both.

The United States did not commit the military resources necessary to secure the withdrawal of the Syrian army and the suppression of the potential opposition of various Lebanese factions to Amin Gemayel's government. It needed Israel's military power to attain those ends, but it was unwilling to give Israel sufficient incentive to cooperate. Israel's government needed at least a peace agreement with Lebanon to justify its costly war, but the United States advised Gemayel to hold back because it did not want to arouse negative Arab reaction at a time when it was still seeking Arab support for the Reagan Plan (an Arab summit in September had neither rejected nor accepted the plan, but King Hussein was trying to secure support for the plan from the PLO's Arafat, under the cover of an alternative plan adopted by the summit). When the Israeli government threatened to redeploy its forces without regard to Gemayel's intertests, the Americans advised him to negotiate but to drag his feet and delay.

By the spring of 1983, the attempts to salvage the Reagan Plan had finally failed and the report of the Kahan commission on Sabra and Shatila had led to the censure and punishment of several senior Israeli officers, the dismissal of Sharon from his defense post and his replacement by the suave, American-educated Moshe Arens. These developments impelled the administration to seek in earnest an Israeli-Lebanese pact that would lead to Israel's withdrawal, which in turn would meet the condition that Syria had set for its own withdrawal. In May 1983, Secretary of State Shultz personally mediated a Lebanese-Israeli agreement that was, in his view, sufficiently short of peace to protect Gemayel's government and anticipate Syrian objections, but was close enough to peace to satisfy Israel and allow it to withdraw its forces. He then took the agreement to Damascus to confirm Syria's promise to withdraw.

By that time, however, the circumstances that had induced Syria to contemplate withdrawal had changed, and President Assad accordingly relented. On the one hand, the Soviets, prompted by the direct American military involvement and eager, under a renewed leadership, to regain some of the credibility they had lost by their earlier passiveness, more than replaced Syria's losses of equipment in the war. They provided it with advanced weapons, including SAM 20 missiles, and, as an added deterrent, sent Soviet personnel to man the advanced arms they provided and train the Syrians in the use of these weapons. On the other hand, it had become apparent to Assad that the United States was unwilling to commit its own resources to support its policy, and that the rift that had developed between the United States and Israel, coupled with Israel's apparent loss of stomach for war, made it unlikely that the two would concert action to drive his army out of Lebanon by force. Consequently, Assad not only refused to withdraw, but also rejected the May 1983 agreement *in toto* and vowed to bring about its abrogation; and he began a discrete campaign to force unilateral and unconditional withdrawal of the Israelis and of the Americans as well.

Assad's calculations proved correct, and his campaign succeeded entirely within a year or so. The upheaval that had forced Sharon out had also caused Begin to lose the will to act; he lapsed into a state of despondencey for several months before resigning in September 1983. Before he had quit, his government had settled on a defensive policy of shortening supply lines by partial withdrawal in the face of American entreaties not to do so, and bracing for a long stay in south Lebanon in the faint hope that the United States might find a way to overcome Syria's resistance or otherwise enforce the May 1983 agreement.

The United States, for its part, ran afoul of most Lebanese armed factions, who saw it as seeking to reimpose on them Maronite domination under the guise of a national government. They began by fighting the government's forces with Syrian assistance and incidentally hit marines positions; and after American forces retaliated, they turned against the American presence itself. Their attacks reached a tragic climax in October 1983, when a truck loaded with explosives was detonated in the heart of the U.S. Marines' compound, killing 241 servicemen—more than 17 percent of the marine contingent—in one blow. The United States responded by firing battleship guns on Syrian positions, the Syrians returned fire, the United States struck with aircraft, the Syrians shot down two of the attacking planes, and for a moment it looked as though the exchange of blows would escalate to a full war. However, when President Reagan considered that possibility, his advisers were sharply divided, and the review of the situation only set the ground for the withdrawal of the U.S. Marines and American disengagement from Lebanon the following February.

The disengagement of the United States led Gemayel to abrogate the May 1983 agreement in an endeavor to conciliate Syria. This reduced Israel's policy under Begin's successor, Yithak Shamir, to hanging on in south Lebanon in the face of increasing attacks by Syrian-supported Shi'ite militias and a mounting toll of casualties in the hope of being able eventually to trade withdrawal for practical security arrangements, without which the withdrawal would amount to a politically disastrous admission of total defeat. Shamir's problem, however, was that the Lebanese government could not enforce any security provisions; the Syrians who could enforce security provisions would not discuss a trade off; and the local Shi'ite militia was only willing to offer general assurances based on good faith in exchange for withdrawal. His struggle with the dilemma was, fortunately for him, interrupted by a successful opposition motion in the Knesset on March 22 for early elections, which were set for July 1984.

The elections resulted in an absolute tie, with neither the Labor party nor Likud party able to form a coalition. In the end, the two major parties and their allies agreed to form a government of National Unity based on a peculiar distribution of offices and a limited program that included working for a prompt withdrawal from Lebanon. The government assumed office in September, and, after vainly exploring its options for three months, decided in January 1985 on unilateral complete withdrawal with security measures in a narrow strip adjacent to Israel to be enforced by an Israel-supported local militia assisted by Israeli advisers. The evacuation was completed on June 6, 1985, on the third anniversary of the invasion.

From the perspective of Israel in the fall of 1987, the results of the

Lebanon War were almost entirely negative. None of the objectives entertained by Begin and Sharon was achieved, not even the modest ones that they had used as a ploy to gain authorization for their venture. For, by 1987 the PLO was back in Lebanon, playing once more an important, if no longer or not yet dominant, role in the kaleidoscopic power politics of the country. And the PLO was back even in the south in sufficient strength to fight the Shi'ite militia to a standstill on the turf the latter came to claim as its own. The price paid by Israel included 654 soldiers killed and 3,873 wounded, 1.5 to 5 billion dollars in war costs, and the breakdown of the precious national unity with which Israel had faced wars since its creation. One possible positive outcome is that the Israeli leaders may have learned a lesson about the unpredictablity of war and the limitations of sheer military power. At any rate, the war surely consumed Israel's surplus power for some time to come and thus cancelled one of the strategic consequences of the Egyptian-Israeli peace.

Syria's Quest for "Strategic Parity." Already after the conclusion of the September 1978 Camp David accords that laid the grounds for the Egyptian-Israeli peace treaty signed in March 1979, Syria had given utmost priority to the task of rebuilding a strategic balance with Israel. For the short run, such a balance was seen as essential to deter Israel from attacking or pressing Syria; for the longer run it was seen as creating an indispensable condition for an eventual settlement of the conflict on terms favorable to Syria.

Just what those terms were was never made quite clear, but what was clear was that they had to be different from what the Camp David accords held out for Syria. At best, these would have restored the Golan to Syrian limited sovereignty in exchange for normalization of relations with Israel and for Syria's becoming another client of the United States, third or fourth in rank after Israel, Egypt, and perhaps Saudi Arabia. What Syria wanted was a settlement that would leave it free to maneuver between the superpowers and among the Arab countries for maximum autonomy and advantage; and such a settlement was possible only if it was negotiated from a position of at least equal strategic strength with the opponent, Israel.

Strategic strength, in Syria's conception, had to go beyond a capacity to deter Israel to acquiring a war option against it. Not one that would seek to destroy Israel's capacity to resist dictation—that was precluded by Israel's assumed possession of nuclear weapons—but one that could inflict on it a serious enough defeat to compel it to concede a desirable settlement. The acquisition and exercise of such an option required, in turn, an array of interrelated conditions, including Arab diplomatic and material support, vast financial resources, access to advanced weapons, and international (mainly Soviet) backing; and underlying them all, keeping Egypt isolated and preventing other Arab parties from seeking a separate settlement.

Syria's pursuit of strategic balance and its attendant conditions since 1979 was sustained through many tribulations before coming to a pause or a halt in 1987. By then Syria had definitely acquired a strong deterrent against Israeli pressure as well as against outright attack, but it had fallen short of gaining the option of initiating war. That outcome does not suffice to prompt it to force a showdown, but it may make it less reluctant than it had been to contemplate negotiations for a settlement if a move developed in that direction. Barring such a move, the situation favors a continued stalemate, which because of Assad's failing health and the pivotal role of his leadership, may not be advantageous to Syria.

Syria's quest for strategic balance went through many ups and downs but these can be reviewed in terms of three phases:

1. In 1978 Syria sought to promote an *Arab* counterbalance to Israel, hinged on a Syrian-Iraqi alliance. After a major initial success, the endeavor failed. Syria then salvaged elements of the success and incorporated them in a new endeavor, starting in 1980, that sought to achieve *Syrian* "strategic parity" with Israel.

Right after the Camp David accords, Assad reached out in desperation to his mortal foe, Saddam Hussein of Iraq, and the two concluded an agreement in principle to merge their countries. Assad also seconded Saddam Hussein in steering two Arab conferences held in Baghdad in November 1978 and in March 1979 to adopt resolutions that ostracized Egypt and committed the oil-rich countries to provide massive annual grants to support Syria, Jordan, and the PLO in their continuing confrontation with Israel. The Soviet Union expressed its support for the Baghdad resolutions.

In 1979 the Syrian-Iraqi unity talks failed. Syria felt that Iraq had tried to exploit its security vulnerability to impose itself on Syria. The two regimes reverted to their traditional mutual hostility. Furthermore, the Soviet invasion of Afghanistan at the end of that year split the Baghdad front between a Saudi-led majority that condemned the Soviet Union, and included some that contemplated strategic cooperation with the United States under the Carter Doctrine; and a minority led by Syria that sought to preserve Soviet good will and avert diversion of Arab attention away from the Arab-Israeli conflict. Finally, Iraq's invasion of Iran in 1980 renewed the problem of diversion with greater intensity, and caused Saudi Arabia to actually request the United States to provide military assistance in the form of AWACS aircraft to help protect it against possible Iranian attacks. That, to Syria, portended Saudi Arabia's slipping into a position of support for the American-sponsored peace process.

In response to these developments, Syria renounced the idea of an Arab coalition to balance Israel and decided, in mid-1980, to seek "strategic parity" by itself, encouraged by the oil-induced economic boom that Syria was enjoying. To meet the need for deterrence in the short run and better secure the arms it needed in the longer run, Syria concluded in October 1980 a Treaty of Friendship and Cooperation with the Soviet Union. As part of an effort to retain Arab financial support and prevent defections to the American-promoted peace process, Syria boycotted an Arab summit that met in Amman in November 1980 to deal with the Iran-Iraq war. Syria also deployed large forces menacingly against Jordan, ostensibly because Jordan considered joining the peace process. Its maneuvers succeeded in obtaining the assurances it desired and renewed commitment of financial support from the oil-rich countries.

2. Between mid-1980 and mid-1982 Syria's quest for parity made substantial headway while overcoming serious problems. In June 1981 it faced the danger of premature war with Israel as a result of a confrontation in Lebanon (Israel shot down Syrian helicopters fighting the Phalanges. Syria deployed SAM missiles, and Israel threatened to attack them if not removed), but Saudi and American mediation defused the crisis. Later that year Syria was able to prevent a move toward premature peace by torpedoeing the Fahd Plan advanced by Saudi Arabia, yet it managed to win specific Saudi support for its quest for parity in exchange for helping to moderate Iranian policy and actions.

The premature war and premature peace moves that were averted in 1981 came to pass in 1982, along with setbacks in all other aspects of Syria's quest for parity. We have already reviewed Israel's invasion of Lebanon, its attack on Syria's army there and the crippling of its air force, the desertion of Syria by the Soviet Union and the Arab countries, America's promotion of the Reagan peace plan and its assumption of a leading role in Lebanon and its mediation of a Lebanese-Israeli agreement. We have also discussed how Syria managed to overcome all these adversities, regain Soviet military support and Arab financial assistance, foil all settlement projects, and end up as the sole outside power in Lebanon.

3. Even before all the adversities had been overcome, Syria had resumed its quest for parity with the acquisition of vast amounts of Soviet arms. The large number of Soviet personnel manning some of the new advanced equipment contributed an element of immediate deterrence while the weapons were assimilated. By 1985 or 1986, Syria had built up a military establishment that matched or surpassed Israel's in terms of sheer numbers. There remained a large recognizable gap in the quality of the weapons commanded by the two sides, and a difficult to assess, but perhaps larger disparity in the quality of the personnel. Nevertheless

Israel repeatedly demonstrated respect for Syria's capabilities by adopting more cautious responses to incidents in which Syria had a presumed or indirect involvement.

For a while, Syria's quest for parity appeared to have advanced so far as to raise the issue of asymmetry in the Syrian-Israeli balance and its destablizing potential. (Syria aimed to balance Israel by itself, whereas Israel had to balance Syria plus contributions from other potential Arab belligerents, making for constant escalation of the arms race and putting a premium on prevention.) However, by the fall of 1987 it had become apparent that Syria's quest had exhausted itself. The oil glut that started in 1982 and the decline of oil prices, especially the precipitous drop in 1986 from $32 to less than $10 per barrel, ended the period of economic prosperity and reduced the flow of remittances and grants from oil-rich countries that had sustained the military buildup. The resulting economic strain actually forced a small but instructive cutback in the military establishment in 1986–1987 for the first time in over a decade.

Another significant development affecting the quest for parity was the accession in the Soviet Union of a new leadership, headed by General Secretary Gorbachev, committed to "new thinking" in domestic and foreign policy. In the Middle East, the new thinking was reflected in attempts to escape the Soviet's exclusive dependence on Syria, to diversify and modulate Soviet relations with countries of the area, including Egypt and Israel, and to seek a settlement of the Arab-Israeli conflict without resort to force.

Far more important was the development that took place in the inter-Arab arena as a result of the eruption of the Gulf crisis and the polarization of relations between Iran and its Arab neighbors. The confrontation reduced or eliminated Syria's role as a moderator of Iranian policy, on which it had cashed in, handsomely for many years. Above all, the confrontation impelled the Saudis and the Gulf countries to reach out to Egypt for help and press, successfully, in the November 1987 Amman summit for ending Egypt's ostracism. Underscoring the significance of that move was the fact that the summit's agenda and resolutions gave first priority to the conflict with Iran. They addressed the Arab-Israeli conflict secondarily, and even then the dominant note was not the usual pledges for continuing confrontation but a call for an international conference to seek a peaceful settlement. The fact that Syria, contrary to its behavior in several previous summits, went along was probably an indication of recognition, half-resigned and half-satisfied, that it had reached the limit in its quest for parity. This, coupled with Israel's retrenchment after its Lebanon misadventure, ended the period of strategic instability resulting from the Egyptian-Israeli peace.

Eruption in the Gulf Arena

Iran's Islamic revolution, like the other major revolutions of modern time, was a climactic moment in the contest of historical forces and, as such, had potential implications far transcending its place of origin for other parts of the world where these forces contend. Iran's revolution represented a triumph of Islamic revivalists, seeking to restore an idealized Islamic polity, in an historic struggle against secularizing modernizers, who have aspired to build and develop national states. It potentially appealed to the vast masses of mostly lower-class Muslims everywhere who have felt aliens in the midst of the imported cultures and political orders promoted by their modernizing rulers, and who yearned to reassert their identity and roots.

Iran's revolution inspired militant fundamentalist activity in many countries, but its full impact was held in abeyance by the inconclusive war it has fought with Iraq since 1980. In 1987, however, it became increasingly apparent that Iran was apt to prevail any moment, and that prospect precipitated new reactions by parties most likely to be affected by such a victory and the delayed consequences of the Islamic revolution. These reactions led to intervention by the superpowers, internationalization of the Gulf conflict, and polarization of relations between the Arab countries and Iran. It also set in motion a realignment of forces and a revision of priorities that completely altered the shape of the Middle East problem.

We have pointed out before that the successful encroachment of Western powers on the realms of Islam in the latter part of the eighteenth century was at the root of a crisis of orientation in the Middle East. That encroachment had generated reponses among Muslim societies, which became articulated in the nineteenth century under the impetus of increasing foreign domination, into two ideological and political currents: Islamic revivalism and secularizing nationalism. In the twentieth century, the two currents evolved and bifurcated, but joined sporadically in endeavors to get rid of foreign control. By the time independence of these Arab-countries was achieved, the two currents had spawned extreme versions that were mutually hostile. Islamic revivalism, intially concerned mainly with reformulating the traditional Islamic belief system to allow greater scope for reason, had generated varieties of fundamentalist currents or movements that aspired to replace the existing political systems with Islamic polities modeled after an idealized original Islamic community-state. Nationalism, intially identified with liberalism, had taken on various authoritarian or radical populistic forms committed to forced-pace modernization.

In general, the Islamic currents had far greater appeal to the tradition-bound masses than the nationalist, and that appeal grew stonger as the chauvinistic and populistic programs pursued by the nationalist governments fell far short of their promise and only intensified the restlessness of the masses by further disrupting the familiar moulds. The nationalists, however, commanded the state's instruments of coercion, and they used them to repress any expression of fundamentalist tendencies they deemed dangerous, and to intimidate the masses and neutralize their sympathy.

Iran's Islamic revolution undermined that syndrome by demonstrating, for the first time in history, that a fundamentalist movement enjoying the support of the masses could overcome all odds and wrest state power from a seemingly omnipotent modernizing regime. This provided inspiration for acts of fundamentalist militancy such as the seizure of the Grand Mosque of Mecca, the assassination of President Sadat of Egypt, the sabotage and terror campaign mounted by the Muslim Brethren against the Syrian regime, the rise of Hizbollah in Lebanon, and so on. However, Iran's example failed to generate similar kinds of upheavals at least in part because its revolution was itself subjected to an attempted repression by radical nationalist Iraq, and because, after repelling that attempt, Iran made the overthrow of Iraq's regime a test of the validity and destiny of its Islamic revolution.[1]

When Iraq decided to invade Iran in September 1980, its rulers, as well as those of other neighboring Muslim countries, had a sense that the accession of the fundamentalists to power in Iran presented a danger to their regimes, but they wrongly assessed what had happened in Iran. They thought that the success of the fundamentalists there was due to fortuitous circumstances, and, feeling encouraged by the ensuing disorganization of Iran's armed forces, thought they could undo it with a decisive "police action." By defeating what remained of Iran's armed forces and seizing its main ports and oil-producing region, the Iraqis and their supporters hoped to bring about the collapse or overthrow of the new regime.

The Iraqis made some gains but fell far short of their target and could not press their attack further. By the end of October, 1980, they had halted and had prepared to trade the gains they had achieved for some kind of favorable settlement. Iran refused to negotiate, but as its initial counterattacks failed, as its regime got caught in domestic struggles and purges, as it became embroiled in a conflict with the United States over the seizure of American hostages, and as it lost its principal source

---

[1] In a dark moment of Iran's war with Iraq, Ayatollah Khomeini said that Allah commands us to do our duty but does not assure us of success. This statement contradicts other statements of his to the effect that successes of the revolution were a sign of Allah's approval, and it suggests, at any rate, that his audience thought so.

of supply of arms and spare parts, it seemed that the war had settled into a stalemate favoring Iraq.

However, in the fall of 1981 Iran began a series of offensives that went on intermittently through the winter, and by the spring of 1982 they had routed the Iraqis and driven them out of nearly all the territory the Iraqis had captured. Iraq sued for a cease-fire and a settlement based on the *status quo ante bellum,* but Iran insisted on the removal of the "godless Ba'thist regime" of Saddam Hussein as a condition for ending the war, and threatened to invade Iraq to achieve that end. Since the Iraqi forces had been routed in the recent offensives, the Iranians, as well as others, expected an attack to succeed quickly, and give the Islamic revolution renewed momentum and irresistible appeal.

Saudi Arabia and the other Gulf countries made frantic efforts to dissuade Iran from attacking. They approached Egypt to intervene militarily on Iraq's side, and when Egypt refused, they tried to promote mediation by third parties, enlisted Syria to use its influence with Iran, and discretely elicited American warnings to Iran. The Iranians appeared, or pretended, to be swayed for a while; but, in July 1982, they attacked in force, seeking to cut off and capture the Basra region. Only the unexpectedly successful resistance of Iraq prevented a major cataclysm.

The Iranians came back again and again. Since that first attack on Iraq in the summer of 1982, they have mounted one or two major offensives every year in addition to many smaller attacks. Some of these operations scored significant successes, albeit at enormous costs in casualties, but none has achieved a breakthrough. Interested third parties and analysts reached the comforting conlusion early in the process that Iraq's superior armament would indefinitely check Iran's superior numbers, and that the war would remain stuck in an unbreakable stalemate until the death of Khomeini opened up a possibility for a political accomodation.

Iraq's leaders, however, apparently knew better. Sooner than others they realized that Iran was deliberately pursuing a grinding war of attrition in which it had a better chance of eventually prevailing because of its larger size, more favorable geostrategic position, stronger cohesiveness, superior morale, and the unquestionable authority of the Ayatollah Khomeini. Iraq's leaders could not admit this fact to their people and allies for fear of being abandoned by them, but their anxiety was reflected in the desperate actions they took to foil Iran's strategy. In 1984, for instance, Iraq resorted to chemical weapons to repel an Iranian offensive, openly sought Egypt's support for its war effort, though Iraq had taken the lead five years before in pressing for the ostracism of Egypt, and moved to restore diplomatic relations with the United States, whom it had denounced as the sworn enemy of the Arabs since 1967.

In an effort to force Iran to end the war or at least change the odds that favored Iran, Iraq used its superior air power and newly acquired Exocet missiles to start, in 1984, a campaign against ships carrying Iranian oil exports, which financed its war-making capability. Iran suffered an initial setback, but eventually devised effective shipping arrangments that enabled it to recover and maintain its rate of exports. In the meantime, Iran had also reacted by attacking the shipping of Iraq's Arab friends in the Gulf in order to compel them to press Iraq to desist from attacking Iranian shipping, and *that* gave Iraq a new reason to persist in its attacks. By provoking Iranian retaliation against third parties it hoped to embroil them more deeply against Iran, that is, "internationalize" the conflict and cause international intervention to end it.

Iraq's gambit seemed to have failed until, ironically, the deterioration of its situation reached a point that could not be ignored by others. Early in 1986 its forces suffered their biggest and most obvious defeat since 1982, as the Iranians broke through south of Basra, captured most of the Fao peninsula, and held it against costly massive counterattacks. In July of that year, the Iraqis suffered another defeat in the Mehran region, and in January 1987 they lost ground in the Basra front but were able to prevent the Iranians from capturing the city only at an enormous cost in casualties. These setbacks finally drove home to interested outside governments the notion that Iraq could go under, and that, in turn, put a different perspective on their view of the "tanker war" and triggered a chain reactions, that brought the Gulf war to the forefront of regional and international attention for the first time.

In January 1987, the Soviet Union, who had for a long time a keen concern about the implications of an Iranian victory for its position in Aghanistan and perhaps for its own Muslim population, condemned Iran for continuing the war and for its anti-Soviet attitude. Shortly thereafter, Kuwait, whose ships had been a prime target of Iranian retaliatory attacks, asked the United States and the Soviet Union to help protect its shipping. The United States tabled Kuwait's request, but when the Soviets agreed in May to charter five of their tankers to Kuwait, the United States followed immediately by offering to put eleven Kuwaiti tankers under American registry and to protect them. The Saudis, who had previously been careful to keep a line open to Iran and avoid too close an association with the United States, agreed to facilitate the operations of the American escort forces. The Iranians retaliated by organizing disruptive demonstrations during the pilgrimage to Mecca, which resulted in hundreds of Iranian and other pilgrims being killed and brought Saudi-Iranian relations into open confrontation. The Iranians also responded by mining the waters of the Gulf, which, in turn, brought in naval forces of several NATO countries to protect their own shipping and to help keep the Gulf waters open. Meanwhile, Iran vowed to make everyone's shipping unsafe as long as its own was made so, and Iran backed up its threat with selective attacks on unescorted ships.

While these developments unfolded in the Gulf arena itself, the powers involved engaged in efforts aimed at bringing the war to an end or to confront Iran if it insisted on its continuation. One interesting result of these endeavors was joint action by the United States and the Soviet Union to put through the UN Security Council a resolution enjoining a cease-fire in the war and threatening sanctions in case of noncompliance, followed by consultations between the two superpowers on a follow-up resolution that would proclaim and enforce an arms embargo against a recalcitrant Iran. Another no less intriguing result was the convening of an Arab summit in Amman in November 1987, which put the conflict with Iran at the top of its agenda and resolutions, ahead of the Arab-Israeli conflict. The resolutions condemned Iran as aggressor, proclaimed the determination of the Arabs to resist it, and called for international sanctions against it. They ended the ostracism of Egypt in an endeavor to enlist its strategic weight against Iran and authorized the restoration of diplomatic relations with Egypt, despite its peace with Israel. The resolutions also supported an international conference with the participation of all parties, including the PLO, to settle the Arab-Israeli conflict peacefully. Syria, Iran's ally, the archantagonist of Egypt, and the proponent of strategic parity, participated in the summit and went along with all the resolutions.

Thus, Iraq's strategy of bringing about the internationalization of the conflict, which did not work when it seemed to be holding Iran at bay, began to succeed when it became apparent that the tide of the war had turned against it. Although the international intervention, the polarization of relations between Iran and the Arabs, and what came to be known as the Gulf crisis seemed to have come about as a result of discrete actions by many actors in response to various specific events, the actions were conditioned by the fear of an Iranian victory and its likely consequences. That is why the actions went beyond the events that had elicited them, and began to reorder priorities and shape a tacit coalition to contain Iran's Islamic revolution. That incipient coalition includes such unlikely partners as the United States and the Soviet Union, Syria as well as Iraq, Egypt and Saudi Arabia, in addition to all the Arab countries (except Libya), and even, however implicitly and remotely (through the rehabilitation of Egypt, cooperation with the United States, and downgrading of the Arab-Israeli conflict), Israel itself.

FOREIGN POLICY LANDMARKS

1945   Formation of the Arab League.
1947   UN resolution to partition Palestine into a Jewish state and an Arab
         state

1948–49   Palestine War (Israel's War of Independence)
1955   Soviet-Egyptian arms deal, the first between the Soviet Union and a Middle Eastern country
1956   Invasion of Suez by Britain and France; Sinai War Between Israel and Egypt
1957   Eisenhower Doctrine
1958   Union between Syria and Egypt, creating the United Arab Republic (UAR)
1961   Syrian secession from the UAR
1962–67   Yemen War with heavy Egyptian involvement
1967   Six Day War
1968–70   The "war of attrition"
1973   October War (Yom Kippur War)
1978–79   Camp David accords and Egyptian-Israeli peace
1979   Soviet invasion of Afghanistan
1980   Iraqi invasion of Iran
1982   Israel invades Lebanon, pulls out in 1985
1987   Iran-Iraq War generates "Gulf crisis"

SELECTED BIBLIOGRAPHY

ABRAHAMIAN, ERVAND. *Iran Between Two Revolutions*. Princeton, N.J.: Princeton University Press, 1982.
AJAMI, FOUAD. *The Arab Predicament*. New York: Cambridge University Press, 1981.
ANDERSEN, ROY, et al. *Politics and Change in the Middle East*. Englewood Cliffs, N.J.: Prentice-Hall, 1982.
BATATU, HANNA. *The Old Social Classes and the Revolutionary Movements of Iraq*. Princeton, N.J.: Princeton University Press, 1978.
BILL, JAMES, and CARL LEIDEN. *Politics in the Middle East*. Boston: Little, Brown, 1979.
FREEDMAN, ROBERT O. *Soviet Policy Toward the Middle East Since 1970*. New York: Praeger, 1982.
HEIKAL, MOHAMMED. *The Road to Ramadan*. London: Collins, 1975.
———. *The Sphinx and the Commissar*. New York: Harper & Row, 1978.
HERZOG, CHAIM. *The Arab-Israeli Wars*. New York: Random House, 1982.
HOLDEN, DAVID, and RICHARD JOHNS. *The House of Saud*. New York: Holt, Rinehart & Winston, 1981.
HOURANI, ALBERT. *Arabic Thought in the Liberal Age, 1789–1939*. New York: Cambridge University Press, 1983.
HUDSON, MICHAEL. *Arab Politics: The Search for Legitimacy*. New Haven, Conn.: Yale University Press, 1977.
KERR, MALCOM. *The Arab Cold War*. New York: Oxford University Press, 1971.
KERR, MALCOLM, and YASSIN, EL SAYED, eds. *Rich and Poor States in the Middle East*. Boulder, Colo.: Westview Press, 1982.
KHALIDI, WALID. *Conflict and Violence in Lebanon*. Cambridge, Mass.: Center for International Affairs, Harvard University, 1979.
LEWIS, BERNARD. *The Emergence of Modern Turkey*. New York: Oxford University Press, 1961.
QUANDT, WILLIAM. *Decade of Decisions*. Los Angeles: University of California Press, 1977.
SAFRAN, NADAV. *Egypt in Search of Political Community*. Cambridge, Mass.: Harvard University Press, 1961.
———. *From War to War*. Indianapolis, Ind.: Pegasus, 1969.
———. *Israel: The Embattled Ally*. Cambridge, Mass.: Harvard University Press, 1978.
———. *Saudi Arabia: The Ceaseless Quest for Security*. Cambridge, Mass.: 1985.
STEPHENS, ROBERT. *Nasser*. New York: Simon & Schuster, 1971.
VATIKIOTIS, P. J. *Politics and the Military in Jordan*. London: Frank Cass, 1967.

VAN DAM, NIKOLAOS. *The Struggle for Power in Syria*. London: Croom Helm, 1979.

WATERBURY JOHN. *The Egypt of Nasser and Sadat*. Princeton, N.J.: Princeton University Press, 1983.

YANIV, AVNER. *Dilemmas of Security: Politics, Strategy, and the Israeli Experience in Lebanon*. New York: Oxford University Press, 1987.

YODFAT, AREYH, and YUVAL, ARNON-OHANA. *PLO Strategy and Tactics*. New York: St. Martin's Press, 1981.

10

The Foreign Policy
of Latin America*

Riordan Roett

INTRODUCTION

The legacy of colonial rule and the growing regional hegemony of the
United States dominated the foreign policies of Latin American states
after their independence.[1] Struggling on the world scene to break their
old patterns of economic and political bondage, they also had to confront
the overarching ambitions of the United States. The twin themes of
seeking greater global influence while struggling for autonomy from the
United States provide the leitmotivs of any study of contemporary Latin
American foreign policy.

Latin America was the first of the "Third Worlds" to achieve independence, long before much of Africa, Asia, and the Middle East, but the
area's insertion into the international system has been erratic. Geographic
location, political and social instability, and economic dependence on the

*I am indebted to Mr. Richard S. Sacks for research and editorial assistance in
preparing this essay.

[1]For the purposes of this chapter, I am defining "Latin America" to include all the
states of the Western Hemisphere except Canada and the United States, even those, like
Guyana and Grenada, which are not "Latin."

industrial world precluded any hope of common foreign policy goals.[2] Indeed, while a shared history and common languages and cultural traditions appear to "homogenize" the states of the region, the reality has been nearly two centuries of conflict and competition.

What is "Latin American" about the region's foreign policy? United by a common desire for economic and social development, all of Latin America wants to retain its national sovereignty and independence. Yet from country to country, the variations in geographic size, demography, wealth, developmental level, and politics are enormous.[3] These national differences clearly influence Latin American foreign policies. As examples of political variation, contrast the English-speaking Caribbean, which achieved independence quite recently and proudly maintains British parliamentary traditions, with neighboring states of Haiti, which has known little but dictatorship, or the Dominican Republic, which has only recently consolidated democratic processes. Only a minority of Latin American states have any hope of achieving regional power, by virtue of their size, location, resources, and level of development. Among the natural "leaders" of the region are Argentina and Brazil, traditional rivals on the Atlantic coast, and Chile and Peru, geopolitically prominent on the Pacific. Mexico has long dominated Central America.

GEOGRAPHY AND HISTORY

The geographical anomalies of Latin America have heavily influenced its economic development and foreign policy. For instance, the proximity of Mexico and of the Central American and Caribbean states to the United States has obviously had a strong effect on national life. Most of the southwestern United States was part of Mexico until the nineteenth century, when the United States annexed almost one-half of Mexican territory.

The continent possesses some of the most awesome natural phe-

[2]In 1983, Latin America was 50 percent more populous than North America (390 million as compared with 259 million, while the world total was 4,677 million). The annual rate of population growth was the highest of any continent (3.5 percent as compared with 3.0 percent in Africa, 1.9 percent in Asia, and 0.7 percent in North America). The population of Latin America doubles every 30 years. Latin Americans are not quite as urbanized as North Americans (65 percent as compared with 74 percent) but much more urbanized than Africans and Asians (only 27 percent of whom live in cities). The GNP figures per capita for South and Central America are low ($2,070 and $1,740 in 1980, respectively), but much higher than for Africa ($760) or Asia ($330), excluding Japan and the Middle East.

[3]For example, while Paraguay has a population of just over 1 million, Brazil has 130 million people and Mexico has 76 million. Annual population growth in Nicaragua is 3.6 percent, but only 0.8 percent in Cuba and 1.5 percent in Argentina. Life expectancy in Puerto Rico is 73 years, but only 50 in Bolivia. Uruguay's population is 84 percent urban, while only 30 percent of Guyana's people live in cities. Per capita incomes range from $601 in Bolivia to $2,250 in Mexico to $4,170 in Venezuela.

nomena in the world. The Amazon River plunges across the continent to the Atlantic coast of Brazil at Belem, and is navigable as far as Iquitos, Peru, 1,600 miles upriver. Giant Brazil, larger than the United States without Alaska, is almost as big as all other South American countries combined. The Amazon Basin occupies about one-fourth of the continent and more than half of Brazil. In turn, 61 percent of Peru, 48 percent of Ecuador, 47 percent of Bolivia, and a large part of Colombia are part of the Amazon Basin.

Each of these four states are bifurcated by the towering Andes, which extend from Mexico in the north to the tip of Chile in the south. With an average height of more than 10,000 feet and reaching a maximum of nearly 23,000 feet above sea level, the Andes are rivaled only by the ranges of central Asia. The Andean presence dictates climate (the principal areas of population would be tropical if not for the altitude) as well as livelihood and export potential for there are deposits of copper, silver, gold, and tin. And it has determined patterns of settlement, favoring the mountains to the humid lowlands.

To the east of the Andes the vast Argentine pampa stretches to the Atlantic Ocean. It is a flat, rich land mass unequaled in the world for its fertility. The transportation and communications potential of the River Plate have influenced the Southern Cone countries (Argentina, Uruguay, and Paraguay) through which it flows, from its Paraguay and Paraná tributaries deep in the continent's heartland to its mouth on the Atlantic at Buenos Aires. Of all the states in South America, only Uruguay is entirely in the temperate zone.

Geography must be combined with history to understand the contextual variables that shape the foreign policy of Latin American states. As the era of discoveries accelerated in the late fifteenth century, the rival claims of Spain and Portugal were partially resolved by a papal decision in 1494. The Treaty of Tordesillas divided the New World unequally between the two powers, and gave Spain the major share of the Western Hemisphere. Portuguese-Brazilian expansion in the intervening years led to claims which doubled the earlier grants. (The Treaty of Madrid in 1750 set the framework for the recognition of Portugal's claim.) While the boundary issue was settled legally, Brazil's continuing land hunger created lasting resentment.

Conflicts in the Americas often reflected European wars and dynastic rivalries. Spanish and Portuguese sovereignty was challenged by the French and the English, who eventually settled North America and much of the Caribbean. By the end of the eighteenth century, after its 1763 defeat by England and the rebellion of Haiti, the French presence in the New World was limited to the Eastern Caribbean and French Guyana. The independence movements that erupted in Spain's empire drew their strength in part from traditional European competition and from the French and North American revolutionary movements.

THE INDEPENDENCE PERIOD

Napoleon's invasion of the Iberian peninsula (Portugal in 1807 and Spain in 1808) was the fuse that ignited the Latin American powder keg. Although the Portuguese royal family evaded the French soldiers and fled to Brazil in British ships, the Spanish monarch did not escape. Without the legitimizing rule of the Spanish king to define political life, Spain's New World Empire began a long and painful process of disintegration. Argentina and Paraguay quickly pressed their independence. Other rebellious provinces were thwarted by royalist forces after the restoration of Ferdinand VII in 1812. When Ferdinand suppressed Spain's new liberal constitution soon after his return to power, the wars of independence in the colonies were renewed. Brazil moved relatively smoothly to independence in 1822 (after the King returned to Portugal) and quickly achieved recognition from both the United States and the European powers.

The struggle for independence led to a series of bloody civil wars.[4] After Napoleon's defeat, the restored French monarchy supported Spain's efforts to regain its New World empire. England refused to help the revolutionaries, contenting itself with a preferred commercial role in Brazilian trade. The Liberal Revolution in Spain (1820) assisted the independence movements, particularly in Mexico and Peru, but, in 1823, France sent an army into Spain to suppress the constitutional regime. Knowing that the British would use their military power to keep Spain and France out, the United States decided it could gain more advantage by acting unilaterally. President James Monroe enunciated the new doctrine in his December 1823 message to Congress:

> . . . that the American continents, by the free and independent conditions which they have assumed and maintain, are henceforth not to be considered as subjects for future colonization by any European powers. . . . We owe it, therefore, to candor and to the amicable relations existing between the United States and those powers to declare that we should consider any attempt on their parts to extend their system to any portion of this hemisphere as dangerous to our peace and safety.[5]

By the late 1820s the European powers had accepted the new status quo in Latin America and the United States had successfully asserted its diplomatic pretension regarding Western Hemisphere independence. All that was left of Spain's empire was the island of Cuba.

As the external threat to their independence receded, the Latin American states fell to squabbling among themselves. Visionary efforts to

---

[4]See John Lynch, *The Spanish-American Revolutions, 1808–1826* (New York: Norton, 1973).

[5]A copy of the full message appears in Ruhl J. Bartlett, ed., *The Record of American Diplomacy* (New York: Knopf, 1964), pp. 181–83.

unify fragments of the old empire collapsed. A united Central America broke into five republics. "Gran Colombia" lost Venezuela and Ecuador. Uruguay became an independent buffer state between Argentina and Brazil in 1828. Political instability and boundary disputes became continuing sources of conflict. Only Brazil escaped, by peacefully negotiating its borders with the strong diplomatic backing of the United States.

The disorder of independence had reduced the economies of the region to chaos. With the old links to Iberia severed, Latin America needed new sources for trade and investment. Expanding opportunities in international commerce enticed the Latin American countries to supply food and raw materials for the European market. The United States could not compete with England in providing badly needed capital and marketing facilities, and British bankers and businessmen were soon dominant.

Although British leadership restored some order to the post-independence economic picture, the international relations of the Latin American states remained chaotic for decades. Both Brazil and Argentina, the rivals of the Atlantic coast, attempted to assert regional hegemony. A standoff was achieved by midcentury at a considerable price: the creation of Uruguay, an English-French blockade of Buenos Aires, the overthrow of the Rosas dictatorship in Argentina, and recognition of an independent Paraguay by Argentina. On the west coast, Chile foiled a Peruvian-Bolivian attempt at confederation when it declared war (1836–1839), and it emerged as the preeminent power on the Pacific.

The long and tempestuous relationship between the United States and Mexico began soon after independence. In 1821, independent Mexico extended from the state of Oregon to the Isthmus of Panama, representing half the population and half the wealth of Spanish America. By the Treaty of Guadalupe Hidalgo (1848), following the Mexican-American War, Mexico lost one-half of its territory to the United States, which had meanwhile annexed Texas. U.S. policy derived in part from the belief that Mexico would be unable to resist an anticipated English attempt to create a buffer to U.S. expansion in the American Southwest.

LATIN AMERICA FROM MID-NINETEENTH CENTURY TO THE TWENTIETH CENTURY

After 1850, while republican forms of government were under attack by local oligarchies and caudillos, the Europeans tried one last time to return. Spain unsuccessfully pressed to reincorporate the Dominican Republic into its empire and fought a bloody, ten-year civil war with Cuban nationalists that ended in 1878. Napoleon III sent Austrian Archduke Maximilian to Mexico to occupy a nonexistent throne; the emperor was executed in 1867. Spain occupied a part of Peru from 1863–1869, alleging financial claims. Within the hemisphere, the American Civil War and the War of the Triple Alliance (1864–1870) erupted. The latter pitted Paraguay against the combined might of Brazil, Argentina, and Uruguay in a bloody war that subdued Paraguay and and left it occupied by Brazil for six years.

In Central America and the Caribbean, the United States and Britain competed for trade, markets, steamboat lines and the right to construct a canal across the Isthmus of Panama. The rivalries over the Isthmus did not end until an independent state of Panama was carved out of Colombia in 1903 and construction of an American canal began.

In the last decades of the nineteenth century, two themes prevailed: a search for modernization and development and the emergence of a genuine subsystem of power politics on the continent. Mexico entered a period of sullen acceptance of its dismemberment, and under Porfirio Diaz created a stable, if despotic, regime that survived until the outbreak of that country's revolution in 1911. Central America and the Caribbean came increasingly under American economic suasion, and the "banana republics" phenomenon and "gunboat diplomacy" became facts of life. In South America, relatively secure from outside intervention, and better positioned to develop its exports, a sorting out of power relationships took place. Chile confirmed her power again by soundly defeating Bolivia and Peru in the War of the Pacific (1879–1883).[6] The conflict deprived Bolivia of its Pacific coast, which has remained an irredentist issue until today. Chile occupied Lima, Peru's capital, for two years, and seized the province of Tarapacá, which possessed extensive mineral wealth. The war also created Latin America's "Alsace-Lorraine": the two Chilean-occupied Peruvian provinces of Tacna and Arica. Unable to agree on the terms for a plebecite, the countries did not resolve the issue until 1929, severely complicating their bilateral relations.

On the Atlantic coast, Brazil's ties with Great Britain continued despite the overthrow of the Brazilian empire in 1889, which began a slow but inexorable linking of Brazil's interests with those of the United States. By the turn of the century, the United States would view Brazil as a special ally on the continent, and Brazilian diplomacy artfully employed United States interests in settling its outstanding border disputes with its Spanish-American neighbors. In partial response to that development, Argentina emerged as the principal antagonist of the United States in the hemisphere, opposing United States pretensions of hegemony whenever possible. Uneasy relations between Buenos Aires and Washington would continue into the twentieth century, exacerbated in turn by the distrust

---

[6]For an excellent overview of Chile's role, see Robert N. Burr, *By Reason or Force: Chile and the Balancing of Power in South America, 1830–1905* (Berkeley and Los Angeles: University of California Press, 1965).

between Buenos Aires and Rio de Janeiro. From the perspective of United States foreign policy, Brazil could do no wrong, and Argentina could do little that was right.

As the United States moved toward Great Power status at the end of the nineteenth century, concern about its primacy in the hemisphere increased, as did willingness to press its claim. In 1895, President Grover Cleveland invoked the Monroe Doctrine in a border dispute between Great Britain and Venezuela over British Guiana (today, Guyana). British reluctance to seek a political solution through negotiation irritated the United States. Secretary of State Richard Olney captured the essence of the new American attitude when he commented that "today the United States is practically sovereign in this continent, and its fiat is law upon the subjects to which it confines its interposition." The British yielded and the dispute was settled by international arbitration. Implicitly, England had accepted the United States assertion of the Monroe Doctrine. The incident heralded the opening of a period of direct American involvement in the affairs of Latin America.

THE UNITED STATES INTERVENES

The American century opened with a series of resounding successes for those who had heard the call of empire. Cuba was independent from Spain, but the 1901 Platt Amendment (in effect until 1934), which permitted the United States to intervene in its internal affairs, made it little more than an American colony. The Venezuelan crisis of 1902–1903, which ended any European pretensions to influence in the affairs of the hemisphere, occasioned Theodore Roosevelt to assert a "Roosevelt Corollary" to the Monroe Doctrine:.

> . . . chronic wrongdoing, or an impotence which results in a general loosening of the ties of civilized society, may in America, as elsewhere, ultimately require intervention by some civilized nation, and in the Western Hemisphere the adherence of the United States to the Monroe Doctrine may force the United States, however reluctantly . . . to the exercise of an international power.[7]

The United States thus took responsibility for forcing Latin American states to respect their international obligations, thus clearly establishing its suzerainty in the hemisphere. Use of the "Big Stick" policy became the rule, not the exception.

---

[7]Quoted in Harold Eugene Davis, John J. Finan, and F. Taylor Peck, *Latin American Diplomatic History: An Introduction* (Baton Rouge, La. and London: Louisiana State University Press, 1977), p. 154.

Increasingly, the United States used the Big Stick. Between 1898 and 1933 there were only three years in which U.S. troops were not stationed in one or more Latin American countries.[8]

To further its economic interests, the United States formulated the concept of Pan-Americanism. Initiated by Secretary of State James G. Blaine in 1889, the short-run purpose was to foster harmonious political relations between the United States and the hemisphere; the long-range goal was to increase investment and trade between North and South America.

The Bureau of the American Republics was the first building block in the intricate Inter-American System that has emerged in the Americas over the last century. The 1889 meeting in Washington led to a series of conferences of American states, often utilized by the United States either to justify its policies or seek Latin American endorsement for actions already taken. "Progressive Pan-Americanism," which made its appearance in the early 1900s, "aimed at expanding trade, building investment opportunities, and tapping sources of agricultural and mineral raw materials in Latin America" while appealing to Latin leaders who desired economic progress, and who accepted both "the need for the participation of foreign interests and capital" and the secondary status which progressive Pan-American policies implied.[9]

By World War I, American investment in Latin America began to grow. From 1914 to 1919, the value of United States investments in the region increased by 50 percent and doubled between 1919 to 1929. The investment growth was concentrated in government and private bonds in Argentina, Brazil, Chile, Colombia, and Cuba. The United States was rapidly overtaking Britain as the largest investor in the region and emerged from World War II on top.

LATIN AMERICA AND THE INTERNATIONAL SYSTEM

The early decades of the twentieth century were filled with irony for Latin America. The slow emergence of Pan-Americanism responded to the century-old wish for cooperation and collaborative action that grew out of the idealism of Simón Bolívar in the 1820s. But as the major states of the region appeared increasingly able and willing to pursue that ideal, U.S. imperial interests—political and economic—stood in the way. The new century brought opportunities for multilateral cooperation with Eu-

[8]Dana G. Munro provides an overview of this period in *The United States and the Caribbean Republics, 1921–1933* (Princeton, N.J.: Princeton University Press, 1974).

[9]Robert Neal Seidel, *Progressive Pan Americanism: Development and United States Policy Toward South America, 1906–1931* (Ithaca, N.Y.: Cornell University, Latin American Studies Program Dissertation Series, January 1973), No. 45, p. 2.

ropean states that were previously not available. Only Mexico participated in the First Hague Conference (1899); a number of states attended the second, in 1907. The Latin American states used the meetings mainly to urge adoption of the Drago Doctrine: to limit the use of force in the collection of damage claims and contract debts. But the essential Latin American demands went unheeded. U.S. intervention continued, and national differences were sufficiently strong to prevent any form of unified political action.

If Latin America needed a reminder of the U.S. will to intervene, it occurred in 1914. A dispute with the United States during Mexico's revolution led President Woodrow Wilson to send troops to occupy the port of Veracruz. As a result of the bombardment and occupation, the government of General Victoriano Huerta fell and others viewed favorably by Wilson took power in Mexico City. The revolution, which ended in 1917, was later enshrined in the Institutional Revolutionary party (PRI) and gave the Mexican government a legitimacy possessed by few others in the hemisphere. Revolutionary legitimacy also meant a staunch defense of Mexican national interests, which led to diplomatic and political confrontations with the United States that continue today.

Latin America was ambivalent about World War I. Of the principal states, only Brazil declared war against the Central Powers. Following the war, Latin American states joined the League of Nations, but they contributed little. Argentina, for example, ignored the League. Brazil withdrew in 1926, when it failed to receive a permanent seat on the council.

The 1930s were a decade of change and conflict in the Western Hemisphere. For the first time in the century, a full-scale war broke out on the continent. The Chaco War (1932–1935) pitted landlocked Bolivia against a similarly landlocked Paraguay over possession of the desert region called the "Chaco Boreal". Weak efforts by neighbors and the League of Nations failed to stop the fighting, which went in Paraguay's favor. But in May 1935 a mediating group composed of Argentina, Chile, Brazil, Peru, the United States, and, later, Uruguay laboriously negotiated a cease-fire and, finally, a peace treaty in July 1938. For his efforts in these negotiations, the Argentine foreign minister received the Nobel Peace Prize.

United States–Mexican relations deteriorated during the 1930s. With the 1934 election of President Lázaro Cárdenas, a wave of nationalism swept the country. Agrarian reforms hurt large numbers of American landowners. Moving quickly to "Mexicanize" the country's economy, Cárdenas nationalized the railways in 1937 and all foreign-owned oil properties the following year, promising indemnification "in due course." Quick-witted diplomatic action by the Roosevelt administration led to a negotiated settlement and became a hallmark of his Good Neighbor Policy.

THE GOOD NEIGHBOR

The Hoover administration (1929–1933) began to repudiate the American habit of intervention with a series of steps that, amplified by the Franklin D. Roosevelt administration (1933–1945), became the Good Neighbor Policy.[10] The new approach made Washington's prestige in Latin America soar to heights not seen since it recognized Latin American independence. After a successful preinaugural Latin American tour, President Herbert Hoover began removing United States troops from Central America and the Caribbean while his Secretary of State, Henry Stimson, effectively disavowed the Theodore Roosevelt Corollary with his 1929 Clark Memorandum on the Monroe Doctrine.

President Franklin D. Roosevelt went further, making nonintervention a pillar of United States foreign policy while satisfying a number of long-standing Latin American political goals. In 1934, Washington ended its military occupation of Haiti and restored Cuba's sovereignty by abrogating the Platt Amendment. In 1936, the United States and Panama agreed to abolish the virtual protectorate that had been in force since 1903. Nonintervention, noninterference, and an economically stimulating tariff deal were reaffirmed at the 1936 Inter-American conference in Buenos Aires. By 1940, after tolerating a wave of expropriations of United States interests, Washington had convinced the region that its respect for Latin American sovereignty was genuine.

LATIN AMERICA AND WORLD WAR II

The Good Neighbor Policy was the high point of United States–Latin American relations in this century, but it soon fell prey to the ideological and security imperatives of World War II and the Cold War. In the end, Washington's strategic thinking about Latin America and the Caribbean remained one-sided. Through the 1920s, the United States assumed the Monroe Doctrine and the Roosevelt Corollary were binding on all other states. U.S. strategists continued to emphasize American interests, to the point of preparing contingency plans for potential destabilization in the hemisphere.[11] Hampered by isolationism at home, the United States did not begin multilateral planning with its neighbors until 1939, but by then the Fascist menace had scared the United States into allocating scarce resources to its traditional European allies.

[10]Irwin F. Gelman succinctly summarizes this period in *Good Neighbor Diplomacy: United States Policies in Latin America, 1933–1945* (Baltimore, Md. and London: The Johns Hopkins University Press, 1979).

[11]John Child, *Unequal Alliance: The Inter-American Military System, 1938–1978* (Boulder, Colo.: Westview Press, 1980), pp. 12–14.

By the late 1930s sympathy for the Axis cause was widespread in Argentina, Brazil, Chile, Paraguay, and Bolivia, and United States strategists focused on Nazi penetration of the hemisphere. After Germany invaded Poland in September 1939, the isolationist logjam was broken and it seemed that the United States would soon be at war. Hemispheric foreign ministers meeting in Panama the same month agreed to establish a 300-mile "security zone" around the continent although this meant the United States Navy would do the patrolling, given the state of Latin American naval forces. The 1938 Declaration of Lima had already approved inter-American consultation whenever a foreign power threatened the peace, security, or territorial integrity of an American republic, despite Argentine objections which had forced a watering down of Roosevelt's calls for "collective defense."

At the beginning the war in Europe appeared to be going against Britain and its allies and many, including the U.S. chiefs of staff, believed that the Western Hemisphere would become the next target of Axis aggression. The foreign ministers reconvened in Havana in July 1940 to approve a clear statement of collective defense. Although foreign ministers met for a third time in Rio in January 1942 to create the Inter-American Defense Board (IADFB), it never performed more than a purely symbolic role. Brazil soon emerged as the strongest supporter of the U.S. war effort. In exchange for development aid and arms, the Brazilians provided vital bases and sent an expeditionary force to Italy in 1944. Aside from Brazil, only Mexico actively supported the United States by sending 300 troops to the Far East in 1945.

The 1942 Rio meeting was the last of its kind during the war. Global strategies for maintaining peace in the postwar world increasingly appealed to the United States and Latin American preferences for regional cooperation received little attention in Washington. Amid preparations to found the United Nations, the United States finally bowed to pressures for an Inter-American meeting but effectively excluded Argentina by insisting that only active participants in the war effort attend. Convening in Mexico City early in 1945, the meeting drafted plans for a comprehensive charter for the Inter-American System, to be considered at Bogotá the following year.

The one notable accomplishment of the Mexico City meeting was the Act of Chapultepec, which for the first time in the history of Inter-American agreements sanctioned the use of armed force (but only until the end of the war). The signatories declared they would consider an attack against any state in the Hemisphere as aggression against them all, and they approved using armed force in retaliation.

As the United States wrestled with the issue of regional versus global organization, Latin American states were becoming preoccupied with their economic future. The war had broken their traditional commercial and trade ties with Europe and ruined the European economies. With its usual economic and financial linkages gone, Latin America looked to the United States for support in postwar economic planning, but the United States offered little solace.

The Latin American states were correct if they assumed that the rapidly deteriorating relationship between the United States and the Soviet Union would determine their political and economic fate. As the war ended, the Cold War began. The recovery of Japan and Western Europe and the containment of Eastern Europe and the Soviet Union were uppermost of Washington's priorities.

THE POST–WORLD WAR ERA

The San Francisco Conference met from April to June 1945 to draft a charter for a United Nations that would maintain "international peace and security." The Latin American states had to go along with Washington's global approach in order to protect their concern for regional cooperation. Six of the seven Latin American states that had not yet declared war on the Axis did so by March 1, 1945, guaranteeing their right to attend, but Argentina, which missed the deadline by declaring war on March 27, needed Soviet approval. The Soviets obliged, but only after Washington agreed to allow White Russia and the Ukraine to participate as independent states in the United Nations.

The struggle for a compromise that emphasized globalism but protected regional interests was resolved by Dr. Alberto Lleras Camargo of Colombia and Senator Arthur Vandenberg of the United States in Article 51 of the UN Charter, which upheld "the inherent right of individual or collective self-defense if an armed attack occurs against a member of the United Nations, until the Security Council has taken the measures necessary to maintain international peace and security." The right to regional action was preserved without limiting the Security Council's ability to intervene in a crisis.

With the United Nations launched, hemispheric issues returned to center stage. Although the 1945 Chapultepec conference had mandated another meeting to prepare a permanent collective security agreement, deteriorating relations between Argentina and the United States after the rise to power of General Juan D. Perón in late 1945 made it impossible to reach a consensus on the appropriate next step. As maneuvering continued, Washington's attitude toward regionalism grew more positive. Confronted by a recalcitrant Soviet Union in the Security Council, able and willing to use its veto, regional approaches to peacekeeping became increasingly attractive. Meanwhile, encouraged by the lavish amounts of U.S. aid for Western Europe and Asia, the Latin states had started to insist on U.S. economic support. Old suspicions about U.S. goals in the hemisphere reemerged, not only in Argentina, but also in Mexico and other states.

By the time the Rio Conference got under way in August 1947, the United States wanted a strong treaty reflecting the polarization of world politics that would allow it to get on with higher global priorities having guaranteed the security of its backyard. With the Latin delegations demanding a regional Marshall Plan, Secretary of State George C. Marshall, who headed the U.S. delegation, stalled by getting nonmilitary issues postponed until the forthcoming conference in Bogotá.

The delegates finally concluded the Rio Treaty, a collective security arrangement which amplified Chapultepec accords and created a permanent military alliance among the states of the hemisphere. While the United States viewed the document primarily as an instrument it could use to thwart Soviet ambitions in the hemisphere, the Latin signatories saw it as having much broader application. But the treaty established neither a military command nor any planning mechanism, and it did not mention how the new collective security agreement would be enforced. Again, this issue was postponed for the Bogotá meeting, which was to be the last effort at creative institution building in the postwar era.

As the United States and Latin America prepared to meet in the Andean capital in March 1948 for the Ninth International Conference of American States, demands for United States economic and financial help in reducing Latin reliance on single crops and raw material exports emerged with greater frequency. In the Latin view, the United States had gotten what it wanted at Rio and now they wanted Washington to help them build local industries and improve their standards of living. Latin wishes for reciprocity on the scale they desired were to go unfulfilled. Led by Argentina and Mexico, the March 1948 meeting in the Andean capital was often bitter and recriminatory.[12] In the postwar world the private sector would be left to resolve the economic and social needs of the hemisphere and direct, private investment by U.S. financial institutions became the predominant source of foreign capital.

The U.S. desire for an Inter-American Defense Council was

---

[12]As if to underscore the growing consciousness for social justice in Latin America, the preparatory stages of the Bogotá conference were interrupted on April 9, 1948 by the assassination of Jorge Eliézer Gaitán, the charismatic leader of Colombia's Liberal party who had made explicit populist appeals to the poor. Gaitán's outraged supporters blamed his murder on the ruling Conservatives and invaded the Capitol within hours of Gaitán's death looking for Laureano Gómez, the Conservative party leader. As foreign minister, Gómez was presiding over the conference, which luckily was in midday recess when the mob arrived. The riots that swept Colombia after Gaitán's murder caused an estimated $500 million in material damages and claimed 1500 lives. See J. Lloyd Mecham, *The United States and Inter-American Security, 1889–1960* (Austin, Tex.: University of Texas Press, 1961), pp. 300–317, for an account of the Bogotá conference and the Bogotazo.

thwarted by the Latin American delegations, which could agree only to create an Advisory Defense Committee, subordinate to the Rio Treaty, which has never met. The meeting also ratified the Inter-American Defense Board as a continuing agency, but gave it no authority or power.

The conference then went on to approve its most lasting achievement, the Charter of the Organization of American States (OAS), which created a regional body to complement the work of the UN. The conference also concluded the ill-fated Treaty on Pacific Settlement (known as the Pact of Bogotá) for the resolution of intrahemispheric disputes, which the United States never ratified, and only nine Latin states eventually ratified it.

During the 1950s, Latin America's foreign policies were closely tied to the United States. Beginning in January 1952, the U.S. concluded a series of bilateral military agreements with individual Latin American states in support of hemispheric defense. The states agreed to stockpile U.S. military equipment as a strategic defensive reserve and to cooperate with the U.S. in limiting trade with countries that threatened the security of the continent.[13] As the decade progressed, Washington's Military Assistance Program expanded to encompass U.S. military missions in eighteen countries with up to 800 military personnel in each mission, training of Latin American soldiers in U.S. military schools, a virtual U.S. monopoly on arms sales, and the creation of a unified regional command for Latin America in the Panama Canal Zone.

Mexico emerged as a determined dissenter from many U.S. foreign policy goals in the Americas during the 1950s, particularly on the issues of nonintervention and U.S. support for military regimes. Argentina, under the dynamic nationalist leadership of General Perón, continued its independent foreign policy, attempting to forge links with other actors in the international system and unsuccessfully seeking to limit United States freedom of action in the hemisphere. Neither Mexico nor Argentina possessed the resources to fully develop an autonomous position in world affairs. Internal instability and fiscal mismanagement quickly vitiated the Perón regime, which fell in 1955. Mexico's more aggressive foreign policy masked a civilian-authoritarian state that permitted little domestic dissent. Foreign policy served to co-opt dissident Mexican political groups, frustrated in their efforts to modify domestic policy. The foreign policies of other major actors—Brazil, Chile, Peru, Colombia, and Venezuela—generally supported United States policy during the decade. Traditional border rivalries and territorial claims were quiescent. Elite groups continued to dominate the foreign policy process. Low levels of literacy and a concern with social and economic survival among the mass population left little time or inclination for foreign policy.

[13]Ibid., chap. 4.

The most dramatic assertion of U.S. predominance in the region came with the CIA-sponsored overthrow of the government of President Jacobo Arbenz Guzmán of Guatemala in 1954. Elected president in 1951, Arbenz moved to implement a program of wide social and economic reform that threatened established foreign economic interests as well as those of the local elites. Concerned about the perceived communist threat in Guatemala, the Eisenhower administration used the Tenth Inter-American Conference in Caracas in March 1954 to force through a resolution condemning communist influence in the Americas. Guatemala voted against the resolution; only Mexico and Argentina abstained, while the other states of the OAS voted in favor. Using an arms shipment to Guatemala from the Soviet bloc as an excuse, United States-backed exiles led by Colonel Carlos Castillo Armas invaded Guatemala in June 1954. Guatemala's futile efforts to seek support from either the OAS or the UN were frustrated and ended abruptly when the Arbenz regime fell.

Only at the end of the 1950s could Latin American leaders reassert economic and social development as important priorities. In 1958, the overthrow of dictators in Colombia and Venezuela and the election of a constitutional president in Argentina after three years of military rule opened a period known as the "twilight of the tyrants." Brazil's President Juscelino Kubitschek, in 1958, proposed that the United States help organize a hemisphere-wide program of economic development which he termed "Operation Pan-America." The Eisenhower administration politely turned down the idea, but President John F. Kennedy remembered it a few years later when he proposed the Alliance for Progress. Further pressure for a change in U.S. policy came from Vice-President Richard M. Nixon's ill-fated trip to Latin America in 1958 and the subsequent overthrow of the Cuban dictator, Fulgencio Batista, on January 1, 1959, by Fidel Castro.

Responding to Kubitschek's initiative, Latin American foreign ministers who had gathered informally in Washington pushed for the creation of an inter-American financial institution for economic development and a committee to recommend additional measures for economic cooperation among the states of the hemisphere. This "Committee of Twenty-One," as it was later known, succeeded in founding the Inter-American Development Bank with U.S. support at the end of 1959. An "Eisenhower Plan" of $500 million in development aid was proposed to the Committee of 21 in 1960 and endorsed in the Act of Bogotá by the states of the region. With John Kennedy's inauguration in 1961, the Alliance for Progress, announced in March at the White House, became the bridging mechanism for new efforts to seek social and economic change in the hemisphere. It was multilateralized with the enactment of the Charter of Punta del Este in August 1961 by the American ministers of economic affairs, meeting in Uruguay. The charter signaled an important watershed in United States-Latin American relations, promising "to enlist the full energies of the peoples and governments of the American republics in a great cooperative effort to accelerate the economic and social development" of the continent, to maximize levels of well-being "with equal opportunities for all, in democratic societies adapted to their needs and desires."[14]

FOREIGN POLICY SINCE 1959: UNCERTAINTY, DRIFT, AND FRUSTRATION

The Cuban Revolution of January 1, 1959 opened a new chapter in the international relations of Latin America. With hindsight, the seeds of destruction of the old order had been apparent long before Castro's entrance into Havana. Unwilling to respond to hemispheric development needs, the United States had also refused to accept political deviations, such as the Arbenz regime in Guatemala. In general, the United States was hostile to change but accepting of dictatorships, which seemed to pose no threat to its interests.

Cuba's new status as an aggressive exporter of revolution and as a potential Soviet base meant not only that the United States and its hemispheric allies faced a security problem. It also implied the decline of American hegemony and the rise of a new generation of Latin leaders seeking new solutions for old problems while trying to throw off American tutelage. But change has come slowly. Hemispheric cooperation has increased, but efforts at integration have drifted. In general, Latin American states could not insert themselves into the international system without appearing as United States surrogates. United States efforts to limit external penetration of the hemisphere started with the failed Bay of Pigs invasion of 1961 and the 1962 Cuban Missile Crisis and are continuing today with support for Central America's anti-left forces to counter Soviet and Cuban aid to the guerrillas. Latin America's frustrations about slow economic and social development have grown while regional peacekeeping has fizzled. A period of interstate competition and conflict has reopened as Washington's hemispheric security system loosened. Irredentist claims have reappeared as the growing potential for intrahemispheric conflict climaxed in the 1982 Falkland's War.

Lurking always in the background is the region's severe financial crisis. The oil price rises of the 1970s and the external debt crisis of the early 1980s have produced slow economic growth and sharply deflationary austerity programs. Economic crisis and growing social tensions

---

14Quoted in G. Pope Atkins, *Latin America in the International Political System* (New York: Free Press, 1977), p. 344.

caused by rising debt, falling exports, and shrinking economies have become preoccupations of Latin American foreign policy in recent years. Private commercial banks and the International Monetary Fund (IMF) have become important actors in the foreign policy planning of all of the states of the region.

With the blighted hopes of the last decade a common theme, the Latin countries have turned increasingly to Third World and North-South forums to establish a "dialogue" between the North and the South. How the international system responds to the frustration, drift, and uncertainty in Latin America and the Caribbean will shape both North-South relations and the hemisphere's future role in world affairs.

AN UNCERTAIN AUTONOMY

Most efforts at forming regional or subregional mechanisms for consultation, development, and governance in the hemisphere prior to 1959 have crumbled before the hegemonic power of the United States. The desire for common action dates back to Simón Bolívar's attempts to unify the continent to defend its interests against all outsiders, including the United States. Weakening U.S. leadership and the emergence of increasingly assertive states such as Brazil, Venezuela, and Mexico have strengthened that drive. In addition, the smaller states have sought refuge and support in subregional groupings, hoping to find their own identity in hemispheric entities.

The Caribbean Free Trade Association (CARIFTA) decided to move toward a common market in 1973 by creating the Caribbean Community (CARICOM) and, soon after, a Caribbean Development Bank, the Caribbean Investment Corporation, and the Caribbean Food Corporation, but world recession in the 1970s reduced the area's exports and frustrated efforts at integration.[15] The recovery of the economic integration efforts of CARICOM will depend directly on the economic recovery of the developed countries.

The Latin American Free Trade Area (LAFTA), created by the 1960 Treaty of Montevideo (with Argentina, Brazil, Bolivia, Colombia, Chile, Ecuador, Mexico, Paraguay, Peru, Uruguay, and Venezuela participating), was to become a free trade association by 1973. That objective was postponed until 1980 by the Caracas Protocol of 1969. LAFTA worked relatively well in spurring intraregional trade, which increased from 7 percent of all trade in 1961 to 13 percent in 1978. The degree of integration varied. In 1978, exports from Argentina, Bolivia, Chile, Paraguay,

---

[15]Intraregional exports increased from $500 million in 1980 to only $530 million in 1981. The region's total exports fell from $5.6 billion in 1980 to $5.2 billion in 1981.

and Uruguay to LAFTA countries represented about one-quarter of total exports, while for Mexico and Venezuela (the two biggest oil exporters of the region) this proportion was less than 8 percent. The Latin American Integration Association (ALADI) replaced the 1960-vintage LAFTA in 1980. The new association aims at promoting and regulating trade, economic complementation, and expanding markets through economic cooperation. An alternative to the free trade area envisioned in 1960, the 1980 treaty opts for areas of regional tariff preference and grants preferential treatment to the less developed countries. However, the current economic crisis and the fall in trade have thrown the future of the plan into doubt.

Colombia, Chile, Bolivia, and Ecuador formed the Andean Group with the Cartegena Agreement in 1969.[16] Venezuela officially became a party to the agreement in 1973. The Cartegena Agreement envisioned three basic mechanisms for economic integration: first, trade liberalization to build up a large market (while protecting local production) and common external tariffs; second, industrial programming; and, third, coordinated economic policies. After a promising start the Andean Group faltered in 1976 when Chile withdrew over a difference about a common foreign investment code. In 1980, an Andean Tribunal of Justice began to monitor, interpret, and unify legal provisions and enforce the obligations derived from the integration process, but the Andean Parliament, established in 1979, has not been ratified. An Andean Reserve Fund, created in 1978, has helped countries with balance of payments difficulties. Ongoing territorial conflicts between Ecuador and Peru have slowed the work of the pact, and Bolivia temporarily suspended its participation in 1980 for political reasons. By 1982, pressured by the world economic crisis, countries began to adopt protective short-term policies that undid their commitments to liberalization and the common external tariff. These measures and the failure to decide on the agreement's fundamental mechanisms (for example, the Common External Tariff, Sectoral Programming, Industrial Rationalization, and Agricultural Programming) meant a significant reduction in integration activities and doubts about their viability.

The Organization of American States (OAS) has proven to be the most disappointing mechanism for furthering Latin America's search for autonomy. Following its creation the organization served to justify American interventions in Guatemala in 1954 and the Dominican Republic in 1965. At times of crisis, the OAS has played a marginal role in conflict resolution in the hemisphere, again illustrated during the war between

16For a recent analysis of Venezuelan and Colombian foreign policy, see Bruce Michael Bagley, *Regional Powers in the Caribbean Basin: Mexico, Venezuela and Colombia.* The Johns Hopkins Central American and Caribbean program, Occasional Paper No. 2, January 1983.

Argentina and Great Britain in 1982, the United States invasion of Grenada in 1983, and the ongoing regional conflict in Central America. The specialized organs of the OAS have made large contributions to the social, legal, and cultural life of the hemisphere, but are they sufficient to justify its continued existence?[17]

Many states, such as Brazil, prefer to pursue bilateral relations with their neighbors and do not view the OAS multi-lateral approach with sympathy. Small states have not been able to use the organization to protect them from intervention by the United States or any other major state. The political goals of the OAS remain undefined, although the principles of nonintervention, respect for sovereignty, mutual security, and the peaceful settlement of disputes are highly admirable. But the OAS has neither military might to enforce its decisions nor the political legitimacy in the hemisphere to expect peaceful compliance with its directives.

Because the OAS is ineffectual, Latin American political leaders have resorted to ad hoc consultations to deal with the regional crises of the early 1980s. With formal institutions found wanting, personal diplomacy was in vogue. In June 1984 the eleven-nation Cartagena Consensus Group formed to respond to Latin America's mounting financial obligations to creditors in the industrial countries. The Cartagena group issued several fruitless pleas for help from the North.

A group called "Contadora," composed of Colombia, Venezuela, Panama, and Mexico, tried to mediate the conflict in Central America by finding a solution acceptable both to the United States and to the Sandinista regime in Nicaragua. A "support group" which included Argentina, Brazil, Peru, and Uruguay joined the original four in July 1985. Contadora's efforts atrophied as the Reagan administration made clear that it opposed anything less than the removal of the Sandinista regime. U.S. funding for the anti-Sandinista guerrillas, or Contras, eliminated any role for Contadora until 1987, when Costa Rican President Oscar Arias's initiative pledged the five presidents of Central America to seek a negotiated, political settlement for the region's wars.

When the eight presidents of the Contadora "process" met in Rio de Janeiro in December 1986 as the "Group of Eight," they called a summit meeting for November 1987 in Acapulco, Mexico, the first summit of Latin leaders ever held outside the U.S.-dominated OAS.

The Group of Eight issued a communiqué at the end of their talks called the "Acapulco Commitment to Peace, Development and Democracy." It dramatically recommended collective negotiations with the creditor nations in order to reduce debt service by having it reflect the real

[17]See Tom J. Farer, ed., *The Future of the Inter-American System* (New York: Praeger, 1979).

market value of the debt. In addition to strongly endorsing the Arias Plan, the summit called for the readmission of Cuba into the OAS, which, the Eight stated, was due for a sweeping overhaul. Finally, the Eight proposed an economic recovery program for the Central American countries and agreed to meet again at the end of 1988 in Uruguay.

Whether the Group of Eight will be any more successful than its predecessors remains to be seen. But the Acapulco meeting showed that the democratic leaders of Latin America felt frustrated by United States reluctance to work with them to strengthen civilian, democratic regimes by relieving the debt burden. Strongly in favor of a negotiated, political settlement to the wars in Central America, the presidents stressed that they were acting for Latin America, and not against anyone, but they obviously were looking increasingly to themselves for regional leadership and no longer to the United States.

A SENSE OF DRIFT

The Latin American states have often participated in the activities of Third World groups, but have little to show for their enthusiasm. The United Nations Conference on Trade and Development (UNCTAD) appealed strongly to Latin American and Caribbean states, but yielded little in the way of substantive concessions on trade and finance from the industrialized countries. Latin Americans, notably Raul Prebisch, the former head of ECLA, directed UNCTAD until the 1970s, when the direction of UNCTAD moved to the African and Asian states. Since that time, Latin American participation has been perfunctory.

Over the years, Latin American raw material exporters have joined various producer associations, such as OPEC, without greatly affecting their market relations with the North. OPEC (the Organization of Petroleum Exporting Countries) includes Latin states, such as Venezuela, a charter member that played an important role in OPEC's early days, and Ecuador, a small producer. Mexico, not a member, cooperates with OPEC. At the moment, Latin America does not play a major role within OPEC.

Despite international linkages at the public and private levels, Latin America's efforts to achieve political and economic autonomy were adrift by the early 1980s. Latin leaders have demanded more respect from the United States and the industrialized countries, particularly in multilateral efforts to capture the attention of the North. Yet the economic crisis of the 1980s frustrated their efforts to cut their dependence on U.S. trade and private capital, and the crisis interfered with plans to increase trade with the Third World.[18] Latin hopes that Western Europe might provide

---

[18]A thoughtful assessment of the status of the North-South debate is contained in Roger D. Hansen, ed., *The "Global Negotiation" and Beyond: Toward North-South Accommodation in the 1980s* (Austin, Tex.: Lyndon B. Johnson School of Public Affairs, 1981).

an alternative to the United States have proven groundless. Common Market policy has sharply limited Latin American exports to Europe, and Europe has not offered easy finance terms for the hemisphere's foreign debt. At times individual European states, such as Spain under Prime Minister Felipe González, try to identify with Latin America, but cordial state relations produce mainly rhetoric and little substance in the crucial areas of trade, aid, finance, and autonomy in Latin American–United States relations.

As world power began to shift subtly at the time of the Cuban revolution around 1960, hemispheric politics have been transformed. Among the major changes were the emergence of South American authoritarian regimes featuring autonomous development goals and more independent foreign policies; the development of world economic conditions that led to the Latin American debt crisis of the 1980s; the reassertion of U.S. security interests in Central America and the Caribbean; and an increase in "power politics" to settle disputes. Although the United States remains the region's most powerful state, its ability and willingness to intervene outside its Central American and Caribbean "backyard" is diminishing.[19]

AUTHORITARIAN REGIMES AND FOREIGN POLICY: BRAZIL AND PERU

With the establishment of a secure Marxist state in Cuba, the dynamics of internal politics in Latin America changed dramatically. Cuba immediately began to export revolutionary tactics, and Latin leftists and guerrillas took heart from Castro's efforts to replicate his revolution elsewhere in the hemisphere. The Alliance for Progress quickly lost its original purpose of supporting development and became more concerned with the internal security of the countries in which it operated. Two examples of Brazil and Peru will demonstrate the different paths taken in Latin America in the 1960s as a result of a perceived surge of leftist or subversive activity.

Traditionally, Brazilian foreign policy complemented that of the United States. Washington saw Brazil as a valuable counterweight to normally hostile Argentina, and its tutelage benefited Brazil in a variety of ways, from the consolidation of its borders to aid for its initial industrialization phase. While the two states divereged at times (Kubitschek's 1958 call for a new inter-American development effort was one), only the "independent" foreign policy of the Quadros (1961) and Goulart (1961–

[19]See Lars Schoultz, *National Security and United States Foreign Policy toward Latin America.* (Princeton, N.J.: Princeton University Press, 1987).

1964) administrations disturbed the superficial harmony of interests between the United States and Brazil. When the Brazilian political system unraveled, the armed forces intervened to restore order in 1964 with tacit support from the United States. The first three years of military rule, under President Humberto Castello Branco, appeared to be a return to the halcyon years of Brazilian-American collaboration. Only when his successor, President Artur da Costa e Silva, took office did Brazil's foreign policy innovations become evident.

World political and economic conditions were favorable to the country's new goals. Far more nationalist than its predecessor and determined to lead Brazil to greatness, the new government of Brazil would no longer accept a junior partnership with the United States, which was too preoccupied with Vietnam to assess Brazil's international ambitions accurately. "Benign neglect" meant Latins could begin to seek their fortune in world affairs; Brazilians were the most successful. By 1970, the military government's stabilization program had restored vitality to the economy. Brazil's economic "miracle" included a remarkable 27 percent annual increase in exports between 1968 and 1973, a search for new markets and a reduced future role for the United States.

As Brazil grew too rich to qualify for United States foreign aid, new investment funds came from West Germany and Japan. Export markets in other industrial countries and in the third world beckoned. Brazil rapidly diversified its traditional exports of agricultural commodities to include increasingly sophisticated agro-industrial products and manufactured goods. In 1967 Brazil refused to sign the Tlatelolco Treaty prohibiting nuclear weapons in Latin America; the next year it rejected the Treaty of Non-Proliferation of Nuclear Weapons (NPT), arguing that the industrialized world was attempting to "freeze" the existing international order, leaving no room for upwardly mobile states like Brazil. Unilaterally, Brazil claimed a 200-mile wide territorial sea around its coastline. After abandoning its traditional support for Portugal's colonial policy, Brazil became the first state to recognize the Marxist MPLA regime in Angola.

American-Brazil relations got steadily worse. The United States notified Brazil in 1974 that it could not guarantee the processing of nuclear fuel for Brazilian nuclear reactors. Deeply affected by the 1973 oil price increase, Brazil felt betrayed and quickly turned to West Germany, with whom it negotiated a multimillion dollar agreement to develop a comprehensive nuclear power program. Public efforts early in 1977 by then Vice-President–elect Walter Mondale to prevent the West German–Brazilian accord led to open hostility between Brasília and Washington, which increased with President Jimmy Carter's human rights policy. The American–Brazilian military agreement was broken off soon after Carter's inauguration.

While Africa and other Third World countries had been a principal focus of the military governments of 1968–1974, by the late 1970s Brazil turned back to Latin America. President João Figueiredo (1979–1983) continued the policies of his predecessor, President Ernesto Geisel, with a dramatic policy of rapprochement with Brazil's traditional rival, Argentina. After a series of presidential visits, the two states agreed to seek areas of mutual cooperation and opened a dialog on joint development initiatives. Brazil's pursued rapprochement with Latin America by initiating a treaty to integrate the Amazon basin. Signed in 1980 by all Amazon basin states, the agreement calls for a long-term program of mutual development, putting an end to the specter of Brazilian expansionism and unilateralism in the area and opening a new era of cordial relations with Venezuela, often Brazil's wary neighbor in the northern part of the continent.

A felicitous coincidence of regime change, world economic expansion, and coherent foreign policy goals marked Brazil's distinctive approach to international relations in recent decades. The old fears of Brazilian expansion have disappeared as cooperation has increased between Brazil and its neighbors. Brazil maintains cordial relations with Japan and Western Europe, although it identifies with the Third World, a priority it complements with its growing diversity of economic investment and export markets. While Brazilian-American relations are proper, the dependency of just a few decades ago is gone forever.[20]

The restoration of civilian government in March 1985 and the continuing debt crisis have led to confrontations between Brazil, its international creditors and the governments of the industrial countries, especially the United States. In particular, Brazil's position on computer technology has caused the United States to retaliate, under pressure from companies denied access to the Brazilian market. Other U.S. manufacturers, arguing successfully that Brazil fosters unfair trade practices, have asked for and received further retaliation. In February 1987 Brazil announced a unilateral moratorium on debt payments. The issue was resolved temporarily in late 1987 after months of negotiation, but a permanent solution has yet to be reached that is satisfactory both to Brazil and to its creditors.

Although Brazil still has major problems to solve in the areas of social and economic reform, the country has had greater success in asserting its presence on the world stage than Peru. The Peruvian armed forces introduced populist structural reforms of the country's economic and social systems shortly after they seized power in late 1968. The

[20]For an overview, see Riordan Roett, "Brazilian Foreign Policy," in *Brazil: Politics in a Patrimonial Society*, 3d ed. (New York: Praeger, 1984), chap. 8. Also, John D. Wirth, et al, eds., *State and Society in Brazil* (Boulder, Colo.: Westview Press, 1987).

military's experience in quelling an insurgency in the Andean highlands in the mid-1960s had convinced them of the need for modernizing reforms and of the inability of Peru's typically weak democratic regimes to carry these reforms out. From the start, the regime of General Juan Velasco Alvarado was as eager to alter Peru's international relations as it was to redefine class relations in Peruvian society.[21]

The new government proved its economic nationalism and defended its sovereignty by expropriating the United States-owned International Petroleum Company (IPC) without compensation. To defend Peru's fishing industry a 200-mile territorial sea was rigorously enforced and U.S. vessels were seized. The regime excluded foreign capital from a wide variety of economic areas. It also opened diplomatic and commercial relations with the Soviet Union, the People's Republic of China, and Cuba. It broke the U.S. arms monopoly, and when Washington refused to sell Peru advanced weapons, the government got them from France and the USSR, among others.

Peru's experiments with a radical foreign policy showed how much ground the United States had lost in South America. Arms shipments from other suppliers, including the Soviets, took place without incident. The expropriation of United States companies was left to negotiation. Aggressive Third World diplomacy projected Peru internationally as never before or since.

NEW ECONOMIC REALITIES

Financial crisis is the essential issue in Latin America's relations with the international system in the 1980s. The 1973 and 1979 oil price rises, when combined with the worldwide recession of the early 1980s, devastated Latin America's exports. Moreover, loans for billions of "petrodollars," borrowed in the 1970s at low interest rates, began to fall due in the early 1980s. Loans negotiated in more recent years have been at substantially higher rates of interest and for far shorter periods of time. In some instances long-term debt obligations and short-term loans have matured at the same time. As markets closed both in the developed and the underdeveloped world, Latin American export earnings fell, and foreign exchange dried up. The situation was even worse for oil-poor countries like Brazil and Chile, which had to face both rising oil bills and rising debt obligations.[22]

[21]For more detail about recent change in Peru, see Cynthia McClintock and Abraham F. Lowenthal, eds., *The Peruvian Experiment Reconsidered* (Princeton, N.J.: Princeton University Press, 1983) and Riordan Roett, "Peru: The Message From Garcia," *Foreign Affairs,* 64 (2), Winter 1985/86.

[22]See Pedro-Pablo Kuczynski, "The Outlook for Latin American Debt," *Foreign Affairs,* 66 (1), Fall 1987.

The financing of Latin America's debt is spread among the industrial countries as follows:

	Brazil	Mexico	Argentina	Chile	Peru
U.S. banks	34%	36%	60%	47%	60%
Japanese banks	16	17	15	9	11
British banks	13	9	7	10	10
French banks	7	7	6	3	12
German banks	7	7	9	6	3

As discussions continue about refinancing the debt, Latin states need new loans to finance interest payments and future productive investment. By the end of 1987, Latin America accounted for $400 billion of the more than one trillion dollars loaned to the Third World. Brazil leads the continent with a staggering $113 billion, followed by Mexico with $108 billion and Argentina with $54 billion.

Latin America's future is tied to economic expansion in the industrial world, lower interest rates, new trade opportunities, and reasonable prices for its raw material exports. None of these conditions were favorable in the late 1980s. Moreover, the private commercial banks have signaled that they will lend new money to Latin America only to pay outstanding interest. Private investment has dried up, given the slow down of the Latin American economies and the drop in internal demand. Volatile oil prices have benefited Brazil, but have devastated Mexico and Ecuador.

The Reagan administration has had little success solving the debt crisis. Collective efforts stalled in the mid-1980s when the industrial governments and the private commercial banks began a tactic of quarantining major errant debtors. When Argentina, Mexico, or Brazil were close to balking at servicing their debt, that country would be "quarantined" while special arrangements were worked out to insure that it would not "contaminate" the other two big debtor states in the region.

A more promising approach was unveiled by United States Treasury Secretary James Baker at the annual World Bank–IMF meeting in Seoul, South Korea in October 1985. The Baker Plan called for internal reforms to complement new private commercial bank lending to Third World governments. New lending by the multilateral development institutions (such as the World Bank) would then follow. When the plan had clearly failed at the time of the annual economic summit in Venice in June 1987, Baker offered a "menu of options" for debt management which included a mix of debt-equity swaps, expanded trade finance, and exit bonds to allow smaller banks to avoid making new loans. But by the end of 1987 the menu of options had little concrete support.

By the beginning of 1988 many observers agreed that the Latin American debt crisis was worsening and that conventional remedies adopted after 1982 were not going to work. Economic austerity in Latin America has reduced demand for United States exports dramatically. While United States exports to most other areas of the world are rising, shipments to Latin America have tumbled by 26 percent in 1986 to $31.1 billion, down from $42.1 billion in 1981. In 1986 the four largest debtors (Brazil, Mexico, Argentina, and Venezuela) were importing 30 to 50 percent less than in 1981.

The Big Three of Latin Debt (1987)[23]

	Debt	Growth	Inflation
Brazil	$113	3.0%	350%
Mexico	108	1.0%	150
Argentina	54	2.0%	170

The debt crisis not only has shrunk markets in Latin American and the Third World, it also has accelerated a rush of exports to the United States, and it has intensified competition for American markets for exporters outside Latin America. In 1981 the United States took one-third of exports from developing countries. By 1986 the figure had risen to 60 percent. Since 1982 the United States has been the only expanding market in the industrial world. Trade surplus countries, mainly West Germany and Japan, eagerly bought Latin America's cheap commodities, but used formal and informal barriers to keep Latin American manufactured products out.

Stiff competition among Latin American exporters for access to the U.S. market has put intense pressure on the U.S. Congress to keep imports out, especially those from Third World and Latin American countries. Congress has begun to explore alternatives to the present debt crisis and passed a trade bill at the end of 1987 that would create an international debt management agency to buy Third World debt at discounted prices. The administration opposes such policies, but growing support for them in both parties implies Congressional action in 1988. U.S. lawmakers are acutely aware that new policy initiatives are needed. The United States will no longer be able to absorb surplus production in the Third World if it wants to eliminate its trade deficit.

The high cost of debt servicing was starting to carry a prohibitive political price in Latin America by the beginning of 1988. Needed social

[23]Alan Riding, "A Widening Gyre on Latin Debt," *New York Times*, December 28, 1987.

reforms and investment have been postponed. Democratic governments have been weakened by their perceived inability to deliver goods and services. More extreme groups have come forward to demand a moratorium on debt payments or a full scale default. For the first time since the debt crisis began in 1982 the big three were all in economic crisis. Burdened by a combined debt of $280 billion, all three countries are suffering from high inflation, minimal growth, and mounting unemployment. Earlier efforts to seek solutions at the government level had failed. The June 1984 Consensus of Cartagena, written by the democratic leaders of Latin America, produced few concrete results.

Responding to the deterioring debt climate, three important banks wrote off part of their Latin American loan portfolios at the end of 1987.

By early 1988 the Latin American debt crisis was creating a no-win situation for the private commercial banks in the United States. Industrial country governments were unwilling to agree to direct negotiations with the Latin American governments. Those governments, in turn, were willing to challenge the international financial system in ways they had never dared contemplate earlier in the decade, ranging from Brazil's unilateral moratorium on debt servicing in February 1987 to the meeting in Acapulco in November of the same year.

With elections in key countries in Latin America in 1988 and 1989, as well as presidential election in the United States in 1988, the debt issue appears to be at a dramatic turning point. Resolving the debt issue is vital to the future development of Latin America, which, in turn, will directly affect the relationship the United States seeks to build with the hemisphere in the future. Most importantly, the debt issue has become firmly linked to social development and the maintenance of civilian, democratic regimes. The stakes are high. How political leaders throughout the hemisphere resolve the debt question will influence the hemisphere's growth and development for decades to come.

U.S. SECURITY CONCERNS

Although Cuban efforts failed to instigate successful revolutionary movements in the early 1960s (in countries like Venezuela), twenty years later U.S. national security concerns about its "backyard" have reemerged. While Cuba sporadically supported guerrilla movements in Colombia, Bolivia, and elsewhere into the 1970s, Cuba's foreign policy has grown increasingly international. With Africa the principal focus, Cuban troops are supporting revolutions in more than a dozen states.

Cuba became more interested in Central America after the 1979 overthrow of the Somoza dictatorship in Nicaragua. El Salvador's guerrilla war, a result of repressive military rule and harsh social conditions, provided another flash point of interest to Cuban foreign policy. The United States supported the Sandinista revolution in Nicaragua until it became increasingly Marxist and less tolerant of internal dissent. At that point Washington brought pressure on the Sandinista government to hold elections and to respect fundamental democratic processes. The Nicaraguan government's response was that decades of inequity, supported in part by U.S. acceptance of Somoza, required drastic social and economic reform. Political change would follow at an undetermined point in the future.

The Reagan administration took office in January 1981 determined to stop the spread of revolutionary doctrine in Central America and the Caribbean. The new administration accused the Soviet Union of using surrogates (Cuba and Nicaragua) to support the Marxist guerrillas in El Salvador and to destabilize Honduras, Costa Rica, and Guatemala. By 1982 the United States was providing massive military assistance to the Honduran government to bolster its ability to resist the perceived marxist threat and to provide a launching point for thousands of "Contras," irregular anti-Sandinista troops, supported by the Central Intelligence Agency. A perceived Marxist threat in the Caribbean led to the U.S. invasion of Grenada in late 1983, allegedly at the request of the English-speaking states of the Eastern Caribbean.[24]

Rapid militarization in Central America and the establishment of Marxist governments in the Caribbean caused the countries of the regions to become increasingly concerned about the continuing impact of armed conflicts. When the OAS and the UN did not respond effectively, Panama, Colombia, Venezuela, and Mexico took the initiative. Seeking a regional solution to the conflict, representatives from the four countries met at the Panamanian island of Contadora and became known as the "Contadora Group." Throughout 1983 the four states sought to draft a regional peace plan that would aid the withdrawal of all foreign military advisers from the region and the creation of mechanisms to restore and monitor peace.

Although the United States acknowledged the usefulness of the Contadora Group, it seemed to prefer bilateral diplomatic and military policies in Central America and the Caribbean, rather than yield to regional or multilateral approaches which it saw as benefiting Nicaragua more than the United States. With regional actors willing to assume greater responsibility for peace, the "Contadora process" offered a hemispheric strategy to deal with Marxist states and created new negotiating space between Latin America and the United States. Without firm U.S. support, however, the peace process cannot succeed.

[24]See the collection of essays about the crisis in the hemisphere, "Hemispheric Crisis: Issues and Options," in *Foreign Policy*, 52, Fall 1983.

Suddenly, in August 1987, two events redefined the debate about regional peace in Central America. Seeking to gain the diplomatic initiative, the Reagan administration announced a bi-partisan peace proposal that was backed by the Speaker of the House of Representatives, Jim Wright of Texas. The Wright-Reagan plan called for a regional cease-fire within 60 days, a timetable that was to end on September 30 when $100 million in aid to the Contra expired. If Nicaragua failed to comply with the plan the administration would be in a strong position to ask Congress for new funding for the Nicaraguan "freedom fighters".

A few days later the presidents of Honduras, Nicaragua, El Salvador, Guatemala, and Costa Rica, meeting in Guatemala City, startled the Reagan administration by signing an historic regional peace agreement calling for cease-fires in the area's conflicts and democratic reforms that would require Nicaragua to open its internal political process. The August agreement followed an earlier effort by Costa Rican President Oscar Arias Sánchez to have the political leaders of the region assume greater responsibility for resolving the crisis. For that reason, and because of the critical role he played in Guatemala, the agreement is usually called the "Arias Plan".

The agreement had appeal, offering amnesties for government opponents in each of the five countries, cease-fires in the region's wars, democratizing reforms, a halt to military aid for insurgents, and renunciation by each country of the use of its territory for the staging of armed struggle against any of the other countries. These measures were to take effect simultaneously within ninety days of the August 7, 1987 signing. Key to the plan's success would be the creation of "commissions of national reconciliation" in each country to oversee, in a verifiable manner, "an authentic democratic, pluralistic and participative process" to safeguard human rights and national sovereignty.

Specifically, the agreement would establish complete freedom of the press, political rights for the opposition, and free and regular elections at the municipal, legislative, and presidential levels under international supervision. Under the plan a newly conceived Central American Parliament would meet in 1988. Aid for "repatriation" or relocation of combatants and for their "reintegration into normal life" would be allowed.

Public and political support for the Arias Plan was overwhelming. Speaker Wright quickly backed away from the bipartisan plan and endorsed the Guatemala agreement. Implementation moved ahead with surprising speed, and President Arias visited Washington in September 1987 to drum up support for the regional peace effort. However, in a speech to the OAS in October, President Reagan reiterated his backing of the insurgent Nicaraguan Contras. While praising the Arias initiative, Reagan termed it "insufficient" for U.S. security concerns, stating that "Soviet bloc and Cuban forces must leave" the region.

On October 13 the Norwegian Nobel Committee announced in Oslo, Norway that President Arias, had won the 1987 Nobel Peace Prize. Arias was the fourth Latin American to win the prize in its eighty-six year history. But in late 1987 his peace plan had stalled. An initial cease-fire in El Salvador and discussions between the guerrillas and the Duarte government collapsed after two Salvadoran human rights activists were murdered. Discussions between Guatemalan guerrillas and the government drifted, while the mediation efforts of Cardinal Miguel Obando y Bravo, the Archbishop of Managua, appeared doomed without more flexibility from the two protagonists.

The key issue in moving the Arias Plan ahead was progress in both Nicaragua and El Salvador conflicts, which so far have resisted efforts to call a cease-fire or to move forward with the Arias Plan agenda. The Arias initiative ran up against two immovable ideological forces, the Sandinistas and the Reagan administration. At the beginning of 1988 further progress seemed tied either to an agreement at the superpower summit or to U.S. presidential elections later in the year.

Renewed U.S. sensitivity to threats to its security by outside states reminds many observers of the Roosevelt Corollary. The concern in the U.S. government and the response in Latin America clearly indicates that the past is not forgotten. The Latin American states understand the need for appropriate foreign policies that will restore peace to the region while providing adequate safeguards for U.S. security interests and ensuring respect for the sovereignty of all the region's states.

REGIONAL DISPUTES

With the gradual diminution of the U.S. presence in Latin America and the increasingly aggressive foreign policies of many states in the 1970s, smoldering disputes have burst into flame. While the Inter-American Security System more or less controlled the arms supply to Latin America, territorial disputes were conditioned by Washington's largess, which was never sufficient to instigate full-scale war. New arms purchases from other states, including Latin American manufacturers, depended on favorable trade balances. Eager to demonstrate their ability to defend national sovereignty, military establishments have sought to settle old scores.

The dispute between Argentina and Chile over small islands in the Beagle Channel dates from 1881. Chile has occupied and governed the islands since the end of the last century. In 1977, after a series of incidents, an arbitration award went to Chile. Argentina refused to accept the award and opened negotiations with Chile which were inconclusive. By 1978 the countries had deployed troops and naval forces and were at the brink of war. At the last minute the dispute was referred to papal mediation that finally ended in a permanent settlement in November

1984. Under the agreement, the disputed islands go to Chile in return for limits on Chilean maritime rights in the area.

Antarctica presents a potential area for conflict. Both Argentina and Chile have established claims there, and Brazil is thinking about pursuing one. As scarce natural resources exert pressure on Third World development, the 1959 treaty that postpones the issue of sovereignty over the Antarctic continent, which is thought to be rich in oil, natural gas, and minerals, now appears threatened. Other potential territorial disputes in the hemisphere include the Ecuadorean-Peruvian claims to disputed land in the Amazon that led to an outbreak of hostilities in 1981; conflict among Bolivia, Chile, and Peru over Bolivia's desire for an outlet to the sea, which had been lost by Bolivia in the nineteenth century War of the Pacific; Venezuela's claim to two-thirds of the state of Guyana; Guatemala and Mexico's dispute over the state of Belize in Central America; Colombia and Venezuela's conflict over the Gulf of Venezuela, thought to be rich in petroleum; and, notably, the dispute between Great Britain and Argentina about the sovereignty of the Falkland or Malvinas Islands in the South Atlantic.

The 1982 war between Great Britain and Argentina shows how precarious foreign policy issues are in Latin America. The Argentine claim to sovereignty is a long-standing one, as is British occupation of the islands. In early 1982 an aggressive military government in Argentina, seeking to bolster its waning popularity, decided to strike, and they invaded the Folklands. Negotiations with the British had collapsed. Argentina may have expected at least tacit U.S. support because of Argentina's backing of U.S. policy in Central America. Reacting too late to warlike signals from Buenos Aires, the Reagan administration tried to warn Argentina of the repercussions of armed action. In response to the Argentine invasion the government of Prime Minister Margaret Thatcher dispatched a task force of thirty-five ships to retake the islands. After Secretary of State Alexander Haig's "shuttle diplomacy" had failed, the United States supported the British position. Argentina got support from its fellow Latin American states at the OAS. Peace efforts by a variety of intermediaries failed.

The Malvinas war did have one lasting result—the collapse of the military regime in Argentina that led to the restoration of democracy and the democratic election of President Raúl Alfonsín at the end of 1983. The war showed that armed conflict is one of the few issues that can arouse public interest in Latin America and that military governments which lose such conflicts will retain little legitimacy. Yet the mismanagement of the war, more than its loss, motivated Argentinians to repudiate the armed forces and seek a return to democracy.

More than at any time in the last fifty years, the potential for regional conflict is high in the hemisphere. The continuing guerrilla war in

El Salvador and the action of U.S.-armed Contra forces along the Honduran-Nicaraguan border, and within Nicaraguan territory, confirms that observation. The U.S. armed invasion of Grenada, supported politically and tactically by the states of the English-speaking Caribbean, strongly indicates the willingness of states in the area to resort to force. The sporadic armed conflicts between Ecuador and Peru, and the potential threat of war between Chile and Argentina, as well as the devastating war over the Falkland (or Malvinas) islands, substantiate the volatility of current foreign policy disputes in the Americas.

Ranging from the reassertion of U.S. security interests in its "backyard" to irredentist claims on the continent, the use of force is on the rise. Not only does the United States not have the capacity to contain conflict on the continent, it is deeply involved in the armed struggles of Central America and the Caribbean. Regional institutions have been found wanting once again, unable to provide anything more than a forum for debate, while, in the case of Grenada, they did not even serve that function.[25]

PROBLEMS FOR THE 1990S: DRUGS AND IMMIGRATION

While this chapter has dealt primarily with state-to-state foreign relations, two policy issues of increasing importance in the Western Hemisphere need to be highlighted. The first is the traffic in drugs and the second is the rising tide of illegal immigration to the United States, primarily from Central America and the Caribbean states.

The U.S. Congress has taken action recently in both areas. In 1986 it passed the "Omnibus Drug Enforcement, Education, and Control Act" out of growing frustration that many nations, primarily in Latin America, were selling larger and larger quantities of illicit drugs in the United States. The new law automatically suspends U.S. aid to countries shipping drugs to the United States unless the president certifies annually to Congress that the country is making significant progress in stopping the flow. The law allows Congress to override the certification process. The United States has no tougher automatic foreign sanctions law on the books.

Congressional concern has focused primarily on Mexico, but Colombia, Peru, Bolivia, and other countries are increasingly in the spotlight. A State Department report, issued in late 1986, stated that Mexico's production of marijuana had risen by more than 25 percent that year, while the acreage planted in poppies used to make heroin had grown by one-third in the same time period. Mexico is the largest single-country source of

[25]For a thoughtful consideration of these issues, see "Governance in the Western Hemisphere," (New York: Aspen Institute for Humanistic Studies, 1982).

heroin and marijuana to the U.S. market. The U.S. government also believes that 30 percent of all cocaine entering the United States passes through Mexico. A group of drug traffickers in Colombia, known as the "Medellin Cartel" (named for the Colombian city in which they operate) sells cocaine by the ton and controls 80 percent of the U.S. market, earning as much as $6 billion a year.

Under increasing pressure by the U.S. to control production and shipment, Latin governments argue that with Americans clearly willing to spend large amounts on drugs, the demand for drugs is as much an issue as the supply. They also claim they lack the resources to find and close down the drug dealers, who often are linked to powerful political forces and operate in remote areas of the interior out of effective control by the capital city.

There is plenty of blame to go around. Americans consume drugs in huge quantities, yet the United States has shown itself unwilling to punish its own consumers. Still, Latin American supply routes have grown dramatically since the 1970s. Moreover, with their enormous economic influence, drug lords operate with impunity in most Latin American societies. Drug money often represents a significant segment of the "informal economy." The drug question will not disappear. It promises to grow in importance and will challenge the combined ingenuity of both Latin and North American political leaders to find a comprehensive, hemispheric response.

The U.S. Congress, after years of discussion and debate, also passed a comprehensive immigration law in 1986. The major provisions of the law include an amnesty program for illegal aliens who have resided in the United States continuously since January 1, 1982, and civil and criminal penalties for employers who hire illegal aliens in the future. Alien farm workers who can prove they worked in U.S. agriculture for ninety days in the year that ended May 1, 1986 also got amnesty.

Congress was goaded to act because of the growing inability of the federal government to control its borders. Of the 3 to 5 million illegal aliens living in the United States, 55 percent come from Mexico alone, with other Latin countries accounting for another 22 percent. According to estimates about one-fifth of the entire population of El Salvador now lives in the United States mostly as illegal aliens.

The 2,000-mile border with Mexico is the most attractive point of illegal entry, even for immigrants from Asia and other regions of the world. The problem is aggravated by the inability of the U.S. border patrol to control the frontier. The patrol is understaffed and overwhelmed by the sheer numbers of immigrants. The issue has become a thorny domestic political problem in many states, with accusations being made that illegal immigrants are taking jobs away from American citizens. The new legislation seeks to stop the practice of hiring illegals.

The new law has created concern in Latin America as well. A surge of immigrants back into the region will place a heavy burden on most governments. Unemployment is already very high. Social service demands will increase. And workers' remittances from the United States, sent back to families in dollars, will stop. Moreover, the law will eliminate an important escape valve. For years, unemployed young people in Latin America have been able to come to the United States to work and to establish a career. If they are forcibly kept at home, their discontent will eventually manifest itself politically and create instability in the region.

Neither the drug issue nor illegal immigration have obvious solutions. Both have domestic and foreign implications, and both have aroused heat and passion on both sides of the border. Relatively new on the agenda of United States-Latin American relations, these issues will not simply disappear. Indeed, most specialists believe that both will grow worse, regardless of legislation, as long as few opportunities exist at home for employment and career advancement and as long as civil war and political instability plague Central America and the Caribbean.

CONCLUSION

The basic dilemmas of formulating independent positions in foreign policy continue to frustrate the states of Latin America. An increase in U.S. security concerns in the Caribbean and Central American region highlights Latin impotence when confronted with U.S. determination and will. The Contadora group failed in its attempts to mediate a settlement in Central America. The Arias Plan of five Central American presidents appeared stalemated at the start of 1988.

The profound economic crisis that affects all the states of the hemisphere has demonstrated their continued dependence on the United States and the private commercial banks who provide the lion's share of the region's loans. The Acapulco agreement signed by eight Latin American presidents in November 1987 is strong on rhetoric, but whether it will lead to action is another question. At issue is Latin America's five years of austerity. The Latin leaders have not yet identified a set of policy instruments or amassed the political will to confront the United States and its industrial allies on the critical issues of trade, investment, debt financing, and commodity prices.

A complex web of regional and subregional hemispheric institutions appears unable to clarify goals or to overcome internal dissension, scarce resources, and deep divisions between military and democratic regimes. The hemisphere's ties with the Third World are strong but based on rhetoric since they comprise poor countries that can offer little help to each other. Latin America finds itself closer to the United States than it ever imagined possible in the optimistic days of the 1970s when autonomy seemed increasingly possible.

A danger is that the deep economic crisis may provoke unexpected reactions in Latin America—such as debt moratoriums or the replacement of democratic regimes with nationalist governments. Either event may herald a period of deep distrust between the United States and the region. Moratoriums would directly threaten the U.S. economy and the American banking system. Nationalist regimes in Latin America might decide to take measures to protect their countries that would strike directly at U.S. economic and investment stakes in the hemisphere. Desperate states with nationalist regimes might well seek to redress irredentist territorial claims. A period of border conflict and the settling of old scores would be difficult to control given the fragility of existing regional institutions. U.S. influence has diminished significantly, particularly on the South American continent, nor would U.S. diplomatic intervention necessarily achieve any more success than it enjoyed during the 1982 Falkland Islands War in the South Atlantic.

The hemisphere has once again witnessed the assertion of U.S. security interests in Central America and the Caribbean. After the skillful negotiation of the new Panama Canal treaties in the 1970s, for example, and the very useful role played by the Andean states in 1979 in removing the Somozas from power in Nicaragua, there was every reason to believe that the United States sought a partnership with the hemisphere in solving regional problems. Quickly, with the election of President Reagan and the appearance of a perceived security threat, the balance changed. Not even the skillful diplomatic efforts of the Contadora states or of President Arias have settled the profound differences between the United States and Nicaragua. An earlier attempt by Mexico to find a moderate solution to the differences between the United States, Nicaragua, and Cuba had failed also.

There is now a hiatus in Latin America's search for autonomy in world affairs. Problems of subversion and possible bankruptcy have moved to the top of the hemispheric agenda for the foreseeable future. Latin America will continue to seek marginal degrees of autonomy. Some efforts will be successful; bolder initiatives will encounter the dilemma of debt and the reality of ideology. From the perspective of U.S. foreign policy, it is essential to remember that

> geographic and historic factors, and the international role these dynamic countries can play, especially the "new influentials" all make a constructive relationship with them of profound consequence to the United States. That in turn requires being relevant to national concerns and situations. For the larger countries, relevance means being responsive and helpful to their central anxieties—trade, access to capital, debt management, economic and

social development. For revolutionary situations it means help in fostering moderate solutions of internal conflict and "drying up the ponds."[26]

That is the challenge the hemisphere confronts in the 1990s. The United States remains profoundly important to the states of Latin America. In turn, the region is an essential element in defining the national security interests of the United States. Interdependence is obvious; what is lacking is the guiding spirit or dynamics needed to transform old antagonisms and perceptions into a new reality of hemispheric cooperation that is the best guarantee of Latin America's eventual emergence as a serious actor in world affairs.

FOREIGN POLICY LANDMARKS

1947   The Rio treaty (Inter-American Treaty of Reciprocal Assistance) is signed by the United States and the Latin American nations; a collective security agreement, the Rio treaty served as a model for other mutual defense pacts like NATO.
1948   Founding of the Organization of American States (OAS).
1954   The CIA helps overthrow the Jacobo Arbenz regime in Guatemala, whose program of moderate social and economic reform was viewed as subversive by the Eisenhower administration.
1959   Fidel Castro overthrows President Fulgencio Batista of Cuba and opens a new era in Latin American politics; Castro defies the United States and, with the backing of the Soviet Union, establishes the first Marxist state in the Western Hemisphere.
1961   A CIA-sponsored invasion of Cuba at the Bay of Pigs fails to unseat Castro.
1961   The Alliance for Progress is begun by the Kennedy administration as a response to the Cuban revolution.
1962   The Cuban Missile Crisis is a strategic victory for the United States. The Soviet Union agrees to withdraw its missiles from Cuba in return for a U.S. pledge not to invade Cuba.
1964   Onset of military-authoritarian regimes in Brazil.
1965   The United States intervenes in the Dominican Republic in an attempt to prevent "another Cuba".
1966   Onset of military-authoritarian regime in Argentina.
1967   The death of Cuban leader Che Guevara in Bolivia at the hands of the Bolivian army ends the myth of guerrilla invincibility.
1968   A populist-reformist military regime is started in Peru.
1973   The overthrow of Chilean President Salvador Allende unleashes a long era of brutal repression and destroys the idea of a "peaceful transition" to democratic socialism in Latin America.
1973   Onset of military-authoritarian regimes in Chile and Uruguay.
1976   Another military-authoritarian regime is founded in Argentina.

[26]Viron P. Vaky, "Hemispheric Relations: Everything is Part of Everything Else," *Foreign Affairs*, 59 (3), "America and the World 1980," 1981.

1977   The signing of the Panama Canal Treaties marks a milestone in U.S. relations with Latin America. The United States agrees to transfer the canal to Panama by the year 2000, with administrative control to be given to Panama in 1988.

1979   The Sandinista National Liberation Front forcibly overthrows the dictatorship of General Anastasio Somoza in Nicaragua.

1982   The Latin American debt crisis begins as Mexico narrowly averts default.

1982   The Argentina-British (Malvinas or Falklands) war in the South Atlantic results in defeat for Argentina and serves as a catalyst for the restoration of democracy in Argentina and the election of President Raúl Alfonsín in 1983.

1983   The first meeting of the Contadora Group, which tries to find a solution to the Central American wars independent from U.S. policy.

1983   The United States invades Grenada and unseats an unpopular Marxist dictatorship.

1987   The Arias Peace Plan is launched by the Nobel Prize-winning Costa Rican president in an effort to end the armed conflict in Central America.

1987   The Acapulco Declaration of eight Latin American presidents seeks a political dialog with the industrial countries for Latin America's pressing problems.

SELECTED BIBLIOGRAPHY

ATKINS, G. POPE. *Latin America in the International Political System.* New York: Free Press, 1977.

BAGLEY, BRUCE MICHAEL. *Regional Powers in the Caribbean Basin: Mexico, Venezuela, and Colombia.* Washington, D.C.: The Johns Hopkins School of Advanced International Studies, Central American and Caribbean Program (Occasional Paper No. 2), 1983.

BURR, ROBERT N. *By Reason or Force: Chile and the Balancing of Power in South America, 1830–1905.* Berkeley and Los Angeles: University of California Press, 1967.

CHILD, JOHN. *Unequal Alliance: The Inter-American Military System, 1938–1978.* Boulder, Colo.: Westview Press, 1980.

DAVIS, HAROLD EUGUENE, JOHN J. FINAN, and F. TAYLOR PECK. *Latin American Diplomatic History: An Introduction.* Baton Rouge, La. and London: Louisiana State University Press, 1977.

FAGEN, RICHARD R., and OLGA PELLICER, eds. *The Future of Central America: Policy Choices for the U.S. and Mexico.* Stanford, Calif.: Stanford University Press, 1983.

FERRIS, ELIZABETH G., and JENNIE K. LINCOLN, eds. *Latin American Foreign Policies: Global and Regional Dimensions.* Boulder, Colo.: Westview Press, 1981.

"Governance in the Western Hemisphere: Background Papers." New York: Aspen Institute for Humanistic Studies, 1982.

GRABENDORFF, WOLF, and RIORDAN ROETT, eds. *Latin America, Western Europe and the United States: A New Atlantic Triangle.* New York: Praeger, 1984.

HARTLYN, JONATHAN, and SAMUEL A. MORLEY, eds. *Latin American Political Economy.* Boulder, Colo.: Westview Press, 1986.

KRYZANEK, MICHAEL J. *U.S.–Latin American Relations.* New York: Praeger, 1985.

LEVINSON, JEROME, and JUAN DE ONIS. *The Alliance that Lost Its Way: A Critical Report on the Alliance for Progress.* Chicago: Quadrangle Books, 1970.

LOWENTHAL, ABRAHAM F. *Partners in Conflict: The United States and Latin America.* Baltimore, Md. and London: The Johns Hopkins University Press, 1987.

LYNCH, JOHN. *The Spanish-American Revolutions, 1808–1826.* New York: Norton, 1973.

MUÑOZ, HERALDO, and JOSEPH S. TULCHIN, eds. *Latin American Nations in World Politics.* Boulder, Colo.: Westview Press, 1984.

MIDDLEBROOK, KEVIN J., and CARLOS RICO. *The United States and Latin America in the 1980s.* Pittsburgh, Pa.: University of Pittsburgh Press, 1986.

PHILIP, GEORGE. *Oil and Politics in Latin America: Nationalist Movements and State Companies.* Cambridge: Cambridge University Press, 1982.

ROETT, RIORDAN, ed. *Brazil in the Seventies.* Washington, D.C.: American Enterprise Institute, 1976.

SCHOULTZ, LARS. *National Security and United States Policy toward Latin America.* Princeton, N.J.: Princeton University Press, 1987.

SELCHER, WAYNE A., ed. *Brazil in the International System: The Rise of Middle Power.* Boulder, Colo.: Westview Press, 1981.

SILVERT, KALMAN H., STANLEY HOFFMAN, RIORDAN ROETT, et al. *The Americas in a Changing World: A Report of the Commission on United States–Latin American Relations.* New York: Quadrangle/New York Times Books, 1975.

WESSON, ROBERT, ed. *U.S. Influence in Latin America in the 1980s.* New York: Praeger, 1982.

WIARDA, HOWARD J., and HARVEY F. KLINE, eds. *Latin American Politics and Development.* Boulder, Colo.: Westview Press, 1985.

WOOD, BRYCE. *The Dismantling of the Good Neighbor Policy.* Austin, Tex.: University of Texas Press, 1985.

11

Scandinavia:
Diversity amidst Security,
Prosperity, and Solidarity

Bengt Sundelius

To outsiders, the Scandinavian* countries appear to form a distinct community of nations that share great prosperity, unusual political stability, innovative social programs, and foreign policies supportive of global order and justice. Scandinavians take great pride in these features, but they often see them less as regional characteristics and more as distinct policies of their own native countries—Denmark, Finland, Iceland, Norway, or Sweden. Although accepting the group identity of Scandinavia, the peoples of these small nations with a total population of 22 million are mainly struck by the many differences between them.

Less than a hundred years ago, Scandinavia was a place to leave for a better future in the New World. Since that time, the mining, forestry, farming, and fishing communities of the North have been transformed into advanced industrial countries with all of the material comforts and accompanying social problems of modern times. Not only have Americans of Scandinavian descent found contemporary Scandinavian life in-

*The terms *Scandinavian* and *Nordic* are used interchangeably to depict the five states examined here. Although Scandinavia is the more commonly used term in English, most natives prefer the latter term as a more encompassing characterization for the region. This is symbolized in the regional parliamentary body, the Nordic Council. The author gratefully acknowledges the valuable assistance of Don Odom of the International Graduate School, University of Stockholm, in the preparation of this chapter.

triguing, but also students of government, social welfare, economic management, and industrial relations have discovered that the experiences of these nations are worthy of closer examination.

To students of international affairs, Scandinavia has often seemed less fascinating and less controversial than many of the troubled spots around the world. Scandinavia's distinctive mark—stability—seldom attracts much journalistic or even scholarly interest. Located on the fringe of the continent, the study of these states generally contributes little to an understanding of important European economic and security developments. Being small, their role in world affairs has been overshadowed by more important actors. Still, if one prefers international order and stability over conflict and turmoil, then it may be worthwhile to examine how in this region, despite its location on the border of East and West, such features have come about.

The happy circumstances, however, that have kept Scandinavia out of the limelight of world affairs for some time may be a thing of the past. Increasingly, the strategic interests of the superpowers are focused on the North Atlantic and the adjacent land areas. While some of the historic problems of the European continent now seem to have reached a static condition, the clashing interests of the major powers may have shifted to the North. According to many strategists, the next global war may not be won in Scandinavia, but it could very well be lost there.

The stakes for the United States in these developments are considerable. Changing priorities have already resulted in a higher American profile in this region. Historically, the Soviet Union has long recognized its strategic interests in Scandinavia. Although the Soviet presence has been felt for many years, during the last decade it has become much more visible. In the future, Scandinavia may not only serve as an illustration of a well-balanced, low-tension area, but also as an example of how such stable patterns can erode and turn into an arena for superpower rivalries.

FROM CONFLICT TO COMMUNITY

Historically, Nordic relations have been characterized as much by conflict and rivalry as by neighborliness and cooperation. During the Middle Ages efforts to form one unified Nordic state failed at the hands of Swedish separatists and, instead, two distinct entities emerged. Denmark, Norway, and Iceland composed one unit and, at first, it dominated the region. Sweden and Finland constituted the other unit.

A traditional struggle for regional hegemony continued into the eighteenth century between Sweden and Denmark. There were numerous wars fought, alliances formed, and provinces conquered and reconquered all in a quest for supremacy. This rivalry was aggravated by the temporary power vacuum in northern and central Europe. Prussia and Russia emerged, however, and began to dominate the political scene at the expense of both Denmark and Sweden.

By the end of the Napoleonic Wars, some drastic changes in the political configuration of the Nordic region took place. The Swedish province of Finland, seized by Russia in 1809, was turned into a semi-autonomous province until Finnish independence was achieved in 1917. The intense shock over the loss of one-third of its territory profoundly affected Sweden and resulted in a coup d'état and a new constitution. As a provision of the Congress of Vienna after the Napoleonic War, Norway was given to Sweden in 1814 as compensation for the loss of Finland. However, Norway was never totally integrated as a part of Sweden, as Finland had been, but was instead attached in a union under a joint monarch. The Norwegians retained their own constitution, government, and central administration. Only in foreign policy did the Swedish government represent the Norwegians.

This Norwegian-Swedish union never penetrated from the political and constitutional level down to the economic, cultural, and social levels. Instead, the two societies developed separately during the nineteenth century. Growing cultural, social, and economic differences, increased political conflicts throughout the nineteenth century until in 1905 the union was finally dissolved.

Denmark kept only Iceland, Greenland, and the Faroe Islands after 1814. Iceland would remain a Danish colony until a grant of autonomy in 1918 and would only achieve full independence in 1944. Although the other islands have remained under Danish sovereignty, they have been granted increased autonomy in recent years.

The period between 1800 and the end of World War II has thus been described as an era of Nordic political disintegration, as the two traditional entities in the region were split into five separate nation-states. Further, since 1814 the Nordic region has not experienced any internal military conflicts. This fact contrasts sharply with the tradition of frequent wars prior to that time. Even though the Nordic region was divided into many smaller entities, these small countries acted in unison against greater power interference. Since that time violent solutions have been avoided whenever serious conflict has arisen. For example, Norway peacefully seceded from the union with Sweden in 1905; the Swedish-Finnish dispute over the rights to the Åland Islands was settled peacefully in 1921; and conflicting Norwegian and Danish claims to eastern Greenland were adjudicated by the Permanent Court of International Justice in 1933.

Great power intervention in the region was to be avoided, even if it meant making sacrifices to the neighboring countries. Slowly, these separate decisions in favor of compromise solutions established a tradition of peaceful regional relations. For example, all of the Scandinavian countries stayed neutral during World War I in spite of strong sympathies with the different parties to the war. Similarly, prospects of war among Scandinavian countries are no longer entertained. Thus, a "pluralistic security community" has slowly developed, where dependable expectations of peaceful settlements of regional disputes are found. It is interesting that this condition was not reached until the region was politically divided into several states, which as individuals were reduced to small power status.

SECURING FIVE NATION-STATES

Norway

Norway is a traditionally pro-British nation of 4 million people controlling an important coastline on the North Sea. From independence in 1905 until 1940 it pursued a policy of neutrality. During World War I, the German and British navies competed for dominance in Norwegian coastal waters. Under pressure, the government generally leaned toward the British. This would later prove to be costly in the second round of the British-German Conflict. On April 9, 1940, Germany launched a daring surprise attack by sea and air to preempt British plans for mine laying. After two months of fighting, Norway was occupied for five years. The king escaped into exile in London and became the symbol of resistance.

At the end of the war, Norway for a short time returned to its traditional foreign policy orientation and attempted to perform the role of international bridge-builder, which included support of the newly formed United Nations. In fact, Norway's foreign minister, Trygve Lie, became the first UN Secretary General. In 1948, the government faced the familiar choice of balancing its allegiances. Norway could either join the emerging Atlantic Alliance, or it could stay out of the bloc confrontation through an alliance with neutral Sweden and Denmark.

Since 1945 Norway has shared a 125 mile land border with the USSR in the far north. It feared political pressures similar to those felt by other Soviet neighbors at that time. A firm Western defense commitment to Norway was seen as a strategic necessity as well as a logical extension of the wartime collaboration with the Allies. Since joining the Alliance, Norway has been one of the most steadfast NATO members. Today, government officials note that the widely supported Alliance commitment represents a longer tradition than the previously held position of neutrality.

From the first days of its NATO membership, Norway has attempted to balance the deterrence function of the alliance with an emphasis on its defensive purpose. For example, the government has ruled out the stationing of NATO troops on its territory or the presence of any nuclear weapons in peacetime since 1949. Denmark has also followed this policy, making Scandinavia, in effect, a region free of nuclear weapons throughout the postwar period.

This concern for "reassurance" is intended to avoid turning strategically vulnerable Norway into a more exposed target area in the event of war. Norway does not want to give the appearance of serving as an offensive arrow close to the vital Soviet military complex on the Kola peninsula. Norway's military presence north of the 62d parallel is, therefore, deliberately kept very modest. Along this border area shared by NATO and the Warsaw Pact, few incidents similar to those along the German border have occurred.

A policy of restraint in combination with a firm alliance commitment has solid public support in Norway. The various "reassurance" schemes are very important as in some ways they represent a continuation of the legacy of neutrality and bridge-building. While the Left tends to emphasize this dimension more than the Right, it is an important element of the Norwegian foreign policy profile that all groups can embrace. At times, the left wing of the dominant Labor Party has demanded that the government pursue various confidence building schemes more vigorously. For example, during the early 1980s, a prior Finnish proposal for the creation of a Nordic nuclear weapons free zone reappeared with great intensity in the Norwegian debate. Also, alliance agreements to strengthen the military preparedness of NATO defenses have been controversial. Like the other Scandinavians, the Norwegians have been as concerned with avoiding involvement in conflict as with being well prepared should a crisis develop.

Denmark

During the last century, the Danish international position has been largely shaped by its dynamic neighbor to the south. Without a natural frontier against Germany, this tiny territory, comprising one peninsula off the Continent together with several flat islands, is easily overrun from the south or from the sea. After losing successive wars to Prussia and Austria in 1864, the government embarked on a policy of neutrality and appeasement through World War II.

Although occupied during the last war, Denmark emerged relatively undamaged, and the regular government machinery remained intact. The Danish king, who stayed behind to share the burdens of his people, became a symbol of calm and patience through his daily outings on horseback through the streets of Copenhagen. The country was spared any serious fighting in 1945, but one of the Danish outer islands, Bornholm, was, in fact, liberated by the Red Army. The Russians soon withdrew from this potentially valuable holding in the western part of the Baltic Sea.

With the emerging Cold War, Denmark joined NATO after the collapse of the plans for a Scandinavian Defense Alliance. Less enthusiastic than Norway in this choice, Denmark has remained an ally, but has been less supportive than most members. The United States was anxious for Danish membership due to the strategic importance of its Arctic holding in Greenland, as well as for its control of the gateway to the Baltic Sea.

Because of the NATO alliance and the postwar division of Germany, the pressures on Denmark from the south have virtually ceased. Now, the defense of Denmark proper is the concern of a NATO command dominated by allied West German forces. Of course, the economic surge of the vibrant West German society remains a factor for an advanced industrial nation of only 5 million people. This is best manifested in the Danish membership in the European Community since 1973.

The term "Denmarkization" has been coined in NATO circles to depict a state that fails to live up to its alliance commitments. To a greater extent than, for example, Norway, the precarious Danish economy has set limits to the financial support for the joint defense effort. In addition, a complex domestic political situation with a popular majority favoring a left-leaning security policy but a political majority favoring conservative domestic policies has in recent years made Denmark notorious for its "footnotes" to many NATO declarations. The impression has been given abroad that the country does not take its alliance obligations very seriously. In fact, it appears to enjoy a status of free rider within the joint defense structure.

The strategic importance of Denmark's vast Greenland territory, however, is as evident today as it was during the formative years of the alliance. NATO installations in Greenland have so far not been seriously questioned. However, the leadership of the autonomous Greenland region has during recent years shown greater independence, and, for example, it pulled out of the European Community in 1985. It may be that in the future, the strategic pressures on Denmark will come from the north rather than from the south. In this the Danish and Norwegian governments have a joint interest in the "Nordpolitik" of the Western alliance.

Iceland

Iceland shares the cultural, social, and political traditions of Scandinavia, yet its tiny population, one-sided economic dependence upon fishing, and isolated geographic location produce some vast differences from the other Nordic nations. The central foreign policy problem for Iceland has been how to reconcile a strong sense of independence with its strategic value as a bridge between North America and Europe. Attaining nation-statehood only in 1944, the Icelanders are highly sensitive to infringements on their sovereignty and cultural identity. Proud of the heritage of the Viking Sagas and acutely aware of their isolation, they are torn between the obvious need for cooperation and their negative experience with colonial interference.

During World War II, the Allies occupied Iceland. This protection was not entirely unwelcome, as the obvious alternative was even less appealing. Since the war, the U.S. has maintained a military presence at Keflavik, and Iceland later joined the Atlantic Alliance. The approximately 4,000 Americans stationed in Iceland represent, within the context of a native population of only 230,000, a potential disruptive force to the nation. Because of this, the American profile is kept low and several measures have been used to shield the local inhabitants from unwanted intrusions. At the same time, the NATO base represents a major military and financial asset to a small economy. Not only does it relieve the government from any expenses for defense, but also it generates significant purchasing power to the local economy as well. The NATO facility has also served as a useful bargaining chip in securing vital economic concessions in the fishing sector.

Iceland has prevailed in three "Cod Wars" in which more powerful alliance members acceded to Icelandic demands for fishing rights within a 200-mile economic zone. In these negotiations, the small but committed state could force the terms of agreement through the implicit threat about the future of the strategically vital Keflavik base. The Icelandic government has cultivated good relations with the Soviet Union, which maintains a large diplomatic mission in Reykjavik, and the Soviet Union has been a reliable source of oil.

With the military buildup in the North Atlantic, NATO's access to Iceland, for surveillance purposes and as a support base, remains essential to its defense posture. In fact, the Norwegian policy of not permitting a permanent basing of NATO forces in peacetime may be credible only as long as the Icelanders are willing to accept an American base on their territory. Thus, Iceland helps solve a Norwegian domestic policy dilemma, supports the deterrence function of the alliance, and contributes to NATO reassurance in the North. Obviously, the Icelandic government has managed to make the most of its strategic assets and has turned vulnerability into bargaining strength.

Finland

Finland, like Denmark, has been preoccupied with developing a mutually acceptable relationship with a neighboring Great Power. After some 600 years as part of the Swedish kingdom and 108 years as an autonomous province of Imperial Russia, Finland, a nation of about 5 million people, became independent in 1917. After independence and a brief but violent civil war, Finland adopted a stiff posture toward the new

Soviet state. Centuries of border wars had left a legacy of suspicion. It followed a pro-German line, but it fell victim to the Molotov-Ribbentrop Pact of 1939 and had to fight alone against the Red Army during the winter of 1939–1940.

Soviet ambitions to install a "people's government" in Helsinki, similar to those in the Baltic states, failed. The Finnish government at the end of World War II, however, was forced to accept major territorial losses and to pay substantial war reparations. Under the leadership of President Paasikivi, Finland embarked on a new relationship with its powerful neighbor to ensure that it would never again face another conflict with the Soviet Union.

Adopting a Danish approach to its major security problem, the Finnish government has through the postwar years strived to gain the confidence of the Soviet leadership. Based on the assumption that Soviet interests in Finland are defensive and strategic, and not offensive and ideological, considerations for the legitimate security needs of a major power would not jeopardize the Finnish domestic system, based on Western economic values and democratic ideals.

This policy of good neighborliness is symbolized in the 1948 Finnish-Soviet Treaty of Friendship, Cooperation, and Mutual Assistance. In its title, it parallels several Soviet pacts with Eastern European nations at that time, but its significance has obviously been quite different. The notion of pursuing neutrality outside the power blocs draws on this agreement from the Cold War era. It has been seen less as a restriction on Finnish security policy than as an opportunity to develop an independent foreign policy profile.

Soon after the Communist take-over of Czechoslovakia in 1948, a delegation of Finnish officials arrived in Moscow for negotiations on a treaty of cooperation with the Soviet Union. The Finnish leaders were summoned to lay the foundation to a constructive future relationship with the Superpower neighbor. Soviet Foreign Minister Molotov received the delegation and quickly agreed to work from a Finnish draft to a treaty text.

Experts agree that three elements of the 1948 treaty are of particular importance. First, the contracting parties agreed to "confer with each other if it is established that the threat of an armed attack" is present. This wording is interpreted to mean that both governments must accept this notion of an existing threat. Secondly, Finland's first obligation is to "fight to repel the attack" and any Soviet assistance "will be subject to mutual agreement between the contracting parties." Thirdly, in the preamble to the treaty the Finnish "desire to remain outside the conflicting interests of the Great Powers" is acknowledged. This formula has been the point of departure for the Finnish quest for neutrality between East and West.

At the April 1948 signing ceremony, Stalin characterized the new agreement as a point of transition from a state of mistrust between the two states to a new spirit of mutual confidence. At regular intervals, this pillar of Finnish–Soviet relations has been renewed and over the years the agreement from the Cold War era has come to symbolize a stable relationship of mutual trust unaffected by the many turns of Soviet–American relations.

With the peaceful coexistence offensive of the mid-1950s by the post-Stalin leaders in the USSR, Finland could more vigorously pursue neutrality, as was the case with the newly declared neutral Austrian state. Fears of direct Soviet intervention in the domestic life of Finland faded after the return of the Porkala penninsula outside Helsinki in 1955. Like other Europeans neutrals, Finland has played a role in fostering more harmonious East-West relations. Its efforts seem to be appreciated in Western capitals as well as in Moscow. Certainly, the détente era of the 1970s opened up new opportunities for such a role. The Finnish search for legitimacy as a democratic neutral was crowned in 1975 when—in a thirty-five-nation summit meeting—the "Helsinki Accords" laid the foundation to the now permanent Conference on Security and Cooperation in Europe (CSCE) negotiations. Finland had by then also served on the Security Council of the United Nations. The young state has overcome the disadvantages of its geography and is recognized worldwide as a member of the community of European democracies.

Yet, the Finnish relations with the Soviet Union have not been without problems. The most serious crisis occurred in 1961, when the Soviet government requested consultations in accordance with the 1948 pact. West German activities were cited as a potential threat to Finnish security. Through skillful diplomacy by President Urho Kekkonen, the matter was dropped before any consultations were held.

Among Western commentators unfamiliar with Finnish–Soviet relations, the concept "Finlandization" has been coined to depict a policy of appeasement toward preponderant Soviet power. In contrast to the Finnish postwar experience, this prejorative term suggests an image of a narrowing West European margin of political maneuver in the face of a growing Soviet military dominance. The "Finlandization" term was introduced during the détente era of the early 1970s to dramatize an underlying warning against a growing Soviet threat to Western Europe. However, the logic behind this catchword fits poorly with the postwar reality of Finland. In fact, a process of "Finlandization," taken in for what it really is, may strike many peoples along the Soviet border as a welcome prospect. Throughout the years Finland has enjoyed a widening relm of maneuver and independence.

It is paradoxical that the Soviet Union through time seems to have gained a considerable stake in a harmonious relationship with democratic and capitalistic Finland. The attention given to this small state by the

Soviet leadership is exceptional and seems to go beyond considerations based only on bilateral relations. From the Soviet viewpoint, the Finnish solution can be offered as a model for relations with other West European states. Sceptics, then, can here clearly observe that it is possible to deal with, and benefit from, close and cooperative relations with the Soviet Union.

Thus, the Soviet leadership may be as eager as are the Finns to find mutually acceptable solutions to bilateral problems. The position of the small nation is strengthened. It is curious that while Sweden during the 1980s has experienced a period of tension with the Soviet Union over territorial violations, the Finnish government seems to have been spared such problems.

The U.S. government has always shown considerable empathy and respect for Finland. Its leaders have been well received in Washington, while no Swedish prime minister was granted an official White House visit from 1961 until 1987. The U.S. government seems to have appreciated the relatively low-key approach to global issues adopted in Helsinki. The U.S. and Finnish governments have not engaged in the type of diplomatic spats that at times have characterized United States–Swedish relations and President Reagan planned to visit Helsinki on his way to the Moscow summit in May 1988. Among many Americans, Finnish neutrality is appreciated, while Swedish neutrality is resented.

Sweden

Over the last century, Sweden has benefited from the cushioning effects of its Scandinavian neighbors. While these states have been drawn into the pattern of conflict and cooperation in Europe, Sweden has more often remained outside such activities. A policy of splendid isolation has been combined with the perhaps better known quest for international understanding. Possessing relatively strong economic and military attributes, Sweden, a nation of 8 million people, could long afford such a stand. The superior resource base, representing almost half of the total GNP in the region, has given Sweden dominance in the Nordic arena. In a larger context, Sweden is small and defines itself as a leading small state.

After World War I, Sweden enjoyed an optimal security position. With Germany defeated, the new Soviet state weak, Finland and the three Baltic states independent, and with Denmark and Norway strengthened but friendly, Sweden did not face any serious strategic concerns. Within the immediate security environment Sweden even appeared as a major player.

A benevolent policy was adopted that included acquiescence to a League of Nations ruling granting the Swedish-speaking Åland Islands to the new Finnish state against the clear wishes of the inhabitants. Similarly, the various international disarmament schemes of the period between the World Wars found support in Sweden. In 1925 Sweden set an example for other nations by greatly reducing its own defenses. Like others, notably in the United States at the time, prominent Swedes placed great faith in the abilities of statesmen to create a stable and just world order through international law and diplomacy.

By the mid-1930s, this happy situation was replaced by the rise of Nazi Germany, the consolidation of the Soviet regime, and the collapse of the League. Joining the other small European states, Sweden declared its departure from the collective security system and its return to the traditional defense posture; namely, armed neutrality. During the war, the government's primary objective was to keep the nation out of the conflict that had caused so much suffering in the other states of Europe.

In this respect, the government was successful, but at the expense of being forced at times to interpret the obligations of neutrality in less than acceptable ways. For example, the Swedish government provided assistance to its war-torn Nordic neighbors, allowed German troop transfers across its territory, and facilitated the return of Allied airmen stranded after missions over enemy territory—all apparent deviations from a strict definition of neutrality. The other neutrals of World War II were forced to accept similar compromises as well. At the war's end, Sweden could not join in the celebrations of the Allies, but it continued to assist the victims of war. Clearly, Swedish values were served by the victory, but it is an open question whether the Allied cause would have been better served through Swedish combat participation.

Like the United States, Sweden entered the postwar period from a position of strength. The industrial base was intact and the defense force was formidable. This set the stage for the relative economic and military weight of Sweden over the next thirty years. Sweden joined the United Nations in 1946 after some debate over the compatibility of membership with the policy of neutrality. The second UN Secretary General, Dag Hammarskjold, was recruited from Sweden in 1953. In 1948, an effort was made to keep the Scandinavian region out of the Cold War through a Scandinavian Defense Alliance outside the blocs. At the time, Swedish military might was still sufficiently impressive that such a defense pact could be regarded as a meaningful choice.

When Denmark and Norway opted for membership in the Atlantic Alliance, Sweden returned to its traditional stand of splendid isolation. The resulting formula—freedom from alliances in peacetime, aiming at neutrality in the event of war—remains the cornerstone for Swedish security policy to this day. Even a different internal resource base and vastly changed international conditions for armed neutrality have not undermined the domestic support for this doctrine. In the public mind, this posture has spared the country the devastation of war since 1814 and it has become almost axiomatic.

Possibly, the Swedish postwar security choice facilitated the Finnish effort to avoid the fate of the other nations along the Soviet border. The creation of a neutral buffer in the North, guarded by an impressive air force, may have reduced tensions in an otherwise sharply divided Europe. The peacetime utility of the Swedish posture can easily be appreciated when one compares Scandinavia with the record of bloc confrontation in Central Europe. The wartime credibility of armed neutrality is more open to question because of the fast developing and unpredictable nature of modern warfare.

The comparatively modest Swedish defense force should be sufficient to deter an attack based upon the assumption that neither bloc could—in a crisis—devote most of its military resources to a marginal country. In other words, the cost of an attack would be seen as too high relative to the strategic advantages of controlling the territory. Clearly, the level of conflict preparedness of the armed forces and the ability to foresee any hostile moves are crucial to the credibility of the Swedish policy. Considerable investment has been made in a mobile air force and advanced means of intelligence collection.

During the postwar period the Swedish government has—in addition to its commitment to armed neutrality—continued to promote international understanding and cooperation. Swedish involvement in multilateral initiatives rests on the belief that security can be enhanced both by national defense and by an international milieu less conducive to conflict. A strong commitment to the United Nations, including its multinational peace-keeping forces, an active role in international development issues, and a vocal concern about superpower armaments and their involvement in local conflicts in the Third World, can be understood in these terms.

Closer to home, a major concern has been how to help transform a conflict prone Europe into a setting of greater stability. Active in the Helsinki process and in the development of confidence-building measures, together with the other European neutral and nonaligned states, Sweden recently hosted the Stockholm Conference on Disarmament in Europe. Inspired by the work of the Palme Commission on Common Security, the government has proposed the establishment in Central Europe of a border zone free of nuclear weapons. Similarly, the arms buildup at sea is viewed with concern, and the Strategic Defense Initiative is regarded as a destabilizing element in East-West relations. During the 1980s more emphasis has been placed on the European setting compared to other regions and to global issues.

SLIDING TOWARD THE FRONTLINE?

The security interdependence of the five states of the north has been mutually recognized. The Danish and Norwegian policies of non-basing of NATO forces in peacetime are seen in Sweden and Finland as positive gestures to reduce the local Atlantic Allied presence. On the other hand, Icelandic tolerance of a large American base on their territory may facilitate the Danish and Norwegian choices. Swedish armed neutrality offers Finland a shield in the West and may strengthen her relationship of trust with the security conscious USSR. At the same time, a strong Swedish air force provides a buffer for the defense of Norway. Finnish neutrality in combination with the Danish and Norwegian choices help cushion the Swedish pillar.

Although the security postures selected are clearly based upon calculations of national interest and considerations of domestic politics, the governments often acknowledge that their positions are interlinked and that they have been well served by this pattern. It is not as evident, however, that the benefits to European stability have been as clearly understood by the superpowers. A number of current strategic developments, shaped by the interests of the bloc leaders, may through time erode this favorable setting for regional stability. It is possible that the northern flank could be transformed into a Nordic frontline in the struggle between East and West.

Recent developments in the North Atlantic, have placed Scandinavia at the center of naval interests. A growing Soviet fleet has operated out of the Kola base complex in close proximity to the region for some time. The Soviets understandably developed an acute sense of security for the area surrounding the considerable forces they have amassed at this ice-free port. Although presumably not targeted at the neighboring Scandinavian nations, the nuclear weapons located there play a significant role in the broader strategic picture. Thus, the North Cape is of great interest to NATO planners and to the new American Forward Maritime Strategy. This new element undermines the Norwegian policy of reassurance toward the USSR and complicates the plans for oil and gas exploration in these waters. The defense of northern Finland and Sweden is affected as well, and this has resulted in an upgrading of the local forces.

Traditionally, the U.S. military commitment to European defense has depended on NATO control of the North Atlantic for reliable transoceanic shipment of men and supplies. The Soviet Northern fleet has gradually extended the scope of its operations far out into the North Atlantic. Naturally, NATO planners view this development with concern and have urged a greater Allied presence in these waters and coastal areas to counter the Soviet advance. The strategic posturing of both sides has moved closer to Scandinavia, complicating the traditional strategy of keeping the tensions as low as possible in the area. In current war scenarios, the North figures prominently as a potential combat zone in a super power confrontation. For example, Soviet control of the extensive Swedish air base system could significantly strengthen Soviet ability to fight for dominance of the North Atlantic skies. According to one scenario, the defense of the long Norwegian coastline would be impossible if Norway were cut off through an advance in the Trondheim area.

Also the strategic role of the Baltic Sea has changed. Traditionally, the USSR has promoted the notion of a closed sea, where the largest maritime power could dominate the waters and shorelines. Sweden and the NATO allies have insisted on the Baltic's status as an international sea open to all states. As a result of the division of Europe in 1945, the Soviets now control an immense coastline stretching from the Finnish border in the east to the West German border south of Denmark and west of Sweden. During recent years, several major ports and naval shipyards have been constructed by the Soviets along the Baltic coast. It is not surprising, considering the industrial base of the region, that these installations serve as major overhaul and construction facilities for the vast Soviet global fleet.

The USSR seems to place great emphasis upon the control of the surrounding waters or at least their denial to others. Soviet security concerns may even be intensified by continual NATO surveillance patrols in the Baltic. The offensive Soviet submarine activities along Swedish coastlines, and the increased Allied presence in the Baltic make plain the growing tensions in the area during the 1980s. Since October of 1981, when the famed Soviet Whiskey Class submarine equipped with nuclear weapons beached just off the Swedish coast, underwater activities have been a steady source of tension between the Soviet Union and Sweden. In spite of diplomatic protests in 1981 and 1983, all indicators point toward continued intrusions. Although the inability to repel such activities may not be considered a serious national security failure, it has clearly left many questions about the credibility of Swedish armed neutrality. This issue has also sparked a rather intense domestic debate over the proper response to this new type of threat. When one considers these and related developments, it is not surprising that few Swedes view the Baltic as a "sea of peace," as it is sometimes called by Soviet officials.

Innovations in weapons technology have also affected the strategic posture of Scandinavia. A NATO launching of sea-based cruise missiles across the territories of Sweden and Finland may facilitate reaching targets in the USSR but could also create serious political dilemmas for these neutrals. Doubts about the ability or the determination of these governments to resist such territorial violations could motivate preemptive moves by the other bloc. The pressures on the credibility of Swedish armed neutrality may be greater today than during the earlier postwar years, when the Swedish defense force was significantly larger. Allied concern over the region's role during a crisis or war may also lead to peacetime demands that would be difficult to reconcile with the domestically popular reassurance policies of Denmark and Norway. The preferred pattern of regional confidence and stability could collapse as broader strategic interests clash in the North.

Such unwelcome developments may even be unaffected by a superpower agreement on force reductions in Central Europe. In fact, one could imagine that the bloc confrontation would simply shift arenas and increasingly focus on the maritime and air related dimensions relevant to Scandinavian security. Even with a reduction of global and of European tension levels, the strategic setting of the North could continue a slide toward greater instability. The strategic interests of the major powers may once again, as in 1939–1940, converge on five small states that so far have fared rather well on the quiet flank of East-West relations.

SAFEGUARDING PROSPERITY

During the last thirty years the "prosperous corner" of Europe has enjoyed living standards comparable to, or even exceeding, the U.S. level. Within the last century, five separate, small economies have developed rapidly and are now generating a remarkable level of affluence. The factor of economy of scale—considered so important to the growth of the U.S. economy and one of the objectives of the European Community— was not present in Scandinavia. How, then, did the Scandinavian countries compensate for their smallness? Traditionally, Scandinavia has sought international markets both for trade expansion and for investment opportunities. Welfare at home and competitiveness abroad have been the twin pillars of Scandinavian economic policy.

Scandinavia actively participates in international economic affairs, but refuses to merely adjust its domestic economies or its social structures to the whims of the international marketplace. The principles of Western capitalism have served only as a necessary means toward fulfillment of the social and political aspirations of governments that have been largely dominated by the moderate Left. Four levels of international economic relations have been the focus of external strategies for necessary material gains; namely, the global reach, the Atlantic partnership, the European base, and the Nordic Community. During the postwar period, the European base has dominated and has involved the greatest controversy within the Scandinavian nations.

Global Reach

Like other Western economies, Scandianvia has also greatly benefited from the U.S. sponsored economic order since Bretton Woods.

From their inception, Scandinavia has supported the free trade doctrine of GATT, multilateral financial management through the IMF, and global development programs by the World Bank. Today, the governments have reaffirmed their faith in multilateral solutions in spite of increased pressures for regionalization and bilaterism. Often support is given to Third World demands for international reform to better reflect the political realities and the development needs of today. The value of these international organizations is not only viewed in economic terms, but also as stabilizing elements in a turbulent global political system.

Possessing strong industrial structures—and in the case of Sweden a worldwide network of multinationals—Scandinavia has favored the international trade liberalization of the GATT era. In spite of strong competition from Japan and the newly industrializing countries (NICs), Scandinavia maintains an overall free-trade posture in the belief that new economic giants have more to offer as prospective customers than as fierce competitors. It is believed that deliberate up-market shifts both in production and in export profile can sustain the small, but specialized, Scandinavian manufacturers' competitive edge against the efforts of larger firms.

The usefulness of "smallness" in international trade is well illustrated by a special "Nordic clause" in the Multi-Fiber Arrangement (MFA) that regulates textile trade. Here, the Scandinavian position has achieved international acceptance: small and import-vulnerable economies require greater protection from low-cost imports than is usual. The strategy of promoting global free-trade norms, while also negotiating selected agreements to safeguard vulnerable economic sectors, is not unique to Scandinavia. The task may be easier, however, for the small open economy, because the consequences are usually minor for other parties and for the regime principles. Scandinavia's image of adherence to free trade and to economic globalism may well conceal the face of what is, indeed, a hard-nosed businessman.

Atlantic Partnership

The birth of the European Recovery Program and the advent of the Cold War signaled the rise of the Atlantic partnership in the foreign economic polices of the North. The Marshall Plan covered all the Nordic countries, except Finland. However, trade opportunities were restricted by the U.S. strategic embargo against the USSR.

Finland moved cautiously in matters of foreign trade throughout the 1950s and only joined the seemingly apolitical OECD in 1969. Finland has maintained a close trade relationship with the USSR and has balanced its economic profile more evenly than the other European neutrals. After 1952, with the fulfillment of the burdensome obligations of war reparations—largely in the form of industrial output—to the USSR, Finland's eastern neighbor has become a stable and profitable market for

Finnish industry. The Soviets, in turn, have supplied oil. Trade with the East accounts for approximately 20 percent of Finland's annual trade volume, and has helped balance the effects of Western markets upon Finland. For example, during the recession and rising oil prices of the 1970s, the Finnish economy experienced speedy growth.

Norway's Atlantic relationship is based upon a seafaring tradition. During the war years, the large Norwegian merchant fleet served the Allied cause. The shipping industry has brought valuable foreign currency earnings to a Norwegian economy usually beset by a trade deficit. The new offshore gas and oil industry has offered important opportunities for Norway and its Atlantic partners. American oil companies were instrumental in the early exploration of the remote North Sea fields. Norwegian ownership and technical know-how has developed substantially since then, but Stavanger—Norway's oil capital—is still known for its American "colony."

The growth of the oil sector during the 1970s, when prices were high and demand steady, drastically changed the Norwegian economy and the financial base of the government. At last Norway could catch up with the traditionally superior economic levels of Sweden and Denmark, and a sense of vulnerability was transformed into great optimism. However, rising production costs combined with falling prices has dampened the initial "oil fever" somewhat and the government has had to reassess its ambitious spending plans. Still, it is expected that with gradual exploitation of oil, and mainly natural gas, in the northern waters, Norway can enjoy offshore income for perhaps another century.

The decade of the 1980s has witnessed a new American determination to prevent the transfer of high-technology to the East. This sustained effort has brought the Atlantic dimension back into prominence in international trade. The Nordic neutrals, especially, have felt pressures to conform to the export regulations of the Alliance. In fact, several front-page stories headlining technology leakage through Sweden have appeared in the world press with the result being tighter national controls. Finland has maneuvered cautiously between its obvious desire for advanced technology and the equally pressing need to safeguard the credibility of its neutrality. Scandinavian industry has, to a large extent, found the new procedures cumbersome and trade restrictive.

Nordic Community

Before addressing the crucial and currently topical European dimension, an overview of the Nordic aspect of Scandinavian foreign economic policy is in order. The record of Nordic cooperation is, indeed, impressive in many respects. In the 1950s the foundations were laid through the actions of the Nordic Council that resulted in a common labor market, a passport union, and a social security union facilitating transborder moves. Many of the items in the current plan for further European integration have, in fact, already been implemented in Scandinavia.

In the economic sector, however, the results have been less noteworthy in comparison with the achievements of the European Community. The prospects for Nordic economic cooperation were discussed throughout the 1950s until these negotiations were overtaken by the establishment of the European Free-Trade Association (EFTA) in 1959. Intensive talks were held between 1968 and 1970 in an attempt to form a Nordic Economic Union (NORDEK) that would have advanced the region far beyond the accomplishments of the European Community. Because Europe remained the preferred option for several of the nations involved, the plans for NORDEK collapsed at the very last moment. A series of agreements were concluded during the 1970s that have, in effect, completed many of the ostensible goals of the NORDEK package, yet outside of its economic core and ambitious insitutional framework. Among others, a Nordic Council of Ministers with a permanent secretariat and budget, and a Nordic Investment Bank were established.

During the 1980s, industrial expansionism and production integration transcended the Nordic borders to give substance to the idea of a unified Nordic home market for local firms. The focus of demands shifted to the removal of remaining economic barriers and to further improvement of the infrastructure on a Nordic scale. Inspired by continental developments, plans for such a revitalization of Nordic economic cooperation have been accepted by the governments. A current concern is how the emerging European harmonization process will affect Nordic standards that have already been implemented—Nordic standards that often go beyond those expected on the Continent. A common goal is to protect regional achievements even while accepting the obvious need to move closer to the European arena.

The European Base

It has become apparent to the Nordic nations that prosperity cannot be maintained within the confines of the immediate region, or by links with distant continents. Although Scandinavians have often been reluctant Europeans, the European market remains the most important of their international economic interests. To a greater extent than other peoples, Scandinavians have refused to identify Europe with the European Economic Community, but have instead insisted upon a wider circle of members. The Scandinavians—and not only the neutrals—envision a Europe that stretches beyond the Elbe and the Danube. Yet, the economic core of this landscape centers on Brussels, and Scandinavia, like the USSR, has had to come to terms with the European Community.

By 1972, the negotiations between the Community and the Scandinavian governments resulted in agreements. Denmark's EC membership was ratified in a referendum in October 1972, and it entered the Community together with Great Britain and Ireland in January 1973. Fifty-four percent of the Norwegian voters rejected membership in a September 1972 referendum. This surprising verdict resulted in a government crisis and in a renewal of negotiations for a free-trade agreement. An Icelandic trade agreement on industrial goods was held up until 1976 awaiting settlement of bilateral conflicts over fishing rights. Sweden abandoned hopes for membership or a customs union, but settled for a free-trade agreement. Finnish negotiations resulted in a free-trade agreement in June 1972. This, however, was not signed until the government concluded a parallel treaty with the COMECON in July 1973.

The choices of Finland and of Sweden to remain outside of the Community can be explained in terms of the desire to safeguard their neutrality. However, other motives also played a part, as illustrated by the Norwegian turn around. Certain outspoken segments of Scandinavian voters remained in opposition to the aspirations for European unification and feared supranational controls over local social and economic conditions. Such sentiments were voiced within the leading social democratic parties, and also served as a divisive element among the nonsocialist parties. The governments that did not seek membership were saved from intense domestic controversies such as those characterizing the Danish and Norwegian EC debates. Following the events of these dramatic years, Scandinavian relations with the Community, by and large, developed smoothly over the next decade.

The most obvious result of the agreements between the Scandinavians and the EC was the gradual establishment of a free-trade area. Norway has significantly increased its trade with Europe, and this trade now accounts for around 70 percent of Norwegian exports. The EFTA, as a whole, buys more from the Community than the United States and Japan combined. Finland has been the fastest-growing Scandinavian importer of EC goods. Finnish Eastern trade has also grown to the extent that its net trade balance is essentially unchanged. Almost half of total Swedish trade is with the Community, although during recent years, Sweden has developed a major export market in the growing Norwegian economy and later in the United States. Denmark's new relationship has involved far more than trade, and has added a new dimension to most aspects of public policy. Particularly, the traditionally crucial agricultural sector has been affected by the Common Market agricultural policy. In addition, the costly regional development programs in Greenland have drawn on EC funds.

The nonmember states have also participated in many of the Community programs for scientific and technical research and development, and they have cooperated in the cultural and educational areas as well. For example, Sweden has been an active partner in the European Space Program and in the French-inspired EUREKA project. In contrast, they have remained outside the European Monetary System centered around a strong Deutsche Mark. With the exception of the Danes, the Scandinavians have joined Europe *à la carte,* that is, selectively. Critics often point out that they have gained most of the benefits of cooperation without incurring the obligation of membership.

The EFTA survived the departure of the United Kingdom and Denmark in 1973 when they joined the Common Market. Following the loss of Portugal in 1986, for the same reason, membership was reduced to six small and mostly neutral states located in Northern and in Central Europe. When the Single European Act was adopted in 1985 (see Chapter 8), it became apparent that the outsiders, not only in Scandinavia, would again have to assess their relationships with this evolving community numbering some 320 million people. Many Scandinavian industrial leaders have pressed for closer ties and even for Community membership to ensure continued market access and participation in research and development efforts.

In contrast, many labor leaders have viewed the standards and practices of a Community beset with high unemployment, continuous budget crises, and a more marked capitalist profile, with some suspicion. One major fear is that closer ties with the Community would lead to a pullback from some of the achievements of the past that benefited workers and consumers. It is expected that by the mid-1990s, the Scandinavians must again redefine their roles in the continuing European experiment with economic integration.

PROMOTING GLOBAL WELFARE

The Scandinavian countries are said to pursue highly progressive policies toward the Third World. The Nordic model of development assistance policy is generally characterized by annual aid volumes that—when measured as a proportion of GNP—are among the highest in the industrial world. A sizable portion of this aid is free from any donor country purchase requirements. The least developed nations have received special consideration and rural projects with long-term development effects have been emphasized. Humanitarian assistance to national liberation groups in southern Africa and support of so-called progressive regimes has been given. For good reasons, the Nordic image has been one of progressive, generous, and committed partners in the global development process.

Yet, a more careful examination reveals that each Nordic state has established a distinct development policy. In contrast to most prominent development aid-granting countries, the Nordic nations lack a significant colonial heritage. Their unusually high aid commitment cannot be explained by a colonial background or by the strategic interests of a major power. Rather, the domestic experiences of peaceful political development during the last century of significant and rapid socioeconomic change have heavily influenced current attitudes toward economic and social progress in less developed countries. The successful Nordic transformation from poor, rural societies to highly advanced, postindustrial nations has also helped to form dominant political attitudes toward global development problems. The strength and political prominence of the Scandinavian labor movement has also shaped government views on socioeconomic progress and international solidarity.

Like other Western nations, the Nordic commitment to development assistance began with the founding of the United Nations Technical Aid Program (EPTA) in 1949. By 1952, three of the Nordic countries were also involved in bilateral programs. Finland remained outside of these developments during the first half of the 1950s, but after membership in the United Nations in 1955, it became more actively involved and in 1957 entered into a limited bilateral cooperation program with India.

Important growth for Nordic development policies ensued during the 1960s. Official program objectives were presented, new assistance agencies were created, and the 1 percent of GNP target for development was introduced. Multilateral aid still figured prominently as the best channel for assistance and was, perhaps, the only feasible way to spend the quickly growing funds. Scandinavian support of the UN development effort, however, is still very significant compared to most states. Together, the Scandinavian countries provide about one-fourth of the funds for the UN Development Program (UNDP), as well as disproportionally high sums for such other agencies as the FAO, WHO, and UNICEF. The creation of new national agencies for bilateral aid, more explicit development criteria, and greater interest in the possible economic consequences from such massive outflows of assistance have shifted domestic attention to bilateral programs.

Over the decade, the Nordic development assistance policies matured into a common approach that differed from the prevailing standards of the OECD countries in several respects. First, the great bulk of the assistance was given as outright grants rather than in the form of loans. The emphasis was on a few program countries selected for their potential for fulfilling certain assistance objectives. Preferences of the recipient nation formed a major part in determining the focus for bilateral aid. A substantial share of the transfer consisted of untied grants for import financing. The dominant part of all aid was, in fact, unrestricted and could be used for local needs, such as health and educational program. Both in the receiving and donor country, a clear differentiation was made between assistance and export financing.

Scandinavians have earned considerable worldwide respect for high quality development aid policies. This profile complements Scandinavian support in international forums for such Third World demands as the proposal for a New International Economic Order. The designation, "Like-Minded Countries," was coined during the 1970s to depict Scandinavia, together with Holland, as Third World partners in the effort to reform the global system through multilateral negotiations in several arenas. The international stature of these small states has grown as a result of this positive record.

Nordic development assistance policy, a traditionally protected policy area, seems to have become more integrated with the overall economic and commercial objectives of these nations. In Scandinavia, it is more accepted now than in the past that such global resource transfers may also bring benefits to the donor. The net cost of these impressive programs is reduced considerably through the type of measures adopted recently. Perhaps such innovations are necessary to maintain broad popular support for the public expenditures required to uphold the famed one percent target.

TRANSPOSING THE DOMESTIC EXPERIENCE

This chapter has shown how the surrounding favorable international setting has influenced the development of postwar Scandinavian foreign relations. This element, conducive to the security, the prosperity, and the global stature of these five small states, also helps explain their diverse foreign policies. Within this external context, unique historical experiences and distinct domestic features have shaped each national foreign policy profile. For reasons of space, limited attention has been paid to the domestic influences upon foreign policy formulation. However, rapid socioeconomic transformation, the peaceful emergence of stable democracies, the growth of the active state responsible for public welfare and economic management, technological innovations, and cultural changes during the last century have profoundly affected the external relations of these societies.[1]

The approach to international affairs in many ways reflects the salient features of Scandinavian domestic life. An examination of the internal dynamics of these states, then, is essential in understanding the external objectives and the strategies selected to attain them. Clearly, Scandinavian hopes for global understanding, nonviolent solutions to security dilemmas, and adherence to principles of international law and organization are inspired by the comparatively tranquil regional develop-

[1]Students wanting to pursue the domestic dimension of the Scandinavian experience are referred to the chapter on Scandinavia in Professor Macridis's companion volume, *Modern Political Systems: Europe*, 6th and forthcoming 7th Ed. (Englewood Cliffs, N.J.: Prentice-Hall,1987).

ments during the last century. The quest for global solidarity parallels the ideals of the influential Scandinavian labor movement. The belief in managed market solutions to international economic problems draws upon successful experiences at home that have combined economic growth with shared affluence. The international bridge-building apsirations reflect the dynamics of national consensus formation, whereby sector demands are transformed into broad coalitions composed of leading parties and interest groups.

In most states, whether large or small, the domestic experience is readily transposed upon the international arena in the belief that conditions abroad are sufficiently similar to allow for such analogies. For example, the so-called American way of life has, at times, been promoted as a model for the conduct of very complex international political and economic relations.

Scandinavian efforts to project their national experiences on the world arena have less impact on world politics than the behavior by the bloc leaders. But, after surveying the foreign policies of these five unusually civil states, advocates of world order and justice may regret the limited attention the international community has paid to the Scandinavian foreign policy experience.

FOREIGN POLICY LANDMARKS

1948–49	Establishment of the postwar Nordic security pattern: Denmark, Iceland, Norway join NATO; Finland concludes a mutual cooperation pact with the USSR; Sweden pursues freedom from alliances.
1951	The pattern of postwar Nordic security is completed by the United States–Icelandic agreement on the status of the Keflavik base.
1952	The Nordic Council is established, and it is followed with conventions on a passport union, a common labor market, and a social security union. A mandate to explore the potential for a Nordic Common Market is given.
1955	The Soviet Union withdraws from Finnish soil and Finland joins the United Nations and the Nordic Council.
1956	Urho Kekkonen becomes president of Finland.
1959	The European Free Trade Association is established and inter-Nordic trade grows significantly.
1961	The Finnish-Soviet Note Crisis. Danish, Norwegian, and Swedish applications to the European Economic Community.
1962	The Nordic commitments are manifested in the 1962 Helsinki Agreement on Nordic Cooperation.
1962	The national development assistance programs begin.
1963	The Kekkonen plan for a Nordic nuclear weapons free zone is launched.
1968	A Danish initiative for a Nordic Economic Union (NORDEK) is initiated.
1969	First major oil discovery in Norway.
1970	Iceland joins EFTA; NORDEK plan fails.

1970–73	Relations with the EEC are adjusted; the Nordic commitments are strengthened through the establishment of a Nordic Council of Ministers, joint Secretariats, and additional Nordic conventions.
1973	Denmark joins the EEC; Iceland, Norway, and Sweden conclude free trade agreements. Finland concludes an economic cooperation agreement with the COMECON and a free trade agreement with the EEC.
1975	A thirty-five-nation summit meeting in Finland results in the Helsinki Accords on Security and Cooperation in Europe (CSCE); Norway becomes a net exporter of oil.
1978	The Kekkonen plan for a Nordic nuclear weapons free zone is renewed.
1979	The NATO dual track INF decision is followed by a prolonged Scandinavian debate over the merits of a Nordic nuclear weapons free zone.
1981	The Kekkonen era is over in Finland; the first Soviet submarine incident in Sweden, "Whiskey on the Rocks," is followed by further territorial violations and Swedish diplomatic protests.
1984–86	The Stockholm Conference on Disarmament in Europe, when a thirty-five-nation agreement on confidence building measures is concluded.
1985	Greenland leaves the European Economic Community.
1986	Swedish Prime Minister Olof Palme is assassinated, he is followed by Ingvar Carlsson.
1987	Ingvar Carlsson is granted an official White House visit, only the second such invitation in thirty-five years.

SELECTED BIBLIOGRAPHY

The primary academic journal devoted to Scandinavian foreign relations is the quarterly *Cooperation and Conflict*, published since 1965. The Nordic Political Science Associations sponsor *Scandinavian Political Studies*, formerly a yearbook, but since 1978 a quarterly. Some major Scandinavian language journals are also important: *Internasjonal Politikk* is published by the Norwegian Institute of International Affairs, *Internationella Studier* by the Swedish Institute of International Affairs, and *Ulkopolitiikka* by the Finnish Institute of International Affairs.

The Norwegian Institute of International Affairs publishes valuable articles and documentation in the annual *Norsk Utenrikspolitisk Årbog*. The Finnish counterpart is the *Yearbook of Finnish Foreign Policy*. The Danish Institute of International Affairs publishes the annual *Dansk Udenrigspolitisk Arbog*. The Swedish version is titled *Fred och Säkerhet*. *International Studies in the Nordic Countries*, a biannual newsletter published by the Nordic Cooperation Committee for International Politics, Stockholm, is the best source to follow current research, workshops, conferences, and publications in the field.

General Overviews and Regional Relations

ANDERSON, STANLEY. *The Nordic Council: A Study in Scandinavian Regionalism.* Seattle, Wash.: University of Washington Press, 1967.

ANDRÉN, NILS. *Power Balance and Non-Alignment: A Perspective on Swedish Foreign Policy.* Stockholm: Almqvist och Wiksell, 1967.

BERNER, ÖRJAN. *Soviet Policies toward the Nordic Countries,* Lanham, Md.: University Press of America, 1986.

Essays on Finnish Foreign Policy. Helsinki: Finnish Political Science Association, 1969.

HASKEL, BARBARA. *The Scandinavian Option: Opportunities and Opportunity Costs in Postwar Scandinavian Foreign Policies.* Oslo: Norwegian Universities Press, 1976.

HOLST, JOHAN JÖRGEN, ed. *Norwegian Foreign Policy in the 1980s.* Oslo: Norwegian Universities Press, 1985.

JACOBSON, MAX. *Finnish Neutrality.* London: Hugh Evelyn, 1968.

LINDGREN, RAYMOND. *Norway-Sweden: Union, Disunion and Scandinavian Integration.* Princeton, N.J.: Princeton University Press, 1959.

LUNDESTAD, GEIR. *America, Scandinavia and the Cold War 1945–49.* New York: Columbia University Press, 1980.

SCOTT, FRANKLIN. *Scandinavia.* Cambridge, Mass.: Harvard University Press, 1975.

STENELO, LARS GÖRAN. *The International Critic.* Lund: Studentlitteratur, 1984.

SUNDELIUS, BENGT. *Managing Transnationalism in Northern Europe.* Boulder, Colo.: Westview Press, 1978.

SUNDELIUS, BENGT, ed. *Foreign Policies of Northern Europe.* Boulder, Colo.: Westview Press, 1982.

VÄYRYNEN, RAIMO. *Stability and Change in Finnish Foreign Policy.* Helsinki: Department of Political Science, University of Helsinki, 1986.

WENDT, FRANTZ. *Cooperation in the Nordic Countries.* Stockholm: Almqvist och Wiksell, 1981.

Security Policy

ALLISON, ROY. *Finland's Relations with the Soviet Union, 1944–1984.* London: Macmillan, 1985.

BJÖL, ERLING. "Nordic Security," *Adelphi Papers*, No. 181. London: International Institute for Strategic Studies, 1983.

COLE, PAUL, and DOUGLAS HART, eds. *Northern Europe: Security Issues for the 1990s.* Boulder, Colo.: Westview Press, 1986.

EINHORN, ERIC. *National Security and Domestic Politics in Postwar Denmark: Some Principal Issues 1945–1961.* Odense: Odense University Press, 1975.

FLYNN, GREGORY, ed. *NATO's Northern Allies.* London: Croom Helm, 1985.

GILBERG, TROND, et al. "USSR and Northern Europe," *Problems of Communism*, Vol. 30, No. 2 (March–April 1981):1–24.

GRÖNDAL, BENEDIKT. *Iceland from Neutrality to NATO Membership.* Oslo: Norwegian Universities Press, 1971.

MAUDE, GEORGE. *The Finnish Dilemma; Neutrality in the Shadow of Power.* London: Oxford University Press, 1976.

"Nordic Security Today." In special issue of *Cooperation and Conflict*, Vol. 17, No. 4 (1982).

NUECHTERLEIN, DONALD. *Iceland, Reluctant Ally.* Westport, Ct.: Greenwood Press, 1961.

SUNDELIUS, BENGT (ed.) *The Neutral Democracies and the New Cold War.* Boulder, Colo.: Westview Press, 1987.

VÄYRYNEN, RAIMO, *Conflicts in Finnish-Soviet Relations: Three Comparative Case Studies.* Tampere: Tampere University, 1972.

VLOYANTES, JOHN, *Silk Glove Hegemony; Finnish-Soviet Relations 1944–1974.* Kent, Ohio: Kent State University Press, 1975.

International Economic and Development Policy

ALLEN, HILARY. *Norway and Europe in the 1970s.* Oslo: Norwegian Universities Press, 1979.

DOHLMAN, EBBA. *Economic Security and Swedish Trade Policy.* Oxford: Oxford University Press, forthcoming in 1988.

FRUHLING, PIERRE, ed. *Swedish Development Aid in Perspective.* Stockholm: Almquist och Wiksell, 1986.

HANCOCK, DONALD, ed. "Scandinavia and the European Community." In special issue of *Scandinavian Studies*, Vol. 46, No. 4 (1974).

MILJAN, TOIVO. *The Reluctant Europeans; The Attitudes of the Nordic Countries Towards European Integration.* London: Hurst, 1977.

"Nordic Aid to Underdeveloped Countries." In special issue of *Cooperation and Conflict*, Vol. 5, No. 2 (1970).

"The Nordic Countries and the New International Economic Order." In special issue of Cooperation and Conflict, Vol. 14, No. 2 and No. 3 (1979).

"Petroleum and International Relations: The Case of Norway." In special issue of *Cooperation and Conflict*, Vol. 17, No. 2 (June 1982).

UNDERDAL, ARILD. *The Politics of Fisheries Management: The Case of the Northeast Atlantic.* Oslo: Norwegian Universities Press, 1980.

The Foreign Policy Process

BURGESS, PHILIP. *Elite Images and Foreign Policy Outcomes.* Columbus, Ohio: Ohio State University Press, 1968.

DÖRFER, INGEMAR. *System 37 Viggen.* Oslo: Norwegian Universities Press, 1973.

GOLDMANN, KJELL, et. al. *Democracy and Foreign Policy: The Case of Sweden.* Aldershot, England: Gower, 1986.

HART, THOMAS. *The Cognitive World of Swedish Security Elites.* Stockholm: Esselte, 1976.

HVEEM, HELGE. *International Relations and World Images; A Study of Norwegian Foreign Policy Elites.* Oslo: Norwegian Universities Press, 1972.

KARVONEN, LAURI, and BENGT SUNDELIUS. *Internationalization and Foreign Policy Management.* Aldershot, England: Gower, 1987.

ÖRVIK, NILS. *Departmental Decision Making.* Oslo: Norwegian Universities Press, 1972.

TAYLOR, WILLIAM, and PAUL COLE, eds. *Nordic Defense: Comparative Decision Making.* Lexington, Mass.: Lexington Books, 1985.

Index